AdvancED Flash on Devices

Mobile Development with Flash Lite and Flash 10

Elad Elrom, Scott Janousek, Thomas Joos

friendsof

DESIGNER TO DESIGNER™

an Apress® company

AdvancED Flash on Devices: Mobile Development with Flash Lite and Flash 10

Credits

Lead Editors	**Senior Production Editor**
Clay Andres, Tom Welsh	Laura Cheu
Technical Reviewer and Contributor	**Compositor**
Nancy Nicolaisen	Molly Sharp, Lynn L'Heureux
Editorial Board	**Proofreader**
Clay Andres, Steve Anglin, Mark Beckner,	April Eddy
Ewan Buckingham, Tony Campbell,	
Gary Cornell, Jonathan Gennick,	**Indexer**
Michelle Lowman, Matthew Moodie,	Brenda Miller
Jeffrey Pepper, Frank Pohlmann,	
Ben Renow-Clarke, Dominic Shakeshaft,	**Artist**
Matt Wade, Tom Welsh	April Milne
Senior Project Manager	**Cover Image Designer**
Sofia Marchant	Bruce Tang
Copy Editor	**Interior and Cover Designer**
Heather Lang, Liz Welch	Kurt Krames
Associate Production Director	**Manufacturing Director**
Kari Brooks-Copony	Tom Debolski

I would like to dedicate this book to my wife Jordana, who motivated, inspired, and accommodated me—while taking care of our seventeen-month-old baby girl—as I worked long nights to create this book. I also would like to dedicate the book to my mother Elena and brother Lior; I am lucky to have them in my life and to receive their love and support.

—Elad Elrom

This book is dedicated to my mother and father, who take an interest in my life even though they might not always understand all the technology and geeky stuff. I love you. Thanks also to my older brothers Jeff and Paul for always giving good, sound, real-life advice to a younger sibling.

—Scott Janousek

I would like to dedicate this book to my parents, who are always there for me—whether I'm playing in a soccer game or writing a nerdy book. Thanks for always believing in me. Also, I would like to thank my younger brother Brecht, who is doing a great job of becoming a sports teacher. I hope you finish college soon, so you can get all those young people in good shape. I am proud to have you by my side, together with Mom and Dad. I love you all.

—Thomas Joos

CONTENTS AT A GLANCE

CONTENTS

PART TWO FLASH LITE PLATFORM OVERVIEW

Chapter 2 Flash Lite Platform Fundamentals 29

PART THREE AIR APPLICATIONS FOR MULTIPLE SCREENS AND MOBILE INTERNET DEVICES

Chapter 10 **Adopting AIR for Mobile Devices** **385**

Chapter 11 **Developing Cross-Platform Air Applications** **431**

PART FOUR FLEX APPLICATION RUNNING FLASH 10 ON MOBILE DEVICES

Chapter 12 Mobile Applications and Development Strategies . . . . . . 483 with Flex 4 and Flash Catalyst

FOREWORD

The technology landscape has never been more exciting, and it has also never been more confusing. Everywhere you look, you see a number of ways to connect to your friends and consume digital content. Mobile devices, your living room consumer electronic devices, PCs, laptops, and netbooks are all increasingly connected and capable of providing a full web experience. All of this is very good news for Flash developers. Flash continues to let developers and designers create rich Internet applications across multiple screens. At Adobe, we have been working very hard on the next generation of the Flash Player for mobile devices as well as for cutting-edge areas, like the digital living room.

One of the core promises of the Flash Player has always been to provide a consistent experience for the user regardless of the operating system or the browser. In a world where not only the operating systems but the hardware and screen sizes are all different, that promise is even more important. You have to be able to reach your customers on whatever device they're using, while still providing the rich user experience that users now expect. There is no better or more efficient platform for creating rich content that will run everywhere than Flash.

Up until now, there hasn't been a book that covers the wide range of the Flash platform, so this book is sorely needed. The breadth of the platform means that Flash developers are under more and more pressure to deliver across all multiple environments. The fact that Flash accounts for over 85 percent of video streamed on the Web means that the traditional Flash world is colliding with other media, and the skill demands on a Flash developer have never been more diverse. Part designer, part developer, and part rich-media guru, the Flash developer needs to have many tools available. This book does a great job of covering the budding mobile space, the browser space, and the desktop space all the while providing tips and tricks to use the tools and technologies of the Flash platform.

This book couldn't have a stronger set of authors. Elad Elrom is a rising star of the Flash development world. He brings a fresh perspective, a strong background, and an inherent knack for the more subtle aspects of the Flash platform. He's been involved very early in a number of Adobe products, providing feedback and ideas to ensure that the platform remains cutting edge. Scott Janousek needs no introduction in most Flash circles. He came early to the world of Flash mobile and has watched it go through many, many iterations. He has built some of the most compelling Flash Lite demonstrations out there and has been a constant resource for the community when it comes to Flash on mobile devices. Having him author a book like this, at a time when Flash on mobile devices has never been more exciting, is a resounding endorsement of both what's inside and what's coming for Flash developers.

The multiscreen experience brings many challenges and many opportunities. As a Flash developer, you've got a leg up on the rest of your competition. The combination of great tools, great services, and a formidable rich media infrastructure means you can target these devices with next-generation user interfaces and media. This book will be a great resource as you navigate the waters of multiscreen and mobile development with the Flash platform.

Ryan Stewart

ABOUT THE AUTHORS

Elad Elrom is a technical writer, technical lead, and senior Flash engineer. As a technical writer, Elad wrote books covering Flash technologies. He maintains an active blog (http://www.elromdesign.com/blog) and has spoken at several conferences regarding the Flash platform. He has helped companies follow the XP and Scrum methodologies to implement popular frameworks, optimize and automate built processors and code review, and follow best practices. Elad has consulted for a variety of clients in different fields and sizes, from large corporations such as Viacom, NBC Universal, and Weight Watchers to startups such as MotionBox.com and KickApps.com.

Scott Janousek is a technical writer, software developer, training instructor, community evangelist, worldwide speaker, and CEO. He is also the owner of Hooken Mobile, a mobile design and development company based in the United States, in the suburbs of Boston, Massachusetts. Scott is an Adobe Certified Flash Designer and Developer as well as a recognized Flash mobile expert. In addition to working with Flash Mobile, he is also currently creating native applications for the iPhone, webOS, and Android platforms. As an active and contributing member of the Adobe Flash Mobile User Group, Boston Flash Platform User Group, Mass Mobile, and Mobile Monday Boston (momoBoston), Scott is passionate about mobile and devices and works with the Flash platform across all sorts of devices and gadgets. For more information about Scott and his latest mobile and device endeavors, check out his personal blog at http://www.scottjanousek.com/blog/.

Thomas Joos is a mobile consultant who graduated with a degree in multimedia and communication technology from the Technical University West–Flanders. As a result of his passion for mobile, Thomas specialized in Flash Lite development and mobile concepts and design. In December 2008, he won an Adobe Max Award for Rock Werchter Mobile, the only mobile entry that made it into the European finals. Thomas is always on the lookout for any mobile opportunities that could add value to a client's online campaign, experience, or communication platform. Fueled by his interest in mobile design and concepts, combined with a strong technical knowledge in Flash Lite, Thomas offers a wide variety of mobile consultation, from technical training sessions and workshops to brainstorming meetings, and he's constantly looking for mobile platform opportunities for clients and their online strategies. For more information about Thomas, you can check his personal blog at http://www.thomasjoos.be.

ABOUT THE TECHNICAL REVIEWER

Nancy Nicolaisen is an author, a researcher, and a former computer science professor, specializing in the design and development of small and embedded mobile-device–based solutions. Her three programming books have been printed in five languages. She writes feature and analysis content for Internet-based publishers including Jupitermedia, CodeGuru, and Faulkner Information Services and has published hundreds of feature articles, columns, and analyses in internationally circulated publications including *BYTE*, *PC Magazine*, *Windows Sources*, *Computer Shopper*, *Dr. Dobb's Journal of Software Engineering*, *Microsoft Systems Journal*, *DataBased Advisor*, and *Telecom Advisor*, and for McGraw-Hill/DATAPRO Research Corporation.

Look for her first consumer-oriented book, *Getting Started with Netbooks*, which will be published by friends of ED in 2009. *Getting Started with Netbooks* is a plain-language guide to shopping for best fit and value in your new ultra-mobile computer and learning how to get the most out of the connected mobile lifestyle using cloud computing services and innovative accessories.

ABOUT THE COVER IMAGE DESIGNER

Bruce Tang is a freelance web designer, visual programmer, and author from Hong Kong. His main creative interest is generating stunning visual effects using Flash or Processing.

Bruce has been an avid Flash user since Flash 4, when he began using Flash to create games, web sites, and other multimedia content. After several years of ActionScripting, he found himself increasingly drawn toward visual programming and computational art. He likes to integrate math and physics into his work, simulating 3D and other real-life experiences onscreen. His first Flash book was published in October 2005. Bruce's folio, featuring Flash and Processing pieces, can be found at www.betaruce.com and his blog at www.betaruce.com/blog.

The cover image uses a high-resolution Henon phase diagram generated by Bruce with Processing, which he feels is an ideal tool for such experiments. Henon is a strange attractor created by iterating through some equations to calculate the coordinates of millions of points. The points are then plotted with an assigned color.

$$x_{n+1} = x_n \cos(a) - (y_n - x_n^p) \sin(a)$$

$$y_{n+1} = x_n \sin(a) + (y_n - x_n^p) \cos(a)$$

ACKNOWLEDGMENTS

This book, as you can imagine, is the collective effort of a whole team over at friends of ED, and I would like to thank each and every one of you for the superb team effort in getting this book out in a relatively short amount of time. Specifically, I would like to thank Clay Andres for helping make an idea into this book. Without Clay sharing my enthusiasm, this book wouldn't have been possible.

I would also like to thank Tom Welsh, who made sure to speak what's on his mind about keeping readers' interest and ensuring the high quality of this book. Also, thanks to Nancy Nicolaisen for an excellent technical review and the contribution of the first few pages in Chapter 15, as well as many ideas in this book's chapters. Also, thanks to Sofia Marchant for ensuring that this book stayed on track and for overcoming obstacles.

I would like to thank Adobe evangelists Jason Knell, Ryan Stewart, and Kevin Hoyt for helping me keep in touch with changes that were made in Adobe's line of products and inspiring me while writing this book.

Special thanks go to the Adobe Strobe Team, and in particular to Christine Yarrow and Sumner Paine, who were kind enough to allow us publishing and never-before-seen information about the framework.

I would like to thank my coauthors Scott Janousek and Thomas Joos, who worked day and night to make deadlines while juggling busy schedules and personal lives.

Finally, I would like to thank the mobile and Flash communities for being active and helping inspire much of this book's material, as well as for keeping up with the fragmented mobile ecosystem.

Elad Elrom

Many thanks to Alessandro Pace, Dale Rankine, Mark Doherty, and many other passionate leaders in the worldwide Adobe community for the hours spent evangelizing Flash on mobile and devices over the years. The Flash mobile (and especially the Flash Lite) community is a tight-knit group of great people who are always willing to share opinions, resources, ideas, and knowledge. It has been really great to be a part of the community over the past few years.

To my coauthors, Elad and Thomas, thanks, guys, for hanging in there as we put in all those long hours to make this beast of a book actually happen (finally).

I also want to give big props to the friends of ED team for managing the whole book's process and getting it out to readers, despite many of the obstacles we've encountered along the way. The publishing team at friends of ED rocks!

Scott Janousek

I would like to thank the entire multimedia and communication technology (MCT) crew at the Technical University of West–Flanders for doing a fantastic job providing high-quality and new-media–related education. Going for MCT was one of the best decisions I made and really helped me find out what I wanted to do. Special thanks go to Koen De Weggheleire, who has always inspired and motivated me to get the most out of my projects and my goals.

Many thanks to my coauthors Elad Elrom and Scott Janousek, who worked so hard to make this book great. Besides that, I would like to thank you both for taking me under your wings. Even though there were lots of late nights and long hours, it was a wonderful experience, and I am very proud of the result.

To the entire friends of ED crew, thanks for managing the whole book's process and doing a great job getting this book out to readers. It was a real pleasure working with all of you.

Thomas Joos

INTRODUCTION

The idea of writing this book emerged from the last book Elad coauthored called *AdvancED Flex 3*. In the previous book, Elad wrote an 80-page chapter about mobile devices. Before that book was printed, the team realized that writing a chapter covering Flash Lite may not be suitable for a Flex 3 book, and the chapter was dropped. After a conversation with Clay Andres in Manhattan about trends, technology, Flex, and mobile, Elad and Clay decided that they should do the extraordinary and combine Flash Lite with emerging technologies, taking into account the release of Flash Player 10 on mobile devices; they also decided to include the hard-to-keep-up-with changes to Flash Lite.

Shortly after, Elad was connected with Scott Janousek and Thomas Joos, who shared his vision and helped create this book—it includes theory, relevant real-life examples, as well as never-before-seen tutorials and information on how to develop applications for mobile devices using the Flash platform.

Mobile devices are the most frequently used devices worldwide, and today, the mobile ecosystem is undergoing an exciting revolution. Amid all these changes is the Adobe Open Source Project, which is moving from an idea into a reality with the availability of Flash Player 10 and Adobe Integrated Runtime (AIR) for mobile devices. These exciting changes open up new possibilities for mobile developers and allow you to create cross-platform applications that share code across the devices.

The book is a good starting point if you're a developer interested in getting involved in mobile development using the Flash platform, and it's an equally a great resource for taking mobile development to the next level and moving to more advanced topics and understanding where mobile development is going. This book is suitable for many individuals, whether you're a current Flash Lite developer who wants to push the limits and better understand the mobile ecosystem or a Flex developer who's been reluctant to develop applications for mobile development because you refused to write your code in ActionScript 2.0. This book is also suitable if you're a developer who has never used the Flash platform to develop a mobile application but wants to be part of the exciting possibilities.

The book offers you unparalleled insight into the mobile development world, which is known for being rewarding, as well as complex, fragmented, and rapidly changing. The chapters in this book will cover different versions of Flash content using Flash Player 1.1, 2.0, 2.1, 3.0, 3.1, 9.0, and 10.0. Topics covered in this book include desktop and mobile development using AIR, as well as differences between desktop and web development—as well as how to take these differences into consideration in mobile development. This book includes information regarding existing platforms, content providers, and aggregators that are part of the worldwide mobile ecosystem. It also talks about the communities and desktop and online tools to make your life easier, and it offers exciting tutorials for concepts such as deploying Flash on the iPhone and developing mobile applications using Flash Catalyst, Flex, and AIR.

We believe that this book is a great resource but also a window into the future of mobile development: it addresses not only challenges that mobile developers face today but the new challenges developers will be facing in developing applications with Flash Player 10 and AIR for mobile devices. Our hope is that this book will inspire you to start developing applications for mobile devices.

Layout conventions

To keep this book as clear and easy to follow as possible, the following text conventions are used throughout.

- Code is presented in `fixed-width` font.

- New or changed code is normally presented in **`bold fixed-width font`**.

- Pseudo-code and variable input are written in *`italic fixed-width font`*.

- Menu commands are written in the form Menu ➤ Submenu ➤ Submenu.

- Where we want to draw your attention to something, we've highlighted it like this:

> *Ahem, don't say we didn't warn you.*

- Sometimes code won't fit on a single line in a book. Where this happens, we use an arrow like this: ➥.

  ```
  This is a very, very long section of code that should be written all ➥
  on the same line without a break.
  ```

Part One

MOBILE DEVELOPMENT LANDSCAPE

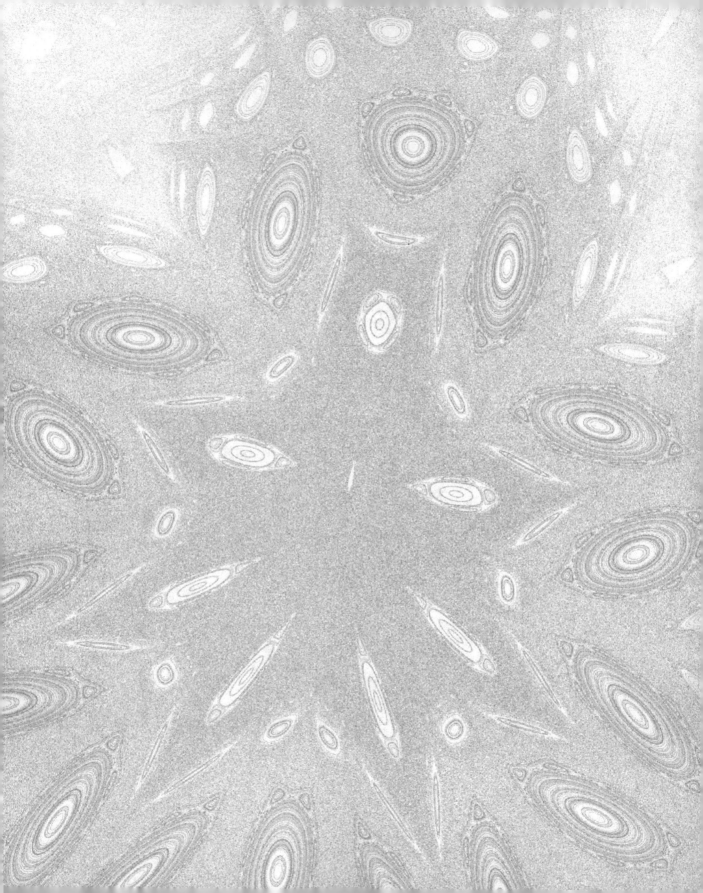

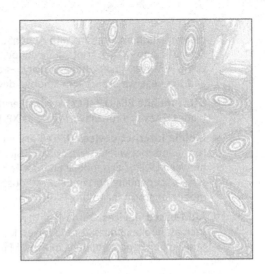

Chapter 1

THE MOBILE AND
DEVICE LANDSCAPE

Mobile devices are undergoing an exciting revolution today due to the rapid increase in network subscribers as well as the increase in experienced designers, which results in better user interface and hardware innovations such as touch screens. According to *Mobile Magazine*, over a billion people will have a mobile device connected to a 3G network with a fast Internet connection by 2010. As the mobile device changes, consumers' expectations of their mobile devices increase as well.

Amid all these changes, the Adobe Open Source Project is moving the Flash Player from a licensed model to an open source model to compete with other mobile technologies. The announcement of the availability of Flash 10 and Adobe Integrated Runtime (AIR) for mobile devices opens new possibilities to mobile developers.

Many different mobile devices are in use today, including the following:

- **Mobile phones** are the most commonly used electronic devices worldwide. The mobile phone started as a mobile device capable of making phone calls, but recent years have seen a real transition from pure voice to data. Today, mobile phones include many more features than just the ability to make calls and have turned into what are called "smart phones," which include more-capable CPUs and larger memory to support multimedia and other programs that we usually use in our desktops or on the Web. Up until now, mobile phones only supported Flash Lite (FL) and the development was limited to creating Flash applications with ActionScript 1.0 or 2.0, which was a major drawback to many Flex, AIR, and ActionScript 3.0 developers who didn't want to create applications using legacy code. However, smart phone prototypes that run Flash 10 on their web browsers already exist, and this year, we expect some mobile devices to support Flash 10 and Adobe AIR.

- **Ultra-mobile PCs (UMPCs)** are smaller than laptop computers and have wireless access capabilities. They can run Linux, Windows XP, Windows Vista, or Windows 7 operating systems.

- **Mobile Internet devices (MIDs)** are multimedia handheld computers capable of connecting to the Internet wirelessly, playing music, and showing videos and images. They bridge the gap between UMPCs and mobile phones. They can use the Linux or Windows XP or Vista operating system, depending on the CPU. Although these devices are not very popular, they are a good mobile platform for testing Flash 10 and AIR applications.

- **ARM-based devices** are devices that have ARM architecture, which can be found in devices such as mobile phones, set-top boxes, MIDs, TVs, automotive platforms, MP3 players, and many other mobile and computing devices. Many of these devices will support Flash 10 and AIR.

Addressing fragmentation

As technology progresses, our mobile devices have better CPUs and more memory, but one challenge remains unsolved: fragmentation.

Fragmentation is mostly caused by OEMs, which decide what goes into mobile devices, what is enabled or disabled, and generally what ends up in consumers' hands. Fragmentation occurs mostly in software. For instance, the OEM may decide to disable Bluetooth sync or multitouch capabilities.

Another challenge is that each device is based on a different platform or operating system and may have different browser specifications and/or networks. Creating an application that can work on many platforms has become challenging and costly.

> *In this book, we will refer to applications that can work on many platforms as cross-platform, multiplatform, multitarget, or multiscreen applications. Often, these applications implement and run on several computer platforms, which can be different mobile operating systems but also different computer platforms such as PCs, Macs, or even web clients.*

The Adobe Open Screen Project (http://www.openscreenproject.org/) is an initiative that is focused on solving fragmentation by connecting partners and striving to address a "write once, run anywhere" (WORA) paradigm. Recently, the project is becoming a reality with the release of Flash Player 10 on many operating systems such as Linux, 32/64-bit, Mac OS X, and Solaris. The Adobe Open Screen Project made an announcement that Flash Player 10 will be available royalty-free to all, and Open Screen partners such as ARM, Nokia, and Intel are adopting Flash 10 and AIR.

> *Chapter 2 covers more details about the Adobe Open Screen Project, especially how it ties into Flash Lite and the roadmap to Flash 10 across mobile and other devices.*

We believe that, as a developer, you can start taking advantage of these innovative changes today and build your application in the Flash 10 environment, so your application will be ready to support many devices. As more and more platforms, browsers, mobile manufacturers, and others support Flash 10, your application will be ready and hopefully deployed with few changes, giving the user the same user experience across many platforms. Figure 1-1 shows the same application running on a computer, TV, laptop, smart phone, and MID.

Figure 1-1.
An Open Screen Project marketing diagram showing the same application running on different devices

That paradigm is already in use by some leading companies today. As an example, take a look at an application called ShifD, which enables the user to update information from the desktop, MIDs, UPMCs, and on the Web using AIR and Flex (see Figure 1-2).

Figure 1-2.
The ShifD application across different devices

With all these exciting innovations, and as we build our next-generation applications today, let's keep in mind that there are still very limited mobile devices that support Flash 10 and Adobe AIR. Therefore, building mobile applications using Flash Lite is still applicable and will be relevant in the coming years. Learning Flash Lite for the first time, as well as understanding it better, will remain very useful and current skills for some time, so a large portion of the next few chapters of the book are devoted to Flash Lite.

Getting to know the devices

In the following sections, we'll explore devices available for use with Flash Lite in some detail. We'll explain more about each of these as they appear in examples and discussions throughout this book.

Mobile phones

As mobile phones advance, phones are being used for more than just making and receiving phone calls. In fact, they are now more personalized and cater to our needs. We can upload music, play games, view videos and photos, surf and shop on the Internet, write e-mails, take pictures, use GPS to get directions, and access a variety of games and applications to keep in touch with our social network and entertain ourselves.

In the mobile phone world, different operating systems are available on different phones. The most popular ones are Symbian, Windows Mobile, iPhone, and Research In Motion (RIM).

For each operating system, developers can write in the operating system's native language, which is usually Java or C++ (including variations such as Objective C for the iPhone). Developers can also choose a platform to leverage and develop multiplatform mobile applications and port the application to different devices. Currently, the two most popular platforms used to write mobile applications across many devices are Flash Lite and Java Micro Edition (ME).

Macromedia (now Abobe) got in the game early with the release of Flash Lite version 1.0 in 2003. Flash Lite 1.0 was created with the intention of supporting non-PC devices and its use spread rapidly. By 2012, according to Strategy Analytics, about 1.4 billion phones are expected to support Flash Lite (see Figure 1-3).

We will cover the different types of mobile phones' operating systems and platforms and how they tie in with Flash. In Chapter 2, we will also give you an overview on how to set emulators on popular devices, so you can test your applications without purchasing a single device. We are also going to set up your environment and get ready to develop mobile applications.

150,694,000 Americas
364,284,000 APAC
100,499,000 CALA
218,742,000 Western Europe
 73,007,000 Central Europe
 82,023,000 Japan

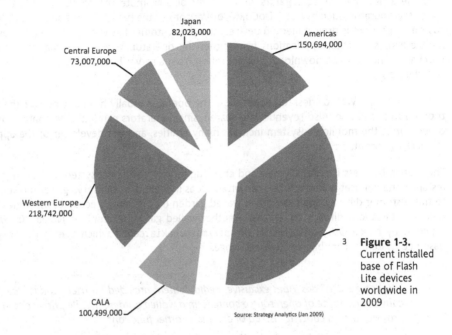

Japan
82,023,000

Central Europe
73,007,000

Americas
150,694,000

Western Europe
218,742,000

CALA
100,499,000

Source: Strategy Analytics (Jan 2009)

Figure 1-3.
Current installed base of Flash Lite devices worldwide in 2009

Navigating the mobile phone development ecosystem

When developing mobile phone applications, the business practices are different from desktop or Internet applications, so it's useful to identify and understand the mobile paradigm and the different players, which are illustrated in Figure 1-4.

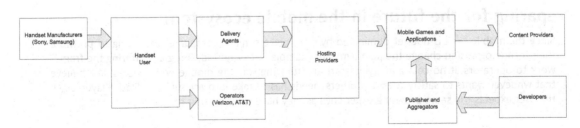

Figure 1-4. The mobile ecosystem

An ecosystem is an environment where plants, animals, and so forth are operating together in harmony. The mobile ecosystem is a business model of the different entities working together in the distribution of mobile content.

The model essentially works as follows: a mobile developer creates an application and can either sell it or use a publisher or aggregators who can test and promote the application. At the same time, either the operator (such as AT&T, DoCoMo, or Verizon) or the manufacturer sells a mobile device to a customer. Content is preinstalled on devices, and the customer has the option to purchase additional mobile games or other applications from either the operator or a delivery agent. Once content is purchased, the user can download the application from a server hosted by a mobile-hosting provider or a third party.

Unlike building a Web or desktop application, the operator usually has control over the content distributed to the phone. Also revenues are shared, since operators can limit the content on devices. In other words, the mobile ecosystem includes many entities, and the developer of the application has to share the profit.

The mobile business is relatively new and changing rapidly, so the ecosystem can change quickly. For instance, the handset manufacturers can often act as independent delivery agents and sell the content to the customer directly, such as Apple's walled garden (i.e., its closed ecosystem), iTunes, used to sell mobile applications directly to iPhones. Another walled garden example is Nokia's (now legacy, and replaced by Nokia OVI Store) MOSH (http://mosh.nokia.com/), which uses a public, community-based ecosystem for mobile content exchange.

> *"Walled garden" describes exclusive media content provided for users and is ideologically the opposite of open source content. In a walled garden, mobile phone operators provide custom content instead of common carrier functions.*

Understanding the mobile ecosystem is essential when getting into mobile development. For more details, there is an excellent and more detailed PDF on Adobe's Developer Connection site that explains how mobile ecosystems work:

www.adobe.com/devnet/devices/articles/mobile_ecosystem.pdf

In Chapter 2, we'll cover the Flash Lite ecosystem and content distribution systems in some detail, for those readers interested in how to monetize your development efforts in the mobile realm.

Preparing for the future in the mobile ecosystem

Since the mobile field is not yet dominated by giant players, many companies are trying to promote their technologies and change the paradigm. For example, with Android, Google is offering the framework to operators at no cost and trying to restructure the way the mobile world works. We believe that whoever wants to satisfy their customers' needs has to take into account the Flash Player, since the user expects the same browsing experience as they have when surfing the Web.

For instance, the Apple iPhone currently has its own software development kit (SDK) and doesn't have support for either Flash Lite or Java ME. Apple doesn't want to install Flash Lite on its operating system, but Adobe is showing a real commitment and is currently working on a Flash Player 10 that would be built specifically for the iPhone (we think this will be an optimized version of Flash Player 10 that includes extra APIs specifically for the iPhone and eliminates APIs that consume too many resources).

> *A mobile SDK is a set of tools that help developers create applications on a platform. It usually includes emulators and application programming interfaces (APIs) as well as an integrated development environment (IDE) or other helpful utilities.*

MID and UMPC devices

A MID is a multimedia mobile device, capable of accessing the Internet wirelessly, that is bigger than a smart phone but smaller than a UMPC. A couple of examples are shown in Figure 1-5. A MID is capable of running the Linux operating system with dual-core processors. It can even run Windows XP or Vista. Adobe released Flash 10 on Linux, so some MID devices are capable of running Flex and AIR applications.

Figure 1-5. The Samsung Q1 UMPC (left) and the Aigo P8860 MID (right)

UMPCs and MIDs are not selling as well as the manufacturers had hoped, at this time. According to market research groups, only about 11 million of these devices will be sold by 2011. We included them in this book because they can be used as testing platforms. You can use them to view your Flash 10 and AIR applications on smaller and less-capable devices than desktop PCs. By porting applications to these devices, we can prepare for the highly anticipated devices that will come to the market in 2009 and will support Flash 10 and AIR.

Digital home consumer electronics

Adobe is working to enable Flash in the digital home by focusing on products such as digital TVs, set-top boxes, Blu-ray, DVDs, and IPTV. Adobe is working closely with the two major players, Intel and Broadcom, to enable Flash on their chips.

Integrating Flash onto Intel chips

Calsoft Labs, Intel, and Adobe have been working on an evaluation port for customers looking to develop devices using Intel's Canmore media processor chip, which is also known as CE 3100 and is an X86-based system on a chip (SoC). The chip is targeted toward consumer electronics products such as digital TVs. The media processor offers leading-edge consumer electronics features for high-definition video support, home-theater quality audio, and advanced 3-D graphics. The chip offers performance, flexibility, and compatibility with Intel Architecture (IA) hardware and software.

In August 2008, Intel and Yahoo announced plans to codevelop the Yahoo Widget Channel, a technology that would allow TVs to connect to the Internet to access widgets, bits of software that would allow adding widgets to digital TV—think of the widgets you have for your personal computer.

> We talk about Flash Lite Mobile and device widgets in Chapter 5, when we explore working with Nokia S60 Web runtime widgets and when working on the Chumby nonportable consumer electronics device.

Samsung Electronics, Intel, and Yahoo put two key pieces of their plan in place to connect TVs to Internet-equipped widgets this year. Samsung agreed to support the technology inside of selected 2009 TVs, and Adobe said that it would port a version of its Flash Lite technology to the Intel Media Processor CE 3100, a key component in Yahoo Widget Channel–compatible set-top boxes.

Integrating Flash onto Broadcom chips

Broadcom is one of the major players in the set-top box and digital TV markets. Broadcom and Adobe Systems have announced that they will work together to integrate Flash into Broadcom's latest digital television and set-top box system-on-a-chip platforms: Adobe Flash Lite 3.0 will be supported in Broadcom's BCM3549, BCM3556, BCM7400, and BCM7405 solutions.

ARM-based devices

ARM-designed architecture is based on utilizing 32-bit Reduced Instruction Set Computer (RISC) processors, which consume less power than regular processors. ARM can be found in almost every mobile consumer electronics including PDAs, mobile phones, MP3 players, set-top boxes, MIDs, TVs, automotive platforms, calculators, and other mobile computing devices. Adobe announced that Flash 10 and AIR would be supported by the most recent ARM chip (ARM11). This marks the first release of Flash 10 and AIR on a smart phone and will potentially satisfy Apple's requirement to provide a fully functioning Flash Player for the iPhone, since the iPhone uses the Samsung ARM 1176 processor.

Getting to know the operating systems and platforms

Today's mobile phone operating systems and platforms available for developers consist of the major competitors Flash, Java ME, Symbian, Windows Mobile, Blackberry/RIM, as well as smaller competitors such as iPhone, BREW, Android, and Palm. Currently, the Symbian operating system dominates the market (see Figure 1-6).

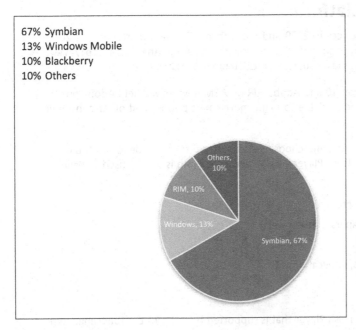

67% Symbian
13% Windows Mobile
10% Blackberry
10% Others

Figure 1-6.
Mobile device shipments worldwide by operating system, according to a 2007 Canalys press release (http://www.canalys.com/pr/2008/r2008021.htm)

Natively compiled vs. interpreted development languages

Applications can be developed natively for any operating system, usually in C or C++. There is an advantage to developing applications in the phone's native language: you gain speed and reduce the size of the compiled file, and you can access all the device capabilities. The main disadvantage is portability—you cannot port your content to other platforms. You'll also experience a long development cycle, since C++ requires much more code, due to the requirement of managing memory on C++ and other coding standards that make development more tedious.

To easily port applications across different platforms and build multiplatform applications, you might want to develop on platforms such as Flash or Java ME, which run on top of the mobile device's native operating system.

These are the benefits of using interpreted language over native language:

- You can port the application on several devices with few or no changes to the code.
- You can develop in your familiar IDE and don't need to learn new tools.
- Programming is easier, for instance C and C++ require memory management.
- You can leverage and use your existing code base or application.

Understanding the Flash platform

Flash Lite is expected reach 1 billion devices in 2009 and more than 2.5 billion by the end of 2010, which is about 46 percent of phones shipped globally, according to Strategy Analytics (http://www.strategyanalytics.com/default.aspx?mod=ReportAbstractViewer&a0=3727).

Additionally, the availability of Flash Player 10 and Adobe AIR on ARM devices will help Adobe ensure the full version of the Flash Player will be available to many more smart phones and other consumer electronics devices.

Each phone is based on an operating system, and choosing the platform to use depends on the operating system of the phone as well as the Flash Player version available. Flash is usually used to develop the following:

- Standalone Applications (games, etc)
- Personalized Content (e.g. wallpapers, screensavers)
- User interfaces
- Mobile Web content (games, ads, applications)

Working with Flash Lite

Flash Lite is an optimized version of the Flash Player that is supported by some of the following, common mobile platforms:

- Symbian operating system
- Windows Mobile operating system
- Binary Runtime Environment for Wireless (BREW) platform

Additionally, many OEMs and operators are shipping Flash Lite–enabled devices, including Chumby, BenQ, China Mobile, iRiver, KDDI, Kodak, LG, Motorola, Nokia, NTT DoCoMo, Samsung, Sony Ericsson, and Verizon Wireless.

As mentioned before, Flash Lite gives you tremendous value when developing. It allows access to about 80 percent of the phones worldwide (see Figure 1-6). By using the Flash Lite platform, you are not dependent on the operating system APIs and can leverage "write once, run anywhere" development practices, since an application can be ported easily to different operating systems, oftentimes with no changes, rather than developing new applications for each operating system.

The Flash Lite architecture (see Figure 1-7) is an optimized version of Flash and includes the following components:

- **Device APIs**: Flash Lite has access to some mobile phone services such as SMS, battery level, and others by utilizing the fscommand() and fscommand2() functions.

- **Network**: HTTP and HTTPS calls can be made to retrieve data, using getURL(), and e-mail, using mailto. Other APIs, such as loadMovieNum(), loadVariables(), and loadVariablesNum(), can be used to load data and media during runtime. XML and SWX are both supported in Flash Lite 2 and 3.

- **Drawing API**: This API allows dynamic or statistical creation of vector graphic and animations.

- **Dynamic data**: External XML data can be loaded and parsed directly, as well as using a proxy to bridge when needed.

- **Persistent data**: You can store local or mobile shared objects in the system directory of the mobile phone to retain the states of applications.

We'll cover more about Flash Lite in Chapter 2, when we cover the fundamentals of getting up to speed with the Flash Lite platform. We'll talk about Flash Lite player versions, player features, tools, packaging, and even content distribution and ecosystems for the platform.

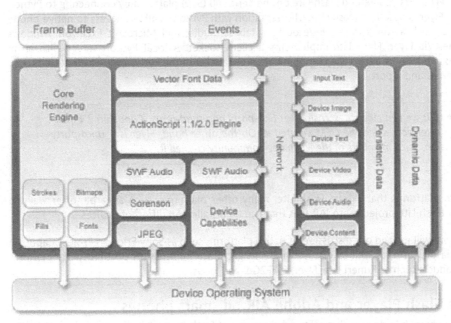

Figure 1-7. Flash Lite 3.1 architecture (courtesy of Adobe Systems)

Extending Flash Lite

Although we can access mobile device functionality, such as SMS and signal strength, using fscommand() and fscommand2(), we don't get full access to all the phone services. Other platforms extend Flash Lite features and give your application control over these "missing" device APIs. They allow us to use Flash and Java to create a powerful environment where you can enjoy both worlds and create a more powerful mobile user experience. Here are some examples of these additional services:

- Support for web services
- Threading
- Mobile payment
- Network connectivity using Bluetooth
- Security, such as encryption
- Access to native device APIs to tap into device hardware such as camera, accelerometer, GPS and more

Here are some examples of the platforms that add functionality to Flash Lite:

- **Capuchin**: This bridge created by Sony Ericsson connects Flash Lite with Java ME. The platform includes an API that allows Flash Lite to communicate with Java ME to access mobile services APIs. It works like this: All the device events are forwarded to Flash Lite, and you can then set listeners for events you are interested in. The communication between Flash Lite and Java ME is made through an intermediate class that sends and receives requests.
- **Flyer**: Flyer lets you extend Flash Lite on the Series 60 (S60) platform by connecting to Python script. Flyer is based on Flash Lite 2.1 integration with Python. It allows access to native phone services such as the camera, Bluetooth, database, audio, and Microsoft Excel on Windows Mobile. Via Flyer, Flash Lite implements a client socket. A local Python server with an IP address and a port allows the communication channel with the Python server identified by an IP address and a port.

> Note that we can classify extensions as first-party and third-party. Capuchin is a first-party extension, since the OEM created it. On the other hand, Flyer is a third-party extension, since members of the Flash Lite community created it.

In addition to platforms that extend Flash Lite, many other platforms, such as Jarpa, offer ways to package your Flash Lite projects into JAR files that can be installed on different devices.

In Chapter 7, we will expand our discussion of native platforms such as Sony Ericsson Project Capuchin and the Nokia platform, as well as discuss where to get more information on third-party platform extension products such as Kuneri Lite, Flyer, SWF2Go, and Janus.

Using the Flash Player and Adobe AIR on smart phones

There are already mobile devices that offer a full version of Flash Player 9 in the browser, such as the Nokia N810. As mentioned before, due to the continuous work of the Open Screen Project, Flash 10 and AIR will be soon available on high-end smart phones, such as those based on Symbian or on ARM processors, like T-Mobile's (Android based) G1 and Windows Mobile.

Understanding the Java ME platform

The Java Micro Edition (ME) platform (http://java.sun.com/javame/index.jsp), which is sometimes referred to as J2ME, is developed by Sun Microsystems. Java ME is an open source collection of APIs and a popular platform to develop games for mobile devices. It has a deep market penetration, since it is built into Symbian, which makes it instantly available to a large market segment. As shown in Figure 1-8, the Java ME architecture is made up of two components:

- Connected Limited Device Configuration (CLDC)
- Mobile Information Device Profile (MIDP)

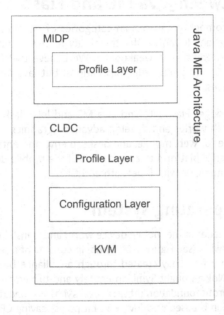

Figure 1-8.
Java ME architecture

CLDC includes the minimum set of configurations and libraries to operate the K Virtual Machine (KVM) and consists of the KVM, configuration, and profile layers. The advantage of the architecture, which is also a drawback, is that the KVM is configured to each profile: it's flexible to work with any device, but developers cannot just port their applications to any device, and modifications are sometimes necessary. Here are some technical details on the three layers:

- **KVM**: This layer is the implementation of the Java Virtual Machine (JVM) and is customized for a particular device's operating system. It supports a particular Java ME configuration. The KVM is small (50–80KB), uses little memory, and was designed for mobile processors with features such as multithreading and garbage collection.
- **Configuration**: This layer includes the minimum APIs available on all mobile devices and being used by the profile layer. Java Specification Requests (JSRs) define revisions of the Connected Device Configuration (CDC) specification. You can find a list of all the JSRs here: http://jcp.org/en/jsr/all.
- **Profile**: The CDC profile layer includes the minimum APIs available on a defined group of devices. Profiles are built for specific configurations, and applications are built for specific profiles. A device can support many profiles, and the application can be ported to any device that supports the profile.

> MIDP is a set of Java APIs that handles user interface and persistence data such as database and networking. MIDP sits on top of the CLDC.

Exploring the relationship between Java ME and Flash

In the mobile world, Java ME and Flash are competitors in certain categories of development, such as games. They are similar in many ways; for example, both offer the ability to create multiplatform applications. However, each platform has its strengths and weaknesses. We believe that Flash Lite is stronger when it comes to creating UIs, games, and multimedia applications, but Java ME is a more powerful platform for coding and device services.

As we mentioned before, Project Capuchin bridges Flash Lite and Java ME and lets Flash Lite access Java ME APIs, allowing developers to enjoy both worlds and develop advanced graphics, multimedia, and animated applications using the same code for web, mobile, and desktop environments with Flash Lite, as well as using the APIs of Java ME's powerful platform to access most of the mobile device hardware and software, such as the ability to communicate with Bluetooth and GPS.

Understanding the Symbian operating system

The Symbian operating system is currently the leader in the mobile device world and is installed in about 67 percent of the mobile devices shipped worldwide (see Figure 1-6). Symbian consists of a set of frameworks and an open operating system. Symbian was initially created through an alliance between Sony Ericsson, Nokia, Motorola, and Psion. In 2008, Nokia bought Symbian entirely and turned the operating system's development over to an affiliated nonprofit foundation (http://www.symbianfoundation.org/), and the software is available royalty free. Symbian is based on ARM, a 32-bit power-saving CPU, includes multitasking and memory protection, and follows the Model, View, Controller (MVC) design pattern. At the time of this writing, all Japanese device manufacturers run Symbian. Examples of manufacturers that have mobile models that use the Symbian operating system are Samsung, Sony Ericsson, LG, Sharp, and Motorola.

These are the main advantages to developing with Symbian:

- **Large distribution**: Close to 300 million Symbian-equipped mobile phones shipped in the first quarter of 2008, according to Symbian's limited financial statement.
- **Flexible platform**: Symbian is a flexible operating system that's easy to use for many developers. The Symbian OS supports many platforms, and you can develop applications in many other platforms such as Flash Lite, Java ME, OPL, Python, Visual Basic, and Perl. Additionally, you can use many different IDEs, such as Visual Studio, Eclipse, or the Java Wireless Toolkit.

The main disadvantage to working with Symbian phones is that applications must be digitally signed: Symbian version 8.1 allows installation of applications with restriction to some APIs. Symbian phones were once prey to many hackers, and phones were attacked by many viruses. Now, since Symbian version 9.x, you are required to pay a fee and digitally sign applications using Symbian's program before your applications can access most of the operating system APIs.

Exploring the relationship between Symbian and Flash

Symbian has embraced Flash, and future Symbian releases will include Flash 10 and Adobe AIR. Today, many of the phones that run the Symbian operating system are shipped with Flash Lite 2.1 preinstalled. Although Flash Lite doesn't have access to all Symbian APIs, some third-party development tools and platforms, such as Kuneri Lite, can extend Flash's capabilities. Nokia S60 Platform Services is another way to extend Flash Lite on newer S60 Symbian-based devices (we cover this in Chapter 7).

> *A good number of Symbian-based Nokia S60 devices support the Adobe Distributable Player Solution, which allows a Flash Lite 3.1 player to be installed (in conjunction with a Flash Lite application). We'll talk more about this in Chapter 3, when we discuss Flash Lite 3.1 features and capabilities.*

Understanding Windows Mobile

The Windows Mobile operating system is based on Microsoft's Win32 API. The current version, Windows Mobile 6.x, includes integration with Microsoft products such as Internet Explorer Mobile and Office Mobile, which includes applications like Outlook, Excel, and Word. The Mobile edition also includes Microsoft SQL 2005, Windows Live, and many other desktop products in compact and optimized versions to fit mobile devices. In 2007, 11 million Windows Mobile devices were shipped, and in 2008, about 20 million, according to Microsoft's chief executive officer Steve Balmer. Figure 1-9 shows the HTC smart phone using Microsoft Mobile.

Figure 1-9.
HTC Advantage X7501
Quadband GSM running
the Windows Mobile
operating system

Exploring the relationship between Windows Mobile and Flash

Flash Lite 2.1 has been supported since the release of Windows Mobile 5. The future release of Windows Mobile will include Flash Player 10 and Adobe AIR, as was exhibited at Adobe MAX 2008. There is already a working version of Flash Lite 3.1 for Windows Mobile.

A significant amount of Windows Mobile devices support the Adobe Distributable Player Solution, which allows a Flash Lite 3.1 player to be installed in conjunction with a piece of Flash Lite content. We'll talk more about this in Chapter 3, when we discuss Flash Lite 3.1 features and capabilities.

Understanding the Adobe Mobile Platform

Adobe's own Mobile Platform (`http://www.adobe.com/mobile/platform/index2.html`) was created for operators, OEMs, and content providers to allow them to deliver multiplatform mobile content and create a source of revenue. Mobile Platform is basically vanilla flavored and allows operators to brand and tailor the product to fit their exact needs.

The Adobe Mobile Platform solution is a special case in the overall Flash Mobile Platform from Adobe. Primarily, this platform is used by Qualcomm in its BREW mobile platform. It differs from the Flash Lite platform that runs on Symbian and other platforms that we'll cover in Chapters 2–8. We will not cover the Adobe Mobile Platform in this book, but may talk about it on the companion website at: `http://advancED.flashmobilebook.com/` at a future time and date.

The platform consists of a front end and a back end (client and server). Currently, the Mobile Platform allows integration of two applications:

- **Adobe Flash Home** was created for delivering dynamic home screens. It's a vanilla-flavored product that can be customized and personalized to deliver live data to create revenue for operators, content providers, and so on.
- **Adobe Flash Cast** was built for delivering rich content by pushing content in an occasionally connected data model. Flash Cast is also another white label product and includes client and server capabilities to provide subscribers access to data such as news, images, and videos games.

Note that the Adobe Mobile Platform is currently available for operators and OEMs. A developer can create content for the platform by partnering with a content provider, but the technology is very much still a niche one; it's not widely used by many partners.

Flash Home and Flash Cast are part of the Adobe Mobile Experience Suite, shown in Figure 1-10, and they allow the creation of subscription-based services that let mobile users subscribe to a channel. Each channel can be customized to the user's needs and can include any data or multimedia, such as music, news, and TV shows. Adobe also provides professional services such as technical support, customization, and training.

Verizon Wireless has created Dashboard, a portal using Flash Cast. Verizon Wireless expects Dashboard to become more and more available as new phones come to market. Developers and brands can create a channel, which is basically a collection of widgets, and can submit the channel to a content provider or directly through Verizon. See Figure 1-11. For more information, visit http://www.adobe.com/devnet/devices/verizon.html.

The applications are multiplatform and support different operating systems. Users can update each brand of application over the air and provide an on-device catalog for users.

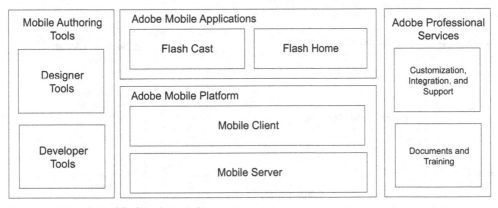

Figure 1-10. Adobe Mobile Experience Suite

Figure 1-11. Verizon Wireless Dashboard content

Understanding BREW

Binary Runtime Environment for Wireless (BREW) was developed by Qualcomm and started as a platform to sit on top of the operating system, like Java ME does. The technology evolved into an independent operating system by providing all the capability operating systems need. BREW allows developers to port applications across to all Code Division Multiple Access (CDMA) devices (making it multiplatform), as well as other air interfaces such as Global System for Mobile communications (GSM). BREW's native language is C/C++, and it supports both Flash Lite and Java ME. Figure 1-12 shows the BREW architecture.

The mobile air interface is the radio frequency (RF) communication link between the mobile station and the active base station. As the subscriber moves from one cell to another in the system, the active base station changes. Each changeover is known as a handoff, and the quality of the RF depends on many variables such as terrain and obstructions, such as steel frames.

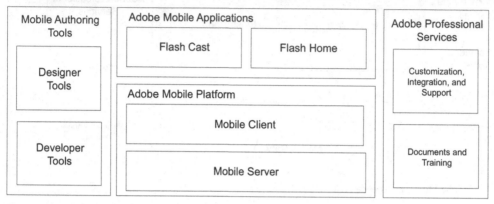

Figure 1-12. BREW architecture

The main advantage to using BREW is that it's air-interface independent. Since BREW runs between the application and the device's operating system, it allows the developer to create an advanced application independent from the system-level interface.

BREW's main drawback is that applications must be digitally signed. The platform allows the carrier to have control over content by forcing developers to digitally sign and test their applications. Obtaining a digital signature is expensive (each costs at least $400) and does not guarantee that the carrier will approve the application.

Exploring the relationship between BREW and Flash

Flash Lite is available on BREW and gets downloaded over the air (OTA) when needed, if Flash Lite is not already installed on the device. As a Flash Lite developer, you will use the BREW billing system and get paid for every download. The revenue share gets split between the operator, you (the developer), and any other parties involved. At the time of this writing, BREW supports Flash Lite 2.1 and is only available in the United States through Verizon Wireless.

The over-the-air (OTA) mechanism allows you to automatically update mobile devices. It requires the device software and hardware to support the feature—the device must be OTA capable. Many other terms are used in relation to OTA such as "firmware over the air" (FOTA) for updating the mobile firmware and "over-the-air parameter administration" (OTAPA) for changing settings of services.

There are two ways to get the Flash Lite content to the BREW phone:

- **Directly**: Digitally sign the application as a BREW developer, which will cost you about $400.
- **Indirectly**: Partner with content provider (publishers or aggregators) such as Atom Entertainment, Smashing Ideas, or Zed (also known as Mobigamez) to distribute and sell your content.

> The Adobe Mobile Platform solution is the next-generation technology Qualcomm is using on their BREW Mobile Platform. Flash Lite 2.1 for BREW differs technically from the Adobe Mobile Client, which is part of the overall Adobe Mobile Platform solution. Adobe Mobile Client uses a specialized mobile Flash Player model instead of using Flash Lite.

Understanding the iPhone SDK

While many phone manufacturers and operating systems, such as Sony Ericsson and Windows Mobile, were having a hard time meeting their own distribution projections, Apple revolutionized the cell phone industry with the release of the iPhone. The iPhone has become a fashion accessory and provides a large and easy-to-use touch screen user interface (see Figure 1-13).

The iPhone operating system, like Mac OS X, is based on the Mach kernel and the native language is Objective C, which is C with dynamically typed (known as Smalltalk) style messaging. The iPhone's user interface is created using core animation from Mac OS X version 10.5 and PowerVR MBX 3-D hardware. Applications for the iPhone can be bought directly from the iTunes Store.

At the time of this writing, there are two versions of the Apple iPhone based on the Internet connection:

- 2G Internet access through Wi-Fi or GSM/EDGE network.
- 3G fast Internet access of 3.6MB per second through third-generation UMTS/HSDPA.

These are the advantages of using the iPhone:

- **Popularity**: Apple had sold only about 5.7 million iPhones by April 2008 (according to Steve Jobs in *MacWorld's* January 2008 edition), which is insignificant in the mobile world. However, it is gaining popularity and exceeding expectations.
- **Multitouch-screen interface**: The iPhone supports a multitouch screen, and most of the phone capabilities can be controlled using it.
- **Developers set application prices**: Developers get to set the price of the application and get 70 percent of profits from application sales.

Figure 1-13.
The iPhone 3G

In comparison to other devices, these are the drawbacks to the iPhone:

- **Limited extensibility**: The iPhone currently has its own SDK, which, at the time of this writing, supports neither Flash Lite nor Java ME. The lack of support for Flash results in an incomplete browser experience. The iPhone also lacks support for many YouTube videos, since only about 10,000 videos are H.264 codec, and the rest are FLVs.

- **Reliance on iTunes**: The iPhone's operating system will not run software that has not been approved by Apple and purchased from the iTunes Store. Although software applications like JailBreak (http://www.iphonehacks.com/jailbreak_iphone/) allow you to install unauthorized applications, if you choose to do so, these applications can stop working with phone updates.

- **Unlocking and activation requirements**: The iPhone cannot be used with all carriers, since the SIM is locked and can only be activated with an authorized carrier. Although there are hacks to overcome this restriction, it results in not maximizing its distribution to the mainstream.

Exploring the relationship between the iPhone and Flash

Adobe is currently working on a Flash Player version for the iPhone that will satisfy Apple requirements, as mentioned before. Although no version has been released at the time of this writing, you port Flash content on the iPhone by combining the Enhance Your Experience Graphical Toolkit (eyeGT) with the b.Tween framework, which are 3rd party developer tools outside of both Adobe and Apple.

The b.Tween framework converts AcionScript-based applications into native C/C++ applications. The conversion requires very few changes to the ActionScript code and doesn't require the operating system runtime, allowing these applications to run on the iPhone. In Chapter 4, we will cover how to build and convert a Flash Lite applications to be ported for the iPhone.

Understanding the AOL Open Mobile Platform

The AOL Open Mobile Platform (http://dev.aol.com/api/openmobile) was announced in 2008 and was aimed at building a new development platform that will allow developers to build and distribute applications across different mobile device operating system such as BREW, Java, Linux, RIM, Symbian, and Windows Mobile.

The platform consists of three parts: an XML-based markup language, an optimized device client, and an application server. AOL will provide the tools and source code necessary to deploy.

Developers will be able to integrate applications and build on the platform with third-party APIs such as AOL's open APIs, AIM, AOL Mail, AOL Video, MapQuest, and others. Monetization will be achieved by deploying applications through AOL's Platform A advertising platform.

Exploring the relationship between the AOL Open Mobile Platform and Flash

It's not clear whether the platform will include Adobe Flash, since the announcement was made and no other information is available at the time of this writing.

Using Research In Motion (RIM) on the Blackberry

The Research In Motion (RIM) operating system is proprietary, and some functionality is unavailable unless developers digitally sign their applications with RIM. RIM doesn't check the quality or the security of code when developers digitally sign applications, so there are no restrictions on developers. It supports Java ME, and other APIs for mobile devices.

> *Wireless Application Protocol (WAP) is the standard provided by the Open Mobile Alliance (http://www.openmobilealliance.org/) and brings the Web to mobile devices through the use of the WAP gateway proxy that sits between the mobile phone and the Web.*
>
> *Wireless Markup Language (WML) is an XML markup language for WAP. It's the HTML of the mobile devices and specifies the protocol stack and application environment for browsing the Internet.*

Internet connection is available through WAP and developers can create cards (pages) in WML; WAP will convert regular sites to WML before displaying them on browsers.

Exploring the relationship between the Blackberry and Flash

At the time of this writing, there have been some rumors about Blackberry devices supporting Flash Lite 3 and Flash 10, but no support for Flash is available yet.

Understanding Android

Android is a newcomer in the mobile world and consists of a platform and operating system based on the Linux kernel. Android was developed by the Open Handset Alliance, of which Google is the main member. Android is almost fully open source, but a few parts of the Android SDK are closed. The first phone running Google Android was T-Mobile's G1, released in September 2008; see Figure 1-14.

Figure 1-14.
T-Mobile's G1 with the
Android operating system

The primary advantage to using the Android platform is that it's provided free to both the handset manufacturers and the application developers. As we explained previously, Google and the Open Handset Alliance are hoping that restructuring the current mobile ecosystem will give Android a competitive advantage over other operating systems.

The main drawback to Android is that it's not completely open source—some APIs in the Android SDK are closed.

Exploring the relationship between Android and Flash

Currently, Flash is not installed on the platform, but Adobe has shown a demonstration of a G1 working with Flash 10 at Adobe Max 2008. Keep in mind that Google's own sites, such as YouTube and Google Videos, contain quite a bit of content using the FLV format, which can only be played with the Flash player, so we believe that Google plans to include the Flash Player 10.

Understanding Palm Pre

Palm Pre is a multitouch smart phone from Palm, Inc. Though not yet released at the time of this writing, it has received very positive feedback from both users and reviewers. The Palm Pre is using a new operating system called webOS, which is based on Linux and offers true multitasking of applications. Multitasking allows the device to offer some cool features, such as the ability to view tabs as actual applications instead of image snapshots, as in the iPhone. The Pre has many features that are on par with the iPhone such as the interface and the touchscreen, and it runs an ARM 600 MHz Cortex A8 CPU and the Texas Instruments OMAP3430 microprocessor and image processor. It includes 7.4GB of storage and uses cloud services. Additionally, the Pre will be in the first generation of smart phones to use electromagnetic induction, which allows you to wirelessly charge your phone.

Exploring the relationship between Palm Pre and Flash

At the Mobile World Congress in Barcelona in 2009, Adobe announced that Palm has joined the Open Screen Project. Pre is expected to support Adobe's Flash 10 version for mobile devices, but no release date was set at the time of this writing.

Figure 1-15. Palm Pre device and its Safari cards

Summary

As the Adobe Open Screen Project is becoming a reality, we have an opportunity to create the same application experience across different platforms, and you can be part of these changes and build exciting applications.

Understanding the mobile landscape—the different players, tools, hardware, platforms, and operating systems—can help you while building applications. You can create and prepare applications today that work across different platforms, as well as create applications that have the foundations to be deployed on new devices with few or no changes.

In this chapter, we gave you an introduction to the mobile world, and we covered the mobile ecosystem. We explained the available devices such as phones, smart phones, MIDs, UMPCs, digital television, set-top boxes, and ARM-based devices.

We also introduced you to the major mobile operating systems and platforms and their relationships with Flash. We covered the Flash platform, Java ME, Symbian, Windows Mobile, Adobe Mobile, BREW, iPhone, AOL Open Mobile, RIM, Android, and Palm Pre platforms.

In the next chapter, we will dive deep into all the different versions of Flash Lite and the capabilities available in each version of Flash Lite. We'll also talk about the tools, products, and services that make up the Adobe Mobile Platform and device platforms. Toward the end of the next chapter, you'll get your feed wet by building and testing a Flash application targeted for mobile and devices.

Part Two

FLASH LITE PLATFORM OVERVIEW

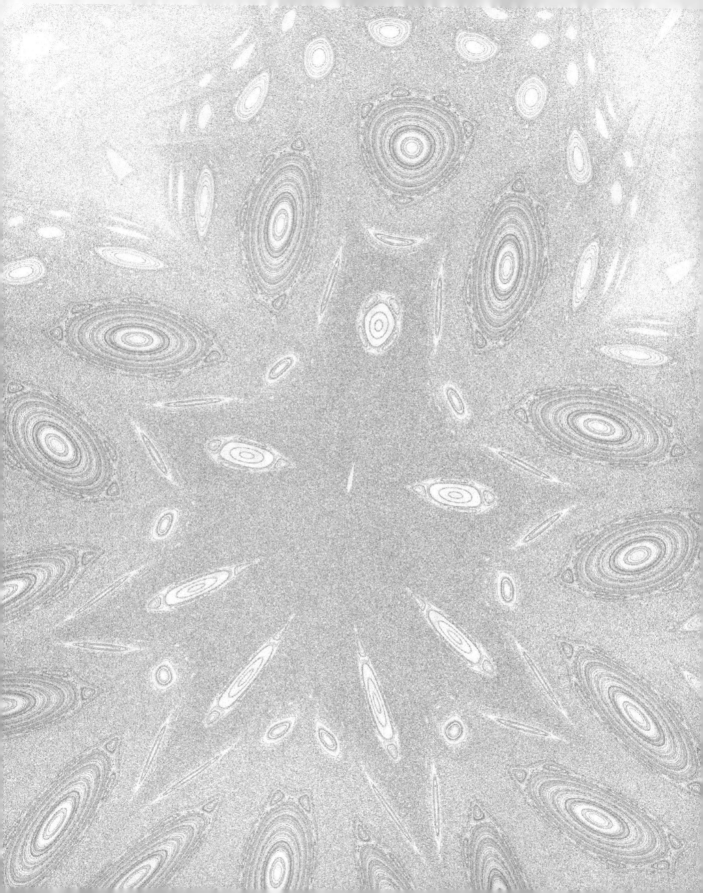

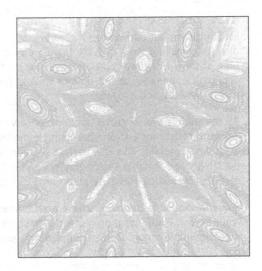

Chapter 2

FLASH LITE PLATFORM FUNDAMENTALS

In Chapter 1, you were given an overview of the ever-expanding landscape of mobile devices, platforms, and operating systems. This included discussions about Symbian, Windows Mobile, Android, BlackBerry/RIM, iPhone, Linux, BREW, and other mobile and device platforms.

If you think the number of development choices in the world of mobile is a bit overwhelming, well, frankly, it is! The sheer number and range of devices ranging from PDAs, mobile phones, MIDs, and other consumer electronics gadgets to suit each region's taste and culture is quite staggering, even for those working in the industry for *years*.

Thankfully, in mobile application development, the Flash Lite runtimes make it far easier to code between all of those platforms and devices, without having to deal with a lot of the time-consuming (and costly) native application porting and some of the nasty mobile development challenges we discussed in Chapter 1 (e.g., portability and device fragmentation issues).

Realizing multiscreen user experiences

It should be no surprise after reading the previous chapter that the world of mobile devices is, at last, starting to converge with and heavily complement the functionality of the PC desktop with functionality (such as web browsing, e-mail, and gaming).

Mobile devices far outnumber PCs worldwide. According to research conducted by the Gartner research firm (www.gartner.com) in 2007, there are over 3.5 billion cell phone subscriptions worldwide. At the time of this writing, we think we can safely say there are *millions* more, even despite the tough global economic conditions, at this time of writing. There is no doubt in our minds that 2009 *is* the year of mobile, devices, and gadgets!

As the mobile world grows, technology-savvy consumers want take advantage of their connected worlds through not just one but multiple mediums and across multiple screens, and much of it, they want while mobile! This is a perfect solution for our dear and beloved friend Flash because of its portability and scalable vector graphics support (we'll talk more about this later in this chapter, in the section, "Evaluating Flash Lite player pros and cons").

Some in the Flash community have even termed using Flash to fill this proverbial hole in the wall as "multiscreen Flash," or more correctly "multitarget Flash," which refers to the ability of Flash to run across multiple target devices and platforms relatively seamlessly, regardless of its screen size.

> *For more information on Adobe's take on what the significance of multiscreen Flash, or multi-target Flash, is please refer to the video titled: "Experiences that Scale Across Devices" that can be found at:* https://xd.adobe.com/#/videos/video/144.

We've already previously touched on the concept of Flash being used for multiscreen mobile user experiences in Chapter 1, but it's important to recognize that Flash Lite plays a huge part in the current reach into not only numerous mobile device platforms but also set-top boxes and other consumer electronics devices like iRiver and Chumby.

> *When we refer to "mobile and devices" in this book, we mean portable devices like cell phones as well as consumer electronics devices, such as TVs, portable game consoles, and portable media players.*

Through this book, you'll see real examples of where Flash Lite can be used to provide the kinds of fluid and highly responsive experiences mobile and device users have come to expect. You'll see how Flash and Flash Lite can be leveraged for user interfaces and applications, as well as how you can begin to target the next generation of mobile devices for AIR and Flash 10 development (see Chapters 9–14).

Getting up to Speed with Flash Lite

In this chapter, we continue our journey with Flash across mobile devices with Flash Lite platform development. In upcoming sections of this chapter, you'll get a bit more acquainted with some of the nuisances of Flash Lite development including the products, tools, services, development language (i.e., ActionScript), and environments involved.

Unfortunately, we can't cover every single platform, device, or mobile development nuisance (e.g., nasty fragmentation issues) that come up with Flash Lite. However, this chapter will attempt to explain a lot of what you need to know about the Flash Lite platform in a very concise format and give you hints at where to search for answers when you hit a brick wall with a Flash Lite–related problem or you just have a question about getting your content to market.

If you already know Flash and ActionScript (i.e., you're a hard-core desktop Flash, AIR, or Flex developer), the majority of this chapter will seem like review; feel free to skip ahead to Chapter 3 or even Chapter 4 (especially if you are a Flash Lite "veteran"). On the other hand, if you're new to the world of Flash, (e.g. a Java Mobile Developer, for instance), keep reading this chapter, as we'll point out the essentials and give you some pointers on the quickest way to get up to speed in developing with Flash Lite.

Either way, this chapter serves as a stepping-stone into the aspects of Flash development unique to the Flash Lite platform and offers some useful knowledge to help you tackle some of the more advanced topics later in this book.

> *Even if learning Flash Lite is not your main goal for reading this book and you're more interested in learning about Flash 10 and AIR, this chapter is intended to serve as a quick overview of Flash Lite platform fundamentals in a condensed format.*
>
> *A resource that we highly recommend when starting out with Flash Lite development is the URL http://www.adobe.com/go/4it, which links into a Getting Started with Flash Lite page composed and maintained by Adobe. It has links for documentation, tutorial videos, and much more.*

Now, let's talk about the Flash platform and how it's evolved. We'll cover products, tools, and services from Adobe, third-party companies, and even Flash community organizations and developers themselves. We'll also discuss how the Flash Lite platform came about, where it is now, and how you can take advantage of it.

The Flash platform

Over the past several years Flash has evolved significantly, in terms of its capabilities and its various uses. Flash is no longer strictly for animation and games. It's also being leveraged for video and rich Internet application (RIA) development, as well as for 3-D visualizations and top-selling console games using Flash for their game user interfaces!

How did Flash end up on devices? To make a long story short, Macromedia created Flash, Flash got adopted onto Pocket PC devices, and then Flash Lite 1.0 emerged as a successful replacement (first appearing in Japan through NTT DoCoMo, a mobile operator) as far back as 2003.

Flash Lite was, and still is, an optimized Flash player that runs within unique constraints, such as low memory, low processing power, as well as other unique mobile and device challenges (e.g., small screen size and short device battery lifespan). Macromedia was acquired by Adobe in 2006, and the rest, so to speak, is history.

Today, Flash Lite versions 1, 2, and 3 all exist in the mobile marketplace, across millions of devices worldwide from dozens of OEMs who support it, including Nokia, Sony Ericsson, and others contributing to the Open Screen Project.

Understanding the importance of the Open Screen Project

According to Adobe and its project partners, the Open Screen Project is "an industry-wide initiative, led by Adobe with the participation of industry leading companies, with one clear vision: enable consumers to engage with rich Internet experiences seamlessly across any device, anywhere." The idea is to have all those participating in this project working to provide a consistent runtime environment for open web browsing and stand-alone content applications, by leveraging the power of the Adobe Flash Player, Adobe AIR, and other Adobe mobile and device technologies that use the SWF binary delivery format for Flash (we'll cover much more about SWF in coming sections).

One of the main goals of the project is to have Flash content running across desktops, mobile phones, television set-top boxes, and other consumer electronicss as seamlessly as possible. Again, we refer to this as multiscreen Flash, and it is one of the many benefits of using Flash as opposed to other native development platforms such as C++.

With Flash, a game or an application written for one device platform can be ideally run on another platform or device, with few tweaks or changes to the source content. This is one of the promises of the Open Screen Project.

There is a growing number of industry partners, including ARM, Chunghwa Telecom, Cisco, Intel, LG Electronics, Marvell, Motorola, Open TV, MTV Networks, NBC Universal, Nokia, NTT DoCoMo, Qualcomm, Comcast, Samsung Electronics, Sony Ericsson, Toshiba, and Verizon Wireless, to name just a few companies. For more information, see http://www.openscreenproject.org/.

> In 2008, Adobe and Nokia started the Open Screen Project Fund that allows developers and companies to submit business plans and potentially be awarded portions of the $10-million-dollar fund to jump-start their ideas for products, services, and tools surrounding Flash on devices. We'll cover this further in our "Distributing and Monetizing Flash Lite content" section later in this chapter.

Exploring the Flash Lite platform

We talked a little bit about the Adobe Mobile Platform in Chapter 1. Flash Lite is just one piece of that evolving platform, but it's an important piece, if not a crucial part of it—even with Flash 10 and subsequent Flash Player technology (i.e., AIR and Flex) coming to devices in the long term.

If you're a developer looking into Flash on mobile and devices for the first time, it's essential to recognize that many devices in today's mobile marketplace are *already* running Flash Lite. It's a fact that cannot be ignored in our opinion, with millions of devices shipping with Flash Lite already preinstalled, or, through the Adobe Flash Lite Distributable Player. There's no waiting involved to get started *now* developing Flash mobile content! Just use Flash Lite!

> We will talk about the Adobe Flash Lite 3.1 Distributable Player more in Chapter 3 when we discuss aspects of Flash Lite 3.1 in more detail.

Flash Lite penetration statistics

It's hard to believe that in 2003 and 2004, only a few million handsets shipped with Flash Lite, and most of them were in Japan. If we jump forward to 2008, the number of mobile and devices supporting Flash was close to one *billion* worldwide. That's quite an impressive number, compared to say an arguably competing technology, such as Microsoft Silverlight, which (at the time of this writing) has yet to ship on a single, actual physical device.

> *You may be wondering exactly how these numbers of users break down and how you can take advantage of Flash Lite in the worldwide ecosystems today. We've got good news for you. This information is available!*
>
> *In 2007 and 2008, an independent marketing company called Strategic Analytics put out some reports containing the forecast for Flash Lite–installed across devices. This data was further compiled into simplified charts, so that information can be better scrutinized.*
>
> *According to Strategy Analytics, there are just about 1 billion Flash-enabled mobile devices worldwide in various regions (this is likely to be well over 1 billion by the time this book reaches the shelves).*
>
> *For more information about Flash Lite platform forecast numbers, please refer the white paper entitled "1.5 Billion Flash-Enabled Handsets to be Shipped in Next Two Years" at http://www.strategyanalytics.com/default.aspx?mod=ReportAbstractViewer&a0=4267.*
>
> *If you are looking for free compiled data (we don't blame you, given the price tag on the above link!) based on the forecast, check out the "Flash Lite Forecast" PDF over at http://www.flashmobileblog.com/ (just search on the main web page). This gives some handy data organized by Flash Lite version, region, and device models.*

Due to the worldwide penetration of Flash Lite, and strength in numbers, a majority of business opportunities are likely to be found within the Flash Lite realmat this time of writing. It will take some time before newer Flash Player technology (i.e., Flash 10, AIR, and eventually Flex) becomes readily available across devices. For this reason, in our opinion, if you want to be successful in addressing the largest amount of end consumers with Flash content, you need to be thinking about leveraging Flash Lite first and foremost, and Flash 10 secondarily, in your mobile game plan.

Of course, this book covers both halves of the spectrum—Flash Lite in Chapters 2 through 8 and Flash 10 in Chapters 9 through 14—as the roadmaps for both products are converging. We recommend that you take a very hard look at Flash Lite and see how it can help make your mobile and device projects and ideas a reality. You can do a lot with Flash Lite, despite its limitations and device constraints! As you read through this book, you'll see examples of how these challenges can be met (especially Chapter 4, which covers tips and tricks to Flash Lite development).

As we stated in Chapter 1, at the time of this writing, Flash 10 for SmartPhones is still under development by Adobe. This new player runtime is highly anticipated by most desktop developers. Devices to ship with Flash 10 implementations will follow (e.g., Flash is coming to Android and webOS, which is what the Palm Pre runs) soon thereafter. Chapters 9 through 12 cover Flash 10 and AIR across mobile devices.

However, on the flip side, millions of devices run versions of Flash Lite, right now, so keep reading this chapter if you want to get started immediately with Flash on mobile and devices and the consumers that have them!

Before we get into the coding aspects of the platform, it's important to talk a bit about the actual Flash Lite run-time player, which we introduced earlier in Chapter 1 but explore in a bit more detail here.

Evaluating Flash Lite player pros and cons

The Adobe Flash Lite player is an optimized, lightweight runtime environment intended for mobile phones and other portable, embedded, and consumer electronics devices. The player allows these non-PC devices to run Flash Lite content. It's not without its pros and cons though, compared to other mobile runtimes, and in this section, we explore a few of the ones that come immediately to our minds (but there are probably others as well).

Here are some of the advantages to using the Flash Lite player over competing mobile runtimes found today:

- **Friendly development environment**: Adobe Creative Suite and Device Central (and the Device Central SDK) provide a nice environment for rapid mobile software prototyping and interactive testing across a wide range of target devices and platforms.

  Device Central can save up to 80 percent (according to our estimates) of testing time by reducing the amount of time spent transferring files to and from devices for testing! In terms of Flash Lite, it's the best thing since sliced bread!

- **Vector support**: In addition to bitmap support, Flash Lite offers rendering of vector graphics that allow for scaling, rotation, and transformations with loss of image quality.

- **Content portability**: Flash Lite is one of the best mobile runtimes out there for migrating desktop content to mobile format with less effort. It might be a stretch to call it "write once, run anywhere (WORA)" but it's as close as a mobile developer is going to get to porting content seamlessly!

  You can take content from one device and with minimal tweaks and changes, have that same content run on another Flash Lite device platform. Flash Lite 1.1 to Flash Lite 3.0 offers the best restriction on APIs and allows for ports to occur. It's not true WORA, but it's as close as you're going to get!

- **Small file size**: Because of its SWF binary file format (which we cover in the next section), file size for Flash Lite content is kept very low, which is ideal for mobile device conditions where memory is a precious developer resource commodity due to a device's format factor (and price). We'll talk more about SWF files and the MovieClips, buttons, and graphic symbols that make up SWFs later in this chapter.

The disadvantages of the Flash Lite player follow:

- **Learning the tools**: For newcomers to the Flash platform, it takes some time to learn the Flash IDE (Integrated Development Environment), timeline, and associated concepts like MovieClips and buttons (we'll cover these later in this chapter). However, learning the ActionScript programming language is easier than other native languages (e.g., Symbian C++, and Objective-C), given its similarities to the popular web development language JavaScript (i.e., ActionScript is an ECMAScript-based development language).

> *On the plus side of things, with actionScript, you do not have to worry about challenging native coding concepts such as memory management and can instead focus on developing applications. This is a real win for developers looking to build applications much more quickly.*

- **Fragmentation**: Device fragmentation still exists across Flash Lite–enabled device platforms (typically across APIs but bugs can crop up causing incompatibilities between models and versions). The number of versions of Flash Lite can be a problem, since each version's capabilities differ, and ActionScript support is different between Flash Lite versions. For example, some legacy security policies are incompatible with Flash Lite 3.

- **Developer adoption rate**: Flash Lite was adopted by OEMs and data providers (i.e., operators using Flash Cast server technology). Early in its evolution, early adopter developer numbers were low because there were relatively few distribution paths for generating revenue from Flash Lite content. This changed by 2008, after Adobe switched focus from the original licensing model of the Flash Lite player to the Adobe Open Screen Project (http://www.openscreen-project.org/—the focus shifted from selling the Flash Lite runtime to OEMs to helping developers build content (i.e., applications) for the millions of devices with Flash Lite players installed in the worldwide marketplace.

Now that you've heard some of pros and cons of the Flash Lite runtime, it's time to turn our attention to some of the details of the player architecture.

Flash Lite player architecture

Although the architectures of Flash Lite versions 1.0, 1.1, 2.0, 2.1, 3.0, and 3.1 vary slightly, they have core pieces that are common.

All Flash Lite players have a core rendering engine, as well as an ActionScript engine (see Figure 1-7). Since this book caters more toward the developer crowd, we'll also be focusing much more on the ActionScript 2.0 side of things, rather than the designer mindset (however, Chapters 6 and 8 will appeal to you, designers).

There are many working components that compose the player, including the ActionScript 1.0 or 2.0 engine, core rendering engine, as well as various media components such as graphics, audio, text, and video to interact with lower level device APIs present on devices.

Flash Lite versions 1.1, 2.x, and 3.x also support dynamic and persistent data, as well as vector rendering and event management. There are quite a lot features for a small player architecture that, incidentally, fits in less than a couple megabytes in total size—pretty impressive! We'll try to cover how these features can be applied to Flash Lite projects as we move through this chapter and into subsequent chapters on Flash Lite in this book.

But what would this optimized Flash Lite player be without all the tools required to design, develop, test, and even deploy the application content that developers slave night and day over? Let's cover some of the tools that make it possible to generate the mobile content that makes Flash Lite really shine.

> *For the purposes of this book, we mainly stick to Flash Lite 2.x and 3.x, except in this chapter, where we do cover some Flash Lite 1.1 since some people might be porting content or working in unique situations (e.g. Flash Cast 1.2).*

Introducing Flash Lite products, tools, and services

Just like the Flash platform is composed of Flash Player 10, AIR, Flex, and other tools, the Flash Lite platform also contains several products and services. Some of these are available to developers directly (e.g., Adobe Creative Suite CS3 and CS4), while others are not, except by collaboration with Adobe (e.g., Adobe Flash Cast and Adobe Flash Home).

If you're a long-time Flash developer, you'll need no explanation for these products. In case you're coming from the mobile development world or are otherwise new to Flash, Adobe Creative Suite (CS) is the integrated development environment (IDE) for creating desktop and web Flash, as well as Flash Lite content (images and videos) and SWF-based applications (we'll talk about SWF files later in this chapter).

Adobe Creative Suite 3 and 4

Adobe Creative Suite consists of several products. The ones that offer mobile workflow support are Illustrator, Photoshop, Captivate, After Effects, Premiere, Dreamweaver, Fireworks, and Flash.

If you're wondering what version of Adobe Creative Suite to get, it really comes down to your needs. In our opinion, when developing Flash Lite 1.1 or 2.x content, CS3 is a valid choice. For Flash Lite 3.0 and 3.1, however, it really makes sense, going forward to utilize CS4, because of the new features of Adobe Device Central CS4 (which we will discuss more, shortly).

With mobile and device content, using the IDE in CS3 or CS4 can be very beneficial to workflow, because working with visual assets and media is easier than working strictly with a code-based work-flow (e.g., compiling ActionScript projects from Eclipse). CS3 and CS4 (the newer version of the two, just to be very clear) are commercially available to use for projects. For more information, see http://www.adobe.com/products/creativesuite/.

> *There are loads of excellent resources on getting up to speed with Adobe CS3 and CS4. However, this book does not concentrate on teaching you the Flash IDE, CS3, or CS4 from a visual stand-point. For more resources, please see a book such as* Foundation Flash CS4 for Designers *(ISBN: 978-1-4302-1093-1).*

Flash CS3 and CS4

The Flash IDE is the development environment present in CS4 for working with both Flash and Flash Lite. As you work through Chapters 3–8, you'll use this tool as the crux for much of the Flash Lite development discussions in this book (we'll also provide examples using Open Flash alternatives such as MTASC). For more information about Flash CS4, see http://www.adobe.com/products/creativesuite/flash.

Device Central CS4

Device Central is an emulator that can be used to test mobile and device content, particularly Flash Lite, before it needs to be pushed onto actual devices for testing.

As we progress through later chapters on Flash Lite in this book, we'll explore many of the time-saving features of Device Central CS4, including the newly added SDK, as well as some of the built-in tools like performance and memory panels that allow developers to save time while testing their mobile content, such as performance panel, memory monitoring panel, automated scripting, and more. We'll cover a lot of this in Chapter 3 when we talk about the Flash Lite 3.1 workflow.

For more information about Adobe Device Central (including access to device profile updates to extend Device Central's available devices), go to http://www.adobe.com/products/creativesuite/devicecentral. There are also some great video tutorials covering Adobe Device Central on tv.adobe.com (just search on "device central").

Adobe Captivate CS4

Adobe Captivate CS4 is one the newest products added to CS4 and is used to author and produce e-learning video content. With the Captivate product, it's possible to rapidly author e-learning content (e.g., corporate or classroom training) with interactivity, scenario simulations, and quizzes. Captivate is part of the overall Adobe eLearning Suite. It supports video export to Flash Lite 3 native Flash video (FLV) format, so mobile e-learning content can be created. We'll talk more about Flash 10 and Flash Lite 3 video in Chapter 15, when we cover how device and native video work across Flash-enabled devices.

Flash Cast

We briefly mentioned Flash Cast in Chapter 1, and we'll continue our discussion here.

Flash Cast is essentially a native mobile client application and set of back-end servers that deliver Flash Lite SWF-based content. The content is delivered over the air (OTA) at periodic intervals through a channel metaphor, where users can subscribe to content they wish to consume (e.g., sports, news, and stock channels).

If you are thinking that Flash Cast is like push technology, you are not far off. If you want to get specific, it's actually periodically pulling content data. Basically, Flash Cast is push technology for mobile devices (especially cell phones in Japan). Flash content is periodically delivered down to user's phones using scheduled pull calls from the Adobe Mobile Client front-end user interface on the device to a remotely network connected Flash Cast server.

With Flash Cast, it's possible to create mobile experiences where subscribed real-time data is streamed down over the air onto consumers' devices without the need for searching out the content directly.

Newer versions of Flash Cast utilize the Adobe Mobile Client, which is a specialized Flash Lite player within the Adobe Mobile Platform (see the "Exploring Adobe Mobile Client" section in this chapter for more information).

> *In this book, we will not cover Flash Cast in depth. Although it is an innovative (and admittedly an advanced) product, it is still primarily only used behind the scenes by operators (such as NTT DoCoMo's iChannel in Japan, Chunghwa Telecom's Channel Me service in Taiwan, Telenor in Sweden, and Verizon Wireless in the United States, which calls it Dashboard). Adobe keeps Flash Cast under lock and key, and it remains very proprietary technology. Contact Adobe if you are interested in developing for the Flash Cast platform.*

If you want more information about Flash Cast, please see http://www.adobe.com/products/flashcast/ or if you are in the United States and interested in Verizon's Dashboard, see http://www.vzwdeveloper.com/.

Flash Home

This is a client-server solution for operators and OEMs that allows for rich, dynamic mobile home screens to be delivered to handsets and other platforms. By allowing for customized screens and live data, devices that support Flash Home technology can feed users information such as news and entertainment services. Flash Home can provide users with a mobile experience that integrates custom call logs, messaging, and device indicators such as battery and signal, so that a much more personalized experience is possible on mobile device idle screens.

> *Flash Home utilizes the custom Adobe Mobile Player for playing back SWF-based content. We will talk about this type of specialized Flash Player for mobile devices later in this chapter.*

For developers, the chances for working with the Flash Home product/service remain mostly in the hands of OEMs. To date, there has been little available publically to developers. In the future, as the platform evolves, there may yet be opportunities for Flash Lite developers to create custom animations and other highly personalized content for devices with Flash Home. Nevertheless, this proprietary product is something important to include in our discussion of the overall Flash Lite platform, since it allows for highly personalized mobile experiences to be created. For more information about Flash Home, you can go to http://www.adobe.com/mobile/solutions/flashhome/.

Adobe Mobile Application Builder

Adobe Mobile Application Builder is a user interface to manage the development of Flash Lite content for Flash Cast. It is a replacement to the legacy Flash 8 extension for authoring Flash Cast channel content.

The user interface to Mobile Application Builder (MAB) looks very similar to Device Central CS4, and it reuses a lot of the same IDE. However, it also has some differences that allow Flash Lite content to be published for Flash Cast. Since we will not cover Flash Cast in this book, we will not be covering MAB in any depth (but we still think it's cool).

For future reference, developers interested in acquiring MAB and developing Verizon Wireless Dashboard Flash Lite channel content using MAB can submit their inquires to the Verizon Wireless Developers Program (http://www.vzwdevelopers.com/).

Adobe Mobile Application Packager

This latest tool from Adobe allows Flash Lite developers to create packaged Flash Lite content that can be deployed. At the time of this writing, both .cab for Microsoft Windows Mobile and Nokia .sis formats are the most current supported deployable packaging formats.

> We'll cover more about Adobe Mobile Packager in Chapter 3 when we talk specifically about the Flash Lite 3.1 player runtime.

Adobe Flash Lite 3.1 Distributable Player

The Adobe Flash Lite 3.1 Distributable Player is a newer Flash Lite player technology that is a native mobile application installed onto supported devices (currently Windows Mobile 6 and Nokia Series 60). It essentially installs the Flash Lite 3.1 player onto the supported target device when launched (if there is not a Flash Lite 3.1 player installed already).

The Flash Lite Distributable Player allows itself to be bundled together (we'll talk about packaging later in this chapter) with Flash Lite developer content such as games and applications (in SWF format) and allows for the Flash Lite player to be delivered and installed OTA (if it is not already installed or if a newer player version is available).

Previously, with Flash Lite 1.0, 1.1, and 2.0, the Flash runtime was always preinstalled before devices were shipped to end users.

> We'll talk much more about the Distributable Player in Chapter 3, where we explore Flash Lite 3.1, or you can check out http://labs.adobe.com/technologies/distributableplayer/.

The underlying delivery method of all Flash Lite content, regardless of player version is the SWF file format, so we'll cover that next.

Working with the SWF file format

"SWF" stands for "Shockwave Flash" and is pronounced "*swiff.*" SWF is an open format for composing rich multimedia user interfaces on a number of platforms, including mobile and devices.

SWFs run within the Flash Lite player when they are executed. Typically, this involves launching a SWF through a mobile user interface or mobile device catalog (think "App Store"), which is sometimes known as an operators deck. SWF files have the file extension .swf, although Flash Lite SWF files are sometimes packaged into other mobile formats (we'll talk about packaging formats such as .sis, .nfl, and others later in this chapter).

Although Flash is most well known for its vector animation capabilities, it can also play back video and provide powerful, interactive experiences for users. During playback, SWF supports text rendering and audio, as well as probably some of the best video capabilities found in today's connected world (we'll look at working with Flash and Flash Lite Video in Chapter 15).

SWF files have typically been optimized to be small because of the constraints of the early Web (before 2000), where network bandwidth was much less than it is by today's standards (we have high-speed fiber instead of dial-up modems for PCs, for one thing!).

The SWF format is well suited to the unique device constraints found on many handsets and other devices that permeate mobile markets around the world (i.e., devices with limited processor speed, limited available memory footprint, and low network bandwidth).

Publishing SWFs

To generate SWF files, there are essentially two core workflows: compiling via the Flash IDE and compiling with open source Flash compilers, like Motion-Twin ActionScript Compiler (MTASC) and Eclipse.

> *In this book (depending on the material covered), we may opt to use the Flash IDE publishing method for some of our Flash Lite examples. This is merely our preference for the material covered, not necessarily a reflection on which approach is right or wrong to use. Other times, we'll be using an open source compiler (particularly in Chapters 9 through 14).*

Compiling through the Flash IDE   Adobe Flash (either CS3 or CS4) is used to take media assets (such as graphics, sound, and video), plus ActionScript code, and compile an end result SWF to be deployed onto Flash-enabled devices. When working within the IDE, the .fla source file is used to store all the assets of the Flash application (e.g., MovieClips, graphics, buttons, text, sound, and video).

In this book, many of our Flash Lite walkthroughs will be with the Flash IDE. Contrary to popular belief with hardcore ActionScript developers, using the IDE makes a lot more sense for less-code-intensive content such as animations, especially where the ActionScript is particularly sparse (e.g., screensavers and wallpapers).

Open source compilers   MTASC is an open source ActionScript compiler available for use publishing Flash Lite SWFs. Although Flash Lite player versions cannot be specifically targeted as with the Flash IDE (there's no dialog option as there is in Flash CS products), it is possible to compile Flash versions such as 7 and 8 that are largely compatible with Flash Lite 2.x and Flash Lite 3.x, respectively.

For a comprehensive list of open source Flash projects, such as MTASC, it's best to refer to the community-driven resource, OSFlash, at http://www.osflash.org/ (the projects are maintained at http://osflash.org/open_source_flash_projects/).

> *We'll talk more about using MTASC more in Chapter 5, when we cover developing Flash Lite widgets for the Chumby (a Wi-Fi–enabled, Linux-based, open source, touch-screen device).*

Online ActionScript compilers An online compiler for Flash Lite is located at http://www. flashlitegenerator.com/. It can be used to generate SWF files dynamically at runtime over an available Internet connection. The online compiler allows for SWF files to be created. At this time, the Flash Lite generator web site service is only offered to a select pool of clients who have a relationship with the creator of the site, Kuneri.

Deploying SWFs

The SWF file is the most common delivery format for Flash. Most Flash Lite–enabled devices will render a .swf if it is copied over to a supported device. For the most part, Flash Lite 1.1 files will run within a Flash Lite 2.x and 3.x player, making Flash Lite versions *typically* backward compatible (note that Flash Lite 3 security changes come into play with versions 1.1 and 2.x running inside of the Flash Lite 3.x player runtime).

Advantages When deploying straight SWF files, there is no need for an extra step in packaging. The content will run whenever the SWF is loaded in the Flash Lite player on a device. The SWF can be run as a stand-alone Flash file, or in some cases, the SWF will be loaded by a mobile web browser off a remotely located web server. Deploying SWF content in this manner might be good for sending content for quick testing, but typically when distributing Flash Lite content, the end result will be packaged into a mobile delivery format. We cover these formats later in this chapter in the "Packaging Flash Lite Content" section.

Disadvantages One disadvantage of SWF format is that the user must remember where the SWF resides on a device in order to run it. Oftentimes, the location of SWF content on devices is not straightforward (e.g., the SWF is sometimes stored in an obscure file path location or in a message inbox). Users need an easier way to find content on a device. SWF files do not have a user customizable icon, so users will be looking at the default system icon for SWF at best, which is not a great experience compared to other mobile content delivery methods. However, these problems can be solved by packaging up Flash Lite content into custom file formats that are not SWF based. Packing provides an installation mechanism (see the "Packaging Flash Lite Content" section of this chapter) for Flash Lite content that is easier for users to install and run.

One of the other disadvantages of SWF format is that there is limited protection of SWF content from those who wish to copy it. Digital rights management (DRM) and forward locking are not supported by Flash Lite, natively, but can be provided by OEMs, for example, Nokia, who choose to implement them.

In addition to the copy protection problem, SWFs are also not encrypted and can be decompiled, and the source code can be retrieved easily.

Another caveat is that SWFs do not allow direct certificate signing but must be packaged in the .sis packages required by some content aggregation intake systems (e.g., the Nokia OVI Store). Again, we'll talk more about packaging later in this chapter.

In terms of Flash Lite, it's important to know the SWF file format and how it is leveraged on various mobile and portable devices, in various regions worldwide. Unlike Flash SWF files on the Web running on PCs, Flash Lite across non-PC devices has many use cases (e.g., screensavers, wallpapers, and ring tones) and thus supports many Flash Lite content types.

Exploring Flash Lite content types

Traditionally, on the Web (*not* the mobile Web, mind you!), Flash has been used within the confines of a web browser for content such as advertisements (Flash banner ads), rich Internet applications (RIAs), games, video (both streaming and progressive clip downloads), and even 2-D and 3-D data visualization.

On portable and mobile devices, up to this point, Flash Lite has been leveraged differently due to unique device constraints such as memory, CPU, screen size, and performance. Flash Lite acts as a Swiss Army knife for rich mobile media content. Since 2004, various OEMs have been using Flash Lite to solve their mobile user experience needs (e.g., user interfaces, animated ring tones, etc.). To accommodate these needs, Flash Lite content types were created.

Content types include screensavers and wallpapers as well as applications and even special cases for device OEMs like user interfaces, animated ring tones, and more (see the "OEM-Specific Flash Lite Content Types" section). Based on the targeted device platform (and sometimes the specific model), devices running Flash Lite often support, and therefore are able to render, one or more Flash Lite content types.

The definitions and operations of these content types are up to the OEMs. However, some of them are common across multiple device platforms. The most prevalent Flash Lite content types, which appear on many devices and platforms, include the stand-alone player, browser, screensaver, and wallpaper types.

> *In Device Central CS4, Flash Lite content types have been consolidated from Device Central CS3 down to a few core content types. For instance, Sub LCD content does not appear in CS4, since it falls under stand-alone content that happens to run on secondary screens.*

Nokia Series 60 (S60) devices typically support stand-alone, browser, and screensaver content types, while BREW devices support mainly Flash Lite application content and sometimes screensavers.

Using Device Central CS3 or CS4, you can get the supported content types for a particular device by looking at the Flash tab under its Device Profile.

Supported content types for devices are always in flux, so it's critical to look to Device Central to determine what is and isn't supported before projects even leave the planning phase. Always plan your target device sets (and addressable world markets) for your content early!

It is important to remember that not all devices support all content types, and it's up to the OEM which content types are and are not supported. For example, Chaku Flash (i.e., animated ring tones) has been utilized on some handsets available in Japan, but this content type is not supported by default on Western Flash Lite–enabled devices (well, not without adding a third-party product like, Kuneri Lite, which allows Flash Lite to be tapped into low-level device APIs).

Primary content types

Content types also vary by Flash Lite version. Most Flash Lite content types unique to Japan are Flash Lite 1.1 based. All other content types appear in Flash Lite 1.1, 2.x, and 3.x.

Here is a breakdown of some of the content types available today:

- **Stand-alone player**: This is the most common Flash Lite type. Typically, an icon (often an .svg graphic) launches the Flash Lite SWF on a device.

  Stand-alone content can either launch full screen or allow for soft key labels to be displayed. SWF files can reside on the device storage (e.g., memory card or device memory) or within on-device message inboxes (e.g., Nokia Message Inbox).

  Stand-alone SWF content will be packaged into another mobile delivery format, such as .nfl, .sis, .cab, and other archive file types (we talk about these later in this chapter).

  Common platforms that support stand-alone content are Nokia Series 40 (S40) and S60 and Windows Mobile, though other OEMs do allow Flash Lite to run from launch icons.

- **Browser**: An important component of mobile is the ability to view web-based content from a mobile device to offer a pleasant Web-surfing experience. For example, the latest S60 devices from Nokia support Flash Lite 3 video playback inside the default S60 device browser, thus giving users the ability to watch optimized video clips from services such as YouTube).

  Nokia supports Flash Lite in its S60 mobile browser, Opera has support in newer versions of its browser, and Sony provides support in their Mylo and PlayStation Portable (PSP) web browsers (yes, the PSP *does* support Flash—Flash Player 6 to be exact, *not* Flash Lite). Many other OEMs are starting to utilize Flash inside of mobile web browsers as well, such as the recent HTC Hero, Android based device.

  Historically, Flash Lite content found in Japan has been browser based and is used for user interfaces of mobile web sites, games, and other use cases within their *Keitai* (i.e., mobile culture).

  More and more OEMs are deciding to leverage Flash and Flash Lite in a browser context, as more devices come preinstalled with mobile web browser capabilities; for example, newer Archos Portable Media Players support Flash content running inside their onboard web browser.

- **Screensaver**: Just as desktop machines have screensavers, some mobile devices offer support for animated idle screen content. This allows end users to personalize their mobile device with cool Flash screensaver animations. In addition to Flash animation, Flash Lite screensaver content often includes clocks, calendars, and other notification information (e.g., battery life and signal strength). Nokia, Sony Ericsson, and other OEMs support screensaver content types depending on the device models. Often, OEMs will have preinstalled Flash Lite screensaver content before a consumer buys a phone, so selling screensavers in the marketplace is not easy.

> *Kuneri Lite (a company specializing in Flash Lite, located in Finland) has a service called Pikkoo that allows developers to upload Flash-based screensavers and wallpaper to a community distribution and sharing site. More information about Pikkoo can be found at http://www.pikkoo.com/.*

- **Wallpaper**: Some devices also support Flash Lite wallpaper, which allows customization of backgrounds. Since wallpapers often are overlaid with important device information such as date/time, signal, and so on, it's important to design wallpapers so that these elements are not obscured. Nokia and Sony Ericsson are both proponents of Flash Lite wallpaper, but it is less popular than screensaver content.

> *"Reactive" describes screensaver and wallpaper content that changes (i.e., reacts) to the variable status of a device. This often includes such things as battery life, signal strength, or even GPS coordinates. For example, when a battery is low on a device, a Flash Lite screensaver might display a skull-and-cross-bones animation, and when it is full, it might display an animated smiley face.*

OEM-specific content types

Some OEMs decide to create their own Flash Lite content types that are *very* region and device specific. Unique use cases of Flash Lite SWFs include the following:

- Address book employs Flash Lite to allow users to associate a SWF with entries in their device's address book application. DoCoMo and VodafoneKK (Japan only) are currently the only OEMs offering this content type.

- Alarm uses Flash Lite to let the user select a SWF file to play for a device's alarm. KDDI and VodafoneKK (Japan only) are currently OEMs offering this content type.

- Application is primarily used within the Flash Lite 2.x for BREW. For all intents and purposes, it is similar to the stand-alone content type, in that it's meant for deploying applications on BREW-specific devices (e.g., Verizon Wireless with LG, Motorola, and other devices).

> *Flash Lite for BREW uses .mod and .mif files, not SWF files, when run on BREW devices. These files are generated using the Flash Lite BREW postprocessor. We will not cover Flash Lite for BREW in this book, since the Adobe Mobile Client is now supported on the new BREW Mobile Platform. If you're interested in leveraging Flash Lite on the BREW Mobile Platform, you can visit the Adobe support page at http://www.adobe.com/devnet/devices/verizon.html.*

- Calling history uses Flash Lite to display an image or animation associated with entries in a user's address book, along with name and phone number. KDDI (Japanese Casio devices only) is currently an OEM offering this content type.

- Calling screen displays Flash Lite animation when the user receives a call or makes one. KDDI (Japan only) is currently an OEM offering this content type.

- Chaku Flash was a content type supported by Japanese devices (KDDI) that allowed animated Flash content to be played back on incoming calls. It was also known as "animated ring tones with Flash Lite."

> *The Kuneri Lite API offers a plug-in that allows Nokia S60 devices to support animated Flash Lite ring tones. Please refer to http://www.kunerilite.net/ for more information.*

- Data box uses Flash Lite to render content in a device's data box application and allows a user to manage and preview multimedia files on the device. DoCoMo, KDDI, and VodafoneKK (Japan only) currently offer the data box content type.

- Data folder uses Flash Lite to render content in the device's data folder application, which lets the user manage and preview multimedia files on a device. KDDI (Japan only) is currently an OEM offering this content type.

- Icon menu uses Flash Lite to allow a user to select custom icon menus for the device's launcher application (used by the UI launcher content type). KDDI (Japanese Casio phones only) is currently an OEM offering this content type.

- Image viewer uses an image viewer application that lets the user manage and preview multimedia files on the device, including SWF files. This content type was adopted by various OEMs in Japan.

- Receiving or incoming call supports playing Flash Lite animations on receiving an incoming voice call on a supported device. DoCoMo, KDDI, and VodafoneKK (Japan only) are currently OEMs offering this content type.

- Sending mail/mailer uses Flash Lite to display an animation when a user sends or receives an e-mail message. KDDI and VodafoneKK (Japan only) currently offers this content type.

- Multimedia uses Flash Lite to preview SWF files (as well as other multimedia file formats). KDDI (Japan only) currently offers this content type.

- My Picture uses the My Picture application to allow users to manage and preview SWF files on a device, as well as other image file formats. DoCoMo (Japan Only) is currently the OEM offering this content type.

- Open EMIRO allows Flash Lite content to be displayed when the device is returning from stand-by mode. This is similar to the wake-up screen content type. KDDI (Japanese Casio devices only) is currently an OEM offering this content type.

- SMIL player uses Flash Lite to preview SWF files (and other multimedia file format). KDDI (Japan only) is currently an OEM offering this content type.

- Standby screen, like wallpaper, allows Flash Lite content to render on a device's wallpaper. DoCoMo and KDDI (Japan only) are currently OEMs offering this content type.

- Sub LCD allows Flash Lite content to display if a device has a secondary screen on supported flip phones. KDDI (Japan only) is one OEM to utilize this content type previously on Flash Lite 1.1 devices. Nokia devices also support playback of Flash Lite content on secondary screens across some S40 and S60 devices. However, Nokia does not utilize the Sub LCD content type; Nokia merely uses the stand-alone content type in the context of the secondary screen.

- UI launcher uses Flash Lite to display the device's launcher application (i.e., the application that allows users to start other applications).

- Wake-up screen supports for Flash Lite content on the screen displayed when a device boots up from the off state (i.e., the phone's boot splash screen). DoCoMo (Japan only) is currently an OEM offering this content type.

Content types are available when publishing from Flash CS4 and testing in Device Central CS4.

In this book, we'll be concentrating primarily on the stand-alone player and browser content types, since they are specific to creating mobile applications, rather than OEM-specific media content.

If you are interested in some of the other OEM-specific content types, you can check out our blog (http://advancED.flashmobilebook.com/blog/) to read about what device manufacturers are doing with content types as newer Flash devices come to market.

Depending on what kind of Flash Lite content you are using, your final deployable file will be in several kinds of packaging formats (we will discuss mobile and device packaging file formats later in this chapter, as they are unique to the Flash Lite and world of mobile content distribution).

Learning the building blocks of Flash-based content

We've now talked about the SWF format and various Flash Lite content types but haven't yet covered what the essential building blocks of Flash are—that is, what's inside of a SWF that makes it play animation, video, sound, or display text. When symbols are dragged or added via ActionScript to the Flash Lite application, those symbols become known as "instances" (i.e., instances of the added visual objects).

If you are already a Flash Lite developer, or are coming from a Flash background, feel free to skip this section, which is a short review of the essential building blocks used to create applications and content using Flash (and thus, Flash Lite).

The following essential pieces are used to build up a Flash application (whether with the Flash IDE or via an open source Flash SWF compilation alternative such as FlashDevelop or Eclipse):

- Symbols
- The Flash timeline
- Frames
- Layers

Symbols

Creating visual content within Flash Lite applications boils down to essentially working with three core media assets: MovieClip, graphic, and button, and each of these is called a symbol:

- **MovieClip**: You can think of MovieClips as miniature Flash movie timelines. Essentially, they store other visual assets like graphics, buttons, and shapes. Traditionally, MovieClips in Flash on the Web were used for animations. However, with Flash Lite, MovieClips are used to do everything from store data and animate Flash Lite game assets, to create fade and wipe effects for Flash Lite productivity applications.

It's possible to add, and target, MovieClips with ActionScript code to make them interactive. For example, the following simply assigns a 50 percent alpha value to a MovieClip called `mymovie_mc` on the Flash stage (where visual elements are stored):

```
// set alpha value of the mymovie_mc instance (i.e., MovieClip) to 50%
mymovie_mc._alpha = 50;
```

- **Graphic**: The least complex of symbols in Flash is the graphic asset. A graphic symbol can act as a MovieClip but has some inherent limitations; for example, you can't attach ActionScript code to make the symbol scriptable.

  The graphic symbol is mainly used for traditional animation purposes (e.g., tweening and frame-by-frame animations). In Flash Lite content, a graphic symbol is used for timeline-based animations, such as fading, and other graphic effects, such as game explosions. The graphic symbol can contain bitmap and/or vector graphics.

  Graphic symbols should be used in situations where memory overhead is a concern, and where using a MovieClip might be considered overkill (because the asset does not need to be scripted dynamically by ActionScript code).

- **Button**: Traditionally, Flash on the desktop has had the capability of user input interaction from a screen, which usually meant a mouse, and therefore, Flash supports clickable button symbols. Depending on the version of Flash Lite, buttons are used for a few different purposes.

  In Flash Lite 2.x and 3.x, buttons are utilized for touch-screen, user-interface elements. However, in Flash Lite 1.1 specifically, buttons are most commonly used for device key interaction (i.e., what are known in the Flash and Flash Lite communities as "key catchers"). You may be wondering why buttons are used for device key interaction in Flash Lite 1.1. The short answer is because of the legacy Flash 4 ActionScript support.

The Flash timeline

The Flash timeline (see Figure 2-1) is possibly one of the most challenging concepts for new developers learning Flash when leveraging the Flash CS3 or CS4 IDE.

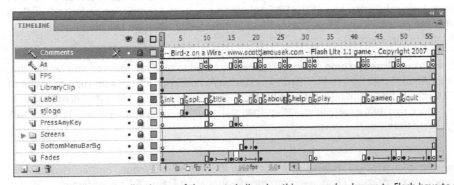

Figure 2-1. The Flash timeline is one of the most challenging things new developers to Flash have to face.

Flash timelines are linear representations of application state when working on Flash content inside of the Flash IDE. If you've ever seen a roll of film, it's a good analogy to what a timeline is in Flash—a sequence strip of individual frames that, when executed, makes up a movie (or in our case, the compiled SWF).

Frames

A timeline is composed of frames, which are essentially individual storage slots for other Flash contents. Frames (and the content they contain) are typically executed in a linear fashion during SWF playback. During development within the Flash IDE, there is a play head, which is a visual indicator of the frame being executed at any given time on a particular timeline.

You'll often hear Flash Lite developers speak of "FPS" and how various decisions affect FPS, and thus performance. Though FPS specifically refers to the "frames per second" of playback, what developers are truly concerned with is the amount of strain put on a CPU while a piece of Flash Lite runs on a device. As more computations hit the device CPU, the Flash Lite player will drop the frame rate currently playing.

Typically, 16–20 FPS is a decent playback rate. However, many early Flash Lite 1.1 devices had 6–7 FPS. Some of the very newest devices have CPUs capable of rates approaching 30 FPS. Times have changed! Ultimately, FPS performance comes down to the clock speed of a CPU inside a device and how it's managed both internally by the operating system and by Flash Lite.

For more information about FPS, and even access to some FPS speedometers (prebuilt performance-reporting objects that can be used to diagnosis bottlenecks in Flash Lite applications), please see http://advancED.flashmobilebook.com/links.html#FPS.

Layers

Within the Flash IDE, it's possible to layer frames on top of one another, giving the illusion of depth. Within both Flash and Flash Lite, layering timeline assets is common. When creating a piece of Flash Lite 1.1 content, it's not uncommon to find dozens of layers on the timelines inside of a .fla Flash Lite source file.

After compilation, layers cease to exist, as the content is published into the SWF file format. Layers are a convention for developers to arrange and manage assets more easily on Flash timelines.

Each MovieClip contained in a SWF has its own independent timeline. Each timeline can be controlled and played back during the execution of the SWF, using some custom ActionScript commands such as stop(), play(), and gotoAndPlay() (we'll cover these in more detail when we talk about working with Flash Lite 1.1 later in this chapter).

These commands can be inserted onto individual frames, attached to buttons, inserted into MovieClips, or placed within ActionScript source files (such as external ActionScript library #include or inside of ActionScript 2.0 .class files). This makes it possible for Flash timelines to be controlled via ActionScript code for much more dynamic experiences, rather than static animations that play from start to finish, the same way, every time.

> For a comprehensive book on working with the Flash IDE, timeline, symbols, and other design, and visual-oriented aspects of Flash, we recommend Foundation Flash CS4 for Designers (ISBN: 978-1-4302-1093-1).

Animating the timeline

Timelines allow designers and developers to arrange visual assets, such as bitmap or vector graphics, onto a visible stage area within Flash CS4. There are essentially three different approaches for animating content on the timeline:

- **Frame-by-frame**: If you follow Disney at all, you know that film animation started off using cel-by-cel–based production techniques for animation. With Flash, a similar method of animating is used. Frames are essentially cels, in loose terms. Frames are contained on layers, which are layered on the timeline.

- **Tweening**: Tweening refers to taking a MovieClip and/or graphic symbol from one position and moving it to another over an interval of time on the Flash timeline without resorting to creating each and every independent frame. Tweening acts as a shortcut to animate objects within the Flash timeline and is common for animation effects (e.g., fading MovieClips in and out) or moving objects within content (e.g., mobile games). The animations themselves are most often called tweens and are very common within Flash circles (regardless of the device being targeted).

> In Chapter 6, we'll talk about reusable Flash Lite user interface component libraries that offer tweening capabilities. Also, in Chapter 7, we'll take a look at the eyeGT and b.Tween frameworks for porting Flash content to the iPhone, which also takes a timeline-based approach to arranging visual assets.

- **ActionScript**: In addition to the previous methods of animation, it is also possible to animate Flash visual assets such as MovieClips using ActionScript code. Using ActionScript to animate content in Flash Lite can cause a performance penalty since the device CPU needs to be continually calculating updates. Depending on the target device, it can sometimes be beneficial to stick to frame-based animation, rather than code-based animation via ActionScript.

For instance, to move a MovieClip right, you would use the ActionScript code `mymovie_mc._x += 5;`, which would move the MovieClip five pixels to the right of its current location. By combining the following statements, a simple tween can be made:

```
// moves the mymovie_mc clip to the right from its initial location
onEnterFrame = mymovie_mc._x += 5;
```

> If you are looking for an excellent book on animating with ActionScript, we recommend you check out Keith Peter's Foundation ActionScript 3.0: Making Things Move! (ISBN: 978-1-59059-791-0). We'll cover more about ActionScript-based animation when we cover tweening in Chapter 6 with our user interface discussions.

As you move through this book, you may note we use any one of these three methods of animation for our Flash Mobile content depending on the situation (the tools used, platform developed for, Flash Lite version, etc.).

This book covers developing Flash Lite content from a developer's point of view focusing on ActionScript. However, if your interest lies in creating traditional animations across devices, we highly recommend Foundation Flash Cartoon Animation *(ISBN: 978-1-59059-207-6), which covers working with timeline animations, very heavily.*

Animating text

When working with Flash, there are three different kinds of text:

- Static refers to text that does not change and is often used within Flash Lite content for user interface labels and other content that does not ever change.

- Dynamic refers to text inside of a piece of Flash Lite content that frequently changes. The data is often loaded into Flash Lite content via query string variable format, XML, or sometimes local files (in the form of shared objects).

- Input refers to text entry fields that allow users of Flash Lite applications to enter data. Depending on the device, input text in Flash Lite can take the form of T-9 input (predictive text), physical QWERTY, or even virtual (touch-screen) user interfaces.

Working with sound

One of Flash's biggest strengths on the desktop has been audio playback support. This is especially true of the Flash 10 player and additional ActionScript 3.0 APIs. With Flash Lite, however, sound support remains fragmented and is one of the more challenging elements of working with mobile, regardless of device platform chosen.

Devices support all kinds of various sound formats, MP3, AAC, MIDI, MFi, and SMAF to name but a few. To combat this, Flash offers up two different methods of dealing with sounds:

- Native sound refers to imported sound assets that are embedded into the SWF and play back the audio without hardware assistance. In Flash Lite 1.1, sounds are typically embedded and controlled on the timeline, while in Flash Lite 2.x and 3.x, there is support for the ActionScript 2.0 Sound object.

- Device sounds are unique to Flash Lite and do not appear with Flash on the desktop and Web (unless we're talking about the mobile Web, that is!). Hardware-specific chipsets are embedded on some devices for high-quality playback of supported formats such as MIDI, MFi, and SMAF. To utilize device sounds in Flash, each sound must be mapped to a local native sound during development (since device sound formats such as MFi are not supported within the Flash IDE for playback).

Since sound is a not a particularly friendly topic for mobile device development in general, we won't be devoting a lot of time to its discussion in this book. We offer many online resources for working with sound in Flash Lite across various device platforms, such as Nokia, Sony Ericsson, and other OEMs at http://advancED.flashmobilebook.com/ links.html#sound.

Working with video

Since Flash Player 6 for Web, it has been possible to render video within Flash content using the On2 and VP6 video codec technologies. Flash video on the Web is a considered a major video delivery mechanisms for major broadcasting networks, as well as for other companies doing streaming media (BrightCove, Vimeo, and others).

Flash Lite 2.x and 3.x offer similar support for video playback across mobile and other support devices using device video and native Flash video formats.

- **Device video**: Starting with Flash Lite 2.0, it is possible to render video on supported mobile devices using device video. However, this is not Flash video content playing within the context of a Flash Lite application. Rather, with device video, the Flash Lite 2.x runtime makes calls out to the default video player installed on a device for playback. Video is loaded by that external player and played as an overlay on top of the existing Flash Lite application according to properties assigned to the video (video format, dimensions of video, etc.).

  For example, with Nokia S60 devices running Flash Lite 2.x, device video is handled by the Real Player media player. With newer Flash Lite 3.x devices from Nokia, however, native Flash Video is supported. The default video renderer with Flash Lite 2.x will vary depending on the device and platform used by the OEM. With Flash Lite 3.x, the video plays within the Flash Lite player itself, just as it does on the desktop or Web.

- **Native video**: When targeting devices with Flash Lite 3.0 and 3.1, native Flash Video is supported (unless an OEM has a very specific reason for *not* supporting it).

  We use the term "native" here to refer to video playback directly within the Flash Lite player itself. The advantage with native or device video is that video content is rendered *within* existing Flash content (i.e., the SWF). This allows for seamless playback and a user experience where there is no distinction between the video playing and the Flash Lite interface that surrounds it.

  Flash Lite versions 3.0 and 3.1 support both the On2 and VP6 codecs. Flash Lite 3.1 adds support for H.264 (when devices are able to support it). When working with video, there are three methods of delivery: embedded video is inserted onto Flash timelines, progressive video is made up of downloaded clips, and streaming video offers live playback (e.g., a live webcam feed).

  Going forward, Flash video will be one of the many features of Flash Lite and future Flash players that will help drive mobile video consumption, due to its video quality and ability to play seamlessly across millions of devices, both on the Web and on mobile devices.

> *Chapter 15 deals with device and native Flash video in some detail. Flash Lite 2.x device video, Flash Lite 3.x native video, and Flash 10 video support on smart phones are also covered in Chapter 15.*

- **ActionScript**: ActionScript is an ECMAScript-based scripting language that almost all Flash developers use today. You can use it to control animations, play videos, control games, dynamically update a user interface, build a next-generation desktop RIA, rotate a 3-D object in space, and anything else you can think up to code.

For a comprehensive list of ActionScript keywords and commands and how they are supported when working on any version of Flash Lite, please consult the document mobile_solutions_as_reference/mobile_solutions_as_reference.pdf located in the Adobe Developer Connection articles area at http://www.adobe.com/devnet/devices/articles/ and then searching for "mobile solutions as reference". You can also find it by going to our companion website at: http://advancED.flashmobilebook.com/links.html#mobile_solutions_as_reference.

When it comes to Flash content, it's all controlled by ActionScript. In the Flash Lite world, it's no different. ActionScript 2.0 drives much of the interactive content such as casual games and other mobile applications out there.

At the time of this writing, Adobe offers support for the following major versions of ActionScript:

- **ActionScript "0.5"**: Flash Lite 1.1 supports a mix of Flash 4 and Flash 5 style syntax that some in the Flash Lite community refer to as "ActionScript 1.0" but really is more like "ActionScript 0.5," since the language does not support some ActionScript 1.0 features.

  Working with this version of ActionScript is typically a bit of a learning curve for existing Flash developers because it requires stepping back to another coding world very different from ActionScript 2.0 and 3.0. We'll cover Flash 4 ActionScript in more detail in the "Exploring Flash Lite 1.1" section later in this chapter.

- **ActionScript 1.0**: Adobe Mobile Client for the Qualcomm BREW-based mobile platform utilizes ActionScript 1.0 (not to be confused with Verizon Wireless, who offers Flash Lite 2.1 support for handsets). For the purposes of this book, we will not cover ActionScript 1.0.

If you are interested in developing for Adobe Mobile Client using ActionScript 1.0, we recommend checking out the Adobe Mobile Solutions ActionScript guide at http://www.adobe.com/devnet/devices/articles/adobe_mobile_solutions_actionscript_language_reference.pdf.

- **ActionScript 2.0**: Currently Flash Lite 2.x and 3.x support ActionScript 2.0. In this book, we'll cover some examples of using class-based development for Flash Lite projects with Flash Lite 2.x and 3.x. Later in this chapter, we'll discuss some of the pros and cons of using timeline-based, functional, and class-based ActionScript within Flash Lite projects.

- **ActionScript 3.0**: There are no versions of Flash Lite that support ActionScript 3.0 at the time of this writing. However, Adobe is currently working on Flash 10 for SmartPhones. We cover more about Flash 10 in Chapters 9 through 15 when we discuss AIR across smart phone and other MID class devices.

We cover ActionScript 2.0 throughout this book assuming you have some familiarity with class-based development and principles of object-oriented programming. However, if this is not the case, one excellent resource for learning about the object-oriented aspects of Flash with ActionScript 2.0 is Object-Oriented ActionScript For Flash 8 (ISBN: 978-1-59059-619-7). Another good in-depth resource for ActionScript 3.0 development is Object-Oriented ActionScript 3.0 (ISBN: 978-1-59059-845-0).

We now turn our attention to discussing the various Adobe Flash runtimes available that work across feature phones, smart phones, MIDs, and other consumer electronics devices.

Understanding the Flash Lite versions

Since mobile devices have a much longer shelf life than desktop PCs, it's important to recognize that each Flash Lite version exists for a much longer time on devices. This is typically due to the fact that most users don't upgrade their mobile devices as often as developers would like. Thus, the versions of Flash Lite found in global marketplaces vary from region to region, and device to device. From Flash Lite 1.0 to 3.1, it's good to know the pros, cons, and differences between each version of Flash Lite, as well as how they differ from Flash on the desktop PC environment.

Contrary to popular belief, Flash Lite was not the first attempt at Flash across mobile devices. Prior to Flash Lite, Macromedia (which merged with Adobe in 2006) targeted the realm of Windows Mobile PDAs that ran Pocket PC. This was known as Pocket PC Flash and was made up essentially of Flash 5 and Flash 6 running on supported PDAs. Pocket PC Flash was all the rage for a year or two, but it never achieved status across other devices. Perhaps Macromedia didn't have the muscle to work into other devices, or perhaps it was just too early. For all intents and purposes, Pocket PC is a distant footnote in the history of the evolution of Flash on devices.

Introducing the Flash Lite runtime versions

In the next sections, we cover the various Flash Lite runtime players out on the market at this time of writing, our thoughts about them, as well as their significance, from Flash Lite 1.0 to Flash Lite 3.1. Here is a basic timeline of evolution of Flash Lite before we dive into specifics:

- **Flash Lite 1.0**: Flash Lite 1.0 was embedded into millions of handsets with NTT DoCoMo in Japan, which utilized Flash Lite content via the iMode service. Early implementations of Flash Lite 1.0 lacked the features required to create serious applications, so much of the content remained within the animation, games, wallpaper, and screensaver content that is still popular in the landscape of *Keitai* (i.e., Japanese mobile culture) today.

- **Flash Lite 1.1**: Flash Lite 1.1 fixed a lot of things lacking in the previous Flash Lite 1.0 bits ("bits" is the slang industry term for shipped mobile software). Things absent such as data loading capabilities, as well as more Flash 4 scripting support, and the ability to tap low-level device APIs (e.g., accessing battery level and signal strength) were added. Flash Lite 1.1 reached a more global audience outside of Japan Keitai into other world markets, like Europe.

- **Flash Lite 2.0 and 2.1**: Flash Lite 2.0 followed with support for Flash Player 7 support, ActionScript 2.0 support, and many other features, such as XML support. Version 2.1 is a point release to 2.0 that adds support for XML sockets, as well as other features and even bug fixes. Flash Lite 2.x made its way into yet more worldly markets including the United States (e.g., Verizon Wireless).

- **Flash Lite 3.0 and 3.1**: Flash Lite versions 3.0 and 3.1 represent the latest (at the time of this writing) Flash players optimized for mobile and devices. Features include support for native Flash video and major player performance enhancements. Today, Flash Lite 3.x reaches a worldwide audience on hundreds of device platforms, millions of devices, and potentially a billion mobile users.

Although Flash Lite 1.0 was the first version, we'll start our discussion with Flash Lite 1.1. Flash Lite 1.1 was the first version of Flash Lite that developers worldwide could take advantage of and represents the new baseline for Flash Lite developer (Flash Lite 1.0 is essentially defunct in the marketplace, except perhaps in Japan on some very, *very* old handsets!).

Exploring Flash Lite 1.1

Even though Flash Lite 1.1 has been replaced by Flash Lite 2.x and Flash Lite 3.x, there is still a good deal of work being done with this version given its massive worldwide penetration rate. For this reason, we cover some of the basics you need to know about working with Flash 4 syntax found in Flash Lite 1.1. There is a good deal of 1.1 content out, and it needs to be ported to Flash Lite 2.x and 3.x.

> *We'll cover more Flash Lite 2.x and Flash Lite 3.x in subsequent chapters when we start to work with some of the neat widget frameworks and extend Flash Lite to do things like tap into a device's contact list.*

Since the early days of Flash Lite 1.0, ActionScript has been available for use by developers seeking to leverage scripting capabilities. However, with version 1.0, only basic ActionScript commands such as gotoAndPlay(), stop(), and play() were available. It wasn't until Flash Lite 1.1 that it was possible to create external data-loading routines via loadVariables() and not until Flash Lite 1.1 could developers create reusable pseudo functions, more commonly referred to as "function clips" within the older Flash generation of developers.

> *For a comparison between Flash Lite 1.1 and more current Flash Lite versions, please visit http:// www.adobe.com/products/flashlite/version/flashlite_feature_comparison.pdf.*

Let's talk about some basic Flash 4 you'll need to recall (remember, Flash 4 came out in the 1990s), if you plan to either port existing code or projects from Flash Lite 1.1 to Flash Lite 2.x or 3.x.

Working with Flash Lite 1.1 variables, function clips, and pseudo arrays

When working with Flash Lite 1.1, the basic ActionScript fundamentals are very similar to ActionScript 2.0. However, here we lay out the differences with Flash 4 syntax found in Flash Lite 1.1. Let's start with variables.

Variables

When working with Flash Lite 1.1, you really only have three kinds of data types to work with when using variables in your application, game, or other piece of code. You have access to Strings, Numbers, and Boolean primitive types. Booleans can also be mimicked by using 1 or 0. Also remember that var is unnecessary in Flash 4 syntax, so you just define the variable outright.

```
// In Flash Lite 1.1, it all comes down to numbers
// and strings in terms of available data types
myNumber = 5 ;
myString = "test";
myBoolean = (isFriendOfEdReader) ? 1 : 0;
```

Functions and function clips

One oddity that most developers new to Flash Lite notice is that no real functions exist within Flash Lite 1.1. No functions whatsoever exist in Flash Lite 1.0. However, both Flash Lite 2.x and 3.x do support function. With Flash Lite 1.1, developers must use what are called "function clips" (see Figure 2-2) to achieve reusable bits of code that functions allow for.

To create a function clip in version 1.1, in the past, we've found it is a good practice to store all function routines in a MovieClip with an instance name. Place this MovieClip off stage, and in the Flash timeline, create a separate layer to store the function clip instance, so it's easy to locate later on. Typically, the layer is named functions, functionClip, or something similar.

Inside the function MovieClip, you create reusable code snippets by inserting ActionScript code into unique frames that have labels corresponding to the actions. These names can be thought of as the function names and are used to execute all of the ActionScript contained within the indicated frame. Each frame label should also have some sort of stop() contained in them to prevent run over into subsequent function labels on the timeline.

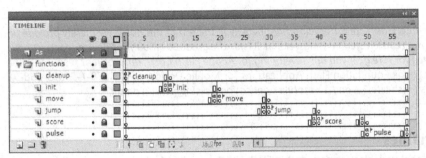

Figure 2-2. This sample function clip defines several functions. The spacing between frames is for readability.

To run a function contained in a function clip, the clip containing the label must be named and executed. This is done by the call() function that is part of Flash 4 syntax.

```
// calling a function in Flash Lite 1.1. Yes, that's a full colon to
// separate the MovieClip from function name.
call( "functionclip_mc:executeMyFunction" );
```

Pseudo arrays

It is important to note that built-in array data types are not supported Flash Lite 1.1. It is possible to simulate arrays, however. One trick is to build pseudo arrays by using a series of named variables that contain all the array elements in separate variables:

```
// building an pseudo array in Flash Lite 1.1
rgb0 = "red";
rgb1 = "blue";
rgb2 = "green";

// access an element from the pseudo array
trace( "rgb" add "0" ); // this will output the value "red"
```

Here is a simple way to access a pseudo array dynamically at runtime:

```
// populate during runtime
rgb0 = "red";
rgb1 = "blue";
rgb2 = "green";
for ( i=0; i <3; i++ ) {
 trace( eval( "rgb" add i ) );
}
```

Reviewing Flash Lite 1.1 ActionScript syntax

Dozens of commands, keywords, and properties were added as part of the Flash 4 ActionScript support provided in Flash Lite 1.1. This enabled developers to begin to create cool applications, casual games, and mobile user interfaces.

> *We won't go into Flash Lite 1.1 development heavily in the rest of this book; we merely provide an overview. If you're interested in using version 1.1 for the greatest amount of device reach or have a specific need for it (e.g., if you are developing for Adobe Flash Cast), an excellent resource is the Friends of ED book* Foundation Flash Applications for Mobile Devices *(ISBN: 978-1-59059-558-9), which covers Flash Lite 1.1 and 2.x mobile application development in detail.*

Global variables

A number of global variables are provided in Flash Lite 1.1 (many of which are read-only):

- $version returns the Flash Lite player being used (e.g., FL 8,1,56,0 is returned for a compiled Flash Lite 1.1 SWF rendered within a Flash Lite 3.0 player).

- _cap4WayKeyAS returns true or false, depending on whether a four-way navigation (up, down, left, and right device key interactions) is supported.

- _capEmail returns whether or not it is possible to send e-mail on a device using the getURL() command:

  if (_capEmail) { getURL("mailto:authors@flashmobilebook.com"); }

- _capLoadData returns true or false depending on whether the device can load local or external variables via loadVariables() and loadVariablesNum().

- _soundbuftime is the amount of time allocated for buffering device sounds before playback.

- _capStreamSound, in some early devices running Flash Lite 1.1 that can stream sounds, returns true; otherwise, false.

- _capCompoundSound returns true if the device supports playback of multiple sounds, which relies on built-in device chips. Otherwise, this returns false.

- _capMFi returns true or false depending on if the device supports MFi, which is a sound format for (mostly) Japanese devices.

- _capMIDI returns true or false on whether the MIDI sound format is supported on the Flash Lite device.

- _capMP3 returns true if the device can play MP3 sound files. Otherwise, it returns false.

- _capSMAF is true if the device can play files in the SMAF device sound format; otherwise, it's false.

- _capSMS indicates that sending SMS messages is possible with Flash Lite if this capability property is true. If it's not able to, the value is false.

- _capMMS this property will be true if a device can send MMS messages. Otherwise, it's false.

- _focusrect controls the Flash Lite focus rectangle and can be true or false. By default, when text fields and other user interface elements are added to a Flash Lite application, a focus rectangle (which is typically yellow) surrounds these elements. It is built-in functionality to make it easier for users to know what is selected (or not selected) inside of Flash Lite content. Typically, in Flash Lite application content, regardless of the version, _focusrect will be set to false, and a developer-defined focus system will be implemented.

- _global allows you to get and set variables globally within a Flash Lite application. Often, it is considered a bad practice (due to memory overhead) to use _global variables when developing Flash Lite 2.x or 3.x applications. It remains an option for creating quick global variable access in Flash Lite.

```
// set a global debugging flag for a Flash Lite 1.1 application
_global.DEBUG = true;
```

MovieClip properties

In addition to the global Flash Lite 1.1 properties we talked about in the previous section, there are several properties that are part of MovieClips symbols. These include

- _currentframe contains the current frame number on which the Flash timeline is at a particular time, for a specific MovieClip. For example, mymovie_mc._currentframe might return the value 20, if the Flash timeline playhead was currently at frame 20.

- _totalframes returns the total number of frames for a timeline for a MovieClip.

- _framesloaded remains from the Flash 4 days and can be used when creating preloaders. With Flash Lite, it's often not used unless the Flash Lite SWF is run within a browser context or the SWF is loading in external assets.

- _root refers to the top-level MovieClip in a Flash Lite application when dealing with Flash scope.

> *In Flash Lite 2.x/3.x, accessing _root for variables, with, for example, _root.myvariable is frowned upon, because it defeats the purpose of reuse by hard-coding variable names. However, for Flash Lite 1.1 content, and sometimes even quick Flash Lite 2.x or 3.x content (like screensavers and wallpapers), using _root, although not a best practice, can be handy where code reuse is less of a priority.*

- _parent, when dealing with nested MovieClips in Flash Lite, refers to the parent, or referenced, MovieClip from inside another MovieClip (if such a MovieClip exists).

- this, a keyword, refers to the current symbol in which the Flash timeline is running. It is used in Flash Lite 1.1 but more frequently in Flash Lite 2.x or 3.x when utilizing ActionScript 2.0. We may occasionally use the this statement in this context in future chapters, when developing with Flash Lite 2.x or 3.x and ActionScript 2.0-based classes.

- _levelX represents stacked level areas in a specified MovieClip. Depending on the Flash Lite application, there could potentially be _level0, _level1, and so on inside of legacy Flash Lite 1.1 applications. These can be used to stack objects contained on Flash timelines on top of one another (e.g., level0 has a background image, and level1 might have user interface elements).

> *In Flash Lite 2.x or 3.x, developers often opt for using MovieClips instead of levels. Typically, you'll see levels used in Flash Lite 1.1 content for loading variables using loadVariables() or stacking visual elements on top of each other. It is also used to target SWF loading for loadMovieNum() commands.*

- _x, a variable, returns the x coordinate location of a MovieClip in Flash Lite content.

- _y, a variable, returns the y coordinate location of a MovieClip in Flash Lite content.

- _xscale is the percentage, from 0 up, to use when scaling MovieClips on the x axis. Setting the value to 100 represents 100 percent: the MovieClip shown at its original size scaled in the x direction (i.e., width).

- _yscale follows the same conventions as _xscale except in the y direction (i.e., height).

> *Scaling bitmaps can cause performance issues in Flash Lite content and is not recommended.*

- _width returns the width of a MovieClip.

- _height returns the height of a MovieClip.

- _rotation can be used to rotate a MovieClip, and values range from 0 to 359 degrees:

```
// make the mymovie_mc MovieClip spin clockwise
tellTarget( mymovie_mc ) { _rotation +=1; }
```

Rotating bitmaps instead of vectors can result in performance issues and is not generally recommended.

- `_target` refers to the path to a specified MovieClip inside Flash Lite content (e.g., `_level0/mymovie_mc`).

- `_name` refers to the name of a specified MovieClip instance inside Flash Lite content (e.g., `mymovie_mc`).

- `_visible`, if set to false, hides the MovieClip from the user when Flash Lite content is run. If the `_visible` property is set to true, the MovieClip is visible. When you set MovieClips to `_visible = false`, they still will consume some overhead in terms of memory and some performance if left on the redraw area of the Flash Lite content. A trick is to place unused Flash Lite 1.1 MovieClips offstage when they are not in use to conserve a bit of CPU overhead.

- `scroll` indicates the current scroll value of a text field. For example, a value of 1 means the text field in a Flash Lite application has not yet been scrolled and is at the very first line.

- `maxscroll`, when dealing with text fields, indicates the number of lines that the Flash Lite text field can scroll. It's primarily used for multiline text field entry.

- `_quality` is a shortcut for the fscommand2 setQuality command we will cover later in this chapter. By setting this value to `"HIGH"`, `"LOW"`, or `"MEDIUM"`, the Flash Lite player will change the quality of the content presented (sacrificing or improving overall performance of the Flash Lite content running). When set to low, there is no antialiasing for content, so typically, the quality level will be set at least to a medium setting.

  ```
  _quality = "HIGH"; // other values are "LOW" and "MEDIUM"
  ```

  In various Flash Lite player implementations, OEMs (Nokia, for example) will set the default quality rendering to "MEDIUM", so it's best to set the quality level before beginning Flash Lite content. Typically, you'll set `_quality` to "HIGH" to render the best quality content. However, a legacy trick with Flash Lite is to use this property to shift between low and high values when additional processing speed is needed, for example, if you're loading data while a Flash timeline tween is happening simultaneously.

- `_highquality`, if true, will set the Flash Lite player into rendering quality at its highest setting, with antialiasing of rendered content.

When working with Flash Lite 1.1, the keywords, operators, and commands covered in the following sections exist.

Operators

Primitive operators such as *, /, +, and - are supported in Flash Lite 1.1.

With string concatenation, developers must use the add command, and not the + command as is possible with ActionScript 2.0. This is often the source for many bugs! "a" + "b" does not equal "ab" in Flash Lite 1.1! This would be written as "a" add "b".

You'll see the add command a lot within legacy Flash 4 and Flash Lite 1.1 content.

Keywords and built-in functions

In addition to operators, you should know several keywords and built-in functions in Flash Lite 1.1:

- trace(*expr*) is perhaps one of the most often used statements in all Flash Lite (or Flash for that matter) applications. trace takes in an expression and outputs for debugging purposes. With desktop Flash, there are other more productive tools for debugging such as XRay (http://osflash.org/xray). For Flash Lite 1.1, 2.x, and 3.0, trace remains the quickest and easiest built-in solution for finding bugs in applications.

```
// adds variable a with b and displays the value in the
// Flash output window
trace(a+b);
```

When working with Flash Lite inside of the Flash IDE, setting break points within ActionScript is not supported, so tracing is one option for debugging.

- call(*targetmovie:frame*) allows ActionScript contained on a specified MovieClip frame to be executed. A target frame label must also be specified that exists in the target MovieClip. Flash Lite 1.1 does not support built-in functions. Flash Lite 2.x or 3.x support ActionScript 2.0 and therefore support the keyword function).

With Flash Lite 1.1, the alternative to using functions is call statements. This routine allows functions to be simulated. Given a frame label name on a timeline, the call statement allows ActionScript contained on a particular labeled frame to be executed.

Passing parameters is not supported by call but can be mimicked by setting and maintaining ActionScript variables defined in the Flash Lite 1.1 application.

```
// instruct the library_mc MovieClip to execute the ActionScript
// contained on the "debug" frame label
call("library_mc:debug");

// contained within a library_mc MovieClip, on a frame
// labeled with "debug"
trace("foo!");
```

In Flash Lite 1.1, to simulate a library of functions, a custom MovieClip is often created to store frame labels for each individual function call.

- play() and stop() have already been covered with the Flash timeline basics. With Flash Lite 1.1 content, you'll often find numerous stop and play commands on various timelines, inside MovieClips, and in other spots.

- gotoAndPlay(*expr*) and gotoAndStop(*expr*) are two additional commands for controlling the timeline. These are essentially the same as the previous stop() and play(), but the former will jump to a particular frame number or labeled frame. The latter will jump to a frame and then stop on that frame in the timeline (until a play() command is issued again for that particular MovieClip).

```
gotoAndPlay(2); // goto frame 2 and continue playing the SWF
gotoAndStop("quit"); // goto the frame labeled "quit" on the timeline
```

- nextFrame() and prevFrame() are available to go to the next and previous frames when called from a current frame (rather than utilizing the gotoAndPlay() and gotoAndStop() commands). These commands take no arguments.

- nextScene() and prevScene() are similar to the previous commands and allow you to move between defined scenes of a Flash Lite application. These commands take no arguments.

> *We personally recommend staying away from leveraging Flash scenes when developing mobile content in any version of Flash Lite. It's much easier managing scope and assets in one main timeline (one scene) with multiple frame labels, rather than trying to split a Flash Lite application across multiple scenes. This is just a tip from us.*

- tellTarget(*target*) is perhaps one of the most important routines in Flash Lite 1.1 syntax, as it makes it possible to instruct other MovieClips to perform various actions. The target parameter is a MovieClip. tellTarget instructs the MovieClip to perform actions on the target MovieClip specified.

```
// update the variable called gameover inside of game_mc to a
// value of 1
tellTarget( game_mc ) {
    gameover = 1;
}
```

> *In Flash Lite 1.1, there is no notion of dot syntax hierarchy as found in ActionScript 2.0 and other object-oriented languages. For example, in Flash Lite 1.1, to change the _x location of a MovieClip, a tellTarget must be used. Using code like mymovie_mc._x = 10; will not compile! tellTarget("mymovie_mc") _x = 10; will work.*

- loadVariables(*URL*), available since Flash Lite 1.1, supports data-loading capabilities. This command loads up the timeline with variables loaded in from an HTTP query string formatted with name/value pairs. For example, if a text file called data.txt containing the string "&a=1&b=2&c=3" existed, a developer could load that data, using a loadVariables("data.txt"); command. The end result would be the variables a=1, b=2, and c=3 on the timeline that called the loadVariables() command.

> *When using Kuneri Lite (a third-party Flash Lite extender framework) and targeting Flash Lite 1.1, loadVariables(URL) is utilized to pass data back and forth between the Kuneri Lite server and the Flash Lite player.*

- loadMovie(*SWF, MovieClip*) and unloadMovie(*SWF, MovieClip*) allow you to load and unload external SWF files into the currently running SWF. When creating Flash Lite 1.1 applications, it is often preferable to have a core SWF that loads or unloads external SWF assets at runtime (e.g., have different menu SWF files depending on a user interface selection made in a Flash Lite application).

SWF movies are loaded into either the current timeline or MovieClip that is specified. The second parameter of the load and unload calls is a target MovieClip that must exist on the Flash stage at runtime.

```
// loads a custom menu into the menu_mc MovieClip
// that is available on the stage
loadMovieNum("menu1.swf", menu_mc);
```

We recommend utilizing loadMovie() and unloadMovie() for large Flash Lite 1.1 applications where there are many pluggable pieces of an application. For example, perhaps in a Flash Lite 1.1 game that has multiple levels of play, each SWF loaded could be a distinct level in the game.

- loadMovieNum(*SWF, level*) and unloadMovieNum(*SWF, level*) are essentially the same commands as the previous ones, except that SWF files are loaded into levels instead of MovieClips.

```
// loads a game level 1 into the current .swf running
loadMovieNum("gamelevel1.swf", 1);
```

- getTimer() is a built-in function that returns the number of seconds that have elapsed since the Flash Lite application was launched in integer format. It's handy for creating timeouts and is used often in casual Flash Lite games.

  This routine can also be used for debugging purposes to troubleshoot performance issues (by capturing a timer before a function begins and then after it finishes, and computing the elapsed time difference). We've used it for that use case on a few Flash Lite projects before. elapsedTime = endTime: startTime will result in elapsed time that can be used to find potential performance bottlenecks in Flash Lite applications.

- getURL(*method*), which was one of the additions from Flash Lite 1.0 to the 1.1 runtime, allows a device to open a new SMS, MMS, mail message, or web URL if there is a default browser installed on the device (and it supports the target method). Common examples you'll find in Flash Lite 1.1 content are getURL("sms:555-5555"); and getURL("http://scottjanousek.mobi");.

- stopAllSounds() offers a way to stop all sound playback from occurring in a Flash Lite 1.1 application (if any sounds are playing, that is). It is typically used within a frame of a Flash Lite 1.1 game.

  When working with Flash Lite 2.x or 3.x, you'll most likely be working with the Sound object, so this routine is unique to Flash Lite 1.1 content.

- duplicateMovieClip() and removeMovieClip() are two methods to add and remove MovieClips from the Flash library onto the visible area of a running Flash Lite application.

```
// takes an existing box MovieClip on the Stage and makes a
// duplicate called boxcopy_mc
duplicateMovieClip("box_mc", "boxcopy_mc", 1);
```

  In Flash Lite 2.x or 3.x, attachMovie() replaces the duplicateMovieClip() as a means of adding MovieClips to the stage area of a Flash Lite application.

- getProperty(*instance,parameter*) and setProperty(*instance,parameter*) allow you to retrieve properties:

```
// set the x coordinate of the box_mc MovieClip to 200
setProperty("box_mc",_x,"200");
```

- eval(*expr*) is useful for executing ActionScript expressions at runtime. For example, eval(1+1) will return the value 2.

  eval is very useful for evaluating dynamic variables in Flash Lite 1.1 and is used heavily when creating games and other applications. For example, currentball_mc = eval("ball" add i add "_mc"), where i = 1, would allow a developer to dynamically target the ball MovieClip, ball1_mc, on the stage at runtime for a game.

- int(*Number*) will convert a given number into integer format. With Flash Lite 1.1 content, you're mainly dealing with String, Number, and Boolean data types. This allows for some basic conversion.

- random(*Number*) is a built-in function that picks a whole number from 0 to the value in the expression and returns it for use. A majority of Flash Lite 1.1 casual games utilize the random routine.

```
// pick a random number from 0 to 100 and assign to variable num
num = random(100);
```

In Flash Lite 2.x or 3.x, the random() function is replaced by the Math object in ActionScript 2.0. The Math object is much more complex and offers a huge range of computations, such as Math.sin, Math.floor, and other useful mathematical routines.

- length(*expr*) is useful when dealing with strings. The length() routine will return the total number of characters contained in a specified text string. Often, in Flash Lite 1.1, it is used for error checking text input fields.

```
mystring = "foo";
len = length(mystring); // len is equal to 3
```

- substring(*s*,*idx*,*c*) is another useful routine in the substring function, which allows for strings to be modified. Again, this is useful whenever text input or manipulation comes into play.

- chr(*Number*) takes in a number and returns the equivalent ASCII character value.

- ord(*String*) takes in a String value and returns the equivalent ordinal number value.

- set(*expr*,*variable*) is an odd bit of syntax you may run into with Flash Lite 1.1 content. This command is a legacy way of setting variables. It's useful for setting dynamic variable expressions such as set("myvar" add total, a+b);.

- IfFrameLoaded() is merely alternative syntax for the _framesloaded property we discussed previously. Use it to determine if a particular frame within a Flash Lite 1.1 application has been loaded or not.

- mbchr(), mblength(), mbord(), and mbsubstring() offer support the conversion of an ASCII code numbers to multibyte characters, but we've never used these in our Flash Lite projects.

- toggleHighQuality() is merely a legacy method of setting quality to high as can be done with quality = "HIGH", fscommand setQuality, and _highquality = true;. If you're working in the Flash Lite IDE, you'll be using fscommand. In open source alternatives, such as with MTASC, you'll be using the other two methods (_quality and _highquality) so that no compilation errors occur.

- fscommand(*"Launch"*, *expr*) is a legacy command that allows external device commands to be executed from within Flash Lite (e.g., launching a video player). Some OEMs allow external applications to be launched on Flash Lite 1.1 devices (e.g., Nokia S60). You may see launch commands in older Flash Lite 1.1 content that has specifically hard-coded application paths such as to media players, browsers, and other applications.

> When working with Flash Lite 2.x or 3.x, you'll have to seek out alternatives for launching applications, as the launch command, fscommand("Launch", expr) has been deprecated.
>
> For instance, on the Nokia S60 Platform, there are S60 Platform Services and third-party tools such as Kuneri Lite (we talk about these in Chapter 7 when we cover how to extend Flash Lite capabilities on some mobile platforms).

- if, else, and else if conditional statements are supported:

```
if ( a == 1 ) { /* is a is 1 */ }
  else if ( a == 2 ) { /* if not a is 1 and a is 2 */ }
  else { /* otherwise a does not equal 1 or 2! */ }
```

In Flash Lite 2.x or 3.x, these are the same, regardless of whether you're using ActionScript 1.0 or 2.0.

- switch and case statements are also supported in ActionScript, even as far back as Flash Lite 1.1. This allows you to construct lengthy conditional logic such as the following:

```
switch(a) {
  case 1:
  trace("a is 1");
  break;
  case 2:
  trace("a is 2");
  break;
  default:
  trace("a is not 1, and it's not 2");
  break;
}
```

- for, do while, and while are supported with all versions of Flash Lite. These are typical of what is found in other languages and follow the same ECMA standard syntax. Here are some examples:

```
for(i=0;i<10;i++){ /* do stuff */ }

do {
  // stuff to do
} while (notdone);

while ( notdone ) {
  // stuff to do
}
```

- break is a keyword statement used to jump out of if, while, or for loops. In the switch statement example, you see an example of break after each case statement that ensures each case expression is executed only once.

> In Flash Lite 2.x and 3.x, some of these Flash Lite 1.1 properties are still valid, but others have been deprecated. By using the Adobe Live Help inside of the Flash IDE (About ➤ Help), you can determine which of these properties have equivalent syntax in Flash Lite 2.x or 3.x.

Using the fscommand2 API

Although some primitive device-level API commands were present in Flash Lite 1.0, version 1.1 extends the number of device system commands. fscommand2 is a unique command to Flash Lite; it allows you to make calls accessing various device-level APIs. These are things like getting the signal strength level of a device, getting battery life remaining, getting the connection status of a network, or setting up the device soft keys that are present on many mobile devices.

A typical fscommand2 has the following syntax:

```
// get remaining battery life
batterylevel = fscommand2( "GetBatteryLevel" ) ;
if (batterylevel > -1 ) trace("batterylevel is " add batterylevel);
```

There are a few things to note about fscommand2. The commands execute immediately. There is usually a return value with either an error status number or a success flag (typically a 0 value). Also, not all devices support every fscommand2. If an fscommand2 is not supported, a negative value (typically a −1 value) is usually returned to inform the application that the device cannot get the value returned from an fscommand2.

Here are the most common fscommand2 calls you should know:

- FullScreen sets the size of the display area to be used for rendering.
- GetBatteryLevel returns the current battery level.
- GetDevice sets a parameter that identifies the device on which Flash Lite is running (e.g., "Nokia N97").
- GetDeviceID sets a parameter that represents the unique identifier of the device (e.g., the serial, or IME, number of most mobile devices.
- GetFreePlayerMemory returns the amount of heap memory, in kilobytes, currently available to Flash.
- GetMaxBatteryLevel returns the maximum battery level of the device.
- GetMaxSignalLevel returns the maximum signal strength level as a numeric value.
- GetMaxVolumeLevel returns the maximum volume level of the device as a numeric value.
- GetNetworkConnectionName returns the name of the active or default network connection.
- GetNetworkConnectStatus returns a value that indicates the current network connection status.
- GetNetworkGeneration returns the generation of the current mobile wireless network (such as 2G, or second generation of mobile wireless).
- GetNetworkName sets a parameter to the name of the current network.
- GetNetworkRequestStatus returns a value indicating the status of the most recent HTTP request.
- GetNetworkStatus returns a value indicating the network status of the phone (i.e., whether there is a network registered and whether the phone is currently roaming).
- GetPlatform sets a parameter that identifies the current platform, which broadly describes the class of the device (e.g., Symbian).

- GetPowerSource indicates whether or not a device is plugged in for power charging.

- GetSignalLevel returns the current signal strength as a numeric value.

- GetTotalPlayerMemory returns the total amount of heap memory, in kilobytes, allocated to Flash Lite.

- GetVolumeLevel returns the current volume level of the device as a numeric value.

- Quit causes the Flash Lite player to stop playback of an application and terminates it.

> *Unless your Flash Lite application is a special case, like the screensaver or wallpaper content types, you are going to always want to have a Quit command present in your Flash Lite content.*

- ResetSoftKeys resets the soft keys to their original settings (e.g. "Options" and Quit").

- SetSoftKeys remaps the soft keys of a mobile device. Recall that soft keys are the custom buttons found on many mobile devices. Typically, these consist of LSK (left soft key), RSK (right soft key), and sometimes MSK (middle soft key). Flash Lite has support for setting the labels using this command. However, Flash Lite content typically runs as full-screen mode using the fullScreen command, hiding the soft key labels during playback of SWFs. Typically, RSK is used to quit mobile applications, but that is not always necessarily true.

```
// sets the LSK label name to "options" and the RSK to the label "quit"
fscommand2( "setSoftKeys", "options", "quit");
```

- StartVibrate starts the phone's vibration feature.

- StopVibrate stops the current vibration, if any.

> *Many of these commands have been deprecated in Flash Lite 2.0 and beyond, but the equivalent functionality can be achieved in Flash Lite via newer means, typically by accessing the System.Capabilities object that ActionScript 2.0 supports. Deprecated fscommand2 commands include GetDateDay, GetDateMonth, GetDateWeekday, GetDateYear, GetLanguage, GetLocaleLongDate, GetLocaleShortDate, GetLocaleTime, GetTimeZoneOffset, GetTimeSeconds, GetTimeMinutes, GetTimeHours, Unescape, and Escape.*
>
> *For more information about these commands, please see the Flash Lite ActionScript reference at http://livedocs.adobe.com/flash/9.0/main/flashlite2_as_reference.pdf.*

A complete list of APIs and functionality can be found in quite a number of places. The most convenient is inside of the Help contained in Adobe Creative Suite 3 and 4. To access this, you simply go to Windows ➤ Help in Flash CS4.

Accessing the Flash Lite 1.1 syntax reference sheet

Scott Janousek (one of the authors of this book) has also created a "Flash Lite 1.1 API Cheat Sheet," available at http://www.flashmobilebook.com/downloads/FlashLiteCheatSheet.pdf that you can use as a reference when you are developing Flash Lite 1.1 content. It is a bit dated, having been created in 2005, but nevertheless, it is useful for those still working in a Flash Lite 1.1 world, for example, with Flash Cast.

In addition to the cheat sheet provided as a companion to this book, we also wanted to mention an ongoing community endeavor from Adobe. Although, at the time of this writing, Adobe's book is far from finished, it is entitled *Flash Mobile and Device Cookbook*, and it will be available from the Adobe web site (http://www.adobe.com/cfusion/communityengine/index.cfm?event=homepage&productId =3). This additional resource contains all kinds of little tips and tricks accumulated from experienced designers and developers from the Flash Lite community.

Knowing the Flash Lite error codes

Depending on the version of Flash Lite you are working with, error codes returned on actual devices may differ. In addition, on some devices, no error codes or very generic ones may be displayed. For instance, on the Chumby consumer electronics device (which we talk about in Chapter 5), there are no error code prompts displayed (at least not at the time of this writing).

- 1: Out of memory—indicates the Flash Lite player has run out of memory
- 2: Stack limit reached—indicates that MovieClips or other assets have exceeded the nesting level allocated for a Flash Lite player
- 3: Corrupt SWF data—usually means that the Flash Lite player is trying to play an incompatible published SWF file (e.g., user is trying to play a Flash Lite 3.0 game on a device that only supports Flash Lite 1.1)
- 4: ActionScript stuck—occurs when ActionScript enters an infinite loop
- 5: Infinite ActionScript loop—typically happens when an infinite loop occurs accidently within Flash Lite content
- 6: Bad JPG data—happens when an incompatible JPG is used in Flash Lite (typically a progressive JPG)
- 7: Bad sound data—occurs when a loaded sound is otherwise corrupt
- 8: Cannot find host—happens when a host cannot be loaded on a load call (e.g. loadMovie())
- 9: ActionScript error—a generic ActionScript error
- 10: URL too long—specified URL is too long (e.g., a getURL() that targets a URL that has a long query string)

Additional resources to learning Flash Lite 1.1 include two great documents from Adobe:

- http://livedocs.adobe.com/flash/9.0/main/flashlite1_gettingstarted.pdf
- http://livedocs.adobe.com/flash/9.0/main/flashlite1_developing_apps.pdf

An additional video tutorial from Adobe covering Flash Lite 1.1 basics is provided at http://www.adobe.com/devnet/devices/articles/flash_lite_video_training.html.

There are still use cases for developing with Flash Lite 1.1, such as Flash Cast development and publishing content within the Japanese market. However, for all intents and purposes, Flash Lite 2.x and 3.x are the most attractive options for Flash Lite development, due to player feature enhancements as well as support for ActionScript 2.0.

Exploring Flash Lite 2.0

With the introduction of Flash Lite 2.0 comes support for many (although not all) Flash Player 7 capabilities. Among these are support for much of the ActionScript 2.0 scripting language, loading and parsing of XML, the ability to store and retrieve persistent data, improved display and handling of text and fonts, shape drawing through an API, dynamic loading of multimedia content and playback using on-device codecs, and other features.

> For a comparison between Flash Lite 1.1 and Flash Lite 2, please visit http://www.adobe.com/products/flashlite/version/flashlite_feature_comparison.pdf.

Although not all of the ActionScript 2.0 scripting language is supported in Flash Lite 1.1, many of the basic loops, operators, and other fundamentals are. As you will see later in this chapter, as well as in subsequent chapters, ActionScript 2.0 allows you to create object-based mobile applications, games, and other content so long as you are careful about memory utilization and performance variations between devices.

For instance, it is very easy to create a complete framework using the Model, View, Controller (MVC) design pattern, but on some devices, that may consume considerable memory, leaving less left for other application tasks like loading data, video, and sound. When working with Flash Lite 2 and above, serious consideration is needed as to how much memory will be allocated and consumed by an application, which depends on target devices supported. Some developers will even take a Flash Lite 1.1 approach to creating content since it incurs less memory overhead, with no addition costs for using ActionScript 2.0 objects.

If you're creating a simple screensaver that has little, if any, code and that code will never be reused, there is little advantage to using ActionScript 2.0 over the Flash 4 syntax found in Flash Lite 1.1. However, if you're creating a mobile application framework that will be developed by a large team of developers or your project is part of larger set of work, there is more reason to take an ActionScript 2.0 route. We'll talk more about reuse of ActionScript frameworks in Chapter 6.

> Comprehensive documentation covering ActionScript 2.0 with Flash Lite 2.0 is provided by Adobe at http://livedocs.adobe.com/flash/9.0/main/flashlite2_as_reference.pdf.

Handling text and fonts

The ability to modify text color, size, and other properties of text combined with improved font rendering capabilities was added in ActionScript 2.0. This also included the first introduction of support for right-to-left languages, such as Arabic and Hebrew.

Supporting compressed SWF formats

Although Flash Lite 2.0 added support for the compressed SWF format, you should be careful of utilizing compressed SWF, as there is a performance hit in the decompress phase of the process during playback on devices.

Incorporating XML support

In Flash Lite 1.1, loading local and remote data relied on using either the loadVariables() or loadVariablesNum() function calls. In Flash Lite 2.0, XML capabilities were added to the runtime, allowing you to load and parse (typically small) XML files.

loadVars() was also added in Flash Lite 2.0, allowing for an alternative means to load simple query string data. This can be utilized for loading large sets of data where there is too much memory overhead with XML loading and processing.

> For a good (but, admittedly, a bit dated) resource on working with parsing and loading XML documents with Flash and ActionScript 2.0, please see Foundation XML for Flash (ISBN: 978-1-59059-543-5).

Loading and playing back dynamic media

More sophisticated images, sound, and video playback capabilities were added for devices in Flash Lite 2.0. In addition to loading the SWF format, as was possible in version 1.1, support for loading external .gif, .jpg, and even .png graphical formats was added. In addition, playback of popular audio and video formats, such as 3GP and MP4, was added. This lends to a much richer mobile user experience due to the media capabilities of Flash Lite. Synchronized device sound was also added in version 2.0, which allows for animation to be synchronized to sound data in some supported device sound formats such as MIDI, SMAF, and other mobile audio formats.

> We'll cover working with media later in Chapter 15, where we talk about working with Flash Video across mobile and non-PC devices.

Persisting data

The ability to locally store and retrieve small pieces of data, such as custom saved preferences, high scores, and usernames was first provided through the notion of mobile shared objects (MSOs). Much like local shared objects (LSOs), their Flash cousins in the Flash desktop player, MSOs offered an easier means of persisting data on devices without a needed trip to an external web server to save and load data or the need to load third-party products to allow data to be saved.

A good resource for walking through MSO is provided on Adobe's Developer Connection site at http://www.adobe.com/devnet/devices/articles/persistent_data.html.

Playing device video

Video is another feature that was added with Flash Lite 2.0, as part of the dynamic media loading functionality. Device video allows developers to play supported video formats, such as 3GP, MP4, and other video supported on target devices. However, the Flash Lite 2.0 player does this by making a call out to the default media playback on a device to render the video content. For instance, on many popular Symbian S60 devices from Nokia, the default player is the Real Player. Ultimately, however, it is the device manufacturer that decides if and how this is supported.

> In Chapter 15, we explore how to play back embedded, progressive, and streaming Flash video inside of Flash Lite and Flash 10 applications.

Accessing the Drawing API

Another cool feature that was added as a consequence of Flash Player 7 support is access to the Flash Drawing API. This allows developers to dynamically create, on screen, very simple drawings using a predefined set of methods. Creating filled circles, boxes, lines, and other polygon shapes is possible with this Drawing API. One caveat, however, is that this takes a good deal of processing CPU power. So, when you're dealing with Flash Lite, and especially Flash Lite 2.x, you'll need to pay close attention to CPU utilization for your mobile content both within Device Central and on actual, physical target devices.

Using the fscommand2 additions

A few fscommand2 commands were added to Flash Lite 2.0, in addition to those existing in the API from Flash Lite 1.1 that we covered earlier in this chapter:

- SetFocusRectColor sets the color of the focus rectangle to any color. The color value is not specified in hexadecimal format, as you might expect. Instead, setFocusRectColor takes in RGB values. For instance, to set the current focus rectangle to red, the values would be 255,0,0, respectively.

  ```
  // set focus rectangle to red
  status = fscommand2("SetFocusRectcolor", 255,0,0);
  ```

- SetInputTextType specifies the mode in which the input text field should be opened (e.g., numeric, alpha):

  ```
  status = fscommand2("SetInputTextType", "dial_txt", "Numeric");
  ```

- ExtendBacklightDuration extends the duration of a backlight for a specified period of time (in seconds). This is often useful for Flash Lite applications that may be used in indoors or at night so that the content can be viewed most easily.

  ```
  // extends the backlight of a device (if supported) for 45 seconds
  status = fscommand2("ExtendBacklightDuration", 45);
  ```

Some Flash Lite content types, such as screensavers and wallpaper, do not necessarily support the ExtendBacklightDuration fscommand2 command. It is best to consult Adobe Device Central for device-specific Flash profile information to find out whether this specific command is supported.

> In Chapter 7, we'll talk about some of the ways Flash Lite can be extended using custom APIs from various OEMs, such as Nokia's S60 Platform Services and Sony Ericsson's Capuchin APIs.

Let's move onto talking about dealing with errors in Flash Lite.

Introducing the Flash Lite 2.0 error codes

Error codes between Flash Lite 1.1 and Flash Lite 2.0 are different. Flash Lite 2.x versions have more error conditions due to the capabilities added into the player (note that Flash Lite 3.x shares the same error codes as Flash Lite 2.x).

> In Chapter 4, we'll cover some of our best tips and tricks on how to best avoid some of these errors as well as address other unique Flash Lite challenges, such as optimization and performance. The supply of trips and tricks are numerous, though, so we encourage you to visit our web site at http://www.flashmobilebook.com/errorcodes for further details.

Here are the Flash Lite 2.0 error codes (error codes 5 and 9 are omitted because they don't exist):

- 1: Out of memory—indicates that the Flash Lite player has exhausted all memory when running a Flash Lite application
- 2: Stack limit reached—thrown when the nesting of MovieClips or other assets exceeds the allowed limit set by the player (deep nesting of assets should be avoided in Flash Lite)
- 3: Corrupt SWF data—typically indicates that the Flash Lite player and loaded Flash Lite content are incompatible (e.g., a user is trying to run a Flash Lite 2.0 game inside a Flash Lite 1.1 player)
- 4: ActionScript stuck—means that the Flash Lite player has stopped executing ActionScript code
- 6: Bad image data—indicates that a loaded image is not supported by the Flash Lite player (e.g., a TIF is loaded, but the Flash Lite player does not support this format on the target platform)
- 7: Bad sound data—usually means an incorrect Sound format was loaded and was not able to play
- 8: Root movie unloaded—the _root MovieClip attempted to be unloaded, which is not allowed
- 10: URL too long—a loadVariables or similar command was issued with an excessively long URL causing the Flash Lite player to complain
- 11: Insufficient memory to decode image—not enough memory is allocated to display an image inside a Flash Lite application
- 12: Corrupt SVG data—indicates that scalable vector data is corrupted so the Flash Lite player can't read it
- 13: Insufficient memory to load URL—indicates that this is not enough memory to load in a specified URL in a Flash Lite application

In Flash Lite 2.x and Flash Lite 3.x, error codes 5 and 9 are not defined. We know it is bizarre, but that's just the way it has been (we've never gotten proper explanation on why this is, either).

Additional resources to learning Flash Lite 2.0 include the following two great documents from Adobe, a getting-started document and a developing applications document:

- http://livedocs.adobe.com/flash/9.0/main/flashlite2_gettingstarted.pdf
- http://livedocs.adobe.com/flash/9.0/main/flashlite2_developing_apps.pdf

Exploring Flash Lite 2.1

Very shortly after releasing Flash Lite 2.0, the 2.1 point release was released to a select few OEMs to place onto new devices (specifically targeting the Qualcomm BREW Platform first). Essentially, the version 2.1 player offered additional Flash Player 7 capabilities, new features, and various bug fixes exposed in the previous Flash Lite 2.0 player.

> For a comparison between Flash Lite 2.0 and Flash Lite 2.1, please see http://www.adobe.com/products/flashlite/version/flashlite_feature_comparison.pdf.

New features included in 2.1 include:

- **XML socket support**: The main difference between Flash Lite releases 2.0 and 2.1 is that XML sockets have been added. XML sockets provide real-time communication between the Flash Lite player and a remote server through a designated port. This allows for chat applications, as well as other uses where the Flash Lite player needs to communicate directly to a server in real time. Using XML sockets, it's possible to create multiuser chats, games, and other applications (assuming there is a good enough network connection, that is).

- **Multiplatform support**: Flash Lite 2.1 extended support across Symbian, Qualcomm BREW 2.x/3.x, and Microsoft Windows Mobile 5. The number of OEMs adopting Flash Lite jumped considerably between versions 1.1 and 2.x.

- **Inline text support**: Support for text input fields that render Flash Lite content was added in version 2.1. Previously, in Flash Lite 2.0, a user entered text into an input field through a native operating text input dialog, which was not the best user experience. Inline text support allows mobile users to enter in text for an application text box directly, without the need for odd-looking pop-up prompts.

These Flash Lite 2.1 features remain in the Flash Lite 3.x player as well. However, not all OEMs include this functionality into their respective players. It's a good idea to check device profile information in Adobe Device Central for each target device you plan on deploying applications and content to.

Support for Flash Lite 2.1 was adopted by Qualcomm and introduced to the Verizon Wireless BREW mobile ecosystem around 2006. There are very specific nuances to developing for Flash Lite 2.1 for BREW, which are described over at Adobe's Developer Connection site at http://www.adobe.com/devnet/devices/brew.html.

> In this book, we'll be focused more on the next generation of Flash on the mobile BREW platform, which will be mentioned in Chapter 7, and not Flash Lite for BREW.

Flash Cast is leveraged by Verizon Wireless through its custom Dashboard implementation. Verizon Dashboard (not to be confused with the Apple Widget framework) is a mobile client and service for Verizon Wireless customers to get real-time information pulled over the air via custom SWF channel content.

Verizon Dashboard is a push and polling mechanism for bringing Flash Lite SWF content down into the Flash Cast client where it can be viewed and interacted with by mobile users in an occasionally connected manner. It's possible to have channels that seamlessly push stock quotes, sports scores, and other data.

Flash Lite version 1.1 is still supported in Verizon Dashboard SWF content, even though it is running in a Flash Lite 2.1 context. We will not be discussing Flash Cast in any detail in this book, as it is a fairly complex and detailed environment that would easily fill its own book. However, for more information, you can visit http://www.adobe.com/mobile/solutions/flashcast/.

> *In 2006,* Foundation Flash Applications for Mobile Devices *(ISBN:978-1-59059-558-9) was one of the very first technical books to focus on Flash Lite application development for mobile devices; it concentrated on Flash Lite 1.1 and Flash Lite 2.0.*
>
> *Although some of the book's contents may be dated in terms of tools and Flash Lite devices mentioned, the discussion about the ActionScript and building content in Flash Lite is still useful if you are looking to target across a greater range of handsets that support 1.1, 2.x, and even 3.x.*
>
> *In its more than 500 pages,* Foundation Flash Applications for Mobile Devices *covers many topics ranging from creating mobile applications and casual mobile games, to other content types like screensavers and wallpapers.*

Exploring Flash Lite 3.0

The Flash Lite 3.0 runtime ships on a growing number of Nokia handsets (S40 and S60), various phones in Japan (via the NTT DoCoMo operator network), and consumer electronics devices (Chumby, iRiver, etc.). In terms of features and support, essentially the changes from Flash Lite 2.1 to 3.0 boil down to the following new core capabilities:

- **Flash video support**: Perhaps one of the most anticipated features of Flash Lite 3 has been the support for native Flash video playback for mobile and devices. In Flash Lite 3.x, support has been added for playback of .flv files directly within Flash Lite content leveraging the ON2 Technology's VP6 and Sorenson codecs. It is possible to load Flash video clips using progressive as well as live streaming.

> *In Chapter 15, we'll take a look more closely at Flash video across mobile and other devices supporting Flash Lite 3.x, including how to load progressively and stream live Flash videos to devices. We'll also touch more on some of the new features of Flash video support added in Flash Lite 3.1 in Chapter 3.*

- **Performance improvements**: Arguably one of the best features of Flash Lite 3.0 is the performance gain and overall playback optimization.
- **Lazy loading**: Flash Lite 3.0 supports lazy loading of various internals, which means that the runtime tries to be efficient about the way it loads various libraries and components. Based on the particular content type being run on a device (screensaver, stand-alone, etc.), the player

will determine if particular Flash Lite player modules need to be loaded at runtime. Player start time and performance has been greatly improved due to this feature.

- **Memory management improvements**: Although Flash Lite 3.0 still does not support user-defined garbage collection, it has gotten better about how resources are allocated and deallocated during playback, so memory management has improved.

- **Flash 8–based security model**: Flash Lite 3.0 adds the Flash Player 8 security model for loading local and remote assets (e.g., text data, video, and audio). When publishing legacy Flash Lite 1.1 or 2.x content, it is important to recognize that Flash Lite 3 has a new publish setting for Flash Lite 3.0 that restricts the loading of external data. More information about the Flash 8 security model can be found at http://www.adobe.com/devnet/flashplayer/aticles/ flash_player_8_security.pdf.

The error codes for Flash Lite 3.0 and 3.1 are the same as Flash Lite 2.x. Please revisit the Flash Lite 2.0 section, "Introducing the Flash Lite 2.0 Error Codes" section of this chapter for the list of error codes you may encounter when building Flash Lite 3.0 and 3.1 applications.

Exploring Flash Lite 3.1

Flash Lite 3.1 tacks on a few additional features and capabilities:

- **Flash Lite 3.1 web browsing**: Access to the Web on mobile devices is now a necessity rather than a luxury. To enhance the user experience for browsing the Web, several Open Screen Project participants, such as Opera Software (with its Opera browser) and Nokia (with its S60 browser) have added Flash Lite plug-in support directly into their available browser technology.

    When supported, Flash Lite 3.1–enabled devices are able to browse SWF content that has been compiled up to Flash 9 (with limitations). Adobe provides guidelines on how to publish Flash Lite SWF content for web consumption, as well as how existing published Flash 9 content will render within the Flash Lite 3.1 browser.

    You can download these guidelines at http://www.adobe.com/devnet/devices/articles/ web_browsability_guidelines.pdf.

- **H.264 support**: Flash Lite 3.1 adds high-definition mobile videos encoded with the H.264 format for device platforms that support it.

> *We'll cover more about how to take advantage of the H.264 format in Chapter 15, when we cover working with Flash video across mobile and other devices supporting both Flash Lite 2.x, 3.x, and Flash 10.*

- **ActionScript extensions**: With Flash Lite 3.1 comes the ability to extend Flash capabilities via custom-built extensions. Previous to Flash Lite 3.1, Adobe and OEMs referred to this technology as man-machine interface (MMI), and it allowed device manufacturers to more easily allow communication between Flash Lite (typically user interfaces) and native device capabilities. This was accomplished using OEM-specific fscommand2 syntax (which we do not cover in this book, since it is not general public knowledge).

Extensions are essentially application plug-ins that authorized developers (typically those working for or with OEMs) to allow the communication between Flash Lite content and native applications or services running on devices. For example, you might hook up a Flash Lite user interface to respond to built-in device events, such as interception of an incoming phone call or reading and writing text files.

In this regard, you can think of ActionScript extensions as plug-ins for extending Flash Lite capabilities on devices supporting Flash Lite 3.1.

> We'll cover more about extending Flash Lite capabilities through APIs in Chapter 7 when we discuss Nokia S60 Platform Services and Sony Ericsson's Project Capuchin. However, ActionScript extensions, at the time of this writing, remain a feature of Flash Lite that only OEMs can access.
>
> If an SDK for creating ActionScript extensions, or other related material should become publicly available in the near future, we'll be sure to discuss it on our companion web site at http://advancED.flashmobilebook.com/chapter7/.

- **Distributable player support**: Flash Lite 3.1 is the first Flash Lite runtime from Adobe that allows OTA updates. Previous versions of Flash Lite had to be preinstalled across devices, which meant long deployment turnarounds for newer versions of Flash Lite to reach users.

  With the Flash Lite 3.1 Distributable Player, it is now possible to package SWF content, distribute it, and not have to worry about whether the Flash Lite 3.1 player is installed on the target device. With the Distributable Player, it will be installed, if it's not already present.

  Adobe Mobile Packager is used to package your SWF with the Flash Lite 3.1 Distributable Player, and it currently supports Symbian S60 and Windows Mobile (and possibly more by the time you read this).

> If our feature discussion on Flash Lite 3.1 here seems brief, it's because we devote our entire Chapter 3 to the features and capabilities of the runtime.

Let's move on to discussing another, less-well-known custom Flash player implementation called Adobe Mobile Client.

Exploring Adobe Mobile Client

Flash Lite is not the only runtime that is part of the overall Adobe Mobile Platform. Adobe Mobile Client (AMC) is another Flash runtime optimized for a wide range of devices. AMC is used for presentation of data services and data-enabled user interfaces, such as those found in the Flash Cast and Flash Home products.

AMC is a Flash 6–based player with support for a subset of ActionScript 1.0 and 2.0, and it supports many of the familiar features supported in Flash Lite including vector graphics, bitmap transparency, rotation, scaling, frame-based animation, UTF-8 support, text input, dynamic text, as well as native device and vector fonts.

AMC also has an object-based extension mechanism that allows for integration of device APIs, such as call logging, memory management, browser, media players, productivity software, and more.

For more information on the Adobe Mobile Client, you can visit the documentation (over 300 pages) at http://www.adobe.com/devnet/devices/articles/adobe_mobile_solutions_actionscript_language_reference.pdf.

> We will not be covering Flash development with the Adobe Mobile Client in this book, since it is tightly integrated into Flash Home and Flash Cast, which are both proprietary Adobe solutions. However, in the future, we may discuss it on our companion web site located at http://advancED.flashmobilebook.com/.

Exploring ActionScript

In this section, we'll talk a bit more about ActionScript 2.0 and specifics about how that technology ties in with Flash Lite. Don't expect this to be a comprehensive section on everything there is to know about ActionScript. That would easily be hundreds pages. See *Foundation ActionScript for Flash 8* (ISBN: 978-1-59059-618-0) for an in-depth look at the language.

Using ActionScript 1.0

Typically, when you're developing for mobile and devices, using ActionScript 1.0 syntax is rare. Although Flash Lite 1.1 does target ActionScript 1.0 during publishing, it's essentially Flash 4 syntax, or what we like to call "ActionScript 0.5." It does not support many of the features of ActionScript 1.0.

However, some devices on the market support ActionScript 1.0 because of the Flash Player 6 that it uses. For example, the PSP supports Flash 6 content that runs within the confines of the preinstalled Sony web browser. Thus, when you go to develop a game or other application for the PSP, you should target Flash 6 and ActionScript 1.0 settings.

However, most of the time with mobile devices, you'll find that the majority of your time will be spent either targeting Flash Lite 1.1, or Flash Lite 2.x and Flash Lite 3.x across Nokia, Sony Ericsson, and other mobile devices. This means you'll be working primarily with "ActionScript 0.5" and ActionScript 2.0. For this reason, we will not cover much ActionScript 1.0 in this book.

Using ActionScript 2.0

To use the Flash CS IDE, or not to? That is the question. Well, the answer is, "It depends."

Really, it comes down to personal preference (do you prefer working within an ActionScript editor?), how your development team operates (is it a team of 1, 5, or 10?), the kind of content you are creating (are you creating cute screensavers or a hard-core application?), and how much you will gain by using ActionScript 2.0 class frameworks (will you reuse the Flash Lite content elsewhere or on other target platforms?). These are all points to address when debating whether to go with a full-blown ActionScript 2 framework for Flash Lite projects.

Choosing an ActionScript 2.0 editor

What text editor to use for Flash Lite development is typically left up to you; use whatever set of tools you are most comfortable with.

With Flash Lite 1.1 development, there are no real advantages to working outside the Adobe Flash CS4 built-in ActionScript editor pane. Because of the Flash 4 syntax, lack of modularized external ActionScript class files, and the smaller set of APIs with Flash Lite 1.1, there are no advantages to using an external editor besides preference.

When it comes to working with ActionScript 2, however, you're more likely to want to use an external text editor. More elaborate code hinting, search and replace capabilities, as well as other niceties like color coding and syntax hinting can be helpful. Some other ActionScript editors when working with Flash Lite are explored in the following sections.

Flash Creative Suite 4 ActionScript editor pane   As we mentioned, when developing for Flash Lite 1.0 and 1.1, there is not much advantage to using an external ActionScript editor. Adobe Flash CS4 offers the default CS ActionScript pane environment for working with Flash 4–style code. The ActionScript editor pane (see Figure 2-3) offers some compelling features such as built-in help for Flash Lite 1.x, 2.x, and 3.x, code hinting, line numbering, and target path insertions based on timeline assets. All of this is fine for developing simple content such as Flash Lite screensavers or other less sophisticated content types.

However, for more complex ActionScript 2.0–based development with Flash Lite 2.x and 3.x, most developers tend to choose other editors, such as FlashDevelop, Eclipse, or Sepy, that offer more compelling features.

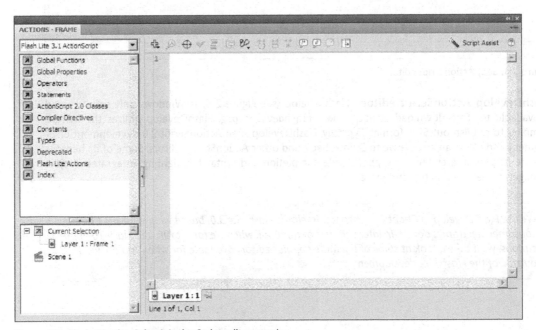

Figure 2-3. Flash Creative Suite 4 ActionScript editor panel

Sepy ActionScript editor Sepy is cross-platform for OS X and Windows (see Figure 2-4). It is open source and available for free download at http://sourceforge.net/projects/SEPY. Sepy is a good choice for developers who need a free ActionScript editor that is cross platform and offers many features that help with ActionScript 2.0 workflow (e.g., integrated CVS and SVN, a shared object reader, an XML reader, JavaDoc support, and more).

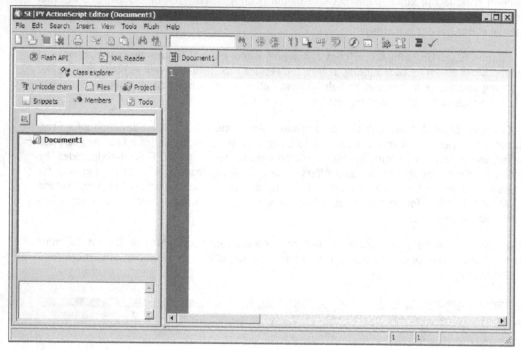

Figure 2-4. Sepy ActionScript editor

FlashDevelop ActionScript editor FlashDevelop (see Figure 2-5) is Windows-only software and is available for free download at http://www.flashdevelop.org. FlashDevelop utilizes the MTASC compiler to publish out SWF format. Typically, FlashDevelop is an ActionScript 2.0 development environment and offers an alternative to Eclipse, Sepy, and other ActionScript editors. Some of its benefits include its plug-in architecture support, code completion and syntax highlighting, integrated project manager, project templates, and more.

> We use FlashDevelop in Chapter 5 when we develop a Flash Lite 3.0–based widget for the Chumby consumer electronics device. In later chapters of this book when we target AIR and Flash 10 applications, we'll take a look at some of the more popular editors available for when you are working outside of the Flash Lite development world.

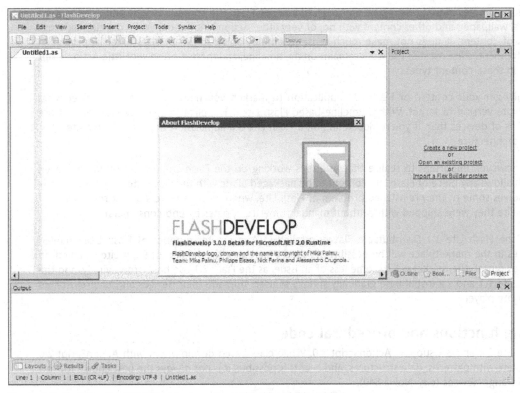

Figure 2-5. FlashDevelop 3.0.0 (the latest version at the time of this writing)

Developing via the timeline vs. classes

There are essentially three different approaches to working with Flash Lite. Which path you choose depends on a number of factors, including which version target devices support, as well as the complexity of the mobile or device project you're working on. Other factors might include the total number of team members, how a code base might potentially be reused across multiple projects, and the target device sets and the highest versions of Flash Lite that they support.

The approaches can be based on the following three aspects of development:

- Timeline
- Functions and procedural code
- Class

Working with the timeline

For projects that do not involve a lot of code, Flash Lite 1.1 timeline-based development can be used to maximize the range of devices that support Flash Lite. A Flash Lite 1.1 timeline-based approach to development can be used to attain a larger total number of addressable devices on the market, yet offer ActionScript support on embedded frames and in #include files.

Perfect examples of using a timeline approach to building Flash Lite content include animated screen-savers, wallpaper, and other content with no, or very little, ActionScript code. When developing these types of content, it does not make much sense to employ an ActionScript class-based approach to development, since most of the work remains on the timeline, and there is often very little ActionScript at all in these content types.

To fully get your content or Flash Lite application to market, you need to carefully consider what Flash Lite version to target. With a timeline-based Flash Lite 1.1 application, you can hit many more millions of devices than if you're depending on a Flash Lite 3.0 application that has a complete MVC class architecture.

It is, however, important to realize that Adobe is working on the Flash Lite 3.1 Distributable Player, which allows any piece of Flash Lite content to be packaged along with the Flash Lite player. Essentially this solves some of the preinstalled problem of Flash Lite, where devices were stuck at the version of Flash Lite they were shipped with (without manual firmware updates by end consumers).

With the Flash Lite 3.1 Distributable Player installed OTA, a greater number of Flash Lite–enabled devices in the marketplace will be possible. As time progresses, the version of Flash Lite installed on devices out on the market will become less of an issue, as the Flash 3.1 use base grows virally, and the Flash Lite 1.1 and 2.x install base gradually shrinks as users upgrade their devices and/or preinstalled Flash Lite players.

Using functions and procedural code

Flash Lite 2.x and 3.x support ActionScript 2.0. While class-based development with ActionScript 2.0 complete with patterns, data structures, and events *is* possible, it is *not always* the best choice for low to midrange devices (e.g., Nokia S40).

You should keep in mind the device constraints, such as low memory and less powerful CPUs, found on many mobile devices supporting Flash Lite. Power management, or managing performance and memory effectively, is a crucial piece of Flash Lite development. Using an ActionScript 2.0 class-based approach to projects may get you code reuse, but at what costs? CPU and memory overhead! You need to be careful of introducing significant performance lag in your applications due to heavy ActionScript processing.

For this reason, sometimes, it can be better to take a function-based or procedure-based approach to developing Flash Lite content. With functions, you get the benefits of reusable code, and these snip-pets can be assembled in external ActionScript library files, contained on the first frame of a Flash Lite application, or inserted into a MovieClip that may be reused across projects.

Consumers of applications don't care if the code is in ten functions or twenty, but they do care if the application crashes with an out-of-memory error or is annoyingly slow! It's important to test early, and often, and to always keep device limitations and potential bottlenecks in mind.

Memory and CPU are perhaps the greatest challenges to address with mobile development right along with screen size constraints and user input methods (e.g., stylus, touch screen, buttons, or QWERTY keyboard). Try to keep this in mind when planning out your project before the development phase even begins.

For high-end devices, such as newer S60 smart phones from Nokia (e.g., N97 and 5800), as well as other embedded, MID, and high-end consumer electronics devices (e.g., Chumby), class development and object-oriented programming starts to make more sense. These devices typically have more memory and available CPU.

Developing classes

For mobile applications that will be reused across projects or that involve multiple team members, it makes sense to take a look at class-based development if the target devices support Flash Lite 2.x and 3.x. Typically, more memory and CPU is going to be needed, so the lowest common denominator needs to be chosen from the get-go if there are multiple target devices. Memory and CPU requirements should be determined before development begins.

During developing, a close eye should be kept on memory to gauge how well an application is utilizing memory and/or CPU during its execution through early, middle, and even late stages of project development.

If you're lucky enough to be dealing with only one target device, it becomes much easier to manage memory requirements for Flash Lite content, because there is one, consistent device with the same memory and CPU specifications.

Some handy tools for keeping track of memory and CPU usage are to take advantage of the Performance and Memory panels in Device Central CS4 (we'll talk about Device Central more in Chapter 3 and beyond).

Another tip is to utilize the fscommand2 command GetFreePlayerMemory and GetTotalPlayerMemory to determine how much memory is actually being consumed by Flash Lite during runtime on a physical device (Device Central simulation will not catch every memory leak!).

You might also benefit from using FPS monitors and memory usage monitor components, such as the ones provided in the Nokia Oxygen framework at http://wiki.forum.nokia.com/index.php/ Oxygen_-_The_Flash_Lite_Developers_Kit.

> *In Chapters 9 through 14, when we get into talking about working with AIR and Flash 10 on high-end smart phones and more powerful MIDs, you'll be utilizing class-based ActionScript development a lot more frequently than with lower-end Flash Lite 2.x and 3.x devices.*
>
> *Although we would love to spend hundreds pages on talking about working with object-oriented programming (OOP) in Flash Lite with ActionScript 2.0, unfortunately, we cannot. If you are unfamiliar with OOP and class-based development, we recommend the next best alternative. Pick up Foundation Object Oriented Flash 8 (ISBN: 978-1-59059-619-6).*
>
> *We also recommend checking out Chapter 4, where we discuss some tips and tricks for working with Flash Lite; you'll learn how to best optimize your mobile content across mobile devices.*

Exploring the Flash Lite CDKs

Since the inception of Flash Lite, there have been a few CDKs that can be leveraged by developers looking to create Flash Lite applications based on common assets, code, and frameworks (rather than building applications from scratch). Reusable components and other tools are often essential to building successful applications both quickly and more efficiently. Here, we explore some of those options publicly and/or commercially available to the broader Flash Lite community.

Introducing the Flash Lite CDKs

These CDKs can be leveraged with both Flash Lite 1.1 and Flash Lite 2.0:

- **Adobe Flash Lite 3.1 Distributable Player Solution CDK**: http://tv.adobe.com/#pg+15313
- **Adobe Flash Lite 2.0 CDK**: http://www.adobe.com/cfusion/entitlement/index.cfm?e=flashlite2cdk
- **Adobe Flash Lite 1.1 CDK**: http://www.adobe.com/cfusion/entitlement/index.cfm?e=flashcdk

> We'll cover more about the Flash Lite 3.1 Distributable Player Solution CDK in Chapter 3 when we talk about Adobe Mobile Packager and the Flash Lite 3.1 Distributable Player.

Both the Flash Lite 1.1 and 2.0 CDKs from Adobe contain tips, techniques, interface elements, examples, and tutorials on how to leverage Flash Lite 2 for mobile phones and devices.

Several other very device- and region-specific Flash Lite CDKs are available at http://www.adobe.com/devnet/devices/development_kits.html. These CDKs are for working with legacy iMode, Motorola, Sony Ericsson, Windows Mobile, Pocket PC, Nokia, KDDI, Sony CLIE, and other device platforms. Since the previous CDKs are legacy platforms, we will not cover them further in this book.

Introducing the Device Central CS4 SDK

As we have already discussed, Device Central CS4 (see Figure 2-6) is the newest testing and device emulator available. Previous to Device Central CS4, Device Central CS3 served as Adobe's successor to the Flash 8 mobile emulator. Today, developers have the luxury of using Device Central CS3 or CS4, which allow streamlined testing from Flash and other tools directly into Device Central for quick and efficient testing workflow.

> In Chapter 3, we'll discuss the Device Central SDK in more depth, including where to find more information on getting started creating custom automated scripts and custom tasks to do things like send Flash Lite content automatically to connected Bluetooth devices, as well as explore many ways to improve workflow in Adobe Creative Suite 4.

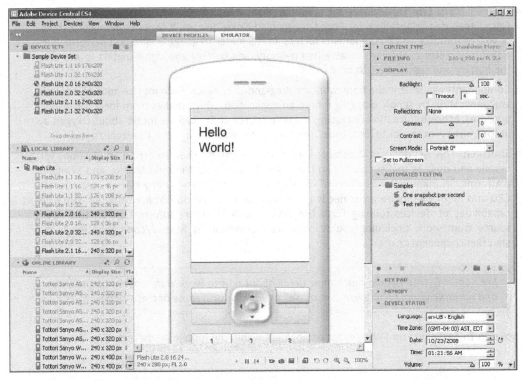

Figure 2-6. Adobe Device Central CS4

Introducing Flash Lite visual component sets

Some visual component frameworks known (and publicly available) for Flash Lite follow:

- **Adobe Experience Team (XD) prototyping components**: Although a work in progress, these visual user interface components for Flash Lite 1.1 and Flash Lite 2.x have been graciously donated to the Flash Lite development community and are available for download at http://flashmobileblog.com/examples/.

  The components include examples for list, slider, tile, navigation model, and gapper components that can be utilized for Flash Lite 2.x and 3.x development. There are also carousel menu, story, and scroll bar components for Flash Lite 1.1.

  Provided in the Adobe XD Flash Lite component set is an image-handling (loading/unloading) example that uses the TileMenu component, as well as a NavModel component that demonstrates creating device UIs for multiscreen applications.

  We'll explain more about the Adobe XD components in Chapter 6 when we cover Flash Lite frameworks.

> *The Adobe Experience Team components are not supported by Adobe and are merely intended for prototyping and noncommercial use by developers.*

- **Oxygen Flash Lite Developers Kit**: This is a set of free components and libraries to use in Flash Lite–based applications for Flash Lite–enabled Nokia devices. It includes debugging tools, as well as reusable visual components such as an FPS meter to gauge application performance, a memory meter to display available free memory, and battery and signal meters to monitor the battery and signal strength on devices.

  Components available in the framework are drag-and-drop ready. Each may be added to a Flash Lite application by simply dragging it onto an application, which makes them ideal for testing purposes. More information (including example source code) can be found about Oxygen at http://wiki.forum.nokia.com/index.php/Oxygen_-_The_Flash_Lite_Developers_Kit.

- **Shuriken**: This ActionScript 2 component framework can be used to create applications for mobile and devices that support Flash Lite 2 like the Chumby, Windows Mobile, and Symbian platforms. Shuriken is a collection of visual GUI components and utility classes that address CPU and memory requirements needed to run on devices that do not have the performance capabilities of devices running Flash Lite 3.x or Flash 10. More information on this open source framework (including source code) can be found at http://code.google.com/p/shurikencomponents/.

> In Chapter 6, we'll go into much more detail about how to work with some of these CDKs and reusable visual component sets, as well as working with some of these with Flash Lite.

Let's move on to packaging up SWF files for deployment within the mobile landscape.

Packaging Flash Lite content

One the most unique aspects of working with Flash across devices, including mobile ones, is the way content is delivered to end users. Packaging Flash Lite content across devices depends on various factors, including the target device, operator or carrier, and sometimes even the region in which the content is deployed.

Understanding Flash Lite packaging formats for SWFs

Here, we discuss some of the common mobile and device packaging formats for Flash Lite SWFs:

- NFL, or Nokia Flash Lite packaging, is a standard for packaging Flash Lite content to address the S40 platform. NFL is supported by only S40 fifth-edition and newer phones, so for previous S40 devices, you must use SWFs to distribute your content on the platform. More information about NFL can be found at http://www.forum.nokia.com/info/sw.nokia.com/id/384a5c01-70fe-480d-86bc-627f92d3ed7c/Series_40_Nokia_Flash_Lite_NFL_Package_Format.html.

- SIS, or Symbian Installation Source, is an installable file format for the Symbian operating system that allows applications to be loaded on Symbian-based devices. Developers who target Nokia S60 devices are the most likely to use .sis files.

SIS files can be Symbian certified in various degrees (which means that the content has gone through significant external certified testing) and can provide extra functionality, such as getting rid of Symbian install warning pop-ups for security.

Although Nokia and Symbian provide tools, many popular pieces of software will export to SIS format and offer more elegant user interfaces and wizards to make SIS package creation much easier (see the next section for more information). The SIS format is not exclusive to the Flash Lite world, and it can be used to package Symbian, Java, or other executables to be loaded on S60 devices.

Also, SIS files allow Flash Lite content to be installed within the software applications folder user interface (the specific name varies across devices), with a custom graphical icon for launching it (e.g., Nokia uses Scalable Vector Graphic, SVG, icons on S60 devices).

One point about SIS files is that sometimes aggregators and content providers require those files to be securely signed. The party responsible for that is www.symbiansigned.com. Nokia's OVI Store, for example, requires Flash Lite SIS content to be signed. We'll talk more about OVI when we discuss Flash Lite Mobile ecosystems later in this chapter, in the section, "Distributing and monetizing Flash Lite content."

- CAB, Microsoft Windows Cabinet, files are a native compressed archive format similar to .zip format. Similar to Symbian SIS files, CAB files support compression and digital signing as well. Microsoft offers support for Flash Lite 2.x and 3.x across many of its Windows Mobile 6 smart phones and other devices. Because of this, CAB is a valid packaging file format for SWF files on the Windows Mobile Platform.

  Adobe Mobile Packager has the option to generate CAB files containing the Flash Lite 3.1 Distributable Player installer and any deployable SWF files. We'll talk more about this in the next chapter.

- JAR, Java archive, files can package SWF files by using both Jarpa and SWF2JAR. JAR files are analogous to .zip files within the Java development world (although the actual archive encoding process is different). JAR files can be created using the jar command that is part of the Java Development Kit (JDK) that is freely available from Sun Microsystems and the resulting file typically ends in the .jar extension. JARs are not exclusive to Flash Lite content; they can be used for Java or other development platforms. Both SWF2JAR and Jarpa are software products that allow for JAR packaging of Flash Lite content. More info about the JAR file format can be found at http://en.wikipedia.org/wiki/JAR_(file_format).

- WGZ, or Widget Zip, is basically a renamed .zip file that contains predefined assets, such as a manifest file, an icon graphic, and Flash Lite SWF files that compose the package (see Figure 2-7). WGZ is the standard packaging for Nokia Web Runtime S60 widgets.

> We'll talk about the Nokia Web Runtime (WRT) in Chapter 5, when we explore how to develop Flash Lite widgets for the S60 platform. Nokia WGZ files can be used for packaging not only Flash Lite content but other development platforms as well (Java, Symbian, etc.). We'll cover creating WGZ files in Chapter 5 when we build a Nokia WRT S60 widget using the third-party widget IDE called Aptana.

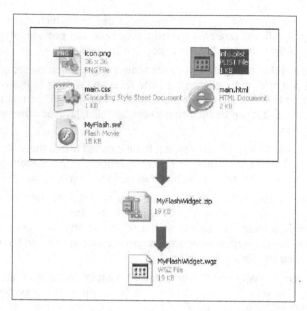

Figure 2-7.
File contents of a Nokia
WGZ file for WRT

Packaging file formats and methods for Flash Lite content

The following sections cover some of the available packaging solutions for Flash Lite–enabled mobile and devices today.

Custom SIS

To learn how to create a SIS file from scratch, a great resource is the tutorial over on Adobe's Developer Connection site at http://www.adobe.com/devnet/devices/articles/creating_sis_files.html.

Custom NFL

As we discussed earlier, NFL is Nokia Flash Lite packaging and is unique to the Nokia S40 platform. If you're not using a third-party GUI tool, such as SWF2NFL or W'd-get-it, you can follow these instructions for creating the archive manually at the command line: http://www.forum.nokia.com/info/sw.nokia.com/id/384a5c01-70fe-480d-86bc-627f92d3ed7c/Series_40_Nokia_Flash_Lite_NFL_Package_Format.html.

SWF2SIS

This legacy Flash Lite packager created by BlueSkyNorth allowed Flash Lite 1.1 or 2.0 applications, games, and other content types to be bundled in SIS format for second-edition Nokia devices. Today, it's largely unused, as third-edition Nokia devices are much more prominent in the marketplace. More information can be found at http://www.blueskynorth.com/swf2sis/. For third-edition S60 devices, you should consider using SWF2Go, SWFPack.com, or some of the other SIS packaging tools listed in this section.

SWF2Go Professional

This third-party Flash Lite packager supports packaging for Nokia S60 devices. SWF2Go version 2.0 is a professional SIS installer and SWF launcher toolkit. It's compatible with Flash Lite 1.1, 2.x, and 3.x and works with Symbian third-edition devices (Symbian versions 9.1, 9.2, and 9.3+). Version 2.0 of the product produces Symbian-signed and express-signed SIS installers containing Flash Lite content.

In addition to packaging, SWF2Go supports Python S60 and Net60 runtimes, so that Flash Lite can be extended to create more-powerful applications (e.g., allowing a Flash Lite application to pull on-device calendar information or tap into current GPS location coordinates).

> *Although we don't cover working with SWF2Go to extend Flash Lite applications in Chapter 7, we do cover working with Nokia S60 Platform Services and Sony Ericsson Capuchin. If you are interested in extending your Flash Lite content, please see Chapter 7.*

Another useful feature offered with this product is the ability to create trial versions of SWF content (with splash screens and "Buy now" reminders). SWF2Go offers an elegant, step-by-step wizard interface for constructing SIS files.

More information about this Flash Lite packager can be found at http://www.swf2go.com/.

SWF2JAR

The SWF2JAR software utility tool (see Figure 2-8) allows you to package your SWF files into JAR format on Sony Ericsson devices. The main purpose of this tool is to allow Java and Flash Lite developers a means to package any applications that take advantage of Capuchin.

> *We'll talk more about Project Capuchin and how to use SWF2JAR in our discussion of extending Flash Lite in Chapter 7.*

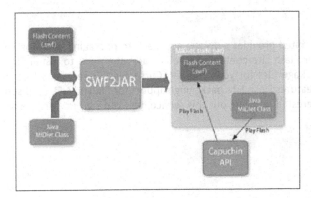

Figure 2-8.
Sony Ericsson's SWF-2JAR allows SWFs to be bundled with Java midlet class files inside a JAR file.

Jarpa

The Jarpa Project is an open source, community-driven project to allow Flash Lite content in SWF format to be packaged into a .jar file (see Figure 2-9). Jarpa predates Sony Ericsson's SWF2JAR tool and is not specific to the Sony Ericsson platform. For more information on Jarpa, check out the Google code project at http://code.google.com/p/jarpa/.

Figure 2-9.
Jarpa Project: how
the Jarpa packaging
system works

At this time of writing, the community authors of Jarpa have announced that they will no longer support this product in the future. Use Jarpa at your own discretion.

SWFPack.com

This third-party product from Kuneri Limited provides a unique approach to packaging, allowing you to log in to a web site to package your Flash Lite content. This eliminates the need to install SDKs, Perl, and the like to create custom package files for your content. Currently, this service is free for use if you're a Flash Lite developer. It features Flash Lite packaging support for SIS and NFL (and soon perhaps even CAB) files. If you are interested in trying out this service, you can sign up for free and access it at http://www.swfpack.com/.

Forum Nokia Flash (and Flash Lite) packager

This is yet another online packaging tool that is actually based on the SWFPack.com solution. It is provided by Nokia and allows developers to output packaged Flash Lite content for S40 and S60 devices. It can be accessed at http://www.forum.nokia.com/Resources_and_Information/Explore/Web_Technologies/Flash_Lite/.

> *As we understand it, Nokia has licensed at least some of the SWFPack.com code. Hence, the similarities between SWFPack.com and Nokia's online packaging service.*

SWF2NFL

SWF2NFL is a freely available tool that allows you to package your Flash Lite content for S40, fifth-edition phones using the NFL packaging format. The application (see Figure 2-10) is actually an AIR-based application packager. More information can be found at http://www.moket.com/swf2nfl/.

Figure 2-10.
SWF2NFL: an AIR-based tool for packaging Flash Lite content into the NFL format

Adobe Mobile Packager

This Flash Lite content packager represents Adobe's first effort to provide the Flash Lite development community with a packager for Flash Lite SWF files.

> *In the next chapter, we'll point to some video tutorials that cover the process of packaging Flash Lite 3.1 content with Adobe Mobile Packager.*

Currently, Symbian S60 and Windows Mobile platforms are supported (see Figure 2-11). The packager allows Flash Lite 1.x, 2.x, and 3.x content to be packaged into both SIS and CAB files via an easy-to-use interface.

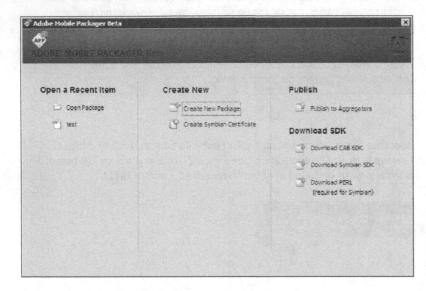

Figure 2-11.
Adobe Mobile Packager's splash screen

Adobe Mobile Packager differs from some of the other packaging solutions available in that the actual Flash Lite 3.1 player gets installed *along with* the Flash Lite content to be packaged. This enables supported devices without Flash Lite already installed to download the latest Flash Lite player OTA.

To use Adobe Mobile Packager, you must have either the Microsoft CAB SDK or Symbian SDK to create the required CAB or SIS files (see Figure 2-12). Active Perl also has to be installed. All of the installation procedures are laid out in the documentation provided by Adobe after you download the Adobe Mobile Packager setup.

During the extraction process of the packaged file, both the File Lite content and the Flash Lite 3.1 player are installed (if necessary) onto the device.

> *At the time of this writing, Adobe Mobile Packager is Windows-only software, but on a Mac, you can install and run it via Bootcamp or virtualization software such as Parallels from VMWare (we have used Parallels with no issues).*

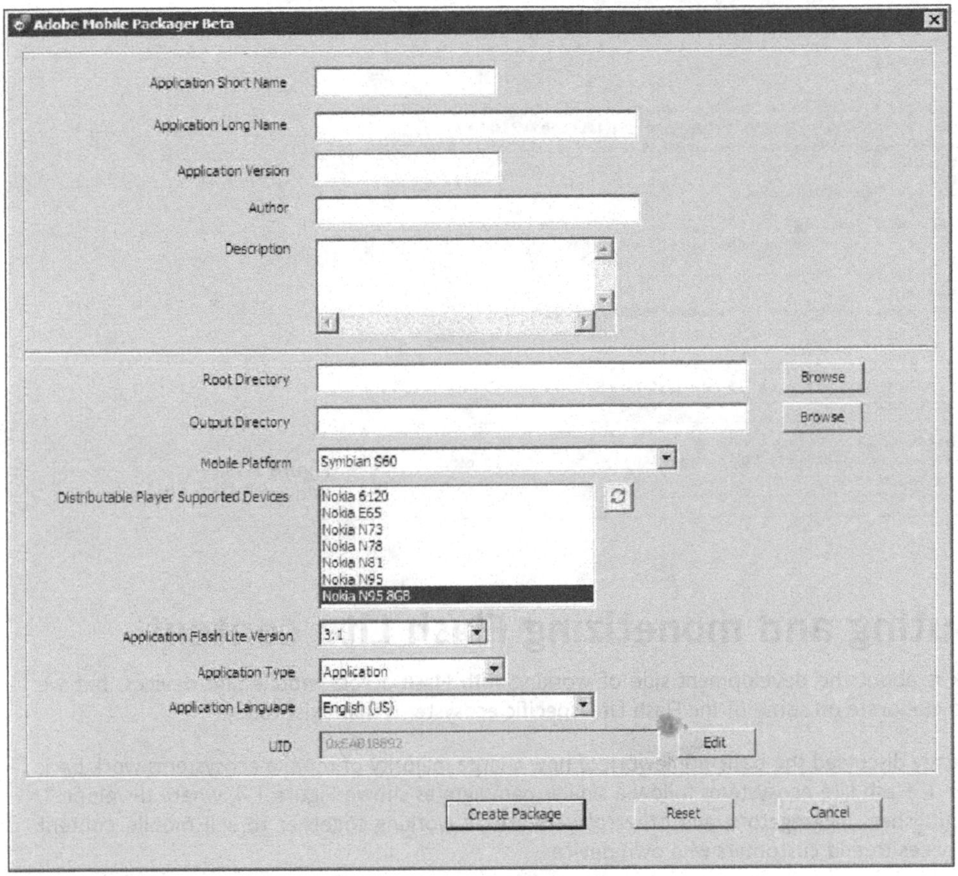

Figure 2-12. Configuring the target device platforms in Adobe Mobile Packager (BETA)

W'd-get-it

This community tool (see Figure 2-13) allows packaging of Flash Lite SWF content for Nokia S60 WRT (WGZ files) as well as NFL packaging for S40 fifth-edition devices. It is currently a Windows-only tool and is available for free download at http://mobilewish.com/applications/wd-get-it/.

Once content is packaged, the next step is to get it out onto markets or to distribute content to mobile and devices. After all, developing content might be fun, but you'd like to get paid for all the hard work put into content development.

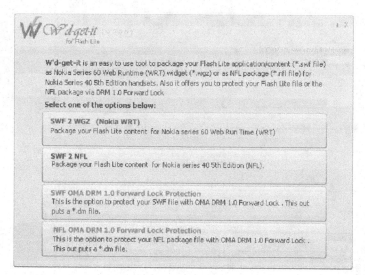

Figure 2-13.
W'd-get-it Flash Lite packager

Distributing and monetizing Flash Lite content

This book is about the development side of working with Flash across mobile and devices, but we wanted to elaborate on some of the Flash Lite–specific ecosystems that exist today.

We've already discussed the basic framework of how a large majority of mobile ecosystems work back in Chapter 1. Flash Lite ecosystems follow a similar paradigm as shown Figure 1-4, where developers, content publishers, aggregators, and other players are all working together to sell mobile content and/or services to end customers who own devices.

For more information on mobile ecosystems, a publicly available white paper from Adobe and Strategic Analytics called "How Mobile Ecosystems Work" is provided at http://www.adobe.com/devnet/devices/articles/mobile_ecosystem.pdf. It is a good primer on how mobile content distribution works and gives you insight into possible business opportunities with Flash Lite (although admittedly it's a bit outdated, as it was written in 2008).

Of course, one important part of distribution is also the monetary aspect of selling mobile content, otherwise known as monetization.

Monetization with mobile content, in general, is a tricky business full of unique challenges due to the fragmentation of the marketplace, mobile content consumption in different regions, and mobile cultures, as well as other factors. An entire book could be written about making money with Flash and mobile.

This section breaks down some of the basics you need to know with an emphasis on working with third-party aggregators and content providers. However, we make no claims here as to which companies will provide the best return on your investment of time and energy when distributing Flash Lite content.

> *For a more comprehensive list of content providers, aggregators, or other Flash and Flash Lite business opportunities in the mobile realm, we recommend you check out the web site http://www.flashmobilebook.com/links.html#companies.*

Introducing Flash Lite content aggregators and providers

Some of the aggregators and active content providers out there that we have heard of and/or have previous experience with are explained in the following sections (note that these are presented in no particular order of preference).

Zed

Zed is a mobile entertainment and products company primarily based in Europe. It is known for acquiring and integrating smaller mobile development companies. One such company Zed acquired in 2008 was Mobitween, an early Flash Lite game company based in France.

As part of the merger, Zed now owns the user-content–generated, Flash-based game service called ugenGames. It also owns Mobigamz, which aggregates third-party content through its content provider program. See http://www.zed.com/, http://www.mobitween.com/, http://www.ugengames.com, and http://www.mobigamz.com/ for more information about how Zed is leveraging Flash Lite.

> *As we'll discuss in Chapter 3, Zed is one of several companies allowing Flash Lite 3.1 content to be packaged for delivery through the Flash Lite 3.1 Distributable Player.*

ThumbPlay

This relative newcomer to the Flash world distribution scene is a New York–based mobile entertainment content company called ThumbPlay. ThumbPlay is one of several mobile companies invested into the initial Adobe Flash Lite 3.1 Distributable Player solution and is one of many routes for you to get your Flash Lite content to market. For more information, please see http://www.thumbplay.com/.

> *We'll also cover ThumbPlay more in Chapter 3 when we talk about the Flash Lite 3.1 Distributable Player solution.*

GetJar

GetJar is a mobile content company with a slightly different model to existing revenue-sharing models based on content for sale. It offers content to Java, Symbian, Windows Mobile, Blackberry, Palm, as well as Flash Lite–enabled devices, but instead of charging full price for the download, it relies on advertising featured along with content. More information can be found at http://www.getjar.com/.

> *GetJar is another company that is part of the initial launch of the Adobe Flash Lite 3.1 Distributable Player solution, so we'll cover them more in Chapter 3 too.*

Nokia MOSH

The Nokia MOSH content portal site is an open source, free, and experimental content distribution community for all kinds of mobile content available for Nokia platform devices. MOSH content is made up of audio clips, videos, games, applications, screensavers, wallpapers, themes, and other media assets developed and submitted by users worldwide. It also includes a smattering of Flash Lite content for S60 devices (with some compatible S40 content).

From our perspective, MOSH was an early marketing tool intended for developers so that Nokia could evaluate emerging content for its various ecosystems (e.g., Nokia Download!). MOSH was useful for end user feedback and for getting marketing attention. Developers used it as a stepping-stone to get prominently featured on Nokia Download! and sometimes get preinstalled across Nokia devices.

> *During of writing of this chapter, MOSH has been phased out and will be replaced by Nokia's new mobile application store, called OVI. We anticipate some content off of MOSH will migrate into the OVI Store over time. We still mention MOSH here, as a good example of an experiment for mobile content distribution.*

MOSH is located at `http://mosh.nokia.com/`, but by the time you read this, it will most likely have been redirected to the OVI Store (which we discuss next).

Nokia OVI Store   Currently, the OVI Service is a site for collecting, storing, and sharing media assets (photos, videos, etc.) uploaded by users from a desktop PC or their Nokia device (you can think of it as a Flickr or YouTube service created by Nokia for S40 and S60 devices). You can find out more about OVI at `http://www.ovi.com/`.

> *Here's a fun bit of mobile trivia to try to stump your friends and colleagues: "ovi" means "portal" or "doorway."*

One new piece of the OVI service will be its much-anticipated store, set to launch as early as May 2009 (knock on wood). The OVI Store is "MOSH version 3.0" with a lot more bells and whistles, plus an actual monetary incentive for revenue sharing from uploaded content (think "iPhone App Store for Nokia devices")! The store is a self-service online publishing tool for developers to submit, distribute, and monetize their mobile content for Nokia devices (Nokia S60 Symbian-based devices and others). This includes Flash Lite content such as productivity applications, games, screensavers, and other Flash-based content. If you are interested in publishing content to the OVI Store, you can get started and register at `http://publish.ovi.com`. Later this year when the store launches, the content will most likely be available for consumers to download at `http://store.ovi.com/` as well as through an on-device application yet to be defined. We're imagining the latter will be similar to the Nokia Download! application found on many S60 devices.

Nokia Software Market and Nokia Download!

Nokia Software Market is a business-to-consumer marketplace that connects developers and their products directly to millions of users with Nokia devices. Developers marketing products through Nokia Software Market can get support from Forum Nokia, an online community created to bring together professional developers working with technologies and platforms supported by Nokia mobile devices.

The Nokia Download! client is a preinstalled native application found on many S60 and newer S40 devices. This on-device application allows consumers to access a portal containing hundreds of pieces of content that can be downloaded and installed directly onto the device. Some of the content is free, though the majority is not. If you're interested in targeting Nokia devices with Flash Lite content, you should take a hard look at http://www.forum.nokia.com/main/go_to_market/overview.html.

All of the players we have mentioned in this section work in some shape or form with Flash Lite content. By the time you read this book, there will likely be more options, so we invite you to check out http://advancED.flashmobilebook.com/links.html#ecosystem for the most current list.

Verizon Wireless Get It Now

Since Flash Lite 2.1 for BREW was released, it has been possible to distribute Flash Lite content through the built-in content catalog feature on Verizon Wireless mobile phones, called Get It Now. The Get It Now solution is viable for larger mobile companies, but for smaller mobile companies and individuals, it is (in our opinion) much more feasible to approach the third-party content catalogs we mentioned previously. More information about the Verizon Get It Now service and the road to distributing content with this solution can be found at http://www.vzwdevelopers.com and http://www.adobe.com/devnet/devices/verizon.html.

Smashing content

As a subsidiary of Smashing Ideas, Inc., Smashing Content started back in the Flash Lite 1.1 days and has since evolved to acquire BlueSkyNorth (a longtime Flash Lite casual games company) out of the UK region.

At the time of this writing, Smashing Content is another method of getting Flash Lite content targeted for the BREW platform out onto devices on the Verizon Wireless network. The company has a similar content catalog application to Shockwave Games, although it appears to be more open to third-party content than Shockwave Games, and has a dozen distributors. For more information, see http://www.smashingcontent.com/.

Shockwave Games (Atom Entertainment)

Originally, this company developed casual games for the desktop but has now ported many of those games into Flash Lite format. It maintains a casual games catalog on the Verizon Wireless BREW content catalog deck from third-party developers. For more information, check out http://www.atomfilms.com/.

Moket Content Network

This is a Flash Lite–based content provider service offering from Moket Limited, located in Australia. The Moket Content Network (MCN) was created to fill the need for smaller mobile businesses, as well as individual developers, to get their mobile content—games or applications, wallpaper, or screensavers—into various Flash Lite distribution channels. More details and information about getting started with the Moket Content Network can be found at http://www.moket.com/mcn/.

Handango

This mobile content distributor is located at: http://www.handango.com/. Essentially, it's an aggregator for the millions of Symbian- and Windows Mobile–based devices out there. Handango has been around for many years, even prior to the introduction of Flash Lite. In fact, the Handango distribution site delivers many types of mobile platform content (including Flash Lite) to millions of users across many popular mobile platforms. Developers can join the Handango Content Partner Program to find out if it's a viable solution to get your Flash Lite content and applications through the web to mobile devices.

Voeveo

This New Zealand–based content distribution company is another relative newcomer. It is actively seeking new Flash Lite games, applications, and other content. Check it out at http://www.voeveo.com/.

Mobibase

Mobibase is a global mobile content aggregator, based in Paris, with a growing Flash Lite content catalogue of wallpaper, screensavers, animations, and casual mobile games targeting millions of mobile consumers. The company is looking to expand its catalog with Flash Lite content to provide to carriers and mobile publishers. You can submit your content, get qualified to sign a licensing agreement to work with Mobibase, or just find more information at http://www.mobibase.com/.

ClickGamer

ClickGamer has a similar model to Handango and is a direct-to-consumer portal site catering to a number of device platforms including Windows Mobile, Symbian, Palm, Java ME, RIM, and others. It aggregates Flash Lite content, and developers can join this network to reach out to its customers at http://www.clickgamer.com/.

FunMobility

FunMobility, a leading provider of innovative wireless community and media services in the United States, deals with Flash Lite content as well many other platforms and media services. For more information about this company and its endeavors, head on over to http://www.funmobility.com.

Chumby Network portal

Chumby is a hackable, Linux-based, open source, consumer electronics device; it's a nonportable, Wi-Fi–enabled, touch-screen Internet appliance that sits on your desktop. The device runs Flash Lite 3.0, but the player is updateable via firmware updates OTA through its Wi-Fi connection.

At the time of this writing, all the content on Chumby is free for users to subscribe to and access (no direct monetization method for developers is provided Chumby Industries). However, just recently, Chumby has announced plans to scale its online content distribution system into other consumer electronics devices such as set-top boxes, PCs, and other screen formats besides the cuddly-looking Chumby device.

Chumby Flash widget content is essentially composed of SWF files that run inside a channel framework (much like a TV), where users add and remove their favorite games, applications, news, and other widgets. More information on working with Chumby can be found at http://www.chumby.com/developers/ and http://www.chumby.com/developers/flash/.

> In Chapter 5, when we talk about developing Flash-based widgets, we'll cover Chumby and how to develop for this unique platform that runs Flash Lite version 3.0.

Iguana Mobile

This content provider and aggregator located in Singapore deals with a lot of Nokia-based content on S60 devices. More information about this company can be found at http://www.iguanamobile.com/, and its content portal is at http://www.iguanamobile.com/main/.

Aggregating content for Flash 10 and AIR applications

Later in this book, we'll cover designing and developing Flash 10 and AIR applications. It's still very early with Adobe working on these to get them into suitable mobile versions, so no tangible ecosystems exist quite yet. However, we see no reason why Adobe's AIR Marketplace (http://www.adobe.com/cfusion/marketplace/) will not be extended to support mobile content and applications when it's appropriate.

Adobe did have the legacy Flash Lite Exchange (http://www.adobe.com/devnet/devices/articles/mad_exchange.html), which developers took advantage of in the early days of Flash Lite 1.1. This helped many developers to market and promote their mobile content until ecosystems were established.

We anticipate the same happening when AIR makes it ways onto Flash-enabled devices. However, these are merely our thoughts on the matter. We make no guarantees on how things play out! We also fully anticipate that many of the players we've mentioned previously working with Flash Lite (e.g., Nokia, ThumbPlay, and Zed) will gradually begin to shift to Flash 10 and AIR. Many we suspect will be offering Flash 10 and AIR content as these technologies start to make their way onto shipping handsets and other devices. There is no doubt there will be new players and we'll try to post about them on http://advancED.flashmobilebook.com/links.html#ecosystem as they appear in the future.

Distributing via direct-to-customer and consultation models

Publishing content to various ecosystems and working with content providers and aggregators is not for everyone. Besides often taking a cut of developer profits, these systems can be time consuming to implement and demand many more resources to manage projects. For example, you often need to devote your own time not only to development but to sales, marketing, and support.

Another route to take is to sell content directly to customers or consumers. This often means consultation, work for hire, training, and similar activities. This model is not something to be overlooked and can be an option for independent developers who don't necessarily have aspirations to grow large mobile companies. Many members of the Flash Lite community have taken this path. However, it's up to you to make decisions about how you go about trying to make money off your efforts with Flash in the mobile and device landscape.

Introducing the Open Screen Project Fund

In early 2009, Adobe and Nokia launched an initiative called the Open Screen Project Fund. Essentially, it's a $10-million market development fund created to stimulate and accelerate products, services, and content that leverage the Adobe Flash platform across mobile, desktop, and other consumer electronics devices.

Developers and companies can submit their most innovative business ideas in hopes of being awarded a bit of seed money to get those ideas into production. Submissions are reviewed by a panel of judges (currently from Adobe and Nokia) who can award portions of the $10 million if the idea is worthy of investment. Not everyone will be selected.

For more information about this initiative, see http://openscreen.forum.nokia.com/ or http://www.openscreenproject.org/developers/get_started.html.

At the time of this writing, there is no end date for the fund, but by the time this book reaches your hands, selection will be well underway. Since the allotted $10 million will be distributed among submissions, it's best to get your ideas into them as soon as possible!

Joining Flash mobile and device development communities

One of the great things about the Flash platform is the community of designers, developers, and other professionals within it (such as yourself). Just like Flex, AIR, and other Adobe products have a community of followers, Flash on mobile and devices does as well.

Although we'll cover much in this book, we have found that the best way to learn mobile technology, given it's fragmentation across so many devices and platforms, is to become part of the active development groups for open discussions about technical issues, business opportunities, and other topics. There are several ongoing Flash and Flash Lite communities we recommend that you become a part of as you journey into the world of Flash across mobile and devices. To that end, we've compiled the following list of online communities you might like to check out:

- **Adobe Mobile and Device User Groups**: Several user groups are sponsored by Adobe around the world in major cities. At the time of this writing, some active Flash Mobile user groups include:

  - **BAMaDUG, the Boston Adobe Mobile and Device User Group (US)**: http://www.flashmobilegroup.org

  - **UKMaDUG, the United Kingdom Mobile and Device User Group (UK)**: Search http://groups.adobe.com to find and register for this group

  - **IndiMaD, the India Mobile and Device User Group (India)**: http://www.indimadgroup.com

  - **AMaDUG, the Adobe Mobile and Device User Group (Italy)**: http://mobile.actionscript.it/

  - **Poland**: http://www.flashlite.com.pl/

  - **SMaDUG, the Spain Mobile and Device User Group (Spain)**: http://www.blocketpc.com/index.php

- **Flash Lite Yahoo list**: This is an excellent way for developers to communicate with one another via e-mail list. This list is primarily for those new to Flash Lite, but many Flash Lite veterans read this list and sometimes answer technical questions. To join, go to http://groups.yahoo.com/group/FlashLite/.

- **Flash mobile Google list**: Another user group list for developers and other professionals working in the Flash Lite space is http://groups.google.com/group/Flashmobilegroup Though this is the BAMaDUG, anyone can join provided you give a few details about yourself, specifically your name, what you are doing with Flash Lite, and where you are from.

- **Adobe user group forums**: If you prefer newsgroups to e-mail lists, the Adobe user group forums are available at http://forums.adobe.com/ (look for the Mobile and Devices User Group tab on the page).

There are several lists, including ones covering platforms such as Nokia, Samsung, Sony Ericsson, Windows Mobile, and BREW. There is also a dedicated Flash Lite 2 development list, where experts often field questions for not only Flash Lite 2.x, but also 1.1 and 3.x.

Other lists include a Flash Cast list and one on the Flash Player SDK, as well as a generic Flash handhelds group. These provide an excellent forum to get threaded feedback from developers working in the Adobe mobile products available today.

- **Blogs**: There are so many blogs covering Flash Lite across device platforms that we cannot list them all here. However, a good resource for a growing list of Flash Lite developer blogs and their focuses (games, embedded devices, etc.) can be found at our site at http://advancED. flashmobilebook.com/links.html#blogs.

- **Adobe Groups site**: A great resource for finding and connecting with fellow Adobe professionals is the newly launched Adobe Groups site at http://groups.adobe.com/. By registering and then searching for "Flash Lite" or "mobile," you can find many individuals working within the mobile space using Adobe products (e.g., designers using Photoshop and Fireworks to mock up mobile designs or hard-core ActionScript developers doing Flash Lite).

- **Facebook**: A growing number of Flash Lite and Flash mobile groups are at www.facebook.com. Just search for "Flash Lite" to get the most current list.

- **Twitter**: Another great resource of communicating with other Flash Lite developers in the community is to join www.twitter.com (the micro blogging site). Thomas Joos (one of this book's authors) has compiled a list of Flash Lite professionals worldwide and it is available at http://vilebody.wordpress.com/2009/02/18/follow-more-active-flash-on-mobile-guys-on-twitter/.

Summary

In this chapter, we gave you an introduction to the Flash Lite platform, including associated products and services. We covered everything from the Adobe mobile tools (Creative Suite, Device Central, and the Flash IDE) to Flash Lite–based services such as Flash Cast and Flash Home.

You learned about the different versions of Flash Lite (1.1, 2.0, 2.1, 3.0, and 3.1), various Flash Lite content types (e.g., screensavers and wallpaper), and some of the differences between desktop and mobile ActionScript code (e.g., the fscommand2 API). We also explored a good deal of Flash Lite 1.1 so that you can address as many handsets as possible in the worldwide market, and we provided references to some CDKs that are available to help you in your Flash Lite design and development needs.

This chapter also explained a bit of what is happening within the Flash Lite development world, as well as some methods of getting your Flash Lite content packaged with various mobile formats (e.g., SIS and NFL) and distributed to existing worldwide players like content providers and aggregators that exist in the Flash Lite ecosystem today.

Finally, we gave you some ways to get involved in the Flash user communities that are actively working with Adobe mobile and device technologies such as Flash Lite.

In our next chapter, we dive further into what specifically Flash Lite 3.x has to offer in terms of features compared to its predecessors. We'll cover some of the capabilities possible with the latest Flash Lite version 3.1, including some discussion on Adobe Mobile Packager and the Adobe Flash Lite 3.1 Distributable Player. We'll also cover Device Central CS4 and its SDK.

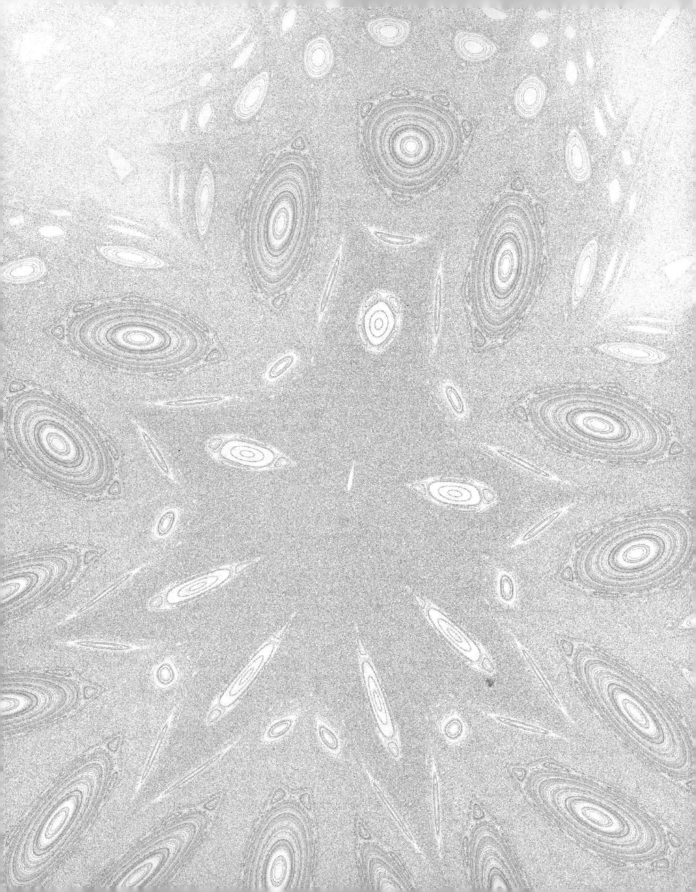

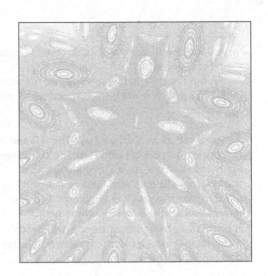

Chapter 3

FLASH LITE 3

In the previous chapter, we talked quite extensively about the Flash Lite platform and its fundamentals (e.g., Device Central, fscommand2, ActionScript, the Flash IDE, open source Flash). We also discussed a bit about the evolution of Flash Lite and some essentials you need to know when targeting older devices running Flash Lite 1.1. We covered the tools and services available for packaging and distributing Flash Lite content in various mobile ecosystems today.

Now, let's turn our attention to working with the newest Flash Lite player, version 3.1 at the time of this writing. In this chapter, we'll cover many of the new features in Flash Lite 3.0 and 3.1 and walk through creating a Flash Lite 3 video application using the same Eclipse-based development style we used in Chapter 2. Finally, we'll introduce you to the new Adobe Device Central CS4 SDK, which allows you to create reusable testing tasks and plug-ins to better enhance the Flash mobile and device development workflow.

As you saw in the previous chapter, Flash Lite is a very sizeable topic, just because it spans so many devices and platforms. With that in mind, our goal in this chapter will be to get you up to speed with Flash Lite 3 features first. Toward the end of the chapter, we'll walk through an application you will build with Flash Lite.

> *An additional resource to this chapter is the Adobe Flash Lite 3 video training provided at http://www.adobe.com/devnet/devices/articles/flash_lite3_training_video.html. Check out this resource, before you dive into the more advanced topics we cover in this chapter and later in this book, as it will help you understand the basic Flash Lite 3.x capabilities.*

As you'll see as we explore Flash Lite 3.0 and 3.1, the feature set is pretty sweet, and a lot of cool things are now possible with Flash Lite compared to versions 1.1 and 2.x. As we discussed in Chapter 2, Flash and Flash Lite have a long lineage across various mobile and device platforms stretching back to the Macromedia days with Flash running on the Pocket PC platform. We touched on the Adobe Flash platform roadmap back in Chapters 1 and 2, so you should be aware that although Flash Lite is, for all intents and purposes, an interim thing (i.e., we'll only use it until Flash 10 can be rolled out successfully to a *large* number of devices worldwide). However, you must realize that, in the grand scheme of the mobile world, older software versions tend to stick around a lot longer on devices than on the desktop PC platforms.

There are literally millions of Flash Lite–capable devices out there running Flash Lite 1.x, 2.x, and now 3.0 and 3.1. A lot of consumers simply don't upgrade their phones or devices as much as developers would like them to. Plus, not all device hardware will be capable of running Flash 10 given current existing device constraints (e.g., memory and CPU). Thus, it's important to seriously consider Flash Lite as a viable target development platform for mobile applications on devices supporting the runtime, at this time of writing.

> *As you will see in this chapter, the Adobe Flash Lite 3.1 Distributable Player seeks to address the problem of Flash Lite player version stagnation by adding the capability to phone home to Adobe, ask if there are updates, and update itself OTA with the latest version of the Flash Lite player. It's a pretty slick feature, adopted from the similar way recent desktop Flash players work.*

Getting to know Flash Lite 3.0

In 2008, the specifications for the Flash Lite 3.0 player were sent to various OEMs, including Nokia, Sony Ericsson, and others participating in the Open Screen Project. Today, Flash Lite 3.x exists pre-installed on millions of handsets and other devices worldwide (e.g., Nokia S40 and S60, iRiver, and Chumby), and that number seems to be growing as more OEMs participate in the Adobe Open Screen Project.

We already talked a bit about Flash Lite 1.1 and 2.x in the previous chapter, so we're going to cruise right into talking about Flash Lite 3.0. First, we'll cover some of the features of Flash Lite 3.0 and what they offer to developers who are working and publishing Flash Lite content.

Improving performance

With version 3.0 of the Flash Lite player, Adobe added new player performance improvements and alterations to the runtime engine. These include graphics rendering acceleration as well as changes to the way runtime memory allocation is handled. There are two major changes you should be aware of:

- **Graphics rendering acceleration**: With significant changes, text scrolling, vector translations, and animated vectors with opaque fills are now rendered much more quickly and efficiently than in previous versions of the Flash Lite runtime.

- **Runtime memory reduction**: The Flash Lite 3 player supports lazy loading during SWF content playback. This means that only the resources required to render the first frame of any movie are loaded at startup. All other Flash Lite player resources are loaded as needed in the execution of a published SWF. The effect of this change is a noticeable improvement in startup time of Flash Lite content over Flash Lite 2.x versions.

If you have been working with Flash Lite 2.x content, you will notice these two enhancements when playing back legacy Flash Lite 1.x and 2.x content within the Flash Lite 3 player, as the performance when rendering SWF content is apparent.

Enhancing video capabilities

Starting with Flash Lite 3.0, support for native Flash video (FLV) playback was added into the runtime environment. Support for both ON2 VP6 and Sorenson codecs were added to Flash Lite 3.x.

With these additions, you can play back video that has been optimized for mobile and devices regardless of whether or not the device supports a specific video format (such as MP4 and 3GP). Unlike device video in previous versions of Flash Lite 2.x, FLV is also now rendered directly within the Flash Lite player, regardless of the video format, since the data is now in the FLV format.

Since the FLV format allows playback within the confines of the Flash Lite player, there is now support for embedded video on the timeline, progressive download of video from a local or remote server (over HTTP), and streaming video from a remote server via RTMP connections.

Later in this chapter, we'll cover an example of using FLV playback for a Flash Lite 3 YouTube application.

> In Chapter 15, we're going to be covering more about Flash video on mobile and devices, including progressive and streaming video from an external source down to a mobile Internet-connected device.

Browsing web content

Flash Lite 3 supports playback of a majority of Flash 8 web content available today through the Flash Lite browser content type found across many devices. Keep in mind that there may be some loss of overall fidelity in the content accessed due to the processor and memory requirements needed to render it.

Flash 8 features may not be supported due to these device constraints. Certain features of Flash 8 may scale back to optimal settings when playback occurs on a Flash Lite 3–enabled device because of processor or memory demands.

Flash 8 features such as bitmap caching, blend modes, bitmap filters, and enhanced strokes or gradients are all good examples of this. If a SWF contains any of these features, it will render these assets without the expressiveness to maintain a more responsive and convenient user experience on a Flash Lite 3 device.

Table 3-1 describes the Flash 8 content and features that are supported, partially supported, or not supported.

Table 3-1. Flash Lite 3 Web Content Support

Capability	Supported	Support Details
Flash 8 basic HTML tags	Yes	The Flash Lite player can now recognize and play back most Flash 8 content, with some loss of fidelity.
Security enhancements	Yes	The Flash Lite security model is now consistent with the desktop player's security model. For local file security details, please download the comprehensive Adobe Flash Player 8 security white paper at http://www.adobe.com/devnet/flashplayer/articles/flash_player_8_security.pdf.
Flash Video	Yes	The Flash Lite player now supports Flash Video (FLV) using versions of the ON2 VP6 and Sorenson codecs optimized for mobile devices. It also supports RTMP client implementation (one-way, not two-way real-time implementations). See Chapter 15 of this book for more details about working with Flash Video across mobile and devices.
HTML base tag	Yes	The base tag allows Flash Lite to behave in a manner similar to the Flash Player on the desktop.
FlashType text	Partially	Complete support is not critical to displaying content. Text is rendered but without full FlashType implementation.
Bitmap caching, effects, and enhancements	No	These features are not implemented because most require floating-point support or make excessive demands on processor or memory resources.
Focal gradients	No	These gradients are not implemented, because they are processor intensive and not critical to displaying content.

The "Adobe Flash Lite 3.1 Web Browsability Mobile Guidelines for Developers" document is a must-read for developers looking to leverage Flash Lite within the browser context. The document is available on the Adobe Developer Connection site at http://www.adobe.com/devnet/devices/articles/web_browsability_guidelines.pdf.

In Chapter 5, we'll cover working with Nokia S60 Flash Lite widgets running inside the S60 browser using Web RunTime.

Local file security

With Flash Lite 3 comes some additions to security that we need to discuss, as these impact you in your task of correctly publishing SWF content.

Recall that Flash Lite 2.x SWF files were relatively devoid of any kind of internal player security model. In 2.x, local SWF files were allowed to interact with and unload data from other SWF files, whether local or remote. This was a potential security vulnerability whereby an untrusted SWF might be loaded and able to access private data on a device and send it back to the malicious content author via HTTP connection. In Flash Lite 3.0, a security model consistent with Flash Player 8 has been added: all SWF files are placed in a SWF sandbox where they are loaded by the Flash Lite player. Each SWF file is loaded into a specific sandbox depending on where it was loaded from.

For example, SWF files downloaded from a network are placed in a remote sandbox based on the domain where the SWF originated. SWF files loaded over a network can read the data from their domain of origin only and cannot access the data from other domains, unless permission to access those domains is specifically given to SWF files that have requested it. For instance, by default, a Flash Lite SWF file from http://www.friendsofed.com cannot communicate directly with a SWF file loaded from http://www.apress.com without defining a policy that outlines cross-domain permission rules. In other words, a SWF file from http://www.friendsofed.com may read from a remote server at Apress if a policy file exists on http://www.apress.com that permits access from the http://www.friendsofed.com domain.

A Flash Lite SWF file in http://www.friendsofed.com may cross-script (i.e., access) another SWF in another domain, like http://www.apress.com, if the SWF in http://www.apress.com calls the System.security.allowDomain method with a parameter specifying the name of the domain(s) requesting access (e.g., friendsofed.com).

SWF files from a local file system are placed into three different kinds of security sandboxes in Flash Lite 3.0:

- **Local with file system**: SWF files may read (e.g., using XML.load) from files on local file systems, but they may not communicate with the network in any way.

- **Local trusted**: SWF files may read from local files, interact with any server, and script any other SWF file. In Flash Lite 2.1, all local files are effectively in this sandbox.

  If you are developing on Nokia devices, particularly S60, there is a folder called trusted. Typically, this is in the \Data\Others\Trusted directory on a device. Installing SWF content in this directory allows the content to run without Flash Lite 3 security measures in place. Some popular third-party extenders offer this feature (e.g., SWF2Go and Kuneri Lite).

- **Local with networking**: SWF files are allowed to communicate with other local SWF files with networking enabled and send data to servers (e.g., using XML.send).

This new security scheme affects the functionality of almost all ActionScript that involves data loading or cross-scripting, including extremely common functions like getURL, loadMovie, loadMovieNum, LoadVars, LoadSound, XMLSocket.send, and XMLSocket.load. For a comprehensive list of all API functionality that is affected by security, please see the "Flash Player 8 Security-Related APIs" PDF on the Flash Player Developer Center page at http://www.adobe.com/devnet/flashplayer/articles/flash_player_8_security.pdf.

These are some of the important *differences* that exist between the Flash Lite 3 and Flash Player 8 security models:

- Trust management is done by the host application in Flash Lite.
- No trust configuration files are required in Flash Lite.
- SWF file developers, manufacturers, and carriers must make all security decisions in Flash Lite. There is no user-mediated trust or settings manager. However, the host application may provide a mechanism by which users can make limited security decisions. For example, the host may allow users to designate a particular SWF file as trusted.
- Prohibited operations fail silently; no dialog box is displayed in Flash Lite.

When publishing to Flash Lite 3.0 and 3.1, note the new Publish Settings window security option in Flash CS4 (see Figure 3-1).

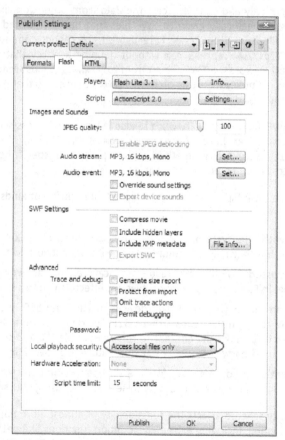

Figure 3-1.
The Flash Lite 3.x Local playback security drop-down in Flash CS4 Publish Settings

Managing content

A new feature in Flash Lite 3 is the ability to store metadata inside of published Flash Lite SWF files for content management purposes. This is possible because Flash Lite 3 is based on the Flash Player 8 SWF specifications, which allow for embedded metadata within published SWF files.

When publishing Flash Lite 3.x content (such as through the Adobe Flash CS4 IDE), you can enter in metadata within the publish SWF settings. Go to File ➤ Publish Settings ➤ Flash, and under the SWF Settings label, check Include XMP Metadata. Click the File Info button to get access to the panel containing metadata, and click the Mobile SWF tab (see Figure 3-2).

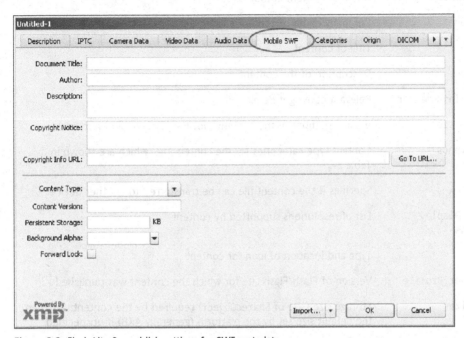

Figure 3-2. Flash Lite 3.x publish settings for SWF metadata

After the SWF is published, this metadata may be extracted from the SWF, and can be used to categorize or otherwise manage Flash Lite content stored by content providers, aggregators, operators, and even OEMs on the device.

Examples of uses for embedded data in SWFs are on-device content catalogs built by operators for organization purposes (e.g., splitting up games and productivity applications into different categories). It can also be used by Flash Lite content aggregators who want to segment SWF content to make searching and discoverability easier for its customers on their mobile application store fronts (e.g., Nokia OVI).

> The metadata that is saved within Flash Lite 3 published SWF files can be accessed and read using third-party SWF extraction tools. Some of these are listed at http://osflash.org/open_source_flash_projects under the SWF Readers heading.

Flash Lite 3.x offers several metadata properties that can be defined for each published SWF (see Table 3-2). However, these properties may differ depending on the OEMs that are implementing a Flash Lite 3 player—some, or perhaps all, of these properties may not be available to your specific target device.

Table 3-2. Flash Lite 3.0 Metadata Tags

Title	Description
Content Author	Name of content author
Company Name	Company name of content author
Title	Title of content
Description	Description of the content
Copyright Information	Relevant copyright details
Content Version	Version number of the content (*not* the Flash version number)
Content Type(s)	Content type categories for the content file, which are shown in Table 3-3
Forward Lock	Specifies if the content file can be transferred to another device
Supported Display Resolutions	List of resolutions supported by content
Icon	Type and location of icon for content
Flash Player Profile	Version of Flash/Flash Lite for which the content was published
Storage Size	Storage size (size of SharedObject) required by the content; assigned the default size set by the platform (generally 4KB) if unspecified
Background Alpha	Preferred alpha value and blend mode for the background transparency feature
Looping	Specifies looping behavior, whether content repeats indefinitely or stops after the last frame
Default Quality	Quality level at which the content should be played

Content developers can use the Content Type property to further segment content and how it might be utilized and segmented on supported devices.

The specific content types may look familiar, as they conform to some of the types of content we talked about earlier in Chapter 2 (stand-alone, screensaver, wallpaper, etc.). The embedded metadata content types for Flash Lite 3.0 (see Table 3-3) more accurately describe each specific use case of how the content will be leveraged on a device. For instance, there is an Icon type, which might be used for a custom animation for launching Flash Lite content, or the Shutdown application content type, which is an animation played before a device powers down.

Another place where you can now specify metadata is within the Description tab (see Figure 3-3). Here, you can specify the Document Title, Description, and other fields (note that in Adobe Flash CS3, these fields are found in the Document Properties dialog).

Table 3-3. Flash Lite 3.0 Content Type Metadata

Metadata Content Type	Description
Screensaver	Flash animation that is shown when a device-specified timeout occurs
Ringtone	Animation played when phone is receiving an incoming call
Background	Animated wallpaper that is displayed behind the idle/home screen
Game	Interactive game
Application	Stand-alone application
Presentation	Presentation converted to a Flash movie
Icon	Flash-based animated icon
Movie	Animated Flash movie
Skin	Skin or theme for the phone or a single application
Startup	Startup animation
Shutdown	Shutdown animation
Other	Flash content that does not fit into any of the other types

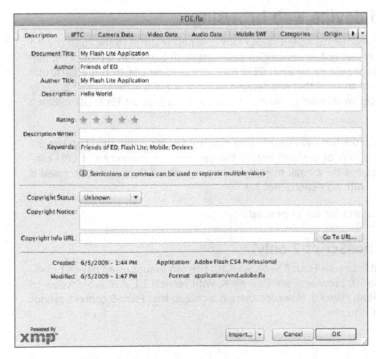

Figure 3-3.
Document Description
tab in Flash CS4 IDE

Getting to know Flash Lite 3.1

As we discussed in the previous chapter, at the time of this writing, Flash Lite has both a major 3.0 version and a point release of 3.1. Flash Lite 3.1 adds a slew of cool and powerful features to the runtime that can be leveraged by developers to create new, more compelling mobile and device experiences.

With the Flash Lite 3.1 Distributable Player available, the Flash Mobile community should see a lot more adoption of Flash Lite, much more so than Flash Lite 3.0 (even though version 3.0 is preinstalled on many devices by various OEMs). Flash Lite 3.0 and 3.1 are increasing in numbers, as devices start to ship in 2009 and beyond. We'll talk much more about the Adobe Distributable Player Solution later in this chapter when we cover the Flash Lite 3.1 Distributable Player and Adobe Mobile Packager software.

Flash Lite 3.1 offers a variety of features to improve web-browsing ability, performance, and video capabilities, as well as ActionScript extensions.

> *ActionScript extensions allow developers to extend the capabilities of Flash Lite 3.1–supported devices. However, at the time of this writing, the technology is propriety and only available to mobile and device developers who have very close ties to OEMs (i.e., developers who work for them!). For this reason, unfortunately, we will not be able to cover ActionScript extensions in this book. On the bright side of things, we'll cover how to extend Flash Lite using Nokia S60 Platform Services and Capuchin in Chapter 7 of this book.*

Enhancing mobile and device web browsing

In terms of mobile web browsing, Adobe has added some really cool new features to the Flash Lite 3.1 player. It's important to remember that not all device OEMs support Flash Lite 3.1 as a browser implementation. This is a choice made separately by each OEM that adopts Flash Lite to run a particular device. Nokia is a good example of an OEM that has decided to support Flash within its S60 browser found on millions of Nokia devices worldwide. However, LG does not yet support Flash Lite within a browser context.

According to Adobe, 91 percent of the top 500 Internet sites now will render within the Flash Lite 3.1 player. Of course, not all sites will look or perform exactly the same due to memory and CPU constraints imposed on some devices, but the overall majority will now render if the content accessed is comparable to a Flash 8 or 9 SWF with no ActionScript 3.0.

Let's explore some of the new features for better browsability.

Supporting Flash 9 (ActionScript 2 only)

In Flash Lite 3.0, it was only possible to view Flash 8 SWFs via Flash Lite run in supported device browsers (e.g., Opera Mobile and Nokia S60 browsers); see Figure 3-4. With version 3.1, it is also possible to view SWF content published to Flash Player 9. However, there is a caveat: that Flash 9 content cannot contain any ActionScript 3.0–specific code.

A large amount of Flash 9 sites will still play back with Flash Lite 3.1 if they don't contain any ActionScript 3. Flash Lite 3.1 announces itself as a Flash 9–capable player and automatically scales back on high performance features encountered during SWF playback.

When web sites containing Flash 9 content are loaded, the Flash Lite 3.1 player will evaluate the SWF and render the SWF content, but only if it contains only ActionScript 2.0 compiled code. If use of ActionScript 3.0 is encountered within a Flash 9 SWF, the Flash Lite player will display a user-friendly error icon informing the user of the incompatibility.

We recommend that you refer to the "Adobe Flash Lite 3.1 Web Browsability Mobile Guidelines for Developers" document, which discusses details on how Flash Lite 3.1 treats existing Flash 8 and 9 web-based SWF content: http://www.adobe.com/devnet/devices/articles/web_browsability_guidelines.pdf.

Figure 3-4.
The friends of ED web site with Flash banner on a Nokia 5800 (S60 with Flash Lite prein-stalled)

Using the LocalConnection class

In ActionScript 2.0, the LocalConnection class lets you develop one or more SWF files that can send instructions to each other *without* the use of fscommand2() or JavaScript. LocalConnection objects can communicate only among SWF files that are running on the same device, but they can be running in different Flash Lite applications. LocalConnection objects can also be used to send and receive data within a single SWF file, but this capability is not used very often because there are not a lot of advantages to doing so.

The Flash Lite 3.1 implementation of the LocalConnection object supports communication among SWF files running in the same process (e.g., in the same browser window). This may be useful if, say, you have an advertisement banner done in Flash Lite and a Flash Lite game on a page that interacts with the banner. With Flash Lite 3.0, this was not a possibility, but with Flash Lite 3.1, it is!

On most Flash Lite 3.1 devices, more than one SWF may be open at any given time. You could have a Flash Lite casual game open and keep that running in the background while starting up a Flash Lite RSS reader application. With LocalConnection, it's possible to communicate between these two individual SWF files, assuming you've done the planning and included the code that allows the interaction to happen.

When using the LocalConnection object, there are essentially two methods to send and receive data. The first is LocalConnection.send(), and the second is LocalConnection.connect().

Now, let's have some fun exploring this capability on mobile devices. We'll do an example of two individual Flash Lite 3.1 stand-alone SWFs communicating through a LocalConnection object.

Implementing the LocalConnection class   Our example here demonstrates two independent SWFs communicating one property value. The first SWF will run through a bunch of alpha values, while the second SWF intercepts those alpha values and changes the background color accordingly. Let's get started.

1. First, create your first source file, and call it A.fla.

2. Next, change the default background color. Select Modify ➤ Document, and then select another color such as #cccccc (you can pick any color you'd like).

3. Next, create a simple text box on the screen. Inside of the first frame of A.fla, add the following preamble ActionScript that we've talked about before:

```
// Set to full-screen mode, quality to high,
// and make sure no text field focus is enabled
fscommand2("fullScreen", true);
fscommand2("setQuality", "high");
_focusrect = false;
```

4. Next, we're going to define some variables to keep track of our alpha value as it fades in and out. These go in the first frame of the A.fla movie.

```
direction_bool:Boolean = false;
var fadeinterval_num:Number = 10;
var fadeamount_num:Number = 1;
```

The first line determines whether the fade is increasing or decreasing. The second defines how fast the fade happens, and the third tells the amount of fade to increment by (effectively how bright the background will get over the time the application runs).

5. In our next step, we define the localConnection object, which we simply call sending_lc. Our currentalpha_num variable keeps track of the current value to assign the background to at any given time.

```
var sending_lc:LocalConnection = new LocalConnection();
var currentalpha_num:Number = 0;
```

6. For debugging purposes, create a simple text field to output the alpha values; center the text field on the screen.

```
this.createTextField( "alphavalue_txt", 1,
                    (Stage.width/2)-50,
                    (Stage.height/2)-10, 100, 20 );

alphavalue_txt.text = currentalpha_num;
```

7. Now for the crux of this small application, we need to set up our connection to the second SWF via LocalConnect. Here, we simply give a name for the pipe, fadelocal, which acts as a memory pipe that both SWFs tune into, and thereby communicate. The second parameter is the function to call in our upcoming second SWF we named changeAlpha(). Finally, the currentalpha_num is the update alpha variable being sent continuously into the second SWF, B.swf:

```
sending_lc.send("fadelocal","changeAlpha",currentalpha_num);
```

8. Now, we need to set up the logic to control how the fade occurs. Here, we are simply checking to see if the alpha fade goes above or below 100, or 0, and then when it does, our fade just reverses direction. The effect of this is a strobe light (depending on the fadeamount_num and fadeinternal_num specified above). Here is the code, which is set up as a function so it can be called later:

```
function setAlpha():Void {
currentalpha_num += (direction_bool) ➡
?1*fadeamount_num:-1*fadeamount_num;
if (currentalpha_num<0) {
 currentalpha_num = 0;
 direction_bool = true;
  } else if (currentvalue_num > 100) {
  currentalpha_num = 100;
  direction_bool = false;
 }
}
```

9. Our next step is to add some error-checking code. The onStatus() routine does some basic error checking for us here:

```
sending_lc.onStatus = function(info_obj:Object) {
 switch ( info_obj.level ) {
  case 'status':
    alphavalue_txt.text = currentalpha_num;
    break;
   case 'error':
    alphavalue_txt.text = "Not Connected!";
    break;
  }
}
```

10. Finally, just set a timer to fire off periodically. We could have done this using the timeline, but instead, we're using setInterval(). The function setAlpha() gets fired off sending our alpha values into the B.swf depending on the number of milliseconds assigned to fadeinternal_num:

```
fadeid_num = setInterval(setAlpha,fadeinterval_num);
```

11. Great, now we're done with A.swf, which sends out values. We need to create B.swf, which receives those values via the localConnection object.

12. Create b.fla. On the first frame insert the following preamble as before:

```
// Set to full-screen, quality to high, get rid of text field outlines
fscommand2("fullScreen",true);
fscommand2("setQuality","high");
_focusrect = false;
```

13. Now, we need to define some global variables. These will be used to determine the height and width or our screen dimensions used to color our background that we create.

```
var maxX_num:Number = Stage.width;
var maxY_num:Number = Stage.height;
```

14. Next, we need to color our background, so that we have something to fade in and out of as the two SWFs communicate. Here, simply create a MovieClip called background_mc and fill it with a color of black, 0x000000:

```
this.createEmptyMovieClip("background_mc", 1);
with (background_mc) {
 beginFill(0x000000, 100);
 lineTo(maxY_num 0);
 lineTo(maxX_num, maxY_num);
 lineTo(0,maxY_num);
 endFill();
}
```

15. Now, set up your LocalConnection object to receive events coming from A.swf as follows:

```
var receieving_lc:LocalConnection = new LocalConnection();
receieving_lc.changeAlpha = function(currentAlpha_num:Number) {
 _root.background_mc._alpha = "Alpha value is " + currentAlpha_num;
}

receieving_lc.connect( "fadelocal" );
```

16. You're finished! Check for any syntax errors, and let's move onto testing.

Unfortunately, we can't use Adobe Device Central CS4 to test this application, since it only allows one instance of a mobile application to test at any one time.

Instead, we'll open A.swf and B.swf on the PC desktop by right-clicking, selecting Open As, and then selecting the latest desktop Flash Player that can be utilized on your PC (if you need to, simply visit www.adobe.com to download the latest Flash Player).

After opening *both* A.swf and B.swf, you should see the interaction between A and B as depicted in Figure 3-5.

Figure 3-5.
A.swf controlling the B.swf
alpha fade value, with
both SWFs published as
Flash Lite 3.1 content

Identifying use cases for LocalConnection   Where would you utilize the LocalConnection feature? Some use cases for this might be communicating between two or more SWF files on a mobile web page. Perhaps you have a SWF containing a mobile advertisement and you want to communicate with another SWF on the page or a login SWF. You can even extend the communication so that the two SWFs are not necessarily in the same domain. You can do this with LocalConnect objects. By utilizing allowDomain(sendingDomain:String) within the receiving object, you can even specify which domains are valid. Utilizing the LocalConnection object in stand-alone content is useful for those developing user interfaces and on-device integration. This is very unique to each OEM.

> *You might imagine, in our previous example, that have a whole Flash Lite user interface on a device, where LocalConnection is used to communicate between parts of the user interface that are loaded. We might have wallpaper running on a primary display that communicates with a Flash Lite menu that exists on the device. LocalConnection can provide communication between SWFs outside of implementing potentially costly low-level man-machine interface (MMI) instructions that were previously done with Flash Lite 1.1 and Flash Lite 2.x.*

Enhancing HTML browser support

Flash Lite 3.1 also includes some feature enhancements that make rendering web content a better experience. Some of those features include HTML text, getURL _target, WMode, and CSS support. Let's cover some of these.

- **HTML text-handling tags**: Flash Lite 3.1 has support for a few HTML text-handling tags that were not previously supported in Flash Lite 3.0. Flash Lite 3.1 includes support for the use of text as links and support for the <img> tag.

- **Hyperlinks**: The HTML anchor tag, <a>, which is used to create hypertext links, is now supported in Flash Lite 3.1. This means links can be embedded in Flash Lite to kick off additional browsers on a mobile device.

> *On a mobile device, opening new browser windows within a Flash Lite application is discouraged. Not only is doing so memory intensive, it can cause the user to lose focus on what is going on. Open only one web browser link to navigate to a specific item.*

- **Embedded external images**: HTML text fields in Flash Lite 3.1 support the HTML <img> tag. This tag can pull in images either from the local file system or external remotely located image files to be rendered within the HTML text. JPG, GIF, and PNG graphic file formats will render, if the device supports the image type needed. Querying System.capabilities.imageMIMETypes can determine what image formats are available on each specific device.

  The <img> tag can also pull in a local or remote SWF file or MovieClip (an id attribute is needed to target the MovieClip inside the SWF). When these loaded assets are brought in via the <img> tag, they become accessible via ActionScript and can be controlled and manipulated (e.g., you can modify the _visible, _x, and _y properties). HTML text fields in Flash Lite 3.1 also support multiline, wordWrap, and other properties (take a look at Flash Help inside of the Flash CS3 or CS4 IDE for a comprehensive list).

- **Cascading Style Sheets (CSS) support**: Prior to Flash Lite 3.1, text formatting via CSS styles (a feature found in the desktop Flash 8 player) was not supported. With version 3.1, both externally loaded CSS files and inline styles via ActionScript are now supported. This CSS feature allows you to modify the text contained in Flash Lite applications to conform to the overall design style of the Flash Lite content.

- getURL _target **support**: The target parameter is an optional parameter that is passed into the getURL() ActionScript command, for example, getURL("http://www.friendsofed.com/", '_new'). It is used to load a document into the browser window or HTML frame specified by the target name.

  In versions of Flash Lite before 3.0, the _target parameter was not supported in Flash Lite because no mobile Internet device browsers supported this feature. This has changed, however, as browsers have been rapidly enhancing their capabilities as mobile users do much more Internet surfing on their devices.

  To follow suit, with Flash Lite 3.1, the optional _target parameter support has now been added to the player. It is now possible to target several window names, including

  - "", the empty string, denotes _self, the default value for the currently opened browser window.

  - _new specifies the current frame in a new browser window.

  - _blank specifies a new browser window.

  - _parent specifies the parent of the current frame.

  - _top specifies the top-level frame in the current browser window.

  - _self specifies the current document that is opened running the original Flash Lite application. This option is also used if no parameter is given at all and acts as the default target window.

  > *There must be frames in the browser window for all of the _target parameters to work as specified. If there are no frames in the browser, _blank works as expected— it opens the URL in a new blank window. However, the _self, _parent, and _top parameters open the URL in the same window.*

- **WMode Support**: WMode is a new feature of Flash Lite 3.1. By specifying this parameter in the context of a browser and its HTML text for embedding SWFs, you can manipulate the background of the HTML page that contains the Flash Lite content. By utilizing WMode, you can set the background color or background image that shows through the Flash Lite movie embedded on the HTML page. The value of WMode can be window (the default), opaque, or transparent:

  - window plays the application in its own rectangular window on a web page; it indicates that the application has no interaction with HTML layers and is always the topmost item.

  - opaque makes the application hide everything behind it on the page.

  - transparent makes the background of the HTML page show through all the transparent portions of the application and can slow animation performance.

- **Support for scale, salign, and align**: Flash Lite 3.1 offers support for JavaScript parameters that define how the Flash Lite content gets scaled, positioned, and aligned when embedded in an HTML page within a supported mobile device:

  - scale defines how the SWF file is placed in the browser window when width and height values are percentages. Its values can be showall, noborder, or exactfit.

  - align determines how the SWF file is positioned within the browser window. Its values can be L (left), R (right), T (top), or B (bottom).

  - salign specifies where a scaled SWF file is positioned in the area that the width and height settings define. Its values can be TL (top left), TR (top right), BL (bottom left), or BR (bottom right).

Using the new HTML capabilities

What better way to see the new HTML capabilities put into the Flash Lite 3.1 player than by an example? Here, we'll be mocking up an application that will spawn mobile browser windows based on links a user clicks. We'll also add a WMode parameter so the background shows up (i.e., the friends of ED logo).

1. First, we are going to create our Flash Lite file that will load as one part of an HTML document. Our SWF will act as a mobile advertisement for a mock friends of ED mobile web site. Open a brand-new FLA, and call it FOE.fla for simplicity.

2. Next, we should change the Flash output file in the Formats tab (see Figure 3-6). It's under File ➤ Publish Settings.

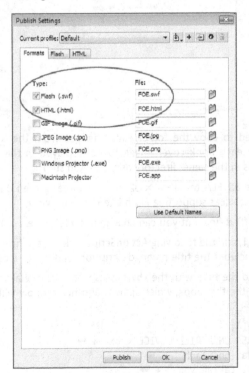

Figure 3-6.
Under Publish Settings, to get an HTML file that will display our Flash Lite SWF, we must select that format.

3. Next, click the HTML tab (see Figure 3-7), and make sure that the Window Mode is set to Transparent Windowless (we'll want to test out the WMode parameter in later steps). This will allow our HTML background graphic to actually show through the Flash content to demonstrate this new window mode feature added in Flash Lite 3.1 (it's also supported on desktop Flash players).

Figure 3-7.
Under the Publish Settings HTML tab, set Window Mode to Transparent Windowless.

4. Before creating the FLA, you'll need to copy the folder called images from the Chapter 3 source code folder, which contains each book cover image to be displayed in this example (9781430216063.jpg, etc.). Keep this in the same directory as the FLA in step 1.

5. Set the dimensions of the Flash Lite 3.1 FLA to 240px × 320px, our target screen dimensions and a popular size for many mobile devices supporting Flash Lite in the browser.

6. The default background color (#ffffff) is fine, but you can change it if you'd like.

7. Now, in the Flash Lite SWF on frame 1, add the following ActionScript code that defines an array containing book information. This includes the title name, description, and image location.

Note all the HTML format applied to the title, with the <b> tag, as well as the relative links to the images, and the target _new for the first book, which spawns another window will load up our companion site for this book.

```
var books_arr:Array = new Array();
books_arr[0] = "<b>AdvancED FLASH ON MOBILE DEVICES</b>" + ➥
"<br>The follow up to the Foundation Flash " + ➥
"Applications on Mobile Devices, taking you " + ➥
```

```
"further along the road to becoming a Mobile " + ➡
"Flash Master.<p><img src='images/9781430216087.jpg'>" + ➡
"<br><br><a href='http://www.flashmobilebook.com/' " + ➡
"target='_new'><b>www.flashmobilebook.com</b></a>" + ➡
"<br><a href='http://www.friendsofed.com/' target='_new'>" + ➡
"<b>www.friendsofed.com</b></a>";

books_arr[1] = "<b>AdvancED ActionScript 3.0 Animation</b>" + ➡
"<br>The follow up to the best-selling Foundation" + ➡
" ActionScript 3.0 Animation, taking you further " + ➡
"along the road to becoming an ActionScript Master" + ➡
"<p><img src='images/9781430216087.jpg'>";

books_arr[2] = "<b>HTML and CSS Web Standards Solutions</b>" + ➡
"<br>A Web Standardistas' Approach HTML and CSS Web " + ➡
"Standards Solutions: A Web Standardistas' Approach." + ➡
"<p><img src='images/9781430216063.jpg'>";

books_arr[3] = ➡
"<b>The Essential Guide to Flash CS4" + ➡
" AIR Development</b>" + ➡
"<br>This book allows you to get started with" + ➡
"the essential aspects of " + ➡
"developing Adobe AIR applications using " + ➡
"the Flash CS4 IDE." + ➡
<p><img src='images/9781430215882.jpg'>";

books_arr[4] = ➡
"<b>The Essential Guide to Dreamweaver " + ➡
"CS4 with CSS, Ajax, and PHP</b><br>" + ➡
"Concentrates on getting the best out of " + ➡
"Dreamweaver CS4, in a pragmatic, practical fashion." + ➡
+"<p><img src='images/9781430216100.jpg'>";

books_arr[5] = ➡
"<b>Flex 3 Component Solutions</b>" + ➡
"<br>Build Amazing Interfaces with Flex " + ➡
"Components Flex 3 Component Solutions:" + ➡
" Build Amazing Interfaces with Flex " + ➡
"Components.<p>" + ➡
"<img src='images/9781430215981.jpg'>"; ➡

books_arr[6] = ➡
"<b>Foundation XML and E4X for Flash " + ➡
"and Flex his book provides Flash and Flex " + ➡
"developers with a coverage of XML and E4X " + ➡
"from the ground up." + ➡
"<p><img src='images/9781430216346.jpg'>";
```

8. Next, we set an index variable that will keep track of the current display book that is being rotated. This variable is

```
var bookIndex_num:Number = 0;
```

9. We'll also define an empty string that will store the HTML that we load up later:

```
var html_str:String = "";
```

10. Now, we'll create an HTML-based text field in Flash Lite dynamically through ActionScript and set some of its properties. Here, we want to let Flash know it's an HTML-based text field as well as enable the wordWrap and multiline parameters. Also we change the color of the text.

```
this.createTextField("html_txt", 1, 0, 0, 240, 320);
with ( html_txt ) {
 html = true;
 multiline = true;
 wordWrap = true;
 textColor = 0x000000;
}
```

11. We start with the first book item to be displayed before the rotation of other books starts, by assigning the first element of the array to the HTML text field.

```
html_txt.htmlText= books_arr[ 0 ];
```

12. Now, we add the setInterval() command, which rotates the books displayed one by one in the HTML text field. Here, we are rotating at an interval of every 3000 milliseconds—every 3 seconds the user will see the next book in the array.

```
bookrotateID = setInterval( rotateBooks, 3000 );

function rotateBooks():Void {
 if ( bookIndex_num >= books_arr.length-1 ) bookIndex_num = 0;
 html_txt.htmlText = books_arr[ ++bookIndex_num ];
}
```

13. Now that we have our Flash Lite SWF published, it's time to add our custom background to demonstrate the WMode functionality. You already have a FOE.html page from when you defined publish settings in steps 2 and 3. Now, just make the following modification to your FOE.html page by changing the wmode parameters to transparent:

```
    <object classid="clsid:d27cdb6e-ae6d-11cf-96b8-444553540000" ➥
codebase=http://download.macromedia.com/ ➥
pub/shockwave/cabs/flash/swflash.cab#version=8,0,0,0" ➥
width="240" height="320" id="FOE" align="middle">
    <param name="allowScriptAccess" value="sameDomain" /> ➥
    <param name="allowFullScreen" value="false" /> ➥
    <param name="movie" value="FOE.swf" /> ➥
    <param name="quality" value="high" /> ➥
    <param name="wmode" value="transparent" /> ➥
    <param name="bgcolor" value="#ffffff" /> ➥
    <embed src="FOE.swf" quality="high" ➥
      wmode="transparent" bgcolor="#ffffff" ➥
      width="240" height="320" ➥
```

```
   name="FOE" align="middle" ➥
   allowScriptAccess="sameDomain" ➥
allowFullScreen="false" ➥
type="application/x-shockwave-flash" ➥
pluginspage="http://www.adobe.com/go/getflashplayer" /> ➥
</object>
```

Great, now that both parts are completed (see Figure 3-8), it's time to test! Unfortunately, at the time of this writing, no mobile devices have shipped with Flash Lite 3.1 with browser support. To remedy this situation for our test, we'll merely run our example within a desktop browser, such as Microsoft Internet Explorer or Mozilla Firefox (both of which must have at least Flash Player 9 installed). We'll get similar behavior to what we might expect on a Flash Lite 3–1–enabled handset.

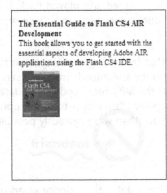

Figure 3-8.
The friends of ED rotating advertisement page displayed in a browser

Video enhancements

Some of the new enhancements with Flash Lite 3.1 to video follow:

- **Postprocessing**: Flash Lite 3.1 supports video post processing (using the Video object's smoothing and deblocking properties), which results in a higher quality of display of video files on devices. We'll see this in Chapter 15, when we go into more depth about working with Flash video on mobile and devices.

- **H.264 support for Flash video**: One of the coolest new features with Flash Lite 3.1 is the support for the H.264 video format for mobile devices that are able to support it. Like the desktop Flash Player version 9.2, Flash Lite 3.1 is able to play back Flash 7, 8, and 9 SWF files that use Flash video, by replacing the FLV file with an H.264 one on the server (Flash Media Server or HTTP).

- **Streaming video seek functionality**: Flash Lite 3.1 now supports seek functionality when streaming Flash video. Prior to version 3.1, version 3.0 only supported minimal video seeking support, and seeking to a forward or backward position relative to the current head position was supported only for small HTTP videos.

  Flash Lite 3.1 supports the ability to seek within large FLVs: seeking backward is always supported, but seeking forward is supported with some limitations. Forward seeking only works for the portion of the stream that has been downloaded so far. If an attempt is made to seek to a position beyond the end of the downloaded stream, the video continues to play from the current head position of the current video.

  The seek functionality is used along with the NetStream class. NetStream.seek() is used to seek forward or backward in the HTTP video stream.

> *If you're interested in working with Flash video and the newest features of Flash Lite 3.1, you can skip ahead to Chapter 15. In that chapter, we cover working with Flash video in both Flash Lite 3.1 and the upcoming Flash 10 player.*

In our "Working Working with Flash Lite 3.x" section of this chapter, we'll walk through a Flash Lite 3 video application.

MP3 streaming support

One of the new multimedia features added into Flash Lite 3.1 is the ability to stream MP3 audio files using the ActionScript Sound object. In previous versions of Flash Lite 2.x and 3.0, MP3 files had to be downloaded completely before they could be decoded and played back. If there was not enough memory to be allocated, errors would result during playback and cause an unsatisfactory audio experience.

In Flash Lite 3.1, progressive streaming sound is supported by loading audio data over an HTTP connection or local file system protocol. This means audio can be streamed from a web server or local file storage into a device for playback, if the device supports the MP3 audio codec. The data in the MP3 is decoded and processed as it is downloaded, which allows the Flash Player to better optimize memory consumption and allows larger MP3 files to be played back than was previously possible in Flash Lite 2.x and Flash Lite 3.0.

Graphic API additions

Although device constraints such as memory and CPU are still a top priority when developing for Flash Lite–supporting devices, version 3.1 supports APIs that you can use to increase expressiveness by translating, rotating, scaling, and skewing images in content.

The flash.display and flash.geom packages found in Flash 8 are now available in Flash Lite 3.1. The flash.display package supports the BitmapData class, which can be carefully used to create bitmaps of arbitrary sizes, and flash.geom supports classes and methods that can be used to perform pixel manipulations, including translating, rotating, scaling, and skewing.

The "Adobe Flash Lite 2.x and 3.x ActionScript Language Reference" documentation provides complete details about using these packages. Here are some of the supported classes in Flash Lite 3.1:

```
Flash.display.BitmapData
flash.gem.Point
flash.geom.Matrix
flash.geom.ColorTransform flash.geom.Rectangle
flash.geom.Transform
```

Keep in mind that using these classes will typically incur a pretty steep memory or CPU penalty. Therefore, it is recommended that you test heavily both inside Adobe Device Central CS4 and on-device for memory and CPU bottlenecks when utilizing these classes within your Flash Lite 3.1 content.

ActionScript enhancements

Some of the new ActionScript features supported by Flash Lite 3.1 follow.

ActionScript extensions   In Flash Lite 1.1, if developers or OEMs wanted to extend the capabilities of Flash Lite, they were looking at building their own custom solutions. Typically, they created a custom interface layer between Flash Lite and the lower level device operating system, and communication was handled via MMI.

With the introduction of Flash Lite 2.x, the Flash Lite community saw the introduction of third-party Flash Lite Extension software packages. Extenders allow developers to add capabilities to the base functionality of Flash Lite. Kuneri Lite, Flyer, Janus, and SWF2Go were among the first products to allow developers to reach outside the confines of the Flash Lite player to do interesting things, such as take photos, acquire GPS location coordinates, or even figure out device orientation via an accelerometer.

With Flash Lite 3, it is now possible for third-party developers to add features and ActionScript APIs to Flash Lite using a custom static or dynamically linked library file, through a new feature called ActionScript extensions.

The extensions feature allows you access to device-level functions contained in custom dynamically linked libraries (DLLs) via ActionScript APIs. You can now interact with APIs exposed on devices by writing a DLL that bridges the capabilities of the device with the Flash Lite player. The end result is Flash Lite applications that can access a device's file system, use GPS data, take photos, or tap other low-level device API functionality not normally exposed by the Flash Lite player during runtime without additional third-party software (e.g., Kuneri Lite).

ActionScript extensions are available to third-party developers only if extensions have been enabled by device manufacturers. You must consult the device OEMs for this information, as it is not currently publicly available.

> In Chapter 7, we'll take a look at how to extend Flash Lite by using this third-party software. However, at the time of this writing, working with ActionScript extensions is primarily only available to developers who work for specific device OEMs utilizing this feature.

setTimeout and clearTimeout functions   The ActionScript 2.0 setTimeout and clearTimeout global functions were not supported in Flash Lite 3.0 but are supported in Flash Lite 3.1. The setTimeout function is used to run a specified function after a specified delay interval (in milliseconds). The clearTimeout function will immediately terminate a pending setTimeout call if it is active and running. If you're familiar with the setInterval command in ActionScript 2.0, you will notice similarities between these two commands.

Here is a simple example of using this command that makes a call to delay a user prompt dialog.

```
function openURLAfterPause(url_str:String):Void {
 getURL( url_str, "_new" );
}
setTimeout(openURLAfterPause,1000,"http://www.flashmobilebook.com");
```

Using setTimeOut or clearTimeOut in conjunction with inline input text can cause problems for time-sensitive applications, such as online quizzes or games, because background processing of all ActionScript (including the timer) is paused when text is being input by the device user.

Shared objects   Although local shared objects (LSOs) were added to Flash Lite as early as version 2.0, in Flash Lite 3.1, some significant changes have been made to their behavior.

First off, the rules for storage of local shared objects in Flash Lite 3.1 are now fully compatible with those of Flash Player 8 on the desktop. Prior to Flash Lite 3.1, the location of the shared object was derived from the name of the SWF, so shared objects could not share data no matter where the SWF files were located. When working with subdomains, this limitation didn't make much sense, but protecting top-level domain-named SWF files was not an issue. For instance, a SWF named a.swf could not be accessed by b.swf regardless of the location of the SWF files on a device file system.

In Flash Lite 3.1, the location of the shared object is now derived from its URL, instead of its file name, so /data/A.swf located on a device can access shared objects stored by /B.swf.

Another change in Flash Lite 3.1 is that if a SWF file was modified, even if the file name remained in the system, any associated shared objects with that SWF would be treated differently than the original ones. This is no longer the case. In Flash Lite 3.1, a SWF file's shared objects are treated the same as long as the URL or sandbox is the same, even if the SWF file has been modified or renamed.

Also, prior to 3.1, two different versions of a SWF file could not access each other's shared objects, but in 3.1, they can. In Flash Lite 2.x, shared objects were only available to locally stored SWF files. SWF files played back in a network browser could not use Flash Lite shared objects.

In Flash Lite 3.0 and later, SWF files running in the network security sandbox can access and store shared objects. All network SWF files in version 3.0 could store and access local shared objects, but access to them was limited to a per-SWF basis. In Flash Lite 3.1, all SWF files originating from the same network domain can access each other's shared objects.

These are the core features that have been added to Flash Lite 3.1. Video is also another big item.

Working with Flash Lite 3.x

Now that we've covered some of what's new with Flash Lite 3, it's time to put some of that knowledge to work. In this section, we'll create a Flash Lite 3 video application.

> *If you are new to Flash and require assistance, remember that we covered a lot of useful places to get up to speed on ActionScript and Flash in Chapter 2.*

We'll be using our Eclipse-based Flash Lite setup from Chapter 2 to create a YouTube video mash-up application.

Explaining mash-ups

Mash-ups are all about combining existing data sources to create new applications. For instance, Jibe (see Figure 3-9) is a company that allows the user to search Flickr, YouTube, and other social media already on the Web. It also allows you to personalize your own channel that can be viewed on your phone or shared with your friends.

The FLV compressed format can be used within a SWF, and YouTube, Google, Yahoo, and other sites are using that format to allow faster downloads. Flash Lite content is distributed over the air (OTA), so the data has to be optimized, since smaller size means faster download to the mobile device.

Creating our Flash Lite 3 video application

In this section, we will build a Flash Lite 3 video application that will let the users search videos from YouTube and play them; the application is shown in Figure 3-10.

Figure 3-9. Jibe mobile phone mash-up

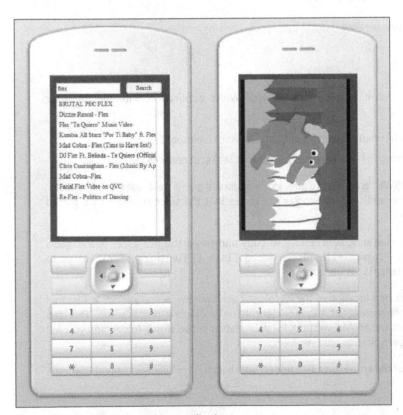

Figure 3-10. Our YouTube mash-up application

125

Let's get started in creating our sample application. Open the Eclipse IDE, and create a new project by selecting File ➤ New ➤ Other ➤ ActionScript ➤ New ActionScript Project. Call the application YouTubeMobileApplication, and click Next followed by Finish. Create the directory src/com/mobile. Now, create an ActionScript class called Main, which will be our entry point for the application:

```
class com.mobile.Main
{
private var movie:MovieClip;
private var textField:TextField;

  /**
   * Default constructor
   */
  function Main(movie:MovieClip)
  {
   this.movie = movie;
  }

  /**
   * Main method assigns this class to the _root.
   */
  public static function main():Void
  {
  Flashout.info("main invoked");
  Trace("test");
  }
}
```

Next, create the Flashout file. Set it as we did in our HelloWorld application, with the following information:

- Path to SWF: [workbench]\YouTubeMobileApplication\src\com\mobile\Main.swf
- Root (main class): [workbench]\YouTubeMobileApplication\src\com\mobile\Main.as

Since we will be compiling our SWF, remember to add, in the additional parms field, -header 240:320:12. You can compile the application and check the logger tag to see that the trace statement we placed is showing correctly.

Since we will be using several classes, it is necessary to copy and paste the MM folder (Macromedia shared scripts and files) from C:\Program Files\Adobe\Adobe Flash CS3\en\First Run\Classes to our application's YouTubeMobileApplication\src.

Now, set the core classes to the new location of the MM folder. Click Window ➤ Preferences ➤ Flashout ➤ Directory of Macromedia's core classes. Set it to [workbench]\YouTubeMobileApplication\src. This step is necessary; otherwise, Flashout and MTASC will look for your classes in the wrong folder, and you will get the following error message: type error class not found.

Create the directories and classes shown in Figure 3-11 under [workbench]\YouTubeMobileApplication\src.

Figure 3-11.
Folder structure of
YouTubeMobileApplication

Next, we need to obtain YouTube videos for the application. We will call the YouTube API and receive an XML list of all the YouTube videos; we'll also deserialize the data and extract the specified FLV selected by a user in the application. The YouTube API provides us with a SWF to play the videos, but to customize our player, it's more beneficial to pull the FLV and create our own player.

The classes are already separated into an MVC framework, so we can easily implement either Cairngorm Mobile Edition or some other enterprise framework for easy maintenance.

Figure 3-12 depicts the YouTube Mobile Application class diagram we use to work with the data provided by YouTube.

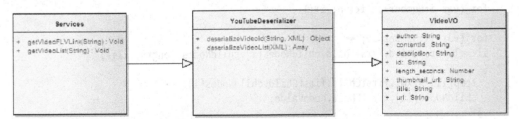

Figure 3-12. YouTube Mobile Application class diagram

A value object (VO) will be created next, so we can create a collection of entries. We will call it VideoVO, and creating one is easy once you know the structure of the YouTube XML data. I downloaded a small

XML sample from the YouTube API and manually decided which fields we are interested in capturing based on our application.

```
class com.mobile.vo.VideoVO {
 public var author:String;
 public var id:String;
 public var title:String;
 public var length_seconds:Number;
 public var description:String;
 public var url:String;
 public var thumbnail_url:String;
 public var contentId:String;
}
```

Now, we need to be able to deserialize the XML response to fit into our VO. The two methods deserializeVideoList and deserializeVideoId iterate through the XML collection and then pass the information to setVideoVO that returns for us a video entry value object. Notice that unlike with ActionScript 3.0, we don't have E4X to help us iterate through the collection.

```
import com.mobile.vo.*;

class com.mobile.helpers.YouTubeDeserializer
{
  /**
   * Deserialize video list results.
   */
   public static function deserializeVideoList(xml:XML):Array
   {
   var xmlString:String = xml.toString();
   var temp:Array = new Array();
   var len:Number = xml.firstChild.firstChild.childNodes.length;
   var video:VideoVO = new VideoVO();
   var videoCollection:Array = new Array();

   for (var i:Number=1; i<len; i++)
   {
   for (var ii:Number= 0; ➡
   ii<xml.firstChild.firstChild.childNodes[i].childNodes.length; ii++)
   {
     temp[ii] = xml.firstChild.firstChild.childNodes[i]. ➡
     childNodes[ii].firstChild.nodeValue;
   }

   video = YouTubeDeserializer.setVideoVO(temp[0],
     temp[1], temp[2], temp[3], temp[5], temp[11], temp[12]);
     videoCollection.push(video);
   }
```

```
    return videoCollection;
}

/**
  * Extract FLV URL from XML.
  */
  public static function deserializeVideoId➡
  (xml:XML, url:String):Object
{
  var temp:Array = new Array();
  var xmlList:String = xml.firstChild.childNodes.toString();
  var len:Number = xml.firstChild.childNodes.length;
  var results:Object;

      for (var i:Number = 0; i<len; i++)
      {
        temp[i] = ➡
        xml.firstChild.childNodes[i].firstChild.nodeValue;
      }

      results = url + "?video_id=" + ➡
      xml.firstChild.childNodes[0].firstChild.nodeValue + "&t=" +
      xml.firstChild.childNodes[1].firstChild.nodeValue;

        return results;
      }

/**
  * Method to set <code>VideoVO</code> type objects.
  */
  private static function setVideoVO(author:String, ➡
  id:String, ➡
  title:String, ➡
  length_seconds:String, ➡
  description:String, url:String, ➡
  thumbnail_url:String):VideoVO
    {
      var video:VideoVO = new VideoVO();
      var vidURL:Array = new Array();

      video.author = author;
      video.id = id;
      video.title = title;
      video.length_seconds  = Number(length_seconds);
      video.description = description;
      video.url = String(url);
      video.thumbnail_url   = thumbnail_url;
```

```
                vidURL = url.split("http://www.youtube.com/?v=");
                video.contentId = vidURL[1];

                return video;
            }
        }
```

The next class we need is a service class that can handle the entire business layer. The class will include the different methods we will be using for that service and will dispatch events upon completion.

Here's the Services class content:

```
        import com.mobile.helpers.YouTubeDeserializer;
        import mx.events.EventDispatcher;
        import mx.utils.Delegate;

        class com.mobile.business.Services
        {
          private static var DEV_ID:String    = "WplekwLy_Nw";
          private static var PROXY_URL:String = "http://YourSite.com/proxy/";
          private static var VIDEO_LIST_PROXY:String = "proxyRequest.php";
          private static var VIDEO_FLV_LINK_PROXY:String = "getVideoId.php";
          private static var FLV_VIDEO_URL:String = ➥
          "http://www.youtube.com/get_video";

          private var methodType:String;
          private var xml:XML;

          public function dispatchEvent() {};
          public function addEventListener() {};
          public function removeEventListener() {};

           /**
            * Default constructor
            */
           public function Services()
           {
             EventDispatcher.initialize(this);

              xml = new XML();
              xml.ignoreWhite = true;
              xml.onLoad = Delegate.create(this, serviceLoadedEventHandler);
           }

           /**
            * Handler for results.  This method will
            * send the different service calls to the
            * appropriate deserializer.
            */
```

```
   function serviceLoadedEventHandler(success:Boolean):Void
{
  if(success)
  {
    var results:Object;
    switch (methodType)
    {
     case "youtube.videos.list_by_tag":
       results = YouTubeDeserializer.deserializeVideoList(xml);
       break;
     case "videoid":
       results = ➡
YouTubeDeserializer.deserializeVideoId(xml, FLV_VIDEO_URL);
       break;
    }

    // set up the event object:
    var event:Object = { target:this, type:methodType };
    event.msgtxt = methodType;
    event.results = results;
    this.dispatchEvent(event);
  }
  else
  {
    trace("Connection Failed: " + methodType);
  }
}

/**
 * Service for method youtube.videos.list_by_tag.
 */
public function getVideoList(tag:String):Void
{
  var vars:LoadVars = new LoadVars();

  methodType = "youtube.videos.list_by_tag";

  vars.method=methodType;
  vars.dev_id = DEV_ID;
  vars.tag = tag;
  vars.page="1";
  vars.per_page="10";

    vars.sendAndLoad( PROXY_URL + VIDEO_LIST_PROXY +
      "?url=http://www.youtube.com/api2_rest", xml, "POST" );
}
```

```
/**
 * Service for method videoid.
 */
public function getVideoFLVLink(videoId:String):Void
{
  var vars:LoadVars = new LoadVars();

  methodType = "videoid";

  vars.method=methodType;
  vars.url="http://www.youtube.com/watch?v="+videoId;

  vars.sendAndLoad( PROXY_URL +
    VIDEO_FLV_LINK_PROXY, xml, "POST" );
  }
}
```

In ActionScript 2.x, you have to attach the event handlers to the event such as this:

```
mc.button.onRelease = function() {
    trace("do something");
}
```

However, that can cause scoping issues, since the function doesn't have access to other members. A good way to solve that problem is to use a delegate class, which allows us to break that tie and create event handlers as independent functions:

```
mc.button.onRelease = Delegate.create(this, releaseEventHandler);
...
private function releaseEventHandler():Void
{
 trace("do something");
}
```

There is a known issue with using a delegate in MTASC. You will receive the following runtime error:

```
mx.utils.Delegate: type error Local variable redefinition.
```

To fix it, replace the following contents of the `mx.utils.Delegate` class

```
static function create(obj:Object, func:Function):Function
{
 var f = function()
 {
   var target = arguments.callee.target;
   var func = arguments.callee.func;

   return func.apply(target, arguments);
 };
```

```
        f.target = obj;
        f.func = func;

    return f;
        }
```

with this

```
        static function create(obj:Object, func:Function):Function
        {
            var f = function()
            {
                var target = arguments.callee.target;
                var func2 = arguments.callee.func;

                return func2.apply(target, arguments);
            };

            f.target = obj;
            f.func = func;

            return f;
        }
```

We will be using proxy requests using PHP and will name the file proxyRequest.php. You can create your own PHP environment on your local machine for testing. The following proxy will allow you to retrieve the XML list of videos from YouTube, since YouTube changes its crossdomain.xml frequently, and we don't want our mash-up to break. See http://www.youtube.com/crossdomain.xml for the format of the cross-domain file and its policy settings.

```
    <?php

    // PHP Proxy to responds to HTTP GET/POST requests

    $url = ($_POST['url']) ? $_POST['url'] : $_GET['url'];
    $headers = ($_POST['headers']) ? $_POST['headers'] : $_GET['headers'];
    $mimeType =($_POST['mimeType']) ? ➥
    $_POST['mimeType'] : $_GET['mimeType'];

    $session = curl_init($url);

    $vars = '';
    while ($element = current($_POST))
    {
                $vars .= key($_POST).'='.$element.'&';
                next($_POST);
    }

    curl_setopt($session, CURLOPT_POST, true);
    curl_setopt($session, CURLOPT_POSTFIELDS, $vars);
```

```php
curl_setopt($session, CURLOPT_HEADER, ($headers == "true") ? ➥
 true : false);
curl_setopt($session, CURLOPT_FOLLOWLOCATION, true);
curl_setopt($session, CURLOPT_RETURNTRANSFER, true);

$response = curl_exec($session);

if ($mimeType != "")
{
                header("Content-Type: ".$mimeType);
}

echo $response;

curl_close($session);

?>
```

We need to create a second proxy, getVideoId.php, to extract the specified FLV file from YouTube.
YouTube doesn't expose the FLV file name in the API, but using the curl method in PHP, we can find
out the location of the FLV file:

```php
<?php
$url = trim($_REQUEST["url"]);

if (strpos($url, "http://www.youtube.com/watch?v=") === 0)
{
    $ch = curl_init();

    curl_setopt($ch, CURLOPT_URL, $url);
    curl_setopt($ch, CURLOPT_HEADER, false);
    curl_setopt($ch, CURLOPT_RETURNTRANSFER, true);

    $info = curl_exec($ch);

    $pos1 = strpos($info, "&video_id=", $pos1);
    $pos2 = strpos($info, "&t=", $pos2);

    $video_id = substr($info, $pos1 + 10, 11);
    $tag_t = substr($info, $pos2 + 3, 32);

    $response  = "<video>";
    $response .= "<id>" . $video_id . "</id>";
    $response .= "<t>" . $tag_t . "</t>";
    $response .= "</video>";

    header("Content-type: text/xml");

    echo $response;
```

```
        curl_close($ch);

}
else
{
    die("Wrong URL or parameters");
}

?>
```

To test that everything's working correctly, we need to change our entry point, Main.class; we will set the class to search for videos based on keywords and retrieve the FLV location:

```
import com.mobile.business.Services;
import com.mobile.vo.VideoVO;
import mx.utils.Delegate;

class com.mobile.Main
{

  private var movie:MovieClip;
  private var textField:TextField;

  /**
   * Default constructor
   */
  function Main(movie:MovieClip)
   {
    this.movie = movie;
   }

  /**
   * Main method assigns this class to the _root.
   */
  public static function main():Void
   {
     Flashout.info("main invoked");
     var Main:Main = new Main(_root);
     searchYouTube("flex");
   }

  /**
   * Method to search YouTube for videos based on tags
   */
  public static function searchYouTube(tagString:String):Void
    {
      var service:Services = new Services();
      service.addEventListener("youtube.videos.list_by_tag",
```

```
      Delegate.create(Main, getVideoListEventHandler) );
      service.getVideoList(tagString);
    }

    /**
     * Event handler that will be used once the list
     * of videos returned with results.
     */
    public static function getVideoListEventHandler ➥
    (event:Object):Void
  {
     var contentId:String = VideoVO(event.results[0]).contentId;
     var service:Services = new Services();

      trace(contentId);
      trace(event.msgtxt);

      service.addEventListener("videoid",
      Delegate.create(Main, getVideoFLVLinkEventHandler) );
      service.getVideoFLVLink(contentId);
     }

    /**
     * Handler to use the video FLV that was returned
     * from YouTube.
     */
    public static function getVideoFLVLinkEventHandler ➥
   (event:Object):Void
      {
        trace(event.msgtxt);
        trace( String(event.results) );
        // play video
      }
  }
```

Now that we are done building the YouTube API, let's go back to Flash Professional to create the user interface pieces.

Create two layers, one called Video and another called List underneath it. Also create an ActionScript layer (see Figure 3-13). Next, drag and drop the following components from the Flash library onto the Stage area (see the components in the Flash library shown in Figure 3-13):

- A Button with the instance name searchButton onto the List layer
- A List with the instance name videoList onto the List layer
- A previewVid with the instance name video onto the Video layer
- A TextInput with the instance name textInput onto the List layer

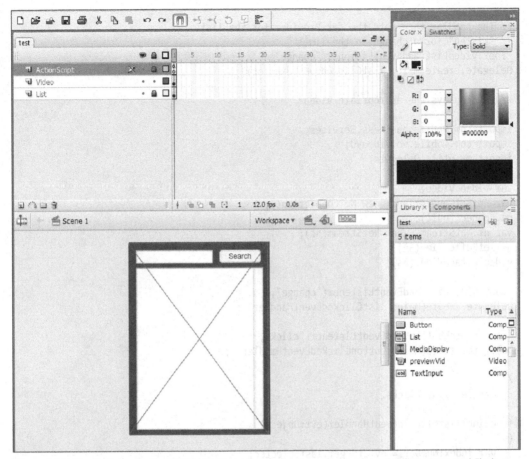

Figure 3-13. The Flash Professional IDE with the video application user interface, timeline setup, and Flash Library items

The ActionScript layer will replace our entry point in Eclipse. Therefore, the methods are going to be very similar, but this time, we will attach them to the components.

Save the FLA in YouTubeMobileApplication\src so we will be able to use the class structure, just as we could in Eclipse.

Once a search is submitted, an event is dispatched and buttonClickedEventHandler is called:

```
_root.searchButton.addEventListener("click",
Delegate.create(Main, buttonClickedEventHandler));
```

In the handler, the service.getVideoList is being called to bring back the results, and once the results are back, they will be handled by getVideoListEventHandler:

```
service.addEventListener("youtube.videos.list_by_tag",
Delegate.create(Main, getVideoListEventHandler) );
```

```
// The handler then sets the dataProvider for the list.
// "Listen" for a change in the list:
_root.videoList.addEventListener("change",
Delegate.create(Main, listClickedEventHandler));

// Which plays the appropriate video?

import com.mobile.business.Services;
import com.mobile.vo.VideoVO;
import mx.utils.Delegate;

var video:Video;
var nc:NetConnection = new NetConnection();
nc.connect(null);
var ns:NetStream = new NetStream(nc);
ns.setBufferTime(5);
video.attachVideo(ns);

_root.videoList.addEventListener("change",
Delegate.create(Main, listClickedEventHandler));

_root.searchButton.addEventListener("click",
Delegate.create(Main, buttonClickedEventHandler));

/**
 * Handler list clicks.
 */
function listClickedEventHandler(evt:Object)
{
   var index:Number = evt.target.lastSelected;
   var contentId:String = ➡
 _root.videoList.dataProvider[index].contentId;

   trace(contentId);

   var service:Services = new Services();
   service.addEventListener("videoid",
     Delegate.create(Main, getVideoFLVLinkEventHandler) );
   service.getVideoFLVLink(contentId);
}

/**
 * Handler search click event.
 */
function buttonClickedEventHandler(evt:Object)
{
```

```
    var service:Services = new Services();
    service.addEventListener("youtube.videos.list_by_tag",
     Delegate.create(Main, getVideoListEventHandler) );
    service.getVideoList(_root.textInput.text);
    }

    /**
     * Event handler that will be used once the list of videos
     * returned with results.
     */
    function getVideoListEventHandler(event:Object):Void
    {
    _root.videoList.dataProvider = event.results;
    _root.videoList.labelField = "title";
    }

    /**
     * Handler to use the video FLV that was returned from YouTube.
     */
    function getVideoFLVLinkEventHandler(event:Object):Void
    {
    trace(event.msgtxt);
    trace( String(event.results) );
    ns.play(String(event.results));
    }
```

Test the application by pressing F12 or Ctrl+Enter to open Device Central. Congratulations, you've got a mash-up video player!

> In Chapter 15, we'll be covering Flash video capabilities more with both Flash Lite 3 as well as Flash 10. This will include a discussion of progressive, streaming, and embedded video.

Now that you have gotten a taste of the capabilities of Flash Lite 3 with native video, it's time to turn our attention to talking about the Adobe Distributable Player Solution.

Exploring the Adobe Distributable Player Solution

In addition to the core features of the Flash Lite 3.1 player that we talked about previously in this chapter, the Adobe Distributable Player Solution (ADPS) focuses on two important challenges with the Flash Lite runtime: improving Flash Lite content distribution, and addressing the Flash Lite player version stagnation that appears across mobile and devices. Let us explain each of these of topics:

- **Content distribution and player market penetration**: You've already read about the various worldwide Flash Lite content distribution mechanisms in Chapter 2. The ADPS offers a new avenue that you can take advantage of to get your mobile content out to market. With the ADPS, Flash Lite applications can be bundled into installable files that allow end users to more easily install content on their supported devices (currently S60 and Windows Mobile).

- **Addressing Flash Player stagnation across mobile and devices**: Up until this time, Flash Lite 1.1, 2.x, and 3.0 have been preinstalled on devices by OEMs, meaning high turn-around times to get new Flash Lite player technology out to market. Updates to the preinstalled Flash Lite player required users to perform unintuitive firmware updates to their device.

  The ADPS addresses Flash Lite player version stagnation by allowing the Flash Lite runtime to be updated OTA on supported devices. After installing the Flash Lite 3.1 Distributable Player, users are much more likely to have the latest version of Flash Lite installed on their respective devices because of its player check technology, which functions as a dial-home-for-updates feature.

  As new runtimes become available from Adobe, Flash Lite (and in the future, possibly Flash 10) player runtimes can be installed via the Distributable Player technology.

> *Since the Adobe Distributable Player is still in its beta version at the time of this writing, we encourage you to visit http://advancED.flashmobilebook.com/ADPS for more information as newer versions become available.*

To address these challenges, the ADPS is composed of two components: the Flash Lite 3.1 Distributable Player and Adobe Mobile Packager.

Downloading the Flash Lite 3.1 Distributable Player

The Distributable Player acts as a unique stand-alone Flash Lite player that installs alongside any pre-installed Flash Lite player (e.g., Flash Lite 1.1, 2.x, and 3.0) or any built-in Flash Lite browser plug-in on a device (e.g., the Nokia S60 browser).

Because the Flash Lite 3.1 Distributable Player is currently in its beta version, it's only available from the Adobe Labs site at http://labs.adobe.com/technologies/distributableplayer/.

At the time of this writing, the Adobe Flash Lite 3.1 Distributable Player is available for Windows Mobile 5 (pocket PCs and smart phones), Windows Mobile 6 Professional, and S60 third-edition devices. A working list of devices supporting the Distributable Player is located at http://labs.adobe.com/wiki/index.php/Distributable_Player:Supported_Devices. However, more platform support may be available by the time you read this chapter, especially if the first official release of the Distributable Player is available. To check what's available currently, visit http://labs.adobe.com/technologies/distributableplayer/.

Using Adobe Mobile Packager

Adobe Mobile Packager, shown in Figure 3-14, is a desktop tool (currently Microsoft Windows only) for packaging SWF application content (i.e., Flash Lite) alongside a player-checker feature, launch icon, and metadata into an installable file format for supported mobile and device operating systems.

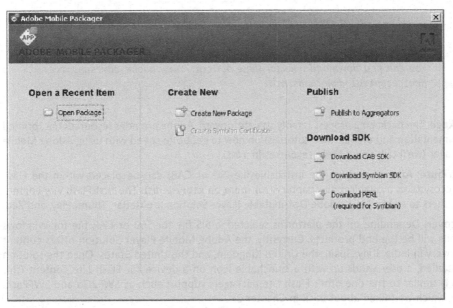

Figure 3-14. Adobe Mobile Packager (beta)

Currently, Adobe Mobile Packager supports Nokia S60 (i.e., smart phones) and devices running Windows Mobile 5 and 6. At the time of this writing, Adobe has certified the Flash Lite 3.1 Distributable Player for the Windows Mobile 5 for SmartPhone, Windows Mobile 6 Standard and Professional, S60 third edition, S60 third edition feature pack 1, and S60 third edition feature pack 2 device platforms. Certification for more devices is likely in the future.

The installable file formats currently supported are .sis for S60 and .cab for Windows Mobile devices.

> Recall that, in Chapter 2, we discussed SIS and CAB mobile packaging formats. The difference here is that the Distributable Player portion is bundled up with the SWF files for delivery, enabling the OTA player check and update mechanism in the Flash Lite 3.1 Distributable Player.

Downloading Adobe Mobile Packager

Currently Adobe Mobile Packager can be downloaded from the Adobe Labs web site at http://labs.adobe.com/downloads/distributableplayer.html.

These are the four basic steps to content distribution with Adobe Mobile Packager:

1. **Create**: Using Flash CS3, Flash CS4, or one of the open source Flash alternatives that we discussed in Chapter 2, create a Flash Lite SWF. When publishing SWF content, any version can be targeted. However, it's best to publish to the Flash Lite 3.1 stand-alone content type. At this time, the Flash Lite 3.1 Distributable Player supports only stand-alone applications, and does not allow for other installable content types (e.g., screensavers, wallpapers).

> *In order to publish Flash Lite 3.1 content from Flash CS4 and test it with Device Central CS4, both the Adobe AIR 1.5 update for Flash CS4 Professional and the Flash Lite 3.1 update for Device Central CS4 must currently be installed. You can find download links for these at http://www.adobe.com/support/devicecentral/downloads.html.*

2. **Package**: The packaging process is fairly straightforward. Adobe provides resources (i.e., printed documentation and online video tutorials) on how to get up to speed with using Adobe Mobile Packager (we'll talk about these resources in a bit).

3. **Distribute**: After packaging, the installable file (SIS or CAB) can be placed within the Flash Lite ecosystems available (see Chapter 1 for more on ecosystems). The first Flash Lite content publishers to support the Adobe Distributable Player Solution are GetJar, ThumbPlay, and Zed.

4. **Discover**: Depending on the platforms selected, a SIS file for S60 or CAB file for Windows Mobile will be the end products. Currently, the Adobe Mobile Player Solution offers content discovery in India, Italy, Spain, the United Kingdom, and the United States. Once the solution is installed, a user winds up with a launchable icon on a device for Flash Lite content (this icon is similar to the one other Flash Lite packagers support such as SWF2Go and SWFPack.com, which we talked about back in Chapter 2).

Accessing Adobe Mobile Packager documentation

Adobe offers some documentation on how to set up and use Adobe Mobile Packager at http://download.macromedia.com/pub/labs/distributableplayer/distributableplayer_usingmobilepackager_en.pdf. Apparently Adobe has not updated the Adobe Labs site since the merger, or at least not the Downloads section, given the Macromedia URLs. Please forgive that.

Adobe also offers video-based tutorials as part of the Flash Lite 3.1 SDK; these cover the Flash Lite 3.1 Distributable Player, the process to package SWF content, and signing that content using the Symbian and Windows Mobile signing processes. You'll find all this information in their *Flash Lite Distributable Player Tutorials* video series, which we talk about next.

Accessing the Flash Lite Distributable Player tutorials

In addition to written documentation resources we've noted, Adobe also provides online video tutorials available to get you up to speed with the ADPS on the tv.adobe.com site:

- *Distributable Player Solution Overview*: This video provides you with an overview of the ADPS and both of its components: the Flash Lite 3.1 Distributable Player and Adobe Mobile Packager. Watch the video at http://tv.adobe.com/#vi+f15313v1002.

- *Mobile Packager Setup*: This tutorial walks through requirements needed to run Adobe Mobile Packager, including the host operating system parameters (Windows XP with service pack 2 or 3), Active Perl (5.6.1 or higher), and the Symbian SDK (third edition or third edition feature pack 1 or 2) or Windows Mobile SDK. More information can be found at http://tv.adobe.com/#vi+f15313v1001.

- *Creating a Mobile Package*: Once your development environment is configured correctly, see this tutorial to find out how to go about the packaging process using the latest mobile packaging tool. The video covers some important tips to using the tool (such as how packaging configurable fields are used and how to name your packaged assets). It also contains a walkthrough using Adobe Mobile Packager. Visit http://tv.adobe.com/#vi+f15313v1004 for the latest tutorial on using the packager.

- *Icon Boot Camp*: This tutorial instructs designers and developers on some of the ways in which Flash Lite application scalable vector graphic (SVG) icon graphics can be created for Symbian-based devices, as well as ICO icon graphics for the CAB format under Windows Mobile. The tools involved in icon creation (e.g., Adobe Illustrator) are also covered, as well as some useful tips and tricks for designing mobile icons. See http://tv.adobe.com/#vi+f15313v1006.

- *Application Signing*: The final tutorial in the series covers how to go about signing SIS and CAB files to be deployed within the distribution opportunities where content providers (e.g., ThumbPlay, Zed, and GetJar) require Symbian signing. See http://tv.adobe.com/#vi+f15313v1003.

> *Adobe can sometimes change the URLs for these tutorials. If you are having trouble locating the tutorials with these URLs, please type the title of the video tutorial specified at the search field located at the top of the page at http://tv.adobe.com.*

You've seen the next-generation packaging that Adobe has created to make packaging and distributing Flash Lite content a bit easier for developers.

It's time now to turn attention to Adobe Device Central CS4 and its SDK, specifically the new features in it that make off-device content (e.g., Flash Lite SWF) testing easier for developers.

Introducing the Adobe Device Central CS4 SDK

Among the myriad of features that Adobe Creative Suite 4 offers to mobile professionals is the new SDK that is included in Adobe Device Central CS4. The Adobe Device Central CS4 SDK is a framework that allows developers to create and reuse exiting plug-ins that extend the tasks that can be used in Adobe Device Central projects.

Using the Device Central CS4 SDK can increase productivity by allowing you to create reusable plug-ins to handle common testing and authoring tasks. In fact, Adobe Device Central CS4 ships with three preinstalled task plug-ins: Bluetooth, CopyFile, and SendToFTP. These can be accessed by opening Adobe Device Central, selecting File ➤ New Project, and right-clicking the wheel cog icon under the Tasks section of the project dialog—see Figure 3-15, and note that the Say Hello World task that is visible is the sample plug-in created after installation and was not preinstalled.

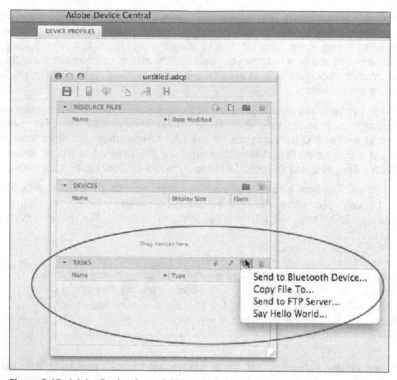

Figure 3-15. Adobe Device Central CS4 preinstalled task plug-ins

With the added SDK, mobile developers can work dynamically and interactively with their mobile content, using a scriptable language (called ExtendScript) to create Adobe Device Central plug-ins. These plug-ins can be created and managed through the Tasks dialog to streamline mobile workflow. This can lead to device content to being tested faster (and potentially more cheaply, given the time savings that some plug-ins and tasks may yield).

Among the preinstalled plug-ins with Adobe Device Central, other possibilities include automatic archiving of Flash Lite content (using a ZIP file), uploading of Flash Lite content to content providers via web services, and automatic Bluetooth access for Flash Lite content to physical devices for testing.

Downloading the Adobe Device Central SDK

The Adobe Device Central SDK does not (currently) ship with CS4, so you must download it from Adobe. It's among several SDKs found at this URL: http://www.adobe.com/devnet/sdks.html.

Exploring the Adobe Device Central SDK

Once you have downloaded the archive, just unpack it and take a look at the directory structure, which should include the following folders and files:

- /Documents/
- /Sample Plugins/
- /Sample WebService/
- ReadMe.txt

The ReadMe.txt file explains what each directory contains, but we'll also explain briefly here. First, the Documents folder contains all the documentation and API information:

- *ADC SDK Programmer's Guide* (ADC SDK Guide.pdf)
- *ADC SDK Programmer's Reference* (ADC SDK Reference.pdf)
- *JavaScript Tools Guide CS4* (JavaScript Tools Guide CS4.pdf)

The Sample Plugins folder contains some very rudimentary code samples to get you started, including Hello World, Create Zip, SendToWeb, and XML MetaData plug-ins. Lastly, the Sample WebService directory contains code for setting up Adobe Device Central to automatically upload mobile content to a web site via a web service.

To learn about how to create plug-ins, start with the *ADC SDK Programmer's Guide* and the sample Hello World application provided in that document. Use the *Programmer's Guide* to understand the Adobe Device Central DOM object reference, which offers access to objects such as Bluetooth, ZIPFile, StatusDialog, and other functionality provided by the SDK.

Installing sample plug-ins

Installing sample plug-ins is very straightforward. Depending on your platform and operating system, you'll need to copy them in the following respective folders:

- **Windows Vista**: Go to Users\%USERPROFILE%\AppData\Local\Adobe\Adobe Device Central CS4\Tasks.
- **Windows XP**: Go to \Documents and Settings\Users\%USERPROFILE%\Local Settings\, and then navigate to Application Data\Adobe\Adobe Device Central CS4\Tasks.
- **Mac OS X**: Go to /Users/%USER/Library/Application Support/, and then find Adobe Device Central CS4/Tasks.

Once installed, the new task should be available in the Projects dialog (see Figure 3-15) within Adobe Device Central, which you can open by selecting File ➤ New Project.

Leveraging Adobe Device Central CS4 plug-ins

Once you've read the *ADC SDK Programmer's Guide* and have a good handle on the ExtendScript language you can start to create your own plug-ins and tasks to help your Flash Lite project workflow.

We have some free plug-ins available that we've created that you can download, reuse, and learn from at http://advancED.flashmobilebook.com/ADC_CS4_SDK_plugins/.

Summary

In this chapter, we looked at Flash Lite 3.x and how you can begin to leverage some of the great features in this powerful mobile and device runtime.

We walked through a sample Flash video application using Flash Lite 3 and the Eclipse Flash Lite development setup we used in Chapter 2. You also got an overview of the Flash Lite 3.1 Distributable Player and Adobe Mobile Packager, which compose the Adobe Distributable Player Solution (ADPS). Toward the end of the chapter, you also read about how to leverage Adobe Device Central CS4 SDK to help improve your testing workflow, and information was provided on how to get started using it.

In the next few chapters, we'll move onto more advanced Flash Lite topics from creating Flash Lite widgets (Chapter 5), to using reusable user interface components and frameworks (Chapter 6), as well as extending device capabilities of Flash Lite on Nokia and Sony Ericsson devices (Chapter 7). In Chapter 8, we'll talk about porting Flash Lite content to the iPhone and how to address working with touch-screen devices.

What about Flash 10? In Chapters 9 through 15, we'll get you prepared for working with Adobe Integrated Runtime (AIR) and Flash 10 on next-generation smart phones and others devices.

Before we get into these advanced topics, though, we'll share some practical tips and tricks when working with mobile content and Flash Lite in our next chapter.

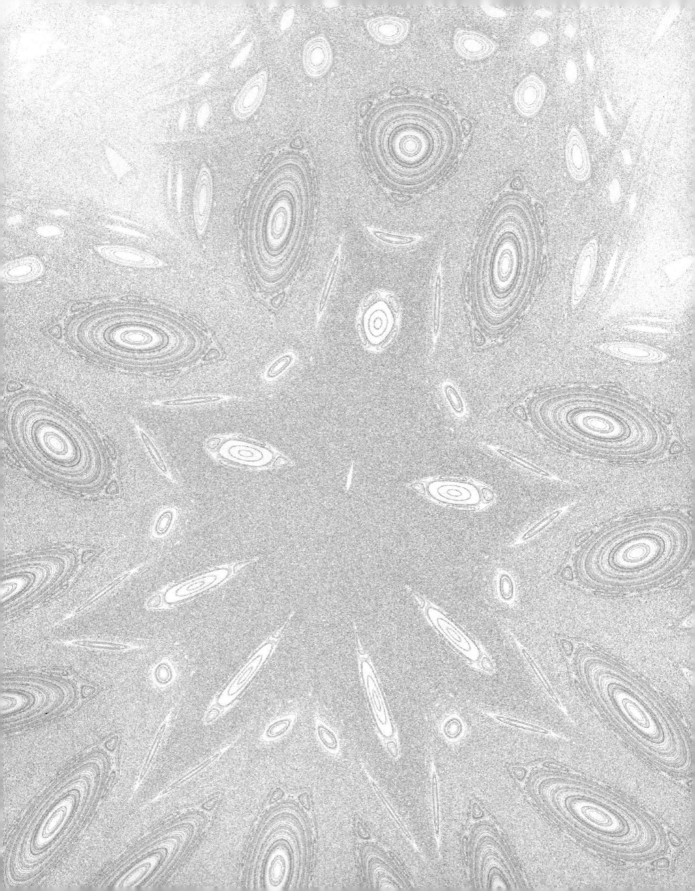

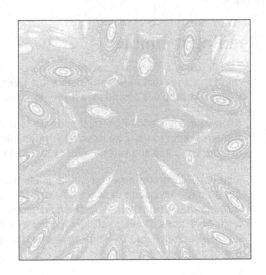

Chapter 4

TIPS AND TRICKS FOR DEVELOPING FLASH MOBILE APPLICATIONS

Even though there are already a few touch-screen–based devices (e.g., the iPhone, Blackberry, Nokia 5800 Express Music, Nokia N97, etc.), the majority of mobile devices are still key based. Mobile applications for these key-based devices are always based on the same flow: navigate to a certain option using the arrow keys and execute a task via the enter key or the soft keys. Guiding the user through the application flow intuitively is crucial to a successful application. Not having to think which key should be pressed makes for a good user experience. That's why we think it is important to create an optimized mobile interface that guides users along the way, and that's exactly what we will handle in this chapter.

Optimizing your mobile user interface

Guiding a user through your mobile application is not always easy. A user who is confused or lost in the interface will quickly shut down your application and most likely never open it again. Before you know it, a negative review is written on a blog somewhere, and via Facebook and Twitter, lots of people end up reading it. That's something we want to avoid, right? Let's have a look at a few tips to help you with that.

Keeping it simple

Mobile users do not like having too many options while navigating through your content. Keep in mind that they feel most comfortable just navigating, selecting something, and performing an action. Keeping it simple is a good idea if you don't want confused users who give up on your application.

Keep your application flow clear and easy to understand by following these basic rules: let people use the arrow keys to navigate or scroll through information or to select some choice or option. Let them use the enter key and soft keys for executing tasks like moving in or out of a section.

Figure 4-1 illustrates how you can optimize your flow by following these suggestions. The arrow keys are used for navigation between different topics (as shown in the left screenshot) or to browse/scroll through the information (as in the right screenshot). The enter key and soft keys are always used to perform actions. The left soft key and the enter key will execute the same task. In this example, they let the user move into a section, while the right soft key will always allow the user to go back or move out of a section.

Figure 4-1.
Marktrock Mobile
keeps it simple.

Visualizing interaction

We try to let our user interact intuitively with our mobile content to improve the application's usability. This does not mean we can't influence which type of interaction seems natural though. When visualizing possible user interaction, you should know that human beings can visualize in two different ways.

As an example of the first way, you can explain which button needs to be pushed for some action to happen. Perfect examples are soft key labels and the little arrow images shown in the Marktrock Mobile screenshots in Figure 4-1. The soft key labels should perfectly explain what task will be executed when those keys are pressed. The tiny arrow images illustrate which arrow keys can be used to browse or scroll through the content.

The second type of visualization is to make clear what happened after a certain key press in order to optimize the application flow. A perfect example is highlighting a list item to show the user the item that's selected after an arrow key is pressed.

Having a smart interface design results in a better user experience. When users notice the visual guides, navigating correctly through the application is easier for them, and the process feels more natural. They feel that they are navigating intuitively, while actually you are guiding them around. Take a look at the following tips to create a smarter interface by visualizing user interaction.

Using soft key labels

Use labels, like "select" and "back," to explain the effect of pressing the left or right soft key. You should consider using the left soft key and the middle enter key for the same task, because this feels more natural and intuitive. If you choose not to, be sure to create a label for the enter key as well. Make sure to place it above the enter key just as the other labels are placed above the soft keys they refer to.

Using arrow visualization

Whenever you expect users to navigate with the arrow keys, you should include subtle arrow visualization. This will help users to understand how to browse or navigate through the content and the flow will feel more natural. Check out the Marktrock screenshot in Figure 4-1 to see an example of arrow visualization.

Highlighting items

Item selection is very important in a mobile application flow, so use highlighting to make clear what item is selected, as shown in Figure 4-2. You can change text colors or move bounding boxes to point out selected items. You can also come up with something more creative, as long as you make sure the highlighted item has a clear visual focus.

Minimizing interaction possibilities

You should always try to minimize the set of interaction possibilities. Using the arrow keys for navigation and browsing combined with two or three soft key actions is more than enough. If you are providing too many tasks or actions together, users get confused and are more likely to get stuck and stop using your application. Consider using step-by-step navigation instead. For example, imagine you're creating a mobile travel guide that allows users to book hotel rooms. When providing an availability schedule, you can let the user select a day first. After the enter or left soft key is pressed to select the day choice, you can display the available rooms. Avoid combining both day and room choices together in one part of the application. This only increases the chance of the users getting confused and no longer using the application.

Figure 4-2.
FITC Amsterdam highlights

Providing extra explanation

Providing explanations about how to use an application can make it much more user friendly. For example, if you are creating a mobile game, you can take the user through a step-by-step explanation on how to use the controls before game play begins. You can also add some extra information in the interface. A label or banner saying "Use arrow keys to navigate" or "Press any key to continue," as shown in Figure 4-3, can make your user interface much easier to understand.

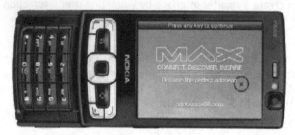

Figure 4-3. The Adobe MAX game's extra information

Minimizing text

If possible, try to avoid using a lot of text. For example, if you are explaining how users should make a cocktail, consider using self-explaining icons instead of writing everything down. A step-by-step visual example is easier to read and follow than just plain text. You can use arrow keys to provide "previous step " and "next step" features to navigate through the steps naturally.

Considering usability: four reasons user context is important

When you start designing your mobile interface, keep in mind what type of user you are targeting. You already know that designing for children requires a different approach than doing so for business people. To have a really successful interface, you should dig a little deeper though. Defining who is going to use your application is a good start, but don't forget finding out when and where they will use your application. Let's have a look at four key things you need to consider.

Light

No matter where and when people are using your application, some kind of light will be affecting the look and feel of your mobile application. That's why it is important to define a user profile and decide where and when your application will be used. Will users be inside a building with artificial lighting or standing outside in the sunlight? Or will they be in darkness that's relieved only by streetlights? Those are some important questions you need to ask yourself because indoor light, sunlight, and streetlights will all have different effects on the application's look and feel. Instead of waiting until your content is used in real life, you should simulate the environmental conditions via Adobe Device Central. Simulating different types of light (indoor and outdoor light for instance) in the emulator will give you a glance at how the content is visualized under a certain type of light.

A conference guide like FITC Toronto Mobile will be used mostly inside a conference building, and users will be surrounded by indoor light. That's why, in Figure 4-4, we chose to use more contrast in the interface combining darker background colors with brighter foreground colors. We avoided using shiny foreground colors, because that would not improve visibility when having an indoor light reflection. You should only use very bright and shiny colors if the application will be used in a relatively dark environment.

Figure 4-4.
The FITC Toronto interface is built with dark colors for use in a hotel surrounded by indoor light.

Time

Knowing how long your user is willing to use your application is important. A conference guide like FITC Toronto Mobile should provide information quickly based on an optimized and rapid navigation; it only needs three or four clicks to get to every kind of information it has to offer. When creating a mobile game, though, you might want to take some time to guide the users through the controls or game rules instead of letting them start playing immediately. Unlike mobile conference guide users, gamers are willing to spend more time with an application to find how the game should be played.

Application awareness

You should always try to define how much awareness your user would like to have produced when using your application. For a game, implementing vibrations, sounds, highlights, and so forth can add value to the game play. Be careful when implementing awareness, though, because sometimes that's exactly what your user does not want! A user attending a conference session or meeting would find it very irritating to have an application beep and vibrate every few minutes. If you do implement application awareness, a good idea is to provide different application profiles. That way, users can set the application to silent mode when they don't want to be disturbed and easily set it back to normal whenever they like.

Movement

Having an idea of any physical movements your user might make while engaged with your application is also important. The more the user is moving around while attempting to use your content, the more static (instead of heavily animated) you should keep your interface and content. Otherwise, the user will miss a lot and probably will not think your application is very user friendly. If your user is walking (or even running), for instance, you should focus even harder on the most important content, so information is available in the blink of an eye. When your user is sitting in a bus or train, a more animated interface can add value to the application, because there is enough time to appreciate it and work with it.

Optimizing for mobile devices

If you are optimizing for mobile devices, basically everything comes down to power management. This is not something a designer is going to automatically identify as an issue, so it should be your first priority to emphasize its importance to the application's success.

Developing for mobile devices requires a different approach than developing for the Web. We have a smaller screen size, limited CPU power, a small amount of available memory, and so forth. A byte here and there may make all the difference, so we need to make our mobile content as efficient and lightweight as possible. We all like to see our mobile content running smoothly and performing well instead of lagging or crashing.

In this section, we are going to talk about how to optimize your Flash Lite content to get better performance. The two most important things to keep in mind during this process are memory management and CPU performance.

Managing memory

One of the biggest challenges of being a mobile developer is keeping control of memory usage. A mobile device is a very limited environment, and in contrast to the desktop, a byte may make all the difference. Let's see how the Flash Lite player handles memory allocation and garbage collection, before we give you some important code optimization tips.

Understanding the static and dynamic memory heaps

If you want to understand how Flash Lite handles memory allocation, it is important to know the player uses two heaps to allocate memory from: a static memory heap and a dynamic one.

Flash Lite reserves a fixed amount of memory from the operating system to create a static memory heap. This memory is reserved when the player starts up, and the size is defined by the device manufacturer. The operating system can optionally provide the player with additional memory called a dynamic memory heap. When Flash Lite launches, it does not reserve any memory for the dynamic heap.

The player responds to all memory requests by trying to allocate memory from the static heap first. If the static heap does not have any memory available, the player tries to allocate from the dynamic heap (in 32KB blocks) and adds it to the static heap. If dynamic memory is not available, the player will throw an out-of-memory error (we covered these error messages in Chapter 2).

> Note that when you are building a Flash Lite 2.x or 3.x application, the player changes this allocation order for rendering objects and JPG images. The player tries to allocate from the dynamic heap first; if there is no available dynamic memory, it will then try to allocate static memory.

Understanding the garbage collector

Garbage collection is a form of automatic memory management that frees up the memory from objects that are not being used. The Flash Lite player will free unused memory by running the garbage collector process every 60 seconds, or whenever memory use increases suddenly by 20 percent or more.

The Flash Lite player frees the memory in two phases, using a garbage collection method called mark-and-sweep. In the mark phase, the garbage collector marks objects that are no longer referenced by the application. It then frees the memory in the sweep phase. Both phases execute every time the garbage collection process runs.

This process is something the programmer cannot trigger explicitly. There is no command or API to start running the garbage collector through code. This does not mean we can do nothing about collecting unused memory, however. It is a good practice to free unneeded memory through code. We can do that by deleting every existing reference to the specific object.

Memory used by timeline or global objects can be freed by using the delete statement or using removeMovieClip(). Memory used by local objects can be freed by setting the referring variable to null. In other words, freeing unneeded memory through code helps the garbage collector to figure out what objects are no longer referenced by the application. This memory will be freed during the sweep phase.

The following code example shows how to free memory from a global and local object:

```
// global var
var mcHeader= new MovieClip(); // creates a MovieClip object
trace(mcHeader); // returns MovieClip object
delete mcHeader; // deletes the object
trace(mcHeader); // returns undefined

// global variable attached to a timeline movie or MovieClip
_container.mcHeader = new MovieClip(); // Creates a MovieClip object.
trace(_global.mcHeader); // Returns the MovieClip object.
delete _global.mcHeader; // Deletes the object.
trace(_global.mcHeader); // Returns undefined.

// Local Variables:

function localVarExample()
{
var mcHeader = new MovieClip(); // Creates MovieClip object.
trace(mcHeader); // Returns MovieClip object
delete mcHeader; // No effect.
trace(mcHeader); // Returns MovieClip object
mcHeader = null; // Sets Object reference to null
trace(mcHeader); // Returns null.
}

localVarExample(); // calls localVarExample() function
```

Keep in mind that memory will not be freed if any ActionScript functions are still referring to the specific object, even when it is deleted through code. This is the case with intervals and listeners. Be sure to clear active intervals using clearInterval() and remove active listeners using removeListener() before deleting the object through code. Otherwise, the memory will not be freed.

The following code example shows how to free memory from an object that has an active listener and interval:

```
function closeScreenIntro()
{
        clearInterval(_exampleInterval); // clear active intervals
        Key.removeListener(myKeyListener); // clear active listener
        delete _screenIntro; // delete _screenIntro movieclip
}

closeScreenIntro() // Calls closeScreenIntro() function
```

Optimizing for efficient memory use

We just introduced you to the most important memory management concepts in the Flash Lite player. Now, it's time to go over a few tips to help you optimize your code and turn your application into a more memory friendly one.

Using external assets If you have a lot of data, you will need to decide the best place from which to load this content in order to keep the file size down. For instance, if you are creating an image gallery, loading thumbnails from inside the Flash library and loading the bigger images externally would be most efficient. You could save them in a local directory (and include that later while packaging), or you could save them online at an external directory. Defining a target user profile might be a good idea to help you decide what to do. If your main target group is made up of active, mobile Internet users, you can go for the online strategy. If not, it would be wiser to go for the external directory and include it while packaging your application.

Let's say you are creating a Flash Lite image gallery for a clothing store to showcase a new collection. Employees at the shop will promote the application and provide a free wireless network. This is a perfect situation for the online strategy. You still might want to store the most important set of images locally though, so users can have a look at them again when they are at home or with friends. As you can see, you are always balancing between local and external. It's up to you to try to make the right decisions.

Artwork optimization When designing mobile artwork for your application, keep the file size down as much as possible when saving. If you are using Adobe Photoshop, use the Save for Web option, and save your images as PNG or JPG files. If you use a JPG file, try to keep the quality as low as possible as long as the result is acceptable. Be sure to minimize the amount of transparency in PNG files, because the player will need to calculate redraws, even for the transparent parts of the bitmap. If you are a Windows or Linux user, using a PNG optimization tool like PNGout or PNGcrush might come in handy.

- **PNGcrush**: PNGcrush is an optimizer for PNG files. It can be run from a command line in an MS DOS window or from a UNIX or Linux command line. Its main purpose is to reduce the size of the PNG IDAT (image data) stream by trying various compression levels and PNG filter methods.

    PNGcrush is open source and may be used by anyone without a fee. You can download it from http://pmt.sourceforge.net/PNGcrush/.

- **PNGout**: You can create smaller image files, match PNG and CSS colors, and edit more types of PNG files with the PNGout plug-in, a file-format plug-in for Adobe Photoshop. PNGout matches PNG and CSS colors by removing the gamma chunk and reads and writes 8-bit indexed and alpha PNG images (i.e., 256 colors with 256 levels of transparency).

  You can download a trial or purchase the plug-in at http://www.ardfry.com/png-plugin.

Clear unused objects   As discussed before, it is very important to remove objects that are no longer needed, so you can reduce memory usage. To help the garbage collector figure out which memory can be freed, you can remove objects programmatically. Make sure to clear active listeners and intervals or else memory will not be freed, even when the object is deleted. For more details, check out the "Understanding the garbage collector" section in this chapter.

If you would like to hide an object (instead of removing it) and use it later on you can put it off stage, make sure to keep it at least 1000 pixels off the edges. Objects placed just off the stage are still added to the rendering queue, and this causes a reduction in performance. By placing the objects very far off the stage, a performance improvement is achieved, as the objects are not added to the queue.

Using a bitmap or vector   You should always try to strike a balance between bitmaps and vectors. Bitmaps usually need more memory than vector graphics, which increases the size of the exported SWF file. Your application will not be scalable any more, but you can easily create a more photorealistic result.

Vector graphics and animations are smaller but put more load on the processor. When you want to use vector shapes, optimize them as much as possible. The more dimensions a shape has, the more the Flash Lite player will have to do to render that shape. Before exporting the movie, select the shape and then choose Modify ➤ Shape ➤ Optimize from the menu tab to optimize it even more.

When possible, stick with flat edges, especially with very small vector shapes. Vector corners are simpler to render than curves.

Initializing your first frame   When developing Flash content on the desktop, preloading all your content at the beginning of your movie seems quite normal. If you use this strategy on a mobile device, chances are quite high your movie will start slowly. Define your content naturally throughout your application so MovieClips or other objects are initialized only when they are about to be used.

Fonts   Embedding fonts means your text will be vectorized when exported to the SWF file. Most of the time, vectorizing creates complicated shapes for Flash to render. Try using device fonts as much as possible to keep the file size down. As an added bonus, device fonts are displayed very clearly on the screen, so they should be easy to read.

Improving CPU performance

As a mobile developer, you are dealing with limited CPU power and battery life. Optimizing your content to improve the performance is a must. We want our users to have some battery life left after running our application! Compared to a desktop or laptop, the capabilities of a mobile device are quite limited. That's why it is very important to keep your content running smoothly and performing well. Unlike when we're developing for the desktop, we really need to focus on battery life. When creating a mobile game, for instance, our user should not run out of battery after playing it a few times.

The following tips will help you to optimize your flash content and ActionScript code in order to keep the CPU from dying of overwork.

Rendering bitmap artwork

Bitmaps are rendered much faster than vectors, so to keep the CPU usage low, you should try to use bitmaps if possible. Minimize the use of vector gradients. Calculating and rendering them is an intensive task for the player. If you must use them, note that linear gradients render faster than radial gradients, and every gradient increases the SWF file size (by about 50 bytes). Also, try to limit the amount of transparency, because the player needs to calculate redraws every frame (even for the transparent parts of the bitmap).

Be aware that the Flash Lite player does not support bitmap smoothing. This means that if you scale or rotate a bitmap, chances are it will not look good. It is best to use bitmaps at their native rotation and resolution. If you have an image that you need to scale or rotate, consider using a vector graphic instead.

Loading XML data

Loading and parsing XML is a very CPU-intensive process. If possible, try to store data in simple name/value pairs, and use Loadvars or precompiled SWF files to load the data. If you would like to use XML, make sure the file is not too big. Consider splitting up XML data into multiple XML files. For instance, when presenting a conference schedule, you could have multiple XML files: one for each day, or even one for each morning and one for each afternoon.

Using gotoAndPlay()

When using gotoAndPlay() to skip frames, remember that every frame between the current frame and the requested frame will need to be initialized before the requested frame can be played. If those frames in between contain lots of content, using gotoAndPlay() could really slow down the process. This means that using different movie clips could be more efficient than using timeline frames.

Tweening objects

Using tweens puts a lot of load on the heap. That's why using keyframe animation to move objects around could be more efficient. If the animation does not look smooth enough, you can use a tween. Because Flash draws an animated region (defines a rectangular bounding box around the area), you should try to avoid overlapping tweens. The Flash Lite player will merge the overlapping area into one large total region, and this merged region impedes performance.

Registering variables and defining functions

Local variables are registered, so getting and setting them, rather than global variables, is much faster for the player. That's why you should use local variables whenever possible. When you are defining a function, avoid using anonymous syntax:

```
// avoid anonymous syntax
myXML.onLoad = function( ) { ... };
// defined functions are more efficient:
function xmlLoadComplete( ) { ... };
myXML.onLoad = xmlLoadComplete();
```

Looping iterations

Using for loops can result in too much CPU overhead while the condition is checked in each iteration. If possible, you should unroll your loop and execute multiple operations individually. Doing so will cause your code to be longer but will result in faster performance:

```
// Simple loop
for(var i:Number=0; i<5; i++){
    myArray[i]+=5;
}
// unroll and execute multiple operations

myArray[0]+=5;
myArray[1]+=5;
myArray[2]+=5;
myArray[3]+=5;
myArray[4]+=5;
```

Using events

When using events, make sure you only listen to the ones you absolutely have to. Avoid using Object.watch and Object.unwatch. Remove event listeners from objects you want to delete using removeListener(), or else memory will not be freed, and the listener will stay active.

Optimizing calculations

Try to avoid using Math functions and floating point numbers. Doing Math calculations at runtime slows down the performance of your application. You should consider using precalculated values, stored in an array. Getting precalculated results from a data table is faster than having them calculated at runtime.

Optimizing a project before publishing it

You can do a few things to optimize your project or workflow and keep your content running smoothly. To remove all your trace statements in the SWF file automatically, go to Publish Settings, and check omit trace action.

To find out which frames or assets are consuming the most SWF bytes, you can also generate a file size report. Just go to Publish Settings, and check generate file size report.

When your SWF file is being published, Flash will generate a text report of assets contained in your final SWF file. You can use this information to get an overview of which frames and/or assets are using most of the SWF bytes. The report contains information about individual byte count for frames, symbols, embedded fonts, bitmap compression statistics, and so on.

Generating a file size report is a perfect way to find out which frames or assets can use more optimization.

Using Oxygen, the Flash Lite Developers Kit

This Flash Lite Developers Kit includes free debugging tools as well as components to be used in applications. To help you debug your Flash Lite content, you could use Oxygen's frames-per-second (FPS) meter and memory meter.

- **FPS meter**: The FPS meter shows the frame rate of the last 10 frames. This could be helpful for optimizing animations for mobile device playback.

- **Memory meter**: The memory meter shows you the percentage of memory being used from the total available memory, and this report always comes in handy.

You can download the Oxygen toolkit at the following web site:

```
http://wiki.forum.nokia.com/index.php/Oxygen_-_The_Flash_Lite_Developers_
Kit#Download
```

If you want to know more about existing Flash Lite user interface components, you should check out Chapter 6!

Testing using mobile emulators

While developing Flash Lite content, you are able to constantly test your application using emulators. In the following sections, we will discuss which tools you can use and how to take advantage of them.

A mobile emulator provides designers and developers with a desktop environment that shows how mobile content will look on different mobile devices. It lets you quickly preview and test your content with different screen resolutions, color depths, and other performance characteristics. It simplifies the mobile authoring workflow before it deploys the content on mobile devices for final testing.

Make sure to check every part or feature of your mobile content on a real device, because emulation is not always 100 percent correct. In the following sections, we are going to discuss Adobe Device Central and DeviceAnywhere.

Adobe Device Central

This Adobe Creative Suite component has all the tools you need to help you preview and test your mobile content across different media formats (including Flash Lite, bitmap, web, and video). Because Device Central is fully integrated with other CS3 and CS4 components, it accelerates your mobile authoring process, allowing you to preview mobile content from other components like Flash, Photoshop, and Illustrator.

With the built-in device library, you have access to detailed device information on a wide range of different devices, including screen size, color depth, and sound availability. Adobe Device Central not only gives you the ability to quickly preview and test your content, it also offers a great means to show your work to other people.

Let's have a look at the top features Adobe's Device Central provides to help you test your application on all kinds of different handsets. For reference, Device Central is shown in Figure 4-5.

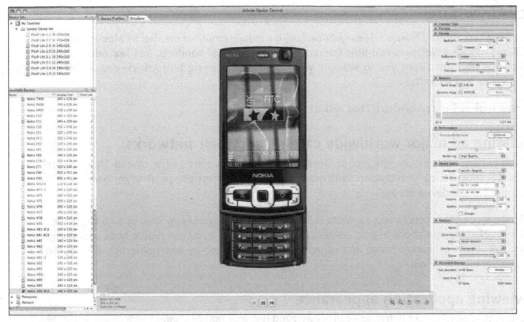

Figure 4-5. Here, we're using Adobe Device Central to preview mobile content using a mobile device skin for the Nokia N95. Some of the phone settings, like network status and backlight timeouts, were changed (see the right panel), and an indoor light is reflecting on the screen.

Using device profiles

Device Central offers detailed information on a whole rang of devices, including things like screen size, supported content types, network options, color depth, and navigation type. By specifying device parameters, you can create a list of device profiles that match your target. It is a good idea to group your profiles by carrier or screen size to have quick access to sets of your favorite or popular devices.

Previewing application appearance and performance

You can preview and test the appearance and behavior of your mobile application using the mobile device skins. Interact with the devices keys to go through your application. Just click a specific key with your mouse to find out if the content will behave like you want it to. You can play with various display conditions, such as backlight timeouts and types of light reflecting on the screen (indoor and outdoor light), to see how your mobile interface will look. You can even play with gamma and contrast settings.

Device Central allows you to estimate how much memory your content is consuming and to look at the behavior of the static and dynamic memory heaps. Changes to signal and battery levels and volume, time, and date settings are also among possibilities offered by Adobe Device Central.

DeviceAnywhere

DeviceAnywhere (http://www.deviceanywhere.com) is a mobile emulator created by Mobile Complete that allows mobile developers real-time interaction with all sorts of handsets. Just like Adobe Device Central, this emulator allows you to simulate your application pressing buttons, viewing animations, playing video, and so forth.

Let's now look at DeviceAnywhere's top features.

Emulating all major worldwide carriers and their networks

DeviceAnywhere can emulate the mobile devices of all major carriers in the United States, United Kingdom, France, Germany, and Japan. With more then 1,500 handsets online, all major handset OEMs are adopted in the device library.

By obtaining remote access to real handsets in live networks via DeviceAnywhere, you no longer need to be in-market for validations of your content and applications. So you can realize huge cost savings, get your products to market faster, and expand your market reach by addressing networks outside your geographical location.

Previewing application appearance

Just like with Adobe Device Central, you can preview and test your mobile content with device inputs like the keypad, touch screen, side keys, and more. Experience device outputs like vibrations, backlight, and sound to find out if the content reacts like you want it to. You can even preview hardware controls like switching power on/off and disconnecting the battery. If your mobile content uses a device Wi-Fi or GPS, you can also test it on your desktop, as long as your chosen device handset supports these features.

Working through best practices tutorials

We've already discussed several tips and tricks to optimize your content and ActionScript code, but in this chapter, we'd like to offer some practical tips as well. That's why the following sections will guide you through some important concepts every Flash Lite developer should keep in mind.

Using persistent data

In this example, we'll show you how to make your application store and receive data, like game scores, user preferences, and login details. Using sharedobject.fla, we will create a simple application that stores a name value to provide you with a personal welcome message the next time you open the application.

Configuring the application

In our first frame, we set _focusrect to false and enable full-screen mode. We create a string variable username where we'll store our name value:

```
_focusrect = false;// standard focus false
fscommand2("Fullscreen", "true");// enable full screen mode
var username:String; // this string will be used to load saved name
```

Checking existing data

When the application starts, we will check for existing data using the SharedObject class. A SharedObject allows users to save and retrieve local data from a device, in this case our user's name.

Flash Lite shared objects could be compared to browser cookies: just like cookies, shared objects are able to contain Booleans, strings, arrays, and integers. Shared objects are located in the system directory of a mobile phone (typically C:\System\Apps\saflash2\).

Let's start with creating a shared object:

```
// shared object check: existing data?
// We create the shared object:
var so:SharedObject = SharedObject.getLocal("so");
```

Because reading and writing shared objects is slow on mobile devices, we will add a listener to make sure the data is only available when it's ready to use. Using the getSize() command we are able to check if the shared object contains any data:

```
// add listener
SharedObject.addListener( "so", loadComplete );
function loadComplete (mySO:SharedObject) {
    if (mySO.getSize()==0 ) {
    // If the size is 0 there is no name being saved
    Selection.setFocus(txtInputName); //set focus on textfield so user can type in
                                 his name
  }else {
    // there is a name
    gotoAndPlay(2);
  }
}
```

If the shared object does not contain data, we set the focus on the input text field so the user can add a name. If the shared object already contains data, the user has already filled in a username, and we go to the next frame to show the personal welcome text message.

Once our user types a name, we need to store this value into our shared object. We create a data attribute called username to do so.

```
// catch text input and store value into shared object
txtInputName.onChanged = function() {
  username=txtInputName.text;
  so.data.username=username; // store username value into shared object
  so.flush(); // write data into shared object
  gotoAndPlay(2); // go to frame 2 and display welcome text message
}
stop(); // stop here so we do not go to frame 2
```

When we move to frame 2, we are going to retrieve the username value from the shared object in order to display our welcome text message:

```
txtName.text=so.data.username; // fill textfield with shared object username value
stop();
```

Loading interactive SWF files

In this tutorial, we'll show you how to build a Flash Lite application using multiple SWF files loaded into the main timeline. We will guide you through local and external SWF access using a few examples, and we will discuss common issues, such as cross-domain policies and interaction between SWF files.

Before we begin, you should know a few things about the Flash Lite player. Unlike Flash Lite 2.x's player, the Flash Lite 3.x player comes with the Flash 8 engine, which means the security sandbox feature is implemented as well. The problem with this security sandbox is that you can't have a local connection (loading local files) and a network connection (loading external files) at the same time. This was no problem using Flash Lite 2.x, therefore, the new security sandbox feature breaks all backward compatibility: a Flash Lite 2.0 application using both local and network access will not work on a Flash Lite 3–enabled device.

Nokia Series 60 (S60) and Series 40 (S40) devices offer a trick that can solve this problem. The folder in C:\data\others\trusted disables the security sandbox and enables applications to communicate both with local and network files. The problem this trusted folder brings is that everything in this directory is visible under Gallery, and sifting through all the files in one place is not a perfect user experience.

There's another problem with the trusted folder: on S60 devices, you can either install your application in the phone's memory or on the memory card. If you have a Flash Lite 3.0 application that should be installed in the trusted folder, you must install the application on the trusted folders of both the phone memory and the memory card, and of course, those trusted folders are located at different paths. In the phone memory, the folder is located at C:\data\others\trusted, and on the memory card, at E:\others\trusted. Because it is not possible to install Symbian applications (.sis packages) to different folders, you can't get your application Symbian signed, so you can't create a Symbian installer for Flash Lite 3 applications using both local and external files. Omitting the application icon does not create a good user experience, so if you are building an application loading only local or only external files, you can consider using Flash Lite 3.0. If you need an application that uses files in both locations, it's probably better to go with Flash Lite 2.x.

Now that you know how to choose your version on Flash Lite, let's get started with our example. First, we will guide you through a Flash Lite 2.0 sample using both local and external SWF files. After that, we'll show you how you can use either local or external SWF files in a Flash Lite 3.0 project.

Using local and external SWF files

In this example, we are creating a Flash Lite 2.0 application that uses local and external SWF files to build the interface. We are using a local header.swf and footer.swf to load into the main timeline. And then we'll show you how to create interaction between the local and the external SWF files.

It all starts with creating `main.swf`. Create a new Flash Mobile FLA file. Choose Flash Lite 2, and use the following code to set the application in full-screen mode and run in high quality and to disable the yellow focus rectangle:

```
// main movieclip config
fscommand2("fullscreen", "true");
fscommand2("setquality","high");
_focusrect = false;
```

To allow the external SWF file access to functions and variables from this timeline, we are using the allowDomain function from the System.security class:

```
// allow any external swf in this directory to access
// vars/functions/etc from the main timeline
// you can change the url to the external location
// that contains your swf file
System.security.allowDomain("http://labs.boulevart.be/ ➡
mobile/tutorials/FlashLite/loading_interactive_swf/");
```

We are going to load our three SWF files into MovieClips on the stage. We are going to load two local and one external SWF files:

```
// ---------------- //
// loading swf files //
// ---------------- //
// loading local footer swf
footer_mc.loadMovie("footer.swf");
footer_mc._x=0;
footer_mc._y=290;
// loading local header swf
header_mc.loadMovie("header.swf");
header_mc._x=0;
header_mc._y=0;
// loading external swf file
content_mc.loadMovie("http://labs.boulevart.be/ ➡
mobile/tutorials/FlashLite/loading_interactive_swf/
content.swf");
content_mc._x=0;
content_mc._y=75;
```

After that, we define the main functions that are going to be called from the loaded SWF files:

```
// --------- //
// functions //
// -------- //

// main functions to be called from loaded swf files
quitApp = function(){
 trace("quitApp called");
 fscommand2("Quit")
}
```

This is actually all we need to do in our main.swf file. We are loading other SWF files to build the interface, and we used the System.security class to allow interaction between our local main.swf and the external content.swf file. We defined a function to be called from inside our loaded SWF files. Let's take care of those local files.

The first local SWF file we need to create is footer.swf. We start by using the System.security class to allow interaction with the parent (main.swf):

```
// ---------------- security ------------------//
System.security.allowDomain(_parent._url)
// root init
var myFooterRoot:MovieClip = this;
```

Next, we define a key listener to have our footer.swf file react on key press events:

```
// footer key listener
var myListener:Object = new Object();
myListener.onKeyDown = function() {
    if (Key.getCode() == Key.RIGHT) {
                trace("You pressed the right arrow key")
                myFooterRoot._parent.header_mc.setText("right key was pressed");

    } else if (Key.getCode() == Key.LEFT) {
                trace("You pressed the left arrow key");
                // switch banner text
                myRoot._parent.header_mc.setText("left key was pressed");
    } else if(Key.getCode() == Key.DOWN) {
                trace("You pressed the down arrow key");
                // scroll down
    } else if (Key.getCode() == Key.UP) {
                trace("You pressed the up arrow key");
                // scroll up
    } else if(Key.getCode()==ExtendedKey.SOFT2){
                // quit
                myFooterRoot._parent.quitApp();
    }
}
Key.addListener(myListener);
```

Let's dive a little deeper into this code. When the right soft key is pressed, we talk to our main.swf to run the previously defined quitApp() function:

```
else if (Key.getCode()==ExtendedKey.SOFT2){
 // quit
 myFooterRoot._parent.quitApp();
}
```

When the right arrow key is pressed, we are going to talk directly to the other local loaded SWF file, header.swf. We are calling the setText() function being defined in our header.swf.

```
if (Key.getCode() == Key.RIGHT) {
 trace("You pressed the right arrow key");
 myFooterRoot._parent.header_mc.setText("right key was pressed");

}
```

Now, let's look at our header.swf. The System.security class is used again in order to allow inter-action. We also define a setText() function that is going to be called directly from inside the footer.swf file.

```
// --------------- security -----------------//
System.security.allowDomain(_parent._url)
// root init
var myHeaderRoot:MovieClip = this;
setText = function(s:String){
 txtURL.text=s;
}
```

Now, you know how to create a Flash Lite 2.0 application using different interactive local SWF files talking to the main.swf or directly to each other. But as you already noticed, main.swf is also loading an external SWF file called content.swf. Let's find out how we can interact with that.

In our main.swf, we used the System.security class to allow interaction between the external SWF file and main.swf. Then we are loading the SWF file into the main timeline using loadMovie.

```
// loading external swf file
content_mc.loadMovie("http://labs.boulevart.be/mobile/ ➥
tutorials/FlashLite/loading_interactive_swf/content.swf");
content_mc._x=0;
content_mc._y=75;
```

Although it is not necessary for this example, generally, having a cross-domain policy on the root directory of your server is a good idea. This is an XML file named as crossdomain.xml containing the following code:

```
<!-THIS FILE ALLOWS FLASH TO COMMUNICATE WITH FILES ON YOUR SERVER ->
<!- http://www.adobe.com/cfusion/knowledgebase/index.cfm?id=tn_14213 ->
<cross-domain-policy>
<allow-access-from domain="*"/>
</cross-domain-policy>
```

When your application is trying to access external data from an XML file or other data source, the Flash Lite player will not load any data unless you have this cross-domain policy implemented in your crossdomain.xml. Again, we are not using external data in this tutorial, but always having this up and running is a good practice.

In our external content.swf file, we use the System.security class to allow interaction. We define a setIMG() function to be called from within the local footer.swf to jump to the right keyframe after pressing the right or left arrow key. Each keyframe showcases a different image.

```
// ---------------- security ------------------//
System.security.allowDomain(_parent._url)
// root init
var myContentRoot:MovieClip = this;
setIMG = function(n:Number){
  trace("set IMG");
  myContentRoot.gotoAndStop(n);
}
stop();
```

That's it! You've now created a Flash Lite 2.0 application using the interactions between both local and external SWF files to build a rich interface.

Next, let's take a look at Flash Lite 3.0, which as we told you before, means dealing with the security sandbox issue. If you need an application using both local and external files, using Flash Lite 2 is better. On the other hand, if you are creating an application using only local or external files, new Flash Lite 3 features could come in handy. A perfect example could be streaming video, and that's exactly the topic of our next example.

Loading external files to stream video in Flash Lite 3

We start by creating a new Flash Mobile movie using Flash Lite 3.0. After your file is created, go to Publish Settings and set the local playback security to Network access only. This makes sense because we are only going to load external files.

First, you should make sure your server has a cross-domain policy. Like we said before, it is a good idea to have a cross-domain policy located on the root directory of your server. Again, this is an XML file containing the following code, named as crossdomain.xml:

```
<!-THIS FILE ALLOWS FLASH TO COMMUNICATE WITH FILES ON YOUR SERVER ->
<!- http://www.adobe.com/cfusion/knowledgebase/index.cfm?id=tn_14213 ->
<cross-domain-policy>
<allow-access-from domain="*"/>
</cross-domain-policy>
```

We start by configuring our application just like we did before:

```
// main movieclip config
fscommand2("fullscreen", "true");
fscommand2("setquality","high");
_focusrect = false;
// root init
var myRoot:MovieClip = this;
```

Just to make sure our SWF file will stream the video, we use the System.security class to allow its domain:

```
// allow any external swf in this directory to access
// vars/functions/etc from the main timeline
// you can change the url to the external location
// that contains your swf file
System.security.allowDomain("http://labs.boulevart.be/mobile/ ➡
tutorials/FlashLite/loading_interactive_swf/");
```

Our next step is to define our soft key labels and create a key listener. We will use both soft keys to play a little video and to shut down the application using the playVideo() and quitApp() functions:

```
// softkeylabels
txtLeft.text="Watch ad";
txtRight.text="Exit";
// footer key listener
var myListener:Object = new Object();
myListener.onKeyDown = function() {
    if (Key.getCode()==ExtendedKey.SOFT1) {
        // play
        playVideo();
    } else if(Key.getCode()==ExtendedKey.SOFT2) {
        // quit
        trace("you pressed quit");
        quitApp();
    }
}
Key.addListener(myListener);
```

In the playVideo() function, we will stream an external FLV file, in this case, a little ad made by Boulevart to hire talented .NET developers. We start by creating a NetConnection and a NetStream. We attach the NetStream object to our video object on the stage. After configuring a buffer time, we can use the play() function to play the external SWF file:

```
// --------- //
// functions //
// -------- //
// playVideo() //
// ********** //
playVideo = function(){
if(!ncVideo){
    ncVideo  = new NetConnection();
    ncVideo.connect(null);
}
if(!ns){
    ns = new NetStream(ncVideo);
}
```

```
    ns.setBufferTime(2);
    ns.play("http://labs.boulevart.be/mobile/tutorials/ ➥
    FlashLite/loading_interactive_swf/boulevart.flv");

    videoHolder._visible = true;
    videoHolder.attachVideo(ns);
    }
```

And finally, we create our quitApp() function:

```
// quitApp () //
// ********** //
quitApp = function(){
 trace("quitApp called");
 fscommand2("Quit")
}
```

You've now finished creating a Flash Lite 3 application streaming external data. Remember to change your publish settings according to the type of file you will be loading (local or external). Always consider using Flash Lite 2 if you are creating an application loading both local and external assets.

Summary

We hope this chapter helps you to push the boundaries of a mobile device and inspires and guides you to create stunning, rich mobile applications.

In the beginning, we discussed the importance of a good interface. You can write the best code ever, but if the interface is not good enough, users are likely to shut down your application and never open it again. Using our guidelines, you are now capable of pushing your interface to another level. Visualize interaction, define a detailed user profile, and keep the user context firmly in your mind when you are designing and working out your application flow.

When all of the creative part is finished, you can start using the CPU optimization tips we provided in order to get your application performing much better and improve the rich mobile experience even more. Making the right decisions takes a little bit of practice when it comes to balancing two options (bitmap or vector graphics for instance), but you should be on the right path now!

Last but not least, make sure to always test, test, and test your content. Using emulators like Adobe Device Central or DeviceAnywhere can help you quickly simulate your content on the desktop. Always do final testing on real devices though, because the simulation does not always correspond with the real performance of your application. That's it for this exciting chapter! In the next chapter, we are going to talk about mobile and device widget development using Flash.

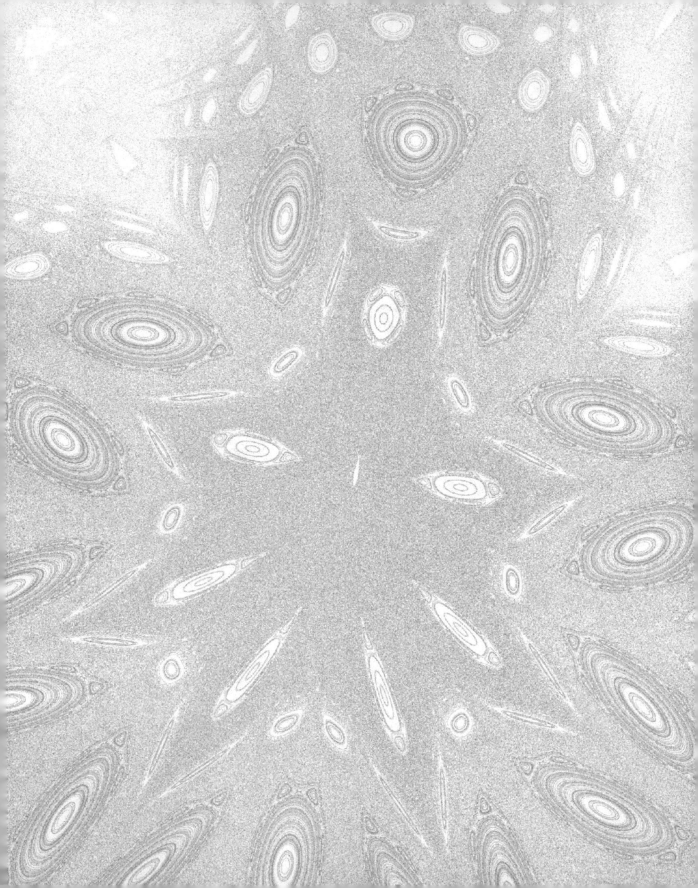

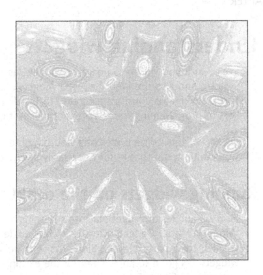

Chapter 5

MOBILE AND DEVICE WIDGET PLATFORMS WITH FLASH

In the previous chapter, we covered some practical and useful tips and tricks you can apply to your mobile application development processes with Flash Lite. We hope you keep these fresh in your mind as we head into this chapter, as well as the chapters to come. Knowing about device limitations, how they affect Flash Lite, and what kinds of workarounds, tips, and tricks are available will help to save tons of time during development and testing!

In this chapter, we'll be shifting gears a bit—we will be entering the exciting world of mobile widgets. We cover two active mobile and device widget platforms that utilize Flash Lite: Nokia Web Runtime for supported S60 handsets, and the Chumby device. OK, the Chumby *isn't* a portable device straight out of the box—but we'll cover why we think it has potential as a mobile widget development platform in the future, according to some announcements about the direction the Chumby platform is taking!

Before we dive into each of these, we'll talk about widgets in general and discuss how they fit into the context of both mobile and desktop computing environments.

Understanding widgets

We're sure you will have heard of widgets, as they have become common across desktop operating systems and also the Web (i.e., web widgets). Just in case you haven't heard, we'll explain. In its basic form, a widget is a just a small, easy-to-install, reusable, single-purpose application that utilizes some sort of programming framework that makes it quick and easy for developers to create.

Often, widgets utilize underlying web-based technology such as HTML, CSS, and JavaScript for application content, but that is not necessarily always the case.

Running widgets on the desktop

Some examples of widget platforms running on the desktop include Apple's Dashboard and Microsoft Windows Vista's Gadgets. On the Web, Google and Yahoo have widget platforms, as do many other smaller, third-party players. Since the idea behind mobile widgets sprung from the idea of desktop widgets, it's good to know some of the existing platforms that are out there, so we've provided some examples in Figure 5-1.

Figure 5-1. Some of the popular desktop widgets: Apple Dashboard, Yahoo Widgets, Google Gadgets, and Microsoft Vista Gadgets

> In Chapters 9 and 10, we'll be taking a look at Adobe Integrated Runtime (AIR) as it applies to mobile and other consumer electronic devices (e.g., MID and TV set-top boxes).
>
> In many respects, using AIR technology is similar to creating widgets using Flash Lite (you're creating small reusable applications). However, with AIR, you have a lot more platform integration, in addition to other differences (e.g., you can use existing HTML, CSS, and JavaScript; Flash; or Flex to develop AIR applications).
>
> As mobile devices, such as smart phones, become more powerful, it will be possible to target both mobile and desktop with AIR technology. We'll talk more about that in Chapters 9 and 10.

Running widgets on mobile and devices

The term "widgets" is a web industry term; it's also a legacy one, stemming from user interface widgets (or at least that's where I came across the term first, long ago). Most modern widget platforms have the same goal: to make it as easy and quick as possible for developers to create small, web-technology–based applications, whether on a desktop PC or a mobile device.

There are many neat native *mobile* widget platforms out there today, too (WidSets, Yahoo, Plusmo, Opera, etc.), but for this chapter, we're going to stick with those that support Flash. In fact, we're going to concentrate most of our efforts on Flash Lite, since this is used most often on the target device platforms we cover in this chapter.

Figure 5-2 is a Nokia N96 device, which supports S60 Flash Lite–based WRT widgets. In Figure 5-3 is the Chumby device, which runs Flash Lite 3–based widgets. We'll cover developing for both of these Flash-based widget platforms in the pages to follow.

Developing widgets with Nokia Web Runtime

Nokia ships hundreds of millions of handsets worldwide, and those devices are being constantly connected to the Internet around the world. It shouldn't be much of a surprise that Nokia has created a mobile widget development platform. In fact, it's called Nokia Web Runtime (WRT), and you can use it to create mobile widgets.

Figure 5-2. A Nokia N96 running a WRT widget that is Flash Lite content

> Those working on the Nokia S60 platform often refer to Nokia WRT widgets as "WRT widgets" or "S60 widgets."

The Nokia WRT allows developers to create front ends for Web 2.0 services. With this technology, it is possible to create desktop-like web experiences and bring them to S60 home/idle screens (see Figure 5-4), as well as allowing for widget applications on Nokia S60 devices.

Figure 5-3. The Chumby desktop Internet appliance supports Flash Lite widgets

Figure 5-4.
One of the most anticipated features of the forthcoming Nokia N97 is its support for widgets on the home screen.

If you have existing web development and design skills, with Nokia WRT, you can make a mobile web experience in just hours or days, rather than weeks, because you're already familiar with the core web-based technologies involved (i.e., HTML, CSS, and JavaScript).

WRT adds a web application runtime environment to the default Nokia web browser found on S60 devices. Developing applications by hooking into web data services, creating mash-ups, or tapping into low-level device APIs is possible with Nokia WRT.

> *With S60 fifth edition's Platform Services (see Chapter 7), you can extend the capabilities of widgets. It is possible to add more personal and context-aware widgets using standard HTML, JavaScript, and Flash Lite.*
>
> *Using Platform Services, developers can gain access to low-level device information, such as accessing locally stored information like calendar and phone book data. By combining the power of Platform Services and Nokia WRT, you can combine information from the Internet and local sources of data, such as GPS coordinates, to provide a much more personalized mobile user experience.*
>
> *Again, we'll talk much more about Nokia Platform Services in Chapter 7.*

It is also possible to port existing mobile and desktop widgets to WRT with some tweaking.

> *Nokia has an article entitled "Porting Apple Dashboard Widgets to S60" available on the Forum Nokia web site, which covers how to port widgets from Apple Dashboard to Nokia WRT. Search* http://www.forum.nokia.com *for the article, or check out* http://advancED.flashmobilebook.com/links.html#WRT *(the original link from Nokia is extremely long to provide here).*

Let's move on to the essentials of widget development with Nokia's WRT!

Learning the basics of WRT

WRT is an extension to the mobile web browser on the S60's third-edition software platform, and it allows instances of the browser to be run as if they are applications. Nokia S60 WRT is available on devices running S60 version 3.2 Feature Pack 2 (FP2) or later (e.g., S60 fifth-edition devices like the Nokia N97, which is shown in Figure 5-5). This brings the total worldwide number of Nokia devices that can run WRT widgets well into hundreds of millions. Like all widgets, WRT widgets are easy to create using web-based technology: HTML, CSS, and JavaScript (and Flash, which we'll cover in a bit!).

Nokia S60 WRT widgets are portable, lightweight applications with the following specific advantages:

- **Extend widgets through Nokia Platform Services**: The Nokia S60 fifth-edition platform further enhances widget development with JavaScript extensions to tap into S60 Platform Services (which, again, we talk about more in Chapter 7).

  Using Platform Services, developers can access user information from the application such as calendars, contacts, logs, messages (SMS/MMS), device location and landmarks, system information, and sensors' data. It's very powerful technology that is comparable to, if not better than, what is available on other mobile device platforms.

- **Easy installation**: Nokia S60 widgets are installed and accessed by users the same as other native S60 applications that are built using Java, Symbian, and even Flash Lite. An S60 mobile device user can easily add a widget to the device's idle screen (the default splash screen) or default Applications or Installation programs folder (see Figure 5-6).

- **Security**: Another benefit of WRT widgets from Nokia is that, unlike native applications written in Symbian C++ and the like, widgets do not need to be signed, since they run in the context of the web browser (which is already sandboxed and provides a default level of security). S60 WRT widgets don't have additional security risks, any more than browsers executing JavaScript technology. A sandboxed security model is applied to WRT widgets as they run inside the Nokia browser. With S60 fifth-edition devices, WRT widgets benefit further from the ability to connect to core applications and capabilities of the S60 platform, such as the phone book, calendar, GPS information, and the like.

Figure 5-5. The home screen on the Nokia N97, enabled with widgets

Figure 5-6. Nokia S60 Applications (or sometimes Installations) folder is where WRT widgets are installed and launched.

Preparing to develop a widget for an S60 device

Before you get started with developing WRT widgets, you'll need to acquire the latest S60 platform SDKs for the Symbian operating system and C++. The SDK contains the emulator, which will aid you in testing later on. To download it, you'll need to go to Forum Nokia at the URL that follows. Be aware that this SDK is available only for Microsoft Windows at the moment:

1. Access the SDK by going to Forum Nokia:

   http://www.forum.nokia.com/

2. Then, find the SDK page by tacking on the URL:

   /main/resources/tools_and_sdks/listings/symbian_cpp_tools.html

   > *You must be a registered developer for Forum Nokia to access the SDK link. Register at http://www.forum.nokia.com if you have not yet done so. Registration for new users is completely free.*

3. On the Forum Nokia download page, you'll want to find and click the S60 Platform SDKs for Symbian OS link. This should bring you to a page where you can download the SDK. Whether you need the third-edition FP2 or fifth-edition SDK, or an even newer one, will depend on your target device. The easiest way to figure out what you need is to use Device Central to see what

the device runs. Simply open Device Central CS4, select a target Nokia device from the Device Central library, and go to the GENERAL tab under the CORE entry, where you'll see an entry for Platform (see Figure 5-7).

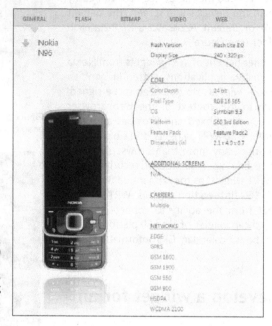

Figure 5-7.
Nokia N96 is an S60 third-edition (FP2) device that runs Symbian operating system 9.3.

Once the correct SDK is downloaded, you'll need to unzip the download and run the included setup.exe file. Depending on whether you have Perl and Java installed, you will be asked to install the latest versions. Both ActivePerl (http://www.activeperl.com/) and the Java Runtime Environment, or JRE, (http://www.sun.com/java/) are free.

> *You do not need to install the ARM tool chain when asked with the SDK; this item is optional. Also, you can safely ignore the warning about the SDK being able to install a default device.*

Once the SDK is installed, you now have access to the S60 SDK emulator, which will allow you to test your widget without running it on a device. We'll cover this in a bit. You can access the Nokia device emulator by going to S60 Developer Tools ➤ SDK ➤ C++ ➤ Emulator (see Figure 5-8).

Exploring the widget files

A Flash Lite WRT widget consists of an icon; an info.plist text file (a configuration file); and CSS, HTML, and SWF files (see Figure 5-8). These are all archived in a WGZ file, which is essentially a renamed ZIP archive containing all the widget assets (see Figure 5-9).

Name	Date modified	Type	Size
icon.png	12/5/2007 12:11 PM	PNG File	4 KB
info.plist	12/5/2007 4:02 PM	QuickTime Prefer...	1 KB
main.css	12/5/2007 4:02 PM	CSS Document	1 KB
main.html	1/9/2009 8:14 PM	HTML Document	2 KB
main.swf	10/25/2007 9:03 PM	SWF File	15 KB

Figure 5-8.
Files needed for a rudimentary Flash Lite widget

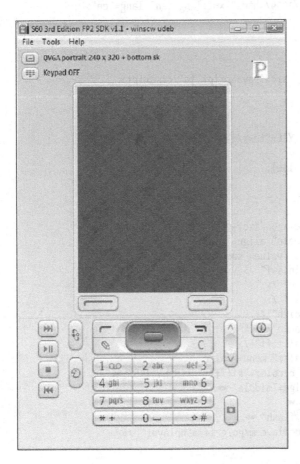

Figure 5-9.
The Nokia S60 Platform SDK gives you a device emulator so that you can test emulated widget content.

The beauty of S60 widgets for the Nokia WRT is that there are not a lot of steps to get an application up and running, and you need only a few files for a rudimentary Flash Lite widget. You basically need a blend of four web technologies to create Flash Lite widgets for Nokia WRT. The anatomy of a typical widget is HTML, CSS, JavaScript, and Flash files. Let's explore each of these.

HTML   Since we're dealing with web widgets, we need—you guessed it—HTML source code. Our HTML markup acts not so much as the presentation layer for the widget's contents but more as a container for our Flash Lite SWF content. Version 4.01 is the recommended specification for widget creation at the time of this writing.

As the following code shows, we also import some CSS and JavaScript files in the HTML header, which we'll talk about shortly. We then make use of an object tag to target a Flash Lite SWF file that contains all our viewable Flash content for the widget.

```
<!DOCTYPE html PUBLIC "-//W3C//DTD XHTML 1.0 Transitional//EN"
"http://www.w3.org/TR/xhtml1/DTD/xhtml1-transitional.dtd">
<html xmlns="http://www.w3.org/1999/xhtml" xml:lang="en" lang="en">
<head>
 <style type="text/css">
  @import url("main.css");
 </style>
 <script type='text/JavaScript' src='JavaScript.js'></script>
</head>
<body>

<script language="javascript" TYPE="text/javascript">
<!--
 widget.setNavigationEnabled(false);
//-->
</script>

<object classid="clsid:d27cdb6e-ae6d-11cf-96b8-444553540000"
 width="238" height="318" id="main" align="middle">
 <param name="allowScriptAccess" value="sameDomain" />
 <param name="movie" value="main.swf" />
 <param name="loop" value="false" />
 <param name="menu" value="false" />
 <param name="quality" value="high" />
 <param name="wmode" value="opaque" />
 <param name="bgcolor" value="#ffffff" />
 <embed src="main.swf" loop="false" menu="false"
 quality="high" wmode="opaque" bgcolor="#ffffff" width="238" ➡
 height="318" name="Finish" align="middle" ➡
allowScriptAccess="sameDomain" ➡
 type="application/x-shockwave-flash" ➡
 pluginspage="http://www.macromedia.com/go/getflashplayer" />
</object>
</body>
</html>
```

CSS The file contains information for controlling the design and layout of a widget's contents and defines how to display HTML information: position, color, background color, and so on. The CSS code can be embedded in the HTML file or stored as an external cascading style sheet.

Within the CSS, the Class selector used to define common style for widget's elements; ID is used to define style for a particular widget's element; and pseudo-class is used to define style for pattern elements.

JavaScript   For non-Flash widgets, JavaScript acts as the logic layer. However, for Flash Lite widgets, all the application logic and functionality is handled by the ActionScript code contained inside the widget SWF.

There are instances where you want the SWF to communicate with the HTML wrapper. There is no simple bidirectional communication mechanism. To facilitate communication between Flash Lite and HTML, you must resort to using the object tag to pass messages into the widget and getURL() to pass messages out of the SWF back to the HTML widget container.

Exploring the info.plist configuration file

We've taken a look at all the previous files that contain some kind of code, but there is also a configuration file that goes along with each Nokia S60 WRT Flash Lite widget.

This file is required to be named info.plist and is contained in the WGZ archive that gets extracted by the device. The file is actually just a text-based XML configuration file, as shown in the following source code:

```xml
<?xml version="1.0" encoding="UTF-8"?>
<plist version="1.0">
 <dict>
  <key>DisplayName</key>
  <string>WidgetName</string>
  <key>Identifier</key>
  <!-- unique string to identity this widget -->
  <string>com.nokia.forum.widget.test</string>
  <key>MainHTML</key>
  <!-- the HTML document which is loaded when icon is selected -->
  <string>main.html</string>
  <key>AllowNetworkAccess</key>
  <!-- allows access to network services from the widget -->
  <true/>
 </dict>
</plist>
```

> *You may have noticed that the XML format in Nokia WRT widgets is a bit funky. The <key> node line is followed by a separate second line that actually defines the value for the key. We are not entirely sure why Nokia decided to implement this strange, inefficient XML markup, but this is what currently works!*

In the preceding code, you'll notice the root node has to be named <plist> and is a required root node. Below this node is a <dict> tag that contains all the configuration details of the Nokia WRT widget. Each <dict> node has some required parameters that need to be defined:

- displayName: The <key> node is used in the display title of the widget and should be something that makes sense to those that will actually run your widget after it is deployed. The value of string gets displayed in the S60 installation menu.

- Identifier: This value is a unique string that acts as an identifier that distinguishes the widget from others installed on a device. It is recommended that this string value use a reversed-domain naming structure to make it as uniquely identifiable as possible (e.g., com.flashmobilebook.widgets.mySampleWidget).

- AllowNetworkAccess: This node parameter allows or denies the widget access to one or more available networks. The valid values for this are true and false.

- MainHTML: This node defines the string value of the file to load first when the widget icon is selected by a user. This value can be almost any file name. With Flash Lite widgets, it will be either an HTML page or a SWF file.

As you might expect, launching an HTML page containing an embedded object pointing to a SWF, rather than just loading the SWF directly, has both advantages and disadvantages. Table 5-1 outlines some considerations on which road to take when launching a Flash-based Nokia widget.

Table 5-1. Pros and cons of launching Flash Lite-based WRT widgets

Launch Method	Pros	Cons
HTML embedded	Ability to add assets around SWF	Content appears in browser context
Direct SWF launch	Widget content appears as stand-alone SWF	Leaves empty (white) blank screen after exit User prompted to save Flash Lite SWF on exit

A <meta> refresh launch is a third way to launch a Flash Lite widget. This involves creating a simple HTML refresh tag contained in the main HTML page. Once launched, the original window will still be open, but it can be customized with custom graphics, instructions, or even a "thank you for using" message: <meta http-equiv="refresh" content="1;url=splash.swf">.

Building a Flash Lite–based WRT widget using Aptana Studio

Although it's completely possible to create a WRT widget using HTML, CSS, and JavaScript alone, the resulting mobile user experience is, frankly, not as exciting or robust as when Flash is leveraged. With Flash Lite, widgets can have animation, video, and other media capabilities found in the Flash Lite player (see Figure 5-10).

When developing widgets (like the one shown in Figure 5-11), the Flash Lite version that can be leveraged will depend on what is installed on the target handsets.

Since S60 third-edition FP2 and fifth-edition devices support the Nokia WRT, it's best to target your Flash Lite widgets for versions for 2.x and 3.x (support for Flash Lite 1.1 handsets is not a concern with WRT, as Nokia is pushing out more smart phones with Flash Lite 2.x and 3.x devices into the global marketplace).

Figure 5-10. A vector-based animation using Flash Lite called "Evil Panda" by Hooken Mobile Inc.

Figure 5-11. Flash Lite Countdown Clock Widget we will create later in this chapter.

In the following sections, we will create, step by step, an example widget using Flash Lite. By leveraging Flash Lite with Nokia WRT widgets, more compelling and attractive mobile experiences can be created. Let's take a look how to go about integrating Flash into Nokia WRT.

You've already read about many of the aspects of Nokia WRT widgets. Now, it's high time we built a widget. There are many editors out there, but one of the noteworthy widget IDEs coming to market at the time of this writing is Aptana Studio.

> Nokia and Adobe also have released a WRT plug-in for Dreamweaver CS4. Please refer to: http://
> www.adobe.com/devnet/dreamweaver/articles/getting_started_nokia_wrt.html if you are
> interested in working with Dreamweaver CS4.

In this section, you'll use a combination of the Flash IDE and Aptana Studio to build, test, and deploy a Nokia WRT Flash Lite widget. The widget is a countdown clock for a Flash conference (specifically, the Boston-based Flash on Tap event).

Since you're already very much acquainted with the Flash IDE, let's jump right in and talk about how the Aptana Studio IDE can be used to create Nokia WRT widgets.

Aptana likes to call its IDE the "premier IDE for Web 2.0." That's a bold statement, yet in some respects, we believe it to be true. Aptana Studio is a cross-platform, stand-alone, Eclipse-based plug-in IDE environment for developing web-based widgets on a number of platforms.

Currently, it supports developing content for the Web as well as mobile deployments, as well as RadRails, PyDev, PHP, iPhone, Adobe AIR, and more. At the time of this writing, Aptana has just launched a version 1.0 of a plug-in for developing Nokia WRT widgets as well. We will take advantage of this IDE.

Downloading, installing, and configuring Aptana Studio

Before any coding can begin, Aptana Studio must be downloaded, installed, and configured to develop and deploy Nokia WRT widgets.

Luckily, it's very quick to get up and running with Aptana. The first step is to download Aptana Studio. There are two choices here: a stand-alone Aptana IDE (see Figure 5-12) or the provided Eclipse plug-in.

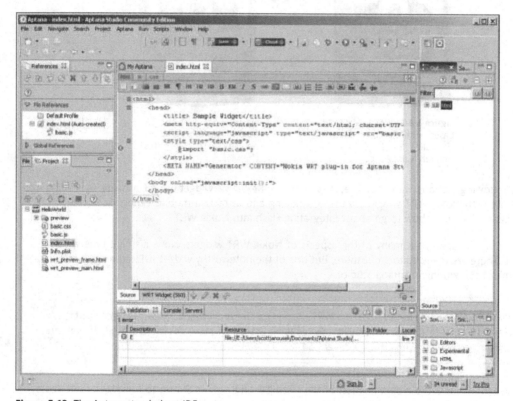

Figure 5-12. The Aptana stand-alone IDE

Both the stand-alone Aptana Studio IDE and Eclipse plug-in are cross platform: they run on Mac, Windows, and even Linux OS environments.

For the example in this section, we will be using native Aptana Studio IDE, as it provides an easy-to-use development environment for Nokia WRT widgets.

Aptana Studio can be downloaded at http://www.aptana.com/studio/download. At the time of this writing, the most current version is 1.2.1. For the purposes of this walkthrough, the stand-alone Windows version of Aptana Studio 1.2.1 will be used (see Figure 5-13).

Figure 5-13. Aptana Studio splash page

Downloading and installing the Nokia WRT plug-in

Once Aptana Studio is downloaded, the Nokia WRT plug-in needs to be downloaded and installed. To do so, click the Plug-ins menu found circled on the splash page (see Figure 5-13). A step-by-step install wizard is provided inside of Aptana to guide the installation process (see Figures 5-14, 5-15 and 5-16).

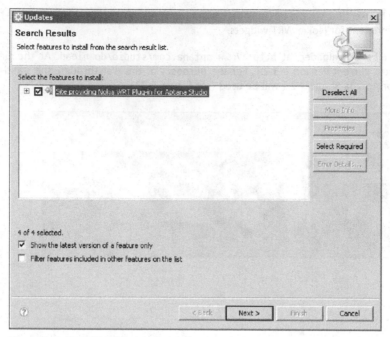

Figure 5-14. Nokia WRT plug-in for Aptana Studio

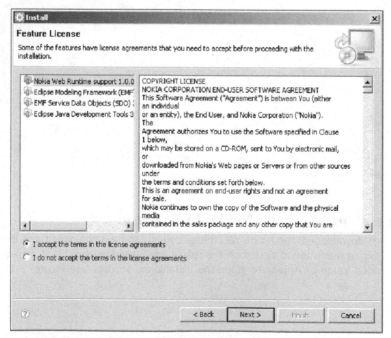

Figure 5-15. Accept the license for the Nokia WRT plug-in.

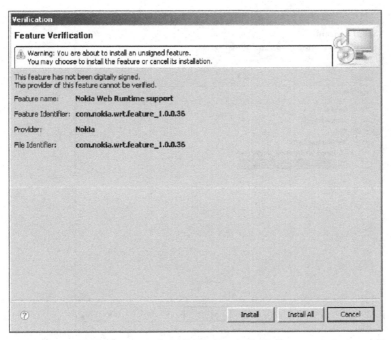

Figure 5-16. Nokia WRT support is added to Aptana Studio.

Once Aptana Studio has been installed and the Nokia WRT plug-in has been downloaded and installed, development can begin.

> Nokia has recently published a comprehensive document for getting started with Aptana Studio. It can be downloaded from the Forum Nokia site at http://www.forum.nokia.com/. Search for "Nokia WRT Plug-in for Aptana Studio Quick Start Guide."

Developing a Nokia WRT widget

To get started developing the Nokia WRT widget, follow the steps in Aptana Studio, once opened.

1. Select File ➤ New ➤ Project. In the New Project wizard (see Figure 5-17), select New Web Runtime Widget (S60). Click Next.

   If the New Web Runtime Widget (S60) selection does not appear, restart Aptana, and verify that your installation was successful.

2. In the New Nokia Widget Project wizard, select Basic Widget Project from the template selections available (see Figure 5-18). Click Next.

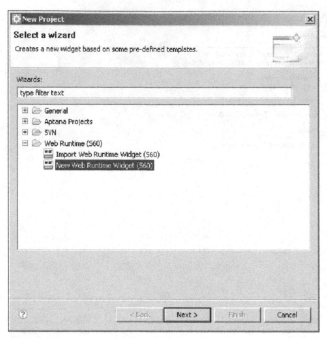

Figure 5-17. After installing the Aptana Nokia WRT plug-in, the New Web Runtime Widget (S60) selection appears.

Figure 5-18. Select Basic Widget Project in the Aptana Nokia widget project wizard.

3. In the Project Name field, enter in FOEWidget. Select a location to store the project, or use the default (see Figure 5-19). Click Next.

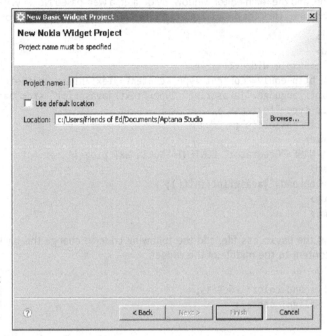

Figure 5-19.
Enter a valid project name (required) and a new project location (optional).

4. In the last dialog, change the Widget name property to FOEWidget and the Widget identifier to com.friendsofED.example.FOEWidget (see Figure 5-20). Click Finish.

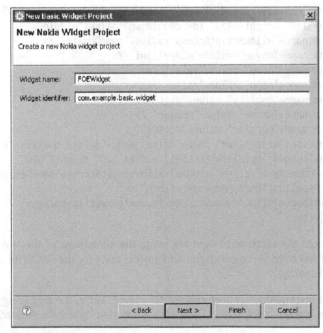

Figure 5-20.
Set the Widget name and Identifier properties.

5. Once the wizard process has been completed, it's time to begin the coding for the widget. The Aptana Studio IDE is divided into several panels, including: File References, Project, Problems, Outline, and the main editor window. By default, a web-based Nokia WRT widget is created. In the Project panel, click the index.html file to reveal the basic HTML skeleton code for a WRT widget:

```html
<html>
<head>
<title>Sample Widget</title>
<meta http-equiv="Content-Type" content="text/html; charset=UTF-8" />
<script language="javascript" type="text/javascript" src="basic.js"></script>
<style type="text/css">
@import "basic.css";
</style>
<META NAME="Generator" CONTENT="Nokia WRT plug-in for Aptana Studio 1.0.0.36" />
</head>
<body onLoad="javascript:init();">
</body>
</html>
```

6. Within the basic.css file, add the following code to change the background color and align the content to the middle of the widget:

```css
body {
 background-color: #6c5635;
 text-align: center;
}
```

7. Now that the HTML shell has been created for the widget, the SWF needs to be inserted. This is done by embedding the SWF in object and embed tags which the S60 browser will execute when the WRT widget is run off a device.

```html
<object classid="clsid:d27cdb6e-ae6d-11cf-96b8-444553540000"
width="240" height="320" id="countdown" align="middle">
<param name="allowScriptAccess" value="sameDomain" />
<param name="movie" value="widget.swf" />
<param name="loop" value="false" />
<param name="menu" value="false" />
<param name="quality" value="high" />
<param name="wmode" value="opaque" />
<param name="bgcolor" value="#6c5635" />
<embed src="widget.swf" loop="false" menu="false" quality="high"
wmode="opaque" bgcolor="#6c5635" width="240" height="320"
name="countdown" align="middle" allowScriptAccess="sameDomain"
type="application/x-shockwave-flash"
pluginspage="http://www.macromedia.com/go/getflashplayer" />
</object>
```

You should note the width and height are set to the dimensions of the Nokia N95 and that a background color has been set to match the background color for the Flash Lite countdown SWF that will be generated shortly.

Now that the placeholder has been created for widget.swf in the preceding code, it's time to create the actual countdown clock SWF in Flash. Let's get started coding the ActionScript for it!

Designing the Nokia WRT widget's Flash Lite content

Now that the HTML-based container has been created, the countdown.swf file needs to be generated. For this example, you can use any environment you wish to generate the SWF (FAME or Flash IDE).

1. Open the Flash IDE (CS3 or CS4 can be used) by selecting Programs ➤ Adobe Master Collection CS3 (or CS4) ➤ Adobe Flash CS3 (or CS4).

2. On the Start page (see Figure 5-21), select Flash File (Mobile), and Adobe Device Central will be launched. Alternatively, just go to File ➤ New ➤ General ➤ Flash File (Mobile).

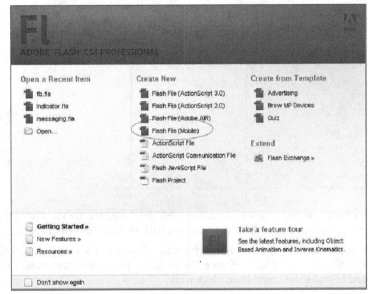

Figure 5-21. Select Flash File (Mobile) on the Flash Start page.

3. Inside Device Central CS3 or CS4, select Nokia N95 8GB from the Local Library on the left panel of Device Central (see Figure 5-22).

> *If no Nokia devices are present within the current local library, drag and drop the Nokia folder from the Online Device Library below Local Library. This will copy down all the latest and greatest Nokia devices and allow you to use them for development.*

4. Next, change Target Flash Player to Flash Lite 2.0 (see Figure 5-23). If you are sure your device is running Flash Lite 3 due to recent firmware updates, you can select Flash Lite 3 in this selection as well. The ActionScript code provided will work in both versions 2 and 3, just not Flash Lite 1.1 (since we utilize ActionScript 2.0 in the example).

> *Most shipping devices supporting Nokia WRT at the time of this writing are running Flash Lite 3, especially those devices running Symbian S60 fifth edition.*

Figure 5-22. The Nokia N95 8GB device is a S60 third-edition FP1 device. With a firmware update, it will run Nokia WRT widgets.

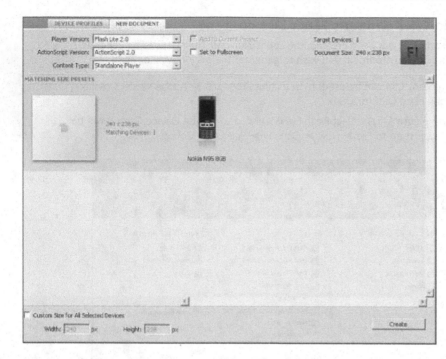

Figure 5-23.
Configuring the
Device Central set-
tings for the Flash Lite
widget for a Nokia
WRT deployment

5. Once the parameters have been added, click the Create button located in the lower right-hand corner of Adobe Device Central to be sent back to Flash (see Figure 5-23).

6. Within the Flash IDE, you will notice the stage dimensions are now set to 240X320, the default screen size of the Nokia N95 (see Figure 5-24). From here, the ActionScript code must be added to make the countdown clock work.

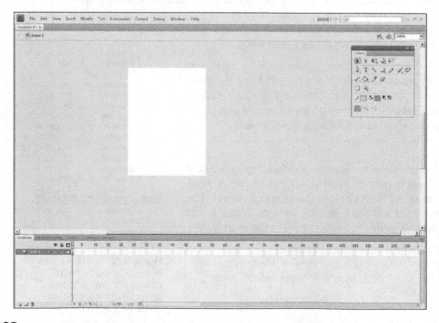

Figure 5-24.
The Flash IDE has
been opened for
the Flash Lite widget
development.

Save the FLA file, and call it `widget.fla`. This will match the `widget.swf` that will be used when the widget HTML page is loaded.

7. First, fill that white background with a nice graphic. Add a new layer below Layer 1, and rename it to Background. Make sure frame 1 of the new Background layer is selected. Choose Select File ➤ Import ➤ Import to Stage. Pick the graphic named `widgetBackground.png` located under `/resources/images/` in Chapter 5. This will bring in the Flash on Tap background.

8. Next, rename Layer 1 to ActionScript. On that layer, enter in the following code:

```
fscommand2("FullScreen", true);
fscommand2("setQuality", "high");

var ndate:Number = 20090528;
var date:Date = new Date((ndate/10000), (ndate/100%100)-1, (ndate%100));

var textformat_fmt:TextFormat = new TextFormat();
with ( textformat_fmt ) {
 bold = true;
 font = "Arial";
}

this.createTextField( "countdown_txt", this.getNextHighestDepth(), ➥
(Stage.width/2)-50, (Stage.height/2)+50, 200, 20);

with ( countdown_txt ) {
 embedFonts = false;
 setTextFormat( textformat_fmt );
 textColor = 0xffffff;
}

function countDown():Void {
 var now:Date = new Date();
 var n:Number = Math.abs((date.getTime() - now.getTime()) / 1000);
 var days = int(n / (60*60*24));
 n = n % (60*60*24);
 var hours = int(n / (60*60));
 n = n % (60*60);
 var mins = int(n / 60);
 var secs = int(n % 60);
 countdown_txt.text = "" + days + " days, " + hours + "h, " + mins + "m, " + ➥
 secs + "s";
}

var timerID_num:Number = setInterval(countDown, 1000);

stop();
```

9. Now, publish the SWF; select File ➤ Publish Settings, and use the settings shown in Figure 5-25.

There is no need to generate an HTML page for this project, as the one generated by Aptana will be used (see Figure 5-26).

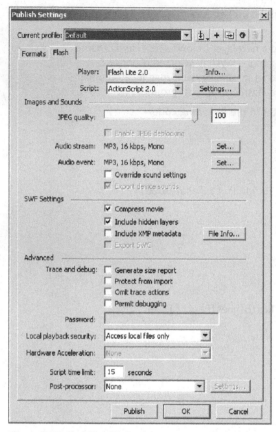

Figure 5-25. Flash Publish Settings are set to Flash Lite 2.0 and ActionScript 2.0.

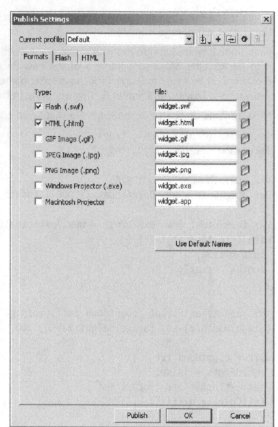

Figure 5-26. There's no need to generate the HTML (only the SWF file), since Aptana already provides it.

Now that the HTML and Flash Lite code have been generated, it's time to package up the widget.

Adding the Flash Lite content to a Nokia WRT widget framework

Once the SWF is generated in the previous section, it needs to be added to the widget. To do this, simply right-click the FOEWidget project in the Project panel, and select File ➤ Import from the top bar menu. In the Import Wizard, select General ➤ File System. Choose the widget.swf file that was created in the previous section from the From directory field (see Figure 5-27).

Now that the widget development is completed, you're ready to package it for deployment on a supported Nokia S60 handset.

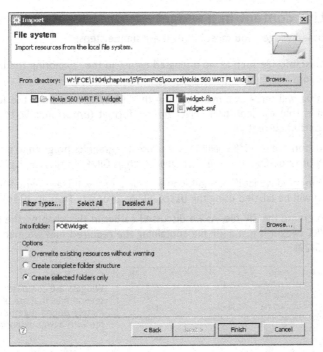

Figure 5-27. Importing widget.swf into Aptana for use within the widget

Packaging a Nokia WRT widget

To package a widget, simply right-click the project, and select Package Widget from the context menu (see Figure 5-28). This option will generate the widget in WGZ format. The WGZ file can then be deployed to a supported S60 handset for installation, as well as further on-device testing. The WGZ file will be output in the directory you specified back in step 3 of "Developing a Nokia WRT Widget" when configuring the Aptana workspace.

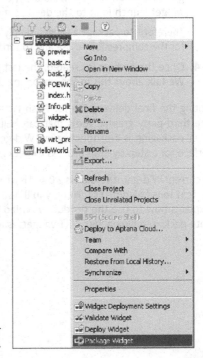

Once the widget is packaged into a WGZ file, it can be transferred to a WRT-supported device (such as the Nokia N95 we targeted earlier). When first running the widget, the user will be prompted to install it. For subsequent use, it can then be launched from the Applications folder on the device.

Although Aptana Studio provides a very quick and easy-to-use packaging system, it's good to know what's going on behind the scenes when it comes to packaging a Nokia WRT widget. Let's take a further look at the packaging process.

Figure 5-28. Packaging a Nokia WRT widget in Aptana Studio.

Packaging Flash Lite content in a widget

To package a Flash Lite-based widget, you must follow these simple steps:

1. First start with a plist.info file such as we discussed earlier in the "Exploring the info.plist configuration file" section.

2. Creating an icon that will serve as a menu icon in the S60 system menu is the first step. The basic requirement is that the icon be in PNG graphic format (unfortunately, the SVG vector format is not supported currently).

   The recommended icon size is 88×88 pixels. You can use any graphics program to create the PNG, including Adobe Photoshop CS4 or a free alternative, such as GIMP (http://www.gimp.org).

   One thing to keep in mind is that if a widget icon is missing or invalid, a generic S60 icon will be displayed; the icon will be labeled using the DisplayName property from its plist.info file.

3. Next, you need to create the ZIP file. As we discussed earlier in this chapter, the final delivery of a Nokia S60 WRT widget is just a ZIP file containing the required files we mentioned previously (see Figure 5-29).

Name	Date modified	Type	Size	Tags
icon.png	12/5/2007 12:11 PM	PNG File	4 KB	
info.plist	12/5/2007 4:02 PM	QuickTime Prefer...	1 KB	
main.css	12/5/2007 4:02 PM	CSS Document	1 KB	
main.html	1/9/2009 8:14 PM	HTML Document	2 KB	
main.swf	10/25/2007 9:03 PM	SWF File	15 KB	

Figure 5-29.
Widgets are composed of several files that are ultimately zipped together in a file with a .wgz extension.

The packaged file *must* have the extension of .wgz. This extension identifies the file as a widget, and when the file is opened, the S60 device will install all the relevant files and add the widget launch icon to the device's menu.

Therefore, to package a widget, simply select all the files and create a ZIP file. Use the default settings for the compression to use and so forth. Then, just to change the final .zip extension to .wgz.

4. Once the archive is created, the last step is to place the WGZ file onto a point of distribution. We talk about this in the upcoming "Deploying and Distributing WRT Widgets" section.

Creating the final delivery file for Flash Lite–based Nokia S60 WRT widgets is easy. Even so, there are some third-party graphic tools that can help streamline the process. One useful option for S60 WRT widget packaging is a product called W'd-get-it (see Figure 5-30). W'd-get-it provides a graphical user interface for a step-by-step process to package SWFs that will be delivered as Nokia WRT S60 widgets.

The current W'd-get-it version is 2.0 and is a free download. You can obtain it at http://mobilewish.com/applications/wd-get-it/. Here, you'll also find the most current documentation available as a PDF; it explains how to use the product. A video tutorial explaining how to use the W'd-get-it packager to create packaged Nokia S60 WRT widgets is also provided.

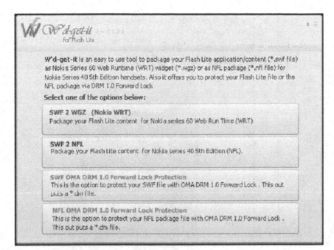

Figure 5-30.
W'd-get-it version 2.0
supports Nokia S60
WRT packaging.

Testing a WRT widget

For testing your Flash Lite widget, you can utilize the following methods: testing with the Nokia S60 platform SDK emulator, testing with Aptana, testing with RDA, and testing with Adobe Device Central. Let's discuss each of these options.

Testing with the Nokia S60 platform SDK emulator

The first option for testing your widgets is by utilizing the S60 platform SDK emulator shown in Figure 5-31. You should have downloaded this earlier in this chapter in the "Preparing to develop a widget for an S60 device" section.

If you launch the SDK emulator (by selecting S60 Developer Tools ➤ SDK Edition ➤ Emulator), you'll see a representation of what the device user interface looks like for your target device platform. Currently, this means it will be either S60 third or fifth edition (see Figure 5-31 and Figure 5-32). The widget SWF file can be loaded into this emulator for testing purposes.

Next, you can simply select File ➤ Open (see Figure 5-33), and choose the WGZ file we created earlier in the "Packaging a Nokia WRT Widget" section (see Figure 5-28).

Figure 5-31. S60 third-edition FP2 SDK emulator

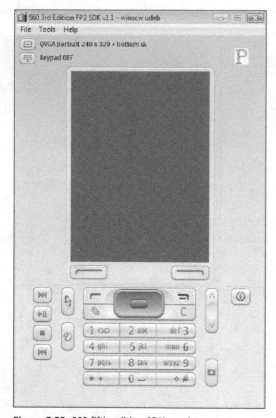

Figure 5-32. S60 fifth-edition SDK emulator

Figure 5-33. The Nokia WRT widget being tested within the SDK emulator

When the WGZ file is executed, it will kick off the widget installation process. During the installation, when you are asked for the location to install the widget, you can select Phone Memory or Memory Card. Either location will work when working within the emulator.

If there are no installation errors, you can open and test the widget from the emulator. To do this, simply navigate to the Installations or Applications menu folder (which one you have depends on the Symbian operating system of the Nokia device), under the S60 programs folder (see Figure 5-34), and locate the application with the name and image you created earlier.

Testing with Nokia S60 handsets

When you're ready, you can test your shiny new Flash Lite widget on your supported, Flash Lite–enabled Nokia S60 handset (see Figure 5-35). Alternatively, you can use RDA to test your widget if you don't have ready access to a physical WRT-widget–supporting device.

Figure 5-34. The Applications folder on the third-edition Nokia N95 (sometimes called Installations on other S60 devices)

Figure 5-35. Flash Lite widget running on a Nokia N95 (S60) handset

You may be wondering what you should do if you make one or more changes to a widget after it is first tested. Of course, you don't want to repackage and reinstall the widget each time! To solve this, you just need to modify the source files directly on disk. But where are they?

Well, dive into driveletter:\Symbian\Symbian Version\SDK Version\ epoc32\winswc\c\private\10282822\. There, you'll find all the unique keys you assigned for your widgets that have been previously installed for use in the S60 SDK emulator.

You'll simply be overwriting the source files in here with your updated development source. You'll then need to reload the widget to see the changes in emulator. After that, you can test iteratively with changes applied to widgets.

Testing with Aptana

Aptana provides a convenient way of testing directly from the IDE (see Figure 5-36). Aptana supports pushing widgets to a selected device for testing via Bluetooth or utilizing the S60 SDK emulator. We already covered installing the S60 SDK earlier in this chapter. These testing options can be found under the Preferences ➤ Webruntime ➤ Deployment menu of Aptana.

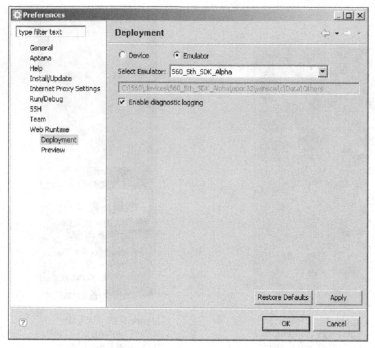

Figure 5-36. Testing the SWF of the WRT widget from Aptana by configuring the S60 SDK emulator (or target device)

Testing with RDA

The third option for testing widgets is the Nokia Remote Device Access (RDA) service that can be used if you don't have access to a supported Nokia handset; see Figure 5-37.

The service allows you access to a wide array of remotely located Nokia devices via an online emulator. This emulator can be accessed through an online connected Java-based application. To get started using Nokia RDA, check out http://forum.nokia.com/ and load the HTML page at /main/ technical_services/testing/rda_introduction.html.

With the application, essentially, you can reserve time slots for selected S60 Nokia devices contained in an available device pool to test on. It's like having the actual device in your hand. Plus, it's free to use; you just need to reserve your testing time slot, because as you can imagine, it's a busy little service offered by Nokia.

> *An alternative to RDA is the Forum Nokia Virtual Developer Lab powered by DeviceAnywhere (http://www.deviceanywhere.com/nokia/welcome.htm).*

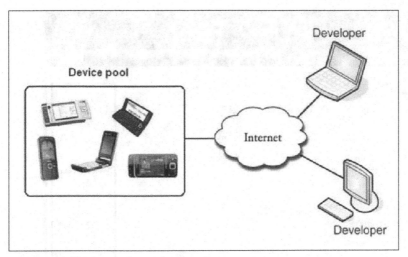

Figure 5-37. Nokia RDA allows you to test mobile applications over the Internet connection.

Testing with Adobe Device Central

Since we are utilizing Flash Lite for WRT widgets, we can utilize Device Central CS3 or CS4 for testing (to a degree). The restriction is that we can only test the Flash Lite SWF itself. We can't test the widget as it works within its widget shell (e.g., HTML or JavaScript). Essentially, we can't test to see how the final widget behaves on a device. However, for testing the content contained *within* the SWF, Device Central can be leveraged just by opening the SWF in Device Central CS3 or CS4.

Deploying and distributing WRT widgets

Once you've created a Flash Lite widget using Nokia's WRT, what do you do with it? How do you get it out to hundreds of millions of potential consumers worldwide? How does one distribute Nokia WRT widgets? At the time of this writing, you can deploy your content through several channels including Nokia MOSH, Nokia Download, or the new Nokia OVI Store (we talked about each of these in Chapter 2). All of these distribution options feature a native Symbian content catalog application that allows consumers to browse, download, and install WRT widgets.

MOSH

Nokia MOSH (http://mosh.nokia.com) is a public, free, ad-based portal for sharing all kinds of Nokia handset content (see Figure 5-38). It is run by Nokia, and currently, WRT widgets can be uploaded to this portal for distribution.

Although MOSH does support WRT widgets, Nokia has announced that MOSH will be phased out at some point in the future. It's best to look at the OVI Store for WRT widget distribution going forward.

Figure 5-38. Nokia MOSH is a web-based portal from which users can download device content (media, games, applications, etc.). Note that it has been made defunct by the Nokia OVI Store.

The OVI Store

OVI is Nokia's newest storefront for mobile application distribution across over 70 types of handsets in over 200 countries. OVI supports both stand-alone Flash Lite content and Nokia WRT widgets. To get started publishing widgets to OVI, visit http://publish.ovi.com/.

Figure 5-39. The Nokia Download! client

Nokia Download!

This is Nokia's premier on-device content catalog (see Figure 5-39). It allows mobile development companies to share their creations with users of the millions of Nokia S60 handsets in the worldwide market. The content is a mixture of free and commercial mobile applications.

Other distribution methods

Other distribution methods for Nokia widgets include serving the WGZ file from a (mobile) web server or sending it via Bluetooth. Distributing widgets off-portal (e.g., via Bluetooth or an external memory card) will work for hard-core developers and technically savvy owners of Nokia devices, but these distribution methods are tough to monetize. They also require significant marketing efforts for users to find and acquire the content, so we do not cover them in this book.

Installing a widget onto a supported S60 device

Installing a widget on supported Nokia S60 devices is fairly straightforward:

1. Find and download a WGZ widget from one of the distribution points mentioned in the previous section.

2. Click the WGZ file.

3. The handset extracts the WGZ file and asks if you want to install it.

4. Specify the storage location when prompted. Installation begins, and the required files are copied from within the WGZ file into the location specified.

5. The new widget icon will appear in the S60 menu Applications folder, and the widget can be launched from there. Once launched, the widget content will appear just like a native application would on S60 devices (see Figure 5-40).

Figure 5-40.
An installed WRT widget
(WeatherBug) running on
a Nokia N95 (an S60 third-
edition device)

In this section, we've looked at Nokia S60 WRT widgets, which can take advantage of Flash Lite to drive a superior mobile user experience. The Nokia WRT is not the only widget platform though! Let's move on to look at how a device called the Chumby is leveraging widgets using Flash.

Developing Chumby widgets

In this section, we're going to take a peek at the Chumby (http://www.chumby.com/). Though Chumby (see Figure 5-41) is not portable, it is a Wi-Fi enabled, Linux-based, consumer electronic device, with touch-screen support that also happens to, you guessed it, run Flash Lite widgets. Specifically, the current Chumby runs Flash Lite 3.0.

One of the cool features of the Chumby is its over-the-air (OTA) self-updating mechanism over Wi-Fi. It's the same idea as the Adobe Flash Lite 3.1 Distributable Player we talked about in Chapter 3 but uses a proprietary method of updates (using P2P connections, actually!) Because of the update feature offered with each shipping Chumby, it may actually run a newer version of Flash by the time you are reading this (i.e., something more recent than Flash Lite 3.0). Neat, huh!

Figure 5-41.
The Chumby spends a lot of time as a passive glanceable information display.

Introducing the Chumby

The Chumby is essentially a stationary Internet appliance that can stream news, music and podcast recordings, photos, social networking, games, weather, videos, sports events, auctions, and classifieds. It also provides an alarm, messaging capabilities, and more. It's a multifaceted media device! Whether the Chumby is tethered to an office, a bedroom, a kitchen, or other location, it's constantly streaming information for your eyes. We classify it as a glanceable device.

Understanding glanceable technology

The Chumby is unlike a lot of other consumer electronic products out there in terms of how you interact with it. We call it a glanceable technology, because it is a device that you place in any location and it feeds you all kinds of data, yet you only interact with it when you glance something of interest and are compelled to look further.

In that respect, the Chumby acts as conduit for information, and it aids you throughout its life on your office desk, bed, or other location in your home or at work (it's important to remember that the Chumby does have an AC power cord, unlike many of the battery-powered devices we've spoken of earlier in this book).

All that wonderful glanceable information is contained inside Flash-based widgets that are displayed on the Chumby's touch screen.

Comparing Chumby and Nokia WRT widgets

Previously in this chapter, we spoke about WRT mobile widgets that ran on Nokia handsets. Chumby widgets are very similar, in that they are small applications that are easy to install and distribute. However, there are some fundamental differences.

First, Chumby widgets are not launched by users clicking application icons. Instead, configured widgets are loaded via Wi-Fi connection across the Internet. Users install Chumby widgets by adding them to a profile that is located on the www.chumby.com network portal site. Widgets are available from a variety of categories including games, weather, and news (see Figure 5-42).

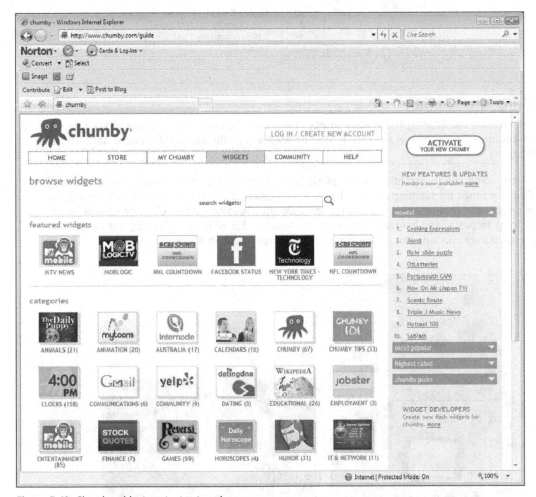

Figure 5-42. Chumby widget content categories

Another difference is that widgets are delivered to a Chumby in channels that users create and assign to their Chumby devices. A channel contains one or more widgets. The channel metaphor that Chumby uses is somewhat similar to that of TV channels, though on the Chumby, users switch channels via a touch-screen control panel user interface (see Figure 5-43).

Figure 5-43.
The Chumby control panel,
which is actually Flash
based

Hacking the Chumby

Did we mention the Chumby is also open source? Well, it is. The open source nature of the Chumby allows consumers to purchase and modify (i.e., hack!) the Chumby through hardware, software, or other means.

Of course, some minor restrictions are in place, but for the most part, the open source nature of the Chumby allows for seemingly endless hacks and modifications—very fun stuff! Figure 5-44 shows some clever modifications. Chumby owners are constantly modifying their Chumby devices. Hacks range from software, and hardware, and even craft-specific hacks! In fact, Chumby Industries thoroughly encourages hacking and personalizing your Chumby to suit your everyday needs!

Figure 5-44. Some modifications include a teddy with an embedded Chumby and a robot with a Chumby head.

The Chumby also acts as a very simple music, radio, and podcast system (see Figure 5-45).

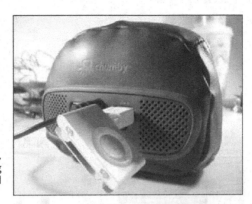

Figure 5-45.
The Chumby playing
music from an iPod

Because of the open source nature of the Chumby, there is community that encourages feedback and knowledge sharing. A good amount of information is available on the Chumby community forums (http://forum.chumby.com/), as well as public wiki pages (http:wiki.chumby.com/). A third site, outside of Chumby, is the Chumby users' Google group (http://groups.google.com/group/chumby-user-group). These are excellent locations for finding out what's new with the Chumby. Community is a huge part that makes it stand apart from other devices on the market.

Accessing online community support resources

Due to its open source nature, the Chumby has a few active locations for resources where developers can get current and in-depth answers to coding questions and the like. Three of these that we personally recommend, at the time of this writing, follow:

- **Chumby Flash developer start page**: http://www.chumby.com/developers/flash
- **Chumby newsgroup Flash widget forum**: http://forums.chumby.com/Flash
- **Chumby widget development wiki**: http://wiki.chumby.com/mediawiki/index.php/Developing_widgets_for_chumby

We recommend that you take a look at these resources, as they provide a good amount of additional knowledge about developing Flash widgets. Plus, these offer the latest material from the folks over at Chumby Industries!

Getting hold of a Chumby

At the time of this writing, the Chumby is available in the United States, Japan, and Australia. A Chumby may be purchased online at http://store.chumby.com/ directly from Chumby Industries (see Figure 5-46), which is based on the west coast of the United States. Unlike other handheld devices we have spoken of up until this point, the Chumby is not yet available in physical stores (to our knowledge anyway).

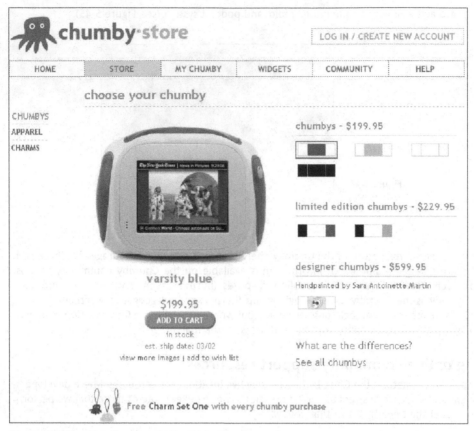

Figure 5-46. The Chumby store at http://store.chumby.com/

Exploring the Chumby

The Chumby device is one of the more unique nonportable gadget devices running Flash. It breaks down into the following pieces.

Software   As we mentioned earlier, the Chumby runs Linux. The Linux version is custom to the Chumby device, and it allows for some really cool possibilities on the Chumby.

Hardware   For the price of a couple hundred US dollars, the Chumby manages to pack a lot of amazing hardware inside. Although the Chumby internals, or guts, are constantly being updated between models as the device evolves from community feedback, it comes with the following components at the time of this writing: a 350-MHz ARM processor, 64MB SDRAM, a 3.5-inch color LCD touch screen, two full-speed external USB 2.0 ports, dual stereo speakers, a headphone jack, and an accelerometer (a motion/force sensor).

Compared to a lot of other Flash Lite mobile devices, the Chumby is actually a beefy little guy with a lot of muscle power in terms of memory and CPU. As you'll see shortly when we talk about the Flash widgets on the Chumby, there is a lot of "developer room" to create widget applications.

User Interface   One of the cool things about the Chumby is that the user interface of the device not only loads in Flash Lite widgets but the device user interface, itself, is actually built in Flash Lite! The entire control panel is Flash based (see Figure 5-47).

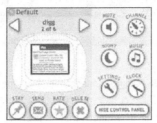

Figure 5-47.
Chumby control panel

OK, so we've talked a bit about some the principles and personality behind the Chumby, so now, let's focus on some widget development!

Getting ready for Chumby widget development

It should be no surprise that developing Flash widgets for the Chumby is quite a lot of fun! However, before we dive into the nuts and bolts of creating Chumby widgets, let's explore some of the unique features and unique differences of Flash widget development on the Chumby.

Flash widgets on the Chumby

Chumby runs a custom port of a Linux-based version of Flash Lite 3. For all intents and purposes, the Flash Player on the Chumby performs similarly to Flash Player 8. Of course, it doesn't nearly approach the performance you get with a Flash 8 running on a desktop PC, but as you'll see, the Chumby offers considerably more CPU power, as well as more addressable memory, than a typical handheld device.

We've already discussed the benefits and features of Flash Lite 3 in Chapter 3. Although not all the Flash Lite 3 features are supported on the Chumby, some key features include native FLV support, which allows you to create video-based Chumby applications and other content (in fact, we'll actually take a look at Flash video in Chapter 15). In the latest version of Flash Lite for the Chumby, you'll also notice performance improvements over previous Chumby prototypes, which had Flash Lite 2.0. Now, let's continue our exploration of some of the unique features of Flash on the Chumby.

Delivering content via channels

Another major fundamental difference between Flash on the Chumby and other Flash mobile platforms is the way in which content is delivered to end users. On mobile devices, typically, Flash Lite content is loaded onto a device via an archive file such as a SIS, an NFL, or a WGZ file, as we talked about previously with Nokia S60 WRT widgets. Common transfer methods include direct mobile download (via an aggregator on the Web or on-device catalogs) or side loading (via Bluetooth or a physical cable).

Unlike Nokia WRT widgets, Chumby widgets are not loaded within a Chumby browser. Instead, on the Chumby, the user interface (which is itself a Flash application) loads in Flash Lite widgets. With the Chumby, Flash content is actually stored remotely on the Chumby Network and brought down to the Chumby device via its Wi-Fi connection. SWFs are stored in a cache on the Chumby and displayed individually in containers called channels (see Figure 5-48).

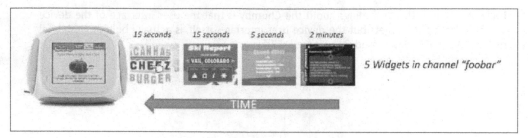

Figure 5-48. Chumby Flash widgets loading into a channel over a period of time

Channels are simply collections of widgets that a user has configured to view from the Chumby Network portal site (http://www.chumby.com/guide/). Each widget contained within a channel also has some configuration properties associated with it. One important one is the duration (in seconds) that a particular widget will run—its play time.

Understanding Chumby input methods and sensor APIs

Currently, the Chumby offers two main methods of user input that Flash developers can take advantage of: touch-screen interaction and the accelerometer hardware component (see Figure 5-49).

There are actually two additional ways of interacting with the Chumby: a built-in microphone and the toggle switch on the top of a Chumby. Microphone access is not currently supported in the Flash Lite 3.0 implementation shipping right now (hopefully, that will change in future versions), so that functionality is not available via ActionScript.

The top switch on the Chumby is used by default to access the control panel. Although it may be accessed via ActionScript, typically it's reserved for the built-in Chumby control panel. See the "Bend switch" section below for more information. Let's cover the touch-screen, accelerometer, bend switch, and microphone inputs on the Chumby.

Sensor	ActionScript

Touchscreen	_rawX = ASnative(5,10); // get the last raw touchscreen X coordinate
	_rawY = ASnative(5,11); // get the last raw touchscreen Y coordinate

Display	_getLCDMute = ASnative(5,19); // get the value of the LCD "mute"
	_setLCDMute = ASnative(5,20); // set the value of the LCD "mute"
	
	_setLCDMute(0); // full on
	_setLCDMute(1); // dim
	_setLCDMute(2); // full off

Speaker	_getSpeakerMute = ASnative(5,17);
	_setSpeakerMute = ASnative(5,18);
	_setSpeakerMute(1);

DC Power	_dcPower = ASnative(5,16);

Accelerometer	_accelerometer = ['ASnative'](5,60);
	version = _accelerometer(0);
	timestamp = _accelerometer(1);
	currentX = _accelerometer(2); currentY = _accelerometer(3); currentZ = _accelerometer(4);
	avgX = _accelerometer(5); avgY = _accelerometer(6); avgZ = _accelerometer(7);
	impactX = _accelerometer(8); impactY = _accelerometer(9); impactZ = _accelerometer(10);
	impactTime = _accelerometer(11);
	impactHits = _accelerometer(12);

Bend Sensor	_bent = ASnative(5,25); // get the "bent" flag (0/1)

Figure 5-49. Sensor and other available APIs on the Chumby

Touch screen

All Chumby devices come with a 3.5-inch color display that provides 320×240 pixels of screen real estate to display content and facilitate user interaction. The following code will return back the precise location of X and Y raw coordinates of a screen touch by a user:

```
_rawX = ASnative(5,10); // get the last raw touchscreen X coordinate
_rawY = ASnative(5,11); // get the last raw touchscreen Y coordinate
```

Since the Chumby is without device keys, using the touch screen coordinates and hit states on MovieClips and buttons are the best ways to detect user touch interaction with objects that are contained with the Flash widget. You can access these states as follows:

```
movieclip.onMouseDown = function() {
 trace( _xmouse, _ymouse );
}

mybutton.onPress = function() {
 trace( "touched the object" );
}
```

> *Mouse coordinates and events are used and simulate screen touches, since legacy Flash and ActionScript 2 does not support multi-touch screen.*

Accelerometer

One of the exciting new features of the Chumby is its support for a built-in accelerometer. Like the accelerometers found in many popular mobile devices, it detects force and movement along the X, Y, and Z axes.

Users can detect these events by utilizing an ActionScript native call, which is much like the Flash Lite fscommand2 API commands we talked about in Chapter 2, except there are raw calls into the Chumby Flash Player. Here's the ActionScript to access the accelerometer:

```
_accelerometer = ['ASnative'](5,60);
version = accelerometer(0);
timestamp = accelerometer(1);
currentX = accelerometer(2);
currentY = accelerometer(3);
currentZ = accelerometer(4);

avgX = accelerometer(5);
avgY = accelerometer(6);
avgZ = accelerometer(7);

impactX = accelerometer(8);
impactY = accelerometer(9);
imoactZ = accelerometer(10);
```

```
impactTime = accelerometer(11);
impactHints = accelerometer(12);
```

Bend switch

Older alpha and prototype Chumby devices feature a unique bend sensor switch that allows developers to detect the amount of squeeze pressure applied to the Chumby. However, recent Chumby devices feature only an on/off switch on the top of the Chumby. Here's the code to access the bend switch:

```
_bent = ASnative(5,25); // get the bent flag (returns 0 or 1 value)
```

Although this switch can be accessed through ActionScript, it does not add much advantage to most widgets, since the button is reserved for bringing the user into and out of the Chumby control panel navigation mode. Mapping actions to the top switch is therefore *not* recommended.

Microphone

Currently, the embedded microphone on the Chumby is *not* accessible via ActionScript, since the version of Flash Lite 3.0 installed on the device does not support the Microphone object (at the time of this writing). Please visit the Chumby forums at http://forum.chumby.com to find out if this changes in the future.

Display

The Chumby API currently allows the display to be dimmed using some native ActionScript calls:

```
_getLCDNute = ASnative(5,19); // get the value of the LCD mute
_setLCDMute = ASnative(5,20); // set the value of the LCD mute
_setLCDMute(0); // display is on
_setLCDMute(1); // display is dimmed
_setLCDMute(2); // display is off

_getSpeakerMute = ASnative(5,17);
_setSpeakerMute = ASnative(5,18);
_setSpeakerMute(1); // mute is enabled
_setSpeakerMute(0); // mute is disabled

_dcPower = ASnative(5,16); // returns if Chumby has plugged power
```

In Figure 5-49, we provide a convenient table of the ActionScript code in the Sensor API for your reference in Chumby development.

Using Chumby variables

Because of the way SWFs are delivered to the Chumby, there are some unique ties from the Chumby Network portal to each individual device that Chumby sells. In fact, each Chumby has a defined Chumby environment where variables can be stored. Some of these are static and some are dynamically changed at runtime. These variables fall, currently, into two categories: widget parameters and widget configuration variables.

Widget parameters

Widget parameters (see Figure 5-50) are static values that act to identity unique properties of a Chumby. These are set by the Chumby itself or on the Chumby Network and sent down to the Chumby as widgets play back in channels.

- _chumby_chumby_name: Name assigned to the Chumby by the owner (e.g., Susan)
- _chumby_widget_instance: Unique GUID assigned to each widget instance (e.g., 12121212-1212-1212-1212-121212121212)
- _chumby_user_name: The Chumby owner's username (e.g., John)

Widget Parameters	
_chumby_chumby_name	Name assigned to Chumby by owner (Ex: "Sue")
_chumby_widget_instance_id	Unique GUID assigned to each widget instance (Ex: 12121212-1212-1212-1212-121212121212)
_chumby_user_name	Chumby owner username (Example: "scott")
Widget Configuration Variables	
this['foobar']	Widgets that have a desktop configuration can set custom variables which each widget instance.

Figure 5-50. Environment parameters on the Chumby

Widget configuration variables

Widget configuration variables are user-defined variables that can be utilized for the duration a widget runs within a particular channel. These are useful for keeping very basic configuration parameters available and are typically set when a user enters in widget configurator variables.

- this['variablename']: Widgets that have a desktop configuration can set custom variables for each widget instance. These are essentially local environmental variables, which you can use to keep persistent little pieces of data in memory for the duration that the channel widgets run. For example, a widget might have a current date value (e.g., 5/5/2009) stored in a custom variable named this['currentdate'], which is leveraged inside a widget.

Using the Chumby fscommand2 API

Although Flash Lite on the Chumby offers some valid fscommand2 APIs (we discussed basic fscomand2 syntax in Chapter 2), some are not supported. In Figure 5-51 is a complete breakdown of the commands and their return values on the Chumby device.

Command	Return Value
FullScreen	-1
GetDeviceID	Unique ID
GetNetworkConnectionName	-1
GetNetworkConnectionStatus	1
GetNetworkGeneration	-1
GetNetworkRequestStatus	0
GetNetworkStatus	-1
GetPlatform	"Linux 2.6.16"
GetBatteryLevel	228
GetMaxBattery	100
getMaxVolumeLevel	100
GetSignalLevel	Number
GetLocalLongDate	-1
GetLocalShortDate	-1
GetLocalTime	-1
GetTimeZoneOffset	0

Command	Return Value
GetVolumeLevel	Number
getFreePlayerMemory	Number
GetTotalPlayerMemory	12,542 KB
ResetSoftKeys	-1
GetSoftKeyLocation	-1
Quit	0
getPowerSource	1
SetInputTextType	0
SetSoftKeys	-1
StartVibrate	-1
StopVibrate	0
GetLanguage	-1
GetTimeHours	Number
GetTimeMinutes	Number
GetTimeSeconds	Number
GetDateDay	Number
GetDateMonth	Number
GetDateYear	Number
GetDateWeekDay	Number

Figure 5-51.
fscommand2 return values on the Chumby

Although these are documented and contained in the downloadable unofficial Chumby reference sheet (see http://advancED.flashmobilebook.com/chumby/), we show them in Figure 5-52 so that you can see what is supported and not supported on the Chumby platform.

Command	Return Value
_compoundSound	1
_capEmail	0
_capLoadData	1
_capMFI	0
_capMIDI	0
_capSMAF	0
_capSMS	0
_capStreamSound	1
_cap4WayKeyAS	1
$version	FL 8,1,52,0

Figure 5-52. Miscellaneous (legacy) properties on the Chumby

Dealing with Flash security on the Chumby

Like other Flash Lite 3 mobile applications, the Chumby inherits the Flash 8 security model. In the Flash Publish Settings window, it is important to always select Access network only from the Local playback security drop-down, as shown in Figure 5-53.

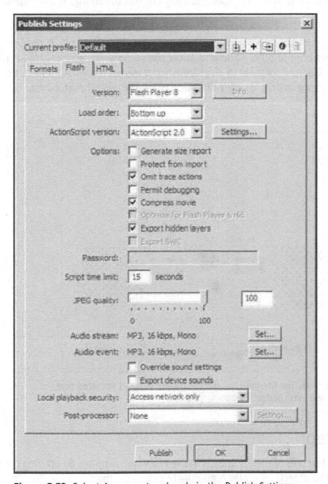

Figure 5-53. Select Access network only in the Publish Settings window for Chumby.

When creating a Chumby application that pulls remote data, you're most likely going to have a crossdomain.xml file that allows the connection to take place. Since Chumby widgets are very commonly loading external assets over Wi-Fi, the cross-domain file is needed, or a server proxy needs to be implemented.

Although we won't go into too many security policies here because of the sheer volume of that material, we do recommend that you read the Flash 8 security paper that details a lot of the rules that must be followed when serving local and remote SWFs: http://www.adobe.com/devnet/flashplayer/articles/flash_player_8_security.pdf.

Working with audio

Each Chumby has two speakers and provides stereo audio playback for both music and sounds (see Figure 5-54). When working with audio on the Chumby, MP3 is primarily the format you want to use. You can embed the audio on the Flash timelines of your widgets or attach it dynamically using ActionScript at runtime. Loading external sounds over HTTP (progressively but not streaming) is also supported.

> *To avoid annoying your users, when creating widgets with sound, allow end users to toggle sound on and off or raise and lower the volume. It's also courteous to have the default sound state set to disabled when a widget is loaded (unless, perhaps, you are trying to grab a user's attention when the widget first loads).*

Figure 5-54. The Chumby has stereo speaker support for streaming music and Flash widgets supporting sound.

Working with video

One of the greatest Flash features of the Chumby is native FLV video support. By utilizing the video, netstream, and netconnection objects, you play high-quality videos on the Chumby with decent playback results (see Figure 5-55). The recommended settings for video on the Chumby are a Flash frame rate set to 12 FPS, video data rate of 220KB per second, and audio set to 32KB (mono) or lower quality.

> *We recommend trying to avoid using the FLV media components provided in Adobe Creative Suite, and instead, build custom classes to drive video playback through external files. The desktop Flash IDE FLV media components have not been optimized for mobile or embedded devices. It's best to keep Chumby widgets as lightweight (both in file size and also processor usage) as possible.*

In Chapter 15, we'll cover how to leverage Flash video across devices.

Figure 5-55.
A Chumby video widget
playing back at 320×240
pixels in native FLV format

Loading and saving data

Sooner or later, you'll want to load and work with data with Chumby widgets. There are really two ways to load and save data on the Chumby: remotely and locally. Which you choose depends on your needs.

Remote data

As with most other Flash Lite 2 and 3 mobile applications, the Chumby offers support for loadVars, loadVariables, loadMovie, XML, and even XMLSocket objects. Chumby even supports the open source SWX data format (http://www.swxformat.org/). Security ties into being able to load data, since the Flash Lite 3 data security model is used with the Chumby (see the "Dealing with Flash Security on the Chumby" section of this chapter).

Persistent data

For persistent data storage, shared objects are not recommended for use on the Chumby. Instead, widget configuration variables should be used. If you remember, we talked about these special environment variables earlier in this chapter. An alternative method for storing persistent data is just to hook up the Chumby to a remote database server via some of the data methods we discussed, for example, loadVars and XML.

Working with widget configurators

Because of the lack of a device keyboard on the Chumby, user input must be done via the touch screen. For character entry, this can be tedious. Tedious text entry also affects the configuration of Chumby widgets. Rather than configure any settings for a Chumby widget on the touch screen device itself, Chumby Industries opted to place widget configuration options on the Chumby web site.

Widget configurators are simply Flash movies that store user configurable variables that allow the user to customize widget behavior. For example, usernames and passwords can be configured on the web server for a widget (see Figure 5-56) or a ZIP code can be entered into a configurator so that a user does not have to select a location every time a weather widget is loaded.

To create a configurator, a Flash 6 or higher SWF needs to be generated with some custom ActionScript code to set parameters that the Chumby understands. Steps for building a widget configurator are laid out on the Chumby wiki pages (http://wiki.chumby.com/mediawiki/index.php/Developing_ widgets_for_chumby#Widget_Configuration_Dialog).

Publishing Chumby SWFs

Depending on your workflow, you'll be publishing Chumby widgets using either Flash Lite 3 or Flash 8. You also have two paths to working with the Chumby: through the Adobe Flash CS4 IDE or an open source option like MTASC.

If you are utilizing the unofficial Chumby device profile with Adobe Flash and Device Central CS4, you'll want to use Flash Lite 3 and ActionScript 2.0 output settings (see Figure 5-57) when creating new widget content.

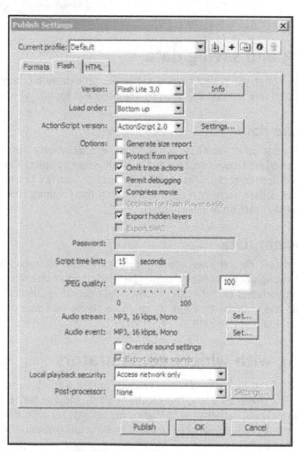

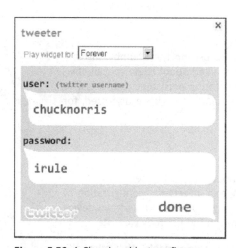

Figure 5-56. A Chumby widget configurator

Figure 5-57. Adobe Flash CS4 Publish Settings (Flash Lite 3.0 is the target within the IDE, but Flash 8 will also work since Flash Lite 3.x is a subset of Flash Player 8.)

Finding tips, tricks, and further resources for Chumby widgets

In addition to the great community support forums Chumby Industries runs, which we talked about earlier, we have created some resources of our own to share with you. We've already talked about one such resource—the unofficial Adobe Device Central CS4 device profile. This resource, and others (e.g., a Chumby wire framing design document, useful for designing and planning widgets) can be found on the advanced companion book site (http://advancED.flashmobilebook.com/chumby/).

Using best practices for Chumby widget development

You've gotten some valuable insight in this chapter on how to develop Flash widgets for the Chumby device. We'd also like to share some best practices we have collected when developing for the Chumby:

- Use _lockroot or use nonabsolute path names for MovieClips that are used in widgets.
- Enlarge the hit areas of button states to maximize the possible hit areas on the touch screen.
- Use large (and easy-to-read) text in widgets.
- Implement cooperative mode, so Chumby widgets don't expire after a set time limit and instead wait for a special flag to be set. For more info, refer to: http://wiki.chumby.com/mediawiki/index.php/Developing_widgets_for_chumby#Cooperative_Mode.
- Keep widget file sizes relatively small (ideally less than 200KB).
- Avoid lengthy Flash preloaders (if you can't avoid them altogether, as they are distracting), but splash screens are OK.
- Utilize the (unofficial) Adobe Device Central Chumby profile for Flash IDE–based development.
- Sound should always be optional to users and *not* a requirement.
- Consider having a version number displayed in the widget (e.g., v 1.21).
- Check out the Chumby one-sheet PDF reference when developing your widgets.

Check the web site we have set up for more suggestions like these: http://advancED.flashmobilebook.com/chumby/.

Now that you have some understanding of the unique API and development considerations for the Chumby, it's time to get writing a widget.

Building a Flash Lite widget for the Chumby

Using the Adobe Flash IDE in Creative Suite for developing Chumby widgets is perfectly acceptable, but the Chumby's open source roots make it a really appealing platform to develop for with open source software. Tools such as OpenLaszlo (an open source Flex-like alternative), MTASC (an open source ActionScript 2 compiler), SWFMill (an XML-to-SWF converter), and SWFTools (SWF modifications tools) can all be leveraged to generate Chumby Flash widget content.

> *Because of the open source community of Chumby developers, it's even possible to compile ActionScript code and output widget SWFs directly on the Chumby itself (using a native Chumby binary of MTASC)! Very cool! For more information, check out http://wiki.chumby.com/mediawiki/index.php/Actionscript. Why would you want to do this? This possibility gives the Chumby the ability to dynamically generate SWF files on the fly, so you can compile custom user interfaces and widgets for home-brewed Chumby hacks that are bootable via USB key or perhaps via the built-in Chumby web server.*

Although we would love to talk about all these tools, we have too much other exciting material to talk about in this book. Instead, we focus on a couple tools out of the lot that we think are practical workflows for open source Chumby widget development.

Check out our companion web site at http://advancED.flashmobilebook.com/chumby/ for more materials about working with the Chumby and other open source tools.

In this example, the open source IDE FlashDevelop is used to develop the ActionScript code for a Chumby widget. You will be using the FlashDevelop IDE and SWFMill to develop a fun Flash Lite 3–based Chumby widget. First, the environment needs to be configured. Let's proceed!

Before development can begin, the environment needs to be properly configured with the open source tools FlashDevelop and SWFMill.

Downloading and installing SWFMill

SWFMill is an open source, command-line–driven XML-to-SWF processor (it actually works in reverse as well, but we do not use it here that way). Essentially, this tool loads in assets (graphics, sounds, etc.) defined in the XML code and generates a SWF with those assets. You can download the latest version of SWFMill at http://osflash.org/swfmill.

Once downloaded and extracted, the simple command-line executable (swfmill.exe on Windows or SWFMill on the Mac, see Figure 5-58) can be run against a properly constructed XML file to generate a SWF.

You'll use the SWFMill tool when you start building the Chumby widget in a bit, but for now, proceed to installing FlashDevelop and the Chumby FlashDevelop template.

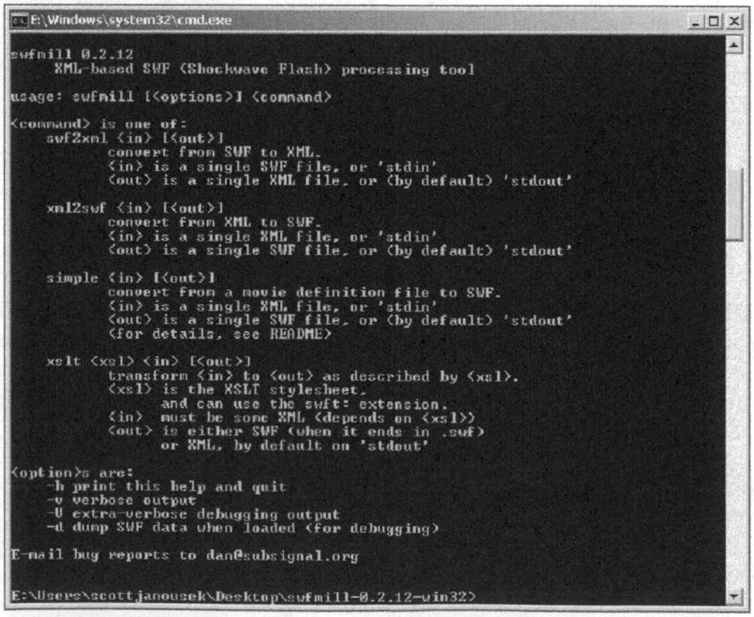

Figure 5-58. SWFMill is a command-line tool for converting assets specified in XML into a compiled SWF.

Downloading and installing FlashDevelop

Before starting the example for this section, you need to acquire a copy of FlashDevelop. At the time of this writing, FlashDevelop version 3.0.0 RC1 is the latest version available for download. The IDE can be downloaded at http://www.flashdevelop.org/ under the Downloads link and then installed onto a Windows machine running Microsoft Windows XP or Microsoft Windows Vista.

> *FlashDevelop is currently supported only under a Windows development environment, so Microsoft XP or Vista is required to follow along with the example using FlashDevelop.*

Once FlashDevelop is installed, it needs to be updated so that it can compile ActionScript 2–based SWF widget content for the Chumby. Luckily, because of the open source nature of the Chumby, a FlashDevelop template has already been created to extend the FlashDevelop environment.

The FlashDevelop Chumby project zip file can be downloaded at http://code.google.com/p/chumbydevelop under the Downloads section of the page at Google Code. Version 0.17 is the most current at the time of this writing.

Once the zip file is downloaded and extracted, a main Chumby development directory will contain a subdirectory called 03 ActionScript 2 - Chumby and another called examples (see Figure 5-59). The 03 ActionScript 2 - Chumby directory should be moved into the FlashDevelop templates directory. On both Microsoft XP and Vista, this should be something similar to C:\program files\FlashDevelop\Templates\ProjectTemplates\.

> *You'll notice that the directory name 03 ActionScript 2 - Chumby fits the convention of some other project templates, including ActionScript 2 and 3. It's important to keep a proper naming convention for the directory so that FlashDevelop knows to load the project template.*

Once the template has been moved into the FlashDevelop directory, it's time to start up FlashDevelop and make sure the installation took hold. Open and launch FlashDevelop by selecting Start ➤ Programs ➤ FlashDevelop ➤ FlashDevelop. On the main Start page, select New Project from the left tab (see Figure 5-60).

> *If FlashDevelop is already open, select Project ➤ New Project to start.*

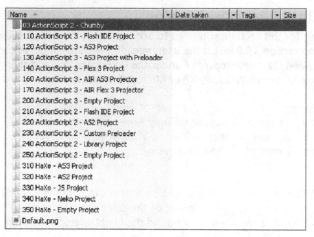

Figure 5-59. File contents of chumbydevelop_0.17.zip extracted

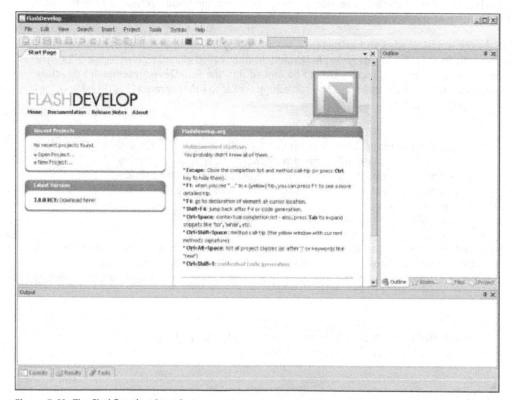

Figure 5-60. The FlashDevelop Start Page

If the Chumby template appears in the New Project window (as shown in Figure 5-61), configuration has been completed successfully. Development can begin!

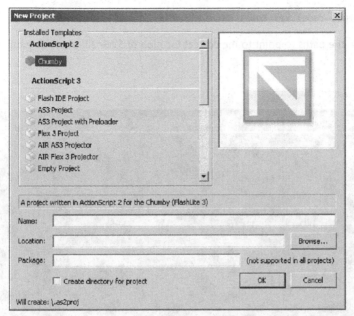

Figure 5-61. The FlashDevelop Chumby template has been installed correctly and is available.

Creating the Asset SWF

When developing Chumby widgets using FlashDevelop, there is no notion of a Flash timeline to store assets such as sounds, graphics, and videos. SWFMill allows a SWF to be created from an XML file where these assets are specified. The following XML file for SWFMill defines a SWF file with the target frame rate and dimensions of the Chumby screen (320×240) and pulls in both a button and sound that will be used later in the widget.

Create the following XML file (or reuse the one provided in the Chapter 5 directory):

```xml
<?xml version="1.0" encoding="iso-8859-1" ?>
<movie width="320" height="240" framerate="12">
 <background color="#000000"/>
 <!-- 1st frame in SWF -->
 <frame>
  <!-- add Assets to the library in the SWF -->
  <library>
   <clip id="buttonID" import="library/button.png"/>
   <clip id="soundID" import="library/Yodel.nmp3"/>
  </library>
 </frame>
</movie>
```

Once the XML file has been created, it just needs to be run through the SWFMill engine (see Figure 5-62). Within the SWFMill directory, simply run the following command from within the /library/assets/ directory for the example in Chapter 5:

```
swfmill.exe simple Yodel.xml Yodel.swf
```

You may need to change the paths to point to the correct location of SWFMill depending on where it was installed or copied.

Figure 5-62. Publishing a SWF containing media assets defined in the specified XML file with SWFMill

Once the Yodel.swf file has been compiled successfully, it should be located in the /library/assets folder.

Developing the Flash Lite Chumby widget

After installing the Chumby FlashDevelop template and creating the asset SWF generated from SWFMill, you can begin developing the Chumby widget. The widget will respond to a touch event on a button and play a sound (actually, a yodel).

The first step is to establish valid parameters for the New Project screen (see Figure 5-63). In this case, the Name should be set to Yodel. Location should be set to a local path where the source and deployment files will be kept. The Package parameter should be kept blank. Select the Create directory for project check box so that work will be contained inside a new directory (Yodel will be used for the directory name, since this is the name of the FlashDevelop project).

Once the project is created, in the Project panel, there will be bin and src directories. The src directory contains the util ActionScript class file, as well as the Main.as ActionScript class. Main.as is the source file where ActionScript for this widget will be placed.

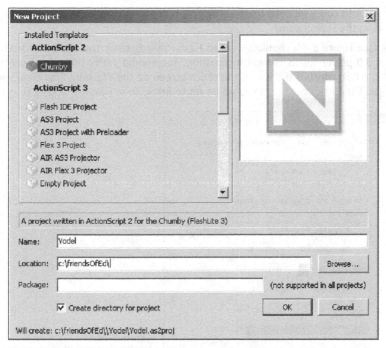

Figure 5-63. Configuring FlashDevelop project parameters for the Chumby widget

> *For simplicity's sake, the ActionScript is being placed directly inside the Main.as file. However, for more complex widgets, a framework should be created that consists of many class files, which create an ActionScript framework.*

The util directory contains several reusable class files that can be used when using the FlashDevelop Chumby template: BarChart.as, Chumby.as, Horizontal.as, Menu.as, UI.as, and VerticalMeter.as.

The Chumby.as class wraps all of the custom ASNative ActionScript calls that tap into the Chumby device hardware (accelerometer, power supply, etc.) into convenient getter and setter function calls such as getDCPower(). All the other classes are for providing a very simple graphical API. For the example, we will only be using the UI.as and Chumby.as classes (the other .as util files can be safely deleted from the project, by the way).

> *The util class files are open source and provided as by the original developer. Using them is up to you and at your own discretion for Chumby widget development. For the example provided here, we will be using them. Support and feedback for these class files should be directed to authors of the FlashDevelop template, rather than us.*

1. Before we get into code, we need to set some properties on the project. Right-click the Project name, Yodel, in the Project panel.

The Target (see Figure 5-64) should be set to Flash Player 8, since the Chumby currently uses a Flash Lite 3.0 player for its current incarnation. You should verify that the Dimensions are set to 320×240 px, which is the size of the touch screen on the Chumby. Framerate should be set to 12 fps. The Background color should be set to black, so in hex, it is #000000.

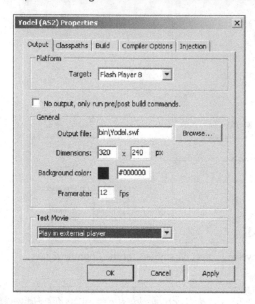

Figure 5-64.
Configuring project properties within FlashDevelop for a target Chumby Flash widget

The Test Movie selection should be set to Play in PopUp, which will open the default stand-alone Flash Player for testing (see Figure 5-65).

> If you have Adobe Creative Suite 3 or 4 installed, you can set the Test Movie selection to Test in external player, and Device Central should automatically be used to preview your Chumby widget. You'll need to acquire and install the Chumby widget, however. You can download it at http://advancED.flashmobilebook.com/chumby/.

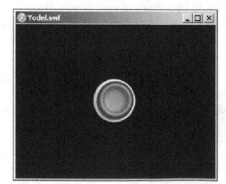

Figure 5-65.
Testing the Chumby widget within the default Flash Player (via a pop-up)

2. To be able to use the assets created with SWFMill, you need to inject them into the project you are creating. To do this, simply go to the Injection tab in the Projects panel (see Figure 5-66). Enter the path to the Yodel.swf file generated from SWFMill earlier, and be sure to check Enable Code Injection. Click Apply when you're finished.

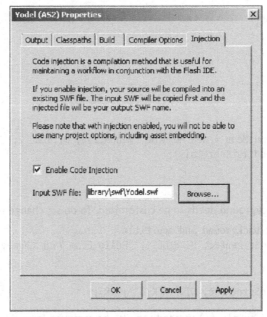

Figure 5-66.
Configuring the Yodel.swf file
(and its embedded assets) to be
injected into the FlashDevelop
Chumby widget project

You should notice that the Yodel.swf file will turn blue to indicate that it will be injected into the Chumby widget SWF when the FlashDevelop project is compiled (see Figure 5-67).

Figure 5-67.
Yodel.swf will turn blue when it
has been properly injected into
the FlashDevelop project.

3. Open the Main.as ActionScript class within the FlashDevelop IDE located under the src folder.

4. Remove the following commented code from the default Main constructor:

```
/*
 * Simple menu
 *
 var menuArray:Array = [
"One",
"Two",
"Three",
"Four",
"Five",
"Six",
"Seven",
"Eight"
];

 var menu:Menu = new Menu(mc, menuArray, UI.BLUE_2, UI.BLUE_3, UI.WHITE);
 menu.addListener(this);

 */
```

5. The background needs to be customized. To do so, change the following code

```
// set background and app title
UI.mainScreen(mc, UI.BLUE_1, "Hello From Your Chumby!");
```

to this

```
UI.mainScreen(mc, UI.BLACK, "", 18);
```

The onMenuSelect() method can also be removed from the Main.as class file.

6. Once the previous steps have been followed, you should have the following code inside the original Main.as file, which acts as the starting point for the Chumby widget:

```
import util.*;

class Main
{
 private var parent:MovieClip;
  function Main(mc:MovieClip)
  {
  // save reference to main movieclip
  this.parent = mc;
  UI.mainScreen(mc, UI.BLACK, "", 18);
 }

 static function main(mc:MovieClip)
 {
  var app = new Main(mc);
 }
}
```

7. Now, the sound needs to be attached to the stage. Recall that the sound has already been injected into the project in step 2, so it just needs to be attached using the SoundID instance name that was used to create Yodel.swf via SWFMill. The sound is loaded, and the volume is set to maximum volume using the following code:

```
var sound_snd:Sound = new Sound();
with (sound_snd) {
attachSound("soundID");
setVolume(100);
}
```

8. Next, the button needs to be tackled. Since the Chumby is a touch screen device, the button just needs to be added to the screen. The button is attached and positioned in the middle of the stage:

```
var button = mc.attachMovie("buttonID", "button_mc", ➥
mc.getNextHighestDepth(), ➥
{_x:(Stage.width/2)-40, _y:(Stage.height/2)-40 } );
```

9. Now, the button needs to respond to press-and-release events. When pressed and released, the button will initiate the playback of the attached sound in step 7 (i.e., the yodel) using the start() method of the Sound object. The button's X and Y coordinates will also shift a bit so the user knows the button has been pressed or released:

```
var button = mc.attachMovie("buttonID", ➥
 "button_mc", ➥
mc.getNextHighestDepth(), ➥
{_x:(Stage.width/2)-40, _y:(Stage.height/2)-40 } );

button.onPress = function() {
 sound_snd.stop();
 sound_snd.start();
  this._x += 1;
  this._y += 1;
}

button.onRelease = function() {
 this._x -= 1;
 this._y -= 1;
}
```

10. Once the code has been entered, it's time to test and compile within FlashDevelop.

In FlashDevelop, use F5 to compile and test the application, and F8 to produce the final output (SWF). Alternatively, to compile the Chumby widget, the publish button (see Figure 5-68) can be used (i.e., the right-facing arrow icon).

Figure 5-68.
Publishing from FlashDevelop requires only a simple button click from the top navigation (the arrow icon).

If the code is entered correctly and no compilation errors occur, and the final Yodel.swf will be created and located in the bin directory of the project (see Figure 5-69).

Figure 5-69.
After publishing, the SWF will be generated and is located in the /bin directory of the project.

> *Check the* output *panel of FlashDevelop for any errors that might occur. The* output *panel will contain the* Build Succeeded *message once no compile-time errors are found. Once no errors are found, it's best to switch* Debug *to* Release *in the dialog shown in Figure 5-68, before the final SWF is pushed to the Chumby device.*

The final published SWF can be uploaded to the Chumby Network so that it can be tested within the Chumby Network. There are alternative means for testing Chumby widgets as well, which we cover next.

Testing Chumby widgets

In the previous section, we stepped through how to complete a Chumby widget. Testing it is our next step. There are a few ways in which to test Chumby widgets. We'll describe each of these methods, and the pros and cons of each, as well as the conditions where they should be used.

Testing without the Chumby device

There are essentially two ways to test without the device (testing content off the Chumby): Virtual Chumby and Adobe Device Central.

Virtual Chumby   The Virtual Chumby (see Figure 5-70) is a simple way of testing your Flash widgets within the context of a web browser. The Virtual Chumby is basically just an embedded Flash movie that pulls in widgets from the Chumby portal. These are loaded not on the actual Chumby hardware device, but contained within HTML pages. The Virtual Chumby allows embedding of the Flash Chumby widget content within HTML pages on social networks such as Facebook and MySpace. For example, the Virtual Chumby Facebook application is located at http://www.facebook.com/apps/application.php?id=2349139814.

> *Things such as accessing the Chumby API, performance feedback, and other on-device items cannot be tested with the Virtual Chumby. The actual Chumby hardware and Chumby Network must be used for things such as accessing the accelerometer or benchmarking the performance of the Chumby widget.*

You can find out more information, including how to set up the Virtual Chumby, at http://www.chumby.com/mychumby.

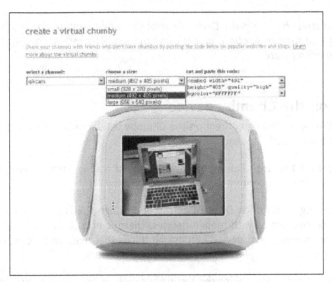

Figure 5-70.
Creating the Virtual Chumby

Adobe Device Central At the time of this writing, no official Chumby device profile exists for Adobe Device Central CS4. However, as we have mentioned, an uncertified Chumby device profile has been created and is maintained by the Boston Adobe Mobile and Device User Group (http://www.flashmobilegroup.org) and the Chumby developer community.

This unofficial Chumby device profile (see Figure 5-71) can be loaded into Device Central CS3 or CS4 and used to test Flash Lite 3 content. It can be downloaded at http://advancED.flashmobilebook.com/chumby/.

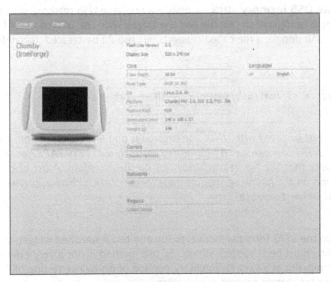

Figure 5-71. The unofficial Chumby device profile for Adobe Device Central (created by Scott Janousek)

> We must stress here that the Device Central Chumby template has not been certified by either Chumby Industries or Adobe. Consider using this template for noncommercial development, since it is in an alpha state.

Testing on the Chumby device

As you can imagine, testing content on the Chumby is tedious and time consuming, as it requires the widget to be uploaded after each change is made.

Single-channel testing   During the final stages of testing Chumby widgets, we recommend that you test your Flash Lite content directly on the Chumby.

Although testing with Adobe Device Central, or through the Flash Player on the desktop, results in quicker workflow, just as with mobile devices, there is no substitute for testing on the real device. Performance, memory, and device APIs are all things that need to be checked on an actual Chumby before rolling out your application on the Chumby Network.

One recommendation for making this testing as simple as possible is to create a separate testing channel on the Chumby Network site. Within that channel, create a test widget that has a maximum play time of forever. The test widget will stay loaded as you test.

> An alternative to single-channel testing is to utilize the sticky widget feature in the Chumby control panel so that, in a multiple-widget channel, the testing widget stays focused for testing until you proceed to another widget.

Testing with a bootable USB memory stick   Creating a bootable USB memory stick with a Flash widget requires just a single configuration text file and the target SWF. The USB must be formatted in the VFAT format. On the USB dongle, a file called debugchumby should be created. Its contents should be as follows:

```
#!/bin/sh
chumbyflashplayer.x -i /mnt/usb/targetWidgetName.swf
```

> The debugchumby file must be saved with UNIX line encodings and line terminations. You should reformat a USB drive to VFAT to make sure it's formatted correctly (FAT16 or FAT 32 are supported but not VFAT). Also note that the file debugchumby has no file extension. A list of compatible USB drives can be found on the following support page: http://wiki.chumby.com/mediawiki/index.php/USB_Flash_Drive_Compatibility.

Once the file is created on the VFAT formatted drive, to run and test a specified widget, the USB drive is inserted and the Chumby must be rebooted. Obviously, this method is not a very time efficient for testing interactively, so it remains as a very rudimentary method of on-device testing of Chumby widgets. This method is better for sharing content than testing.

Testing via your chum list   You can also send a Chumby widget to a friend (i.e., a Chumby chum) for third-party testing before it is made live on the Chumby Network site. Instructions for configuring a chum list (see Figure 5-72), which is essentially a list of friends for sending and receiving widgets, can be found on the Chumby Network portal site at http://www.chumby.com/chums/.

To register your friends as chums, you'll need to exchange your Chumby Network usernames, and both parties must configure their "sent to" and "receive from" lists via the Chumby web site.

Figure 5-72. A Chumby chum list

Testing on an SSH console   With some Linux knowledge, it is possible to set up a secure socket shell (SSH) under Linux to test content via the built-in secure shell daemon (SSHD). Although the most comprehensive and up-to-date instructions are contained on the Chumby wiki, here are the basic steps to set up SSH on the Chumby:

1. Bring up the Chumby control panel by squeezing the top switch on the device.

2. Within the Chumby control panel, select Settings.

3. Enter into Chumby Info.

4. Note the pi symbol (π) in the top right-hand corner. Touch this Easter egg (i.e., hidden feature).

> For other Easter eggs and Chumby hacks, please see http://wiki.chumby.com/
> mediawiki/index.php/Chumby_tricks.

5. Once you're within the hidden menu, select SSHD.

6. Plug a USB dongle into the Chumby, and create the debugchumby file that we talked about earlier. This time, inside the contents of the text file, enter the following command:

```
#!/bin/sh
/sbin/sshd
```

7. Copy the SWF you wish to test onto the USB memory stick.

8. Now, reboot the Chumby with the USB stick.

9. After the boot, telnet to the Chumby device using an SSH client (such as PuTTY):

```
telnet root@<IPAddressOfTheChumby>
```

10. Once you're logged in (no password is needed), the Flash Player must be stopped using the following command:

```
stop_control_panel
```

11. The touch screen and sensors should now be off. Now, just launch the SWF:

```
# chumbyflashplayer.x -i /mnt/usb/<WidgetName>.swf
```

> *Using Ctrl+C allows you to exit the Chumby Flash Player.*

Testing on an external HTTP server   It is also possible to test external Chumby widget content as an external SWF hosted on a remote web server. This involves logging into the Chumby device, as defined in the "Testing on an SSH console" section. Once there, target the Chumby's Flash Player to an external URL:

```
# chumbyflashplayer.x -i http://advancED.flashmobilebook.com/test.swf
```

The security settings will adapt to whatever crossdomain.xml file is located on the external server or fall back on what is defined within the loaded SWFs that are being tested.

Once your widget has been significantly tested via any one of these methods, it's time to move along to deploying the widget on the Chumby Network widget catalog page (http://www.chumby.com/guide).

Deploying a widget on the Chumby Network

Once your widget is developed, it's time to share it! There are a few methods for local and remote sharing of Chumby widget content:

- **USB stick**: All Chumby devices have at least one USB port. Along with storing media files, it's possible to create bootable widgets. To do this, a simple configuration text file is needed on the USB stick, along with your SWF files to be run.

```
#!/bin/sh
chumbyflashplayer.x -i /mnt/usb/targetWidgetName.swf
```

Using USB sticks is, in some sense, like using the game cartridge of old days; your users plug in the stick to play your content. Of course, distributing your content this way limits the amount of users who can get your content, since you must distribute USB sticks to them (which is expensive). However, it's still fun. A much more efficient way to distribute your Flash widget content is through the Chumby Network.

■ **Chumby Network portal**: A much more convenient method to share Chumby widgets is via its network connection to the Internet via Wi-Fi. Currently, Chumby offers a network portal site (http://www.chumby.com/guide/) that acts as a repository of community-submitted content. At the time of this writing, the Chumby Network is a free service in which developers can upload their widgets and share them with other owners of a Chumby device. Uploading widgets to the Chumby Network portal is shown in Figure 5-73.

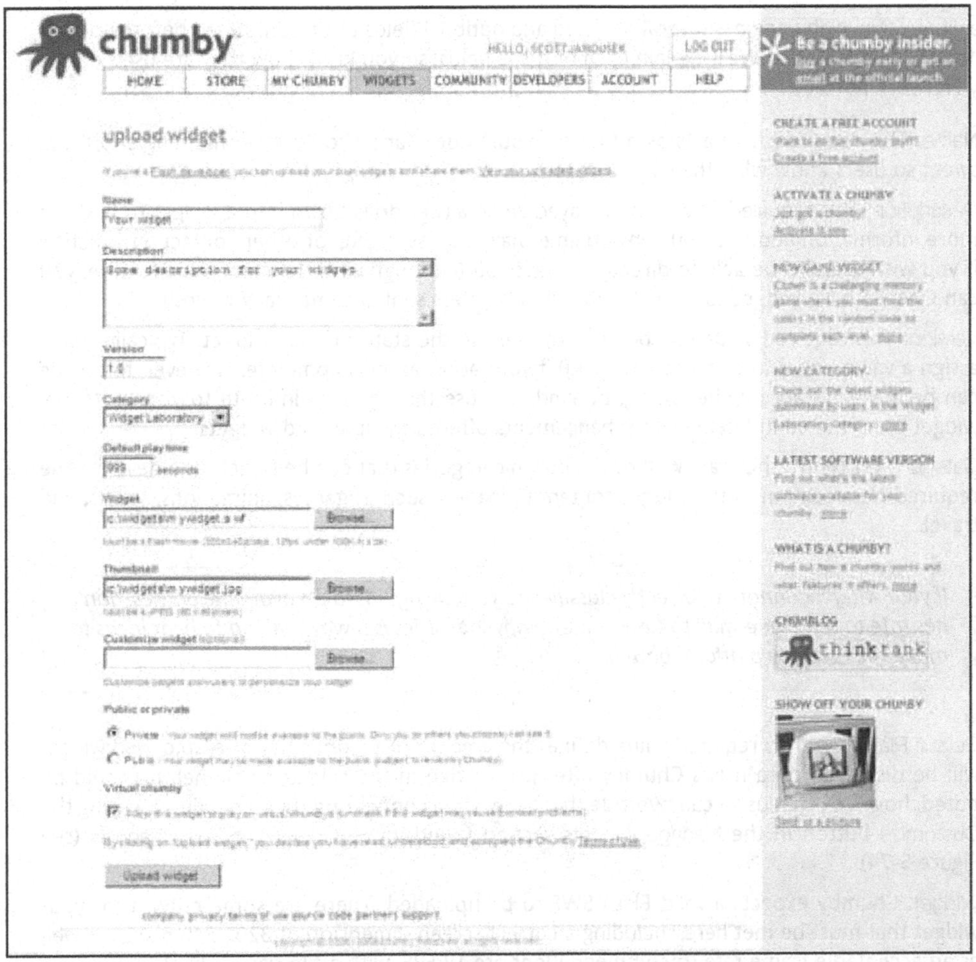

Figure 5-73. Uploading a widget to the Chumby Network portal

In some respects, the Chumby Network store is like the iPhone App Store, but it differs in that there is no obvious marketplace for selling widgets. Currently, the Chumby Network portal is a free service, and widgets are shared without any monetary compensation. However, note that there are alternative methods of monetizing Chumby widgets, such as tying in a subscription-based service or feature or using an ad-based model.

There are the major steps to get your Flash widget up onto the Chumby Network portal. First, you're going to need an account. Typically, if you have purchased a Chumby, you will have already created an account to authorize your Chumby. For users without a Chumby, the URL to register is http://www.chumby.com/account/new and widgets may be uploaded, configured, and viewed on a Virtual Chumby at http://www.chumby.com/mychumby/. Once you're logged in, the page to upload a widget can be found by selecting Widgets ➤ Submit a Widget (or navigating directly to http://www.chumby.com/widgets/upload).

The Submit a Widget web page has several required and optional fields to be completed before uploading the final widget SWF file. We'll explain each of these fields, so you know how they are used on the Chumby Network portal.

- Name: This required field acts as a title for your widget and should be something short and sweet so users know what the widget does.

- Description: This required field gets displayed when a user drills down into a widget to find out more information about it. You can add an e-mail address, a URL, or other contact information if you wish users to be able to directly contact you (although with the comments feature, you can elect to have widget comments submitted by users sent automatically to you).

- Version: This required value can be used to indicate the state of your widget. Typically, you'll assign a value equal to or greater than 1.0 if your application is complete. However, this value can be any arbitrary number string. Be kind, and use this value to indicate to your potential widget users the completeness or enhancements offered by uploaded widgets.

- Category: Currently, there are well over a dozen categories that can be selected to describe the required classification of the widget content uploaded, such as games, animations, sports, and travel.

> If your widget cannot be correctly classified to your liking based on available entries, don't hesitate to send an e-mail to Chumby. Chumby Industries is always willing to hear ideas to make the Chumby platform better!

- Default Play Time: This required value defines the amount of seconds that the uploaded widget will be displayed on a user's Chumby after it is loaded in the selected channel. It should be noted, however, that users can override this value when configuring their channels by using the Customize button in the Manage Widgets section found in My Chumby ➤ My Channels (see Figure 5-74).

- Widget: Chumby expects a valid Flash SWF to be uploaded. There are some criteria for your widget that must be met here, including a correct screen dimension of 320×240 pixels, as well as an acceptable frame rate (recommendations are 12 FPS, with a file size under 100KB).

  Although Flash 4, 5, 6, 7, and 8 files will work, we recommend that you publish your final Flash content as either Flash Lite 3.x or Flash Lite 8 files, as we mentioned previously.

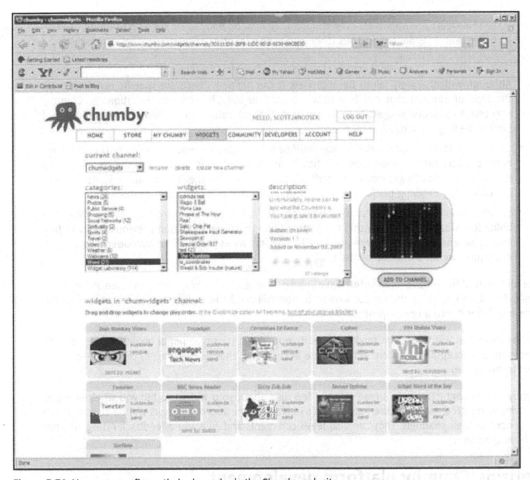

Figure 5-74. Users can configure their channels via the Chumby web site.

- Thumbnail: A valid JPG that is 80×60 pixels is expected. This icon will be displayed on the Chumby Network in the Widgets ➤ Browse Widgets section. The icon you choose should be easy to read and indicate what your application does. The thumbnail image is a required field.

- Customize Widget: Not all Chumby widgets require configuration, so this field is optional. More information about how to add custom parameters to Chumby widgets can be found at http:// wiki.chumby.com/mediawiki/index.php/Chumby_Tutorials#Say_Hello_Using_Parameters.

- Public or Private: This flag toggles whether or not a Chumby widget is visible on the Chumby Network portal. Private should be selected here if a widget is for private use or is still being developed or tested. Production-quality widgets should be marked Public, allowing them to be entered into a review process conducted by Chumby before becoming a live widget that can be added by users to their channels.

Once a widget is uploaded and marked Public, it usually takes a few days to get feedback on a widget and find out whether or not it has passed the review process.

> *Until widgets are approved, even though they may be flagged as* Public *on upload, they will remain invisible to end users (they won't show up on the Chumby widget catalog).*

Although widgets rarely fail to be approved, it can happen. There are specific restrictions on the type of content that can be publicly posted to the Chumby site. Additionally, Chumby may reject uploaded widgets based on widgets that misbehave or otherwise have serious and noticeable bugs that need to be fixed.

- Comments: This flag indicates if e-mail notifications should be sent when Chumby users comment publicly on the widget once it has been uploaded. It is up to you, the developer, to specify if you wish to get real-time feedback on widgets once they're uploaded. Since Chumby is a constantly evolving platform, it is recommended that this setting be enabled.

- Virtual Chumby: We already discussed working with the Virtual Chumby. This setting allows the uploaded widget to be run within the Virtual Chumby. As we discussed previously, this setting should be enabled unless there are specific circumstances in which an uploaded widget may misbehave within a desktop context.

Once all required fields have been entered (i.e., Name, Description, Version, Category, Default Play Time, Widget, Thumbnail), clicking the Upload Widget button will send the widget and its details off to the server and enter it into a review process.

Chumby Industries will take steps to determine if your widget passes minimal quality inspection and adheres to the acceptable content policies (see http://www.chumby.com/pages/terms for specifics about terms of use).

Chumby should contact you via e-mail within a few days about your widget to tell you whether it was approved or rejected, including the reasons if it's rejected. Once approved, users will be able to assign your widget to their channels. They can also leave comments and give you a feedback rating on what you have created!

Monetizing Chumby platform development

Sure, you can have a lot of fun hacking the Chumby device, developing widgets for yourself and your friends, or creating that latest, greatest prototype. But you may be asking, "What are the viable ways of publishing out Flash widgets and generating revenue from the Chumby platform?"

Currently, there is no application store for Chumby. However, creating one has been mentioned in the Chumby forums. One of the exciting things about the Chumby is that the company has plans to roll out its Chumby Network and widget frameworks beyond the Chumby device to set-top boxes, MIDs, PCs, and other devices. This means that, in the future, it may be possible for those device manufacturers to potentially create their own revenue-based models and application stores for Flash widgets. This is exciting news, as it may be possible in the future to develop Flash widgets that run across dozens of devices, all from the Chumby widget platform.

Even though the Chumby platform has yet to spread beyond the device at the time of this writing, there are a few ways to try to monetize your efforts on the Chumby:

- **Working for hire with Flash widget development**: One way of earning money of Chumby widget development is by working for hire to build other companies' products and services targeting the Chumby platform. This often requires porting some sort of existing software application or service into the Chumby framework. Oftentimes, working for hire revolves around quick prototypes, but several major brands have really engaging widgets on the Chumby device, and they sometimes contract out Chumby work.

- **Selling advertising in Chumby widgets**: Offering advertising space, whether on a widget-loading screen or directly in a Flash Lite widget, is another possible way to generate revenue. With Chumby distribution hitting Japan, Australia, and the United Kingdom, in addition to the current United States market, the viability of options is likely to grow in the future. Once a significant number of Chumby devices exist in various regions to justify the advertising dollars (i.e., market penetration is achieved), advertising may be one option to take a hard look at.

- **Offering subscriptions to content**: Again, with the new worldwide markets of Chumby devices, it may be possible to offer a subscription-based service to Flash Lite widget content offered on the Chumby platform.

- **Customizing the device and crafting Chumby accessories**: The idea here is not to focus on the software or widget development the Chumby offers but to sell physical add-ons such as custom Chumby skins or cases, charms, or hardware accessories. For instance, Internode from Australia sells customized Chumby animal skins bundled with their custom widgets sets. If interested in this model, be sure to check out http://chumby.on.net/purchase/ for more details. It'll make you smile a bit.

Summary

In this chapter, we looked at Flash Lite–based widgets on two Flash-enabled device platforms: the Nokia S60 WRT and the Chumby. By combining Flash Lite with the widget platforms for devices with HTML, CSS, and JavaScript (e.g., Nokia S60 WRT), you can very quickly create visually appealing user experiences with the Flash Player driving the user experiences.

For the WRT development in this chapter, we used the Aptana Studio IDE, which allows you to create widgets across not only Nokia WRT but also widgets for Adobe AIR and even non-Flash, web-based widgets for the iPhone. We also covered an open source approach to Chumby widget development using the FlashDevelop IDE, which hooked in with the MTASC ActionScript compiler.

You're now ready to move onto the next chapter, where we take a look at the exciting world of mobile and device user interface components and how to create rich, engaging user experiences using Flash across devices.

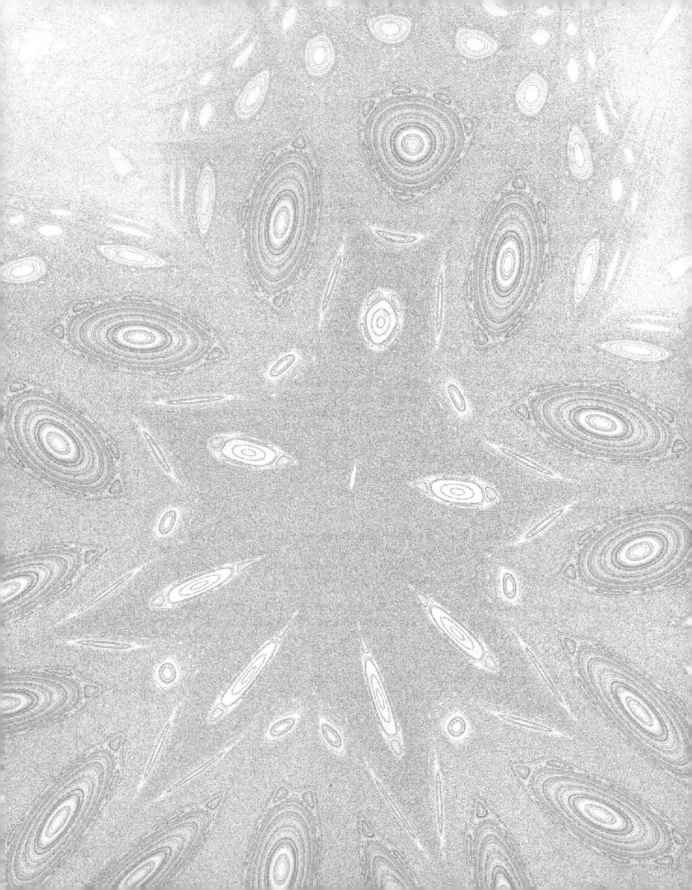

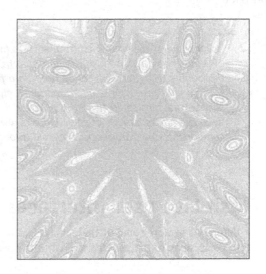

Chapter 6

FLASH LITE USER INTERFACE COMPONENTS AND FRAMEWORKS

User interfaces are one of the most compelling use cases for Flash Lite, due to the speed with which they can be designed, developed, tested, and deployed as well as the visual experiences they bring to consumers.

As you'll learn in this chapter, a number of device OEMs (e.g., iRiver, Sony Ericsson, and LG) utilize Flash Lite user interfaces for these reasons. They have successfully used Flash Lite–based user interfaces (UIs) to improve their time to market, as well as create compelling mobile user experiences across various devices.

In this chapter, you'll learn about some of the component sets and frameworks available for Flash Lite, and how you can get started using them to create UIs more quickly. You'll get an overview of how to leverage reusable third-party Flash Lite UI component frameworks such as Feather, Shuriken, Nokia Components, and the Oxygen Toolkit. You'll also be introduced to some prototype UI components released by the Adobe Experience Team (such as navigation menus and data list interfaces) that can be leveraged in Flash Lite applications.

All of the component sets and frameworks discussed in this chapter help mobile developers develop more compelling Flash Lite applications faster. These reusable frameworks and components allow designers and developers to focus on functionality and features, rather than spending precious time redesigning and re-creating UI elements that have already been built.

Using some of the component frameworks in this chapter can sometimes be both memory and CPU intensive on your Flash Lite applications. Before you use any framework or component sets, thoroughly test your application both on a physical device and in Device Central to make sure memory and processor usage is managed effectively. All of the reusable component sets in this chapter are considered "works in progress" by the respective authors of these community initiatives. During discussions of each initiative, we'll try to point out the strengths and weaknesses of components and frameworks discussed throughout this chapter.

Flash Lite user interfaces

Before we explore some of the popular Flash Lite UI frameworks and component sets, it's important to recap some of the benefits of Flash Lite, when we're talking about mobile and device UIs.

Benefits of Flash Lite with user interfaces

Flash Lite is the perfect candidate when creating mobile and device UIs. Flash Lite has significant advantages over competing technologies (such as J2ME), including the following:

- **Scalable vector and bitmap graphics**: Flash content is vector based, so it scales easily across various screen sizes. However, you can create UIs that blend both vector and bitmap, depending on your requirements.

- **Portability**: A UI designed for one device platform, such as Nokia, can be more quickly ported to another device platform, such as Sony Ericsson, with few (and sometimes no) changes to the Flash Lite UI. This results in a huge time-savings for OEMs and developers alike, who reuse UIs and individual user interface elements and/or UI designs across devices and applications.

- **Backward compatibility**: Flash Lite offers backward compatibility, so that UIs published for Flash Lite 1.1 devices will subsequently work in newer Flash Lite player runtimes (e.g., Flash Lite 2.x/3.x) with minimal tweaks to both existing code and assets.

- **Robust mobile and device development and testing toolset**: Working with the Flash IDE makes it easy to design and develop Flash Lite UIs because of its rich toolset for drawing and animating content. With the Flash IDE, it's easy to prototype UI designs quickly.

  The integration of Device Central with the Flash IDE also makes testing Flash Lite UIs across a range of devices much simpler and less time consuming than testing across a large set of physical devices.

Two device manufacturers utilizing Flash Lite heavily for UIs on devices are LG and iRiver. These two mobile device OEMs (out of several) have greatly improved their time to market because of the aforementioned benefits of the Flash Lite runtime (e.g. the speed of workflow that the Flash IDE and Device Central offers both designers and developers).

One of LG's landmark devices based on Flash Lite was the PRADA phone, which was one of their early touchscreen-based devices utilizing a Flash Lite UI. iRiver's Korean-based U10 and Clix portable media players were also landmark devices for utilizing Flash Lite UIs to drive device experiences, enabling users to listen to music, watch videos, view photos, and even play installed Flash Lite–based games.

Leveraging Flash Lite user interfaces

There are two use cases for UIs for Flash Lite: "on-device" UIs where OEMs use Flash Lite internally for their device platforms, and Flash Lite application content created by developers for public consumption (e.g., Flash Lite content to be distributed within mobile ecosystems).

On-device user interfaces

LG, Sony Ericsson, iRiver, Chumby, and many other OEMs have been using Flash Lite for on-device UIs since early 2004 with Flash Lite 1.1. As of this writing, Flash Lite 2.x and 3.x are leveraged for non-PC consumer devices UIs on dozens of device models from companies like LG, iRiver, and other OEMs ranging from mobile phones (such as Nokia and Sony Ericsson), portable media players (such as Archos), to other consumer electronic devices (such as the Chumby, which we discussed in Chapter 5).

SmartPhones Devices such as Sony Ericsson S500i (Figure 6-1) and LG devices such as the Viewty KU990 (see Figure 6-2) are just a couple of examples (as of this writing) where Flash Lite UIs are being leveraged for more vibrant user experiences on mobile phones.

Figure 6-1. Sony Ericsson S500i (which offers an animated Flash Lite mobile UI)

Portable media players Other device manufactures are also utilizing Flash Lite on other non-PC devices. For example, iRiver has been leveraging Flash Lite for years across many of its Portable Media Players (e.g., U10, E10, Clix, SPINN, and P35). Figure 6-3 shows the Flash Lite 2.x–based UI on an iRiver Clix 2, based on an innovative four-way (up, down, left, right) clickable display (i.e. otherwise known as the iRiver D-Click interface).

Figure 6-2. LG Viewty KU990 (leverages Flash Lite for the UI)

Figure 6-3. iRiver Clix "D-Click" navigation. The Clix is one of many iRiver devices sports a Flash Lite UI.

For a list of (newer) devices supporting Flash-based UIs, please refer to our links page at http://advancED.flashmobilebook.com/links.html#flashliteui.

Consumer electronic devices   With the Open Screen Project started in 2008, more OEMs are beginning to consider Flash for UIs across not only mobile devices but many other consumer electronic devices as well, such as set-top boxes, televisions, and Blu-ray players.

> In addition to mobile devices, with the announcement of Adobe Flash Platform for Digital Home, we believe adoption of Flash and Flash Lite for UIs on TVs, set-top boxes, Blu-ray devices, and other home-based digital electronics is likely to increase over the next few years. For more information, check out http://www.adobe.com/aboutadobe/pressroom/pressreleases/200904/042009FlashDigitalHome.html.

Figure 6-4. Chumby's Internet Appliance features a control panel that is Flash Lite based.

One example of a consumer electronics company taking advantage of Flash Lite is Chumby Industries. The Chumby Internet appliance and Platform which they make leverages a Flash Lite UI (see Figure 6-4). It also supports Flash Lite–based widget content, which we covered in Chapter 5.

User interfaces in Flash Lite applications

You'll recall that in Chapter 2 we discussed how using a class-based approach to developing Flash Lite 2.x and 3.x applications requires special attention to CPU and memory requirements for devices.

Fortunately, there are several third-party Flash Lite developer community projects that can help build UIs more quickly by offering reusable components and easy-to-use, lightweight ActionScript development frameworks.

Creating Flash Lite user interfaces with components and frameworks

In this section, we will introduce you to several freely available UI component sets used in the Flash Lite developer community that are Flash Lite 2.x/3.x based, as well as some that are compatible with Flash Lite 1.1.

> All of the Flash Lite UI interface components and frameworks covered in this chapter are noncommercial products as of this writing. They are available for use under certain open source licensing agreements.
>
> Feather Framework is GPL, which encourages changes and sharing of code. More information about GPL can be found at http://opensource.blocketpc.com/en/license.html.
>
> Shuriken is under the MIT License, which allows for reuse within proprietary software as long as the original license remains intact upon distribution. For further information about the MIT License, please refer to http://en.wikipedia.org/wiki/MIT_License.
>
> You should check source licenses before using any of the components and frameworks mentioned in this chapter for your Flash Lite projects.

Flash Lite Feather Framework

QInteractiva (a Flash Lite and mobile development company based out of Spain) has two evolving open source projects that developers can use to help address the challenges of low memory and restricted CPU performance found on many devices supporting Flash Lite.

The projects are distributed through the BlocketPC site at http://www.blocketpc.com (if you recall, we mentioned this Flash Lite community user group back in Chapter 2). The two projects are

- **Feather Framework**: This is an optimized framework for developing class-based applications with Flash Lite. The framework consists of approximately 23 ActionScript classes, and a few open source projects that have been added, including the ASAP Framework (only classes that are not "hard" on the CPU and memory), TweenLite (a lightweight animation library for Flash), and QueueLoader (a simple class to load images in Flash Lite to avoid the limit of URL load requests per frame in Flash Lite).

- **LayoutManager**: This allows Flash content to fit different screen sizes, and also responds to screen orientation changes on devices (e.g., a user flips a phone from portrait to landscape viewing). LayoutManager allows for nine different registration points to align MovieClips in what are referred to as "virtual layers." It supports absolute or relative values, and can even respond to change the screen size and orientation, such as portrait, landscape, landscape right-handed, or landscape left-handed (helpful for those "lefties" out there).

Both of these projects can be used to save time, and both offer code reusability across Flash Lite 2.x and 3.x applications.

> As of this writing, the Feather Framework is currently in version 0.4.7 and is considered a work in progress. We recommend that developers keep this in mind, as it works to establish a 1.0 status in the Flash community.

Downloading and exploring the Feather Framework

Getting started with Feather Framework is straightforward for those with ActionScript 2.0 experience and familiarity with class-based development (see Chapter 2 for resources on ActionScript 2.0 development).

First, the Feather Framework (featherframework_0_4_7.rar) must be downloaded from the community site: http://opensource.blocketpc.com/en/featherframework/index.html. Once you've downloaded the archive file (currently a .rar file), you must extract the archive using an unrar tool (we recommend www.rarsoft.com, or www.winzip.com for Windows users).

Inside the archive are several directories (see Figure 6-5) that make up the Feather Framework:

Name	Date modified	Type	Size
components.fla	4/28/2009 11:44 ...	Flash Document	512 KB
changelog.txt	4/4/2009 5:46 PM	Text Document	2 KB
license.txt	1/13/2009 12:01 ...	Text Document	2 KB
gs	4/28/2009 11:44 ...	File Folder	
org	4/28/2009 11:44 ...	File Folder	
de	4/28/2009 11:44 ...	File Folder	
com	4/28/2009 11:44 ...	File Folder	

Figure 6-5. Top-level directory for the Feather Framework

Figure 6-6. Feather
FrameworkUI elements

- /components.fla: Contains UI element "skins" that can be reused in Flash Lite applications you build using the Feather Framework (see Figure 6-6). After opening the components.fla inside Flash CS3 or Flash CS4, refer to the Flash Library where they are stored (Ctrl+L on Windows or Option+L on Mac).

- /changelog.txt: Be sure to read the changes, since by the time you read this book the framework may have been improved and/or changed.

- /license.txt: Explains the license agreement (currently open source GPL). Read this carefully before starting to use the Feather Framework in any production-quality work.

- /gs/TweenLite.as: The GreenSock TweenLite animation library (uses ActionScript 2.0). See http://blog.greensock.com/tweenliteas2/.

- /org/asapframework: A partial subset of the ASAP Framework (http://asapframework.org/) that only includes the required classes to help keep memory requirements low. The ASAP Framework is a collection of classes typically used to develop ActionScript 2.0–based web applications, but has been reused in the Feather Framework used in Flash Lite applications.

- /de/betriebsraum/loading/QueLoader.as: An ActionScript 2.0 class that allows images (and other media assets) to be loaded in queue fashion to avoid the URL request limit found in Flash Lite.

- /com/blocketpc/: Contains the components, controllers, managers, models, utilities, and views that make up the base of the Feather Framework. You'll get to see some of these classes in action, when we walk through the Litedays Flash Lite application built using the Feather Framework.

For further in-depth information about the Feather Framework, check out the official API at http://opensource.blocketpc.com/featherframework/doc/index.html.

Examining the Litedays demo application

In this section, you'll walk through one of the demo applications that BlocketPC distributes with the Feather Framework. This is the demo Flash Lite application called "Litedays," an event guide that was created for the Mobile World Congress Event held in Barcelona (the application is actually in Spanish).

> You'll note that the Litedays demo application uses Spanish keywords to describe some of the components of the framework. Given the number of regions that Flash Lite runs in (e.g., Japan and parts of Europe), you'll often come across code that incorporates non-English keywords. Here we'll translate from Spanish to English where necessary.

The Litedays application (see Figure 6-7) leverages much of the Feather Framework. It's ideal for breaking down some of the Feather components and shows how Flash Lite applications can be built using a Model, View, Controller (MVC) development approach with Flash Lite 2.x and 3.x.

Let's get started. First, download the Litedays application at http:// opensource.blocketpc.com/en/featherframework/ under the Downloads header. Extract the file demo_ff_01.zip using WinZip. Once extracted, note litedays.fla and the litedays folder, along with the Feather Framework files.

Open litedays.fla, and select frame 1 on the main timeline. Then view the ActionScript on frame 1, by selecting Windows ➤ Actions.

The code first imports the Application class and instantiates the Application class that is part of the Model of the MVC architecture of the Feather Framework.

Figure 6-7. Litedays Feather Framework demo application

```
import litedays.Application;
this.__proto__ = Application['prototype'];
var app = Application;
app.apply ( this, [] );
```

Next, examine the Litedays Flash Library (see Figure 6-8) and note that it contains many of the Feather Framework components. Select the various MovieClips in the Screens folder, and right-click to view the properties of each. You'll note that each is mapped to a Screen ActionScript 2.0 class (which we'll talk about next). You'll also note that some naming conventions are in Spanish. Not to worry; we'll translate the keywords where needed!

The Screens folder (/litedays/views) of the Litedays demo contains the MovieClips that make up the different screen views of the Litedays application: Evento ("Event"), Home, Inscripcion ("Messages"), Lugar ("Place"), and Talleres ("Workshops"). We'll discuss each of these screen views in a moment.

In viewing each of the screen views in the library, you can see Evento is the information page about the event (in Spanish), Home is the main menu of the event guide, Inscripcion is a screen that allows for SMS messages to be sent, Lugar is a page containing a map of the location of the event, and Talleres is a list interface that gets loaded with event information.

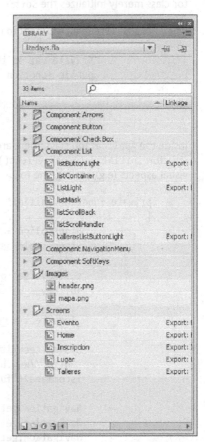

The litedays folder extracted from the demo_ff_01.zip (refer to Figure 6-8) contains the Feather Framework ActionScript classes that drive the application. Application.as contains the code that acts as the main application controller for the demo application. As this is the base of the application, let's walk through each section of the Application.as code base.

Figure 6-8. Flash Library assets for the Litedays Feather demo application

Open Application.as in the Flash IDE or a code editor. As you step through the source, we'll discuss the pieces of the Feather Framework and how they are being leveraged in the sample application.

First, the base ActionScript 2.0 classes of the Feather Framework must be imported into the Flash Lite application:

```
/**
 * @author Administrador
 */
import com.blocketpc.managers.KeyManager;
import org.asapframework.util.ObjectUtils;
import com.blocketpc.managers.AbstractManager;
import com.blocketpc.components.SoftKeysLight;
import com.blocketpc.managers.Navigation;
import com.blocketpc.view.AbstractView;
```

Next, the Application class extends the AbstractView class of the Feather Framework. The constructor class merely initializes the softKeys class that is part of the Feather Framework.

```
class litedays.Application extends AbstractView
{
        private var softKeys:SoftKeysLight;
        public function Application()
        {
                softKeys._visible = false;
        }
}
```

Inside the Application class, there are three methods of interest, in addition to the Application constructor: initialize(), onKeyPress(), and onChangeScreen(). The initialize() method sets up the visual aspects (e.g., scaling, the focus rectangle, full-screen mode), as well as navigation.

```
private function initialize():Void
{
        Stage.align = "TL";
        Stage.scaleMode = "noScale";

        softKeys.setSoftKeys(null, "Salir");
        softKeys._visible = true;

        _focusrect = _global.useFocusRect == false;

        System.security.loadPolicyFile(
          "http://www.blocketpc.com/crossdomain.xml");
        fscommand2("fullscreen", "true");

        Navigation.getInstance().initialize(this);
        Navigation.getInstance().currentScreen = "Home"; ➡
        Navigation.getInstance().addEventListener(➡
        Navigation.ON_CHANGE_SCREEN,
        this, "onChangeScreen");
```

```
            KeyManager.getInstance().addEventListener( ➡
            KeyManager.ON_PRESS_KEY, ➡
            this,   "onPressKey");
    }
```

Let's investigate each of these areas of initialization.

First, the stage size of the Flash Lite application is set so that it does not scale:

```
        Stage.align = "TL";
        Stage.scaleMode = "noScale";
```

It also uses the softKeys class (also part of the Feather Framework) to set the device keys that respond to the LSK (left soft key)—that is, the null value on the default Home screen when the application starts—and the RSK (right soft key) of the application (i.e., Quit), via the setSoftKeys() method of the softKeys class.

When starting up, the application blows up to full screen via the fscommand2, and focusrect is turned off:

```
        fscommand2("fullscreen", "true");
        _focusrect = _global.useFocusRect == false;
```

The application security policy is also modified via the System.security.loadPolicyFile call (which allows external data loading calls):

```
        System.security.loadPolicyFile( ➡
        "http://www.blocketpc.com/crossdomain.xml");
```

The Feather Navigation class is instantiated next, and that object is used to manage all the screen views of the Litedays application. Home is set to the default MovieClip screen view to load on application launch:

```
        Navigation.getInstance().initialize(this);
        Navigation.getInstance().currentScreen = "Home"; ➡
        Navigation.getInstance().addEventListener( ➡
        Navigation.ON_CHANGE_SCREEN, this,
          "onChangeScreen");
```

The KeyManager class that is part of the Feather Framework is used to catch all ongoing key press navigation for the Litedays application:

```
        KeyManager.getInstance().addEventListener(
        KeyManager.ON_PRESS_KEY, this,
          "onPressKey");
```

The onKeyPress() takes care of the right soft key on the Home page (i.e., ExtendedKey.SOFT2), and exits out of the application if it is pressed:

```
        private function onPressKey(evt:Object):Void
        {
                switch (evt.key)
```

```
        {
                case ExtendedKey.SOFT2:
                    fscommand2("Quit");
                    break;
        }
    }
```

Inside the onChangeScreen(), depending on the current screen selected, the softKeys are updated for the application ("Salir" means quit, and "Inicio" means back):

```
    private function onChangeScreen(evt:Object):Void
    {
            switch (Navigation.getInstance().currentScreen)
            {
                    case "Home":
                        softKeys.setSoftKeys(null, "Salir");
                            break;
                    default:
                        softKeys.setSoftKeys("Inicio", "Salir");
                            break;
            }
    }
```

Once the application is started, each of the screen views will be loaded, depending on the navigation buttons pressed. Inside the /litedays/view/ directory are the individual application screens used for the Litedays application (see Figure 6-9):

- Home.as: The initial Home screen with a main menu for the Litedays event
- Evento.as: A description of the event in a scrollable text box
- Inscripcion.as: A screen that allows an SMS message to be constructed and sent
- Lugar.as: A map of the location of the event
- Talleres.as: A scrollable listing of the Litedays agenda through the event
- TalleresListButton.as: A button that allows users to get more information on a particular time slot during the Litedays event

Name ▲	Date taken	Tags	Size
Evento.as			1 KB
Home.as			2 KB
Inscripcion.as			2 KB
Lugar.as			1 KB
Talleres.as			3 KB
TalleresListButtonLight.as			1 KB

Figure 6-9. ActionScript 2.0 screen view classes for the Litedays Feather demo application

Let's examine each of these ActionScript class files, as well as the code they contain to drive each of the Litedays screen views.

Open the Home.as class file located in the /litedays/view/ directory, and note the Feather Framework code used.

First, the Feather class files used are imported, which include Navigation, Abstract Manager, and KeyManager. The AbstractView and also the Feather lightweight ButtonLight class are imported for use:

```
/**
 * @author Administrador
 */

import org.asapframework.events.EventDelegate;
import com.blocketpc.components.ButtonLight;
import com.blocketpc.managers.Navigation;
import com.blocketpc.managers.AbstractManager;
import com.blocketpc.managers.KeyManager;
import com.blocketpc.view.AbstractView;
```

The Home screen is extended from the Feather AbstractView screen class:

```
class litedays.view.Home extends AbstractView
```

For this screen, several buttons are used to navigate the application on key presses:

```
private var evento:ButtonLight;
private var talleres:ButtonLight;
private var lugar:ButtonLight;
private var inscripcion:ButtonLight;
```

The constructor for the Home screen is initially set up to make the screen invisible by setting alpha to 0 (later it will become visible):

```
public function Home()
{
        this._alpha = 0;
}
```

The initialize() method sets the titles of the screen buttons. Each button is assigned an event that sends the appropriate button label name to the onPressButton() method in this screen view (e.g., evento.onPress() makes a call to onPressButton() passing the Evento label name). The open() command makes the Home screen view visible to the end user:

```
private function initialize():Void
{
        evento.title = "Evento";
        talleres.title = "Talleres";
        lugar.title = "Lugar";
        inscripcion.title = "Inscripcion";
```

```
        evento.onPress = EventDelegate.create( ⟼
        this, onPressButton, "Evento");

        talleres.onPress = EventDelegate.create( ⟼
        this, onPressButton, "Talleres");

        lugar.onPress = EventDelegate.create( ⟼
        this, onPressButton, "Lugar");

        inscripcion.onPress = EventDelegate.create( ⟼
        this, onPressButton, "Inscripcion");

        open();
}
```

The onPressButton() method makes a call to the changeToScreen() method that exists in the Application object instantiated from the main timeline of the Litedays application, passing in the name of the button label (e.g., "Evento"):

```
private function onPressButton(section:String):Void
{
        changeToScreen = section;
        close();
}

private function onClose():Void
{
        Navigation.getInstance().currentScreen = changeToScreen;
}
```

For the Evento screen view, the demo application just loads and displays scrollable text about the Litedays event. Open the Evento.as class file located in the /litedays/views/ directory.

First, the Feather Framework classes are imported for use. This includes Navigation and AbstractManager, as well as the KeyManager:

```
/**
 * @author Administrador
 */

import com.blocketpc.managers.Navigation;
import com.blocketpc.managers.AbstractManager;
import com.blocketpc.managers.KeyManager;
import com.blocketpc.view.AbstractView;
```

The AbstractView class is used to extend the Evento screen view:

```
class litedays.view.Evento extends AbstractView
```

In the constructor, Evento(), alpha is initially set to 0, so that the screen will fade in:

```
public function Evento()
{
        this._alpha = 0;
}
```

The initialize() method sets up the KeyManager to listen for any device key presses, and if they are detected it will make a call to the onPressKey() event in the Evento screen view. By default, when a user selects the Evento screen from the Home screen, the open() method is automatically called from the initialize() method:

```
private function initialize():Void
{
        KeyManager.getInstance().addEventListener( ➡
        KeyManager.ON_PRESS_KEY, this, ➡
        "onPressKey");

        open();
}
```

The onPressKey() event handler within the Evento screen view merely checks for an LSK press. When detected, it makes a call to changeToScreen(), which updates the screen view back to the main Home screen and removes the event listener for the key press as well, using the removeEventListener() method on the KeyManager class:

```
private function onPressKey(evt:Object):Void
{
        switch (evt.key)
         {
                case ExtendedKey.SOFT1:
                        KeyManager.getInstance().removeEventListener( ➡
                        KeyManager.ON_PRESS_KEY, ➡
                        this, "onPressKey");
                        changeToScreen = "Home";
                        close();
                        break;
         }
}
```

The onClose() method detects when the close() command has been issued from the onPressKey() method, and switches the view back to the Home screen of the Litedays application:

```
private function onClose():Void
{
        Navigation.getInstance().currentScreen = changeToScreen;
}
```

Inscripcion.as defines the screen view that sends an SMS to a user given the phone number and other user information. Open Inscripcion.as, and as you'll see, first the common Feather class files are imported:

```
/**
 * @author Administrador
 */
import com.blocketpc.components.ButtonLight;
import org.asapframework.events.EventDelegate;
import com.blocketpc.managers.Navigation;
import com.blocketpc.managers.AbstractManager;
import com.blocketpc.managers.KeyManager;
import com.blocketpc.view.AbstractView;
```

Next, the Inscripcion screen view is extended from the AbstractView class:

```
class litedays.view.Inscripcion extends AbstractView
```

Input text fields are added and a send button is defined; these are used later on the screen to send off the SMS to a defined user:

```
private var loader:LoadVars;
private var nombre_txt:TextField;
private var apellidos_txt:TextField;
private var correo_txt:TextField;
private var result_txt:TextField;
private var send:ButtonLight;
```

The constructor class, Inscripcion(), initializes the loader class, which is used to send off the SMS message (you'll see this in a bit). It also does some setup of text fields on the screen, by setting the _focusrect:

```
public function Inscripcion()
{
        loader = new LoadVars();
        this._alpha = 0;
        nombre_txt._focusrect = true;
        apellidos_txt._focusrect = true;
        correo_txt._focusrect = true;
}
```

The initialize() function sets the send button label to enviar ("send" in Spanish). The send button is set to call the sendForm() method when clicked. The open() command opens the screen view when the screen is loaded:

```
private function initialize():Void
{
        KeyManager.getInstance().addEventListener( ➥
        KeyManager.ON_PRESS_KEY, this, ➥
          "onPressKey");

        send.title = "enviar";
        send.onPress = EventDelegate.create(this, sendForm);
        open();
}
```

The sendForm() method loads up the user input text fields, which include nombre (first name), apellidos (surname(s)), and correo (e-mail address). An additional field, called antispam, is for spam checks on the server end of things.

The loader.sendAndLoad() makes a call to a PHP script called sendform_complete.php, which takes in the query string values sent via the loader object. When the script has been executed and the sendAndLoad detects data, it makes a call off the onLoadData():

```
private function sendForm():Void
{
        loader.antispam = "blocketpc";
        loader.nombre = nombre_txt.text;
        loader.apellidos = apellidos_txt.text;
        loader.correo = correo_txt.text;

        loader.sendAndLoad(
        "http://www.blocketpc.com/litedays/php/ ➥
        sendform_complete.php",
        loader, "POST");
        loader.onLoad = EventDelegate.create(this, onLoadData);
        result_txt.text = "enviando...";
}
```

The onLoadData() call merely sets the result text field on the screen with mail enviado (mail sent):

```
private function onLoadData():Void
{
        result_txt.text = "mail enviado";
}
```

The onPressKey() method for this screen view takes care of sending a user back to the Home screen of the Litedays application via the close() method. Before doing that, the Inscripcion view removes the key press event handler and closes the current screen.

```
private function onPressKey(evt:Object):Void
{
        switch (evt.key)
        {
        case ExtendedKey.SOFT1:
                KeyManager.getInstance().removeEventListener( ➥
                KeyManager.ON_PRESS_KEY, ➥
                this, "onPressKey");
                changeToScreen = "Home";
                close();
                break;
        }
}
```

The changeToScreen value is used to update the Navigation class with the current screen that should be loaded:

```
        private function onClose():Void
        {
                Navigation.getInstance().currentScreen = changeToScreen;
        }
```

Lugar.as is the map screen ("lugar" means "place" in Spanish). For this particular demo app, all the screen does is open and close with an image of the Litedays location from Google Maps.

Open Lugar.as. As before, with the Lugar screen view, it first imports the Feather Framework classes:

```
/**
 * @author Administrador
 */
import com.blocketpc.managers.Navigation;
import com.blocketpc.managers.AbstractManager;
import com.blocketpc.managers.KeyManager;
import com.blocketpc.view.AbstractView;
```

The Lugar class extends the AbstractView class:

```
class litedays.view.Lugar extends AbstractView
```

The constructor sets up the screen to fade in by setting the screen to be hidden at first:

```
        public function Lugar()
        {
                this._alpha = 0;
        }
```

The initialize() method listens for any device key presses, and if detected, will make a call to the onPressKey() method in the screen view. The open() call makes the Lugar screen fade in:

```
        private function initialize():Void
        {
                KeyManager.getInstance().addEventListener( ➥
                KeyManager.ON_PRESS_KEY, ➥
                this, "onPressKey");
                open();
        }
```

The onPressKey() function for this screen view simply detects an LSK press, and then switches the view back to the main Home screen view. The onClose() event is called from the close() call when the soft key is pressed:

```
        private function onPressKey(evt:Object):Void
        {
                switch (evt.key)
                {
                        case ExtendedKey.SOFT1:
                                KeyManager.getInstance() ➥
                                .removeEventListener( ➥
```

```
                    KeyManager.ON_PRESS_KEY, this, ➡
                    "onPressKey");
                    changeToScreen = "Home";
                    close();
                    break;
            }
        }

        private function onClose():Void
        {
                    Navigation.getInstance().currentScreen = ➡
                    changeToScreen;
        }
    }
```

The Talleres.as class ("talleres" means "workshops" in Spanish) creates a scrollable list of loaded data items, and allows the user to view workshops that happened at the Litedays event at Mobile World Congress.

Open Talleres.as. This is the last screen view of the Litedays demo application. Let's take a look.

First, the Feather Framework classes are imported:

```
/**
 * @author Administrador
 */

import org.asapframework.util.ObjectUtils;
import org.asapframework.events.EventDelegate;
import com.blocketpc.utils.JSON;
import com.blocketpc.components.ListLight;
import com.blocketpc.managers.Navigation;
import com.blocketpc.managers.AbstractManager;
import com.blocketpc.managers.KeyManager;
import com.blocketpc.view.AbstractView
```

This includes a utils.JSON ActionScript class for loading in externally located data (i.e., "the workshop data"). In addition, ListLight, a lightweight scrollable list control, is used to store the workshop entries after loading them via a LoadVars command.

Next, the Talleres screen view class is extended by the AbstractView class:

```
class litedays.view.Talleres extends AbstractView
```

There are two properties of the Talleres screen view. List is a ListLight visual component, and the dataLoader is a LoadVars object (for loading in the actual workshop data from a remote URL):

```
private var list:ListLight;
private var dataLoader:LoadVars;
```

The constructor of the Talleres class is initialized at alpha of 0, so it can fade in when a user clicks the Talleres button from the Home screen view:

```
public function Talleres()
{
        this._alpha = 0;
}
```

The intialize() method sets up the dataLoader object, and makes a call to load in the workshop data via from the URL that points to the talleres.txt query string-delimited file. Once the external file is loaded, a call to onLoadData() is made:

```
private function initialize():Void
{
        KeyManager.getInstance().addEventListener( ➡
        KeyManager.ON_PRESS_KEY, this, "onPressKey");
        dataLoader = new LoadVars();
        dataLoader.onLoad = EventDelegate.create(this, onLoadData);
        dataLoader.load( ➡
         "http://www.blocketpc.com/litedays/json/talleres.txt");
}
```

The onLoadData() method takes the returned data from the talleres.txt file (in name/value query string pairs), parses the data out, and stores it in the tObj object. That object populates the list Feather component that is part of the Talleres screen.

When loaded properly, the list of workshops stored in the list Feather component contains information about the time, title, and speaker of each workshop:

```
private function onLoadData():Void
{
        var oResult:Object;
        var temp_array:Array = new Array();
        var json:JSON = new JSON();

      · var jsonStr:String = dataLoader.toString();
        jsonStr =➡
        unescape(jsonStr.split("=&onLoad=[type Function]")[0]);

        try
        {
        oResult = json.parse(jsonStr);
                for (var i=0; i<oResult.talleres.length; i++)
                {
                var tObj:Object = new Object();
                tObj.hour = oResult.talleres[i].hora;
                tObj.title = oResult.talleres[i].titulo;
                tObj.autor = oResult.talleres[i].autor;
                temp_array.push(tObj);
                }
```

```
        }
        catch(ex)
        {
                trace(ex.name + ":" + ex.message + ":" + ex.at + ➥
                ":" + ex.text);
        }

        dataLoader = null;
        list.listButtonRender = "talleresListButtonLight";
        list.initialize(temp_array);
        list.setSize(235, 220);
        open();
}
```

As previously discussed, the onPressKey() event brings the user back to the Home screen when the LSK is pressed by calling the close() method. The other device keys, such as Up and Device, are reserved for navigating through the list component used in this screen view:

```
private function onPressKey(evt:Object):Void
{
        switch (evt.key)
        {
        case ExtendedKey.SOFT1:
                KeyManager.getInstance().removeEventListener( ➥
                KeyManager.ON_PRESS_KEY, this, "onPressKey");
                changeToScreen = "Home";
                close();
                break;
        }
}

private function onClose():Void
{
        Navigation.getInstance().currentScreen = changeToScreen;
}
```

The TalleresListButtonLight.as class is used to set the properties of the ListButtonLight visual component. It sets the workshop title_txt, hour_txt, and autor_txt (i.e., "speaker name") text fields in the application through the set data ActionScript setter command. The ListButtonLight component is one of several in the Feather Framework that are useful for displaying data.

```
/**
 * @author Administrador
 */
import com.blocketpc.components.ListButtonLight;
class litedays.view.TalleresListButtonLight extends ListButtonLight
{
        private var hour_txt:TextField;
        private var autor_txt:TextField;
```

```
        public function TalleresListButtonLight()
        {
                super();
        }

        public function set data(obj:Object):Void
        {
                _data = obj;
                hour_txt.text = data.hour;
                title_txt.text = data.title;
                autor_txt.text = data.autor;
        }

        public function get data():Object
        {
                return _data;
        }
}
```

You can give the Litedays application a try by compiling the litedays.fla and moving the litedays.swf to a device supporting Flash Lite 2.x or 3.x (such as a Nokia S60 device).

> *Since this application utilizes device keys, make sure that the target device supports keys for up, down, left, and right, and that it also has support for soft key buttons (left and right soft keys).*

With the Feather Framework, Flash Lite 2.x and 3.x applications such as Litedays can be created in less time due to code reuse. If you are interested in further examples of working with the Feather Framework, visit the developer community page at: http://opensource.blocketpc.com/en/feather-framework. Although Feather has yet to reach version 1.0 status at the time of this writing, you can use it to prototype Flash Lite applications and build Flash Lite 2.x and 3.x applications more quickly.

Downloading and exploring Feather user interface components

Examples of the Feather UI components can be found under the Downloads section at http://opensource.blocketpc.com/en/featherframework. The NavigationMenuLight link points to the demo_ff_02.rar download that contains the examples.

Once extracted, the following examples are contained in the navigation menu folder (see Figure 6-10, from left to right):

- hNav.fla: A horizontal navigation menu
- listNav.fla: A scrollable list of items
- rNav.fla: A partial carousel navigation menu
- vNav.fla: A vertical menu

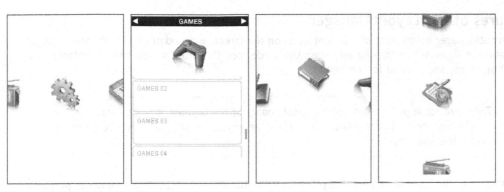

Figure 6-10. Navigation UIs with Feather Framework

All of these sample components utilize the components featured in the components.fla of the Feather Framework (refer back to Figure 6-5).

If you open hNav.fla in the Flash IDE and look at frame 1 on the main timeline, the code to initialize the navigation menu looks like this:

```
navigation.gap = 120;
navigation.initialize(
    ["calendar", "camera", "contacts",
    "explorer", "games", "messages",
    "music", "notes", "radio",
    "settings"]);
```

The Flash Library contains all the assets for navigation, including a MovieClips folder that has each of the icons in the horizontal navigation.

On the main timeline is the NavigationMenuLight component (an empty MovieClip), which maps back to the navigation instance name on frame 1.

The other examples provided in the ff_demo_02.rar file demonstrate the other components in the Feather Framework (components.fla).

Flash Lite BlocketPC LayoutManager

In addition to the Feather Framework, BlocketPC also offers an ActionScript 2.0–based LayoutManager for addressing different target screen sizes and orientations (e.g., landscape vs. portrait) that crop up when you're developing Flash Lite content on mobile devices.

The BlocketPC LayoutManager is a framework system that allows developers to place items on an available screen area, and then send notifications when the available area changes, due to either size or orientation changes. The end result is a Flash Lite application that can run across many target screen sizes and screen orientations.

Features of the LayoutManager

The LayoutManager keeps track of different items on the screen and updates them whenever size or orientation changes. When working with Flash Lite on devices, this often means portrait or landscape for right handed, and portrait for left handed.

> *There are some great visuals of the functionality of the LayoutManager, located at http://opensource.blocketpc.com/en/layoutmanager/ under the* Screenshots *section of the support page.*

LayoutManager allows Flash assets to be placed on absolute or relative positions (either in pixels or percentage values). It currently offers nine registration points from which items will take coordinates. The LayoutManager can be added to projects without heavy integration into existing Flash Lite applications, since it is ActionScript 2.0 class based.

The LayoutManager system consists of six ActionScript 2.0 classes that make up the LayoutManager ActionScript package. Three classes are used for internal management purposes only: LayoutPosition, LayoutOrientation, and LayoutType. Developers work with the remaining three classes—LayoutManager, LayoutLayer, and LayoutItem—in their Flash Lite 2.x and 3.x applications.

Exploring the LayoutManager demos

In the Downloads and Demos area of the LayoutManager support page are four use cases for the LayoutManager (see Figure 6-11). All four of these examples can be downloaded from http://opensource.blocketpc.com/en/layoutmanager/.

The four examples utilizing the LayoutManager are

- **Basic usage**: demo01.rar
- **Headers, contents, and footers**: demo02.rar
- **Table menu with nine options**: demo03.rar
- **Table menu with five options, soft keys, and controls to change the orientation**: demo04.rar

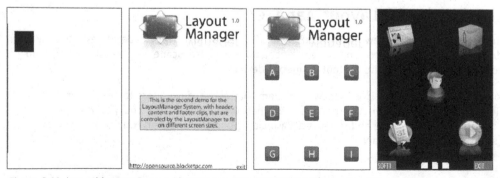

Figure 6-11. LayoutManager Demos (demo01.rar, demo02.rar, demo03.rar, demo04.rar)

Exploring the LayoutManager demo01.rar example

Download demo01.rar and extract its contents. Under the source directory, locate the demo01.fla source file, and open it in the Flash IDE. This example shows how to set up layers and align MovieClips using the LayoutManager.

On the first frame of the main timeline, note the ActionScript. First, the LayoutManager classes are imported that deal with position, orientation, and type of layout:

```
import com.blocketpc.managers.layoutmanager.LayoutManager;
import com.blocketpc.managers.layoutmanager.LayoutType;
import com.blocketpc.managers.layoutmanager.LayoutPosition;
import com.blocketpc.managers.layoutmanager.LayoutOrientation;
```

Next, the screen is set to full-screen mode, and the stage scaling and alignment are set to the defaults. The focus rectangle is also turned off.

```
var status:Number = fscommand2("FullScreen",true);

Stage.scaleMode = "noScale";
Stage.align = "TL";
_focusrect = false;
```

The remaining code checks to see if full-screen mode is supported, and if so, it instantiates the LayoutManager class in the layout variable. From there, a new demoLayer is created and aligned, and its size is set to 100px×100px on the screen. Its position is also set to 0,0 in the X and Y coordinates.

On the main stage area of Flash, note the clip_mc MovieClip. This maps to the MovieClip Test LauoutManager MovieClip in the Flash Library.

The addItem call on the layout applies the layout to clip_mc . Given all the parameters, the final layout is shown in Figure 6-12.

```
if (status != 0)
{
        trace("FullScreen Mode not supported.");
}
else
{
        var layout:LayoutManager = new LayoutManager(this,1);

        layout.createLayer("demoLayer");
        layout.setLayerAlignment("demoLayer", LayoutPosition.MC);
        layout.setLayerSize("demoLayer", LayoutType.ABSOLUTE, ➥
        LayoutType.ABSOLUTE, 100, 100);
        layout.setLayerPosition("demoLayer", LayoutType.ABSOLUTE, ➥
        LayoutType.ABSOLUTE, 0, 0);
        layout.addItem("demoLayer", "demoClip", clip_mc, ➥
        LayoutType.ABSOLUTE, LayoutType.ABSOLUTE, ➥
        LayoutPosition.MC, 0, 0 ,0 ,0, true);
}
```

Figure 6-12. The basic LayoutManager demo (demo01.rar) with its layout configured

Further documentation on how to use the LayoutManager, including the full API, is provided at http://opensource.blocketpc.com/layoutmanager/doc/index.html.

The next component framework for Flash Lite is another developer community contribution; it's called "Shuriken."

Shuriken Flash Lite 2.x component framework

Shuriken is an open source component framework for Flash Lite 2.x. It is currently a developer community-driven project attempting to provide a reusable framework for Flash Lite.

> "Shuriken" (which means "sword hidden in hand" in Japanese) is an ancient concealed weapon used in throwing, stabbing, and slashing enemies. A lot of westerners refer to them as "throwing stars" (apparently, not totally accurate). More info is available for those who are interested in ancient culture and weaponry at http://en.wikipedia.org/wiki/Shuriken.

Shuriken was created because of the lack of Flash Lite 2.x components specifically designed and developed for mobile and device development, where both RAM and CPU are precious resources. It is designed to run on the Flash 8 (or lower) runtime, making it ideal for Flash Lite 2.x and Flash Lite 3.x devices.

Shuriken can be used for developing on devices such as the Chumby, mobile phones, set-top boxes, and game consoles such as the Wii, PSP, or PlayStation 3, which run older versions of Flash (e.g., PSP runs a Flash Player 6).

The overall goal of Shuriken are to provide a working set of Flash Lite components across the lowest common denominator devices. These components are easy to extend, and provide a basic set of visual UI components for developers.

Shuriken was originally released to be used with Flash Lite 2.x, and is compatible with Flayer Player 7 and ActionScript 2.0. Shuriken components have not been updated to take specific advantage of the Flash Lite 3.x player features (e.g., the way it improves upon memory usage and performance enhancements, which we talked about in Chapter 3). However, Flash Lite applications using Shuriken can be run within the Flash Lite 3.x player, since it is an ActionScript 2.0–based component framework.

> *As of this writing, Shuriken components have not been updated since the release of Flash Lite 2.x. For this reason, we will not cover Shuriken in depth in this chapter, other than offering an overview of the component framework and telling you where you can go for more information.*
>
> *However, this is not to say that Shuriken is completely obsolete. This framework still can be used for legacy Flash Lite 2.x platforms where there is sufficient memory and CPU that can be leveraged (such as Chumby).*
>
> *With further awareness and contributions from developers, the Shuriken project could become valuable to developers in the future with Flash Lite 3.x non-PC device platforms, given its open source licensing.*

Currently, Shuriken components can be used in the Flash IDE. The ActionScript 2.0–based code base for Shuriken is supported in the Flash IDE, and movie clips and skins can be applied to component assets within the framework.

As of this writing, Shuriken is an open source MIT License allowing developers to contribute to it and use it within projects.

Downloading and installing Shuriken

The current components are on a Google code repository and can be downloaded at http://code. google.com/p/shurikencomponents/.

To obtain the latest Shuriken components, developers must check out the source code from the Google Code Subversion repository where it resides.

The SVN command-line checkout URL for the Shuriken source code is

```
svn checkout http://shurikencomponents.googlecode.com/svn/trunk/ ➥
    shurikencomponents-read-only
```

There are also stand-alone, desktop IDE, and IDE plug-in Subversion clients available for source control at http://subversion.tigris.org/links.html#clients. Some of the software is open source; others are commercial products.

- **OS X**: Mac Versions is the authors' preferred version control client for most (Flash) developers. It can be downloaded at http://versionsapp.com/.
- **Windows**: TortoiseSVN is a recommended source manager client (actually, it's a Windows file extension to be exact). It can be downloaded from SourceForge at http://sourceforge.net/ projects/tortoisesvn/.

To check out the Shuriken tools using a visual client, simply provide the SVN URL to the source code repository (http://shurikencomponents.googlecode.com/svn/trunk/) and check out Shuriken (see Figure 6-13).

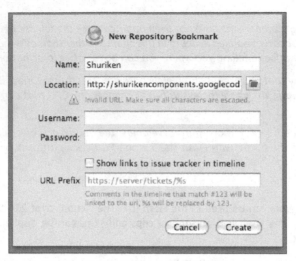

Figure 6-13. Configuring versions with the Shuriken URL to the source code

Exploring the Shuriken components

Once Shuriken has been checked out of the Google repository, it can be integrated into Flash Lite development projects. It consists of a reusable ActionScript 2.0 framework as well as several lightweight components.

The main trunk of the repository contains the following directories (see Figure 6-14):

- /classes/: Contains the Shuriken ActionScript 2.0 framework classes
- /deploy/: Contains the component_examples.zip and shuriken_f8_examples.zip files, which have the visual components Shuriken offers
- /docs/: The official documentation for Shuriken and its API
- /examples/: Contains the sample Flash Lite applications built with Shuriken (Google_Calendar.zip and 360FlexLite.zip), as well as the existing component set example files
- /jsfl/: Contains JFSL scripts that are installed into the Flash CS3 or CS4 IDE by running the Shuriken Tools.mxp file

Examples of all the available components can be found in the shuriken_f8_examples_v3.zip file. Once the zip is extracted, there are two folders:

- /classes/jxl/shuriken/: Contains all the Shuriken framework ActionScript 2.0 class files.
- /flas/examples/: Contains examples of the Shuriken visual UI components (e.g., Button.fla, List.fla, CheckBox.fla, and more).

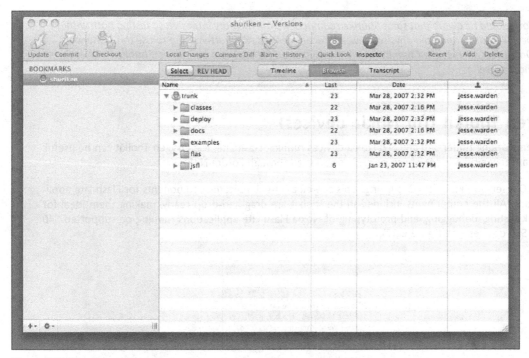

Figure 6-14. Shuriken source code trunk

Documentation for extending Shuriken components can be found at http://code.google.com/p/ shurikencomponents/wiki/Documentation.

In the additional "featured downloads," 360FlexLite.zip (a mobile conference guide) and Google_ Calendar.zip (an application that manages a Google Calendar) are provided as examples of using the Shuriken component set with Flash Lite 2.x applications (see Figures 6-15 and 6-16). These can be downloaded at http://code.google.com/p/shurikencomponents/downloads/list.

Figure 6-15. Shuriken example (360FlexLite mobile guide)

Figure 6-16. Another Shuriken example (Google Calendar application)

> *You should be aware that some Shuriken components are memory intensive, so testing both within Device Central and on a physical device is recommended when attempting to use this framework. On devices such as the Chumby, where memory and CPU are more abundant, Shuriken makes the most sense.*

Oxygen Toolkit (for Nokia devices)

When working under S40 and S60 Nokia devices running Flash Lite, the Oxygen Toolkit can be useful. It is a freely available set of components distributed through Forum Nokia.

The Oxygen Toolkit offers debugging tools as well as visual indicator components for Flash Lite applications. All the components included in the toolkit are drag-and-drop ready, making them ideal for quick testing, debugging, and prototyping of Nokia Flash Lite applications running on supported S40 and S60 devices (see Figure 6-17).

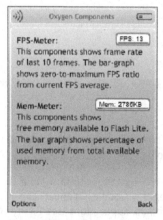

Figure 6-17. Oxygen components

As of this writing, the current version is 1.0. The toolkit is compatible with both Flash Lite 2.x and 3.x, as well as Flash Lite 1.1.

> *Although these components are distributed on Forum Nokia, they may be used for any devices running Flash Lite on other device platforms (such as Sony Ericsson and Windows Mobile). They are not Nokia specific.*

The current Oxygen Toolkit set offers a few components that Flash Lite developers can take advantage of. Let's explore each of them.

Exploring the Oxygen components

Oxygen components currently consist of the following reusable visual indicators:

- **FPS Meter**: A visual component (see Figure 6-18) that can be added to a Flash Lite application to provide a visual indicator of the frames per second (fps) of the last 10 frames currently being displayed in a Flash Lite application.

  The FPS Meter component can help gauge a mobile application's performance (e.g., animation playback and SWF rendering) when testing on a physical device. This component can also help verify the performance statistics that are simulated in Device Central CS4 when testing emulated SWF content.

  As of this writing, this specific component is version 3.0. The component can be used to indentify performance bottlenecks and is useful in optimizing Flash Lite content when it is tested on actual physical devices.

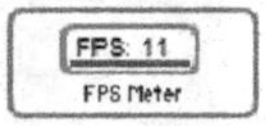

- **Memory Meter**: Displays the number of kilobytes a Flash Lite application is taking to run (see Figure 6-19) while running on a physical device. This component is useful for testing memory usage against the numbers given in Device Central CS4 for further verification that a Flash Lite application is behaving as it should on a physical target device.

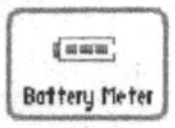

- **Battery Meter**: The Battery Meter visual component displays a battery level indicator, which is computed through the GetBatteryLevel and GetMaxBatteyLevel fscommand2 calls (see Figure 6-20).

- **Signal Meter**: The Signal Meter component displays the current signal strength level as indicated by the device, as reported back from Flash Lite via the fscommand2 GetSignalLevel and GetMaxSignalLevel calls (see Figure 6-21).

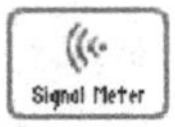

Figure 6-18.
Oxygen FPS Meter component

Figure 6-19.
Oxygen Memory Meter component

Figure 6-20.
Oxygen Battery Meter component

Figure 6-21.
Oxygen Signal Meter component

Downloading and installing the Oxygen Toolkit

The components can be downloaded from http://wiki.forum.nokia.com/index.php/Oxygen_-_ The_Flash_Lite_Developers_Kit. The download Oxygen Toolkit v1.zip contains full source code for all the components as well as an installation package.

The current Oxygen Toolkit consists of

- Oxygen Toolkit - Flash Lite 1.1.fla: The source code for the Flash Lite 1.1 version of the Oxygen components. These components are written using Flash 4 syntax. (We gave an overview of Flash Lite 1.1 features, capabilities, and functionality in Chapter 2.)

- Oxygen Toolkit - Flash Lite 2-3.fla: The source code of the Oxygen components that are compatible with Flash Lite 2.x and 3.x. The components are written using ActionScript 2.0.

- Oxygen Toolkit.MXI: The .MXI file is a configurable file used to create the MXP installable package that loads the Oxygen components into the Adobe Extension Manager, so they can be used within the Flash CS3 and CS4 authoring environment. The MXI is supplied so that custom installations can be created. By default, the MXP installs the Oxygen Toolkits for both Flash Lite 1.1. and 2.x/3.x.

- Oxygen Toolkit.mxp: The .MXP file is an Adobe extension that allows the Oxygen components to be installed within the Flash CS3 or CS4 authoring IDE.

Installing the Oxygen Toolkit components is as easy as double-clicking on the .MXP file. If Adobe Flash CS3 or Flash CS4 is installed, the Adobe Extension Manager will launch and asks if the Oxygen components should be installed (see Figure 6-22).

269

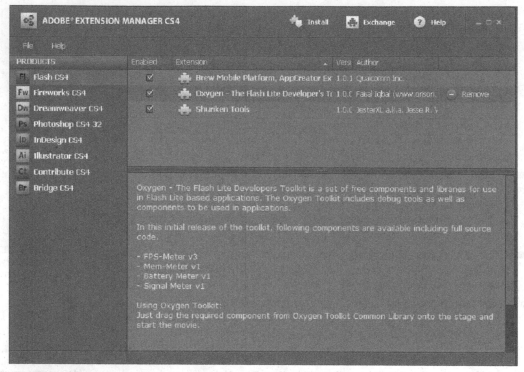

Figure 6-22. Adobe Extension Manager with Oxygen components installed

Using the Oxygen components

Once the components are downloaded and installed, it is a simple step-by-step process to use them with a Flash Lite application:

1. Open Flash Lite CS3 or CS4, and choose to create a new Flash Lite application.

2. Navigate to Window ➤ Common Libraries.

3. Select either Flash Lite 1.1 (i.e., Oxygen Toolkit – Flash Lite 1.1) or 2.x/3.x components (i.e., Oxygen Toolkit – Flash Lite 2-3).

4. Drag and drop the required Flash Lite 1.1 or 2.x/3.x components from the Library window onto the Flash stage (see Figure 6-23).

Figure 6-23. The Oxygen components (Flash Lite 1.1 components and Flash Lite 2.x components)

Let's move on to our next set of UI components available to Flash Lite developers.

Nokia Flash Lite Indicator and List components

The Nokia Flash Lite Indicator and List components are provided for use with S40 and S60 devices supporting Flash Lite.

The components (currently) include the following:

- Device Battery Charge indicator (includes Network Generation)
- Signal Strength monitor
- Dynamic List component

All three components have accessible skin components in the Flash Library. The Signal Strength monitor and Device Battery Charge indicator components react to soft key placement and screen orientation change. The source for each of the components is provided so they may be tweaked.

> *As of this writing, the Nokia Flash Lite 2.x components are a bit memory intensive, requiring around 600KB for the Signal Strength monitor and Device Battery Charge indicator, and approximately 700-800KB for the Dynamic List component (depending on the data loaded). You should keep an eye on the available memory on any target device where you plan to use these components.*

Exploring the Nokia Flash Lite 2.x components

The Nokia Flash Lite 2.x components currently consist of Battery Charge and Signal Strength indicators (see Figure 6-24), and a Dynamic List UI (see Figure 6-25).

Figure 6-24. Dynamic List component

Figure 6-25. Battery charge and Signal Strength indicator components

Downloading and installing the Nokia Flash Lite 2.x components

The Flash Lite Nokia components for Flash Lite 2.x can be downloaded from Forum Nokia at the following URL:

```
http://www.forum.nokia.com/info/sw.nokia.com/id/ ➥
d2336af2-0953-40a6-8dae-b80d368dead1➥
/Adobe_Flash_Lite_2_x_Components_for_Mobile_Development.html
```

or locate the link off our companion site under the Flash Mobile UI Components header:

```
http://advancED.flashmobilebook.com/links.html#uicomponents
```

The Nokia Flash Lite 2.x components currently consist of these files:

- Adobe_FL_2_x_Components_for_Mobile_Development.mxp: This is the Adobe extension that installs the Nokia components into Flash CS3 or Flash CS4.
- /examples/DynamicListExample.fla: Provides a basic vertical list navigation UI.
- /examples/IndicatorExample.fla: Has both a reusable battery indicator as well as a signal strength battery indicator.
- readme.txt: Be sure to take a quick peek in case the component sets have been updated by the time you read this!

Installing the Nokia components is straightforward, and as with the Oxygen components, only requires executing the Adobe_FL_2_x_Components_for_Mobile_Development.mxp file (assuming Flash CS3 or CS4 is installed, along with the Adobe Extension Manager; see Figure 6-26).

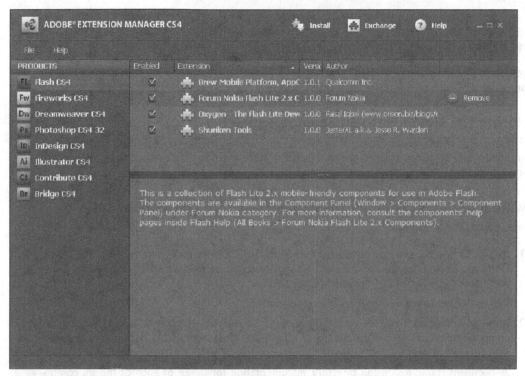

Figure 6-26. Nokia Flash Lite 2.x components installed from the MXP

Using the Nokia components

Once the components have been downloaded and installed, they can be leveraged in Nokia S40 and S60 Flash Lite 2.x applications. The process to use a component is very similar to installing Oxygen Toolkit components, except for a couple of minor differences.

1. Open Flash CS3 or Flash CS4 and start creating a Flash Lite 2.x/3.x application.

2. Navigate to Window ➤ Components ➤ Component Panel (see Figure 6-27).

3. Drag and drop the component to be used onto the Flash Lite application.

For more information, consult the components' help pages inside Flash Help (All Books ➤ Forum Nokia Flash Lite 2.x Components).

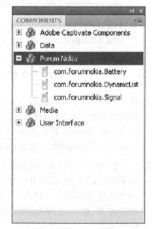

Figure 6-27. Forum Nokia Flash Lite 2.x components installed in Flash CS4

> *For more information, about the Flash Lite UIs on the Nokia Platform, there are always new resources being created on Forum Nokia. Please refer to Forum Nokia for the latest information: http://www.forum.nokia.com/Technology_Topics/Web_Technologies/Flash_Lite/.*

Forum Nokia Flash Lite component set

In addition to the components in the previous section, Forum Nokia has also released a continued set of components for use on Flash Lite 2.x and 3.x projects.

Exploring the Nokia Flash Lite component set

The Forum Nokia components consist of (currently) six reusable UI elements: Button, Contacts, List, Media, Popup, and Scrollbar. These make up the overall component set. Let's walk through downloading and installing the Forum Nokia component set.

Downloading and installing the Nokia Flash Lite component set

To begin, follow these steps:

1. As of this writing, the components are in a version 1.0 beta state and available for download at http://www.forum.nokia.com/info/sw.nokia.com/id/430ed7e3-dae8-481a-a3d7-e00ff8c1624c/Flash_Lite_Components.html.

   The components are downloaded in a zip format.

2. After downloading the Flash_Lite_Components_v1_0_beta_en.zip file and extracting the components, you'll see Documentation, Flash Lite Components, and MyContacts Example Application folders in the Flash_Lite_Components_v1_0_beta_en (the root folder):

   - Documentation: Inside this directory, documentation for usage of each of the six components is provided. You should view each PDF before utilizing any of the intended components for reuse in Flash Lite projects. Each PDF contains source code for how to use each of the components in Flash Lite 2.x/3.x projects.

   - Flash Lite Components: Contains FN FlashLiteComponents.mxp, which will install the Flash Lite component set into Flash CS3 or Flash CS4 (depending on what is installed).

   - MyContacts Example Application: This is a simple example of using the Contacts component to display a list of contacts on a target device.

3. Once the Flash_Lite_Components_v1_0_beta_en.zip archive has been extracted, navigate inside the Flash Lite Components directory and double-click on FN FlashLiteComponents.mxp. This will launch the Adobe Extension Manager and install the component set into Flash CS3 or Flash CS4 (depending on what is installed and used by default).

4. Once the component set has been installed, the Forum Nokia components become available in Flash CS3 or CS4 in the Components dialog (choose Window ➤ Components). The six components are listed under Forum Nokia. (Note: You must have a Flash Lite 2.x/3.x project started that is targeting ActionScript 2.0 for the components to be listed properly in the Components dialog.)

Now that the components are installed, they can be leveraged.

Using the Nokia Flash Lite component set

The MyContacts Example Application inside the Forum Nokia component set download is an excellent place to start. It provides an example of how all components offered can be leveraged together to create a practical Flash Lite application (such as a Contact Manager application that utilizes Nokia S60 Platform Services).

> *In Chapter 7, we'll cover more of Nokia S60 Platform Services, so the MyContacts Example Application in the Forum Nokia component set download is a good way to get a quick taste of the capabilities of extending Flash Lite on S60 Nokia devices (e.g., tapping into the Contacts database on an S60 device).*

Please refer to the Release_Notes.txt file in the MyContacts Example Application folder to see how this component set works using the Forum Nokia Flash Lite component set.

Adobe XD Flash Lite user interface component examples

In addition to the components from Nokia and other Flash Lite community members (e.g., Feather, Oxygen, Shuriken), the Adobe Experience Design Team has also unofficially released a set of reusable Flash Lite UI components, through community channels at http://www.flashmobileblog.com/examples/.

These are extremely lightweight components, created by the Adobe Experience Design Team. The components were used to create mockups and prototype UIs for customers as well as internal projects. Adobe has graciously shared them with the Flash Lite community, in the hope that developers will provide feedback and thus help to improve them.

> *The Flash Lite UI components offered at http://www.flashmobileblog.com/examples/ are not officially supported by Adobe. These components were used internally by Adobe, but the Experience Design Team at Adobe has made these available, free of charge, for the Flash Lite community. These components are offered for educational purposes, and are provided "as is." At this time, there is currently no documentation or support available for them.*

Exploring the Adobe XD Flash Lite user interface components

The current Flash Lite UI components from Adobe include a good number of visual Flash Lite components for reuse. The following Flash Lite 2.x/3.x components are offered (see Figure 6-28, from left to right):

- List.fla: This is a simple vertical list component that can contain multiple entries, and scrolls vertically as more items are added. It provides capabilities similar to the Nokia Flash Lite 2.x Dynamic List component.
- Slider.fla: This is a horizontal menu for images and other icon assets. It utilizes tweening and scaling of items for effect.

- `TileGrid.fla`: This file demonstrates image handling with unloading/loading assets, in a scrollable tile-based grid of icons.

- `NavModel.fla`: This file demonstrates effective use of multiscreen applications. The UI allows for both horizontal tabbing of screens, plus vertical scrolling between list items.

- `Gapper.fla`: This is an example of vertical tween animation of a list of items, similar to the `Slider` component. The items in the list expand and contract depending on whether they are selected.

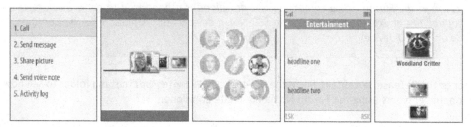

Figure 6-28. Flash Lite 2.x/3.x UI components from the Adobe Experience Design Team

> *The Adobe Experience Design Team Flash Lite 2.x components are less memory hungry than the Nokia Flash Lite components. The XD components have been optimized for low- to mid-range handsets where memory and CPU are precious commodities.*

The Flash Lite UI components from the XD team also offer several Flash Lite 1.1 components (see Figure 6-29, from left to right), including

- `carousel.fla`: This is a simple example of a Flash Lite 1.1 "slider" UI that simulates horizontal tweening between items in a list.

- `displays.fla`: This is useful for battery and signal strength indicators in Flash Lite 1.1 applications.

- `iconmenu.fla`: This is a horizontal menu item that utilizes some very lightweight tweening for added effect.

- `menu.fla`: This provides a scrolling vertical list of items that has an attached scrollbar.

- `story.fla`: This is an example of a scrollable text field using scrollbars.

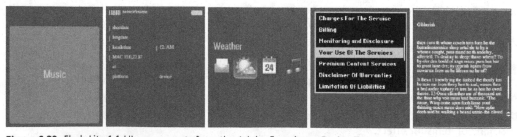

Figure 6-29. Flash Lite 1.1 UI components from the Adobe Experience Design Team

These components give a good insight into how lightweight components (i.e., low-memory UI elements) should be created in Flash Lite.

> *The Adobe Experience Design Team Flash Lite 1.1 components are very lightweight in terms of memory usage, and use less than 400k when published and run.*

Downloading the Flash Lite user interface components

Currently, these can be downloaded at http://www.flashmobileblog.com/examples/ under the Flash Lite UI Component Examples section of the blog.

The archived download file, flashlitecomponents.zip, contains two directories: FL 1.1 - UI examples and FL2.0 - UI examples, respectively.

Using the Flash Lite user interface components

Once the flashlitecomponents.zip is extracted, the .fla source code we discussed in the previous section can be plugged into existing Flash Lite 1.1, 2.x, and 3.x applications.

> *Before using the Flash Lite UI components, keep in mind that these specific components are not officially supported by Adobe, and have been provided for educational purposes, as well as providing feedback to Adobe.*

Summary

In this chapter, you have seen some of the existing interface component sets available for developers to reuse on their Flash Lite projects.

The Feather Framework and LayoutManager from BlocketPC, Oxygen Toolkit, and the Shuriken components are all community-driven efforts. They offer a good base for building simple Flash Lite applications more quickly. Both Nokia and Adobe have also contributed to the Flash Lite community, with their respective component sets, which we covered in this chapter.

Although the component sets in this chapter are "works in progress," these resources can be leveraged to rapidly prototype Flash Lite UIs for applications. Components give developers a good place to start when dealing with UI design and development in Flash Lite applications, without going through the time-consuming process of creating UI elements from scratch for every project (e.g., the drag-and-drop nature of the Nokia UI components).

In the next chapter, you'll learn how to extend Flash Lite capabilities on device platforms such as Nokia S60 using Platform Services. We'll also look at using Project Capuchin on Sony Ericsson devices.

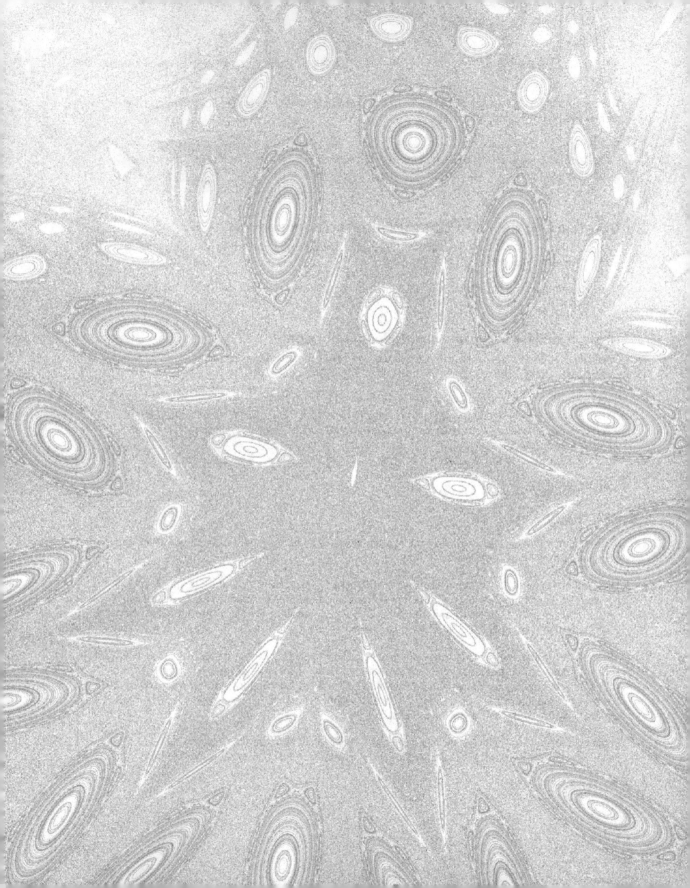

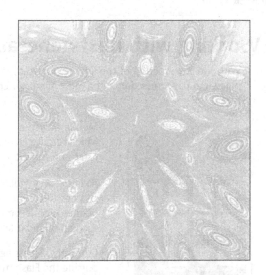

Chapter 7

EXTENDING FLASH ON MOBILE AND DEVICES USING OEM-BASED SOLUTIONS

One of the greatest strengths of Flash is its ability to run across multiple devices and platforms with relative ease compared to other runtimes. We're talking about portability, here, the ability to more easily move Flash content such as applications, games, or user interfaces from one device (or platform for that matter) to another with as few modifications, or tweaks, as possible (sometimes none at all!).

This portability, however, comes at a price. Some developers might even claim that it's a steep price. Because of Flash's history of portability on mobile and devices, until only very recently, it has not always been possible to access low-level device functionality (e.g., camera and Bluetooth) across platforms. This limitation exists because device features and capabilities, especially those tied to hardware components, can vary greatly across mobile devices in the various worldwide mobile markets. This is part of a well-known challenge in the mobile industry known as fragmentation.

Early in the life of Flash Lite across devices, when the Flash Lite player required licensing, Adobe (and even Macromedia before it) made the decision to restrict the use of low-level device APIs for most device manufacturers in an effort to stem the amount of fragmentation of Flash content for devices (and avoid some of the fragmentation lessons learned from J2ME; both past and present). As a consequence, device functionality suffered (e.g., Bluetooth capability is not built into the Flash Lite runtime), yet the number of total devices addressable for Flash was increased worldwide.

Working with next-generation mobile and device APIs

With the introduction of the iPhone, Android, webOS, and other device platforms, the mobile marketplace and consumer demand a more feature-rich experience which continues to evolve at an amazing rate.

Mobile device end users are demanding more-sophisticated experiences, which require applications and content that tap into low-level device features and functionality (see Figure 7-1).

Today's savvy mobile users want applications that tap into location-based services (via GPS), as well as other device sensor hardware such as microphones, accelerometers, cameras, Bluetooth, and even user information such as calendar and contact data on devices.

Currently, accessing each of these device capabilities requires reaching outside the Flash runtime and security sandbox that is in place. Therefore, Flash on mobile and devices must be extended using various APIs provided by OEMs and third-party software vendors. Both of these parties have taken it upon themselves to make it possible to extend the capabilities of Flash and Flash Lite across mobile and devices.

As you read in Chapter 1, with the introduction of the Adobe Open Screen Project, Adobe has done away with previous Flash and Flash Lite player licensing restrictions. It's now possible for companies to leverage Flash however they see fit (with some legal restrictions and provisions, of course).

Figure 7-1. The iPhone has been a catalyst for the adoption of more-sophisticated device experiences throughout the mobile landscape.

> *For instance, the Google Android mobile platform will most likely support Flash on devices similar to the G1 (see Figure 7-2) by the time you read this.*

Because of the Open Screen Project, many device manufacturers and other Open Screen Project partners have introduced very powerful device APIs that are exposed directly in Flash. These APIs allow developers to harness even more capabilities within their Flash applications when addressing mobile and device platforms.

Extending Flash Lite with device APIs

In this chapter, you will learn about various methods that are available to extend the capabilities of Flash on specific mobile and device platforms. Integrating Flash with OEM-based solutions, such as Nokia S60 Platform Services and Sony Ericsson Project Capuchin are covered.

Figure 7-2. The Android-based G1 device offers a sleek experience and powerful phone capabilities.

> *Both Nokia S60 Platform Services and Sony Ericsson Project Capuchin are currently Flash Lite–based, but these will likely evolve into Flash 10 solutions sometime in the future.*

In addition to some popular first-party solutions explained in this chapter, several third-party tools such as Kuneri Lite, Janus, SWF2Go, and Flyer allow developers to tap into low-level device APIs on Flash Lite devices. Because of the overwhelming amount of material, this content will be supplied on the companion web site at http://advancED.flashmobilebook.com/extend, instead of being covered in this chapter.

The third-party material is also provided in an online format because the products are constantly changing and evolving. This is good for developers but not so easy for authors to write about in a book format! Check out the book's companion web site for details on some of these evolving, community-based products.

Without further ado, let's jump right into exploring some of the solutions available today and how to go about harnessing some of the very cool device features that can be tapped by some of these solutions! First up, let's take a look at Nokia S60 Platform Services and how this technology can be used to create powerful Flash Lite–based mobile applications.

Powering Flash with Nokia S60 Platform Services

As you read in Chapters 1 and 2, Nokia is one of the earliest OEMs to support Flash (particularly the Flash Lite runtime) on its range of mobile devices. At the time of this writing, Flash Lite comes pre-installed on Nokia S40, S60, and many of its other popular device platforms (e.g., Nokia N810 tablet runs Flash 9 within a browser context). The Flash Lite versions on these devices vary, but the latest to be preinstalled is Flash Lite 3.0.

> *The latest S60 platform Nokia devices also recently support the Flash Lite 3.1 Distributable Player, but no Nokia devices ship with Flash Lite 3.1 at the time of this writing. Nokia does, however, provide firmware updates (both via OTA and physical cable). Some of these updates are starting to push down Flash Lite 3.x updates to supported Nokia devices as we speak!*

In this section, we'll talk a bit about the API available from ActionScript and then delve into a very quick example of Flash content utilizing some of the new Platform Services APIs for S60 devices.

Introducing S60 Platform Services

Starting with S60 fifth-edition devices, Nokia introduced S60 Platform Services to allow Flash mobile developers to access very powerful, low-level APIs without the need for low-level programming (such as native Symbian coding). Nokia S60 Platform Services is available to Flash via not only the available ActionScript APIs but also other platforms such as Java, Python, and others.

At the time of this writing, Nokia 5800 and N97 (see Figure 7-3) are the first S60 fifth-edition handsets that support S60 Platform Services. By the time you read this page, many more devices should be available (check Nokia's reference site at http://www.forum.nokia.com/devices/matrix_all_1.html for the most up-to-date list of supported devices).

Figure 7-3.
The Nokia N97 and
Nokia 5800 Music
Xpress are Nokia S60
fifth-edition devices

At the time of this writing, Nokia S60 Platform Services is only supported on S60 fifth-edition devices. However, Nokia may decide at a later date to launch on certain S60 third-edition devices. Search forum.nokia.com for the latest updates. (In case you're wondering, there is no Nokia fourth edition. Nokia decided to bypass this number because of negative associations with an unlucky word that sounds like "fourth" and translates to "death" in Chinese).

Getting to know the S60 Platform Services methods

With Nokia S60 Platform Services, developers can tap into powerful device level capabilities. In this section, we'll discuss the functionality provided by Nokia S60 Platform Services on a high level. Later in this chapter, we'll walk through a short example leveraging S60 Platform Services with Flash Lite. There are four core methods when dealing with Nokia S60 Platform Services APIs:

- GetList(): Retrieves a list of Service API–specific objects available for developers to access on a specific device
- RequestNotification(): Registers for notifications of changes to specific service indicated
- CancelNotification(): Cancels an outstanding notification
- Cancel(): Cancels an ongoing asynchronous call that has been imitated

Currently Nokia S60 exposes the following service APIs:

- **Application Manager**: This service allows developers to get an iterable list of any user-installed applications, as well as the available applications on the device, whether they were installed by the user or not. GetList() returns the list. It is also possible to launch an application based on a unique ID (UID) with the LaunchApp() method, as well as launch an application based on its document type using LaunchDoc().
- **Calendar**: As the name might suggest, this service allows developers to tap into creating and managing calendar entries on S60 Platform Services-supported devices. GetList() returns a list of available calendars or calendar data. Add() creates calendars or adds calendar entries to a device.

The Delete() method removes those entries. Import() and Export() have the ability to import and to export both an iCal or the vCal file format (for importing and exporting calendar data).

- **Contacts**: In addition to Calendar, Nokia has opened up onboard contacts, so that personal contact information can be accessed and modified by using S60 Platform Services. Like other services, Contacts has several functions. GetList() returns a list of contacts, contact groups, or contact databases. Add() allows contacts, contact groups, or contact databases to be added to a device. Delete() provides for the removal of those contacts, groups, or database. There also exist Import() and Export() functions that allow contacts to be loaded unto and off of the device in vCard file format. The last method, Organise(), adds a contact to a contact group or removes contacts from a contact group.

- **Location**: Geolocation is a popular device feature within S60 handsets that are equipped with GPS hardware. With the Location service, it is possible to retrieve and calculate location information that is reported by a GPS. GetLocation(), Trace(), and Calculate() are all available methods.

- **Landmarks**: In addition to Location, S60 Platform Services allows for accessing and managing landmarks and landmark categories on supported devices. This means important locations marked by users can be managed. With GetList(), you can retrieve a list of landmarks or landmark categories. New() creates a new, empty landmark or landmark category on the device. Add() adds a landmark or category, and Delete() removes one from the landmark database. Both Import() and Export() functions handle input/output of landmark .lmx files, which are just XML documents containing XML. Organise() adds landmarks to a category or removes landmarks from an existing category.

- **Logging**: This service opens up call, messaging, and data log events, so that they can be read and deleted. GetList() retrieves an iterable list of entries from the device log event database. Properties such as time, destination, direction delivery status, and other events can be retrieved from this database of event log information. It is possible to insert and remove log entries by using the Add() and Delete() functions.

- **Media Management**: In addition to being personal communication devices, Nokia S60 devices are also great media players supporting music, video, and slideshow playback for starters. The Media Management service allows you to tap into things such as images, audio, and even video. GetList() returns a list of media information objects from the media Gallery (the default location for finding audio, video, and graphic files). It is possible to get properties such as Date, Type, FileName, FilePath, and Song, as well as URLs from the files contained in the media Gallery.

- **Messaging**: With this service, you can send, retrieve, and manage messages (SMS and MMS) stored on S60 devices. GetList() retrieves a list of messaging objects from the messaging center. Send() sends an SMS or MMS message to recipients. The ChangeStatus() function will change the message status from Read, Unread, Replied, and Forwarded. Delete() removes a message from the message center.

- **Sensors**: One of the new exciting features of S60 Platform Services is access to various device sensors (e.g., accelerometer). Access to the data reported back from the physical sensor can be accessed by applications. In the case of an accelerometer that means X, Y, and Z as well as force values can be read and interpreted by the application to perform various actions (e.g., play an animation when a device is shaken). FindSensorChannel() searches for sensor channels available on a device. Acceleration, tapping, orientation, rotation, magnetic, and tilt properties can all be polled. The GetChannelProperty() function retrieves sensor channel data. The data can be values of the integer, double, and string data types.

- **System Information**: Access to system information, such as Device, Display, General, and Memory device capability objects, is supported. GetInfo() and SetInfo() are the getter and setter functions for the previous objects. Display information properties that can be queried are ScreenSaverTimeout, UserInactivity, KeyGuardTime, AutoLockTime, AutoLockStatus, Wallpaper, LightTimeout, DisplayResolution, and DisplayOrientation. Device properties are PlatformVersion and PhoneModel and provide device information for users. General properties are InputLanguage, SupportedLanguages, and PredictiveText. Memory information such as ListDrives and DriveInfo may also be accessed through this S60 Platform Services object.

Leveraging S60 Platform Services

Compared to other mobile development environments (e.g., Symbian, C++, or Java) that support S60 Platform Services, in our opinion, Flash offers a far simpler solution to get up to speed and developing more quickly. In this section, you will start development with S60 Platform Services using Flash Lite and ActionScript 2.0.

Before any development begins, however, the ActionScript API class library is required to be downloaded and installed, so it can used within the Flash development environment (Adobe Creative CS3 or CS4). Let's cover that, next.

Installing the Nokia S60 Platform Service APIs

Before you can get started using Platform Services with supported Nokia devices, you must first download and install the Nokia S60 Platform Services ActionScript 2.0 class library.

This is provided from the Forum Nokia site and allows a simple means of creating and manipulating the service objects you read about earlier in this section.

First, download the zipped archive of the ActionScript APIs library at http://library.forum.nokia.com and then traverse to the following directory:

    /topic/Flash_Lite_Developers_Library/

The ZIP containing the classes can be found by entering the file name onto the previous URL and path above:

    ActionScript_library_for_s60_Platform_Services.zip

> If the ActionScript API library cannot be found at that URL, you'll need to search library.forum.nokia.com for the .zip file (Nokia often revamps and moves files around the site).

Next, you'll need to extract and copy the package contents of the ZIP file into the Flash class path folder (you should have either Flash CS4 or Flash CS3 installed).

The path depends on what operating system you are running:

- **Vista**: \Users\%USERPROFILE%\App Data\Local\Adobe\Flash CS4\en\Configuration\Classes
- **XP**: %USERPROFILE%\Local Settings\Application Data\Adobe\Flash CS4\en\Configuration\Classes
- **Mac**: /Users/$USER/Library/Application Support/Adobe/Flash CS4/en/Configuration

If you are running Adobe CS3, merely replace "Flash CS4" with "Flash CS3" in the above paths.

Once the com folder is copied to the appropriate location for your operating system, you should have the following ActionScript class files located under the com\nokia\lib subdirectory: ErrorValue.as, InvalidParamException.as, Iterable.as, Service.as, and ServiceUtils.as (see Figure 7-4).

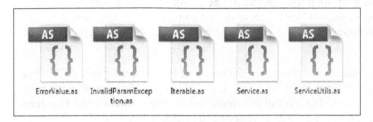

Figure 7-4. Five core source files make up the S60 Platform Services ActionScript 2.0 library.

Now, that you've downloaded and installed the S60 Platform Services API, it's time for you to do our SMS application walkthrough, which demonstrates some of what you have been learning in this section. Let's move on!

If you have incorrectly installed the class files (or skipped that step), when you go to compile the sample application in the next section, you'll get a compile-time error complaining about the missing class files.

Targeting S60 platform Services–supported devices

For our example here, you'll be targeting the Nokia 5800 (see Figure 7-5), since it's one of the first available devices from Nokia to have Symbian S60 fifth edition and supports S60 Platform Services. By the time you read this, many more fifth-edition devices, such as the Nokia N97, should be available for testing and development.

Also, at this time of this writing, Adobe and Nokia have just released a Nokia 5800 Music Xpress device profile as part of the Adobe Device Central CS4 Profile Update 2. If you do not find the Nokia 5800 contained in Adobe Device Central, refresh the Online Device Library in CS4 and drag the Nokia 5800 profile to the local library for use. New or enhanced device profiles are displayed in orange within Adobe Device Central (when updates and enhancements are available).

Figure 7-5.
The Nokia 5800 is one of the first S60 fifth-edition devices on market to support Nokia S60 Platform Services.

Writing an inline SMS application

As you read back in Chapter 2, since Flash Lite 1.1, it has been possible to send SMS, MMS, and even e-mail messages from Flash Lite through a getURL() command like so: getURL("sms:1234567890&body= hello world").

On the Nokia platform, the caveat of using this method has been that it launches the default messaging application dialog on devices such as Nokia. This leads to a somewhat convoluted mobile user experience. The Flash Lite application will behave and look different than the messaging client the device serves up to end users.

By using the Nokia S60 Platform Services and leveraging the power of the Messaging Service API, it is possible to create an *inline* messaging experience for mobile users. By "inline," we mean that the messaging application is confined to *one* application and not spread across two separate ones. This deep device service integration is just one of the powers of utilizing S60 Platform Services.

> With the BREW platform, there is a special case in Flash Lite 2.1, where SMS message can be sent silently without any user prompts. This is a unique case to the legacy Flash Lite player for BREW. Although we will not cover BREW in depth in this chapter, we discuss it on our companion web site at http://advancED.flashmobilebook.com/chapter7.

The inline SMS messenger application will only have two screens for the sake of simplicity. The first screen will be used to enter in message details and the second to send it off.

Let's take a look at how the messaging application is constructed:

1. Locate SMSMessenger.fla in the Chapter 7 downloads, and open it in Adobe Flash CS3 or CS4.

2. Once it's open, examine the Flash timeline and notice that the application is split into two frame label states: init and send. Each layer in the application divides the visual assets into decomposable areas of the application (e.g., soft keys, UI, and text fields).

3. On frame 1 on the ActionScript layer is the ActionScript needed to initialize the application. Open the ActionScript Panel, and take a look at the code.

4. First, the standard Flash preamble is given. However, one difference here is the new fscommand2 command DisableKeypadCompatibilityMode.

   This is a new command for touch-screen–based devices from Nokia that do not necessarily have physical buttons. Essentially, this command enables or disables a virtual keypad depending on the Boolean value specified. Here, we set to true, so no virtual keyboard is displayed, and users must utilize the touch screen to enter text and navigate the user interface:

   ```
   fscommand2( "DisableKeypadCompatibilityMode", true );
   ```

5. Next are the standard commands to set to full-screen mode and assign soft keys. Here, the only soft key assigned is to quit out of the application. The _focusrect is disabled for this application, as some custom events will be used to manage that.

   ```
   fscommand2( "FullScreen", true );
   fscommand2( "Soft keys", "", "Quit" );
   _focusrect = false;
   ```

6. Next up, some variables are defined to keep track of the state of text fields in the application:

```
var currentfocus;
var lastfocus;
```

7. There are two buttons in the user interface: one button to quit the application and another to send the custom SMS message that will be entered:

```
send_btn.onPress = sendSMS;
quit_btn.onPress = Quit;
```

8. There are two text fields for this application. One will hold the phone number that the SMS message will go to, and the other is the custom user-entered message to be sent to that phone number:

```
var phonenumber_str:String = "<phone number>";
var message_str:String = "<your message>";
phonenumber_txt.text = phonenumber_str;
message_txt.text = message_str;
```

9. In step 7, the event handlers were defined for the buttons. sendSMS() is the function that is called when the send button is tapped by a user. Pressing the send button will advance the application to the next frame and run the ActionScript located on the frame labeled with "send".

```
function sendSMS():Void {
 gotoAndPlay( "send" );
}
```

10. In step 5, the soft keys were enabled for this application. Here, a key handler is defined so that when the right soft key is pressed, the application will call the Quit() function:

```
var key_obj:Object = new Object();
key_obj.onKeyDown = function() {
 switch ( Key.getCode() ) {
  case ExtendedKey.SOFT2:
   Quit();
   break;
 }
}
Key.addListener( key_obj );
```

11. The Quit command merely makes a call to the fscommand2 API to exit the application:

```
function Quit():Void {
 fscommand2( "Quit" );
}
```

12. As we said earlier, this application uses some custom focus management. When the application starts, it has some default text to instruct the user to enter a phone number and message, but when the text fields are selected, their focus changes.

```
var listener_obj:Object = new Object();
listener_obj.onSetFocus = function( oldFocus, newFocus ) {
 newFocus.text = "";
```

```
}
Selection.addListener( listener_obj );
stop();
```

13. Now, let's get into the Nokia Platform Services code! Jump to the label entitled "send", or frame 2. Inside that frame, you'll find the ActionScript to send off the SMS message that was entered in the user interface that was defined for the application. Before performing the send, however, the Nokia Platform Services Service class must be imported for use:

```
import com.nokia.lib.Service;
```

> The Nokia Platform Services API should already be installed from the previous section, "Installing the Nokia S60 ActionScript Service APIs." If it is not installed properly, you will generate compilation errors.

14. The next step is to create and instantiate the messaging service class and create a messaging object, messaging_obj, to be used to send the SMS message.

```
var messaging_obj = new Service( "Service.Messaging", "IMessaging" );
```

15. The messaging object must be initialized with a MessageType of "SMS", a To value that is mapped to the phonenumber_txt text field, and a BodyText parameter that maps to the message_txt text field. When all three of these parameters are defined, the messaging object knows where to send the message and what to send.

```
var inParams_obj = { MessageType: "SMS",
 To : phonenumber_txt.text,
 BodyText: message_txt.text
}
```

16. The crux of the application is where the SMS is sent, which is accomplished by calling the Send() method on the messaging_obj object. The parameters from step 15 are specified so that Platform Services knows where to send the message and what to send.

```
var outParams_obj = messaging_obj.Send( inParams_obj );
```

17. The remaining code checks for error conditions returning back from the messaging object. Here, either an error is displayed in the event the SMS cannot be sent or a status message is updated.

```
var errorCode_num:Number = outParams_obj.ErrorCode;
if ( errorCode_num != 0 ) {
 status_txt.text = "ERROR: code = " + errorCode_num +
 ", message = " + outParams_obj.ErrorMessage;
} else {
 status_txt.text = "MESSAGE HAS BEEN SENT to " +
 phonenumber_txt.text + "!";
}
```

18. Once the application is compiled, the SWF can be sent to a Nokia S60 fifth-edition device for testing. For the purposes of this example, the target device is the Nokia 5800 (one of the first Nokia devices to support S60 Platform Services).

Copying the SWF to the target device for testing involves using Bluetooth, PC Suite, or other means. Copying the SWF to the target device for testing involves using Bluetooth, PC Suite, or other means.

We will not be covering how to package the SWF into a SIS file in this section. We covered this material back in Chapters 2 and 3 when the Adobe Mobile and Flash Lite packagers were explained. Refer to those chapters for more information about packaging Flash Lite content on Nokia devices.

19. Once the SWF is on the device, it can be tested by entering in a valid phone number to accept the message (see Figure 7-6).

A valid SIM card must be in the Nokia 5800 in order for the SMS message to be sent.

Figure 7-6. The messaging application leveraging S60 Platform Services APIs on the Nokia 5800

When you run the SWF for the first time, because it is utilizing S60 Platform Services, it will ask the user to confirm the request to send through several permission dialogs (see Figure 7-7). Selecting Allow for this session will allow the application permission to send the message.

Figure 7-7. The default Nokia Series 60 Platform Services security access request prompts

Getting more information on S60 Platform Services

In this section, you've seen how to begin to leverage Nokia S60 Platform Services on fifth-edition devices such as the N97 and 5800. Platform Services allows Flash Lite to be extended to offer very practical and powerful device capabilities that are not typically found in the Flash Lite player: you tap into everything from ordinary information like contacts and calendars to cool things like the accelerometer, GPS coordinates, the camera, and other sensor APIs.

In this section, you've just seen the tip of the iceberg of cool and exciting possibilities with S60 Platform Services. For more information about the Nokia S60 Platform Services API, consult the library at the Forum Nokia site at http://wiki.forum.nokia.com/index.php/S60_Platform_Services, or check out some of the more compelling examples we have at our companion web site for this book at http://advancED.flashmobilebook.com/chapter7.

Now that you've taken a first look at how Nokia is extending Flash on their devices, let's switch gears and talk about how it's possible to make powerful applications on Sony Ericsson devices by combining the power of low-level Java APIs and the great user interfaces and fluid experiences possible with Flash. Onward!

Extending Flash on Sony Ericsson devices

Sony Ericsson is one of the OEMs in the mobile marketplace that is concentrating their efforts on the multimedia aspects of their devices. Features such as high-quality cameras, enhanced music capabilities, and a high degree of personalization are all things Sony Ericsson provides very successfully.

What's more, Sony Ericsson is also serious about the mobile user experience, and thus has lent a lot of time and energy to creating very rich and compelling experiences, as illustrated by the sample Flash Lite screen saver animation, shown in Figure 7-8. This means better and slicker user interfaces to allow users to access all these great device features.

Today, millions of Sony Ericsson devices on the market utilize Flash for user interfaces and other pre-installed multimedia assets, such as wallpapers, screensavers, and even themes.

Sony Ericsson was an early adopter of Flash Lite in the European market. Some of its early devices supported Flash Lite in the browser context as far back as Flash Lite 1.1, and now, Flash Lite 3 devices are just coming to market at the time of this writing. In addition, recently, Sony Ericsson's online developer resources have started to expand.

Getting started with Flash on Sony Ericsson devices

It's worthwhile to take a look at the Flash Lite guidelines Sony Ericsson offers on its Developer World site (http://developer. sonyericsson.com/). This contains some good tips when targeting your mobile application to the Sony Ericsson platform. The one most relevant article is called "Developer Guidelines: Adobe Flash Lite 2.x in Sony Ericsson Feature Phones."

Figure 7-8.
Sony Ericsson C905 running a Flash animation

There is also a guideline that covers Flash Lite 1.1–supporting devices, if you're targeting projects intended for legacy Sony Ericsson devices; search the developer site to find it.

On some Sony Ericsson devices, custom device APIs are exposed that are not found on other Flash devices. One such API allows developers to tap into accelerometer-based data, so that motion and force can be used within mobile games, applications, and user interfaces.

Working with accelerometers on Sony Ericsson devices

An accelerometer is a hardware component that can detect the direction and size of any force applied to a device. Accelerometers are a popular feature on devices from Nokia (e.g., Nokia 5800 and N97), as well as Apple's iPhone, and Android devices such as the G1. Select models of Sony Ericsson devices have accelerometers, as well. At the time of this writing, this includes the K850, W910, C902, W760, W980, and C905 (check your documentation to determine if your target device has one).

What's more, Sony Ericsson offers a custom API for Flash Lite applications to access the accelerometer data via a custom API. The command to tap the accelerometer on these devices is a simple loadVariables with the following syntax:

```
//-- returns back X,Y,Z values from accelerometer sensor into
//-- accX, accY, accZ variables (if supported on target device)
loadVariables("accelerometer://data", _root );
```

As you can see, we're merely making a call to a special device API. Remember that this command is specific to Sony Ericsson devices and and will (most likely) not work on other device platforms! The results come back into the specified movie clip of the second parameter. Here you are simply using _root. The values stored are located in accX, accY, and accZ variables.

Detecting devices

When working with the sensor feedback from accelerometers on Sony Ericsson devices, it's good practice to add device detection code.

This allows the Flash file to run both on the desktop for testing and debugging, as well as providing error checking when the code is run on target devices. As we've already stated, not *all* Sony Ericsson models support accelerometers! There are two ways to detect whether or not it is OK to try to tap accelerometer.

The first method to add the conditional checks is by simply leveraging the Flash Lite fscommand2 API:

```
founddevice_bool = ➡
fscommand2("GetDevice","device") == 0 ? true : false;

ondevice_bool = ➡
fscommand2("GetPlatform","platform") == 0 ? true : false;

if (founddevice_bool && ondevice_bool) {
 if (deviceHasAnAccelerometer(platform)) {
 //-- valid device found, so run our accelerometer code here
 } else {
 trace("Not running on a supported Sony Ericsson device!");
 }
} else {
 trace("Not running on a Sony Ericsson device");
}
```

```
function deviceHasAnAccelerometer(deviceplatform_str:String):Boolean {
 var retVal:Boolean = false;
 for (i in supportedDevices_arr) {
  if (i.toLowerCase() == deviceplatform_str.toLowerCase())
  break;
 }
 return retVal;
}
```

The second, and admittedly less error-prone, way to check whether a device supports the accelerometer is to make the call to `loadVariables` regardless of the device and then check to see if accX, accY, and accZ have valid numeric return values.

The benefit of this second method is its brevity, and using it is acceptable when developing for only one target platform or device. However, leveraging the Flash Lite `fscommand2` API offers a much more robust implementation that could be extended to not only help with dealing with the accelerometer API but also to help with other tasks, for example, tweaking the Flash content for screen orientation on specific devices.

In the following code, a check is made to see if any values are returned from the accelerometer call on a supported Sony Ericsson device (e.g., C905):

```
var sensorCheck_bool:Boolean = true;
onEnterFrame = function {
 loadVariables("accelerometer://data", _root);
 if (sensorCheck_bool) {
  //-- only check sensor once!
  sensorCheck_bool = false;
  if (accX != undefined && accY != undefined && accZ != undefined) {
   //-- sensor is reporting, so continue
  } else {
    trace("No sensor is reporting! Is this a supported device?");
  }
 }
}
```

Accessing the accelerometer

Now that you know the basics of dealing with accelerometer API on Sony Ericsson devices, it's time to walk through an example (see Figure 7-9).

Here, we'll be creating a simple animation that responds to a Sony Ericsson device's orientation (i.e., how the device is being held in the X, Y, and Z space).

1. Open the Gravity.fla source file located in the Chapter 7 folder, under the subdirectory called \Sony Ericsson\Accelerometer inside of Flash CS3 or CS4.

2. On the layer named ActionScript on the main timeline in Gravity.fla is the ActionScript needed to tap the accelerometer natively, using the accelerometer://data call we talked about earlier. Let's step through all the code.

3. First is the typical preamble to set the SWF content rendering quality and full-screen mode, and to turn off the focus rectangle:

```
fscommand2( "FullScreen", true );
fscommand2( "SetQuality", "high" );
_focusrect = false;
```

By default, Sony Ericsson supports wallpaper, screensaver, and browser modes for running SWF content. To run this example as a stand-alone application, it can be wrapped inside of a Java MIDlet. You'll learn about this in our next section, when Sony Ericsson's Project Capuchin is discussed. For testing purposes, run the SWF on the intended device as browser, wallpaper, or screensaver content. Opening (i.e., selecting and clicking on) the SWF on the target device should open the Flash Lite player on supported Sony Ericsson devices.

4. Next, the global variables to keep track of event firing are created. The POLLINTERVAL_num variable is used to determine how fast the accelerometer is checked. POLLID_num is used to keep tracking of the polling.

```
var POLLID_num:Number;
var POLLINTERVAL_num:Number = 0.25;
```

Figure 7-9. Using an accelerometer to detect the direction of gravity

5. Next, some basic error checking is done to see if the SWF is running on a device or whether it is running on the desktop.

```
var deviceplatform_str:String;
status_num = fscommand2( "GetPlatform", "deviceplatform_str" );
if ( status_num != 0 ) deviceplatform_str = "desktop";
```

6. Next, there are three functions for the example. The first, called readValues(), simply loads in the accelerometer variables accX, accY, and accZ via a loadVariables command and specifies the Sony Ericsson–specific accelerometer://data local URL. A call to the function updatePointer() is also needed.

```
function readValues():Void {
 updatePointer();
 loadVariables("accelerometer://data", _root );
}
```

7. The updatePointer() function is the crux of the Gravity example. On the main stage of the example on the GravityPointer layer on the Flash timeline is a simple pointer arrow graphic.

The function changes the _rotation property of the pointer_mc movie clip depending on the position of the values from accX and accY based on a mathematical equation that determines which way the device is orientated.

If the SWF is run from the desktop, the example will try to mimic the orientation by following the location of the _xmouse and _ymouse coordinates of the mouse.

```
function updatePointer():Void {
    if ( deviceplatform_str != "desktop" ) {
```

```
pointer_mc._rotation =
-( Math.atan2( accX, -accY )
* 57.29577951308232087679815481 4105 );
} else {
pointer_mc._rotation =
( Math.atan2( -( _root._xmouse - 120 ), -( _root._ymouse - 170 ) ) )
* -57.29577951308232087679815481 4105;
}
}
```

8. Now that all the functionality has been created to access the accelerometer and move the gravity pointer, it's simple a matter of making intermittent calls to the poll the accelerometer on the device. Here, the setInterval() is used. The readValues() function is called every 250 milliseconds based on the POLLINTERVAL_num specified in step 4:

```
POLLID_num = setInterval( readValues, ( POLLINTERVAL_num * 1000 ) );
```

> We could have used an onEnterFrame() to continually access the data from the accelerometer, but this is very CPU intensive. Depending on your application (game, application, etc.) and its needs, one of the following two methods can be utilized: loadVariables() and onEnterFrame(). For the example given here, a simple polling method is used.

9. The last piece of ActionScript merely stops the application from traversing beyond the first frame of the Flash movie.

```
stop();
```

When compiled and run on a Sony Ericsson device that has an accelerometer and Flash Lite 2 (or greater), the example will adjust the pointer so it always orients to which direction is down.

> Recall that accelerometer://data is unique to Sony Ericsson devices, so if the SWF is copied to a Nokia or other device, the API will be not supported. For other platforms, alternative means for tapping into accelerometer must be used (e.g., Kuneri Lite or Platform Services for Nokia devices).

Now that you've seen some of the built-in APIs that Sony Ericsson offers, it's time to turn our attention to a much more powerful extension technology supported by Sony Ericsson devices—Project Capuchin.

Introducing Project Capuchin

With the Sony Ericsson C905 and subsequent high-end devices, Sony Ericsson has created a technology project called Capuchin that allows Flash Lite to tap into very powerful device capabilities through a new API and mobile development architecture.

Project Capuchin is essentially a way for Flash Lite or Java developers to leverage both the sleek interfaces that are possible with Flash and the powerful device APIs provided by Java. This bridging between Flash Lite and Java on each supported device allows designers and developers to leverage the best of both worlds. Let's get into the nuts and bolts of Project Capuchin.

The name "Capuchin" is based on the association between coffee (from its utilization of the Java platform) and the monkey family (Adobe's open source Tamarin project is named for a monkey).

Let's look at some of the pros and cons of both Java and Flash Lite and why Project Capuchin's attempt to merge the two helps give developers the best of both worlds for creating powerful, compelling applications and is an important technology for the Sony Ericsson platform.

Whether you are a Java or Flash developer, it's best to know how leveraging Project Capuchin can benefit your mobile projects when working on Sony Ericsson devices. So let's consider some reasons why developers choose Java or Flash by looking at their strengths and weaknesses.

These are the pros and cons of Java development:

- Pros
    - Wide platform access via Java Specification Requests (JSRs)
    - Security model includes protected domains offered by MIDP
    - Distribution infrastructure using Java archive (JAR) packaging
    - Wide adoption of development language and platform
- Cons
    - Lack of efficient, designer-oriented tools (which Adobe CS4 offers with Flash and Flash Lite)
    - No rich UI framework (like the one Flash Lite offers)
    - Difficult to keep separation between presentation and service layers
    - Designers dependent on programmers in UI development

And these are the pros and cons of developing with Flash Lite:

- Pros:
    - Easy to learn and use and use the Adobe CS3 and CS4 IDE, which offers fast prototyping and device emulation
    - Large, active, and growing Flash community
    - Lots of education materials in the forums, tutorials, user groups, and books (like this one!)
    - Widespread Flash Lite player adoption on Sony Ericsson and many other device platforms
- Cons:
    - Limited system services access
    - No proper standardized security solution for all supported platforms
    - Limited number of distribution channels (but this is changing! Read Chapter 2 for more information about Flash Mobile and Device ecosystems!)
    - Performance and memory consumption

295

As you will see, by combining the strengths of both development platforms through Project Capuchin, it is possible to create highly compelling mobile applications utilizing both Java and Flash Lite. Before we get into developing with Capuchin, let's take a look at the architecture on how all the pieces work together.

Looking at high-level Project Capuchin architecture

Thus far, we've been talking about how a Project Capuchin–based mobile application works. Here, we'd like to give you a visual of how the Project Capuchin framework works.

Figure 7-10 shows an example of a Project Capuchin–based MIDlet (i.e., a mobile Java application) that accesses accelerometer data. It does this by communicating with the JSR-256 (the Mobile Sensor API), which talks to the accelerometer driver on a particular device. In order for the accelerometer data to be accessible in Flash, its data must be sent to Flash via the Project Capuchin API framework.

As you'll see in a bit, this communication is done with the DataRequest and ExtendedEvents objects in ActionScript and also through some custom Java code utilizing FlashImage and FlashCanvas to display the Flash movie.

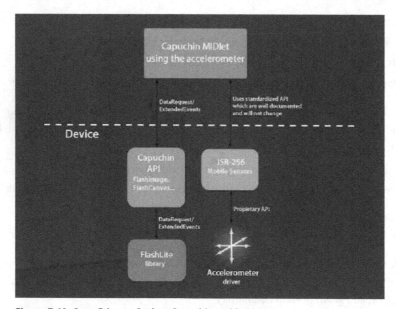

Figure 7-10. Sony Ericsson Project Capuchin architecture

As you can see from the diagram in Figure 7-10, Flash Lite is just one piece of the Project Capuchin framework.

As you'll see later, each Project Capuchin–based mobile application is contained in a JAR file. Once a user downloads and installs that JAR, the Java MIDlet controls the interaction between the Flash Lite user interface and the lower-level JSR through the Project Capuchin APIs provided by Sony Ericsson.

Requests between Java and Flash Lite are bidirectional, meaning that Flash Lite can talk to Java, and vice versa (see Figure 7-11). You'll see this in our upcoming example in this chapter.

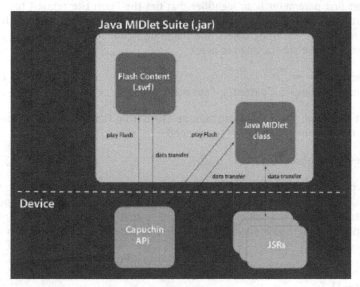

Figure 7-11. Sony Ericsson Project Capuchin architecture

Exploring the use cases for Project Capuchin

There are essentially three use cases for using Project Capuchin in a mobile application:

- **Pure Flash content**: The first use case for using Project Capuchin is to merely package Flash Lite content without providing any kind of Java Service access. By encapsulating Flash games and applications in a MIDlet suite (in a JAR file), it is possible to use the Java ME distribution infrastructure and take advantage of Java security mechanisms. Packaging the content is done with the SWF2JAR utility (which you will read about later in this chapter).

- **Java MIDlet using Flash Lite for parts of the user interface**: It is possible to combine the power of a Java user interface with Flash Lite user interface components. For instance, a 3D Java game could utilize Flash Lite for its main menu or other user interface components.

- **Java MIDlet using Flash Lite for the user interface layer**: In this use case, Flash Lite handles the entire presentation layer, while Java ME is used as a service provider to pass data to the presentation layer. This is the method we'll use in the example we provide in the upcoming Capuchin example.

Passing data between Java and Flash Lite

The power of Project Capuchin is its ability to provide powerful access to device services through Java JSRs that can't be accomplished by any offered Flash Lite APIs. To get access to this data, the Project Capuchin framework offers two ActionScript objects: DataRequest and ExtendedEvents. For one-time loading of data from Java using DataRequest is fine, but where a polling method is needed, it is best to implement the ExtendedEvents method of handling data exchange between Flash and Java.

Using DataRequest

DataRequest is used for asynchronous data transfer between Java and Flash layers (data can be transferred both ways). The first parameter is an identifier that ties the Flash Lite request to the corresponding Java data provider. The other parameters are one or more parameters that can be passed into the MIDlet. To create the requesting object, the following ActionScript can be used (getData, parameter1, and parameter2 are arbitrary names here):

```
var dataRequest_obj = ➥
new DataRequest("getData", "param1", "param2", ... );
```

Once the data request is created, a requesting call must be issued from Flash Lite that asks for the data from the Java MIDlet, in the form of a request() command:

```
var dataRequest_ob.request();
```

Once the MIDlet has processed the requesting command, it sends back the data asynchronously to Flash Lite through an onLoad() event, which must be defined inside of the Flash Lite application. In addition to the data passed back, a status flag is also set, so that minimal error checking can be performed. For example, status_bool in the following code would be true for valid return values or false for invalid values:

```
dataRequest_obj.onLoad = function(status_bool:Boolean) {
 if (status_bool) {
  trace(dataRequest_obj.fromJavaMIDlet);
 }
}
```

On the Java MIDlet end, to pass data back and forth between the Flash Lite application, two Project Capuchin classes must be imported:

```
import com.sonyericsson.capuchin.FlashDataRequest
import com.sonyericsson.capuchin.FlashDataRequestListener;

class testMIDlet extends MIDlet implements FlashDataRequestListener {
 flashImage.setFlashDataRequestListener(this);
}
class synchronized void dataRequested(FlashDataRequest dr) {
 String[] is = dr.getArgs();
 if ("getData".equals[is[0]]) {
  dr.setProperty("fromJavaMIDlet","Hello from Java land!");
  dr.complete();
 }
}
```

As stated previously, the DataRequest object is fine for communicating data asynchronously between Flash Lite and the Java MIDlet through passing of property variables, but for creating and responding to events, Project Capuchin provides a much more elegant method of data exchange—ExtendedEvents.

Using ExtendedEvents

The DataRequest object allows for passing of variables between Flash and Java as properties, but Project Capuchin also offers an alternative means for data exchange, called ExtendedEvents. It implements polling that allows for Java code to more easily notify Flash when data is available. This provides a more synchronized method of data exchange.

With ExtendedEvents, Project Capuchin allows for a listener object to be created in Flash and registered to a corresponding event in the Java MIDlet. When an event happens in the Java MIDlet, it notifies the Flash event listener and allows custom code to be executed in a synchronous manner.

First the event listener must be created and tied to the custom ExtendedEvents Project Capuchin class.

```
var eventListener_obj:Object = new Object();
ExtendedEvents.CapuchinEvent = addListener(eventLsitener_obj);
```

> The property CapuchinEvent is a user-defined variable and can be changed to any label name (e.g., myEvent).

Once the event listener is set up, the event handler must be defined. This is what's triggered from the Java MIDlet when an event occurs.

```
eventListener_obj.onEvent = function(dataFromJava) {
  trace(dataFromJava);
}
```

Inside the Java MIDlet, just like in the DataRequest method, two classes must be imported to use to pass the data between Flash and Java.

```
import com.sonyericsson.capuchin.FlashEventManager;
import com.sonyericsson.capuchin.FlashEventListener;
```

Once the Project Capuchin classes have been imported, they can be put to use by defining the Java event listener. The Project Capuchin MIDlet implements the FlashEventManager class and allows the MIDlet to send data back to the Flash Lite application.

```
class eventMIDLet extends MIDlet implements FlashEventManager {
  FlashImage flashImage;
  FlashEventListener myFlashEventListener;

  eventMIDlet() {
    flashImage.setFlashEventManager(this);
  }
}
```

After the FlashEventManager is defined, it's time to create the logic to define the actual event listener in the Java MIDlet.

```
public synchronized void addFlashEventListener(String name,
    FlashEventListener fe) {
    if ("CapuchinEvent".equals(name)) {
      myFlashEventHandler = fe;
    }
}
```

> The property *CapuchinEvent* is a user-defined value that was defined in the Flash Lite application. The name used must match the listener object property (previously discussed), *ExtendedEvents.CapuchinEvent*. Data can then be exchanged properly between the Flash Lite application and the Java MIDlet.

To send data from the Java MIDlet, the handleEvent method must be called.

```
myFlashEventListener.handleEvent("Data from Java to Flash Lite");
```

Once this method is called, the onEvent() method that was defined earlier in the Flash Lite application will be called, and the code within will be executed. Typically, you will utilize the DataRequest method for simple data one-time property passing. For data that is to be sent periodically (i.e., data that is polled), the EventManager mechanism of data exchange will be used.

Now, that you have an idea of how data is passed to and from Flash Lite and the Java MIDlet, let's get your Project Capuchin environment set up.

Setting up the development environment for Project Capuchin

Before building a Capuchin-based project, a development environment must be established. The steps to do so are explained very well in online documentation provided by Sony Ericsson. Click the Setting up Java environment for Project Capuchin development link, which can be found on the Sony Ericsson developer site (http://developer.sonyericsson.com). This provides the most recent documentation on how to configure the Capuchin development environment.

To develop with Project Capuchin, you need to have several things installed, as laid out in the documentation:

- **Java Runtime Environment (JRE) 1.6 or later**: This can be downloaded at http://www.java.com/en/download/manual.jsp.

- **Sony Ericsson SDK for Java ME**: This can be downloaded at http://developer.sonyericsson.com/site/global/docstools/java/p_java.jsp.

- **Eclipse Software Development Environment (SDE)**: This can be downloaded at http://www.eclipse.org/downloads/.

- **Eclipse ME plug-in**: Installation instructions can be found at http://eclipseme.org/docs/installation.html and http://eclipseme.org/docs/installEclipseME.html.

- **Project Capuchin API (ActionScript classes)**: To download this, search http://developer.sonyericsson.com/ for the keywords "Project Capuchin." In the future, this API may be part of the Sony Ericsson SDK.

> *You will need a Windows-based PC to work with Project Capuchin, since at the time of this writing, Mac development is not supported by Sony Ericsson (the Java SDK that Sony Ericsson provides is only available as a Windows executable). Sony Ericsson also recommends using the Eclipse editor for developing Java ME content. It is possible to substitute, but in this chapter, we will utilize the recommended Eclipse IDE.*

Creating your first Project Capuchin application

Once you have a proper development environment established from the previous section, it's time to get started building a Project Capuchin–based application.

> *Before you get started, we should mention that documentation provided by Sony Ericsson, entitled "Getting Started with Project Capuchin for Flash and Java Developers," is available for download at http://developer.sonyericsson.com/ site/global/docstools/projectcapuchin/p_projectcapuchin.jsp. We recommend that you read through that document and browse and work through some of the examples there. By doing so, you'll be better prepared for what's coming next.*

In following example, we'll cover Project Capuchin from a Flash developer's perspective. Typically, on a Capuchin-based project, one developer will focus on the Java development and the data services layer, while a Flash designer (or developer) concentrates on the front end and user interface.

In this section, we'll only cover the very basics that Flash Lite designers and developers will need to know to leverage the Project Capuchin framework within their projects. Our example will be a premade application, which can be imported into Eclipse and the Flash IDE to follow along.

For the sake of brevity, this will be an overview of what makes up a simple Project Capuchin application. For more detailed walkthroughs, please refer to the tutorials provided by Sony Ericsson at http://developer.sonyericsson.com/ (search for "Project Capuchin").

Downloading, extracting, and installing the Project Capuchin example

Before starting the example, you'll need to download the exercise from the companion web site.

1. The location of the file is http://advancED.flashmobilebook.com/downloads/chapter7/ capuchin_example.zip or within the Chapter 7 folder contained in the friends of ED download file.

2. Once downloaded, extract the contents of the zip into a directory (capuchin_example will work fine).

3. Now boot up the Eclipse editor.

4. Once Eclipse has loaded go to File ➤ Import Existing Projects into Workspace from the General tab (see Figure 7-12).

301

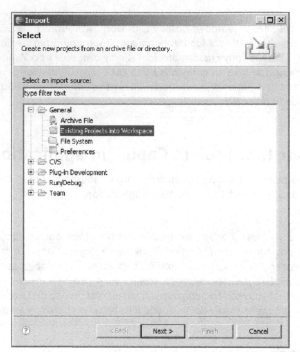

Figure 7-12.
Importing an existing
Java project into Eclipse

5. Next, import the existing Java project from the extracted CapuchinExample.zip folder (see Figure 7-13).

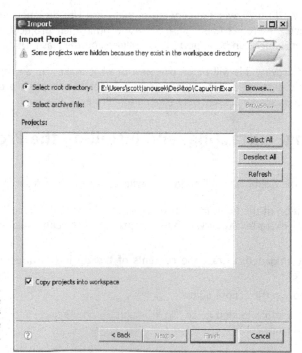

Figure 7-13.
Import the example
Project Capuchin appli-
cation into the Eclipse
workspace.

6. Now, we'll walk through each piece of this sample Project Capuchin application. We'll first discuss the Java portion of the Project Capuchin application. Note the .java MIDlet file located under the src folder, as well as the CapuchinExample.swf file located under the res directory. Also note the CapuchinExample.fla in the main directory; this is the Flash Lite source for the Project Capuchin application (see Figure 7-14).

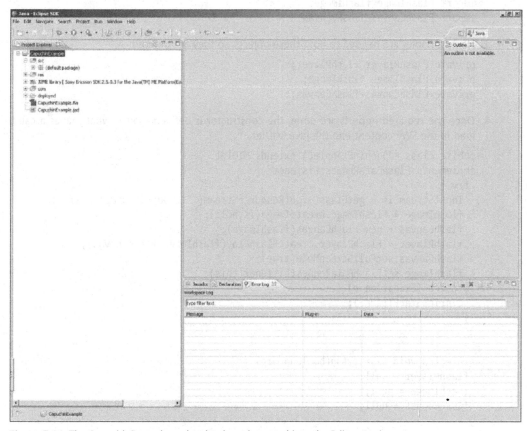

Figure 7-14. The CapuchinExample project has been imported into the Eclipse workspace.

Walking through the Java MIDlet

The CapuchinExample.java file composes the base functionality of a MIDlet. It can be found under the src directory. Opening this file reveals the code that drives the back end of the Project Capuchin application (see Figure 7-15).

1. First, there are several classes that are used to display the mobile application:

```
import java.io.InputStream;
import javax.microedition.lcdui.Display;
import javax.microedition.midlet.Display;
```

As you'll see shortly, the InputStream class provides a load to load up the Flash Lite SWF-based UI. The Display classes provide the means by which the MIDlet displays content on the screen.

2. Next, several Project Capuchin–based APIs are imported; these provide the mechanism to display the Flash Lite content within the Java MIDlet:

```
import FlashPlayer flashPlayer;
import FlashImage flashImage;
import FlashCanvas flashCanvas;
```

3. Next, variables are needed to hold these objects, so they are defined:

```
private FlashPlayer flashPlayer;
private FlashImage flashImage;
private FlashCanvas flashCanvas;
```

4. Once the required imports are done, the constructor is defined. This is what makes a call to load in the SWF content into the Java MIDlet.

```
public class CapuchinExample() extends MIDlet
implements FlashDataRequestListener  {
 try {
  InputStream is = getClass().getResourceStream( "/CapuchinExample.swf" );
  flashImage = FlashImage.createImage(is,null);
  flashCanvas = new FlashCanvas(flashImage);
  flashPlayer = FlashPlayer.createFlashPlay(flashImage,flashCanvas);
  flashCanvas.setFullScreenMode(true);
  flashImage.setFlashDataRequestListener(this);
 } catch (Exception e) {
  e.printStackTrace();
 }
}

protected void destoryApp(boolean arg) {
 flashPlayer = null;
 flashImage = null;
 flashCanvas = null;
}

protected void pauseApp() {}

protected void startApp() {
 if ( flashPlayer != null ) {
  Display.getDisplay(this).setCurrent(flashCanvas);
 }
}
```

```
public synchronized void dataRequested(FlashDataRequest dr) {
  String[] is = dr.getArgs();
   if (is[0].compareTo(new String("exit")) == 0) {
    notifyDestroyed();
   }
 }
}
```

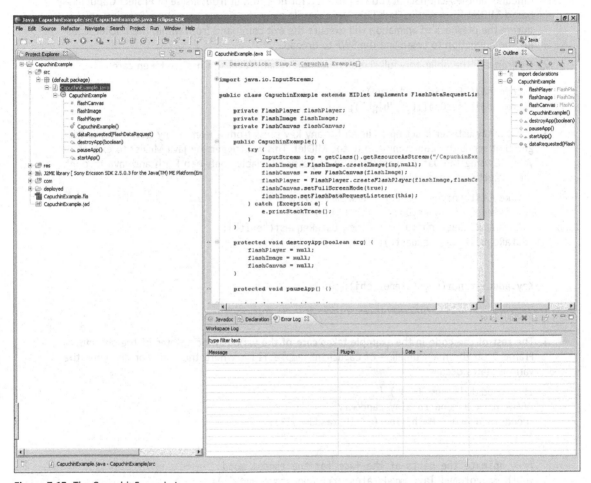

Figure 7-15. The CapuchinExample Java source

Walking through the Flash Lite user interface

Now that you have walked through the Java portion of the Project Capuchin application, it's time to focus attention on the Flash Lite content that is displayed in the application.

1. Open the CapuchinExample.fla found inside the project with Adobe Device Central CS3 or CS4 by selecting Program Files ➤ Adobe Creative Suite CS3 (or CS4). On frame 1 of the Flash timeline, all the ActionScript code is provided for how to quit from inside of Project Capuchin–based MIDlet from within Flash Lite. The example given is a simple animation. Pressing any key during the playback of animation will execute the exit command from within the MIDlet, causing the animation to cease and the SWF to unload.

2. On frame 1, the obligatory full-screen mode and quality level settings are taken care of:

```
fscommand2("FullScreen",true);
fscommand2("setQuality","high");
```

3. Next, a key listener is set up to listen for any key press from a user. If any device key is triggered, it sends the quit command to the MIDlet. This will trigger the Java MIDlet to exit. Here you are using the DataRequest method of passing variables between Flash and Java through the Project Capuchin API.

```
var keyListener_obj:Object = new Object();
keyListener_obj.onKeyDown = function() {
 var dataRequest_obj:Object = new DataRequest("exit");
 dataRequest_obj.request();
}

Key.addListener(KeyListener_obj);

stop();
```

4. The rest of the code in the example takes care of the various mood states of the animation. Frame 2 on the main timeline of CapuchinExample.fla is where the code for changing the various states occurs:

```
if ( moodstate_num != 3 ) {
 //-- pick a mood to play randomly
 moodstate_num = Math.floor( Math.random()*3);
}

//-- animate the parts of the face for the random mood
mouth_mc.gotoAndPlay( moodstates_arr[ moodstate_num ] );
eyes_mc.gotoAndPlay(  moodstates_arr[ moodstate_num ] );
nose_mc.gotoAndPlay(  moodstates_arr[ moodstate_num ] );
```

You can examine the nose_mc, mouth_mc, and eyes_mc MovieClip timelines to get a better understanding of how the basic animation works.

5. When compiling the CapuchinExample.fla (see Figure 7-16), ActionScript 2.0 must be specified (since the Project Capuchin API classes are built using ActionScript 2.0). The Flash Lite version will depend on the handsets that you are targeting (i.e., Sony Ericsson C905 has Flash Lite 2.x preinstalled, right now).

At the time of this writing, Sony Ericsson has only Flash Lite 1.1 and 2.x handsets. However, Flash Lite 3.0 devices may be coming soon, so be sure to check the most current devices' profiles available in the Adobe Device Central CS4 Online Device Library.

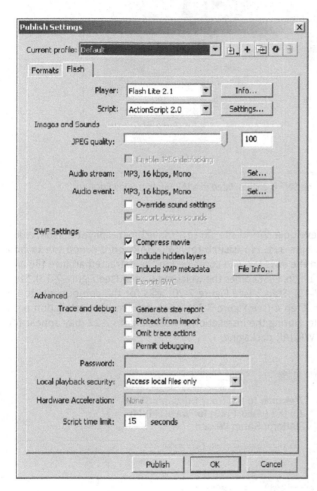

Figure 7-16.
Flash publish settings for a Project Capuchin application (using Flash Lite 2.1 and ActionScript 2.0)

Packaging Flash Lite content with SWF2JAR

The SWF2JAR tool allows you to package your SWFs into a JAR (see Figure 7-17). This JAR is an installation file that allows the respective Project Capuchin–enabled piece of content to be loaded onto a supported device.

The SWF2JAR tool should be installed along with the other tools provided by Sony Ericsson and can be used to package together a MIDlet (e.g., CapuchinExample.jar) and SWF (e.g., CapuchinExample.swf), as found in the previous section.

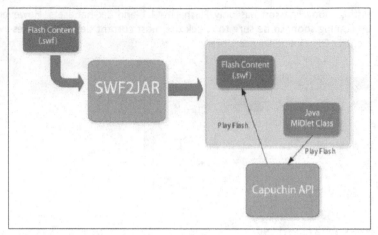

Figure 7-17. Using SWF2JAR, the SWF is encapsulated in a JAR file that Sony Ericsson devices know how to process.

The SWF2JAR utility is located at the Developer World site (http://developer.sonyericsson.com/) and contained in a file named semc_swf2jar_1.1.zip (search for "SWF2JAR" on the web site to find it). Once this file is extracted, merely run the swf2jar.exe contained in the extracted archive file and the step-by-step installation process will begin. First comes the welcome screen (see Figure 7-18). Step 2 is the license agreement (see Figure 7-19). Step 3 (see Figure 7-20) asks for the components to be installed for SWF2JAR; select all of them. Step 4 (see Figure 7-21) is for defining the installation path of SWF2JAR; leave the defaults if possible. During the installation process, Figure 7-22 may appear for confirmation on which JRE to use with SWF2JAR packaging.

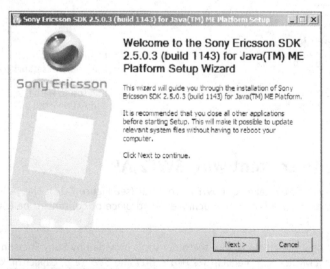

Figure 7-18. SWF2JAR step 1, the welcome screen explaining the requirements to package to JAR format

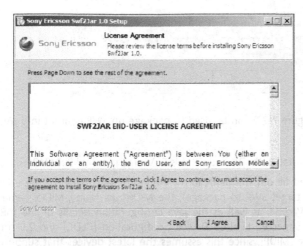

Figure 7-19.
SWF2JAR step 2, the user license agreement

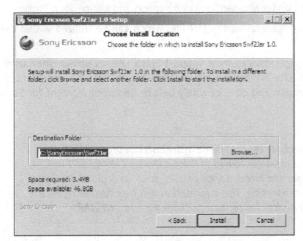

Figure 7-20.
SWF2JAR step 3, the default components for the SWF2JAR installation

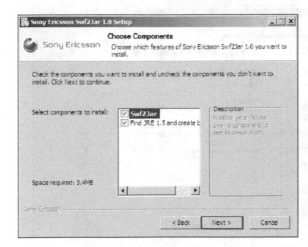

Figure 7-21.
SWF2JAR step 4, the default directory to install SWF2JAR

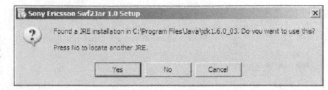

Figure 7-22.
If no JRE is found, this will
need to be installed for
SWF2JAR to work properly.

Once installed, the SWF2JAR tool (see Figure 7-23) can be used to package up SWF content into JAR file format:

1. Open the SWF2JAR tool from its install path. Typically, this is C:\SonyEricsson\SWF2JAR.

2. Find a target SWF to package, and fill out the fields in the Required Fields panel of the user interface: the Flash file path (the target SWF to package), the MIDlet Jar Name, MIDlet name, MIDlet Vendor Name, and MIDlet Version, as well as the Java configuration details of the JAR (typically, these will be 1.1 for Connected Limited Device Configuration [CLDC] and 2.0 for Mobile Information Device Profile [MIDP], since this assumes the latest devices that support Project Capuchin). These are found under Microedition Configuration and Microedition Profile.

3. The Createjar button goes to work generating the JAR file, which can be utilized within the Java distribution.

   Keep in mind that the intended target devices must support Flash Lite, as unlike when using Adobe Mobile Packager, no Flash Lite Player will get installed by default! It's important to choose your target distribution systems and devices wisely before deploying content for Sony Ericsson devices.

> To determine the range of target devices that come with Flash Lite preinstalled, examine the Sony Ericsson device profiles contained in Adobe Device Central CS3 or CS4. Adobe Device Central provides the latest device details, such as regions deployed, operator support, and Flash Lite version. This information will help further refine the possible target Sony Ericsson devices for content packaged using SWF2JAR.

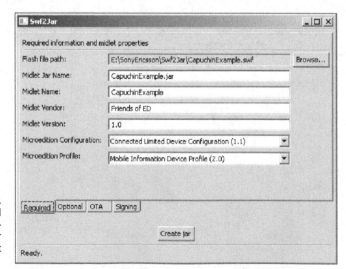

Figure 7-23.
The SWF2JAR utility used
to package SWF applica-
tions, games, and other
content in JAR format

In this section, we will not cover the Optional, OTA, or Signing panels. These offer advanced capabilities that are explained within the documentation from Sony Ericsson. To find more information about these features consult the documentation provided with the download of the SWF2JAR tool. It is found in the C:\SonyEricsson\SWF2JAR directory and should be named ug_swf2jar_r1a.pdf. It's probably a good idea to check it out, as the SWF2JAR tool may evolve a bit over time as it matures.

Getting more information about Project Capuchin

In this section, we've covered some of the essentials of Project Capuchin, but there is much more to the project. The best resource for the newest developer resources for this technology can be found at http://developer.sonyericsson.com/site/global/docstools/projectcapuchin/p_projectcapuchin.jsp.

On the companion web site for this book, at http://advancEd.flashmobilebook.com/extend, we cover further material on Project Capuchin as it evolves and matures on Sony Ericsson devices.

As you've seen in this section, Project Capuchin offers an OEM-based solution to extending Flash on supported Sony Ericsson devices. It allows you to leverage the power of Java while also leveraging the strengths of Flash Lite with user interfaces.

Extending ActionScript in Flash Lite 3.1

In Chapter 3, you read about many of the existing new features of Flash Lite 3.1 including extensions.

Flash Lite extensions are a means for device OEMs to implement plug-in architecture to the Flash Lite player to expand its functionality. However, to date, Adobe has not released any official documentation on how to create plug-ins in the public domain. For this reason, in this book, we will not be covering how to build custom Flash Lite 3.1 ActionScript extensions.

> *In the event that more information becomes publicly available from Adobe on creating custom ActionScript extensions, we will share this information on our companion web site at http://advancED.flashmobilebook.com/extend.*

For more information about extensions for Flash Lite 3.1, contact Adobe directly through its mobile program at http://www.adobe.com/mobile.

Looking forward to Flash 10 and Device APIs

At the time of this writing, Adobe is silently working behind the scenes on all the implementation details for Flash 10 across high-end smart phone devices; that work is known as "Flash 10 for smart phones."

However, the development of this new runtime is still very much a work in progress. Although we love to speculate on all the ways designers and developers will be able to take advantage of low-level device APIs through this new player, please bear in mind that we are only making educated guesses at what support might be provided.

We do believe that when Flash for smart phones does arrive, OEMs will (at least across top-tier devices) be interested in offering low-level device API access (this is especially true of OEMs already offering Flash Lite device APIs). Being able to access GPS, camera, accelerometer, Bluetooth, and other low-level device capabilities is important to creating compelling next-generation mobile applications.

We believe allowing developers' access to these kinds of services will empower them to create much more vibrant mobile user experiences across devices that support Flash for smart phones, just as OEMs such as Nokia and Sony Ericsson provide today with Platform Services and Project Capuchin. At this time, we expect Nokia, Sony Ericsson, and other OEMS planning on supporting Flash 10 to allow the same or similar access to device APIs going forward. However, nothing is set in stone!

By the time you read this, more information about Flash for smart phones should be publicly available to developers. At that time, we will post the latest developments on the companion web site at http://advancED.flashmobilebook.com/flash10. Check there for the latest developments on how Flash 10 is being adopted across various device platforms such as the Palm webOS, Android, and others participating in the Adobe Open Screen Project.

Summary

In this chapter, you had a look at some of the OEM-based solutions available to extend Flash. You learned about solutions offered by Nokia S60 Platform Services and Sony Ericsson's Project Capuchin. Both of these offer the tightest integration and support between Flash and low-level APIs, because they are offered by device manufacturers themselves.

Though you did not get a chance to see solutions from third-party companies such as Kuneri Lite, Janus, Flyer, or SWF2Go in this chapter, these products also can be leveraged on (mostly older) devices where device manufacturers have not yet addressed extending Flash Lite to tap into low-level device capabilities. We do, however, explore some of these third-party products on our companion web site at http://advancED.flashmobilebook.com/extend in several free tutorials. When you get a chance, swing by for the latest and greatest information about extending Flash using these community-driven tools and solutions.

All of these aforementioned options can lead to some very powerful, feature-rich, capable applications and content. By leveraging the combination of Flash and powerful device APIs, designers and developers can create the compelling content that mobile consumers crave.

In our next chapter, we'll take a peek at how to approach getting Flash applications and Flash-like user experiences onto the iPhone by utilizing third-party products (such as eyeGT by leveraging the b.Tween framework). We'll also talk about touch screen experiences found on devices. Let's move on!

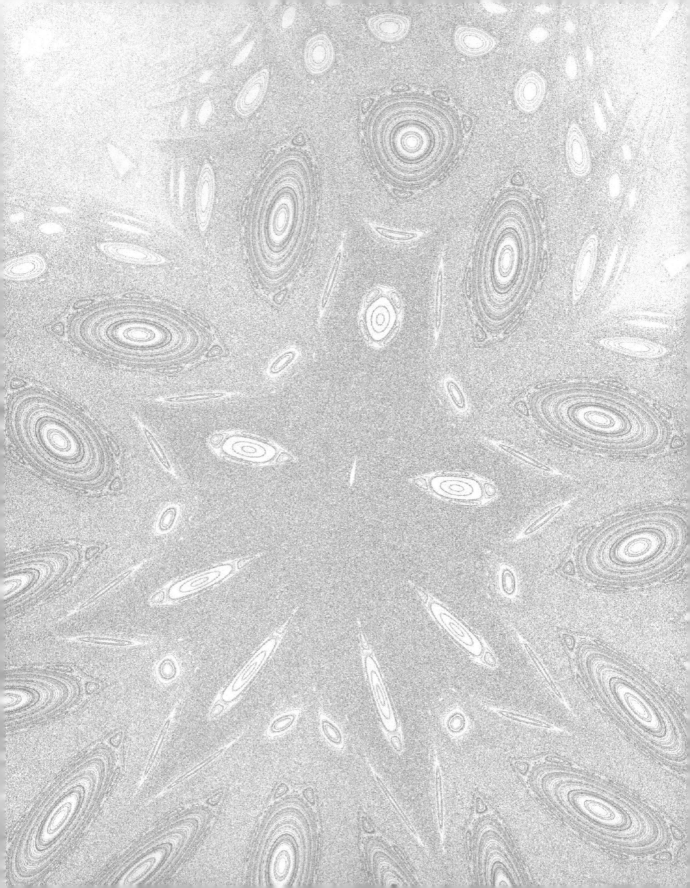

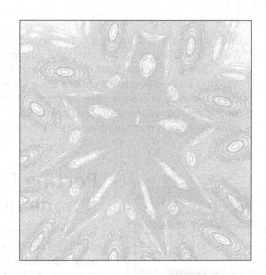

Chapter 8

PORTING FLASH LITE APPLICATIONS TO THE IPHONE USING THIRD-PARTY TOOLS

One of the difficulties in being a Flash Mobile developer at the time of this writing is that the iPhone does not support Flash, so it's not possible to provide an iPhone-optimized version of your mobile content. And that's quite a bummer, isn't it?

According to Adobe's mobile platform evangelist, Adobe is committed to bringing the Flash Player to the iPhone, and while the internal development work has begun, Adobe can't share more details at this point. It is important to note that Adobe needs to work with Apple beyond what is available through the SDK, its emulation environment, and the current license around it to bring the full capabilities of Flash to the iPhone. Adobe thinks Flash availability on the iPhone benefits the millions of joint Apple and Adobe customers and wants to work with Apple to bring these capabilities to the device. Generally, speaking, Apple's policies do not allow third-party developers to release applications that might compete with Apple's own. There are a lot of discussions and theories going on regarding Apple's third-party policy, but why there still is no Flash support is something we might never know. We can only hope that support is available sooner rather than later.

> More info on Adobe's company statement regarding the iPhone can be found at http://flashmobileblog.com/2008/12/31/ adobe-mobile-and-devices-2008-review/.

Does this mean it is impossible to create an iPhone application using your Flash Lite knowledge? Well, yes and no: you can create one, just not directly. In December 2008, Thomas Joos (yes, the same Thomas as on the front cover!) won an Adobe MAX award with a mobile festival guide for Rock Werchter Mobile, which was created using Flash Lite. The cool thing was that the guide was ported to run natively on an iPhone, offering users multitouch screens, Google Maps, and other intuitive tools for finding information about the popular Rock Werchter music festival. Let's take a closer look at how those developers managed to create an iPhone application based from Flash Lite content.

Figure 8-1. Rock Werchter Mobile, an award-winning iPhone application by Boulevart (originally created in Flash Lite)

Porting Flash applications to the iPhone using b.Tween

To get the music festival content running on an iPhone, Thomas worked with Barefoot, a mobile technology and application development company. Barefoot has created a unique development tool called b.Tween based on their in-house Enhance Your Experience Graphical Toolkit (eyeGT) technology, giving developers the opportunity to publish a full spectrum of content in the mobile market. You can take a look at the application in Figure 8-1.

Introducing eyeGT

eyeGT is a highly efficient graphic renderer, capable of handling vector graphics and bitmaps. Besides the basic services of rendering, eyeGT provides a very extensive API that lets you define buttons, animations, hierarchical containers, color, special effects, static text, editable fields, and much more. You can liken it to a Windows GDI+ or Mac OS X Quartz2D, as well as heavily optimized and designed for mobile. You may have heard about other toolkits that do similar things on desktop PCs (like AntiGrain), but eyeGT is in fact very different, not just in terms of speed.

eyeGT is completely self-contained. It does not use any third-party code, like FreeType, for fonts and offers a flat interface to developers, that is, it never returns pointers to objects or requires you to set up complex classes or design schemes. According to Barefoot's chief technology officer Emanuele Cipolloni, it is impossible to create applications with eyeGT that have memory leaks or crashes. Besides efficient memory management, one of eyeGT's greatest strengths is its multiplatform support. eyeGT works on the iPhone, Nokia second and third edition devices, every smart phone and PDA based on Windows Mobile 5 or higher, Sony Ericsson UIQ 2.x and UIQ 3.x devices, and even Nintendo DS (original and Lite) and Sony's PlayStation Portable.

We should also point out that eyeGT is not a Flash-compatible player or virtual machine. It doesn't pick up a SWF file and play it. Barefoot chose not to design a player or virtual machine, because applications would be trapped inside the environment and have no way of accessing the outer world. It would be possible to expand a player with new capabilities to provide those services from within the player, but only virtual machine producers could do it. This would make it very painful for Barefoot to maintain its graphic renderer across all supported devices. Also, a player needs to be present on the hosting platform before the application can be deployed, which is not a problem as eyeGT is self-contained.

Because the vast majority of code that makes up a mobile application is GUI related and not portable to other platforms, Barefoot created a graphic renderer that is able to leverage abstract GUI code, making it portable across various embedded systems. This renderer—eyeGT—allows you to create fully native applications without the typical closed player problems (i.e., limited software API access).

> By the time of publishing Barefoot's technology will not be publicly available. For more info on the technology and tools visit http://www.barefootsoft.com and if you are interested in private beta testing do not hesitate to get in touch with them!

Understanding the inner workings of eyeGT

eyeGT's approach to graphics for embedded systems allows you to treat the display as an advanced and sophisticated canvas. All graphical data is arranged in independent or correlated shapes and organized into prioritized layers. eyeGT allows total control over the way shapes and layers are transformed (rotation, skewing, and scaling) and displayed (normal, translucent, alpha channels, etc.). This means that shapes can decide for themselves how they are displayed on the canvas depending on user-defined parameters like zoom factor, position, and user selections. You can create, delete, and rearrange the contents of a particular layer and its properties and display priority, and even temporary hide layers at any time. Thus, eyeGT provides full control of how the application is presented.

A threefold, sampling, aliasing-reduction algorithm allows for the highest display quality achievable. This all comes with a small memory footprint (only 184KB) for the basic modules compiled for a 32-bit processor and just 280KB for the full library including all multimedia support. eyeGT comes in the form of a very compact shared or static library that can be shipped along with the application without any special setup procedure, and it is invisible to users.

As Figure 8-2 illustrates, eyeGT uses the concept of a canvas (a rectangular zone of the screen of a given width, height, and color depth) in a similar way to some computer-aided design (CAD) programs: the canvas is basically a container where shapes, containers, and other objects are positioned and displayed. The application has no direct access to the canvas, which is the first big difference from the bitmapped mode of other graphical toolkits. The application places visual particles on the canvas, and eyeGT renders them; the application can't draw directly on the canvas.

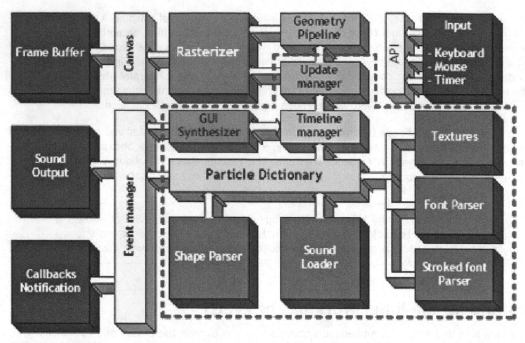

Figure 8-2. eyeGT's modular design (See http://www.barefootmobile.com/blogs/blinky/?p=4 for more information.)

To render something on the screen, the application needs to create a shape, place some drawing commands on it, and place the shape on the screen using the display list. eyeGT uses a dictionary-based system called the Particles dictionary to keep track of every particle (shape, sound, container, button, and so on). It is best to think about the particles dictionary as a storage place for the particle templates and the display list as a list of particle template instances. Figure 8-3 illustrates how the Particles dictionary and display list are related.

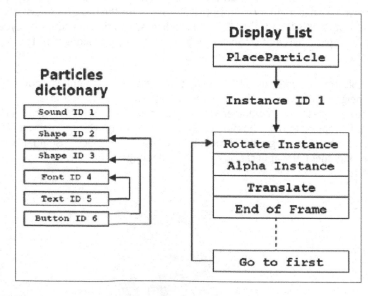

Figure 8-3. The eyeGT Particles dictionary and display list

Converting Flash applications into native iPhone applications

When you need to access features not directly available within the Flash Lite virtual machine, you can use additional solutions and libraries like Kuneri Lite (http://www.kuneri.net) that help extend Flash Lite's capabilities (recall, in Chapter 7, we also covered some of the 1st party solutions such as S60 Platform Services and Project Capuchin). However, such solutions are generally available only for very specific platforms, and Flash Lite might not even be supported on the platform you are targeting. In such cases, you could consider the possibility of porting your work to other platform environments like Java ME or Python. Compared to Flash Lite, though, these alternative platforms offer a substantially downgraded user interface building capability and graphical rendering.

Another alternative is to convert a Flash Lite application into a fully native one, following the hosting platform requirements and UI guidelines. This is a very high-impact solution: it will require you to rearchitect and redesign the entire application, a costly process that has to be repeated for each platform. This is not a solution for every person or company because of a huge time commitment required to develop, debug, and deploy. This is where eyeGT comes in!

Barefoot's eyeGT technology allows you to convert Flash Lite content into native applications for many platforms while keeping the core code platform neutral. Let's see how you can port a key-based Flash Lite game to run natively on an iPhone.

Getting to know the Monster Match game

A basic understanding of what the content is supposed to do is required before you can port the game to the iPhone. Games especially may need some adaptations in terms of graphics or interactivity. In this example, we are going to take a closer look at the Monster Match, provided courtesy of Kooky Panda.

Monster Match is a multilevel strategy game. Three or more monsters are placed in a maze, and each level has a different maze. Each monster can be moved only in a direction where there are no walls or other monsters blocking it. Once the monsters start moving, they cannot be stopped. They stop automatically when they reach another wall, another monster, or the border of the maze. To solve a level, each monster should be placed in the pit that matches its own color. Given the movement limitations, the strategy required to solve the game consists in strategically placing the monsters in a precise order before starting each monster in the direction of the relative pits.

Changing the interface

As illustrated in Figure 8-4, the original game interface has some hints to keypad usage that need to be removed, because on the iPhone, there is no keypad. To move monsters on the iPhone, touch a monster to make him active (originally, pressing the central soft key switched from one selected monster to another). Above the active monster, arrows show the directions the monster can move in. Tapping one of the arrows triggers the monster's movement in that direction. It is entirely up to the developer to choose how to design the touch screen interactions. The best approach, however, is to design games with a touch screen strategy in mind from the beginning.

Figure 8-4.
Changing the Monster
Match interface for
touch screen interaction

Using the reAnimator tool

We are going to launch the reAnimator tool, which comes with the b.Tween framework, and load the MonsterMatch.swf file. Next, we select all the visual elements that need to be touch enabled, such as the arrows and monster MovieClips. No other selections are necessary, as we are exporting the entire game. After you select Convert, the game is fully converted in a few seconds and available to be compiled on the selected platforms (by default the reAnimator exports to Nokia S60 third and fifth edition, Apple iPhone and iPod Touch, Microsoft Windows Win32, and Apple Mac OS X). This process seems almost to good to be true—just press a magical button and the game is converted? More is happening behind the scenes though, so let's start at the beginning and have a closer look at how this conversion process takes place.

Using Barefoot's reAnimator tool, the loaded SWF file is scanned and analyzed. By using a color-coded timeline and custom-sized frame preview (which is shown in Figure 8-5), you can quickly detect how and when various elements are placed on the screen. The reAnimator also provides useful information for cross-referencing shapes, MovieClips, actions, sounds, and so on. These cross-references make it easy to understand the elements of a movie, even if you're not the person who actually wrote it. The reAnimator allows SWF content conversion or extraction by range, by type, and by singular elements, so you can create libraries of elements that can be downloaded and changed at runtime. You can think of them as shared libraries.

Once the conversion project has been set up (by selecting the Convert menu item), the reAnimator creates a project script and passes it to eyeGT's command-line utility called eyeGTConvert, which effectively performs the conversion process. The conversion is divided into two steps so as to provide an option for online (server-based) conversion, which makes this process accessible for every desktop platform.

Using the eyeGTConvert utility results in one or a series of files ending with the .egr extension ("egr" stands for "eyeGT resource"). This is a class representing the behavior of the original Flash content. As mentioned before, these files are ready to be compiled on various environments, as previously mentioned.

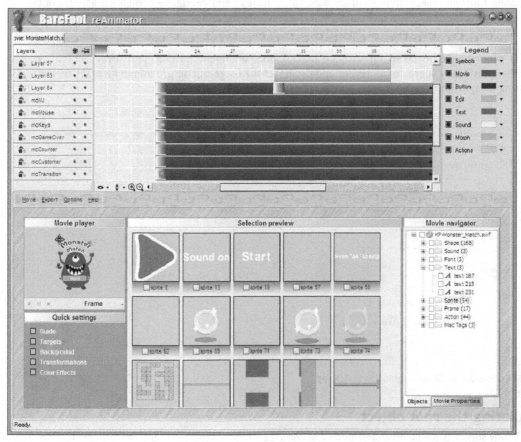

Figure 8-5. The reAnimator tool in action

Porting to the iPhone

The reAnimator exports a MonsterMatch.xcodeproj file, and this should be loaded into Xcode. After selecting the options for the desired installed iPhone SDK version, the converted Flash application can be immediately compiled and launched in the iPhone simulator. Not everything will work magically though. Since the ActionScript code has not been wired up to the respective handlers, the only working code will be the basic actions and the animations within the MovieClips that are not controlled by code.

If you open the CCommonMonsterMatch.cpp file, you will have full access to the platform-independent class CCommonMonsterMatch that encapsulates the entire game. Within that class, you will find the function ActionScriptHandler, where a switch statement detects and handles any ActionScript code that should be executed for each MovieClip and frame.

It is up to you to decide whether to insert code directly into the case statements or to call another function within the class. Generally, using case statements is best when there are very few statements, and calling functions keeps more complex logic easier to read and debug. By comparing actionScript code with the converted C++ or Java code, you can easily see how very similar they really are. Figure 8-6 illustrates this with a code sample of the ported Monster Match game.

Special care should be taken for variable initialization, argument passing, and array access, as ActionScript is pretty liberal in this regard and promotes the usage of bad programming practice, like accessing arrays with negative indexes, which are not tolerated in native code.

```
//All the ActionScript associated to movieclips is handled here
void CCommonMonsterMatch::instancesEvents(U8 EventType, char* Path, U16 Layer, S32 ParticleID, S32 FrameNum, S32 Param3, void* Data)
    {
        if (EventType == evContainerDoActions)
        {
            {
                switch (ParticleID)
                {
                    case 73:
                        {
                            if (FrameNum == 7)
                            {
                                //_root.get_fen = _root.get_fen + 10;
                                get_fen = get_fen + 10;
                            }
                        } break;
                    case 83:
                        {
                            if (FrameNum == 1)
                            {
                                //_root.buNum = _root.buNum - 10;
                                buNum = buNum - 10;
                            }
                        } break;
                    case 88:
                        {
                            if (FrameNum == 1)
                            {
                                //_root.buNum = _root.buNum + 10;
                                buNum = buNum + 10;

                                //_root.shi = true;
                                shi = true;
                            }
                        } break;
```

Figure 8-6. Code example CCommonMonsterMatch.cpp

Emulating the root object

eyeGT fully supports animated and/or nested MovieClips ("MovieClips" are "containers" in eyeGT parlance) but does not support an animated root object like Flash does. To overcome this, the importer class will automatically embed the converted content into another MovieClip that will emulate the root. ActionScript code for the root object is placed directly into the main CCommonMonsterMatch class rather than into the switch statement inside ActionScriptHandler. And ActionScriptHandler will handle only movements between frames of the root. The presence of this extra root-like MovieClip is transparent to the ActionScript code thanks to the specific eyeGT API conceived to help resolve these situations. eyeGT also includes APIs to achieve global transformation of objects placed on the root MovieClip to further help in adapting content to different screen sizes and orientations.

Getting ready to deploy

In theory, the Flash Lite application is now converted into an iPhone project. Via the reAnimator tool, we enabled touch-screen functionality for the required visual elements and automatically ported the basic ActionScript code to run natively. Extra logic can easily be added, for instance, inside the switch statement or via extra functions, to keep your code less complex. This means that our key-based Flash Lite game is ready to be deployed to run on the iPhone, with the official channels offered by the hosting platform (i.e., the App Store). Take a look at Figure 8-7 to see how the iPhone version will look.

Flash on touch-screen devices

We see more and more touch-screen–based devices coming our way. That the most popular of them all, the iPhone, has no Flash support, does not mean we should forget or minimize the way the touch screen is about to dominate the mobile scene. As a mobile developer, it is time to prepare yourself and get comfortable with developing for touch-screen devices. Do I need to tell you that different approaches are required for both developer and designer? Creating a single application available for both touch and keypad devices will cause problems for the developer and the designer, so I thought I'd give you some free advice: get ready for the touchscreen revolution!

Figure 8-7. Our Flash game is ported to iPhone and is ready to be deployed!

Touching things

Using Flash Lite for touch-screen devices means you will have to deal with touch actions that are treated like mouse events. Using mouse handlers like onMouseUp or button handlers like onRelease lets your application react to touch-based input from your user. Even though lots of devices use a stylus, you should consider using a finger as the default way of interaction, because you will avoid clicking and touching problems. Focusing on a stylus means you will have smaller touchable objects, which can cause trouble when trying to press them with a finger.

Also, keep in mind that a key-based interface requires focusing or selecting first, followed by an action. A touch-based approach changes this, because it is possible to skip the focusing part and immediately press the chosen option. We only need to perform the right action after an onMouseUp or onRelease event. Try using those two events, because they are far more user friendly: dragging your finger away from the button or object will cancel the selection if you change your mind. At the time of this writing, the Flash Lite player does not support multitouch interaction, but with a little bit of creativity, everything can be experienced using one single finger!

Designing a touch-based UI

Designing your mobile application's UI and defining its features are good approaches to start off a new mobile project. I think your design process will be smoothest if you start with a clear presentation of your application by answering a few important questions:

- What is your main service?
- What are the main reasons for using your application?
- What are the most important features?
- What type of user are you targeting, and what's his context?

> In Chapter 4, we discussed why our user context is important when trying to build a successful interface, focusing on time, movement, light, and application awareness.

After you have defined your application's goals, features, and target profile, you can start designing your application and work out how the user will efficiently navigate through the application and toward your main features, using only one finger. Creating a detailed wire frame is a good practice for discovering all the differences of a touch screen approach. Of course, creating a wire frame is very platform specific, and this chapter is not focusing on designing or optimizing touch screen UIs. Still, I thought I should warn you not to miss the touch screen UI boat! There is a lot of documentation online if you'd like more information: start with the platform-specific forums like Forum Nokia or Apple's Developer Center to learn more about your favorite touch screen platform. Even though key-based devices are far more prominent, keeping a touch screen approach in mind as you develop your UIs is a good idea.

Summary

Flash on the iPhone is a very popular topic among mobile developers. Although there still is no direct support from Apple, at the time of this writing, Adobe is working on a Flash player for the iPhone, and we hope to see it shipped soon. In the meantime, you can use tools and products like Barefoot's eyeGT technology to reuse your Flash Lite–based core functionality and port it to run natively on other platforms like the iPhone and even extend your application with features like multitouch support. How you target the iPhone is completely up to you, but don't forget that other upcoming touch-screen devices do support Flash (e.g., Nokia Xpress Music 5800, Nokia N97).

Be prepared for a touch screen revolution in the mobile scene, not only in terms of development but also in terms of design and architecture. Keep in mind that you might want to create touch screen versions of your application as well, and no matter which technology you will use, a different approach is required for touch-based UIs!

It's time to get ready for our next chapter, where we will give you a detailed overview of the entire Adobe AIR 1.5 Platform.

Part Three

AIR APPLICATIONS FOR MULTIPLE SCREENS AND MOBILE INTERNET DEVICES

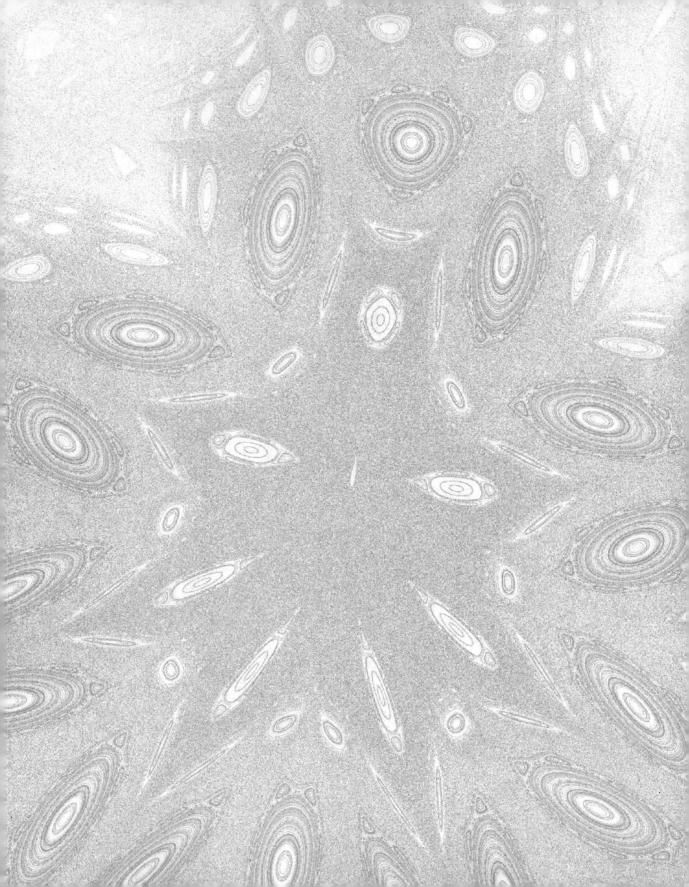

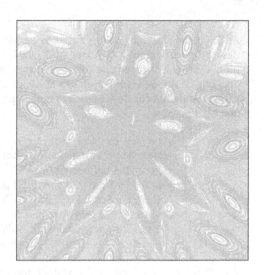

Chapter 9

ADOBE INTEGRATED RUNTIME ON MOBILE DEVICES

The continuing trend is for mobile devices to become as capable as our desktop ones. Additionally, Adobe Integrated Runtime (AIR) availability on mobile devices is expected to increase thanks to the commitment of Adobe partners such as Intel and ARM to release more mobile devices that support AIR.

AIR is a cross-platform desktop runtime that enables the development of desktop applications. It enables you to leverage your existing web development skills to build rich desktop applications, which can be written either in Flash or HTML with JavaScript.

Building applications with AIR allows us to leverage and use our code from web applications. The application can then be deployed platform independent.

Since the release of AIR 1.0 in February of 2008, the technology was adopted very well, and hundreds of applications are currently available for download through the Adobe's AIR Marketplace. In fact, in the beginning of 2009, Adobe announced that over 100 million installations of AIR applications have been installed on desktops. And now, Adobe has released AIR 1.5, which adds new capabilities and is based on Flash Player 10.

At this time of writing, AIR is slated to be adopted and deployed on mobile devices in addition to desktop environments. At Adobe MAX 2007, Intel announced a commitment to create a powerful mobile processor to enable AIR. At the time of this writing, Intel announced the optimization and enabling of Adobe Flash Player 10 and AIR on ARM, which creates new possibilities of creating applications using AIR for devices such as mobile phones, set-top boxes, MIDs, TVs, automotive platforms, and MP3 players.

> *Note that the vast majority of mobile devices will not have the capability to support the full version Flash 10. Flash Lite is likely to evolve over the next year into a Flash 10–compatible player, which will include the capability to write ActionScript 3.0. Flash 10 will be the common target, however, on most devices, Adobe is likely to reduce the API as well as add new mobile-specific API sets such as location and multitouch screen support.*

This chapter is intended to give you an introduction and overview for AIR 1.5. We will give you an overview of the main AIR APIs in general as well as new APIs available for AIR 1.5. AIR is based on Flash Player 10 so we are also going to explore briefly Flash 10 APIs by going over many helpful tips and interesting applications and how they apply when building cross platform applications.

This chapter lays out the foundation for the next chapter where we will continue to explore how to build AIR applications specifically for AIR 1.5 using Flash 10 while taking into consideration the mobile constraints.

Taking a high-level view of the AIR 1.5 platform

The AIR architecture consists of the following components, as shown in Figure 9-1:

- **Network**: The network consists of remote procedure call (RPC) to perform create, read, update, and delete (known as CRUD) operations for a service. The service can be local on the client machine and include a local database or an occasional exchange of data with a remote service while the Internet is connected.

- **Application**: The application can be created as Flash based on two ways:

  - **Flash-based application**: Flash applications can be written in ActionScript 3.0 or Flex, and we can use Flash Catalyst for the front presentation layer. Additionally, we can use HTML content and PDFs (if Adobe reader is installed).

  - **HTML-based application**: HTML applications can be created with and without using JavaScript and not using any Flash. The application can include a Flash component as well as PDF support.

- **Platforms**: Up until the announcement and commitment of Intel and ARM to deploy AIR on mobile, the available platforms were PC, Mac, and 32- or 64-bit Linux. Additionally, with the availability of AIR on UMPC and future availability of AIR on MIDs and smart phones, hopefully by the end of 2009, AIR is expected to be available for deployment on many ARM-based devices, according to Adobe. Also, applications can be deployed on different platforms, which is one of AIR's biggest strengths—it's cross-platform.

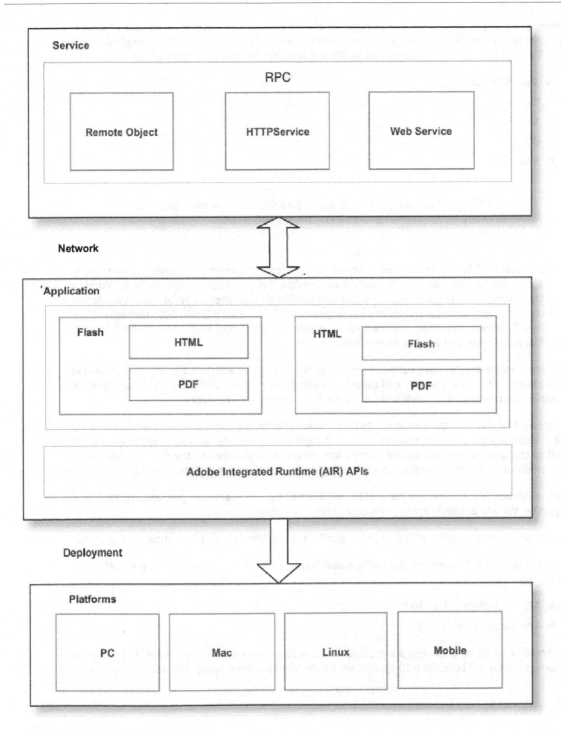

Figure 9-1. AIR architecture

As mentioned earlier, AIR allows you to build desktop applications in Flash or HTML and JavaScript. HTML and Java are made possible via the open source WebKit engine (http://webkit.org/) that renders HTML and executes JavaScript as well as. WebKit supports the following types of files:

- XML HttpRequest
- CSS
- XHTML
- DOM
- SVG

> *Note that with the SVG file format, which is a vector path for pixel graphics, capability is currently not available in Flash through WebKit.*

UMPCs can run AIR 1.5, and we can create applications and deploy them on these devices. These mobile devices have similar constraints as the ARM-based mobile devices. Additionally, Intel's 4G Wireless Broadband Initiative will provide mobile devices with Worldwide Interoperability for Microwave Access (WiMAX) Institute of Electrical and Electronics Engineers (IEEE) standard 802.16e-2005 technology. The initiative will provide nationwide network infrastructure as well as mobile WiMAX-enabled chipsets that will support advanced wireless broadband services.

In general, mobile devices have common constraints that should be addressed in any mobile devices development, and building an AIR application is no exception. In particular, we need to pay attention to mobile constraints such as performance, connectivity, power, and resources.

This means that our AIR application needs to be aware of different hardware constraints and adjust as it is deployed on different platforms or as changes are made. Ideally, your application should adjust to changes and not rely on the device's operating system to adjust to the device's constraints. Additionally, applications are responsible for hiding these issues and constraints from the user.

As we build our AIR applications for mobile, we need to take into account platform, context, and adaptation. We will discuss these in more detail in the next chapter.

The AIR APIs include both the APIs for Flash Player 10 and the APIs for AIR 1.5, as shown in Figure 9-2.

In this section, we will cover the Flash APIs available using AIR 1.5. We prefer splitting the APIs into two categories:

- APIs available for Flash 10
- APIs available for AIR 1.5

You should be aware of which APIs are available for Flash 10 and which belong specifically to the AIR 1.5 platform, so when you build Flash 10 applications for the Web, you know which APIs you can and cannot use.

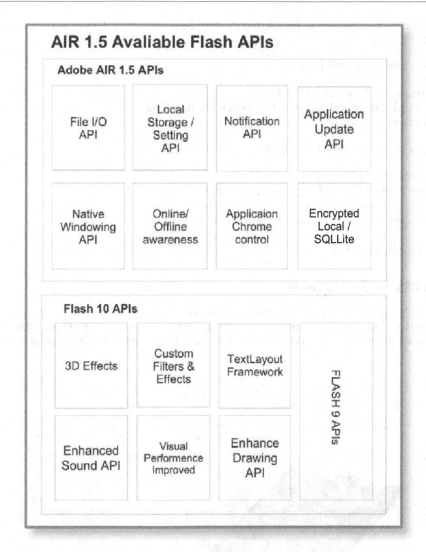

Figure 9-2. AIR 1.5 Flash APIs

Using tips and tricks for Flash Player 10 on mobile devices

AIR 1.5 is utilizing Flash Player 10, which means that all the Flash 10 APIs are available to use, so you should become familiar with all the new APIs and tools that Flash 10 has to offer.

In Flash 10, Adobe has drastically changed many of the APIs and the architecture of the components, as well as adding 3-D capabilities, better video, and better performance. Note that the explanation and examples in this section are written for AIR, but most of them will work in Flex 4 beta if you just change the application tag.

For example, you could change this AIR code

```
<?xml version="1.0" encoding="utf-8"?>
<WindowedApplication xmlns="http://ns.adobe.com/mxml/2009">
</WindowedApplication>
```

to the following, in order to work in Flex 4 beta:

```
<?xml version="1.0" encoding="utf-8"?>
<s:WindowedApplication xmlns:fx="http://ns.adobe.com/mxml/2009"
    xmlns:s="library://ns.adobe.com/flex/spark"
    xmlns:mx="library://ns.adobe.com/flex/halo">

</s:WindowedApplication>
```

Moving objects in 3-D space

Flash Player 10 added a 3-D tool API, which allows you to take any pixel or container and move it around in a 3-D space. It's simple to use and opens up the possibility to create some interesting GUIs. Figure 9-3 shows a little example that demonstrates how easy it is to move a video around a 3-D space.

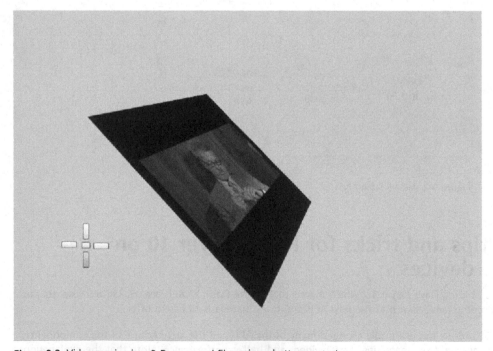

Figure 9-3. Video moving in a 3-D space and flips using a button control

In this minimalist example, we set the FxRotate3D methods attaching them to a VideoDisplay container and use buttons to rotate the container. Take a look at the complete code:

```
<?xml version="1.0" encoding="utf-8"?>
<s:WindowedApplication xmlns:fx="http://ns.adobe.com/mxml/2009"
    xmlns:s="library://ns.adobe.com/flex/spark"
    xmlns:mx="library://ns.adobe.com/flex/halo">

    <fx:Declarations>
        <s:Rotate3D id="rotateXdown"
                target="{video}"
                angleXFrom="0"
                angleXTo="360"
                duration="2000" />

        <s:Rotate3D id="rotateXup"
                target="{video}"
                angleXFrom="360"
                angleXTo="0"
                duration="2000" />

        <s:Rotate3D id="rotateYleft"
                target="{video}"
                angleXFrom="0"
                angleXTo="360"
                duration="2000" />

        <s:Rotate3D id="rotateYright"
                target="{video}"
                angleYFrom="360"
                angleYTo="0"
                duration="2000" />

        <s:Rotate3D id="rotateZright"
                target="{video}"
                angleZFrom="0"
                angleZTo="360"
                duration="2000" />
    </fx:Declarations>

    <s:VideoPlayer
        source="http://thehq.tv/wp-content/uploads/flv/2-13-teaser.flv"
        id="video" width="300" height="300"
        x="200" y="96"/>

    <s:Button id="fxButtonZ"
            label="z"
            click="rotateZright.play();"
            x="119" y="359" height="10" width="14"/>
```

```
        <s:Button id="fxButtonX"
                label="x"
                click="rotateXup.play();"
                x="121" y="330" width="10" height="25"/>
        <s:Button id="fxButtonY"
                label="y"
                click="rotateYright.play();"
                x="138" y="360" width="25" height="10"/>
        <s:Button id="fxButtonY0"
                label="y"
                click="rotateYleft.play();"
                x="86" y="358" width="25" height="10"/>
        <s:Button id="fxButtonX0"
                click="rotateXdown.play();"
                x="121" y="374" height="25" width="10"/>

    </s:WindowedApplication>
```

Let's go through the code. In Flex 4 beta, the Rotate3D tag must be contained within the `<fx:Declarations>` tag since it does not implement mx.core:

```
    <fx:Declarations>
```

After the declarations tag, we can define the Rotate3D tag. Rotate3D is part of the mx.effects API and has properties to attach the effect to an object and define how to rotate the object. In the following code, we rotate an object from 0 to 360 degrees downward:

```
    <s:Rotate3D id="rotateXdown"
        target="{video}"
        angleXFrom="0"
        angleXTo="360"
        duration="2000" />
```

Once all the FxRotate3D tags for each rotation are declared, we need to define the video object. The object sets a video that is 300×300 pixels and positions it at a specified X,Y location. You can use any file format VideoDisplay supports as a video file.

```
    <s:VideoPlayer source="file.flv"
        id="video" width="300" height="300"
        x="200" y="96"/>
```

Last, we need to set buttons so we can rotate the object. To set the button, we can use the FxRotate3D effect we set previously and use the play property to get the effect started.

```
    <s:Button id="fxButtonX0"
      click="rotateXdown.play();"
      x="121" y="374" height="25" width="10"/>
```

Using Pixel Bender for graphics and calculations

If you have cinematic experience, you will be excited to know that Flash 10 allows us to start using Adobe After Effects–like techniques by working with a new tool called Pixel Bender. You can mix your own filters with existing Flash Player filters to create real-time effects.

> *Keep in mind that some of these new features may not be available on mobile devices when Flash 10 becomes available on mobile, since they may consume too many resources. Additionally, even if some visuals features are available, they may drain the mobile battery.*

Up until now, we had to hard-code custom bitmap filters into our code. But this solution is not flexible, since you can't change the filter at runtime. It also takes a lot of native code and is not optimized.

In Flash 10, Adobe added a compiler to handle filters, which is possible through Pixel Bender kernels, which calculate a single pixel at runtime. This is how it works: the Pixel Bender graph uses XML for combining individual pixel-processing operations called kernels. Kernel files are in PBK file format. We can create the PBK XML file using the Pixel Bender toolkit. After our kernel is ready, we can then export it as a bytecode file called Pixel Bender bytecode (PBJ). The PBJ file can then be used in Flash Player 10.

> *A Flex 4 Bender shader contains the Pixel Bender kernels, which use a separate thread from the Flash Player to calculate a single pixel.*
>
> *Additionally, there is another file format called Pixel Bender graphs (PBG), which is supported directly in the Photoshop/After Effects CS4 Pixel Bender extension.*

Pixel Bender can be used for the following graphics:

- **Filters**: You can create a Pixel Bender shader (using the ShaderFilter method) and use the Pixel Bender kernel as a filter on any component based on DisplayObject, just as you use other filters.

- **Fills**: The beginShaderFill method allows you to create custom fills to be used as backgrounds and add to the existing fills built into Flex (i.e., solid, gradient, and bitmap).

- **Blend modes**: By assigning the blendShader property, you can control how DisplayObject is composited and what's beneath it.

- **Calculations:** You can use the Pixel Bender kernel for mathematical calculations.

Creating custom filters with Pixel Bender

Let's take a look at an example of creating custom filters with Pixel Bender.

1. First, download and install the Pixel Bender toolkit from http://labs.adobe.com/downloads/pixelbender.html.

2. Next, download an effect from the Pixel Bender Exchange page: http://www.adobe.com/cfusion/exchange/index.cfm?event=productHome&exc=26&loc=en_us.

3. After the Pixel Bender toolkit download is completed, install and open the filter toolkit (see Figure 9-4), and export it as a PBJ file, which can be loaded at runtime into the Flash Player 10 application.

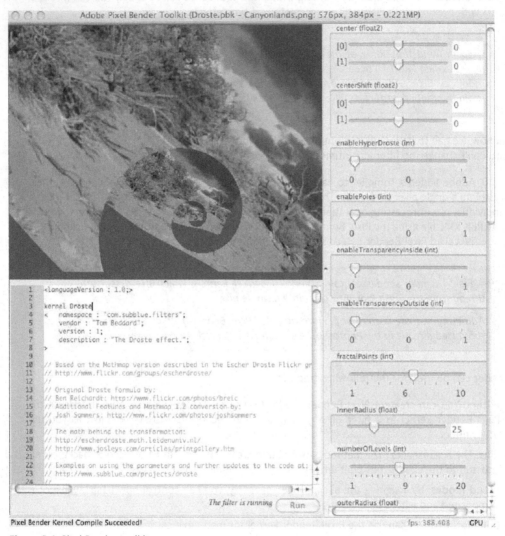

Figure 9-4. Pixel Bender toolkit

Once you have exported the PBJ file, you can use it in Flex 4 beta in several ways. You can use a Pixel Bender shader declaratively in your Flex application, or you can write a Pixel Bender shader and apply it to your Flex component, basically adding its effects to your component's animation sequence.

The following basic example AIR application embeds the TubeView.pbj file. It uses this file as the byte-code source and sets the mine type application/octet-stream. The filter is then used on the image to produce the result shown in Figure 9-5.

```
<?xml version="1.0" encoding="utf-8"?>
<s:WindowedApplication xmlns:fx="http://ns.adobe.com/mxml/2009"
    xmlns:s="library://ns.adobe.com/flex/spark"
    xmlns:mx="library://ns.adobe.com/flex/halo">

    <mx:Image source="img.jpg" width="800" height="600">
        <mx:filters>
            <s:ShaderFilter shader="@Embed(source='TubeView.pbj')"
                radius="300"
                center="50"
                turbulence="80" />
        </mx:filters>
    </mx:Image>

</s:WindowedApplication>
```

Figure 9-5. This AIR application uses Pixel Bender to filter an image.

The filter is placed inside of the image tag and allows us to apply the ShaderFilter filter on the image. The ShaderFilter is the effect we loaded from the Adobe Exchange site.

One thing to remember is that the Pixel Bender toolkit uses the graphics processing unit (GPU). However, Flash Player 10 doesn't use the GPU, since Adobe didn't want to increase the size of the Flash

Player 10, and Pixel Bender toolkit doesn't support any processors or other Intel chips at this point. Due to that difference, a kernel that runs well in the toolkit might not run well at all in Flash Player 10, so you need to test to ensure you get the performance you want.

> The GPU is a dedicated graphics-rendering device. Basically, the GPU is the processor attached to the graphics card and is used to calculate floating point operations and others.

Using Pixel Bender to calculate information

Since the Flash Player is using a single-thread processor, we can leverage Pixel Bender kernels for calculations of data to increase our application performance. As mentioned, Pixel Bender kernels and the Flash Player are running on separated threads, and the kernel is faster than the Flash Player. You can send the request to a separate thread to do the heavy lifting and get an event once completed.

You can use the following math functions in Pixel Bender for calculations:

- sin(x): Sine function
- cos(x): Cosine function
- tan(x): Tangent function
- asin(x): Arcsine (inverse sine) function
- acos(x): Arccosine (inverse cosine) function
- atan(x) and atan(x, y): Arctangent (inverse tangent) function
- exp(x): Exponential function
- log(x): Logarithm function
- pow(x, y): Power of function
- reciprocal(x): Multiplicative inverse function
- sqrt(x): Square root function

Let's create an example of a calculation using Pixel Bender. Open the Pixel Bender toolkit, and create this script to calculate a sine function:

```
<languageVersion : 1.0;>
kernel SinCalculator
<
    namespace : "Your namespace";
    vendor : "Your name or company name";
    version : 1;
    description : "Your description";
>
{
    input image1 src;
    output pixel3 result;
```

```
    void evaluatePixel()
    {
        pixel1 value = pixel1(sin(sample(src, outCoord())));
        result = pixel3(value, 0.0, 0.0);
    }
}
```

The class set pixel1 to do the sine function. Then, we set the result to pixel3, which will output the result. You will need to load an image as a placeholder, since Pixel Bender was not intended to do these calculations. Run the code, and you can export the code for the Flash Player.

To export the code for the Flash Player, select File ➤ Export for Flash Player, then you can save the file as a PBJ and use it in our application.

There is a limit on the number of calculations that Pixel Bender can perform, but we can create a helper class that can handle the communication with Pixel Bender. Let's create a class and call it PixelBenderCalculator.

```
package com.elad.framework.pixelBender
{
    import com.elad.pixelBender.events.PixelBenderCalcEvent;

    import flash.display.Shader;
    import flash.display.ShaderJob;
    import flash.events.Event;
    import flash.events.EventDispatcher;
    import flash.utils.ByteArray;
    import flash.utils.Endian;
```

We should set the event we will be using once we complete the calculations using the event metadata. This step is not necessary but helps us find the event once we add an event listener to this class.

```
    [Event(name="completed", type=➡
"com.elad.pixelBender.events.PixelBenderCalcEvent")]

    public class PixelBenderCalculator extends EventDispatcher
    {
```

We then need to define the PBJ class we will be using; we'll assign a class in our implementation.

```
        public var kernalClass:Class;
```

We also need to define an array, numberCollection, which will hold the collection of numbers we need to do a calculation for, as well as shader and shaderJob.

```
        public var numberCollection:Array;

        private var shader:Shader;
        private var shaderJob:ShaderJob;
        private var input:ByteArray;
```

```
private var output:ByteArray;
private var retCollection:Array;
private var requestsCounter:Number;
private var numberOfRequest:Number;
```

We will also define a const to hold the number of calculations per kernal:

```
private const COLLECTION_SIZE:int = 5000;
```

In our default constructor, we reset the variables, set the kernal class we will be using, and set the collection of numbers we will be performing calculations on. We also define the number of requests we will be making, and since Pixel Bender will produce an error message if there are too many calculations, we will set the number of requests here.

```
public function PixelBenderCalculator➡
(numberCollection:Array, kernalClass:Class)
{
    reset();

    this.kernalClass = kernalClass;
    this.numberCollection = numberCollection;

    requestsCounter = numberCollection.length/COLLECTION_SIZE;
}
```

The reset method just cleaned up our arrays and other data. Since the amount of data may be large, we need a method to destroy the data before we start and after we complete a task.

```
public function reset():void
{
    retCollection = new Array();
    numberCollection = new Array();
    requestsCounter = 0;
    numberOfRequest = 0;
    numberCollection = null;
}
```

This is the method we will be exposing in our API to start the calculations. The method sets the output and input. The input is based on the size of the COLLECTION_SIZE.

```
public function start():void
{
    output = new ByteArray();
    output.endian = Endian.LITTLE_ENDIAN;

    var start:int = numberOfRequest*COLLECTION_SIZE;
    var end:int = ( (numberOfRequest+1)*COLLECTION_SIZE > ➡
numberCollection.length) ? ➡
numberCollection.length : ((numberOfRequest+1)*COLLECTION_SIZE);
```

```
                            input = ➡
convertArrayToByteArray(numberCollection, start, end);
                createShaderJob();
                numberOfRequest++;
        }
```

This method makes the request and is very similar to any loader we would use in Flash. Once we set the ShaderJob, we can define a listener and start the job.

```
            private function createShaderJob():void
            {
                var width:int = input.length >> 2;
                var height:int = 1;

                shader = new Shader(new kernalClass());
                shader.data.src.width = width;
                shader.data.src.height = height;
                shader.data.src.input = input;

                shaderJob = new ShaderJob(shader, output, width, height);
                shaderJob.addEventListener ➡
    (Event.COMPLETE, shaderJobCompleteHandler);
                shaderJob.start();
        }
```

The handler adds the results to the collection. We split our task into parts, and this method starts another request, if needed, which is passed passed to the calculationCompleted method once we complete our task.

```
            private function shaderJobCompleteHandler(event:Event):void
            {
                output.position = 0;
                addByteArrayToCollection(output);

                input = null;
                output = null;

                if (requestsCounter>numberOfRequest)
                {
                    start();
                }
                else
                {
                    calculationCompleted();
                }

        }
```

Once the task is completed, we will dispatch an event to notify that we are done and pass the array containing the calculation results we made in Pixel Bender. We also use the reset method to clean all the data we don't need anymore.

```
private function calculationCompleted():void
{
    this.dispatchEvent( ➥
new PixelBenderCalcEvent(retCollection) );

    reset();
}
```

convertArrayToByteArray is a utility method to convert our array to a byte array:

```
private static function convertArrayToByteArray ➥
(array:Array, start:int, end:int):ByteArray
{
    var retVal:ByteArray = new ByteArray();
    var number:Number;

    retVal.endian = Endian.LITTLE_ENDIAN;

    for (var i:int=start; i<end; i++)
    {
        number = Number(array[i]);
        retVal.writeFloat(number);
    }

    retVal.position = 0;
    return retVal;
}
```

The addByteArrayToCollection method takes the byte array we received from the Pixel Bender kernel, converts the information to a float number, and adds the information to the array we will return to the user. We are checking the data to ensure we are passing three variables, if(i % 3 == 0). Since we had to add three extra pieces of data to pass to the Pixel Bender kernel, pixel3(value, 0.0, 0.0);.

```
private function addByteArrayToCollection ➥
(byteArray:ByteArray):void
{
    var length:int = byteArray.length;
    var number:Number;

    for(var i:int=0; i<length; i+=4)
    {
        number = byteArray.readFloat();
        if(i % 3 == 0)
```

```
                    {
                        retCollection.push(number);
                    }
                }
            }
        }
    }
```

Using this API, we can create a class to implement and check if we achieved any performance gains. We will create two methods: one will call the Pixel Bender kernal, and the other will use the Flash Player for calculations. Take a look at Figure 9-6. We will run a video in the background, while we calculate the result so we can observe performance.

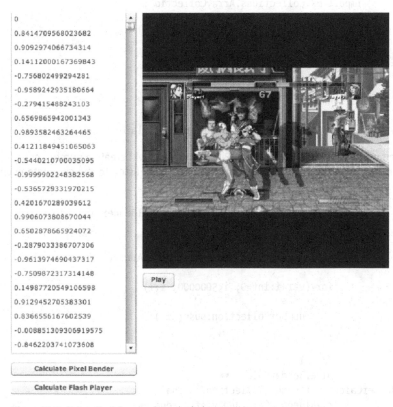

Figure 9-6. Using Pixel Bender for calculations

Let's take a look at the code to create the application in Figure 9-6:

```xml
<?xml version="1.0" encoding="utf-8"?>
<s:WindowedApplication
    xmlns:fx="http://ns.adobe.com/mxml/2009"
    xmlns:s="library://ns.adobe.com/flex/spark"
```

```
            xmlns:mx="library://ns.adobe.com/flex/halo"
            xmlns:local="*"
            width="600" height="650">

            <fx:Script>
                <![CDATA[

                    import com.elad.framework.➡
            pixelBender.PixelBenderCalculator;
                    import com.elad.framework.➡
            pixelBender.events.PixelBenderCalcEvent;

                    import mx.collections.ArrayCollection;
                    import mx.collections.IList;
                    import mx.events.FlexEvent;
```

We define our Pixel Bender class using the following expression:

```
                    [Embed(source="SinCalculator.pbj", ➡
            mimeType="application/octet-stream")]
                    private var kernalClass:Class;
                private var pixelBenderCalc:PixelBenderCalculator;
```

We instruct our method to start the calculations in Pixel Bender; we will create a number collection in the size of 5 million then start the Pixel Bender shader. An event will listen to the complete event we created in the API.

```
                    protected function startCalculatorPixelBender():void
                    {
                        // create a number collection
                        var numberCollection:Array = new Array();

                        for (var i:int=0; i<5000000; i++)
                        {
                            numberCollection.push( i );
                        }

                        // calculate
                        pixelBenderCalc = ➡
            new PixelBenderCalculator(numberCollection, kernalClass);
                        pixelBenderCalc.addEventListener➡
            (PixelBenderCalcEvent.COMPLETED, onComplete );

                        pixelBenderCalc.start();
                    }
```

Once we get the response that the calculation is completed, we can bind the information to a list component.

```
private function onComplete(event:PixelBenderCalcEvent):void
{
    list.dataProvider = new ArrayCollection(event.numberCollection);
    pixelBenderCalc.removeEventListener➡
(PixelBenderCalcEvent.COMPLETED, onComplete);
}
```

This method does exactly what Pixel Bender did, but this time uses the Flash Player, so everything is done on the same thread. This method will be used as a way to test if we gain in terms of performance.

```
            private function startCalculatorFlashPlayer():void
            {
                // create a number collection
                var numberCollection:Array = new Array();

                for (var i:int=0; i<5000000; i++)
                {
                    numberCollection.push( Math.sin(i) );
                }

                list.dataProvider = ➡
new ArrayCollection(numberCollection);
            }

        ]]>
    </Script>
```

Our components include a list to display the results, video player, and buttons. You can test the performance by starting the video, calling the Flash Player, and then comparing the time it took to calculate as well as performance to the Pixel Bender shader.

```
<mx:List id="list" width="200" height="531.5"/>
    <s:Button label="Calculate with Pixel Bender"
width="200" height="20" y="545"
click="startCalculatorPixelBender()"/>
    <s:Button label="Calculate with Flash Player"
width="200" height="20" y="574"
click="startCalculatorFlashPlayer()"/>

    <s:VideoPlayer id="vid" width="355" height="290"
        source="video.flv"
        autoPlay="false" x="209" y="-1"/>
    <s:Button label="Play" click="vid.play();" x="213" y="303"/>

    <local:MemoryDashBoard x="211" y="343"/>

</s:WindowedApplication>
```

The results are astonishing. Using the Flash Player, running the code took 6 to 8 seconds (on an iMac) and the video paused. Using Pixel Bender, the video had a slight glitch, and we received the results back once the task was completed. When the example is running, click to play the video, and use the Flash player button to calculate the results, and you will notice that the video completely stalls while the Flash Player is calculating the results, since we are using the same thread. Run the video again, and the second time, use the Pixel Bender to calculate; you will notice a tiny glitch in the video, but the video keeps playing while the Pixel Bender calculates the number.

Utilizing the Text Layout Framework

Created by the In Design team (http://labs.adobe.com/technologies/textlayout/), the Text Layout Framework (TLF) is Adobe's new Flash framework for dealing with text. The TLF is available in the Flash CS4, Flex 3.2, and Flex 4 SDKs. The new framework consists of a set of classes in Flash Player 10 that brings print-quality graphics to web and AIR applications and allows you to create multilingual web applications using device fonts.

Here are some of the TLF features:

- **Bidirectional text**: Includes vertical text and over 30 writing systems including Arabic, Hebrew, Chinese, Japanese, Korean, Thai, Lao, the major writing systems of India, *Tate-Chu-Yoko* (horizontal text within vertical text), and more

- **Formatting**: Text with inline graphics (images, SWFs, or any DisplayObject) and multiple columns of text with text flow and text selection through these columns, as well as support for vertical text and *Tate-Chu-Yoko* (horizontal text within vertical text)

- **Print-quality typography for the Web**: Allows for kerning, ligatures, typographic case, digit case, digit width, and discretionary hyphens

- **Mouse and keyboard user gestures**: Standard keyboard and mouse functionality for copy, paste, undo, and cut

- **Text metrics**: Includes measurements and offsets of fonts

The architecture of the framework is shown in Figure 9-7. The TLF is the high-level implementation of the Flash Text Engine (FTE). The FTE is a low-level API, so you can come up with your own set of components for FTE. FTE is limited in functionality and offers basic manipulation of text and is the foundation for the TLF.

In Flash Builder 4, there are two SWC libraries that include and provide support for the FTE:

- framework_textLayout.swc includes classes to allow components such as DataGrid or TextField to support the TLF.

- textLayout.swc includes the entire class library to support the TLF.

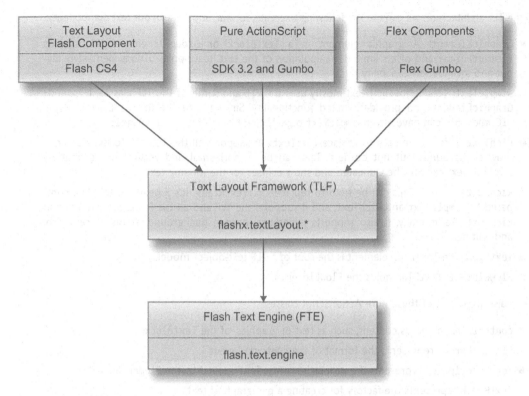

Figure 9-7. TLF architecture

Since the last build of Flex Gumbo, which was given at Adobe MAX 2008 and is available on the pre-release Adobe site, the TLF and components such as TextBox or TextElement have been changed and are no longer available. The best way to check the TLF version is using the BuildInfo class as follows:

```
trace("TLF version: " + BuildInfo.VERSION);
trace("TLF Build number: " + BuildInfo.kBuildNumber);
trace("TLF Audit id: " + BuildInfo.AUDIT_ID);
```

Using Flash Builder 4 beta, we got the following version information:

```
TLF version: 1.0
TLF Build number: 427 (699527)
TLF Audit id: <AdobeIP 0000486>
```

With the TLF architecture, we can use the following to create, format, and control our text components:

- GraphicElement: A graphic element in a TextBlock or GroupElement object extends ElementFormat and offers limited manipulation of the text. It supports UIComponent-style layout and invalidation capability.

- simpleText: This lightweight text mostly uses the FTE and some of the TLF classes; it extends GraphicElement and provides limited functionality. Since it's of the GraphicElement type, UIComponents can have a few simpleText objects share the same DisplayObject.

- RichText: This can be used to replace <mx:Text>. It supports all the TLF text formats and can draw backgrounds but not borders. Text can be in horizontal and vertical but cannot be scrolled. Text can also be truncated and show ellipses for the missing text.

- RichEditableText: This can be used to replace <mx:TextArea>. It's a heavyweight class compared to simpleText and RichText, and it supports the TLF and all the features mentioned in RichText. Additionally, it also supports hyperlinks, border, background, scrolling, selection, and editing.

- TextFlow: The TextFlow element is the root of a TLF text-object model.

- FlowElement: TextFlow holds the FlowElements.

You can also make use of these pure ActionScript classes:

- contentElement holds content, such as text or graphics, of the TextBlock.

- ElementFormat represents the format of the contentElement.

- fontDescription represents the properties of the font applied to the ElementFormat.

- TextBlock represents the factory for creating a paragraph of text.

- textLine is the DisplayObject used for creating a line of text for the TextBlock.

There are three text primitives that you can use: SimpleText, RichText, and RichEditableText.

Let's take a simple example using AIR 1.5:

```
<?xml version="1.0" encoding="utf-8"?>
<s:WindowedApplication
    xmlns:fx="http://ns.adobe.com/mxml/2009"
    xmlns:s="library://ns.adobe.com/flex/spark"
    xmlns:mx="library://ns.adobe.com/flex/halo">

    <s:VGroup>
        <s:SimpleText fontSize="12"
            width="100" x="24" y="309">
            SimpleText</s:SimpleText>
        <s:RichEditableText fontFamily="arial"
            color="0x4697c4" text="RichEditableText" />
        <s:RichText fontFamily="arial"
            color="0x4697c4" text="RichText"  />
    </s:VGroup>

</s:WindowedApplication>
```

The simpleText element extends the GraphicElement and uses the FTE and thus offers limited manipulation of the text:

```
<s:SimpleText fontSize="12" width="100"> Hello, world!</s:SimpleText>
```

Using TLF-based components, you have more control over text, and you can set fonts properties such as style, alpha, antialiasing, and rotation values, as well create custom text components.

```
<s:RichText fontFamily="arial" color="0x4697c4" text="RichText"  />
```

The most advanced text component is RichEditableText; it extends the UIComponent and uses the TLF API. However, it is also the most heavyweight and costly of the three text primitives, since it's based on UIComponent. Take a look at the following code:

```
<s:RichEditableText fontFamily="arial"
     color="0x4697c4" text="RichEditableText" />
```

Notice that the RichEditableText and RichText are UIComponent elements; we don't need to place them in the Group element. Also, once you compile, you will notice that RichEditableText text by default will be scrollable, selectable, and editable.

```
<?xml version="1.0" encoding="utf-8"?>
<s:WindowedApplication
     xmlns:fx="http://ns.adobe.com/mxml/2009"
     xmlns:s="library://ns.adobe.com/flex/spark"
     xmlns:mx="library://ns.adobe.com/flex/halo">


     <s:RichEditableText fontFamily="arial"
          color="0x4697c4" text="RichEditableText" />
     <s:RichText fontFamily="arial"
          color="0x4697c4" text="RichText"  />

</s:WindowedApplication>
```

The TLF's component object model is a tree of FlowElements, such as ParagraphElements and SpanElements (corresponding to <span> tags). What TLF essentially does is create, render, or manipulate the TextFlows classes.

The following SpanElements tags are available to you:

- <a> embeds a link and can include <br>, <img>, <span>, <tcy>, or <tab> tags.
-
 adds a break, so the text will continue to the next line.
- <div> divides text. Inner tags can include <div> or <p> tags.
- <img> adds an image in a paragraph.
- <p> indicates a new paragraph and can include any elements other than <div>.
- <span> creates a run of text in a paragraph and can contain only a <text> tag.

- <tab> adds a tab character to the paragraph.
- <tcy> is used to run horizontal text within vertical text. It can be used for languages such as Japanese and can contain the following tags: <break>, <img>, <span>, or <tab>.

Take a look at the following example, which uses the RichText primitive components as well as SpanElements and TextFlow elements. The example will use the RichText primitive components and add customization (see Figure 9-8).

```
<?xml version="1.0" encoding="utf-8"?>
<s:WindowedApplication xmlns:fx="http://ns.adobe.com/mxml/2009"
    xmlns:s="library://ns.adobe.com/flex/spark"
    xmlns:mx="library://ns.adobe.com/flex/halo">

    <s:Group fontSize="12">
    <s:RichText rotation="12" alpha="0.8" x="50" y="50">
            <s:TextFlow color="0x555555">
                    <s:p>
                            <s:span fontWeight="bold">
                                Just text</s:span>
                            <s:br />
                            <s:a href="http://twitter.com/
                                eladnyc">Elad's
                                twitter user</s:a>
                    </s:p>
            </s:TextFlow>
        </s:RichText>
    </s:Group>

</s:WindowedApplication>
```

Figure 9-8. TLF TextGraphic application output

Notice that, in this example, we have a RichText element that has a TextFlow element. The TextFlow element is the root of a TLF text object model. The TextFlow holds FlowElements such as the ParagraphElements <p> element, the SpanElements <span> element, or the ImageElement <img> element. Essentially, the TLF creates, renders, manipulates, and edits TextFlow elements.

Using the Spark TextArea

Up until Flex 4 beta, Flex offered an out-of-the-box rich text editor called RichTextEditor. It was not that rich, since controlling and manipulating many of the features needed to create a rich text editor could be very challenging. To create the editor, you can just type the following element:

```
<mx:RichTextEditor fontFamily="arial"
    color="0x4697c4" text="RichTextEditor"/>
```

Flex 4 beta offers TextArea, which is based on TextBase. TextArea itself extends the SkinnableComponent Flex 4 core class. It is used as the base class for all the skinnable components, such as Spark's TextInput. Each skinnable component includes a TextView in its skin. It is also part of Adobe's effort to rework the component and separate the view, model, and logic to allow better manipulation and the ability to move to design-centric development.

Let's create an example that uses the Spark TextArea component and gives the user control over some of the text properties:

```
<?xml version="1.0" encoding="utf-8"?>
<s:WindowedApplication xmlns:fx="http://ns.adobe.com/mxml/2009"
        xmlns:s="library://ns.adobe.com/flex/spark"
        xmlns:mx="library://ns.adobe.com/flex/halo"
        width="642" height="427" initialize="initializeHandler(event)">
```

The exportText method uses the toXMLString property, which can export the contents of a Flex 4 TextArea control. In our case, we will post the results in another text area component. The initializeHandler method creates an array that contains a list of all the available fonts names, so we can use them in a drop-down menu.

```
<fx:Script>
        <![CDATA[

                import flash.text.engine.FontDescription;
                import mx.events.FlexEvent;

                [Bindable]
                private var fontDataProvider:Array = new Array();

                private function exportText(evt:Event):void
                {
                        exportTextArea.text = ➡
textArea.export().toXMLString();
                }


                protected function initializeHandler ➡
(event:FlexEvent):void
                {
                        var allFonts:Array = Font.enumerateFonts(true);

                        for (var i:int = 0; i < allFonts.length; i++)
                        {
                                if (allFonts[i].fontType == "device")
                                        fontDataProvider[i] = ➡
allFonts[i].fontName;
                        }
                }

        ]]>
</fx:Script>
```

The following slider controls the width of the TextArea components:

```
<s:HGroup height="408" width="599" left="15" top="5">

        <s:VGroup height="400">

                <mx:HSlider id="widthSlider"
                        labels="Width:"
                        minimum="50"
                        maximum="100"
                        value="250"
                        snapInterval="1"
                        liveDragging="true"/>
```

TextArea allows controlling white space, such as indenting and line breaks; the following slider controls the indent property in the TextArea component:

```
<mx:HSlider id="indentSlider"
                                labels="Indent:"
                                minimum="0"
                                maximum="100"
                                value="0"
                                snapInterval="1"
                                liveDragging="true"/>
```

The textAlphaSlider will be used to control the alpha of the text.

```
<mx:HSlider id="textAlphaSlider"
        labels="Text alpha:"
        minimum="0"
        maximum="100"
        value="100"
        snapInterval="1"
        liveDragging="true" />
```

Margins of text in all directions can be controlled using marginLeft, marginTop, marginRight, and marginButton, as illustrated in the following example:

```
<mx:HSlider id="marginTopSlider"
        labels="Margin top:"
        minimum="0"
        maximum="100"
        value="0"
        snapInterval="1"
        liveDragging="true" />
```

We can control the font size using the following slider:

```
<mx:HSlider id="fontSizeSlider"
        labels="Font size:"
        minimum="0"
```

```
                maximum="100"
                value="16"
                snapInterval="1"
                liveDragging="true" />
```

The following code allows control over aligning the entire text and the last row, as well as control over the font family type:

```
<mx:ComboBox id="fontFamilyComboBox"
dataProvider="{fontDataProvider}" selectedIndex="1"/>

    <s:HGroup>
            <s:SimpleText text="align: " />
            <mx:ComboBox id="alignComboBox"
dataProvider="[start,end,left,center,right,justify]"
selectedIndex="1"/>
    </s:HGroup>
```

We will include the export button to view the text code:

```
        <s:Button id="exportButton" width="200"
        label="export"
        click="exportText(event);"/>
```

The TextArea component binds to all the components that control the properties. Notice that the content tag contains text that includes HTML tags:

```
</s:VGroup>

    <s:VGroup width="336" height="400">

                    <s:TextArea id="textArea"
                        textAlpha="{textAlphaSlider.value/100}"
                        fontFamily="{fontFamilyComboBox.selectedItem}"
                        textAlign="{alignComboBox.selectedItem}"
                        textIndent="{indentSlider.value}"
                        fontSize="{fontSizeSlider.value}"
                        percentWidth="{widthSlider.value}"
                        height="297" width="100%">

                <s:content>
                        <s:p>Lorem ipsum dolor sit amet, ➡
consectetur adipisicing elit, sed</s:p>
                        <s:p>incididunt ut labore et dolore ➡
magna aliqua. Ut enim ad minim</s:p>
                        <s:p>exercitation ullamco laboris nisi ➡
ut aliquip ex ea commodo</s:p>
                        <s:p>dolor in reprehenderit in voluptate ➡
velit esse cillum dolore eu</s:p>
```

```
                        <s:p>Excepteur sint occaecat cupidatat ➥
non proident,  fugiat nulla</s:p>
                        <s:p>sunt in culpa qui officia deserunt ➥
mollit anim id est laborum.</s:p>
                    </s:content>

            </s:TextArea>
```

The second FxTextArea will hold the export contents of a Flex 4 TextArea control once the user clicks the exportButton:

```
            <s:TextArea id="exportTextArea"
                    width="100%" height="83"/>
        </s:VGroup>

    </s:HGroup>

</s:WindowedApplication>
```

See Figure 9-9 for the application screenshot.

To read more about the TLF, see the Adobe wiki at http://opensource.adobe.com/wiki/display/ flexsdk/Spark+Text+Primitives#SparkTextPrimitives-content.

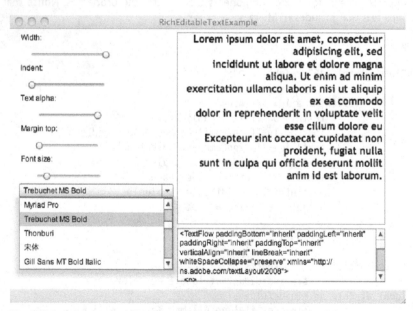

Figure 9-9. Our example AIR application for changing the properties of the FxTextArea component

Creating sound dynamically

Flash Player 10 enhances the sound API and extends the ability to control sound dynamically as well as adding the option to work with more codec.

> *Note that some or all of these new features may not be available on mobile devices when Flash 10 becomes available on mobile.*

Here are some of the new capabilities:

- **Dynamic sound generation**: The sound APIs allow you to create sound dynamically and generate audio applications such as music mixers. You can work with loaded MP3 audio at a low level by extracting audio data and supplying it to the sound buffer. It allows processing, filtering, and mixing audio in real time using the Pixel Bender compiler, which we explained previously.
- **Speex audio codec**: In addition to supporting ADPCM, HE-AAC, MP3, and Nellymoser audio, Flash 10 also supports a new, high-fidelity, open source voice codec called Speex (www.speex.org/), which delivers low-latency voice encoding and adds to the Microphone class.

Using Flash 10, we can create the sound generator shown in Figure 9-10.

Figure 9-10. Sound generator application

Let's look at the code:

```
<?xml version="1.0" encoding="utf-8"?>
<s:WindowedApplication
    xmlns:fx="http://ns.adobe.com/mxml/2009"
    xmlns:s="library://ns.adobe.com/flex/spark"
    xmlns:mx="library://ns.adobe.com/flex/halo"
    xmlns:local="*">

    <fx:Script>
        <![CDATA[

            import mx.events.FlexEvent;

            private var sound:Sound = new Sound();
```

```
                        protected function playSound():void
                        {
                                sound.addEventListener ➥
(SampleDataEvent.SAMPLE_DATA, onSoundReady);
                                sound.play();
                        }

                        private function onSoundReady(event:SampleDataEvent):void
                        {
                                for (var i:int=0; i<2800; i++)
                                {
                                        var random:Number = Math.random();
                                        var data:Number = Math.sqrt( (i*random) )*0.01;

                                        event.data.writeFloat(data);
                                        event.data.writeFloat(data);
                                }
                        }

                ]]>
        </fx:Script>
        <s:Button label="Play" click="playSound()" />
        <local:Visualization type="wave" bars="32"
                        width="100%" height="50%"  x="0" y="38"/>

</s:WindowedApplication>
```

Here is how it's done. The code first sets a new sound instance, which will be used to generate the random sound.

```
        private var sound:Sound = new Sound();
```

Once the user clicks the play button, the playSound event handler is dispatched and sets the listener to start playing the sound.

SampleDataEvent will be dispatched on regular intervals to request more audio data:

```
                        protected function playSound():void
                        {
                                sound.addEventListener ➥
(SampleDataEvent.SAMPLE_DATA, onSoundReady);
                                sound.play();
                        }
```

onSoundReady is the event handler; it needs to fill a ByteArray with sound data. To create sound, we are creating an inner loop with some random numbers that send the ByteArray back to the event data property. The number we assigned gets pushed into the ring buffer, while the sound card feeds from it at the same time and the result is sound playing:

```
        private function onSoundReady ➥
```

```
(event:SampleDataEvent):void
        {
                for (var i:int=0; i<2800; i++)
                {
                        var random:Number = Math.random();
                        var data:Number = ➡
Math.sqrt( (i*random) )*0.01;

                        event.data.writeFloat(data);
                        event.data.writeFloat(data);
                }
        }

        ]]>
    </Script>

    <FxButton label="Play" click="playSound()" />
```

To view the sound, we are using an open source wave visualization component, which will create a graphic to represent the sound, as shown in Figure 9-10. It can be downloaded from this book's Source Code/Downloads page on the friends of ED web site, under the Chapter 9 project.

```
<local:Visualization type="wave" bars="32"
width="100%" height="50%"  x="0" y="38"/>
```

Improving visual performance

Flash Player 10 added new APIs for improving the visual performance, and it's important to be aware of them. However, keep in mind that some of these new features may not be available on mobile devices when Flash 10 becomes available on mobile, since they may consume too many resources. Additionally, even if some visuals features are available they may drain the mobile battery.

Here are some of the new features related to visual performance:

- **Hardware acceleration**: Flash 10 uses a graphic card to paint SWF files, which improves performance.

- **Vector**: Flash 10 brings a new data type called Vector. The new type is similar to an array but enforces elements to be of the same type. You can set the size of the array and other features. The Vector data type increases performance, efficiency, and error checking of data. Here's an example on how to declare a vector: var vector:Vector.<int> = Vector.<int>([10, 11, 12]);. This example generates an array with three numbers. It's easy to see the value of using this type on collections of value objects, since we can enforce and specify the type of the objects.

- **Dynamic streaming**: Flash 10 increases streaming experience. Video streams automatically adjust to changing network conditions, which is key, especially with mobile devices.

- **Color correction**: Flash 10's built-in color correction checks the monitor's International Color Consortium (ICC) color profile and allows you to convert your SWF's color profile to the standard RGB profile. Note that you can only use the new API if the client monitor supports your color profile.

Let's take a look at the code of an application that takes an image and applies color correction; Figure 9-11 shows the final application.

Figure 9-11. Color correction in Flash Player 10

The application we will be building is simple in nature and will include an image and a radio button. Once the radio button is clicked, we will apply color correction.

```
<?xml version="1.0" encoding="utf-8"?>
<s:WindowedApplication
    xmlns:fx="http://ns.adobe.com/mxml/2009"
    xmlns:s="library://ns.adobe.com/flex/spark"
    xmlns:mx="library://ns.adobe.com/flex/halo">

    <fx:Script>
        <![CDATA[
            import spark.components.CheckBox;

            private function isColorCorrectionSupport():Boolean
            {
                var retVal:Boolean;

                if (stage.colorCorrectionSupport == ➥
ColorCorrectionSupport.DEFAULT_ON ||
                    stage.colorCorrectionSupport == ➥
ColorCorrectionSupport.DEFAULT_OFF)
                {
                    retVal = true;
                }
                else
                {
                    retVal = false;
                }

                return retVal;
            }
```

```
                private function onColorCorrection(value:Boolean):void
                {
                    if (value == false)
                        stage.colorCorrection = ➡
flash.display.ColorCorrection.OFF;
                    else
                        stage.colorCorrection = ➡
flash.display.ColorCorrection.ON;
                }

                protected function changeHandler(event:Event):void
                {
                    var selected:Boolean = ➡
CheckBox(event.target).selected;
                    onColorCorrection(selected);
                }

        ]]>
    </fx:Script>

    <s:VGroup>
        <mx:Image source="img.jpg" width="319" height="240" />
        <s:CheckBox change="changeHandler(event)" />
        <mx:Label text="Color Correction" />
    </s:VGroup>

</s:WindowedApplication>
```

The code first checks to see if the client's computer supports color correction. The check can be done using the stage.colorCorrectionSupport property.

```
private function isColorCorrectionSupport():Boolean
{
    var retVal:Boolean;

    if (stage.colorCorrectionSupport == ➡
ColorCorrectionSupport.DEFAULT_ON ||
        stage.colorCorrectionSupport == ➡
ColorCorrectionSupport.DEFAULT_OFF)
    {
        retVal = true;
    }
    else
    {
        retVal = false;
    }

    return retVal;
}
```

The colorCorrection method allows us to toggle on and off the ability to make color corrections using ColorCorrection enumerations custom data.

```
private function onColorCorrection(value:Boolean):void
    {
        if (value == false)
            stage.colorCorrection = flash.display.ColorCorrection.OFF;
        else
            stage.colorCorrection = flash.display.ColorCorrection.ON;
    }
```

We then need an Image component as well as a CheckBox to show an image and switch between the two profiles.

```
<s:VGroup>
    <mx:Image source="img.jpg" width="319"
height="240" />
    <s:CheckBox change="changeHandler(event)" />
    <mx:Label text="Color Correction" />
</s:VGroup>
```

The changeHandler handles the user interacting with the CheckBox component.

```
protected function changeHandler(event:Event):void
{
    var selected:Boolean = CheckBox(event.target).selected;
    onColorCorrection(selected);
}
```

There is another option for correcting colors in a more customized but complex way. You can use the new Flash 10 Matrix3D and ColorMatrixFilter fill to create custom colors.

Using the enhanced Drawing API

The Drawing API hasn't changed much since Flash 6, so in order for us to draw a line, for instance, we have to write a lot of code and basically instruct the player to move from one X,Y location to another to draw. Remember these long blocks of code back in the days of ActionScript 2.0? They looked like these:

```
graphics.moveTo(200, 200);
graphics.lineTo(170, 200);
```

With the new Flash 10 API, drawing becomes much easier: runtime drawings are easier to create with data properties that can be reused. AIR 1.5 and Flex 4 support FXG declarative format and allow converting graphics easily from Adobe Creative Suite. Here's the FXG code to draw a star with a grey solid outline using the Graphics.drawPath.

```
<Path height="100" width="100"
    data="M 87.95 106.25 L 54.19 87.36 19.50 104.47 27.03 66.53
    0.04 38.81 38.45 34.25 56.47 0.02 72.68 35.14 110.80 ➥
    41.70 82.41 67.97 Z ">
```

```
        <fill>
           <SolidColor color="0xf9f2f2"/>
        </fill>
        <stroke>
           <SolidColorStroke color="0x666464" weight="1"/>
        </stroke>
     </Path>
```

Notice that the star uses the drawPath API, which is part of the flash.display. This example is simple, but keep in mind that we can also use the Vector array type in the drawPath and drawTriangles classes to increase performance and to reduce memory usage.

- Graphics.drawPath: Uses a list of drawing commands and coordinates to create a pixel
- Graphics.drawTriangles: Takes Vector data and renders a set of triangles, typically to distort containers and give them a 3-D Z dimension

FXG allows us to easily tweak parts of curves, change styling, replace parts, and use custom filters and effects.

There are many other enhancements, such as these:

- **Winding fill**: Before Flash 10, when two shapes intercepted one another, we had an empty hole. Using the winding fill feature, we can fill that empty area as long as we have the winding in the same direction.
- **UV maps**: "UV" stands for the U and V coordinates and represents a process of making a 3-D model out of 2-D image. These are used in After Effects and other Adobe video products to allow mapping on a 3-D space using a 2-D image. We also gain these features with UV maps:
  - Real perspective
  - Textured meshes in 3-D space
  - Control of the graphics model
  - Read and write rendering

Reading and writing local files

In Flash Lite we are using Shared Objects with limited access to file I/O as well as extensions such as Kuneri Lite to access file system. Additionally, before Flash 10, we needed to use a proxy to read and write to the file system. We would send the request to a proxy, which would handle the task and interact with Flash.

Flash Player 10 exposed two new APIs in FileReference, load and save, which allow you to read and write data on the user's machine. You get information about files such as modification date, creator, and size. However, unlike with AIR's FileStream API, the location of the files will not be visible, and you can only do asynchronous calls.

Asynchronous operations work in the background without waiting for the operation to complete. Thus long processes such as uploading or downloading a large file will not block execution, and the user can keep using the application. Synchronous operations, on the other hand, must complete before the user can interact with the application again.

Let's create an application for loading a file in Flash 10.

First, set the FileReference and the file types:

```
private var fileReference:FileReference;
private static const FILE_TYPES:Array = ➥
[new FileFilter("Text File Format", "*.txt;*.text")];
```

loadFile will be used to allow the user to browse to the location of the file:

```
private function loadFile():void
{
    fileReference = new FileReference();

    fileReference.addEventListener(Event.SELECT, ➥
fileSelectEventHandler);
    fileReference.addEventListener(Event.CANCEL, ➥
function():void { Alert.show("Cancel") } );

    fileReference.browse(FILE_TYPES);
}
```

A second method, called fileSelectEventHandler, will be used to load the file and clean the fileReference for the garbage collector by setting fileReference to null.

```
private function fileSelectEventHandler(event:Event):void
{
    fileReference.addEventListener(Event.COMPLETE, ➥
loadCompleteEventHandler);
    fileReference.addEventListener(IOErrorEvent.IO_ERROR, ➥
function():void { Alert.show("Error uploading file") });

    fileReference.load();
}

private function loadCompleteEventHandler(event:Event):void
{
    var data:ByteArray = fileReference.data;
    output.text = data.readUTFBytes(data.bytesAvailable);

    fileReference = null;
}
```

Run the application, and you will notice that you can use the system to open a file browse window that allows you to choose the location of the file, as shown in Figure 9-12.

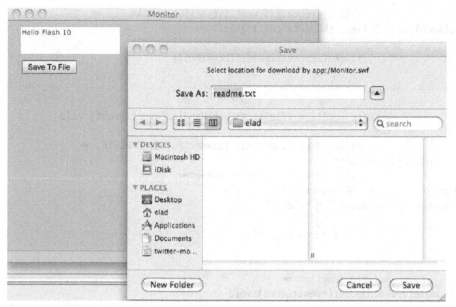

Figure 9-12. Browse and file using Flash 10.

Here's the complete code:

```
<?xml version="1.0" encoding="utf-8"?>
<s:WindowedApplication xmlns:fx="http://ns.adobe.com/mxml/2009"
    xmlns:s="library://ns.adobe.com/flex/spark"
    xmlns:mx="library://ns.adobe.com/flex/halo"
    creationComplete="loadFile();">

    <fx:Script>
        <![CDATA[

            import mx.controls.Alert;

            private var fileReference:FileReference;
            private static const FILE_TYPES:Array =
                [new FileFilter("Text File Format", "*.txt;*.text")];

            private function loadFile():void
            {
                fileReference = new FileReference();

                fileReference.addEventListener(Event.SELECT, ➥
fileSelectEventHandler);
```

```
                        fileReference.addEventListener(Event.CANCEL, ➥
        function():void { Alert.show("Cancel") } );

                        fileReference.browse(FILE_TYPES);
                }


                private function fileSelectEventHandler(event:Event):void
                {
                        fileReference.addEventListener(Event.COMPLETE, ➥
        loadCompleteEventHandler);
                        fileReference.addEventListener➥
        (IOErrorEvent.IO_ERROR, function():void { ➥
        Alert.show("Error uploading file") });

                        fileReference.load();
                }

                private function ➥
        loadCompleteEventHandler(event:Event):void
                {
                        var data:ByteArray = fileReference.data;
                        output.text = data.readUTFBytes(data.bytesAvailable);

                        fileReference = null;
                }

        ]]>
        </fx:Script>

        <s:TextArea id="output" />

</s:WindowedApplication>
```

To write a file, the process is similar. We set a click event that will create a new FileReference instance and set the default file name to be "readme.txt":

```
        private function onSaveClick():void
        {
                fileReference = new FileReference();
                fileReference.addEventListener(Event.COMPLETE, ➥
        fileSaveEventHandler);
                fileReference.addEventListener(Event.CANCEL, ➥
        function():void { Alert.show("Cancel") });
                fileReference.addEventListener(IOErrorEvent.IO_ERROR, ➥
        function():void { Alert.show("Error saving file") });
                fileReference.save(inputField.text, "readme.txt");
        }

        private function fileSaveEventHandler(event:Event):void
```

```
            {
                Alert.show("File Saved Successfully");
                fileReference = null;
            }
```

And the complete code is listed here (see Figure 9-13):

```
<?xml version="1.0" encoding="utf-8"?>
<s:WindowedApplication xmlns:fx="http://ns.adobe.com/mxml/2009"
    xmlns:s="library://ns.adobe.com/flex/spark"
    xmlns:mx="library://ns.adobe.com/flex/halo">

    <fx:Script>
        <![CDATA[

            import mx.controls.Alert;

            import flash.net.FileReference;

            import flash.events.IOErrorEvent;
            import flash.events.Event;

            private var fileReference:FileReference;

            private function onSaveClick():void
            {
                fileReference = new FileReference();
                fileReference.addEventListener(Event.COMPLETE, ➥
fileSaveEventHandler);
                fileReference.addEventListener(Event.CANCEL, ➥
function():void { Alert.show("Cancel") });
                fileReference.addEventListener➥
(IOErrorEvent.IO_ERROR, function():void { ➥
Alert.show("Error saving file") });
                fileReference.save(inputField.text, "readme.txt");
            }

            private function fileSaveEventHandler(event:Event):void
            {
                Alert.show("File Saved Successfully");
                fileReference = null;
            }

        ]]>
    </fx:Script>
    <s:Button label="Save To File"
        x="24" y="62"
        click="onSaveClick()"/>
    <s:TextArea id="inputField" editable="true" x="21" y="9"/>

</s:WindowedApplication>
```

Figure 9-13. Writing a file using Flash 10

Taking a high-level view of AIR 1.5 capabilities

Adobe released AIR 1.5 in February 2009 and added new capabilities to AIR 1.0. AIR 1.5 is based on Flash Player 10 and includes many new APIs, which we covered on the previous pages. In addition to the new APIs that we get automatically since we are using Flash Player 10, additional features are embedded into the AIR 1.5 platform, such as:

- Integration with the SquirrelFish (http://trac.webkit.org/wiki/SquirrelFish) JavaScript virtual machine (VM) into the AIR WebKit HTML engine, which increases performance
- Support for new languages such as Czech, Dutch, and Swedish
- Encrypted local and SQLite databases

In the next pages, we will cover some of the features available since AIR 1.0 as well as some of the new features of AIR 1.5.

Loading HTML and JavaScript to a container

As mentioned earlier, AIR includes the WebKit engine; having a built-in HTML engine allows you to parse and use HTML and JavaScript inside of a container. The AIR HTML content container is accessible using HTMLLoader. The HTMLLoader object allows you to load HTML or PDF pages right from the Web or client local drive using the URLRequest class. You can also attach an HTML string as the container content.

Let's create an HTML container that will load the Yahoo home page. Once loading is completed, we will apply the iris effect. The application includes a creationComplete event to call the onStartup method, which will start loading the web page.

```
<?xml version="1.0" encoding="utf-8"?>
<s:WindowedApplication xmlns:fx="http://ns.adobe.com/mxml/2009"
    xmlns:s="library://ns.adobe.com/flex/spark"
    xmlns:mx="library://ns.adobe.com/flex/halo"
      width="750" height="600"
      creationComplete="onStartup()">
```

We will place the effect in a declaration tag and then set the iris effect to change the scale of the component and set the durations.

```
<fx:Declarations>
        <mx:Iris id="irisEffect"
                target="{component}"
                xFrom="0" xTo="630"
                yFrom="0" yTo="400"
                duration="3000" />
</fx:Declarations>

    <Script>
        <![CDATA[

        import flash.html.HTMLLoader;
        import mx.core.UIComponent;
```

We set the HTML page container, attach it to a component set and and once we receive the onComplete event listener, we can start loading the Yahoo page:

```
private var htmlPage:HTMLLoader = null;

    private function onStartup() : void
    {
        htmlPage = new HTMLLoader();
        htmlPage.width = component.width;
        htmlPage.height = component.height;
        component.addChild(htmlPage);

        htmlPage.addEventListener(Event.COMPLETE, onLoaderComplete);
        htmlPage.load(new URLRequest("http://yahoo.com"));
    }
```

Once the onKeyDown method is called, the application will load the requested page:

```
    private function onKeyDown(event:KeyboardEvent):void
    {
      if (event.keyCode == Keyboard.ENTER)
        htmlPage.load(new URLRequest(txtUrl.text));
    }
```

The handler will be called once the page has loaded, and we can start the iris event, show the component using the visible property, and remove the event listener so the listener will not be called every time to switch to a new page.

```
    private function onLoaderComplete(event:Event):void
    {
        component.visible = true;
        irisEffect.play();
        htmlPage.removeEventListener(Event.COMPLETE, onLoaderComplete);
    }

  ]]>
</Script>
}
```

We set a UIComponent so we can attach our HTML container to a display container and allow selecting other pages or even PDFs in case Adobe Acrobat is installed.

```
    <mx:Form width="100%">
        <mx:FormItem label="Url" width="630">
            <s:TextInput id="txtUrl" width="630" ➥
text="file.pdf"
                     keyDown="onKeyDown(event)" />
        </mx:FormItem>

        <mx:UIComponent id="component"
width="630" height="400" visible="false" />
    </mx:Form>

</s:WindowedApplication>
```

Accessing the local file system

AIR allows you to access the local file system on the client machine the same as native operating system programs. You can do common operations such as reading, writing, moving, and renaming. As mentioned previously, Flash 10 added the ability to save and load files, but using the AIR FileStream API, you have more control over the location of the files and the type of call.

There are two types of calls that you can make: synchronous and asynchronous. The different calls are easy to identify. For instance, some example synchronous calls include File.copyTo(), File.deleteDirectory(), and File.deleteFile(). Their asynchronous counterparts are File. copyToAsync(), File.deleteDirectoryAsync(), and File.deleteFileAsync().

To read files, you set the location through the FileStream, listen to an event, and make the call:

```
    private function readFile():void
    {
        file = new File();
        file = File.applicationDirectory.resolvePath("readme.txt");
        fileStream = new FileStream();
        fileStream.addEventListener(Event.COMPLETE, fileReadComplete);
        fileStream.openAsync(file, FileMode.READ);
    }
```

We need the event handler to receive the file content using readMultiByte, since the format is ByteArray.

```
        private function fileReadComplete(event:Event):void
        {
                fileContent = fileStream.readMultiByte ➡
(fileStream.bytesAvailable, ISO);
        }
```

And finally, just place a handler to handle the result. Here's the complete example:

```
<?xml version="1.0" encoding="utf-8"?>
<s:WindowedApplication xmlns:fx="http://ns.adobe.com/mxml/2009"
    xmlns:s="library://ns.adobe.com/flex/spark"
    xmlns:mx="library://ns.adobe.com/flex/halo"
    creationComplete="readFile();">

   <fx:Script>
    <![CDATA[
        import flash.filesystem.FileMode;
        import flash.filesystem.File;
        import flash.filesystem.FileStream;

        [Bindable]
        private var fileContent:String;

        private var file:File;
        private var fileStream:FileStream;
        private static const ISO:String = "iso-8859-1";

        private function readFile():void
        {
                file = new File();
                file = File.applicationDirectory.resolvePath ➡
("readme.txt");
                fileStream = new FileStream();
                fileStream.addEventListener(Event.COMPLETE, ➡
fileReadComplete);
                fileStream.openAsync(file, FileMode.READ);
        }
        private function fileReadComplete(event:Event):void
        {
                fileContent = fileStream.readMultiByte ➡
(fileStream.bytesAvailable, ISO);
        }

    ]]>
   </fx:Script>

   <mx:Label text="{fileContent}"/>

</s:WindowedApplication>
```

Encrypting SQLite data

AIR 1.5 closes a previously existing security gap. All AIR applications are using the exact same database, so essentially any AIR application can read other applications' tables.

Adobe has updated the framework, which now includes the ability to add additional properties to encrypt your SQLite database. With the new security, you can create an encrypted database, and when attempting to open the database, your code must provide the database's encryption key. Let's now look at how to open and encrypt your database.

First, create a connection and choose the database name you want:

```
protected function initializeHandler():void
{
        connection = new SQLConnection();
        file = ➥
File.applicationStorageDirectory.resolvePath("testEncrypt.db");
}
```

Note that the SQLite database is already installed with AIR; there's no need to install or configure the database.

We will be using the EncryptionKeyGenerator class that was provided with a similar example from Adobe (http://www.adobe.com/devnet/air/flex/quickstart/encrypted_database.html), but you can use other tools such as as3lib to generate the encryption code. Our next method sets the events and opens the connection:

```
private function openConnection():void
{
    var keyGen:EncryptionKeyGenerator = ➥
    new EncryptionKeyGenerator();
    var encryptionKey:ByteArray;
    var password:String = pasTextInput.text;

    if (!keyGen.validateStrongPassword(password))
    {
        output.text = "The password must ➥
        be 8-32 char, " +
        "with one letter lowercase letter, " +
        "one upper case and one number"
        return;
    }

        encryptionKey = keyGen.getEncryptionKey ➥
        (file, password);
        connection.addEventListener(SQLEvent.OPEN, ➥
        openHandler);
```

```
        connection.addEventListener(SQLErrorEvent.ERROR, ➡
        openError);
        connection.openAsync(file, SQLMode.CREATE, ➡
        null, false, 1024, encryptionKey);
    }
            }
```

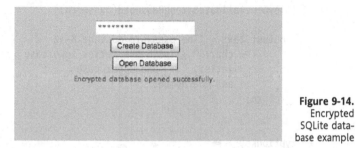

Figure 9-14.
Encrypted
SQLite data-
base example

Here's the complete code:

```
<?xml version="1.0" encoding="utf-8"?>
<s:WindowedApplication
    xmlns:fx="http://ns.adobe.com/mxml/2009"
    xmlns:s="library://ns.adobe.com/flex/spark"
    xmlns:mx="library://ns.adobe.com/flex/halo"
    initialize="initializeHandler()">

    <fx:Script>
        <![CDATA[

            import flash.filesystem.File;
            import flash.data.SQLConnection;
            import mx.events.FlexEvent;

            private var connection:SQLConnection;
            private var file:File;
            private var isCreateDB:Boolean;

            protected function initializeHandler():void
            {
                connection = new SQLConnection();
                file = File.applicationStorageDirectory. ➡
resolvePath("testEncrypt.db");
            }
```

```
                private function openConnection():void
                {
                        var keyGen:EncryptionKeyGenerator = ➥
new EncryptionKeyGenerator();
                        var encryptionKey:ByteArray;
                        var password:String = pasTextInput.text;

                        if (!keyGen.validateStrongPassword(password))
                        {
                            output.text = "The password must be 8-32
                                        char, " + "with one letter lowercase
                                        letter, " + "one upper case
                                        and one number"
                            return;
                        }

                        encryptionKey = ➥
keyGen.getEncryptionKey(file, password);

                        connection.addEventListener(SQLEvent.OPEN, ➥
openHandler);
                        connection.addEventListener(SQLErrorEvent.ERROR, ➥
openError);

                        connection.openAsync(file, SQLMode.CREATE, null, ➥
false, 1024, encryptionKey);
                }

                private function openHandler(event:SQLEvent):void
                {
                        if (isCreateDB)
                        {
                            output.text = ➥
"Encrypted database created successfully.";
                        }
                        else
                        {
                            output.text = ➥
"Encrypted database opened successfully.";
                        }
                }
```

```
            private function openError(event:SQLErrorEvent):void
            {
                    if (!isCreateDB && event.error.errorID == ➡
EncryptionKeyGenerator.PASSWORD_ERROR_ID)
                    {
                            output.text = "Incorrect password!";
                    }
                    else
                    {
                            output.text = ➡
"Error creating or opening database.";
                    }
            }
        ]]>
    </fx:Script>

    <s:TextInput id="pasTextInput" displayAsPassword="true"/>
    <s:Button label="Create Database"
click="isCreateDB=true; openConnection();"/>
    <s:Button label="Open Database"
click="isCreateDB=false; openConnection();"/>

    <mx:Text id="output" />

</s:WindowedApplication>
```

Updating applications and using the notification API

Although the AIR installer application manager can handle updating existing applications, sometimes you want control over the process. For instance, maybe you fixed some bugs in an existing application and you want to alert the users to let them update the application, or maybe you want to change your application certificate.

You can handle these requirements using the Updater class. The Update class, which includes an update method to allow you to point to the user's AIR file and update it automatically. AIR 1.5 updated the Updater API to assist you in updating an existing application. In AIR 1.5, you can actually change the certificate of the application. To update an application, the application ID and the publisher ID should match.

Listening to network changes

AIR is built to run in conditions where the network connection is changing, and this will come in handy on mobile devices. Once the network condition changes, an event is launched—allowing you to create an application that has network connection awareness. In the next chapter, we will be covering device awareness in more detail.

The event we need to subscribe to is the NETWORK_CHANGE event listener. Here's an example of the event listener:

```
air.NativeApplication.nativeApplication.addEventListener ➥
(air.Event.NETWORK_CHANGE, onNetworkChange);
```

Another option is to use servicemonitor.swf, which is included with AIR, to monitor the network connection.

When the Internet connection has changed, the NETWORK_CHANGE event is dispatched. Note that it doesn't ensure that the device is connected to the Internet.

A real-world example would be to listen for connection changes in a web site. For instance, let's assume we want to use a specific service; we can set the URLRequest to point to the service URL, and changes will be tracked:

```
<?xml version="1.0" encoding="utf-8"?>
<s:WindowedApplication
    xmlns:fx="http://ns.adobe.com/mxml/2009"
    xmlns:s="library://ns.adobe.com/flex/spark"
    xmlns:mx="library://ns.adobe.com/flex/halo"
    creationComplete="trackStatus();">

  <fx:Script>
    <![CDATA[

          import air.net.ServiceMonitor;
          import air.net.URLMonitor;

        [Bindable]
        private var networkStatus:String;

        private function trackStatus() : void
        {
            var urlRequest:URLRequest = ➥
new URLRequest("http://yahoo.com");
            var urlMonitor:URLMonitor;
            urlMonitor = new URLMonitor(urlRequest);

            urlMonitor = new URLMonitor(urlRequest );
            urlMonitor.addEventListener(StatusEvent.STATUS, ➥
statusChangeEventHandler);
            urlMonitor.start();
        }

          private function statusChangeEventHandler ➥
(event:StatusEvent) : void
        {
            networkStatus = event.code;
        }
```

```
    ]]>
  </fx:Script>

  <mx:Label text="{networkStatus}"/>


</s:WindowedApplication>
```

We can also use the same technique to listen to a SocketMonitor object to monitor availability of a TCP endpoint. For instance, to listen to changes in a web server, we can place a status change listener on port 80:

```
var socketMonitor:SocketMonitor = ➥
new SocketMonitor('www.YourSite.com', 80);
socketMonitor.addEventListener(StatusEvent.STATUS, ➥
statusChangeEventHandler);
socketMonitor.start();
```

Changing native windowing and chrome control

AIR allows you to control the look and behavior of the native window. You set the properties you want in the NativeWindowInitOptions API and pass it to the window constructor. You can control many properties, but keep in mind that no properties can be changed once the application is started.

There are three types of windows:

- **Normal**: A typical window
- **Utility**: A tool palette
- **Lightweight**: Lightweight window with no chrome

Window chrome refers to the set of controls that allow users to interact with a window. Chrome properties include the title bar, buttons, and border and resize grippers.

AIR allows you to create your own custom window with no system chrome, though you can make the window transparent or even non-rectangular. Creating a window with no chrome requires you to add your own means to handle user interactions such as resizing or adding custom borders.

To create your own chrome, you can specify the new set of chrome in the application header and then implement the new window look.

Let's add an item to the File menu:

```
<?xml version="1.0" encoding="utf-8"?>
<s:WindowedApplication xmlns:fx="http://ns.adobe.com/mxml/2009"
    xmlns:s="library://ns.adobe.com/flex/spark"
    xmlns:mx="library://ns.adobe.com/flex/halo"
      creationComplete="onCreationComplete();">

    <fx:Script>
    <![CDATA[
```

Once the onCreationComplete event is dispatched, we create a new menu item using the NativeMenuItem class and add it to the stage.

```
            private function onCreationComplete():void
            {
                    var menuItem:NativeMenuItem = ➡
    new NativeMenuItem("New Menu");
```

We can place the menu either on the native window menus or the global application menu bar. To find out if our device's operating system supports menus, we can check NativeWindow.supportsMenu and NativeApplication.supportsMenu. Keep in mind that in case the device doesn't support these methods, you cannot change the submenus.

```
            if(NativeWindow.supportsMenu)
            {
                    stage.nativeWindow.menu = new NativeMenu();
                    stage.nativeWindow.menu.addItem(menuItem);
            }


            if(NativeApplication.supportsMenu)
            {
                    NativeApplication.nativeApplication. ➡
    menu.addItem(menuItem);
            }
```

We can then create NativeMenuItem items, assign the name, and add them to a NativeMenu. The event listeners will notify us once the user selects the item.

```
    var item1:NativeMenuItem = ➡
            new NativeMenuItem("item1");
    var item2:NativeMenuItem = ➡
            new NativeMenuItem("item2");
    var subMenu:NativeMenu = ➡
            new NativeMenu();
    item1.addEventListener(Event.SELECT, ➡
            onMenuSelectHandler);
    item2.addEventListener(Event.SELECT, ➡
            onMenuSelectHandler);

            subMenu.addItem(item1);
            subMenu.addItem(item2);
            menItem.subMenu = subMenu;
        }
```

Once the item is selected, we can display the label on a text component:

```
                private function onMenuSelectHandler(event:Event):void
                {
                    var nativeMenu:NativeMenuItem = ➥
        event.target as NativeMenuItem;
                    text.text = nativeMenu.label+" selected";
                }

        ]]>
        </fx:Script>

        <mx:Text id="text" width="200" height="50" fontSize="16"/>

    </s:WindowedApplication>
```

Signing your AIR application

After you complete an AIR application you want to be able to ship and distribute your application. AIR applications are distributed as an `.air` file type that is a zip folder containing the application and all the necessary files. The AIR application allows developers (publishers) to deliver applications while assuring the client that the local machine will not be abused. To achieve that, AIR file require to be digitally signed.

Choosing your digital signing method

AIR offers three options for signing your application:

- Sign with an untrusted certificate, which will result in a warning message during installation of your application. See Figure 9-15. If you are an unverified publisher, this is a good option for testing purposes.

- Sign with a trusted certificate. Once your application is ready for release, it's recommended that you get it signed using an authorized certificate authority (CA).

- Create an AIR intermediate (AIRI) file, which can then be signed by someone within your organization who has the proper credentials. If someone else purchases the certificate, they need to convert the AIRI file into a `.p12/pfx` for the developer to use. An AIRI file can be generated by a CA.

To test your application, you can either sign it yourself or use the AIR Debug Launcher (ADL) tool, which was shipped with the Flex SDK. ADL allows access through the command line.

Signing your application with Flex Builder

The easiest way to sign your application is to use Flex Builder. Select Project ➤ Export Release Version to open the Export Release Build window, shown in Figure 9-15. This window allows you to include source code and other properties.

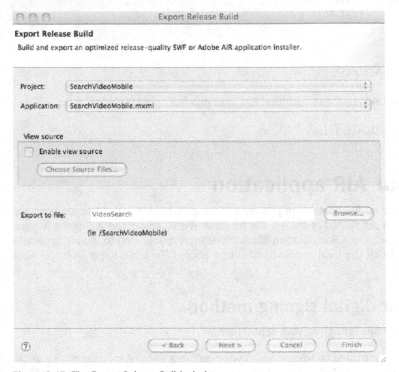

Figure 9-15. The Export Release Build window

Click Next, and in the next screen, you can generate one of the three certificates: an untrusted certificate, a certificate from a CA, or a certificate that's an AIRI file (see Figure 9-16). To sign the application using a CA, just click the Browse button to find your certificate file.

To generate an untrusted certificate, use the Create button, and you can generate your own certificate using the window shown in Figure 9-17.

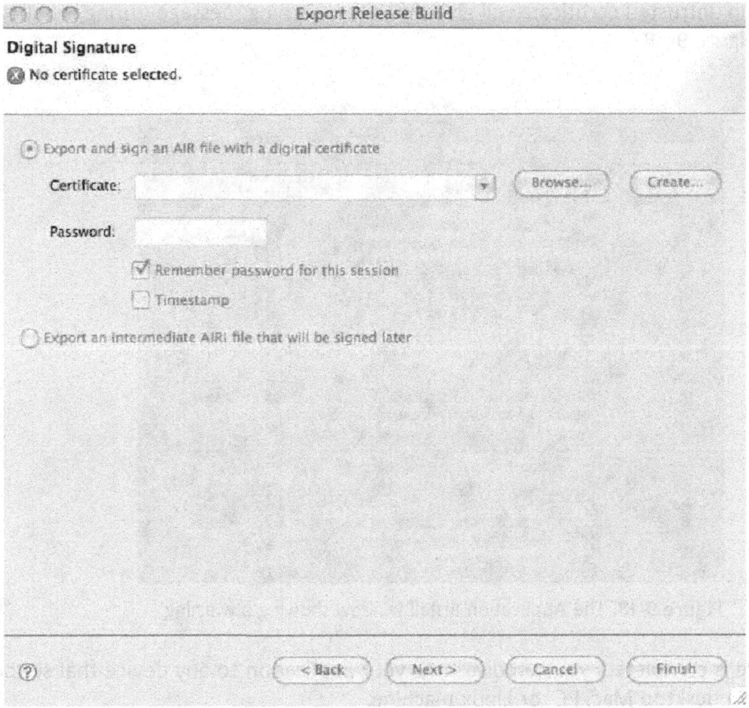

Figure 9-16. Sign your application

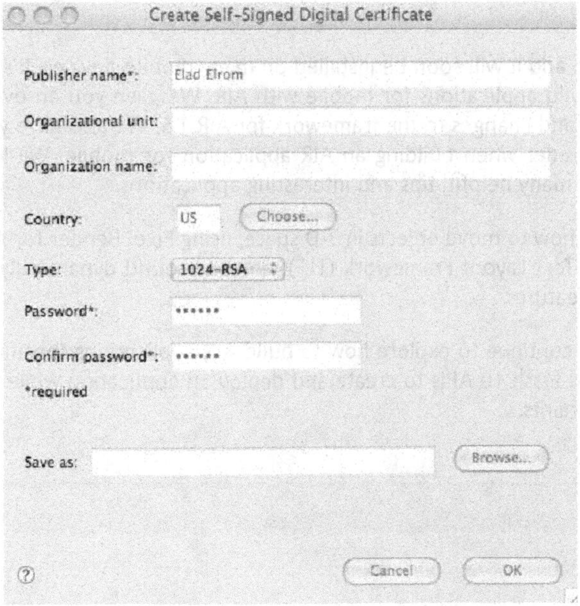

Figure 9-17. Creating a self-signed certificate

Keep in mind that an untrusted certificate will give the user a warning message during installation, like the one shown in Figure 9-18.

Figure 9-18. The Application Install window showing a warning

Once your signature is completed, you can distribute your application to any device that supports AIR such as a UMPC, or a desktop Mac, PC, or Linux machine.

Summary

AIR availability is increasing, and it will soon be installed on many mobile devices. It's exciting to start leveraging our code and build applications for mobile with AIR. We gave you an overview of AIR in general as well as new APIs and changes to the framework for AIR 1.5. We also gave you some pitfalls to look for and tips to consider when building an AIR application for mobile. We looked briefly at Flash 10 APIs by going over many helpful tips and interesting applications.

We specifically showed you how to move objects in 3-D space, using Pixel Bender for graphics and calculations, utilizing the new Text Layout Framework (TLF), creating sound dynamically, accessing local files, and many other new features.

In the next chapter, we will continue to explore how to build AIR applications specifically for AIR 1.5, taking advantage of AIR and Flash 10 APIs to create and deploy an application while taking into consideration the mobile constraints.

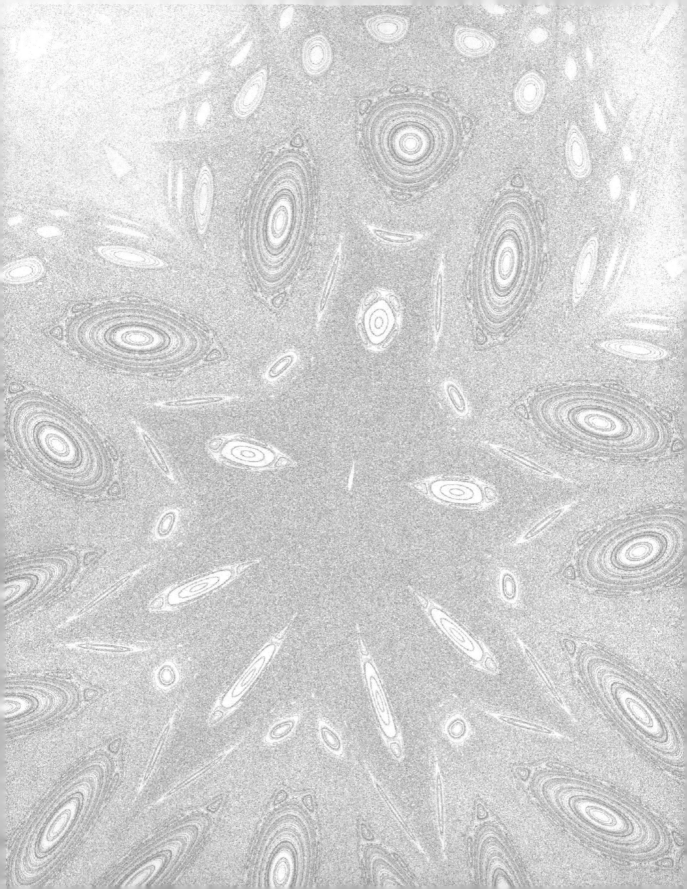

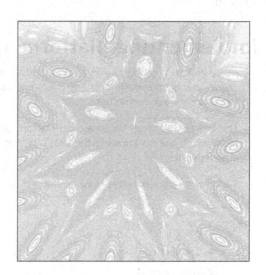

Chapter 10

ADOPTING AIR FOR MOBILE DEVICES

Flash 10 and AIR on mobile will be available on high-end smart phones such as those with the Symbian operating system, Android SDK, or ARM-based processors and will open up new possibilities for mobile developers. As AIR becomes available on mobile devices, you can start taking advantage of these innovative changes today. As more and more platforms, browsers, and mobile manufactures support Flash 10 and AIR 1.5, your application will be ready and deployed automatically, giving the user equivalent experiences across many platforms with no or little changes to your code.

When deploying AIR applications we have to take into account platform and context awareness and have the AIR application adapt to different devices and conditions, and although AIR is not available on smart phones yet, we can prepare today and start building AIR applications on ultra-mobile PCs (UMPCs) and test our AIR application on different operating systems such as Windows, Mac, and Linux. UMPCs are great testing environments, since similar to higher end smart phones, they have limited resources such as less memory, lower CPU power, and lack of video cards, and both mobile devices and UMPCs support touch screens.

In this chapter, we will show you how to use AIR to recognize the device capability and explain best practices to keep track of changes in configuration and how to adapt your application to these changes.

Implementing platform and context awareness

A key goal in creating an AIR application that is deployed on multiple devices is to achieve an application that is independent of any operating system and is adaptable to constant changes in a device (such as network connection).

The key to adopting AIR as a cross-platform application for desktop and mobile is platform awareness, which means knowing the user's system capabilities as well as tracking changes in the user's environment.

Platform awareness refers to obtaining and using information such as the following:

- Bandwidth
- Power
- Connectivity
- Storage
- Security
- Location
- Presence
- Display
- Modality

> *Location awareness and presence are getting popular in mobile devices. Location awareness allows applications to recognize the user's geographical location. Presence allows user to know the status of another user.*

The Flex SDK allows us to get some information regarding the platform awareness, as you will see later in this chapter. Once we have achieved platform awareness, we can adapt a device to a new environment.

For instance, a laptop or mobile device switches to a more power-efficient state by decreasing the display brightness once the battery is low or the device is unplugged. Some more sophisticated adaptations that we may see at some point in the future are a mobile device that recognizes that a user is sitting down in a conference room (using the device accelerometer and GPS) and avoids disturbing the user with unwanted phone calls or even a device that recognizes that a user is on the go (by tracking the GPS movement) and places the phone in speaker mode.

A platform usually adjusts to many changes in the device on its own. For instance, the system tracks network errors and displays an error message. However, our application cannot rely solely on the platform to adjust correctly, and we may want to make changes in the application once changes in the device occur. For instance, our AIR application can go into offline mode once it is not connected to the Internet.

In essence, our AIR application should have the ability to react and adjust during the entire lifetime of the application. It is also responsible for hiding constraints of the mobile device from the user. For instance, a user doesn't know or care that our system has low network download speed and will just stop using an application that delivers choppy video or blame the manufacturer. To keep users happy, we should be aware of changes as well as translate the context. That's where context awareness comes into place.

Context awareness means that once we get information regarding the application platform, we need to translate the information and understand what it means, as well as react accordingly when changes are made in the platform environment.

Our AIR applications should be platform and context aware in order to adapt and deliver a compelling and usable experience to our users. Applications can listen to changes in a platform's logical configuration and environment. For instance, application usage should be possible while on the move and while the device is not connected to the Internet.

AIR offers many APIs to capture system information as well as APIs to capture changes in our device. As AIR increases deployment to mobile devices, it is expected to access other physical conditions such as USB, accelerometer, and GPS.

Currently, we can separate the information available in our application into three categories:

- System capability and support
- User activity
- Changes in the system

AIR captures much of the information, but the information is spread across different APIs. For the example in this chapter, we decided to gather the information into one place and create a singleton manager that allows us to get information at any time, regarding the application condition and capabilities. We will go over the information gathered and then we can start adaptation by using the information to adjust our application to these changes.

To begin, download the project source code:

    http://code.google.com/p/contextawarenessmanager/

Take a look at the different APIs we included in the manager as well as the changes we will be tracking.

Detecting system capabilities

Most of the information regarding the system capability is available through the flash.system. Capabilities API. The Capabilities API provides properties that describe the system and Flash Player that are hosting the application. We will create a value object (VO) that holds the information as well as other properties that we will be using. The default constructor will map the Capabilities properties.

```
package com.elad.framework.vo
{
    import flash.geom.Point;
    import flash.geom.Rectangle;
    import flash.system.Capabilities;

    [Bindable]
    public class ContextVO
```

```
    {
        public function ContextVO()
        {
            avHardwareDisable = Capabilities.avHardwareDisable;
            hasAccessibility = Capabilities.hasAccessibility;
            hasAudio = Capabilities.hasAudio;
            hasAudioEncoder = Capabilities.hasAudioEncoder;
            hasEmbeddedVideo = Capabilities.hasEmbeddedVideo;
            hasMP3 = Capabilities.hasMP3;
            hasPrinting = Capabilities.hasPrinting;
            hasScreenBroadcast = Capabilities.hasScreenBroadcast;
            hasScreenPlayback = Capabilities.hasScreenPlayback;
            hasStreamingAudio = Capabilities.hasStreamingAudio;
            hasVideoEncoder = Capabilities.hasVideoEncoder;
            isDebugger = Capabilities.isDebugger;
            language = Capabilities.language;
            localFileReadDisable = Capabilities.localFileReadDisable;
            manufacturer = Capabilities.manufacturer;
            os = Capabilities.os;
            osName = Capabilities.os.substr(0, 3).toLowerCase();
            pixelAspectRatio = Capabilities.pixelAspectRatio;
            playerType = Capabilities.playerType;
            screenColor = Capabilities.screenColor;
            screenDPI = Capabilities.screenDPI;
            screenResolutionX = Capabilities.screenResolutionX;
            screenResolutionY = Capabilities.screenResolutionY;
            serverString = Capabilities.serverString;
            version = Capabilities.version;
        }

        // track changes
        public var isHTTPAvaliable:Boolean = false;
        public var isNetworkChanged:Boolean = false;
        public var isUserPresent:Boolean = true;
        public var lastUserInput:Number = 0;
        public var isSocketMonitorAvailable:Boolean = false;
        public var windowPositionAfterBounds:Rectangle;
        public var windowPositionBeforeBounds:Rectangle;

        // System Capabilities
        public var getRuntimeVersion:String;
        public var getRuntimePatchLevel:uint;
        public var avHardwareDisable:Boolean;
        public var hasAccessibility:Boolean;
        public var hasAudio:Boolean;
        public var hasAudioEncoder:Boolean;

        public var hasEmbeddedVideo:Boolean;
        public var hasMP3:Boolean;
```

```
                    public var hasPrinting:Boolean;
                    public var hasScreenBroadcast:Boolean;
                    public var hasScreenPlayback:Boolean;
                    public var hasStreamingAudio:Boolean;
                    public var hasVideoEncoder:Boolean;
                    public var isDebugger:Boolean;
                    public var language:String;
                    public var localFileReadDisable:Boolean;
                    public var manufacturer:String;
                    public var os:String;
                    public var osName:String;
                    public var pixelAspectRatio:Number;
                    public var playerType:String;
                    public var screenColor:String;
                    public var screenDPI:Number;
                    public var screenResolutionX:Number;
                    public var screenResolutionY:Number;
                    public var serverString:String;
                    public var version:String;

                    // System support
                    public var supportsDockIcon:Boolean;
                    public var supportsMenu:Boolean;
                    public var supportsSystemTrayIcon:Boolean;
                    public var supportsNotification:Boolean;
                    public var supportsTransparency:Boolean;
                    public var systemMaxSize:Point;
                    public var systemMinSize:Point;

                    // others
                    public var currentAvaliableDrives:Array;
                }
        }
}
```

Detecting system support

Our manager extends the EventDispatcher class, so we can dispatch events to notify our application of changes. We will be using a Singleton design pattern for our manager to ensure we are not creating a few instances of the same class. Let's look at what is needed to create a simple singleton:

```
        package com.elad.framework.utils
        {
            public class ContextAwarenessManager extends EventDispatcher
            {
                public var contextVO:ContextVO;
                protected static var instance:ContextAwarenessManager;
```

```
public function ContextAwarenessManager(enforcer:AccessRestriction)
{
    if (enforcer == null)
    throw new Error("Error enforcer input param is undefined" );
    initializeContextAwareness();
}

public static function getInstance():ContextAwarenessManager
{
    if( instance == null )
    {

        instance = new ➥
        ContextAwarenessManager(new AccessRestriction());
        return instance;
    }
  }
 }
}

class AccessRestriction {}
```

Until recently, ActionScript 3.0 followed ECMAScript, so it currently doesn't support a private class, which is necessary to create the singleton. To stand in for the private class, we have used the AccessRestriction class and created a getInstance() method to retrieve the same class and ensure the class is not created more than once.

Many of the capabilities were mapped in the VO class using the Capabilities API, which is shared by the Flex and AIR applications. Additionally, there are properties that are unique to AIR, so we need to add these to the manager. These properties let us know the system supports items such as menus, dock icons, transparency, and notification cueing on the system.

Let's add these properties to the context manager:

```
private function setSystemSupportCapability():void
{
    contextVO.supportsDockIcon = NativeApplication.supportsDockIcon;
    contextVO.supportsMenu = NativeApplication.supportsMenu;
    contextVO.supportsSystemTrayIcon = ➥
NativeApplication.supportsSystemTrayIcon;
    contextVO.supportsMenu = NativeWindow.supportsMenu;
    contextVO.supportsNotification = ➥
NativeWindow.supportsNotification;
    contextVO.supportsTransparency = ➥
NativeWindow.supportsTransparency;
    contextVO.systemMaxSize = NativeWindow.systemMaxSize;
    contextVO.systemMinSize = NativeWindow.systemMinSize;
}
```

Detecting user presence

An AIR application can detect when a user is actively using the device. There are two states of activity:

- **User present**: An input device, such as a keyboard or a mouse, is in use.
- **User idle**: The user is not using an input device.

Whenever the user uses a keyboard, mouse, or touch screen, the AIR flash.desktop.NativeApplication API will dispatch a userPresent event. If the user is not using the input devices, an idleThreshold will be dispatched, and we can find out how long it's been since the user last employed an input device with the timeSinceLastUserInput property.

```
private function detectUserPresence():void
{
    nativeApp.idleThreshold = idleThresholdTime;
    nativeApp.addEventListener(Event.USER_IDLE, onUserIdleHandler);
    nativeApp.addEventListener(Event.USER_PRESENT, ➡
onUserPresentHandler);
}
```

Next, we'll create the handlers; notice that we can track the time the user last interacted with the system:

```
var lastUserInput:Number = ➡
NativeApplication.nativeApplication.timeSinceLastUserInput;
private function onUserIdleHandler(evt:Event):void
{
    var lastUserInput:Number = ➡
NativeApplication.nativeApplication.timeSinceLastUserInput;
    var event:Event = new Event(USER_IDLE, true);

    contextVO.isUserPresent = false;
    contextVO.lastUserInput = lastUserInput;

    this.dispatchEvent(event);
}
```

Last, we need to dispatch an event so our application can get notified of these changes:

```
private function onUserPresentHandler(evt:Event):void
{
    var event:Event = new Event(USER_PRESENT, true);
    contextVO.isUserPresent = true;
    this.dispatchEvent(event);
}
```

Detecting network connectivity changes

We covered how to recognize network connectivity in Chapter 9 as well as HTTP connectivity. Keep in mind that the network connectivity tracks a change in the network configuration. However, it doesn't tell us what kinds of changes were made, and we cannot rely entirely on information collected by the network changes to know whether we can access the network or not. Take a look at the code that tracks network changes:

```
private function detectNetworkChanges():void
{
     nativeApp.addEventListener(Event.NETWORK_CHANGE, ➡
onNetworkStatusChange);
}

private function onNetworkStatusChange(evt:Event):void
{
     var event:Event = new Event(NETWORK_CHANGE, true);
     contextVO.isNetworkChanged = true;
     this.dispatchEvent(event);
}
```

Detecting HTTP connectivity

Since the NETWORK_CHANGE is not targeted to a specific URL, we can use the HTTP connectivity information to query a specific URL on a web port to let us know whether we can successfully access a specific site. We can detect HTTP connectivity with the following code:

```
private function detectHTTPConnectivity():void
{
     monitor = new URLMonitor(new URLRequest(siteToTrack));
     monitor.addEventListener(StatusEvent.STATUS, ➡
onHTTPConnectivityChange);
     monitor.start();
}
```

Our handler will dispatch either an HTTP_CONNECTIVITY_TRUE or HTTP_CONNECTIVITY_FALSE notification.

```
private function onHTTPConnectivityChange(evt:StatusEvent):void
{
    var event:Event;
    contextVO.isHTTPAvaliable = monitor.available;
    event = (monitor.available) ? ➡
new Event(HTTP_CONNECTIVITY_TRUE, true) :
         new Event(HTTP_CONNECTIVITY_FALSE, true);

    this.dispatchEvent(event);
}
```

Detecting socket connectivity

Detecting socket connectivity allows us to determine whether we can connect to a domain in a specific port. We cannot assume that the user has access to all ports on a domain, since many domains' firewalls and network routers can restrict network communication on ports for security reasons. In case there is a firewall restriction, we can keep track of changes to the socket using the SocketMonitor.

```
public var portToCheck:int;
public var siteSocketMonitor:String;

private function detectSocketConnectivity():void
{
    socketMonitor = new SocketMonitor(siteSocketMonitor,portToCheck);
    socketMonitor.addEventListener(StatusEvent.STATUS, ➥
onSocketStatusChange);
    socketMonitor.start();
}

private function onSocketStatusChange(evt:StatusEvent):void
{
    var event:Event;
    contextVO.isSocketMonitorAvailable = socketMonitor.available;

    event = (socketMonitor.available) ? ➥
new Event(SOCKET_CONNECTIVITY_TRUE, true) :
        new Event(SOCKET_CONNECTIVITY_FALSE, true);

    this.dispatchEvent(event);
}
```

Detecting local drives

AIR applications handle Mac, PC, or Linux operating systems differently in terms of the location of the local drives. We can store an array of files and directories on the operating system. The File.getRootDirectories method will get a listing of the local drives for any operating system and create an array that holds the drives.

```
private function detectLocalDrivers():void
{
    contextVO.currentAvaliableDrives = (contextVO.osName=="mac") ?
        new File('/Volumes/').getDirectoryListing() : ➥
File.getRootDirectories() ;
}

public function refreshLocalDrives():void
{
    detectLocalDrivers();
}
```

Detecting application window movement

AIR applications allow us to detect movement of the application window and location as well as the previous location before we moved the window. The position is of type Rectangle and gives us the exact location of the window on the screen.

```
private function detectWindowedApplicationMovment():void
{
    Application.application.addEventListener(➡
NativeWindowBoundsEvent.MOVING, onWindowedApplicationMovment);
}

private function onWindowedApplicationMovment(evt: ➡
NativeWindowBoundsEvent):void
{
    var event:Event = new Event(NATIVE_WINDOW_MOVED, true);

    contextVO.windowPositionAfterBounds = evt.afterBounds;
    contextVO.windowPositionBeforeBounds = evt.beforeBounds;

    this.dispatchEvent(event);
}
```

Getting the AIR runtime version and patch level

Tracking AIR runtime and patch versions can be very useful. There are many cases when you may need to know the Flash Player, for instance, if we are creating an application that supports Flash Player 10 but only when it's available. Our application can be based on Flash Player 9, and we can still check the Flash Player version and load different modules.

We track these like so:

```
private function setRuntimeInformation():void
{
    contextVO.getRuntimeVersion = nativeApp.runtimeVersion;
    contextVO.getRuntimePatchLevel = nativeApp.runtimePatchLevel;
}
```

Let's take a look at a simple monitor application that can display application information as well as show us live notifications regarding our device. After the container gets created, we can call an init method, which will use the context manager to set the event listeners and start the manager. Figure 10-1 shows the application we created to test the API.

This simple application implements the context manager and gives you an idea of how to track and access the device capability. First, we need to create an instance of the manager. The getInstance() class method is called, so we always use the same class (since we don't need to track the same services more than once).

```
private var ca:ContextAwarenessManager =
ContextAwarenessManager.getInstance();
```

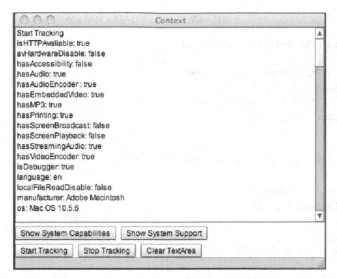

Figure 10-1.
Our AIR application
to test the API

Next, we create an init() method that includes all the properties we would like to track and specify the handlers:

```
private function init():void
{
    ca.addEventListener( ➡
    ContextAwarenessManager.USER_IDLE, onUserHandler);
    ca.addEventListener( ➡
    ContextAwarenessManager.USER_PRESENT, onUserHandler);
    ca.addEventListener( ➡
    ContextAwarenessManager.HTTP_CONNECTIVITY_TRUE, onHTTPConnectivityChange);
    ca.addEventListener( ➡
    ContextAwarenessManager.HTTP_CONNECTIVITY_FALSE, onHTTPConnectivityChange);
    ca.addEventListener( ➡
    ContextAwarenessManager.NATIVE_WINDOW_MOVED, ➡
    onWindowedApplicationMovment);
    ca.addEventListener(ContextAwarenessManager.NETWORK_CHANGE, ➡
    onNetworkStatusChange);
    ca.addEventListener( ➡
    ContextAwarenessManager.SOCKET_CONNECTIVITY_FALSE, ➡
    onSocketStatusChange);
    ca.addEventListener( ➡
    ContextAwarenessManager.SOCKET_CONNECTIVITY_TRUE, ➡
    onSocketStatusChange);

    ca.start();
    textArea.text = "Start Tracking";
}
```

After that, we need to create event handlers to add a message to the TextArea component:

```
    private function onUserHandler(evt:Event):void
    {
        textArea.text += "\nisUserPresent: "+ ➥
ca.contextVO.isUserPresent.toString();
        textArea.text += "\nlastUserInput: "+ ➥
ca.contextVO.lastUserInput.toString();
    }

    private function onNetworkStatusChange(evt:Event):void
    {
        textArea.text += "\nisNetworkChanged: "+ ➥
ca.contextVO.isNetworkChanged.toString();
    }

    private function onHTTPConnectivityChange(evt:Event):void
    {
        textArea.text += "\nisHTTPAvaliable: "+ ➥
ca.contextVO.isHTTPAvaliable.toString();
    }

    private function onSocketStatusChange(evt:Event):void
    {
        textArea.text += "\nisSocketMonitorAvailable: "+ ➥
ca.contextVO.isSocketMonitorAvailable.toString();
    }

    private function onWindowedApplicationMovment(evt:Event):void
    {
        textArea.text += "\nwindowPositionAfterBounds: ➥
"+ca.contextVO.windowPositionAfterBounds.toString();
        textArea.text += "\nwindowPositionBeforeBounds: ➥
"+ca.contextVO.windowPositionBeforeBounds.toString();
    }
```

Here's the button handler called showCapabilitiesClickHandler, which can add the system capability information to the TextArea component:

```
    private function showCapabilitiesClickHandler(event:MouseEvent):void
    {
        textArea.text += "\navHardwareDisable: "+➥
ca.contextVO.avHardwareDisable.toString();
        textArea.text += "\nhasAccessibility: "+➥
ca.contextVO.hasAccessibility.toString();
        textArea.text += "\nhasAudio: "+➥
ca.contextVO.hasAudio.toString();
        textArea.text += "\nhasAudioEncoder : "+➥
ca.contextVO.hasAudioEncoder.toString();
```

```
        textArea.text += "\nhasEmbeddedVideo: "+➡
ca.contextVO.hasEmbeddedVideo.toString();
        textArea.text += "\nhasMP3: "+ca.contextVO.hasMP3.toString();
        textArea.text += "\nhasPrinting: "+➡
ca.contextVO.hasPrinting.toString();
        textArea.text += "\nhasScreenBroadcast: "+➡
ca.contextVO.hasScreenBroadcast.toString();
        textArea.text += "\nhasScreenPlayback: "+➡
ca.contextVO.hasScreenPlayback.toString();
        textArea.text += "\nhasStreamingAudio: "+➡
ca.contextVO.hasStreamingAudio.toString();
        textArea.text += "\nhasVideoEncoder: "+➡
ca.contextVO.hasVideoEncoder.toString();
        textArea.text += "\nisDebugger: "+➡
ca.contextVO.isDebugger.toString();
        textArea.text += "\nlanguage: "+➡
ca.contextVO.language.toString();
        textArea.text += "\nlocalFileReadDisable: "+➡
ca.contextVO.localFileReadDisable.toString();
        textArea.text += "\nmanufacturer: "+➡
ca.contextVO.manufacturer.toString();
        textArea.text += "\nos: "+ca.contextVO.os.toString();
        textArea.text += "\nosName: "+ca.contextVO.osName.toString();
        textArea.text += "\npixelAspectRatio: "+➡
ca.contextVO.pixelAspectRatio.toString();
        textArea.text += "\nplayerType: "+➡
ca.contextVO.playerType.toString();
        textArea.text += "\nscreenColor: "+➡
ca.contextVO.screenColor.toString();
        textArea.text += "\nscreenDPI: "+➡
ca.contextVO.screenDPI.toString();
        textArea.text += "\nscreenResolutionX: "+➡
ca.contextVO.screenResolutionX.toString();
        textArea.text += "\nscreenResolutionY: "+➡
ca.contextVO.screenResolutionY.toString();
        textArea.text += "\nserverString: "+➡
ca.contextVO.serverString.toString();
        textArea.text += "\nversion: "+ca.contextVO.version.toString();
    }
```

The showSystemSupportClickHandler method will display information related to the AIR properties the system supports:

```
    private function showSystemSupportClickHandler(event:MouseEvent):void
    {
        textArea.text += "\nsupportsDockIcon: "+ ➡
ca.contextVO.supportsDockIcon.toString();
        textArea.text += "\nsupportsMenu: "+ ➡
ca.contextVO.supportsMenu.toString();
```

```
        textArea.text += "\nsupportsSystemTrayIcon: "+ ➡
ca.contextVO.supportsSystemTrayIcon.toString();
        textArea.text += "\nsupportsNotification: "+ ➡
ca.contextVO.supportsNotification.toString();
        textArea.text += "\nsupportsTransparency: "+ ➡
ca.contextVO.supportsTransparency.toString();
        textArea.text += "\nsystemMaxSize: "+ ➡
ca.contextVO.systemMaxSize.toString();
        textArea.text += "\nsystemMinSize: "+ ➡
ca.contextVO.systemMinSize.toString();
    }
```

Finally, we can create buttons to start tracking, stop tracking, and show information:

```
<mx:VBox width="100%" height="100%" >
        <s:TextArea id="textArea" width="100%" height="95%" />

        <mx:HBox>
            <s:Button label="Show System Capabilities" ➡
click="showCapabilitiesClickHandler(event)" />
            <s:Button label="Show System Support" ➡
click="showSystemSupportClickHandler(event)" />
        </mx:HBox>

        <mx:HBox>
            <s:Button label="Start Tracking" click="ca.start(); ➡
textArea.text+='\nStart Tracking';" />
            <s:Button label="Stop Tracking" click="ca.stop(); ➡
textArea.text+='\nStop Tracking';" />
            <s:Button label="Clear TextArea"
click="textArea.text=''" />
        </mx:HBox>

    </mx:VBox>
```

Adapting configuration and behavior

Now that we can receive information and notifications from the platform- and context-aware layers, we can have our application modify its configuration and behavior. Adaptive behavior should be guided by user experience and preference. For instance, assume the user starts up the device while traveling; the application should still be able to deliver location-specific and filtered content. As another example, a preferences pop-up could allow the user to set how to handle certain changes in the hardware.

Let's take a look at the YouTube application we built in the previous chapter and configure it to adapt to changes. Recall that the application allows us to view videos online, but once we are disconnected from the Internet, we are unable to view or search for videos. To change this behavior, we need to be able to download files from the Internet, store the information in a database, and once the Internet is disconnected, allow the user to view the videos that were downloaded locally.

Downloading files from a server

Let's create a manager API that can download files from the Internet and onto a local drive. The download needs only two parameters: the file you want to download and the location you want to store it on in your local device.

A downloading API might come in handy in the many ways, including the following:

- Download HTML pages and display them once the device is offline.
- Download multimedia for use offline.
- Process information from a server and store it in a local database.

You can specify the exact location you want to store the file using the desktopDirectory API:

```
var file:File = File.desktopDirectory.resolvePath("C:/temp/myFile.txt");
```

However, I recommend saving the file to a location that is relative to your application, since the application may be deployed in many different operating systems, and saving files in a nonrelative location would make it more difficult to ensure your path is correct. For instance, PC users may have more than one hard drive without necessarily having administrative rights to every drive.

You can use the File API and select the applicationStorageDirectory method, which will map to the location were your .air application is stored:

```
var file:File = ➡
File.applicationStorageDirectory.resolvePath(fileLocalLocation);
```

In the downloadFileFromServer method, we download the file and listen for progress changes and a DownloadComplete event:

```
public function downloadFileFromServer(fileURL:String, ➡
fileLocalLocation:String):void
{
    var file:File = ➡
File.applicationStorageDirectory.resolvePath(fileLocalLocation);
    request = new URLRequest(fileURL);
    fileStream.openAsync(file, FileMode.WRITE);

    stream.addEventListener(ProgressEvent.PROGRESS, ➡
onDownloadProgress);
    stream.addEventListener(Event.COMPLETE, onDownloadComplete);

    stream.load(request);
}
```

Our code's handlers keep track of changes, and once changes are made, we can track changes in a progress bar to keep the user informed:

```
private function onDownloadProgress(event:ProgressEvent):void
{
    var byteArray:ByteArray = new ByteArray();
    var precent:Number = Math.round(bytesLoaded*100/bytesTotal);
```

```
        bytesLoaded = event.bytesLoaded;
        bytesTotal = event.bytesTotal;

        stream.readBytes(byteArray, 0, stream.bytesAvailable);
        fileStream.writeBytes(byteArray, 0, byteArray.length);

        var progressEvent:ProgressEvent = ➡
new ProgressEvent(ProgressEvent.PROGRESS);
        progressEvent.bytesLoaded = bytesLoaded;
        progressEvent.bytesTotal = bytesTotal;

        this.dispatchEvent(progressEvent);
    }
```

Once the download is completed, we need to remove the event listener and dispatch another event to notify the class that will implement this downloading file's API that the download is complete:

```
    private function onDownloadComplete(event:Event):void
    {
        fileStream.close();
        stream.close();

        stream.removeEventListener(ProgressEvent.PROGRESS, ➡
onDownloadProgress);
        stream.removeEventListener(Event.COMPLETE, onDownloadComplete);

        var completeEvent:Event = new Event(Event.COMPLETE);
this.dispatchEvent(completeEvent);
    }
```

To implement the manager, we create an instance of the DownloadManager and set the listeners:

```
    downloadManager = new DownloadManager();
    downloadManager.addEventListener(ProgressEvent.PROGRESS, ➡
onDownloadProgress);
    downloadManager.addEventListener(Event.COMPLETE, onDownloadComplete);
    downloadManager.downloadFileFromServer(videoURL , videoId+".flv");
```

Once the download progress events are dispatched, we can calculate the percent for the ProgressBar component:

```
    private function onDownloadProgress(event:ProgressEvent):void
    {
        var value:Number = event.bytesLoaded;
        var total:Number = event.bytesTotal;
        var precent:Number = Math.round(value*100/total);
        progressBarPercent = percent;
    }
```

Implementing HTTP connectivity awareness

Now that we can download files, we can add an event listener to the context manager and listen to changes in our network so we can switch between online and offline modes. We can implement the ContextAwarenessManager API in our code as follows:

```
var contextAwareness:ContextAwarenessManager = ➥
ContextAwarenessManager.getInstance();

contextAwareness.addEventListener( ➥
ContextAwarenessManager.HTTP_CONNECTIVITY_TRUE, ➥
onHTTPConnectivityChange);
contextAwareness.addEventListener( ➥
ContextAwarenessManager.HTTP_CONNECTIVITY_FALSE, ➥
onHTTPConnectivityChange);

contextAwareness.start();
And take a look at code for the event handler:
private function onHTTPConnectivityChange(evt:Event):void
{
var isHTTPAvaliable:Boolean = ➥
contextAwareness.contextVO.isHTTPAvaliable;
Alert.show("Network status change:"+isHTTPAvaliable.toString());
}
```

Using a database to store information

Our application is now capable of downloading files from servers and recognizing that the user disconnected from the HTTP network. At this point, we want to be able to store the information in a local SQLite database, so the information can be retrieved when needed and after the application session is over.

Storing the information in a SQLite database is the key for working offline. The process for connecting to a SQLite database is as follows:

1. Open a database connection.

2. Execute one or more SQL commands.

3. Close the connection.

To open a SQLite connection you set a new connection and open a SQLite file:

```
var Connection:SQLConnection = new SQLConnection();
var sqlFile:File = ➥
File.applicationStorageDirectory.resolvePath("filename.sql");

try
{
    connection.open(("filename.sql");
}
```

```
catch (error:SQLError)
{
// handle errors
}
```

The next step is to execute a SQL command. We create a SQL statement and execute the command. In the following example, a simple SQL command SELECT * FROM TableName retrieves all the entries from a table:

```
var statement:SQLStatement = new SQLStatement();
statement.sqlConnection = connection;
statement.text = "SELECT * FROM TableName";

try
{
    statement.execute();
}
catch (error:SQLError)
{
    // handle errors
}
```

Last, to close the connection, you call the connection instance and use the close() method:

```
Connection.close();
```

Creating a SQLite manager

Working with an application that has many SQL commands can become challenging; these commands may be initialized from different classes and we may want to keep the database connection open and avoid duplicating code. I have created a SQLite manager that does just that. You can set the database settings and access the manager from anywhere in your application. To download the complete open source code, download SqliteManager from this book's download page of the friends of ED web site.

Let's take a look at the code. Before we define the class, we need to set the event metadata, so we can map to the custom events being used by the class. Each event has an ASDoc comment, so in addition to code hints, you will be able to view information about the event once you get the code hints in Flash Builder 4:

```
/**
 *  Dispatched when the database failed
 *
 *  @eventType com.elad.framework.sqlite.events.DATABASE_FAIL
 */
[Event(name="databaseFail", ➥
type="com.elad.framework.sqlite.events.DatabaseFailEvent")]

/**
 *  Dispatched when a command execution failed
 *
 *  @eventType com.elad.framework.sqlite.events.COMMAND_EXEC_FAILED
 */
```

```
        [Event(name="commandExecFailed", ➥
    type="com.elad.framework.sqlite.events.DatabaseFailEvent")]

        /**
         * Dispatched when a command executed successfully
         *
         * @eventType ➥
    com.elad.framework.sqlite.events.COMMAND_EXEC_SUCCESSFULLY
         */
        [Event(name="commandExecSuccesfully", ➥
    type="com.elad.framework.sqlite.events.DatabaseSuccessEvent")]

        /**
         * Dispatched when the database is connected successfully
         *
         * @eventType ➥
    com.elad.framework.sqlite.events.DATABASE_CONNECTED_SUCCESSFULLY
         */
        [Event(name="databaseConnectedSuccessfully", ➥
    type="com.elad.framework.sqlite.events.DatabaseSuccessEvent")]

        /**
         * Dispatched
         * when the database is ready and you can execute commands
         *
         * @eventType com.elad.framework.sqlite.events.DATABASE_READY
         */
        [Event(name="databaseReady", ➥
    type="com.elad.framework.sqlite.events.DatabaseSuccessEvent")]

        /**
         * Dispatched when creating the database started
         *
         * @eventType com.elad.framework.sqlite.events.CREATING_DATABASE
         */
        [Event(name="creatingDatabase", ➥
    type="com.elad.framework.sqlite.events.DatabaseSuccessEvent")]
```

The manager will extend the EventDispatcher, so we can dispatch events and implement the ISQLiteManager, which is our contract to ensure we have a start method to open a connection and a close connection method:

```
    public class SQLiteManager extends ➥
      EventDispatcher implements ISQLiteManager
```

We need to set variables that we will use across the manager, as well as keep track of the database file name, table name, and the SQL statement to create the database:

```
    public var dbFullFileName:String;
    public var tableName:String;
    public var createDbStatement:String;
```

The following variables are instances of the connection, the statement SQL, and the SQL file:

```
protected var connection:SQLConnection;
protected var statement:SQLStatement;
protected var sqlFile:File;
```

The following variables will be used in case the table doesn't exist and we need to first create the table:

```
protected var repeateFailCallBack:Function;
protected var repeateCallBack:Function;
protected var repeateSqlCommand:String = "";
```

Our manager will be a singleton, so we can ensure we are not opening more than one connection at a time. Since ActionScript 3.0 doesn't have a private class, we will create a second class and enforce that the class doesn't get created more than once.

```
protected static var instance:SQLiteManager;

public function SQLiteManager(enforcer:AccessRestriction)
{
    if (enforcer == null)
        throw new ➥
        Error("Error enforcer input param is undefined" );
}
    public static function getInstance():SQLiteManager
    {
        if( instance == null )
        instance = new SQLiteManager(new AccessRestriction());
        return instance;
    }
}

class AccessRestriction {}
```

The start method sets the database file name, table name, and the create SQL statement. This will allow us to connect to the database, execute commands on a table, and create the table if it doesn't yet exist or has been erased. Additionally, the method allows us to tap into AIR 1.5 capabilities (see Chapter 9) and use password encryption if we want.

```
public function start(dbFullFileName:String, tableName:String, ➥
createTableStatement:String, password:String=null):void
{
    this.dbFullFileName = dbFullFileName;
    this.tableName = tableName;
    this.createDbStatement = createTableStatement;
    var encryptionKey:ByteArray = null;
    connection = new SQLConnection();
    sqlFile = ➥
    File.applicationStorageDirectory.resolvePath(dbFullFileName);
```

```
    try
    {
        if (password != null)
        {
            encryptionKey = ➥
            getEncryptionKey(password, sqlFile);
        }

        connection.open(sqlFile, SQLMode.CREATE, ➥
        false, 1024, encryptionKey);
        this.dispatchEvent(new DatabaseSuccessEvent( ➥

        DatabaseSuccessEvent.DATABASE_CONNECTED_SUCCESSFULLY));
    }
    catch (error:SQLError)
    {
        var errorMessage:String = "Error message:" + ➥
        error.message;

        if (error.details != "")
            errorMessage += ", Details:" + error.details;

        fail(null, errorMessage);
    }
}
```

Notice that we dispatched an event to notify that the database was connected. If the connection failed, we handle the error messages by calling the fail method and placing a trace statement. We use the same open method to connect to the database, and if a password was set, we use the getEncryptionKey method to get a ByteArray that includes the key and pass the array to the connection.open method.

Next, we need a method to close the connection once the download is complete and we don't need a connection anymore:

```
    public function close():void
    {
        connection.close();
    }
```

The testTableExists method is convenient for testing if the SQL commands are executed and ensure that the table exists:

```
    public function testTableExists():void
    {
        var sql:String = "SELECT * FROM "+tableName+" LIMIT 1;";
        executeCustomCommand(sql, this.onDatabaseReady, ➥
    this.createTable );
    }
```

As you can see, the executeCustomCommand passes the createTable method a callback method that will create the table in case it wasn't created before.

```
private function createTable():void
{
    statement = new SQLStatement();
    statement.sqlConnection = connection;
    statement.text = createDbStatement;
    statement.execute();

    statement.addEventListener(SQLEvent.RESULT, onDatabaseReady);
}
```

Next, we'll update the manager so that it can specify common SQL commands, for instance, selecting all the rows in a table or deleting a table.

```
public function executeSelectAllCommand(callback:Function=null, ➡
failCallback:Function=null):void
{
    var sql:String = "SELECT * FROM "+tableName+";";
    executeCustomCommand(sql, callback, failCallback);
}
```

Another example of a common SQL command is the executeDeleteAllCommand method, which creates a SQL command to delete all the entries in the table:

```
public function executeDeleteAllCommand( ➡
callback:Function=null):void
{
    var sql:String = "DELETE * FROM "+tableName+";";
    executeCustomCommand(sql, callback);
}
```

We also need a method to execute a custom command. The method takes a SQL command and a callback method to handle error requests. Using a callback method allows us to handle these requests. We could also leave the callback as null and let the manager handle the request.

```
public function executeCustomCommand(sql:String, ➡
callBack:Function=null, failCallBack:Function=null):void
{
    statement = new SQLStatement();
    statement.sqlConnection = connection;

    statement.text = sql;

    if (callBack!=null)
    {
        statement.addEventListener(SQLEvent.RESULT, callBack);
    }
```

```
        else
        {
                statement.addEventListener(SQLEvent.RESULT, ➡
        onStatementSuccess);
        }

        statement.addEventListener(SQLErrorEvent.ERROR, function():void {
                fail();
        });

        try
        {
            statement.execute();
        }
        catch (error:SQLError)
        {
                this.handleErrors(error, sql, callBack, failCallBack);
        }
    }
```

Some SQL commands will fail if they include certain characters, such as the single quotation mark (which is reserved for SQL commands). For example, take a look at this SQL command:

```
var Sql:String = ➡
"SELECT * FROM Books WHERE bookName='Elad's Flex book';"
```

We can solve that by using a static method to remove the quotation mark:

```
public static function removeBadCharacters(str:String):String
{
        var retVal:String = str.split("'").join("&#8217;&rsquo;");
        return retVal;
}
```

The method finds places with single quotation marks and replaces each with the HTML character code for a single quote. We only implemented the single quotation mark changes but feel free to replace any character by adding a new line with the character you want to change. For instance, to replace the dash, use this line:

```
retVal = str.split("-").join("&#8211;");
```

Last, we need handlers to handle successful and failed statements as well as error messages:

```
private function onStatementSuccess(event:SQLEvent):void
{
        var results:Object = statement.getResult();
        var evt:StatementCompleteEvent = ➡
        new StatementCompleteEvent( ➡
        StatementCompleteEvent.COMMAND_EXEC_SUCCESSFULLY, results);
        this.dispatchEvent(evt);
}
```

```
        private function handleErrors(error:SQLError, sql:String,  ➥
        callBack:Function, failCallBack:Function):void
        {
            trace("Error message:", error.message);
            trace("Details:", error.details);

            if (error.details == "no such table: '"+tableName+"'")
            {
                repeateSqlCommand = sql;
                repeateFailCallBack = failCallBack;
                repeateCallBack = callBack;
                createTable();
            }
            else
            {
                if (failCallBack != null)
                {
                    failCallBack();
                }
                else
                {
                    fail();
                }
            }
        }

        private function fail(event:Event=null, errorMessage:String=""):void
        {
            this.dispatchEvent( new DatabaseFailEvent(  ➥
            DatabaseFailEvent.DATABASE_FAIL, errorMessage) );
            closeConnection();
        }
    }
}
```

Let's create an example that implements the SQLite manager we've just created. Before we do that, we need to set the start method and event handlers and execute a command that selects all the fields:

```
var sql:String =  "INSERT INTO Users VALUES('"+userVO.userId+"','"  ➥
+userVO.userName+"');";
database.addEventListener(SQLiteManager.COMMAND_EXEC_SUCCESSFULLY,  ➥
onInsertSuccess);
database.executeCustomCommand(sql);
```

Now, we can implement the API we just created for a simple application that illustrates how to use the manager. Once we initialize the component, the SQLite database manager calls the initializeHandler method, followed by the readEntries method to read all the entries in the database. We also have the form shown in Figure 10-2; once submitted, it inserts the entry into the database and updates the data grid automatically.

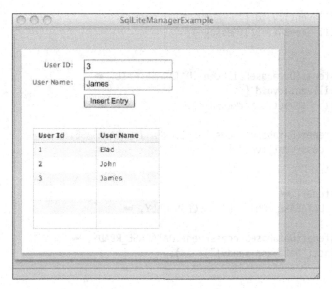

Figure 10-2.
SQLite manager example
AIR application

Take a look at the complete code:

```
<?xml version="1.0" encoding="utf-8"?>
<s:WindowedApplication
xmlns:fx=http://ns.adobe.com/mxml/2009
xmlns:s="library://ns.adobe.com/flex/spark"
    xmlns:mx="library://ns.adobe.com/flex/halo"
initialize="initializeHandler(event)" >

    <fx:Script>
        <![CDATA[

            import com.elad.framework.sqlite.events.DatabaseSuccessEvent;
            import com.elad.framework.sqlite.events.StatementCompleteEvent;
            import com.elad.framework.sqlite.events.DatabaseFailEvent;
            import mx.collections.ArrayCollection;
            import mx.events.FlexEvent;
            import com.elad.framework.sqlite.SQLiteManager;
```

We create an instance to hold an instance of the SQLiteManager class.

```
private var database:SQLiteManager = SQLiteManager.getInstance();
```

The initializeHandler sets event listeners and sets the SQL command that creates the table. The table has two columns, UserId and UserName.

```
protected function initializeHandler(event:FlexEvent):void
{
    database.addEventListener(➥
    DatabaseSuccessEvent.COMMAND_EXEC_SUCCESSFULLY, onSelectResult);
    database.addEventListener(DatabaseFailEvent.COMMAND_EXEC_FAILED,
```

409

```
        function(event:DatabaseFailEvent):void {
            trace("execution fail: "+event.errorMessage);
            });

        database.addEventListener(DatabaseFailEvent.DATABASE_FAIL, ➡
    function(event:DatabaseFailEvent):void {
            trace("database fail: "+event.errorMessage);
            });
        database.addEventListener(DatabaseSuccessEvent.CREATING_DATABASE, ➡
    function(event:DatabaseSuccessEvent):void {
            trace(event.message);
            });
        database.addEventListener( ➡
        DatabaseSuccessEvent.DATABASE_CONNECTED_SUCCESSFULLY, ➡
        onConnectedHandler);
        database.addEventListener(DatabaseSuccessEvent.DATABASE_READY, ➡
        function():void { trace("database ready!"); } );

        // start database
        var password:String = "Pa55word";
        var createTableStatement:String = ➡
    "CREATE TABLE Users(UserId VARCHAR(150) PRIMARY KEY, ➡
    UserName VARCHAR(150))";
        database.start("Users.sql3", "Users", createTableStatement, password);
            }
```

Once the database is connected the handler will call the readEntries method.

```
        private function onConnectedHandler( ➡
            event:DatabaseSuccessEvent):void
        {
            readEntries();
        }
```

The insertEntry method will be called when the user clicks a button to insert the information.

```
        private function insertEntry():void
        {
            var sql:String =  "INSERT INTO Users VALUES(➡
    '"+String(userId.text)+"','"+userName.text+"');";
            database.executeCustomCommand(sql);
        }
```

We can then create a method to insert the information and to retrieve all the fields' data.

```
        private function readEntries():void
        {
            database.executeSelectAllCommand();
        }
```

We now need an event handler to handle the SQL command results. It handles a successful SQL command for inserting information to the database as well as retrieving information. The unsuccessful SQL commands will be handled by the initializeHandler, which will hold listeners and post trace statements on failed commands. You can change the code and split the two into separate classes.

To recognize which SQL command got executed, we first check if changes were made:

```
private function onSelectResult(event:StatementCompleteEvent):void
{
    var result:Array = event.results.data;
    var rowsAffected:int = event.results.rowsAffected;

    if (rowsAffected == 1)
        readEntries();

    if (result == null)
        return;
```

Once we know that a row was inserted, we can also check to see if there are results, meaning that the retrieve command was executed. If there are results we want to add them to the data grid so we can see them on the UI:

```
                var len:int = result.length;
                var dp:ArrayCollection = new ArrayCollection();

                for (var i:int; i<len; i++)
                {
                    dp.addItem( {UserId: result[i].UserId, ➥
UserName: result[i].UserName} );
                }

                dataGrid.dataProvider = dp;
            }

        ]]>
    </fx:Script>

    <mx:Panel x="5" y="5" layout="absolute" height="356">

        <mx:VBox horizontalScrollPolicy="off"
verticalScrollPolicy="off">
            <!-- Form -->
            <mx:Form width="414">
                <mx:FormItem label="User ID:">
                    <s:TextInput id="userId"/>
                </mx:FormItem>
                <mx:FormItem label="User Name:">
                    <s:TextInput id="userName"/>
                </mx:FormItem>
```

```
                    <mx:FormItem>
                            <s:Button label="Insert Entry"
click="insertEntry();"/>
                    </mx:FormItem>
              </mx:Form>
          </mx:VBox>

          <!-- Results -->
          <mx:DataGrid x="19" y="123" id="dataGrid">
              <mx:columns>
                    <mx:DataGridColumn
headerText="User Id" dataField="UserId"/>
                    <mx:DataGridColumn headerText="User Name"
dataField="UserName"/>
              </mx:columns>
          </mx:DataGrid>

      </mx:Panel>

</s:WindowedApplication>
```

Once we implement these capabilities into the YouTube application, we can enable offline awareness and show the videos we downloaded while disconnected from the network.

Take a look at the application in Figure 10-3, and download the complete source code from the friends of ED web site under Chapter 10/VideoMobile.

Figure 10-3.
YouTube application with download and offline capability

Mobile touch and multitouch screen applications

The way users interact with mobile devices is changing. We believe that the tools we use to communicate with our mobile devices, such as keypads and keyboards, will slowly fade away and be replaced with touch and multitouch screen tools allowing the user to engage in a more comfortable and natural experience.

> A touch screen is a display that is aware of the existence and location of a fingertip or a hand. A multitouch screen recognizes more than one finger or hand. The touch screen gives users the ability to use their hands to manipulate data and objects directly on the computer screen.

Multitouch interfaces are powerful in desktop and mobile applications alike, since they can potentially free us from the traditional input devices such as the keyboard and mouse. Apple's iPhone introduced a simple multitouch interface that enables two-finger user gestures to manipulate images and a web browser on the screen and became an overnight hit. Objects can be moved around with a fingertip and scaled by placing two fingertips on the screen edges and either spreading those fingers apart or bringing them closer together. Multitouch user gestures are defined as a user fingertip or hand interaction with the screen to, for instance, scale, move, rotate, or select. The gestures can then be translated into a class object.

Clearly, the future of mobile devices will be related to creating advanced multitouch screen applications, and multitouch applications have already improved devices' user experiences and can be used in the following ways:

- **Web browsing**: Easily surf the Web and scroll through pages.
- **Photo interaction**: Manage, sort, and scale photos.
- **Game play:** Play games as a single player or with several players.
- **Document and e-mail access:** Display, sort, scroll, and scale documents.
- **Workspace organization:** Easily move and delete workspaces.

Understanding the touch screen

The principles of touch-screen technology are quite simple. An array of infrared (IR) light is projected into the side of a screen, and the light is trapped inside the display by the refraction index of the material.

Light-emitting diodes (LEDs) attached to the two sides of the display can detect the IR light. A total internal reflection occurs when the light is inside a higher-index medium and strikes a display surface boundary into a lower-index medium. When the user fingertip touches the surface of the screen, the light is blocked, causing the light to reflect to the back of the display, where a camera captures the light and the device analyzes the information captured by the camera to determine a touch event. See Figure 10-4.

> Total internal reflection (TIR) is used to describe an optical phenomenon. TIR is the reflection of the total amount of incident light at the boundary between two media. What this means in layman's terms is that the light entering gets bent.

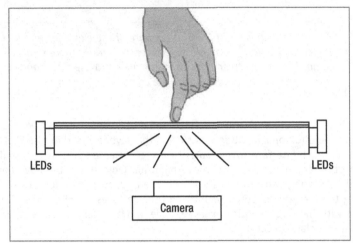

Figure 10-4.
Diagram illustrating how touch screen works

Today, multitouch computer screens can follow the instructions of many fingers and even more than two hands at the same time; they are the ideal input device for mobile development, since mobile devices are typically used on the go and are not connected to a mouse or a keyboard.

To create a multitouch screen application, we need to be able to track gestures. The idea is simple:

1. Register to receive gesture events.

2. Handle gesture events.

3. Interpret the gesture events.

In multitouch development in general, Perceptive Pixel (http://www.perceptivepixel.com/) is leading the way and has developed large screens that respond to several fingertips at once and even to multiple hands from multiple people. Remember the CNN news anchors marking the states each party might win during the United States presidential election in late 2008? They were using Perceptive Pixel technology.

Microsoft is already using Microsoft Surface (http://www.microsoft.com/surface/), which is a 30-inch multitouch and multiuser tabletop display. The technology is in use by many businesses running on Microsoft Vista, which is also installed on many UMPCs and supports touch screens. Vista will support multitouch screens in 2010 according to Microsoft. Additionally, Microsoft recently released a beta version of Windows 7, which can be installed on UMPCs. The beta offers multitouch screen support through the following properties: WM_GESTURECOMMAND, WM_GESTURE, and WM_TOUCH.

You can currently create a multitouch screen application with AIR for Windows 7 on UMPCs by installing Windows 7 Beta with the driver and talking to the .NET classes through a proxy, but this method has not been tested and may cause bugs and security issues.

Some systems are already using AIR to build a multitouch GUI. For example, an open project called Touchlib (http://nuigroup.com/touchlib/) allows you to listen to user gestures and build your own touch screen. At Adobe MAX in Milan, Intuilab (http://www.intuilab.com/) presented an application that takes full advantage of surface computers. The system integrates many types of content such as images, video, web content, Adobe PDFs, Flash, Illustrator, Photoshop, and Microsoft Office.

> *Surface computing is a term used to describe a computer GUI in which traditional input elements such as a mouse and keyboard are replaced with more intuitive, everyday familiar objects. For instance, it's much more natural and intuitive to use our hands to move objects around than learn how to use a mouse.*

Creating a UMPC touch screen application

At the time of this writing, creating a touch screen application on a UMPC is possible, and we can rely on the UMPC device to handle the touch screen. However, you may find that relying entirely on the device is buggy. For instance, the device may prove more sensitive than you'd like; it may register a gesture when your fingertip shifts slightly on the device though you didn't even realize you'd moved.

We recommend implementing your own instructions to register gestures. Take a look at the following class, which gives its own instructions on when to register user gestures. The first step is to create a VO to hold the information we would like to register, such as the X and Y position, the previous X and Y positions, and the length of time since the user gesture started.

```
package com.elad.framework.touchscreen.vo
{
    public class TouchVO
    {
        public function TouchVO(previousX:int=0, previousY:int=0, ➥
        currentX:int=0, currentY:int=0, moveTimer:int=0)
        {
            this.previousX = previousX;
            this.previousY = previousY;
            this.currentX = currentX;
            this.currentY = currentY;
            this.moveTimer = moveTimer;
        }

        public var previousX:int;
        public var previousY:int;
        public var currentX:int;
        public var currentY:int;
        public var moveTimer:int;
    }
}
```

Next, we will pass an instance of the main application, so we can track mouse events. We'll set event listeners, and once the user touches the screen, we can move into a drag state until the user releases that finger; in this way, we can allow the user to move objects around. We then can ignore very small movements and assume that the user didn't mean to move the object.

```
package com.elad.framework.touchscreen
{
    import com.elad.framework.touchscreen.events.TouchEvent;
    import com.elad.framework.touchscreen.vo.TouchVO;
    import flash.events.EventDispatcher;
    import flash.events.MouseEvent;
    import flash.utils.Timer;
    import mx.core.UIComponent;

    public class TouchManager extends EventDispatcher
    {
        private var moveTimer:Timer;
        private var previousX:int = 0;
        private var previousY:int = 0;
        private var component:UIComponent;

        public function TouchManager(component:UIComponent)
        {
            this.component = component;
        }

        public function start():void
        {
            initialize();
        }

        public function stop():void
        {
            component.removeEventListener(MouseEvent.MOUSE_DOWN, ➥
            onMouseDownHandler);
            component.removeEventListener(MouseEvent.MOUSE_UP, ➥
            onMouseUpHandler)
            moveTimer.stop();
            moveTimer = null;
        }

        protected function initialize():void
        {
            component.addEventListener(MouseEvent.MOUSE_DOWN, ➥
            onMouseDownHandler);
            component.addEventListener(MouseEvent.MOUSE_UP, onMouseUpHandler);
        }
```

```
privatefunction startTimer():void
{
    moveTimer = new Timer(100,1000);
    moveTimer.start();
}

private function onMouseDownHandler(event:MouseEvent):void
{
    startTimer();

    component.addEventListener(MouseEvent.MOUSE_MOVE, ➥
    onMouseMoveHandler);

    var touch:TouchVO = new TouchVO(this.previousX, this.previousY, ➥
    event.localX, event.localY, this.moveTimer.currentCount);
    this.dispatchEvent( new ➥
    TouchEvent( TouchEvent.TOUCH_DOWN, touch ) );
}

private function onMouseUpHandler(event:MouseEvent):void
{
    moveTimer.stop();
    component.removeEventListener(MouseEvent.MOUSE_MOVE, ➥
    onMouseMoveHandler);
    var touch:TouchVO = new TouchVO(this.previousX, this.previousY, ➥
    event.localX, event.localY, this.moveTimer.currentCount);
    this.dispatchEvent( new TouchEvent( TouchEvent.TOUCH_UP, touch ) );
}

private function onMouseMoveHandler(event:MouseEvent):void
{
    var isMove:Boolean = isTouchMove(event.localX, event.localY);
    var touch:TouchVO = new TouchVO(this.previousX, this.previousY, ➥
    event.localX, event.localY, this.moveTimer.currentCount);
    if (isMove)
    {
        this.dispatchEvent( new TouchEvent(TouchEvent.TOUCH_DRAG, ➥
        touch) );
    }
}

private function isTouchMove(x:int, y:int):Boolean
{
    var retVal:Boolean = false;
    var ignore:int = 3;
    var isXmoved:Boolean;
    var isYmoved:Boolean;
```

```
            if (previousX != 0 && previousY != 0)
            {
                isXmoved = ➡
                (x > previousX+ignore || x < previousX-ignore) ? true : false;
                isYmoved = ➡
                (y > previousY+ignore || y < previousY-ignore) ? true : false;

                if ( isXmoved || isYmoved )
                {
                    retVal=true;
                }
            }

            previousX = x;
            previousY = y;

            return retVal;
        }
    }
}
```

We have created a simple application that uses the Touch class to move a circle object once the user touches the screen. The application was created using Flash Builder 4 beta for AIR 1.5. Once you touch the screen, a circle will appear, and when you move your finger, the circle moves as user gestures are registered.

```
<?xml version="1.0" encoding="utf-8"?>
<s:WindowedApplication xmlns:fx="http://ns.adobe.com/mxml/2009"
        xmlns:s="library://ns.adobe.com/flex/spark"
    xmlns:mx="library://ns.adobe.com/flex/halo"
    initialize="initializeHandler()">

    <fx:Script>
        <![CDATA[

            import com.elad.framework.touchscreen.vo.TouchVO;
            import com.elad.framework.touchscreen.events.TouchEvent;
            import com.elad.framework.touchscreen.TouchManager;
            import mx.collections.ArrayCollection;

            [Bindable]
            private var arrayCollection:ArrayCollection = new ArrayCollection;

            private var touch:TouchManager;
```

```
protected function initializeHandler():void
{
    touch = new TouchManager(this);
    touch.addEventListener(TouchEvent.TOUCH_DOWN, ➡
onMouseDownHandler);
    touch.addEventListener(TouchEvent.TOUCH_UP, ➡
onMouseUpHandler);
    touch.addEventListener(TouchEvent.TOUCH_DRAG, ➡
onMouseDragHandler);

    touch.start();
}

private function onMouseDownHandler(event:TouchEvent):void
{
    ellipse.visible = true;
    moveEllipse(event.touchVO.currentX, event.touchVO.currentY);
    registerLocation(ellipse.x, ellipse.y, "MouseDown", 0);
}

private function onMouseUpHandler(event:TouchEvent):void
{
    ellipse.visible = false;
}

private function onMouseDragHandler(➡
event:TouchEvent):void
{
        moveEllipse(event.touchVO.currentX, ➡
event.touchVO.currentY);
        registerLocation(ellipse.x, ellipse.y, ➡
"MouseMove", event.touchVO.moveTimer);
}

private function registerLocation➡
(x:int, y:int, type:String, time:int):void
{
    arrayCollection.addItem(➡
{locationX: ellipse.x, locationY: ellipse.y, type: type, time: time});
    dg.dataProvider = arrayCollection;
}
```

```
                    private function moveEllipse(x:int, y:int):void
                    {
                         ellipse.x = x - ellipse.width/2;
                         ellipse.y = y - ellipse.height/2;
                    }


          ]]>
     </fx:Script>

     <s:Group>
          <s:Ellipse height="80" width="80"
id="ellipse" visible="false">
               <s:stroke>
                    <s:SolidColorStroke color="0x000000" weight="2"/>
               </s:stroke>
          </s:Ellipse>
     </s:Group>

     <mx:DataGrid x="341" y="4" id="dg"
 dataProvider="{arrayCollection}" height="410">
          <mx:columns>
               <mx:DataGridColumn
headerText="X" dataField="locationX"/>
               <mx:DataGridColumn
headerText="Y" dataField="locationY"/>
               <mx:DataGridColumn headerText="Type" dataField="type"/>
               <mx:DataGridColumn headerText="Time" dataField="time"/>
          </mx:columns>
     </mx:DataGrid>

</s:WindowedApplication>
```

If you deploy and run the application on a UMPC device, it should look like the one shown in Figure 10-5.

You can enhance the Touch class and include many more user gestures; for instance, you can recognize that the user has moved a finger from left to right or right to left.

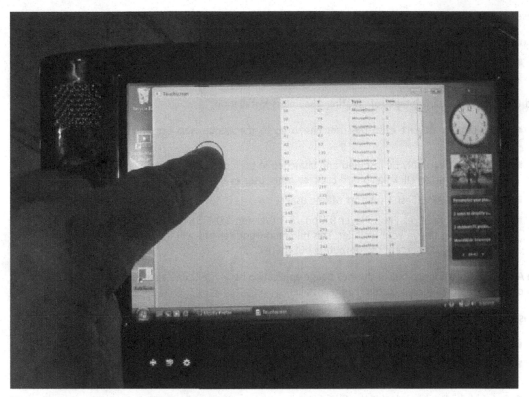

Figure 10-5. Our AIR touch application on UMPC

Creating a seamless installation experience

In Chapter 9, we showed you how to sign and package your AIR application into an .air file. You can also distribute your application via e-mail, flash card, CD/DVD, and more. Additionally, you can distribute your application through the AIR Marketplace at http://www.adobe.com/cfusion/exchange/index.cfm. Note that the AIR application gets installed automatically from the AIR Marketplace web site without the need to first download the .air file or install the AIR runtime.

You can create a web page just like the AIR Marketplace that allows the user to seamlessly detect and install the application during runtime even without the AIR runtime installed. The seamless experience involves creating a badge installer using the Browser API.

You can create a seamless installation for your users in three steps:

1. Detect whether Flash is installed.
2. Install the Adobe runtime if necessary.
3. Install your AIR application right from the page, without needing to first download it to a local drive.

These are the advantages of creating a seamless installation:

- You have better control over the installation experience of your AIR application.
- Seamless installation allows the user to download the AIR runtime installer from the Adobe web site automatically.

And these are the disadvantages of creating a seamless installation:

- If the installer doesn't exist, the user has to go to the Adobe web site and download the AIR installer.
- Applications can only be installed and launched in the context of a user event, meaning it has to follow a button click, keyboard click, or other user event.
- The Browser API doesn't support offline usage.
- The installer requires Flash Player 9 Update 3 (Version 9.0.115), so users without this version won't be able to run your installer. This minimum requirement will mean that the installer will not work on 100 percent of computers out there.

The Adobe SDK provides an out-of-the-box badge application here: Flex SDK/sample/badge/badge.swf. You can also create your own custom badge installer.

To use the badge application, you need to copy three files:

- badge.swf: A sample SWF file that includes the badge installer application
- AC_RunActiveContent.js: Used for pages with multiple SWFs and contains functions that embed your active content based on parameters it receives from the main page
- Default_badge.html: Holds the SWF files

The parameters for the Default_badge.html file are explained in Table 10-1.

Table 10-1. Flashvars parameters on default_badge.html

Parameter	Description	Example	Required
* appname	The name of your application, which will be displayed in a message under the install button if the AIR runtime is not present	myapp	Yes
* appurl	The URL of the .air file on the server	http://mysite/myapp.air	Yes
* airversion	The version of the AIR runtime required to run your application	1.5	Yes
buttoncolor	Takes a six-digit hexadecimal value for the color of the button background or the value "transparent"	0xffffff	No

Parameter	Description	Example	Required
messagecolor	A six-digit hexadecimal value for the color of the text message displayed under the install button	0x1fffff	No
imageurl	The URL of the JPG file to display in the badge interface that can either be a relative path or HTTP, HTTPS, or FTP		No
bgcolor	Sets the badge background color		No

Here's an example of the swfobject tag in Default_badge.html:

```
AC_FL_RunContent(
    'codebase','http://fpdownload.macromedia.com/pub/➥
shockwave/cabs/flash/swflash.cab',
    'width','217',
    'height','180',
    'id','badge',
    'align','middle',
    'src','badge',
    'quality','high',
    'bgcolor','#FFFFFF',
    'name','badge',
    'allowscriptaccess','all',
    'pluginspage','http://www.macromedia.com/go/getflashplayer',
    'flashvars','appname=My%20Application&➥
appurl=myapp.air&airversion=1.0&imageurl=test.jpg',
    'movie','badge' ); //end AC code
```

You can change the settings, such as the background color, in the swfobject tag and open the Default_badge.html file in a browser to see the changes. Figure 10-6 shows the application in action.

Figure 10-6.
The default badge application example

Enabling browser invocation

To allow your application to use the Browser API, you need to enable the application, so it will be able to detect and launch the Browser API. This can be done by specifying <allowsBrowserInvocation> in the application's descriptorXML file.

In src/myapp-app.xml, change the following code

```
<!-- Whether the application can be launched when the
user clicks a link in a
web browser.Optional. Default false. -->
<!-- <allowBrowserInvocation></allowBrowserInvocation> -->
```

to this

```
<allowBrowserInvocation>true</allowBrowserInvocation>
```

Creating a custom badge installer

Adobe provides a default badge.as file. By understanding that code, you can easily create your own badge installer to fit your exact business rules. Let's take a look at the code.

The package extends the MovieClip, since it's pure ActionScript 3 code:

```
package {
    import flash.display.*;
    import flash.events.*;
    import flash.geom.ColorTransform;
    import flash.net.URLRequest;
    import flash.system.*;
    import flash.text.TextField;

    // AIRBadge is our main document class
    public class AIRBadge extends MovieClip {
```

The constructor gets the flashvars parameters and sets default values if none of the optional parameters are set. It uses a loader to load the Browser API and sets an event listener to recognize it once it is loaded.

```
        public function AIRBadge() {
            // Read FlashVars
            try {
                var parameters:Object = ➥
LoaderInfo(this.root.loaderInfo).parameters;
                _messageColor = validateColor(parameters["messagecolor"]);
                _buttonColor = parameters["buttoncolor"];

                if (_buttonColor != "transparent") {
                    _buttonColor = validateColor(_buttonColor);
                }

                _imageURL = validateURL(parameters["imageurl"]);
                _airVersion = String(parameters["airversion"]);
                _appURL = validateURL(encodeURI(parameters["appurl"]));
```

```
                // Make sure the appname does not contain any tags,
                //  by checking for "less than" characters
                _appName = parameters["appname"];
                if ( _appName == null || _appName.length == 0
|| _appName.indexOf("<") >= 0) {
                    _appName = null;

                }
            } catch (error:Error) {
                _messageColor = "FF0000";
                _buttonColor = "000000";
                _appURL = "";
                _appName = null;
                _airVersion = "";
            }
            // Set-up event handler for button
            this.addEventListener(MouseEvent.MOUSE_UP, onButtonClicked);

            // Reset status message text
            root.statusMessage.text = "";

            // Load background image
            if (_imageURL && _imageURL.length > 0) {
                try {
                    var loader:Loader = new Loader();
                    loader.load(new URLRequest(_imageURL));
                    root.image_mc.addChild(loader);
                } catch (error:Error) {
                }
            }

            // Colorize button background movieclip (buttonBg_mc)
            if ( _buttonColor != "transparent" ) {
                root.buttonBg_mc._visible = true;
                var tint:uint = ➥
new Number("0x" + _buttonColor).valueOf();

                var transform:ColorTransform = ➥
new ColorTransform();
                transform.redMultiplier = ➥
((tint & 0xFF0000) >> 16) / 256.0;
                transform.greenMultiplier = ➥
((tint & 0x00FF00) >> 8) / 256.0;
                transform.blueMultiplier = ((tint & 0x0000FF)) / 256.0;

                root.buttonBg_mc.transform.colorTransform = transform;
```

```
                    } else {
                         root.buttonBg_mc._visible = false;
                    }

                    _loader = new Loader();
                    var loaderContext:LoaderContext = new LoaderContext();
                    loaderContext.applicationDomain = ➟
ApplicationDomain.currentDomain;

                    _loader.contentLoaderInfo.addEventListener(➟
Event.INIT, onInit);
                    try {
                         _loader.load(new URLRequest(➟
BROWSERAPI_URL_BASE + "/air.swf"),
 loaderContext);
                    } catch (e:Error) {
                         root.statusMessage.text = e.message;
                    }
          }
```

Installing the Browser API

The Browser API does the heavy lifting of checking if the AIR runtime is installed or not. After the http://airdownload.adobe.com/air/browserapi/air.swf gets loaded, you can check whether or not the AIR runtime was installed.

The getStatus method will return the status of AIR on the user's machine:

```
    varstatus:String = _air.getStatus();
```

There are three states:

- available: AIR can be installed, but it's not currently installed.
- unavailable: AIR cannot be installed on the device.
- installed: AIR is installed.

In our case, we have the message for the button set based on the availability, but you can create a different UI with different functionality.

```
                private function onInit(e:Event):void {
                    _air = e.target.content;
                    switch (_air.getStatus()) {
                         case "installed" :
                             root.statusMessage.text = "";
                             break;
                         case "available" :
                             if (_appName && _appName.length > 0) {
                                 root.statusMessage.htmlText = ➟
"<p align='center'>
```

```
<font color='#" + _messageColor + "'>In order to run " + _appName + ➡
 ", this installer will also set up Adobe¨ AIR.</font></p>";
                            } else {
                                root.statusMessage.htmlText = ➡
"<p align='center'>
<font color='#" + _messageColor + "'> ➡
In order to run this application, this installer
will also set up Adobe¨ AIR.
</font></p>";
                            }
                            break;
                        case "unavailable" :
                            root.statusMessage.htmlText = ➡
"<p align='center'><font color='#" + _messageColor + "'>
Adobe¨ AIR is not available for your system.</font></p>";
                            root.buttonBg_mc.enabled = false;
                            break;
                }
            }
```

Once the user clicks the INSTALL NOW button, the AIR runtime and the AIR application are both installed:

```
_air.installApplication( _appURL, _airVersion );
```

If the runtime and AIR application are not installed, we don't load the AIR file. Take a look at the code that is responsible for this functionality:

```
private function onButtonClicked(e:Event):void {
    try {
        switch (_air.getStatus()) {
            case "installed" :
                root.statusMessage.htmlText = ➡
"<p align='center'> ➡
<font color='#" + _messageColor + "'> ➡
Download and open the AIR file to begin the installation. ➡
</font></p>";
                _air.installApplication(➡
 _appURL, _airVersion );
                break;
            case "available" :
                root.statusMessage.htmlText = ➡
"<p align='center'> ➡
<font color='#" + _messageColor + "'>Starting install...</font></p>";
                _air.installApplication( _appURL, _airVersion );
                break;
            case "unavailable" :
                // do nothing
                break;
```

427

```
                    }
                } catch (e:Error) {
                    root.statusMessage.text = e.message;
                }
                /* clearInterval( _global.installIntId ); */
            }

        // Validate URL: only allow HTTP,
        // HTTPS scheme or relative path
        // Return null if not a valid URL
        private static function validateURL(url:String):String {
            if (url && url.length > 0) {
                var schemeMarker:int = url.indexOf(":");
                if (schemeMarker < 0) {
                    schemeMarker = url.indexOf("%3a");
                }
                if (schemeMarker < 0) {
                    schemeMarker = url.indexOf("%3A");
                }
                if (schemeMarker > 0) {
                    var scheme:String = ➥
url.substr(0, schemeMarker).toLowerCase();
                    if (scheme != "http" && scheme ➥
!= "https" && scheme != "ftp") {
                        url = null;
                    }
                }
            }
            return url;
        }
```

Verify that the color code is a hexadecimal code:

```
        // Validate color: only allow 6 hex digits
        // Always return a valid color, black by default
        private static function validateColor(color:String):String {
            if ( color == null || color.length != 6 ) {
                color = "000000";
            } else {
                var validHex:String = "0123456789ABCDEFabcdef";
                var numValid:int = 0;
                for (var i:int=0; i < color.length; ++i) {
                    if (validHex.indexOf(color.charAt(i)) >= 0) {
                        ++numValid;
                    }
                }
```

```
                                    if (numValid != 6) {
                                        color = "000000";
                                    }
                                }
                                return color;
                            }
```

BROWSERAPI_URL_BASE holds the Browser API URL location and other settings:

```
                    private const BROWSERAPI_URL_BASE: String = ➡
                "http://airdownload.adobe.com/air/browserapi";

                    private var _messageColor: String;
                    private var _buttonColor: String;
                    private var _imageURL: String;
                    private var _appURL: String;
                    private var _appName: String;
                    private var _airVersion: String;

                    private var _loader:Loader;
                    private var _air:Object;
                }
            }
```

For more information regarding seamless installation visit http://livedocs.adobe.com/flex/3/html/help.html?content=distributing_apps_3.html.

Summary

In this chapter, we covered platform and context awareness. We began by explaining what information is your application's responsibility and what you can detect and handle yourself. We continued by creating a manager that listens to changes in device configuration and detects system capability and AIR system support. The manager also notified our application of changes, so we started adapting to these changes in our application. After that, we applied these changes to the YouTube application we built in Chapter 9 and enabled the YouTube application to download FLV video and images files from the Web. We continued by listening to changes in the connectivity and using the SQLite database to store information, and we created a SQLite manager to handle common tasks that are repeated for every SQLite database and can be used in any AIR application.

We also covered mobile touch screen and multitouch screen applications in this chapter. We showed you how to create your own application to register user gestures to give the user a better experience using a touch screen application. We also covered how to create a seamless installation using the default badge application utilizing the Browser API.

In the next chapter, we will continue to work with AIR applications, and we'll give you best practices for building an AIR application that uses dynamic layout to adapt to different devices and cover other topics for deployment of your application across different devices.

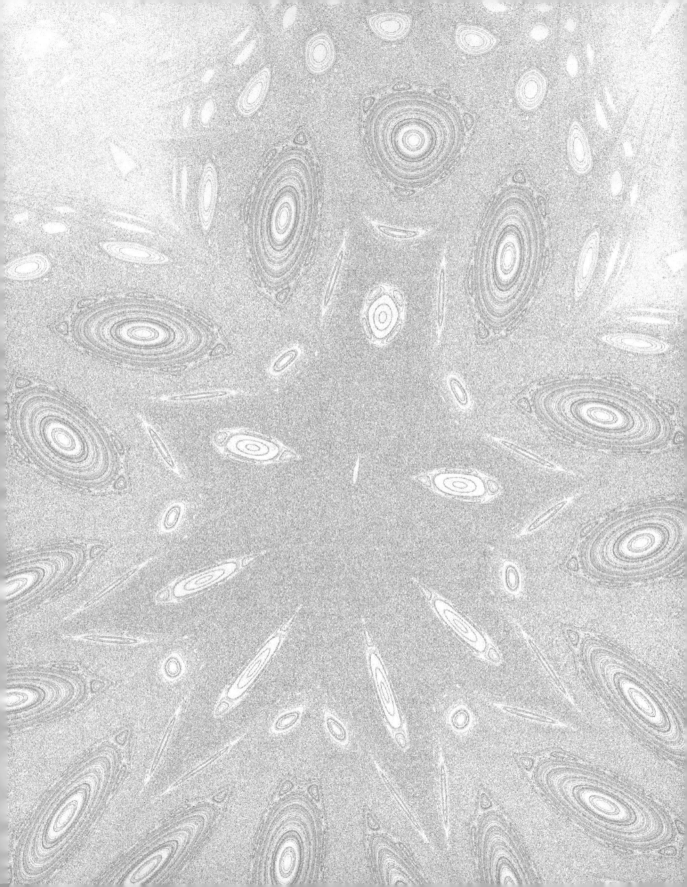

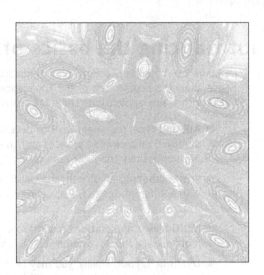

Chapter 11

DEVELOPING CROSS-PLATFORM AIR APPLICATIONS

AIR will soon be available on more types of devices than personal computers and on different operating systems, and these new devices will have various amounts of horsepower. The development architecture of an application that will be deployed on different devices has to take into account creating different views with different functionality. Think about creating a car: all cars have the same basic functionality and parts, such as a steering wheel and an engine. If we can build a car that has the same operating parts, we can potentially switch the body of the car to change its appearance without affecting the functionality.

Creating an application with Flash can be analogous to creating the car. We can split the presentation layer from the logic layer and change the view based on the device the application is deployed on.

In this chapter, we will be start building a cross-platform application. In the next chapter, we will give you an overview of Flash Catalyst, and in Chapter 13, we will continue the application we are building here utilizing Flash Catalyst and explore how to build an application that can be deployed on different devices with a different screen sizes and even different Flash Player versions. Let's get started.

Introducing the basics of dynamic GUIs

Dynamic GUI-based applications are intended to allow us to create a GUI that is easy to change, and hence allow the deployment of the application on different devices. Why would you need different GUIs for the same application? There are few reasons:

- **AIR and Flex**: You might want to develop an application that will be used as a Flex application deployed on a device's browser and an AIR application deployed on the device local drive and have both share the same core code.

- **White labeling**: A company may wish to compete with itself by creating the same application with a different design (i.e., creating a white label product) or may wish to allow others to skin its product.

- **Multidevice application**: You may need to develop an application that will be deployed on mobile, web, and desktop devices, as we will explore in this chapter and in Chapter 13.

- **Dynamic layout**: Finally, you may be creating an application that changes as the user rotates the mobile device. Ideally, we will be able to get a notification from the accelerometer once the user changes the device's position from horizontal to vertical and then we can change the layout. Additionally, we can offer the ability to rotate the application based on user gestures.

In this chapter, we will focus on creating a multidevice application with AIR. Because each mobile phone model has a different screen size, you will likely want to handle that part of the application yourself. You wouldn't want to rely solely on the device OEM to handle adapting applications to fit device screen sizes, because you can get a much better user experience by creating a unique GUI for each device. For instance, let's say you created an application in the size of 800×600 pixels, and the application is deployed on a Nokia mobile device with a device screen resolution of 128×128 pixels that includes a touch screen. Your application will be very difficult to operate using the touch screen, since your buttons are going to be too small.

There are many challenges, for creating dynamic GUI. You need to take into account sceneries such as how the component changes. Besides, you may decide to disable certain components or add different components for different devices. You may also want to build a completely different GUI for each device based on the device capabilities. Some GUIs may not have the same components, since you want the GUI to be lightweight to accommodate a less capable mobile device.

In addition, Adobe's vision is to better separate the presentation layer from the logic layer in the Flex 4 SDK, and this creates additional pressure to ensure the GUI is passive, doesn't include any code, and can be easily changed. Tools like Flash Catalyst can help achieve that goal by providing designers with a new set of tools that they can easily use and allows them to control frames, states, and the visual appearance (pixel) of the application. See Chapter 12 for more details.

The approach you can take is create an advanced custom component in Flex that recognizes the user screen size. Using Flash Catalyst, a designer can create a GUI for the developer, which can be served on one device, but what if you need to create the same application for two devices with different GUIs? For instance, what if you have two devices: one is an iPhone (Adobe already has a version of Flash for the iPhone running on emulation software), and the other is your home computer browser (which has a much larger screen). To accommodate these two devices, two completely different designs are needed, but you still want to keep the same user experience and functionality.

Similarly, each mobile device has a different screen resolution size, and it is a real challenge to create one application that can accommodate all devices. Table 11-1 lists a few examples of different mobile devices of various screen resolutions.

Table 11-1. Examples of mobile phone models for common screen resolutions

Screen Resolution	Phone Models
96×65 pixels	Motorola C350 and Nokia 8910i
128×128 pixels	Alcatel 735, LG 7020, NEC N21i, and Samsung 7250
130×130 pixels	Siemens CF110 and Motorola i670
120×160 pixels	LG SD810 and Samsung SPH-x4900
132×176pixels	Nokia 7650 and Siemens SX1
240×320 pixels	Most smart phones, such as the Nokia N95 or the Samsung SCH-i830
320×480 pixels	iPhone and iPod Touch
480 320 pixels	Blackberry 9000

The following Wikipedia page includes a more complete list of the popular mobile devices and their resolutions: http://en.wikipedia.org/wiki/Mobile_wallpaper.

Understanding the Passive Multi-view design pattern

To create a dynamic GUI, you need to be able to create different views and to create the necessary multi-view experience.

Using Adobe Catalyst, you can create a workflow that includes design responsibility and round-trips to Flash Builder. Flash Catalyst generates a declarative XML code called FXG, and the new component architecture includes the Spark library, which works with Flash Catalyst to some extent and makes building, modifying, and designing custom components easier. We will talk about Flash Catalyst in the next chapter.

The idea is that these base components will allow developers to create and extend core components and focus on their functionality with as little influence and dependency on the layout and display of the components as possible. Adobe hopes that the work of reskinning the Flex components and redesigning the layout, behavior, and new state architecture will be the responsibility of the designer. Ideally, we want to be able to make changes and round-trip with Flex without affecting the underlying code that controls the functionality of the component.

To achieve multi-view functionality, I recommend using a design pattern that is a mix of the Passive View and Factory design patterns called Passive Multi-view. Using the Passive Multi-view design pattern allows you to create different views. All views are using the same base high-level classes, and you can combine them easily with other tools, such as Degrafa, Flex Gumbo, Flex 3, or ActionScript 3.0 with CSS.

We will create an application that uses a music service called the MP3Tunes Music API to demonstrate the design pattern. Once the GUI is ready, you can use a context class to determine the GUI to be deployed based on user's screen size or other factors. For instance, you can create a GUI for touch-screen applications.

Figure 11-1 shows the application we will be building in the next few chapters to deploy the same application on different devices.

Figure 11-1. Our sample application deployed on multiple screens

To explain the Passive Multi-view design pattern, let's take a look at two design patterns from which the pattern is derived:

- Passive View design pattern
- Factory design pattern

Understanding the Passive View design pattern

The Passive View pattern is a derivative of the Model, View, Presenter (MVP) pattern, which itself is a derivative of the Model, View, Controller (MVC) pattern. The Passive View pattern has some similarities to the code-behind implementation, which was very common when Flex 1.5 first came out, and it achieves a complete separation of ActionScript logic and MXML code or MXML and ActionScript component tags.

The passive presentation model allows us to more easily unit test our application, since we can create test cases just for the logic and, if needed, test cases for the view (see Chapter 14 for more information on this).

To better understand the pattern, think of splitting your dirty laundry into two piles, view and presenter. The view characteristics are as follows:

- Application states are part of the view.
- The artwork (pixel) is part of the view.
- The view is passive and is not aware of the presenter.

These are the presenter characteristics:

- The logic is part of the presenter.
- The presenter observes the view's events.
- The presenter updates the view's data.
- The presenter knows about components in the view.
- The presenter holds the data or points to a data class.

By moving all the logic out of the view, the Passive View pattern (see Figure 11-2) can achieve the separation of designer and developer workflows and changing the view is easier. The view class contains only the components and their states—no events, logic, changes, or model.

This pattern works great with Flash Catalyst, since your responsibility as the designer is to create the view (pixel) and behavior (state), so you can copy and paste or import the FXG code into the application and just set the ID property of each component.

Take a look at a Unified Modeling Language (UML) diagram in Figure 11-2 that illustrates the Passive View pattern. The PassiveView class creates a composition based on the Presenter (which holds the logic) and the MainView (which holds the view). As you can see, you can add a SubPresenter and SubView to add components that are part of the main component.

> UML is a modeling language and the industry standard when it comes to creating object oriented programming (OOP) diagrams. Many software applications support creating UML diagrams, such as Microsoft Visio and Visual Paradigm for UML.

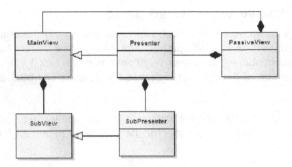

Figure 11-2. Passive View design pattern UML diagram

Understanding the Factory design pattern

Let's take a look at the Factory design pattern. The Factory pattern (see the UML diagram in Figure 11-3) is one of the most basic creational patterns that deals with the problem of creating different products without specifying the exact concrete class that will be created.

You can create different products by creating a separate method for the product abstract class, whose subclasses can override the derived type of product that will be created. The best way to describe that is through an analogy. Think of a pizza restaurant: though it sells different types of pizza—mushroom, bacon, and so on—all pizzas include the same basic ingredients, such as dough, cheese, and sauce.

Take a look at the UML diagram in Figure 11-3. The Creator uses the factory method to retrieve a product, where you can create a design that holds many different types of products that all implement the same interface. The ConcreteCreator holds a switch to select the product.

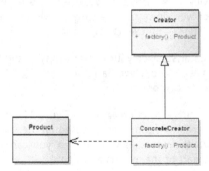

Figure 11-3. Factory design pattern
UML diagram

Putting the patterns together

Now that you have an understanding of these design patterns, we can mix them together, as shown in the UML diagram in Figure 11-4. The Creator uses the Factory pattern to find out which view (product) to use and pushes that view into the Presenter. The SubPresenter and SubView can be used by the main view.

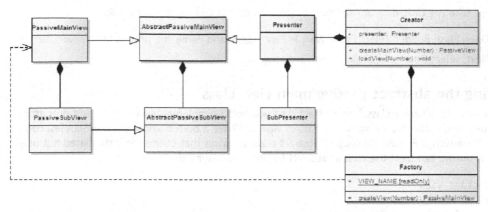

Figure 11-4. Passive Multi-view design pattern UML diagram

Implementing the Passive Multi-view design pattern

Let's create a simple implementation of the Passive Multi-view design pattern. The UML diagram for our example is shown in Figure 11-5. The Creator creates the composition, which consists of a main passive presentation view, passive presentation subview, and two presenters that include the logic.

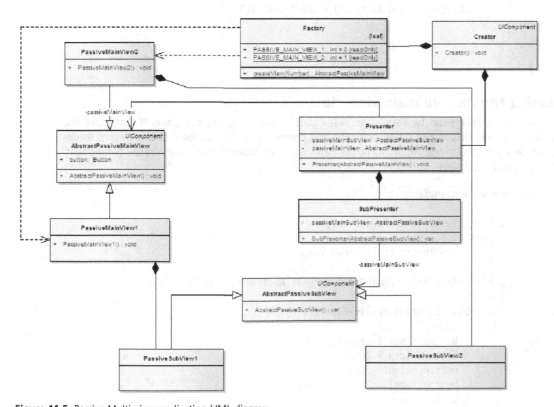

Figure 11-5. Passive Multi-view application UML diagram

437

Next, we'll take the UML diagram and turn it into a functional application using AIR:

1. Open Flash Builder, select File ➤ New ➤ Flex Project, and name the project Multi-viewPattern.

2. Next, select Desktop application (runs in Adobe AIR).

Creating the abstract passive main view class

We start with the abstract class. The abstract class will hold unimplemented methods and properties we will be using in the Passive view. The Passive view will have a button and a passiveSubView component. ActionScript 3 does not support abstract classes, classes that cannot be instantiated but only extended, but we can treat the class as abstract by not instantiating the class.

```
package view
{
    import mx.controls.Button;
    import mx.core.UIComponent;

    public class AbstractPassiveMainView extends UIComponent
    {
        public var button:Button;
        public var passiveSubView:AbstractPassiveSubView;

        public function AbstractPassiveMainView()
        {
        }
    }
}
```

Creating the passive main view class

We're now ready to create the PassiveMainView class, which holds the components that make the GUI. The view will include the states, behavior, and components but not logic, such as event listeners, handlers, or calculations. Additionally, the passive view includes the passiveSubView component, which is a passive subview.

```
package view.mainview1
{
    import flash.events.MouseEvent;
    import mx.controls.Button;
    import view.AbstractPassiveMainView;

    public class PassiveMainView1 extends AbstractPassiveMainView
    {
        public function PassiveMainView1()
        {
            button = new Button();
            button.width = 200;
            button.height = 50;
            button.label = "PassiveMainView1";
            button.x = 0;
```

```
                    button.y = 0;
                    this.addChild(button);

                    passiveSubView = new PassiveSubView1();
                    this.addChild(passiveSubView);
                }
            }
        }
```

The class creates a button and sets the properties as well as adding the passive subview as a child.

Creating the abstract passive subview

The abstract for the passive subview holds a text field, which will be implemented in the passive view class. Keep in mind that you can keep adding passive subviews as you need them.

```
        package view
        {
            import mx.controls.Text;
            import mx.core.UIComponent;

            public class AbstractPassiveSubView extends UIComponent
            {
                public var text:Text;

                public function AbstractPassiveSubView()
                {
                }
            }
        }
```

Creating the passive subview

The passive main view implementation will create a new instance of the Text class and set the properties.

```
        package view.mainview1
        {
            import mx.controls.Text;
            import view.AbstractPassiveSubView;

            public class PassiveSubView1 extends AbstractPassiveSubView
            {
                public function PassiveSubView1()
                {
                    text = new Text();
                    text.y = 60;
                    text.x = 0;
                    text.width = 250;
                    text.height = 20;
                    text.setStyle("color", "0xfa0303");
```

```
            text.text = "ButtonClicked";
            text.visible = false;

            this.addChild(text);
        }
    }
}
```

Next, you'll need to create another view and subview and call them PassiveSubView2 and PassiveMainView2. Change the button text in PassiveMainView2:

```
button.label = "PassiveMainView1";
```

Also change the color of the text field in PassiveSubView2 to 0x032cfa:

```
text.setStyle("color", "0x032cfa");
```

After making these small changes to the properties, we will be able to differentiate between the different views.

Creating the factory class

The factory class will hold a switch and enumeration constants, so we can select one of the two classes that will be used. If you need to add more views, you just create them and add them to the factory class.

```
package
{
    import flash.errors.IllegalOperationError;

    import view.mainview1.PassiveMainView1;
    import view.mainview2.PassiveMainView2;

    public final class Factory
    {

        /**
         * Types enums
         */
        public static const PASSIVE_MAIN_VIEW_1:int = 0;
        public static const PASSIVE_MAIN_VIEW_2:int = 1;

        public static function createView(type:Number): ➡
AbstractPassiveMainView
        {
            var retVal:AbstractPassiveMainView;

            switch (type)
            {
                case PASSIVE_MAIN_VIEW_1:
                    retVal = new PassiveMainView1();
                break;
```

```
            case PASSIVE_MAIN_VIEW_2:
                retVal = new PassiveMainView2();
            break;

            throw new IllegalOperationError ➥
            ("The view type " + type + " is not recognized.");
        }

        return retVal;

    }
  }
}
```

Creating the presenter class

The presenter class will hold the logic for the view. Let's take a look at the logic for the main view class. Create a class, call it Presenter.as, and place it in the view.presenter package.

```
package view.presenter
{
    import flash.events.MouseEvent;
    import view.AbstractPassiveMainView;

    public class Presenter
    {
```

The corresponding view will be attached as the abstract class since we don't want to attach an exact implementation.

```
        private var passiveMainView:AbstractPassiveMainView;
```

The main view holds a subview, so we will attach the logic of the subview in this class.

```
        private var subPresenter:SubPresenter;

        public function Presenter(passiveMainView:AbstractPassiveMainView)
        {
                this.passiveMainView = passiveMainView;
```

Here, we attach the logic of the subview by passing an instance of the subview class to the presenter.

```
                subPresenter = new SubPresenter( ➥
        passiveMainView.passiveSubView);
```

The logic we need is to be able to recognize an event click.

```
                passiveMainView.button.addEventListener(MouseEvent.CLICK, ➥
        onButtonClick);
        }
```

```
                    private function onButtonClick(event:MouseEvent):void
                    {
                        subPresenter.setTextLabelVisible(true);
                    }
                }
            }
```

The subclass of the presenter holds the logic for the subview class and has a method to allow making the text visible.

```
        package view.presenter
        {
            import view.AbstractPassiveSubView;

            public class SubPresenter
            {
                private var passiveMainSubView:AbstractPassiveSubView;

                public function SubPresenter➡
        (passiveMainSubView:AbstractPassiveSubView)
                {
                        this.passiveMainSubView = passiveMainSubView;
                }

                public function setTextLabelVisible(isVisible:Boolean):void
                {
                    passiveMainSubView.text.visible = isVisible;
                }
            }
        }
```

Creating the creator class

The creator class creates the entire composition. It first selects one of the products (view).

```
        mainView:AbstractPassiveMainView = ➡
        Factory.createView(Factory.PASSIVE_MAIN_VIEW_2);
```

Then, the selected product is added to the stage and the logic is applied on the main view.

```
        var presenter:Presenter = new Presenter(mainView);
```

Here's the complete creator class code:

```
        package
        {
            import mx.core.UIComponent;
```

```
import view.AbstractPassiveMainView;
import view.Factory;
import view.presenter.Presenter;

public class Creator extends UIComponent
{
    public function Creator()
    {
        var mainView:AbstractPassiveMainView = ➡
        Factory.createView(Factory.PASSIVE_MAIN_VIEW_2);
        this.addChild(mainView);

        var presenter:Presenter = new Presenter(mainView);
    }
}
}
```

The last step is to attach the creator to the stage.

```
<?xml version="1.0" encoding="utf-8"?>
<s:WindowedApplication xmlns:fx="http://ns.adobe.com/mxml/2009"
    xmlns:s="library://ns.adobe.com/flex/spark"
    xmlns:mx="library://ns.adobe.com/flex/halo"
    creationComplete="creationCompleteHandler(event)">

    <fx:Script>
        <![CDATA[
            import view.Factory;
            import view.AbstractPassiveMainView;
            import mx.events.FlexEvent;

            protected function ➡
creationCompleteHandler(event:FlexEvent):void
            {
                var creator:Creator = new Creator();
                this.addChild(creator);
            }
        ]]>
    </fx:Script>

</s:WindowedApplication>
```

The final view looks like the screenshot in Figure 11-6.

Figure 11-6. Our example Passive Multi-view pattern application

Developing the music player application

Equipped with the knowledge of the Passive Multi-view design pattern, which allows you to create different views, you're ready to create your next sample application. This application will demonstrate to you how to create a cross-platform application that will be deployed on different devices with different screen sizes. The application will be using a music service site called MP3Tunes (http://www. mp3tunes.com). The service allows you to load music files and play them by progressive download from the HTTPS service.

Building the music player API

The first step in building a music player application is to get started with the actual player. The approach will be to create a music player API that is generic enough for use on any application and then use that API to play music files.

The complete code for the music player API can be downloaded from http://code.google.com/p/ eladlib/, which includes the code and an example of a working music player. The API is located under the following folder: com/elad/framework/musicplayer. Let's study the code to understand how it works.

Creating the IPlayer interface

A good place to start is the API's interface. The music player interface, IPlayer, is the contract that our music player will obey. The interface includes methods that the music player needs for pausing the music or playing a track.

```
package com.elad.framework.musicplayer
{
    public interface IPlayer
    {
        function playTrack(songUrl:String, songLenght:Number=0):void
        function pauseTrack():void
        function stopTrack():void
```

```
        function fastforward(timeInSeconds:Number=2):void
        function rewind(timeInSeconds:Number=2):void
        function setVolume(vol:Number):void
    }
}
```

Creating the AbstractPlayer class

The music player's abstract class AbstractPlayer, just like any other abstract class, shouldn't be instantiated. The abstract class will be the parent class (superclass) from which the music player is derived. The class will include methods that any subclass will need, as well as incomplete methods, which will be left purposely unimplemented so each view can implement it differently.

Take a look at the AbstractPlayer code:

```
package com.elad.framework.musicplayer
{
        import flash.events.EventDispatcher;
        import flash.media.Sound;
        import flash.media.SoundChannel;
        import flash.media.SoundTransform;
        import flash.utils.Timer;

    public class AbstractPlayer extends EventDispatcher
    {
```

The Sound class is part of the AbstractPlayer class and lets you load and play an external file. The SoundChannel allows us to assign a song to a sound channel.

```
        protected var sound:Sound;
        protected var channel:SoundChannel;
```

We will use a timer to keep track of the sound position and fileBytesTotal to keep track of the byte loaded.

```
        protected var soundPosition:Timer = null;
        protected var fileBytesTotal:Number;
```

isDownloadCompleted is a flag that indicates whether the download of the file is completed or not.

```
        protected var isDownloadCompleted:Boolean = false;
```

Once the file is downloaded, the pausePosition variable will hold the pause position.

```
        protected var pausePosition:Number;
```

The isPause flag indicates whether the track is paused or not.

```
        protected var isPause:Boolean = false;
```

And the isPlaying flag is used to indicate whether the track is currently playing or not.

```
protected var isPlaying:Boolean = false;
```

Play position, in seconds, will be held by _songPosition. We will be using the underscore to indicate that the variable is private and has a setter and getter.

```
private var _songPosition:Number;
```

The variable _songLength will hold the total song length in seconds.

```
private var _songLength:Number;
```

And the variable _songURL will hold the song we will be streaming.

```
private var _songURL:String;
```

All of the setters and getters are defined in the following code snippet:

```
public function get songPosition():Number
{
    return _songPosition;
}

public function set songPosition(val:Number):void
{
    _songPosition = val;
}

public function get songLength():Number
{
    return _songLength;
}

public function set songLength(val:Number):void
{
    _songLength = val;
}

public function get songURL():String
{
    return _songURL;
}

public function set songURL(val:String):void
{
    _songURL = val;
}

    public function AbstractPlayer()
    {
    }
```

The playTrack method will be used to play a track, based on a given URL. The method handles cases where the user clicks the play button after the song is already playing and where the song was paused. Note that the music file doesn't provide the length of the song right away. The information regarding the length is changing during the progress of the music file, so you can pass the information regarding the length of the song, if you know it. Otherwise, you can retrieve the length information from the PlayProgressEvent. Two parameters are provided: the songUrl, which is the location of the music file, and the songLength downloading music file, which provides the length of the song but after a portion has downloaded rather than right away.

```
public function playTrack(songUrl:String, songLength:Number=0):void
{
    // needs to implement
}
```

Next, we need to be able to pause a playing song; this is achieved by stopping the soundPosition timer and the channel. We also need to set the isPause flag and keep track of our position, so we can resume playing from the same position we stopped.

```
public function pauseTrack():void
{
    soundPosition.stop();
    channel.stop();

    isPause = true;
    pausePosition = channel.position;
}
```

The stopTrack method will be used to completely stop a playing song. We first verify that the song that is really playing by checking soundPosition since the timer get implemented only after the song is playing via

```
soundPosition = new Timer(50);
```

Once the song information is verified, the stopTrack method lets us stop the timer and the channel as well as call resetPlayer, which will handle the logic to reset the player.

```
public function stopTrack():void
{
        if (soundPosition != null)
        {
            soundPosition.stop();
            channel.stop();
            resetPlayer();
        }
}
```

The setTrackPosition method will be used to change the position of the track and will generate the seek capability. When the user seeks to a new position in the song, that newPosition is provided in milliseconds. We then verify that we are not trying to seek to an unavailable position within the song.

```
public function setTrackPosition(newPosition:Number):void
```

```
            {
                    soundPosition.stop();
                    channel.stop();

                    var currentPosition:Number = channel.position/1000;
                    var position:Number

                    if (newPosition<currentPosition)
                    {
                            position = newPosition*1000;
                    }
                    else
                    {
                            position = ➥
        Math.min(sound.length, newPosition*1000);
                    }

                    channel = sound.play(position);
                    soundPosition.start();
            }
```

resetPlayer is used to remove all listener and empty objects once the track has stopped. This method will be implemented in the Player class.

```
        protected function resetPlayer():void
        {
                // needs to implement
        }
```

The fastforward method is used to fast-forward a track. The parameter timeInSeconds represent the fast-forward time we want to seek; the default value is 2 seconds.

```
        public function fastforward(timeInSeconds:Number=2):void
        {
                var currentPosition:Number = channel.position/1000;
                setTrackPosition(timeInSeconds+currentPosition);
        }
```

In addition to fast forward, users may want to rewind a track to a certain position; for that, we'll implement the rewind method. timeInSeconds is the time we want to rewind, and its default value is 2 seconds.

```
        public function rewind(timeInSeconds:Number=2):void
        {
                var currentPosition:Number = channel.position/1000;
                setTrackPosition(currentPosition-timeInSeconds);
        }
```

Finally, the setVolume method adds the capability to adjust the sound volume. The vol parameter is the volume in percentage, and expected values are 0 and 1.

```
    public function setVolume(vol:Number):void
    {
        var transform:SoundTransform = new SoundTransform(vol);
        channel.soundTransform = transform;
    }
  }
}
```

Creating the Player subclass

Now that we've completed the abstract class, we can create the Player subclass; this implementation of the abstract class will complete the unimplemented methods and add capabilities such as the ability to retain event metadata information. The Player class will extend AbstractPlayer and implement IPlayer.

```
package com.elad.framework.musicplayer
{

    Dispatched while downloading a music file in progress
    [Event(name="downloadProgress", ➡
type="com.elad.framework.musicplayer.events.DownloadEvent")]
    Dispatched when music file was downloaded successfully
    [Event(name="downloadCompleted", ➡
type="com.elad.framework.musicplayer.events.DownloadEvent")]
    Dispatched when there is an error playing a track
    [Event(name="playerError", ➡
type="com.elad.framework.musicplayer.events.PlayerEvent")]
    Dispatched when track playing is completed
    [Event(name="trackCompleted", ➡
type="com.elad.framework.musicplayer.events.PlayerEvent")]
    Dispatched while track progress playing
    [Event(name="playerProgress", ➡
type="com.elad.framework.musicplayer.events.PlayProgressEvent")]
    Dispatched when data information is available regarding a track
    [Event(name="id3", type= ➡
"com.elad.framework.musicplayer.events.Id3Event")]

        public class Player extends AbstractPlayer implements IPlayer
        {
Default constructor
public function Player()
{
}
```

playTrack is a method used to play a track based on a given URL. The method handles cases where the user clicks a play button after a song is already playing and where the track is paused.

```
override public function playTrack( ➡
songUrl:String, songLenght:Number=0):void
{
```

In case the song is already paused or already playing, the playTrack method will be ignored.

```
if (isPause)
{
        replay();
        return;
}

if (isPlaying)
{
        return;
}
```

Once the song is playing, the song URL is set and the song length is converted to seconds, in a two-decimal format, using the toFixed method.

```
songURL = songUrl;
songLength = Number((songLenght/1000).toFixed(2));
```

Once we have the URL, we can progressively download the song. The song will start playing as soon as enough data has been loaded. The first step in setting up the progressive download is to create the URLRequest.

```
var request:URLRequest = new URLRequest(songUrl);
```

Next, we create a reference to the Sound class set events, so we can be aware of the following: when the download is completed, any errors that may have gotten dispatched, and of the progress of the download.

```
sound = new Sound();
sound.addEventListener(Event.COMPLETE, ➡
downloadCompleteHandler);
sound.addEventListener(IOErrorEvent.IO_ERROR, ➡
ioErrorHandler);
sound.addEventListener(ProgressEvent.PROGRESS, ➡
downloadProgressHandler);
sound.load(request);
```

Once a sound is created, we create a channel to which we attach the sound, and we track a complete event.

```
channel = sound.play();
channel.addEventListener(Event.SOUND_COMPLETE, ➡
trackCompleteHandler);
```

To make note of the position of the song, we need to set a timer that we will keep aligned with the track—once we pause the track, we should also pause the timer.

```
soundPosition = new Timer(50);
soundPosition.addEventListener(TimerEvent.TIMER, ➡
positionTimerHandler);
```

```
        soundPosition.start();
        isPlaying = true;
    }
```

Next, we should create the resetPlayer method to remove all listeners and empty objects once the track has stopped. It implements the resetPlayer class from the AbstractPlayer abstract class.

```
override protected function resetPlayer():void
{
        this.isPause = false;
        this.isPlaying = false;

        sound.removeEventListener(Event.COMPLETE, ➥
downloadCompleteHandler);
        sound.removeEventListener(IOErrorEvent.IO_ERROR, ➥
ioErrorHandler);
        sound.removeEventListener(ProgressEvent.PROGRESS, ➥
downloadProgressHandler);
        channel.removeEventListener(Event.SOUND_COMPLETE, ➥
trackCompleteHandler);
        soundPosition.removeEventListener(TimerEvent.TIMER, ➥
positionTimerHandler);

        sound = null;
        channel = null;
        soundPosition = null;
}
```

Having stopped the song, users will likely want to resume play at some point. The replay method used internally to resume playing after the pause method was used. We use the pause position, which was captured when the user paused a song, and we start the timer and set the pause flag to off.

```
private function replay():void
{
    channel = sound.play(pausePosition);
    soundPosition.start();

    isPause = false;
}
```

formatTimeInSecondsToString is a static method used to convert a time in seconds to the format 0:00. We are using a static method, since we may need to use this method for other reasons outside the scope of this class, so we'd like the method to belong to the class and not to an instance of the class.

```
public static function formatTimeInSecondsToString( ➥
time:Number):String
    {
        var retVal:String = "";
```

```
                    var timeString:String = (time/60).toFixed(2);
                    var timeArray:Array = timeString.split(".");

                    if (timeArray[1] == 60)
                    {
                            timeArray[0] += 1;
                            timeArray[1] -= 60;
                    }

                    var minutes:String = ➥
(timeArray[0].toString().length < 2) ? "0"+timeArray[0].toString() : ➥
timeArray[0].toString();
                    var seconds:String = ➥
(timeArray[1].toString().length < 2) ? "0"+timeArray[1].toString() : ➥
timeArray[1].toString();

                    retVal = minutes+":"+seconds;

                    return retVal;
        }
```

Next, we'll implement the positionTimerHandler event handler, which is used once the track position has changed. It updates the song length, since the song length information changes as the song is being downloaded, and it sends the PlayProgressEvent event once the track position changes. PlayProgressEvent is a custom event we created.

```
        private function positionTimerHandler(event:TimerEvent):void
        {
        songPosition = Number((channel.position/1000).toFixed(2));
            var totalPosition:Number = ➥
Number((this.sound.length/1000).toFixed(2));

            if (songLength < totalPosition && ➥
isDownloadCompleted == false)
            {
                    songLength = totalPosition;
            }

            if (songLength > 0 && songPosition > 0)
            {
                    // end of song
                    if (Math.round(songLength) == ➥
Math.round(songPosition))
                    {
                            soundPosition.removeEventListener( ➥
TimerEvent.TIMER, positionTimerHandler);
                            trackCompleteHandler(null);
                    }
```

```
                        else
                        {
                             this.dispatchEvent( ➥
new PlayProgressEvent(songPosition, songLength) );
                        }
                    }
                }
```

The download complete handler gets called once the song finishes downloading. With it, we clear our listeners so we will not have memory leaks, update the song total length, and dispatch the DownloadEvent custom event to notify us that the song download is completed.

```
            private function downloadCompleteHandler(event:Event):void
            {
                    sound.removeEventListener(Event.COMPLETE, ➥
downloadCompleteHandler);
                    sound.removeEventListener(ProgressEvent.PROGRESS, ➥
downloadProgressHandler);

                    // set the lenght of the track to the total ➥
position to ensure that the length was entered correctly.
                    isDownloadCompleted = true;
                    var totalPosition:Number = ➥
Number((event.currentTarget.length/1000).toFixed(2));
                    songLength = totalPosition;

                    this.dispatchEvent(new ➥
DownloadEvent(DownloadEvent.DOWNLOAD_COMPLETED, fileBytesTotal, ➥
fileBytesTotal));
            }
```

The ID3 object provides metadata information about the MP3 sound file. ID3 information gets redispatched, so any class that implements our class can retrieve the metadata information.

```
        private function id3Handler(event:Id3Event):void
        {
            this.dispatchEvent(event);
        }
```

Next, we need a method to handle I/O network errors; we will dispatch the PlayerEvent custom event to notify us of these errors.

```
            private function ioErrorHandler(event:Event):void
            {
                    sound.removeEventListener(IOErrorEvent.IO_ERROR, ➥
ioErrorHandler);
                    this.dispatchEvent(new PlayerEvent( ➥
PlayerEvent.PLAYER_ERROR, "Error loading music file, ➥
```

```
        please check cross domain policy and that file exists."+ ➥
event.toString()));
                resetPlayer();
        }
```

If no errors are detected, our progress handler will capture the ID3 information if it's available and dispatch the DownloadEvent custom event.

```
        private function downloadProgressHandler(event:ProgressEvent):void
        {
                this.dispatchEvent(new DownloadEvent(DownloadEvent.DOWNLOAD_PROGRESS, ➥
event.bytesLoaded, event.bytesTotal));
                fileBytesTotal = event.bytesTotal;

                // check if ID3 information is avaliable, needed since id3
                // event doesn't always work correctly.
                if (this.sound.id3.album != null || ➥
this.sound.id3.artist != null || this.sound.id3.songName != null || ➥
this.sound.id3.genere != null)
                {
                        var evt:Id3Event = new Id3Event(this.sound.id3);
                        id3Handler(evt);
                }
        }
```

The track complete handler, which is called once the song is completed, calls the resetPlayer method to clean up the event listeners and timer and to dispatch the custom complete event.

```
        private function trackCompleteHandler(event:Event):void
        {
                channel.removeEventListener(Event.SOUND_COMPLETE, ➥
trackCompleteHandler);
                resetPlayer();
                this.dispatchEvent(new PlayerEvent( ➥
PlayerEvent.TRACK_COMPLETED));
        }

        }
    }
```

The Player class uses four custom events, which hold the constants of the event types and variables we need to pass. For example, PLAYER_PROGRESS stands for the event type:

```
        public static const PLAYER_PROGRESS:String = "playerProgress";
```

Next, we want to store the playPosition and total variables in a custom event, so we will be able to pass the information when we dispatch the event.

```
        public var playPosition:Number;
        public var total:Number;
```

Here's the complete custom PlayProgressEvent event code:

```
package com.elad.framework.musicplayer.events
{
    import flash.events.Event;

    public class PlayProgressEvent extends Event
    {
        public static const PLAYER_PROGRESS:String = ➥
"playerProgress";

        public var playPosition:Number;
        public var total:Number;

        public function ➥
PlayProgressEvent(playPosition:Number, total:Number)
        {
            this.playPosition = playPosition;
            this.total = total;
            super(PLAYER_PROGRESS);
        }
    }
}
```

Creating the music player GUI

Now that we have the API ready, we can create a simple GUI to implement the API and play music to test our API.

First, you'll need to create a new project:

1. Select File ➤ New ➤ Flex Project.
2. For the project name, type MP3TunesAIR.
3. Then, select Desktop application (runs in Adobe AIR) in the New Flex Project window.
4. To create a new MXML application, type GenericMusicPlayer.mxml.

Creating GenericMusicPlayer.mxml

Now that we have the project and the MXML component, our next step is to insert the following code:

```
<?xml version="1.0" encoding="utf-8"?>
<mx:WindowedApplicationxmlns:mx="http://www.adobe.com/2006/mxml">
    <mx:Script>
        <![CDATA[
```

Inside the script tag, set an instance of the Player class, and keep the song URL variables.

```
private var player:Player = new Player();
private var songUrl:String;
```

The playSong method should be called when we want to play a song. To make that happen, we set all the custom events we defined in the Player class and call the playTrack method on the Player class:

```
private function playSong():void
{
      player.addEventListener(PlayProgressEvent.PLAYER_PROGRESS, ➡
onPlayerProgress);
      player.addEventListener(DownloadEvent.DOWNLOAD_PROGRESS, ➡
onDownloadProgress);
      player.addEventListener(PlayerEvent.PLAYER_ERROR, onPlayerError);
      player.addEventListener(Id3Event.ID3, onTrackDataInformation);
      player.playTrack(songUrl);  // songLenght
}
```

The onTrackDataInformation method will display the ID3 object information once the event gets redispatched in the Player class.

```
private function onTrackDataInformation(event:Id3Event):void
{
      songInfoText.text = event.id3.artist+" - "+event.id3.album;
}
```

The onPlayerProgress method will show the progress of the download as the song is loaded and set a slider to move as the progress continues.

```
private function onPlayerProgress(event:PlayProgressEvent):void
{
      songSlider.value = event.playPosition;
      currentTimeText.text = ➡
Player.formatTimeInSecondsToString(event.playPosition);
      totalTimeText.text = Player.formatTimeInSecondsToString(event.total);
      songSlider.maximum = event.total;
}
```

If we happen to get an error due to network or other player errors, the onPlayerError event handler will be called:

```
private function onPlayerError(event:PlayerEvent):void
{
    throw new Error(event.message);
}
```

Next, to handle changes in the slider, we'll implement the dragStartHandler method. It will stop tracking the progress of the song, so we can move the slider thumb without the event changing the position of the track. Otherwise, it will return to the same location when we start to drag the slider.

```
protected function dragStartHandler(event:SliderEvent):void
{
      player.removeEventListener(PlayProgressEvent.➡
PLAYER_PROGRESS, onPlayerProgress);
}
```

The dragDropHandler handler will be called once the user drops the slider. The method will change the song position to the position the user selected and adds the progress event, so the thumb will move as the song plays.

```
protected function dragDropHandler(event:SliderEvent):void
{
      player.setTrackPosition(songSlider.value);
      player.addEventListener(PlayProgressEvent.PLAYER_PROGRESS, ➡
onPlayerProgress);
}
```

Next, the onDownloadProgress method will handle the progress of the song downloaded and display the results on a progress bar.

```
private function onDownloadProgress(event:DownloadEvent):void
{
      progressBar.setProgress(event.bytesLoaded, event.bytesTotal);
}
```

Finally, the dragVolumeHandler method handles the slider for the volume and calls setVolume to change the volume to the new value:

```
                protected function dragVolumeHandler( ➡
event:SliderEvent):void
                {
                        player.setVolume(volumeSlider.value);
                }
        ]]>
</mx:Script>
```

Now that we are done creating the logic, we can create the presentation. Song information, such as the artist name and song name, will be displayed.

```
<mx:Text id="songInfoText" x="10" y="5" text="Artist - song name" />
```

The slider will allow us to use seek functionality with the song. We will be able to see the progress of the download in the progress bar, but keep in mind that we can only seek to a part that was downloaded already.

```
<mx:HSlider id="songSlider"
            y="25" x="10"
            width="400" minimum="0"
            showTrackHighlight="true"
            liveDragging="true"
            thumbDrag="dragStartHandler(event)"
            thumbRelease="dragDropHandler(event)"/>
```

The progress bar will display the progress of the downloaded file.

```
<mx:ProgressBar id="progressBar"
            y="45" x="15"
```

```
                        width="390" height="1"
                        minimum="0" maximum="100"
                         labelWidth="0"
                        direction="right" mode="manual"  />
            <mx:Text y="45" x="420" text="Track Loader"/>
```

We'll also need a couple of text fields to display the elapsed time of the song that is playing and the total length of the song.

```
        <mx:HBox y="30" x="420" horizontalGap="0">
            <mx:Text id="currentTimeText" text="00:00"/>
            <mx:Text text="/"/>
            <mx:Text id="totalTimeText" text="00:00"/>
        </mx:HBox>
```

And of course, we need to add buttons to play, stop, pause, fast-forward, and rewind a song:

```
        <mx:HBox y="60" x="10" horizontalGap="12">
            <mx:Button id="playButton"
                    label="play"
                    click="playSong();"
                    enabled="false" />
            <mx:Button label="pause" click="player.pauseTrack()" />
            <mx:Button label="stop" click="songSlider.value=0; ➥
currentTimeText.text = '00:00'; player.stopTrack()" />
            <mx:Button label="fastforward" click="player.fastforward();" />
            <mx:Button label="rewind" click="player.rewind();" />
        </mx:HBox>
```

Next, we will create a form that will allow us to paste the URL of a song to be consumed by the progressive download. We can provide a URL from either the Internet or from our local network.

```
        <mx:FormItem y="90">
        <mx:FormItem label="Music Url:" />
        <mx:HBox>
            <mx:TextInput id="textInput"
                    width="200" height="20" />
            <mx:Button label="Submit"
                click="this.songUrl=textInput.text; playSong(); ➥
                playButton.enabled=true" />
        </mx:HBox>
        </mx:FormItem>
```

Finally, the volume slider will allow us to change the volume value:

```
        <mx:HSlider id="volumeSlider"
            x="120" y="90"
            width="100" value="1"
            minimum="0" maximum="1"
            liveDragging="true"
            thumbDrag="dragVolumeHandler(event)" />
    </mx:WindowedApplication>
```

Compile and run the application, and you can test the functionality. The application should look like the one shown in Figure 11-7.

Figure 11-7. Generic music player application screenshot

Creating a GUI for a music player application

MP3Tunes is a music service provider (MSP) offering a secure, online music space, so users can access and listen to their song libraries anywhere. The service provides the ability to access song library data, and we will be using an API that connects to the MP3Tunes service and integrates the service with the music player we built. We then can create a skin for the music player to improve the user experience.

Download the MP3Tunes API for ActionScript SWC from here:

    http://code.google.com/p/mp3tunes-as3-api/

Creating the login form

The first step will be to create a login form, so we will be able to log into an account with MP3Tunes. You should create an account with MP3Tunes and upload a few songs so you can test the login form we are creating. For the login form, we will use a TitleWindow component, which allows us to open a pop-up window and close it once we successfully logged into the account.

Create a new component by selecting File ➤ New ➤ MXML Component. Name the class LoginForm. mxml, and add the following code to it:

```
<?xml version="1.0"?>
<mx:TitleWindow xmlns:mx="http://www.adobe.com/2006/mxml"
    close="PopUpManager.removePopUp(this)"
    title="MP3Tunes Login form"
    showCloseButton="true"
    creationComplete="creationCompleteHandler(event)">
```

The title list has a property that we can enable when we want to show the close button, showCloseButton:

```
<mx:Script>
<![CDATA[

        import mx.events.FlexEvent;
        import mx.events.CloseEvent;
```

459

```
import mx.binding.utils.BindingUtils;
import com.elad.mp3tunes.events.MusicEvent;
import com.elad.mp3tunes.Music;
import mx.utils.StringUtil;
import mx.controls.Alert;
import mx.rpc.events.FaultEvent;
import mx.rpc.events.ResultEvent;
import mx.managers.PopUpManager;
```

We create an instance of the music API singleton. The music API class allows exposure to all the methods we need in order to connect to and retrieve information from our library. This singleton class allows us to access other methods after we are connected to the service and even after we close the pop-up window.

```
private var music:Music = Music.getInstance();
```

We will hold an event constant, and once the login is successful, we will dispatch an event to indicate that the user is logged in.

```
// Event const
public static const LOGIN_SUCCESSFULL:String = ➥
"loginSuccessfull";
```

The processLogin method will add the event listeners to the music class to track errors and call the onLogin method on success.

```
private function processLogin():void
{
    music.addEventListener(MusicEvent.LOGIN_SUCCESSFULL, ➥
onLogin);
    music.addEventListener(MusicEvent.LOGIN_ERROR, ➥
function(event:MusicEvent):void {
        Alert.show(String(event.message));
    });

    var user:String = StringUtil.trim(username.text);
    var password:String = StringUtil.trim(password.text);

    music.login(user, password, "3480317529");
}
```

Once a successful login is captured, we will dispatch the custom event, so we can notify the superclass that created the pop-up window that we are logged in and remove this window.

```
private function onLogin(event:MusicEvent):void
{
    music.removeEventListener(MusicEvent.LOGIN_SUCCESSFULL, ➥
onLogin);

    this.dispatchEvent(new Event(LOGIN_SUCCESSFULL));
    PopUpManager.removePopUp(this);
}
```

Once the pop-up window is created, we center the window and add an event listener for the keyboard, so we will be able to track keyboard events—once the user presses Enter on the keyboard, we can open the pop-up.

```
        protected function creationCompleteHandler( ➡
event:FlexEvent):void
    {
        this.addEventListener(KeyboardEvent.KEY_UP, ➡
onKeyboardUpHandler);
        PopUpManager.centerPopUp(this);
    }
```

The onKeyboardUpHandler method is a keyboard handler that will look for an Enter keypress and call the processLogin method to try to log in the user. Using the keyboard handler provides a better user experience, and the user can type the login information and press Enter.

```
        private function onKeyboardUpHandler( ➡
event:KeyboardEvent):void
    {
        if (event.keyCode == Keyboard.ENTER)
        {
            processLogin();
        }
    }

    ]]>
</mx:Script>
```

The presentation component contains a form that includes input boxes for the username and password and a Login button. Once the Login button is clicked, the processLogin method is called. There is also a Cancel button that closes the window, PopUpManager.removePopUp(this). See Figure 11-8.

```
<mx:Form>
    <mx:FormItem label="Email Address">
    <mx:TextInput id="username" width="100%" text=""/>
</mx:FormItem>

<mx:FormItem label="Password">
    <mx:TextInput id="password"
            displayAsPassword="true"
            width="100%" text="" />
</mx:FormItem>
</mx:Form>

<mx:HBox>
    <mx:Button label="Login" click="processLogin();" />
    <mx:Button label="Cancel" click="PopUpManager.removePopUp(this);"/>
</mx:HBox>

</mx:TitleWindow>
```

Figure 11-8. Login
form screenshot

Creating the GUI

We will be creating our GUI using the same architecture we used in the simple Passive Multi-view pattern example. The first step is to define the abstract class, which will consist of all the components we will be using in our GUI.

We will split the GUI into a passive main view and a subview. The main view will hold lists to navigate and select.

The components will be a TileList and an AdvancedDataGrid as well as the AbstractMusicPlayer class, which will be the abstract class for the subview. Notice that, although we are using a TileList, we defined the component as ListBase, which is the base class for the TileList. It's a common practice to use a base class.

The content of AbstractMusicPlayer.as follows:

```
package com.elad.mp3tunes.view
{

    import mx.containers.Canvas;
    import mx.controls.AdvancedDataGrid;
    import mx.controls.listClasses.ListBase;

    public class AbstractMusicPlayerMain extends Canvas
    {
        public var musicPlayer:AbstractMusicPlayer;
        public var tileList:ListBase;
        public var dg:AdvancedDataGrid;

        public function AbstractMusicPlayerMain()
        {
            super();
        }
    }
}
```

The next class to define is `AbstractMusicPlayerMain.as`, which is the subview abstract class. It includes components for the music player such as the buttons, sliders for the volume and song progress, and text fields.

```
package com.elad.mp3tunes.view
{
    import com.elad.framework.musicplayer.Player;

    import mx.containers.Canvas;
    import mx.controls.HScrollBar;
    import mx.controls.ProgressBar;
    import mx.core.UIComponent;

    public class AbstractMusicPlayer extends Canvas
    {
        private var player:Player = new Player();

        // text
        public var songInfoText:Object;
        public var currentTimeText:Object;
        public var totalTimeText:Object;

        // Buttons
        public var playButton:UIComponent;
        public var pauseButton:UIComponent;
        public var forwardButton:UIComponent;
        public var rewindButton:UIComponent;
        public var randomButton:UIComponent;
        public var replyButton:UIComponent;
        public var artistsButton:UIComponent;
        public var albumsButton:UIComponent;

        // sliders
        public var songSlider:Object;
        public var volumeSlider:Object;
        public var trackProgressBar:ProgressBar;
        public var downloadProgressBar:ProgressBar;
        public var volumeProgressBar:ProgressBar;

        public function AbstractMusicPlayer()
        {
            super();
        }
    }
}
```

The next class we will create is `MusicPlayerFactory`. The class will hold constants for each view, and we will create a placeholder for the main view `MusicPlayerMain695x362`.

```
package com.elad.mp3tunes.view
{
    import com.elad.mp3tunes.view.desktop.MusicPlayerMain695x362;
    import flash.errors.IllegalOperationError;

    public final class MusicPlayerFactory
    {
        /**
         * Music player types enums
         */
        public static const WEB:int = 0;
        public static const MOBILE:int = 1;
        public static const DESKTOP:int = 2;

        public static function createView( ➥
musicPlayerType:Number):AbstractMusicPlayerMain
        {
            var retVal:AbstractMusicPlayerMain;

            switch (musicPlayerType)
            {
                case DESKTOP:
                    retVal = new MusicPlayerMain695x362();
                break;
                throw new IllegalOperationError("The view type " ➥
+ musicPlayerType + " is not recognized.");
            }

            return retVal;
        }
    }
}
```

Creating the creator class

The creator will be our entry point class, MP3TunesAIR.mxml. Let's take a look:

```
<?xml version="1.0" encoding="utf-8"?>
<mx:WindowedApplication
    xmlns:mx="http://www.adobe.com/2006/mxml"
    backgroundColor="0xe6e6e6"
    width="695" height="362"
    horizontalScrollPolicy="off"
    verticalScrollPolicy="off"
    creationComplete="creationCompleteHandler(event)">

    <mx:Style source="assets/css/Main.css" />

    <mx:Script>
        <![CDATA[
```

```
                    import com.elad.mp3tunes.view.presenter.➡
        MusicPlayerMainPresenter;
                    import com.elad.mp3tunes.view.AbstractMusicPlayerMain;
                    import com.elad.mp3tunes.view.LoginForm;
                    import mx.managers.PopUpManager;
                    import mx.containers.TitleWindow;
                    import mx.events.FlexEvent;

                    import com.elad.mp3tunes.view.MusicPlayerFactory;
                    import com.elad.mp3tunes.view.AbstractMusicPlayerMain;

                    private var loginForm:LoginForm;
                    private var musicPlayerMainPresenter:➡
        MusicPlayerMainPresenter;

                    // handler after creation complete
                    protected function creationCompleteHandler➡
        (event:FlexEvent):void
                    {
                        loginForm = LoginForm(PopUpManager.createPopUp( ➡
        this, LoginForm, true));
                        loginForm.addEventListener➡
        (LoginForm.LOGIN_SUCCESSFULL, onLogin);
                    }

                    // method to load the view
                    protected function loadView(type:Number):void
                    {
                        var musicPlayerView:AbstractMusicPlayerMain = ➡
        MusicPlayerFactory.createView(type);
                        this.addChild(musicPlayerView);

                        musicPlayerMainPresenter = ➡
        new MusicPlayerMainPresenter(musicPlayerView);
                    }

                    private function onLogin(event:Event):void
                    {
                        loadView(MusicPlayerFactory.DESKTOP);
                    }
                ]]>
            </mx:Script>

    </mx:WindowedApplication>
```

Notice that we create an instance of the LoginForm and of the MusicPlayerMainPresenter presenter:

```
    private var loginForm:LoginForm;
    private var musicPlayerMainPresenter: ➡
    MusicPlayerMainPresenter;
```

The creationCompleteHandler method gets called right after the component event is dispatched and the login window opens. Once the login window is closed, the onLogin method will be used.

```
// handler after creation complete
protected function creationCompleteHandler( ➥
event:FlexEvent):void
            {
                    loginForm = LoginForm(PopUpManager.createPopUp( ➥
this, LoginForm, true));
                    loginForm.addEventListener➥
(LoginForm.LOGIN_SUCCESSFULL, onLogin);
            }
```

onLoginmethod will call the loadView method and pass the type of product we would like to use.

```
private function onLogin(event:Event):void
{
    loadView(MusicPlayerFactory.DESKTOP);
}
```

The loadView method will create the factory product based on the product we choose and the presenter (logic).

```
// method to load the view
protected function loadView(type:Number):void
            {
                    var musicPlayerView:AbstractMusicPlayerMain = ➥
MusicPlayerFactory.createView(type);
                    this.addChild(musicPlayerView);

                    musicPlayerMainPresenter = new ➥
MusicPlayerMainPresenter(musicPlayerView);
            }


        ]]>
</mx:Script>

</mx:WindowedApplication>
```

Creating the skin components

The main view and subview will implement the abstract classes and skin the components. To create the skin, we will be using an Illustrator file. Download MusicPlayer.ai from the Chapter 11 files on this book's Downloads page on the friends of ED web site.

You can see the Illustrator file in Figure 11-9. In the next chapter, you will learn how to convert Illustrator files into declarative XML code that can be recognized by Flex. Meanwhile, we will import the assets into Flash Professional CS3 or CS4 and use CSS to assign them to the components.

One of the simplest methods to create assets in Flash Professional CS3 is to select an object in Illustrator and paste it in Flash Professional. The imported asset will be placed in the asset library in

CS3 and kept as a vector, when possible. See Figure 11-10 that shows the artwork imported into Flash Professional.

Figure 11-9. The music player design in Illustrator

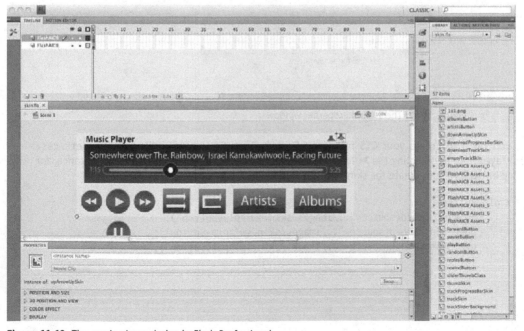

Figure 11-10. The music player design in Flash Professional

We will create a SWF file that can be used in a Flash Builder CSS file. Here's what you need to do. Once you import all your assets into Flash CS3, select an asset, and then select Modify ➤ Convert to Symbol. The Symbol Properties window opens, and you can fill in the information (see Figure 11-11). For Type, select Movie Clip, and in the Linkage area, select Export for ActionScript, and select the name of the class, in our case playButton. Repeat this process for all the assets you want to use in Flash Builder.

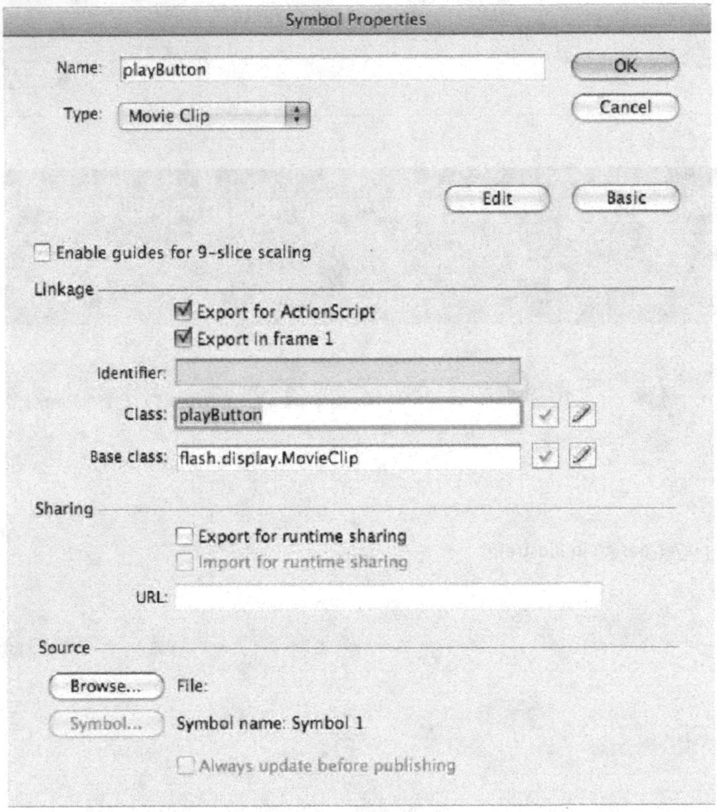

Figure 11-11. The Symbol Properties window

Next, you need to create your CSS file. Open Flash Builder. Create a CSS file under assets/css/MusicPlayer.css by selecting File ➤ New ➤ CSS File. Now, you can use the assets. For instance, for the play button, we can create the skin states as follows:

```
.playButton {
    upSkin: Embed(source="../images/skin.swf#playButton");
    downSkin: Embed(source="../images/skin.swf#playButton");
    overSkin: Embed(source="../images/skin.swf#playButton");
}
```

The complete CSS file follows. The buttons have many states, and since we didn't create all the states, we will just define the common ones as the same assets.

```css
.playButton {
    upSkin: Embed(source="../images/skin.swf#playButton");
    downSkin: Embed(source="../images/skin.swf#playButton");
    overSkin: Embed(source="../images/skin.swf#playButton");
}

.albumsButton {
    upSkin: Embed(source="../images/skin.swf#albumsButton");
    downSkin: Embed(source="../images/skin.swf#albumsButton");
    overSkin: Embed(source="../images/skin.swf#albumsButton");
}

.artistsButton {
upSkin: Embed(source="../images/skin.swf#artistsButton");
downSkin: Embed(source="../images/skin.swf#artistsButton");
overSkin: Embed(source="../images/skin.swf#artistsButton");
}

.forwardButton {
    upSkin: Embed(source="../images/skin.swf#forwardButton");
    downSkin: Embed(source="../images/skin.swf#forwardButton");
    overSkin: Embed(source="../images/skin.swf#forwardButton");
}

.pauseButton {
    upSkin: Embed(source="../images/skin.swf#pauseButton");
    downSkin: Embed(source="../images/skin.swf#pauseButton");
    overSkin: Embed(source="../images/skin.swf#pauseButton");
}

.randomButton {
    upSkin: Embed(source="../images/skin.swf#randomButton");
    downSkin: Embed(source="../images/skin.swf#randomButton");
    overSkin: Embed(source="../images/skin.swf#randomButton");
}

.replayButton {
    upSkin: Embed(source="../images/skin.swf#replayButton");
    downSkin: Embed(source="../images/skin.swf#replayButton");
    overSkin: Embed(source="../images/skin.swf#replayButton");
}
```

```
.rewindButton {
    upSkin: Embed(source="../images/skin.swf#rewindButton");
    downSkin: Embed(source="../images/skin.swf#rewindButton");
    overSkin: Embed(source="../images/skin.swf#rewindButton");
}
```

For the background of the track slider, we will be using an embedded background image. Here's the tag:

```
.trackSliderBackground {
    background-image: ➥
Embed(source="../images/skin.swf#trackSliderBackground");
}
```

For the track slider, we will define the thumb and the track. For the thumb skin, we will be using two progress bars—one to show the track progression and another for the download of the song—so we are using an empty placeholder for the track skin. The empty placeholder is in the size of the track and was created by using a 1×1 pixel.

```
.trackThumbSkin {
    thumbSkin: Embed(source="../images/skin.swf#trackThumbSkin");
    trackSkin: Embed(source="../images/skin.swf#emptyTrackSkin");
}
```

For the download progress bar, we define the bar skin and track skin. The Flex out-of-the-box progress bar contains the track, and the skin inside will fill the track. Since we want to create a bar skin that's a smaller skin than the track skin, as you can see in Figure 11-12, we will keep the track empty and define it separately in trackSkin.

```
.downloadProgressBarSkin {
    barSkin: Embed(source="../images/➥
skin.swf#downloadProgressBarSkin");
    trackSkin: Embed(source="../images/skin.swf#emptyTrackSkin");
}
.trackSkin {
    trackSkin: Embed(source="../images/skin.swf#trackSkin");
}

.trackProgressBarSkin {
    barSkin: Embed(source="../images/skin.swf#trackProgressBarSkin");
    trackSkin: Embed(source="../images/skin.swf#emptyTrackSkin");
}
```

Figure 11-12. Slider graphic

The volume skin will be an HScrollBar component, so we will define the down and up arrow skin. We'll keep the track and thumb empty, since we are not going to implement them in this version of the music player.

```
.volumeSkin {
    down-arrow-skin: Embed(source="../images/skin.swf#upArrowUpSkin");
    up-arrow-skin: Embed(source="../images/skin.swf#downArrowUpSkin");
    trackSkin: Embed(source="../images/skin.swf#emptyTrackSkin");
    thumbSkin: Embed(source="../images/skin.swf#emptyTrackSkin");
}
```

The next custom skin we will create will be the slider track thumb graphic. We chose to create the graphic using the Drawing API. Create a new class here:

```
desktop/components/TrackSliderThumb.as
```

The class will extend SliderThumb, and the default constructor will call the super method to process the logic of the SliderThumb class. The only method we need to update is updateDisplayList. We will override that method and draw a grey border, an outer circle, and an inner circle, as shown in Figure 11-13.

```
package com.elad.mp3tunes.view.desktop.components
{
    import mx.controls.sliderClasses.SliderThumb;

    public class TrackSliderThumb extends SliderThumb
    {
        public function TrackSliderThumb()
        {
            super();
        }

        overrideprotected function updateDisplayList➥
        (unscaledWidth:Number, unscaledHeight:Number):void
        {
            super.updateDisplayList(unscaledWidth,unscaledHeight);

            var x:Number = 0;
            var y:Number = 0;

            // Grey border
            this.graphics.beginFill(0x898989,1);
            this.graphics.drawCircle(x,y,20);

            // outer circle
            this.graphics.beginFill(0x000000,1);
            this.graphics.drawCircle(x,y,18);

            // inner circle
            this.graphics.beginFill(0xffffff,1);
            this.graphics.drawCircle(x,y,9);

            this.graphics.endFill();
        }
    }
}
```

Implementing the AbstractMusicPlayerMain class

Now that we completed creating the skins, we can create the implementation of the music player. The subview, MusicPlayerMain695x362, implements AbstractMusicPlayerMain. We will be using the MusicPlayer as the subview, and it includes List as the TileList and AdvancedDataGridColumn for the DataGrid component.

```xml
<?xml version="1.0" encoding="utf-8"?>
<view:AbstractMusicPlayerMain xmlns:mx="http://www.adobe.com/2006/mxml"
    backgroundColor="0xe6e6e6"
    width="695" height="362"
    xmlns:view="com.elad.mp3tunes.view.*"
    xmlns:player="com.elad.mp3tunes.view.desktop.*"
    borderStyle="solid" borderThickness="3"
    horizontalScrollPolicy="off"
    verticalScrollPolicy="off">

    <mx:VBox>
        <player:MusicPlayer id="musicPlayer" height="200" />

        <mx:Canvas width="100%" height="337">
            <mx:List id="tileList"
                width="173.0303" height="131.36363"
                columnWidth="125"
                rowHeight="125"
                columnCount="4"
                itemRenderer="com.elad.mp3tunes.view. ➥
desktop.components.TileResultRenderer"
                x="15" y="8"/>

            <mx:AdvancedDataGrid id="dg"
                width="466.0606" height="129.31818"
                sortExpertMode="true" x="212" y="10">
                <mx:columns>
                    <mx:AdvancedDataGridColumn dataField=➥
"trackTitle" />
                    <mx:AdvancedDataGridColumn dataField=➥
"artistName" />
                    <mx:AdvancedDataGridColumn dataField=➥
"albumTitle" />
                </mx:columns>
            </mx:AdvancedDataGrid>
        </mx:Canvas>
    </mx:VBox>

</view:AbstractMusicPlayerMain>
```

Notice that `TileList` is rendered by the `TileResultRenderer` class, which includes two labels to display the song name, and count and an image tag.

```xml
<?xml version="1.0" encoding="utf-8"?>
<mx:VBox xmlns:mx="http://www.adobe.com/2006/mxml"
        horizontalAlign="center"
        verticalGap="0" borderStyle="none"
        height="152" width="181">

    <mx:Label text="{data.name}" width="120" textAlign="center"/>
    <mx:Label text="{data.count} song" fontWeight="bold"/>
    <mx:Image source="assets/images/note.gif"
            scaleContent="true"
            autoLoad="true" width="50%" height="50%"/>

</mx:VBox>
```

Implementing the AbstractMusicPlayer class

The subview is `MusicPlayer.mxml`, and it contains the same components as the `AbstractMusicPlayer` class with the skin we created.

```xml
<?xml version='1.0' encoding='UTF-8'?>
<view:AbstractMusicPlayer xmlns:mx="http://www.adobe.com/2006/mxml"
    xmlns:view="com.elad.mp3tunes.view.*"
    width="695" height="200"
    horizontalScrollPolicy="off"
    verticalScrollPolicy="off">

    <mx:Style source="assets/css/MusicPlayer.css" />

    <mx:Canvas width="664"
        height="92.1" x="15" y="36"
        styleName="trackSliderBackground">

        <mx:Text id="currentTimeText"
            fontFamily="Myriad Pro" fontSize="16.7"
            color="0xadacac" letterSpacing="0"
            kerning="true" top="52" left="11" text="00:00" />

        <mx:Text id="totalTimeText"
            text="00:00" fontFamily="Myriad Pro"
            fontSize="16.7" color="0xadacac"
            kerning="true" letterSpacing="0"
            top="52" left="614" />
```

```
<mx:Text id="songInfoText"
    fontFamily="Myriad Pro" selectable="false"
    fontSize="20" color="0xe6e6e6" width="617" height="22"
    top="11" left="15" text="Somewhere over The... "/>

<!-- Track Slider -->
<mx:ProgressBar
    x="72" y="55" styleName="trackSkin"
    width="537" height="7"
    labelWidth="0"/>

<mx:ProgressBar id="downloadProgressBar"
    styleName="downloadProgressBarSkin"
    x="78" y="60"
    width="525" height="7"
    minimum="0" maximum="100"
    labelWidth="0"
    direction="right" mode="manual" />

<mx:ProgressBar id="trackProgressBar"
    styleName="trackProgressBarSkin"
    x="78" y="60"
    width="525" height="12"
    minimum="0" maximum="100"
    labelWidth="0"
    direction="right" mode="manual" />

<mx:HSlider id="songSlider" styleName="trackThumbSkin"
    x="78" y="60" enabled="true"
    width="525" height="12" minimum="0" maximum="100"
    sliderThumbClass="com.elad.mp3tunes.view.desktop.➥
components.TrackSliderThumb"
    />

</mx:Canvas>

<mx:Text fontFamily="Myriad Pro"
    fontSize="20" fontWeight="bold"
    color="0x000000" top="8.104"
    left="11.5" text="MP3Tunes Music Player"/>

<!-- Volume Slider -->
<mx:ProgressBar id="volumeProgressBar"
    visible="false" enabled="false" />
<mx:HScrollBar id="volumeSlider"
    left="619" top="10" styleName="volumeSkin"
    minScrollPosition="0" maxScrollPosition="100" scrollPosition="100"
    width="60"  height="18"/>
```

```
<mx:Button id="forwardButton" buttonMode="true"
    styleName="forwardButton" x="135" y="144"/>
<mx:Button id="rewindButton" buttonMode="true"
    styleName="rewindButton" x="10" y="138"/>
<mx:Button id="randomButton" buttonMode="true"
    styleName="randomButton" x="204" y="138"/>
<mx:Button id="replayButton" buttonMode="true"
    styleName="replayButton" x="296" y="138"/>
<mx:Button id="artistsButton" buttonMode="true"
    styleName="artistsButton" x="392" y="138"/>
<mx:Button id="albumsButton" buttonMode="true"
    styleName="albumsButton" x="547" y="138"/>
<mx:Button id="playButton" buttonMode="true"
    styleName="playButton" x="68" y="134"/>
<mx:Button id="pauseButton" buttonMode="true"
    styleName="pauseButton" x="68" y="134"/>
```

```
</view:AbstractMusicPlayer>
```

Run the application; the results are shown in Figure 11-13.

Figure 11-13. MP3TunesAIR application screenshot

Once the AIR application is completed, we can deploy it on a UMPC device, as shown in Figure 11-14.

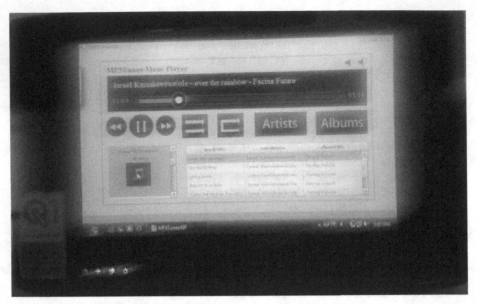

Figure 11-14. MP3TunesAIR deployed on UMPC

Making the application context aware and adaptable

Recall that in Chapter 10 we spoke about context awareness and adaptation. As we build our adaptive application, the behavior will be guided by user experience and preferences.

By identifying the device screen size, we can deploy different views, which will be more suitable for different devices with different screen sizes. For instance, a small screen will require changes in the presentation model for a better user experience, and a larger screen will allow creating an application with larger dimensions that can handle more functionality.

Utilizing context awareness for multiple views

When creating a view for a device, you should consider the amount of screen real estate you can actually make use of. Although a device screen size may be 320X200 pixels, that doesn't mean that we can utilize every pixel for our application. Devices may reserve space for navigation, for example, so even if we expand our application to fit the whole screen, we will not get the full width and height. Device browsers may not utilize the entire screen size, since they may be set to fit a smaller size than the actual device screen.

To test the device to find out the device screen's dimensions before you decide the screen size you want to use for your application, you can create a small application that utilizes the Capabilities API to find out the device height and width as well as draw a border. That way, you can test the width and height and change it until it fits your requirement. Here's a sample application to do just that:

```
<?xml version="1.0" encoding="utf-8"?>
<mx:WindowedApplication
    xmlns:mx="http://www.adobe.com/2006/mxml"
    layout="absolute"
    backgroundColor="0xe6e6e6"
    width="320" height="200"
    borderStyle="solid" borderThickness="3">

    <mx:Text text="screenResolutionX:
        {Capabilities.screenResolutionX}" />
    <mx:Text text="screenResolutionY:
        {Capabilities.screenResolutionY}" y="26"/>

</mx:WindowedApplication>
```

The application will determine and print out the resolution of the screen.

Adapting the application

Once we discover the width and height of the device using the test application, we can create our application and tweak our code to be able to accommodate different devices. We can create two types of views based on the device screen resolution: one for a small screen, MusicPlayerFactory. SMALL_DESKTOP, and one for a large screen, MusicPlayerFactory.LARGE_DESKTOP.

If we take the code of the music player, we can easily modify the onLogin method on our creator class to accommodate to two different views.

```
private function onLogin(event:Event):void
{
    var type:String;

    if (Capabilities.screenResolutionX< 320 && ➥
Capabilities.screenResolutionY< 480)
    {
        type = MusicPlayerFactory.SMALL_DESKTOP;
    }
    else
    {
        type = MusicPlayerFactory.LARGE_DESKTOP;
    }

    loadView(MusicPlayerFactory.DESKTOP);
}
```

Summary

In this chapter, we talked about dynamic graphical GUIs. You learned about the Passive Multi-view design pattern, and then we walked through implementing that pattern. We created a simple example of using the Passive Multi-view design pattern to help you fully understand how to build a multi-view application. We continued by creating a fully working, real-life application that contains a music player API, a GUI for the music player application with a login form, and custom skins. We finished by exploring context awareness and adaptation for multiple views. In Chapter 12, we will cover Flash Catalyst, and in Chapter 13, we will continue exploring adaptation of the music player application using Flash 10 and Flash Catalyst to deploy the application in a web browser.

Part Four

FLEX APPLICATION RUNNING FLASH 10 ON MOBILE DEVICES

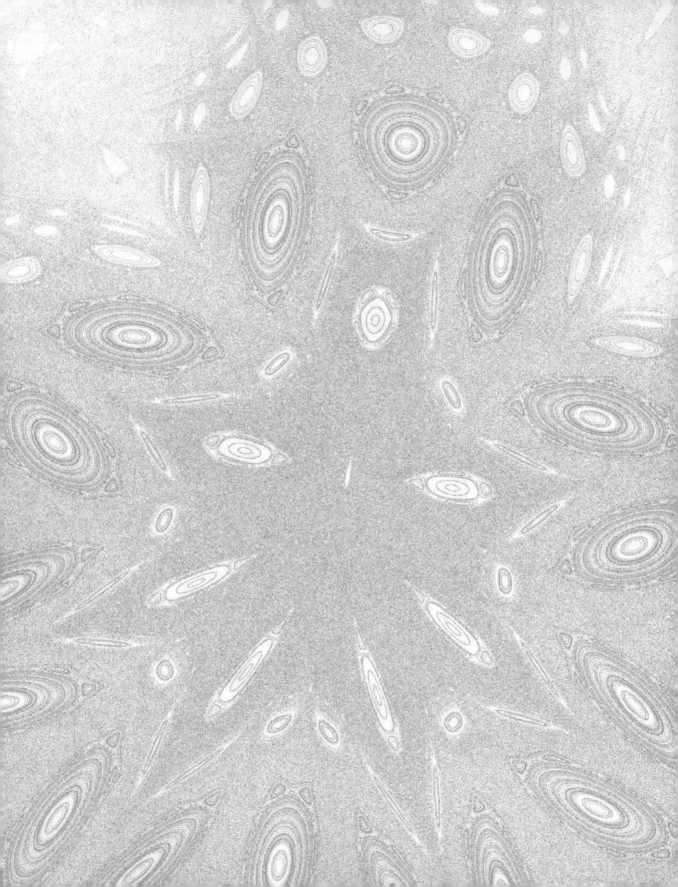

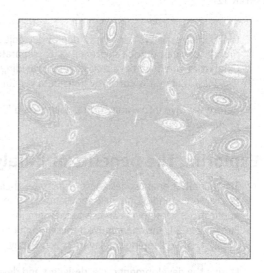

Chapter 12

MOBILE APPLICATIONS AND DEVELOPMENT STRATEGIES WITH FLEX 4 AND FLASH CATALYST

Adobe Flash Catalyst, formerly code-named Thermo, is a design tool for creating Flex application interfaces and interactive content without writing code.

Catalyst allows importing Creative Suite (CS4) graphics and using a familiar IDE to define events, transitions, and motions. When completed, Flash Catalyst outputs either a deployment file or a project file that can be used in Adobe Flash Builder to add logic such as connecting to services.

In this chapter, we'll take a closer look at why Adobe created Catalyst in the first place, and then we'll show you how to create your first application using Flash Catalyst and continue by creating more complex applications using round-trip between developers and designers.

> Flash Catalyst (code name Thermo) is currently in its beta version. Because it's a very early build, features are likely to change and be added in the final build.

Getting to know Flash Catalyst

Adobe's Flash Catalyst will be a powerful additional tool that can help us address the mobile device constraints by creating different skins and states with different functionality, so we can easily deploy an adjusted AIR application to work efficiently on different mobile devices. Adobe's interest is to separate the presentation layer from the logic layer. Flash Catalyst can help achieve that goal by providing designers with a new set of tools that they can easily use. Flash Catalyst is currently in its beta version (that is, right out of the oven).

Before we dive into using Flash Catalyst, we'd like to introduce you to some of the benefits and basics of the tool.

Exploring the benefits of Catalyst

Flash Catalyst enables designers to increase their creative productivity and leverage their existing skills to create a stand-alone Flex application. It also facilitates collaborating in a team when creating Flex applications. Designers can create their graphics using Adobe Photoshop CS4, Illustrator CS4, or Adobe Fireworks CS4, and then convert these graphics into a Flex application by importing the native files into Catalyst, while keeping the layers intact. Catalyst acts as a bridge between Flash Builder and CS4.

During the development cycle, designers and developers can follow a round-trip workflow. Designers can move back and forth between Adobe CS4 and Flash Catalyst and between Catalyst and Flash Builder.

In addition to collaboration, using Catalyst brings the following benefits:

- **Speed**: Expect faster development times for simple to complex projects.
- **Agile workflow**: Designers and developers can work in parallel.
- **Interaction design**: Designers can add interactivity without coding. Catalyst helps bridge technical issues for designers.
- **Consistent graphics**: There's no need to translate graphics to code since Catalyst takes care of that part, and the files created in CS4 convert easily.
- **Easy prototyping**: Catalyst can help create prototype applications.

Getting the tool

Flash Catalyst is in its beta version at the time of this writing. A copy of Flash Catalyst for Mac OS X was given for a trial during Adobe Max 2008. Currently, Catalyst, for PC and Mac, is available for prerelease beta testers only. The final release date and cost have not been announced at the time of this writing.

Separating presentation from logic with Flash Catalyst

Flash Catalyst follows Flex 4 architecture and separates pixels from the plumbing. The new Flex 4 component architecture creates a miniature MVC architecture at each component level and separates the three major parts of the application, that is, data, processing, and presentation:

- **Model**: Represents the data through the life cycle of the application
- **View**: Holds the interface or presentation layer
- **Controller**: Acts as the glue between the view and the model

A designer working with Flash Catalyst is unaware of the separation, which gets created automatically while working with Flash Catalyst. The designer doesn't have to understand or worry about what is being done by Catalyst to create simple applications or provide developers with Flash Catalyst project files.

But why do we even need to separate the presentation layer from the logic layer?

Users' expectations increase as businesses demand more out of our Flash applications. These expectations cause applications to be larger and more complex and to include custom components and many services. Also, as Flex and AIR deploy to more and more devices, we need to be able to easily create different presentation for the same logic, so we can easily create an application that gets deployed on different devices.

The challenge is that the current development cycle is developer centric, and designers are only responsible for creating the pixel discipline and are not involved in any of the Flash experience. Creating Flash applications becomes challenging, since the entire responsibility lies on the developer. Developers are expected to juggle all the application disciplines, such as converting Photoshop .psd files into Flex components, handling data, testing, working with services, coding, and many others.

Adobe is aware of these challenges and has been working in the last few years to close that gap by creating Flash Catalyst. Flash Catalyst reflects Adobe's continual commitment to the Flash framework and the community and can help achieve a new design-centric cycle.

If you've ever tried to extend or skin a Flex component, you know that is not an easy task, and it takes a tremendous level of effort to control every aspect of the component. These challenges led developers to create their own custom components and to the creation of tools and APIs such as Declarative Graphics Framework (Degrafa); see www.degrafa.org for more information.

> Declarative Graphics Framework (Degrafa) allows you to convert Illustrator graphics into a file format called SVG to use as skin graphics.

Using Degrafa is not a seamless process, and often, the code requires tweaking. Flex 4 addresses these issues and allows full control over graphic components. To achieve full control, Adobe had to rework the component architecture. Under the new Flex 4 architecture, components are loosely coupled and split into a miniature MVC architecture.

The programmer is responsible for the model, and the designer can create the visual design as well as the behavior of the component. Using CS4 tools and Flash Catalyst, designers can generate a new file format called Flash XML Graphic (FXG), which includes the component skins as well as the behavior of the different components and the whole application.

> Flash XML Graphic (FXG) is a declarative format based on MXML and is similar to SVG. FXG is supported by Adobe CS4 (Photoshop, Illustrator, and Fireworks). Previously in this book we've mentioned both CS3 and CS4, but only CS4 Photoshop, Illustrator, and Fireworks support FXG.

Exploring Flash's new development cycle

Using Flash Catalyst, Adobe's vision is to make the behavior, such as animation between different states, the responsibility of the designer. It allows designers to control the Flash interaction, choreography of the application, and the appearance without visiting Flash Builder. Once the work is completed, the FXG file format can be provided to a developer, which can integrate it with business logic, data, and services. As the project continues, designers can modify the appearance and interaction without disrupting the workflow.

Under the new development cycle vision, designers and developers can work in parallel. Here's the breakdown of the new responsibilities:

- **Developer responsibilities**: Application logic, processing, data, services, and testing
- **Designer responsibilities**: Frames, states, and visual appearance (pixels) of the application

Designers and developers can work in an agile workflow where both work in parallel development. During the development cycle, designers and developers can follow a round-trip workflow. Designers can move back and forth between Adobe CS4 and Flash Catalyst and then back and forth between Catalyst and Flex Builder, which is illustrated in Figure 12-1.

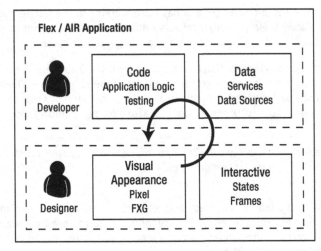

Figure 12-1.
Designers and devlopers
workflow using Catalyst

Visit the Adobe Catalyst online center at the following URLs for tutorials and other valuable information:

http://labs.adobe.com/technologies/flashcatalyst/
http://thermoteamblog.com/

Now that you have a sense of the origins of Catalyst, let's take a look at what can be done with Catalyst and how you can benefit from the Flash Catalyst tool.

Getting started with Flash Catalyst

As we mentioned, Flash Catalyst is a great tool for helping designers and developers bridge their worlds. It can reduce some of the most tedious tasks for the developer and eliminates the need to translate graphics to code, since Catalyst takes care of the heavy lifting. It is definitely fair to say that it makes it a whole lot easier to get artwork out of Photoshop and into an application's visuals. It facilitates development by bridging technical issues for designers.

The round-trip workflow between Adobe CS4 and Flash Catalyst allows designers and developers to work in parallel. The Flash Catalyst IDE was built primarily for the designer, and it is similar in look and feel to Flash Professional and Photoshop. It allows designers to quickly jump in and start using the tool in a familiar environment, all without writing code. However, when you do need to tweak the code, Flash Catalyst has a feature that allows toggling between code view and design view.

Let's get started! Open Flash Catalyst. The welcome window allows you to import an existing project from Adobe CS4 (Illustrator, Photoshop, or Fireworks) or create a new project from scratch (see Figure 12-2). When you import your graphics from Adobe CS4, you can keep your layers intact.

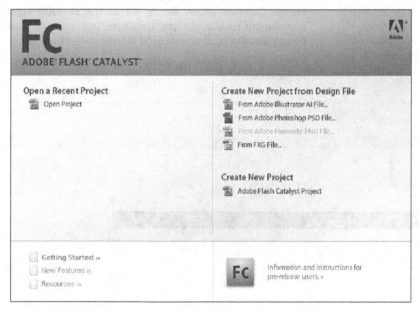

Figure 12-2. Flash Catalyst welcome window

Creating a new Catalyst project

In this section, we will give you an overview of creating a new project as well as importing your Adobe CS4 files. Keep in mind that Flash Catalyst was built with the intention of importing your graphics from CS4, so in most cases, you will be importing the art you have created in CS4 into Catalyst rather than creating your graphics in Flash Catalyst.

Let's start by creating a new project in Flash Catalyst. Select Create New Project ➤ Adobe Flash Catalyst Project, or select from the top menu File ➤ New Project. Type **MyFirstApplication** as the name of your application, and set the project width to **320** and height to **480**. The option for creating an AIR application is disabled in this release, but the final release will likely include an AIR project. Select Web Application (runs in Flash Player). Click OK, and a new application will open (see Figure 12-3).

Figure 12-3. The Flash Catalyst New Project window

The Flash Catalyst work area includes the following panes, which are shown in Figure 12-4:

- **Stage area**: This pane holds the application canvas.

- Pages/States: This pane captures pages and states in an application.

- Tools: This pane includes basic geometric shapes that can be drawn. Once a geometric shape is drawn, a properties window opens automatically and allows you to change properties, as in any other Adobe CS4 product like Photoshop, Flash Professional, or Dreamweaver.

- Components: The view is made of two sections: Common and Project. Common allows you to see all the available common components such as buttons, scrollbars, text input, and others. Project lists the components used in your current project.

- Timelines: This pane is used for creating transitions and sequences.

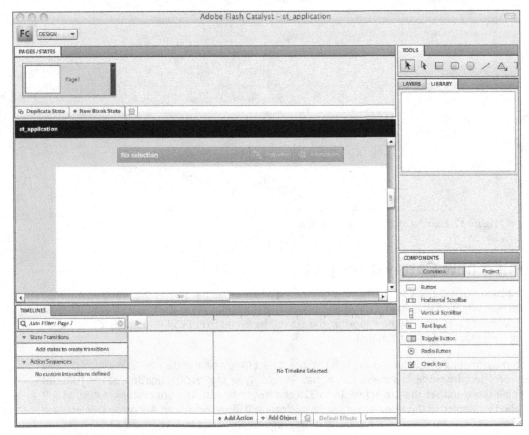

Figure 12-4. The Flash Catalyst work area

Creating your first full Catalyst application

As an example of how to use Flash Catalyst, we will create a simple login form. We will create the design and behavior for the form all within Flash Catalyst and without writing one line of code.

Create a new Flash Catalyst project. Name it LoginForm, and give it a width of 800 pixels and height of 600 pixels.

The work area will open with one Pages/States entry named Page1. Rename the state to SignupState.

Creating graphics

Now that your basic project is created, we'll add some graphics. Choose the Rectangle from the Tools pane, and draw a rectangle in your work area.

The properties window opens automatically and you can set the following properties:

- Fill color: #d1cfcf
- Stroke color: #000000
- Corner radius: 10
- Stroke size: 2

Next, add the login form's text graphic by selecting a text tool. Position it on the top of the box graphic and set the following properties:

- Fill color: #d1cfcf
- Color: #000000
- Font weight: Bold

We'll add the User Name and Password input boxes next. Add a text input tool and square to be used as the input boxes. Position them, and set the following properties:

- Text label
  - Font color: #000000
  - Font size: 12
- Text Input box
  - Width: 136
  - Height: 25
- Background color
  - Fill: Solid
  - Color: #ffffff
- Stroke
  - Fill: Solid
  - Color: #000000

Next, we're creating the Login and Forget Password buttons. Create buttons by placing the round square tool and text. Then set the following properties:

- Background color
  - Fill: Solid
  - Color: #484848
- Stroke
  - Fill: Solid
  - Color: #000000
  - Size: 1
- Corner radius: 10

And change the following properties:

- Text properties
  - Font: Verdana
  - Size: 12
  - Color: #000000
- State Name: **LoginState**

The final result is shown in Figure 12-5.

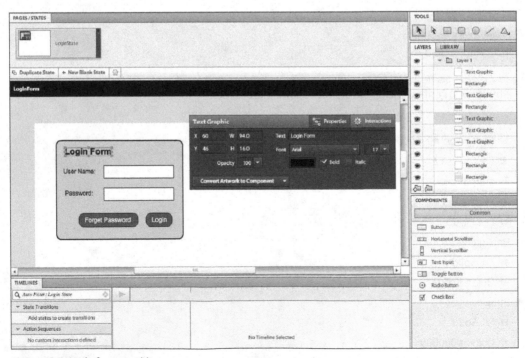

Figure 12-5. Login form graphics

Converting graphics to components

At this point, we have graphics, and we need to convert the graphics into a component. You can do that by selecting the property and then selecting the Convert Artwork to component heads-up display (HUD). Then, set each of the two input boxes to Text Input component. Select each button and Text Input component pair together, and set them to a button component.

To run the project in the browser and observe the results so far, select File ➤ Run Project; you should be able to see the components.

Now, we need to set the button properties (see Figure 12-6). Each button component has four states: Up, Over, Down, and Disabled. Select the button, and in the properties window, set the different states:

- Up: Set the background fill color to #484848.
- Over: Set the background fill color to #262626.
- Down: Set the background fill color to #fc0000.

Since we don't need the button in disabled mode, there is no need to create a graphic for that state.

Run the project, and you can see the button state changing the background color as you hover over or click the component.

Figure 12-6. The Buttons graphic

Next, we will create the forgotten password state. Our login state is ready, and we can now create the next state to change the form when a user forgets a password and needs to retrieve it.

491

To create the Forget Password state click the Duplicate State button in the PAGES/STATES pane to create a copy of the current state, since the two states will be similar. Rename the new state to ForgetPasswordState.

Choreographing the application

When working with Flash Catalyst, creating the behaviors is among the designer's responsibilities. We currently have two states: LoginPage and ForgetPasswordState. We'll start by removing the unnecessary components. Select ForgetPasswordState from the Pages/States window and remove the following elements:

- Password input text box
- Password label
- Forget Password and Login buttons

Next, add a new button to allow the user to retrieve the user's password from a service that we will create later on. Similar to the ForgetPasswordState state, use the same style properties.

We also need to change the User Name text in the label graphic to Email Address and decrease the size of the rectangle box that holds the form to fit the ForgetPasswordState form better.

Flash Catalyst automatically adds effects to fade out and move the components. You can see these changes in the Timelines pane. See Figure 12-7.

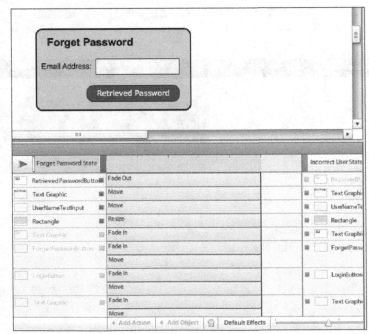

Figure 12-7. ForgetPasswordState effects

Adding actions to the buttons we created

We have completed creating the new behavior, and what we have left to do is to assign an action to the Retrieved Password button so it will let the user switch between the two states. To achieve that click action, select the button, and in the properties window, select the On Click action from the HUD panel, and set the Play transition to state property to ForgetPasswordState.

You can run the application and observe the results of changing to the ForgetPasswordState state and the animation we created. Figure 12-8 shows the two states created.

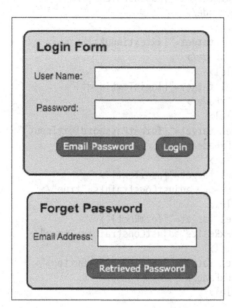

Figure 12-8.
Visuals of the two states created in Flash Catalyst

Switching to code mode

We believe that, for many designers, working with Flash Catalyst will be similar to working with HTML in Dreamweaver. Although you can perform many of the manipulation tasks in design mode using the WYSIWYG tool, you need a deeper understanding to tweak the code, as you must do to complete other tasks. Therefore, most users will slowly explore the code and start to understand FXG and MXML to make their projects more exciting. To switch to code view, select code in the top-left drop-down menu. Let's take a look at the code.

First, we have the application declaration, which sets properties such as width, height, and color:

```
<?xml version="1.0" encoding="utf-8"?>
<FxApplication xmlns="http://ns.adobe.com/mxml/2009"
    xmlns:d="http://ns.adobe.com/fxg/2008/dt"
    width="800" height="600"
    backgroundColor="0xffffff"
    xmlns:th="http://ns.adobe.com/thermo/2009">
```

The states' transitions are defined under the transitions tag that follows. There are two transitions, switching from LoginState to ForgetPasswordState and vise versa. Each transition will make changes in the component in parallel, so once the effect is completed, all the changes are completed.

```
<transitions>
        <Transition fromState="LoginState"  ➥
toState="ForgetPasswordState" d:autoEffect="true">
            <Parallel>
                <Parallel target="{passwordText}">
                    <FxFade/>
                </Parallel>
                <Parallel target="{fxtextinput1}">
                    <FxFade/>
                </Parallel>
                <Parallel target="{loginTextInput}">
                    <FxFade/>
                </Parallel>
                <Parallel target="{forgetPasswordTextInput}">
                    <FxFade/>
                </Parallel>
                <Parallel target="{userText}">
                    <FxMove adjustConstraints="true"/>
                </Parallel>
                <Parallel target="{formRect}">
                    <FxResize adjustConstraints="true"/>
                </Parallel>
                <Parallel target="{retrievedPassButton}">
                    <FxFade/>
                </Parallel>
            </Parallel>
        </Transition>
        <Transition fromState="ForgetPasswordState"  ➥
toState="LoginState" d:autoEffect="true">
            <Parallel>
                <Parallel target="{passwordText}">
                    <FxFade/>
                </Parallel>
                <Parallel target="{fxtextinput1}">
                    <FxFade/>
                </Parallel>
                <Parallel target="{loginTextInput}">
                    <FxFade/>
                </Parallel>
                <Parallel target="{forgetPasswordTextInput}">
                    <FxFade/>
                </Parallel>
                <Parallel target="{userText}">
                    <FxMove adjustConstraints="true"/>
                </Parallel>
```

```
        <Parallel target="{formRect}">
              <FxResize adjustConstraints="true"/>
        </Parallel>
        <Parallel target="{retrievedPassButton}">
              <FxFade/>
        </Parallel>
     </Parallel>
  </Transition>
</transitions>
```

The states tag defines the two states:

```
<states>
     <State name="LoginState" th:color="0xcc0000"/>
     <State name="ForgetPasswordState" th:color="0x0081cc"/>
</states>
```

DesignLayer is a new tag in Flex 4 and adds support for layers and groups. Our layer is placed inside of the tag.

```
<DesignLayer d:userLabel="Layer 1">
            <Rect height="185" radiusX="10" radiusY="10" ➥
height.ForgetPasswordState="126" id="formRect" ➥
width="248" top="32" left="42">
            <fill>
                  <SolidColor color="0xd1cfcf"/>
            </fill>
            <stroke>
                  <SolidColorStroke color="0x000000" weight="2"/>
            </stroke>
      </Rect>
```

The following section contains the components that are included in the two states. Notice that the LoginForm.mxml component includes a reference to the state to be included in, as well as the position based on state, for instance:

```
includeIn=" ForgetPasswordState"
left.ForgetPasswordState="51"
```

The component ID property is generic, and we will change the ID properties once we switch to Flex 4.

```
            <FxTextInput left="127" top="79" skinClass="components.TextInput1" ➥
d:userLabel="UserNameTextInput"/>
            <FxTextInput left="127" top="121" skinClass="components.TextInput2" ➥
d:userLabel="PasswordTextInput" includeIn="LoginState" id="fxtextinput1"/>
            <TextGraphic color="0x000000" left="57" text="User Name:" fontSize="12" ➥
fontFamily="Arial" top="86" text.ForgetPasswordState="Email Address:" ➥
left.ForgetPasswordState="51" id="userText" d:userLabel="UserText"/>
            <TextGraphic color="0x000000" left="60" text="Password:" fontSize="12" ➥
 fontFamily="Arial" top="127" includeIn="LoginState" id="passwordText" ➥
d:userLabel="PasswordText"/>
```

```
                    <TextGraphic color="0x000000" left="60" text="Login Form" fontSize="17" ➥
  fontFamily="Arial" top="46" fontWeight="bold" ➥
text.ForgetPasswordState="Forget Password" d:userLabel="HeaderText"/> ➥
                    <FxButton left="219" top="169" skinClass="components.Button2" ➥
label="Login" d:userLabel="LoginButton" includeIn="LoginState" ➥
id="loginTextInput"/>
                    <FxButton left="87" top="169" skinClass="components.Button1" ➥
label="Forget Password" d:userLabel="ForgetPasswordButton" ➥
id="forgetPasswordTextInput" click="currentState='ForgetPasswordState'" ➥
includeIn="LoginState"/>
                    <FxButton includeIn="ForgetPasswordState" left="123" top="120" ➥
skinClass="components.Button3" label="Retrieved Password" ➥
id="retrievedPassButton" d:userLabel="RetrievedPasswordButton"/>
        </DesignLayer>

    </FxApplication>
```

Some components, such as retrievedPassButton, have a skin class that handles how that button looks. That skin class was created when we converted the graphic into components.

Now that we have completed the application you can download the complete application project from the friends of ED web site and compare your code with ours:

    http://www.friendsofed.com/downloads.html

It's LoginForm_2.fxp in this book's Chapter 12 files.

Creating an application with Flash Catalyst and Flex Builder

To show you an example on how to create a Flex application with Flash Catalyst, we will begin with the application we just created to log in, and we'll add data, services, and additional tasks such as refactoring, as well as do a round-trip between Flash Catalyst and Flex 4. The round-trip can demonstrate how you can keep updating your application with Flash Catalyst. Additionally, this simple application will allow you to understand the basics before building a more complex one.

Our previous Flash Catalyst project was saved as a Flash XML Project (FXP) file, and Flex 4 is capable of opening an FXP project.

In Flex 4 select File ➤ Import FXP. Leave the default settings, and click Finish.

> Flash Catalyst saves the projects in the FXP file format. Flex Builder 4 allows you to import and export FXP files.

Notice that a new project was added, and it is called LoginForm. The new project includes LoginForm.mxml as well as the three button components and the two input box components.

Compile and run the project, and you can see the same results you've seen before.

Refactoring the code

The next step after we import the project from Catalyst is to refactor the graphics' names to be more meaningful, so the application is more readable. If we take a look at the package, we can see the LoginForm class as well as the skin classes. Rename all the skin classes as follows:

- Button1.mxml to ForgetPassBtn.mxml
- Button2.mxml to LoginBtn.mxml
- Button3.mxml to RetrievedPassBtn.mxml
- TextInput1.mxml to UserTextInput.mxml
- TextInput2.mxml to PassTextInput.mxml

Make sure to change the skin class in the FxButtons declaration statement in the LoginForm class:

```
<FxButton includeIn="ForgetPasswordState" ➡
skinClass="components.RetrievedPassBtn" />
```

Rename the ID property of the existing components, so the names are more meaningful, and we will be able to use these components better. If you are using the Flash Builder plug-in, you can select the name by double-clicking it and then right-clicking to get the menu. In the menu under Refactor, choose Rename, and in the New name input box, enter the new name. Then select Update references, which scans the project and changes any places that have the old ID name to the new ID name. Update the references for each of the following components too:

- fxtextinput1 to passTextInput
- textgraphic2 to userNameText
- textgraphic1 to passwordText
- fxbutton1 to loginBtn
- fxbutton2 to forgetPasswordBtn
- fxbutton3 to retrievePassBtn

Adding the user authentication service

In order to authenticate user names, we will create a service that will check if the stored user name and password parameters match the user input and reply with true, false, or an error message if necessary.

Let's create a simple PHP script that authenticates users. The PHP script is simple, because we don't want to distract you from this chapter's subject, but feel free to connect to a database if you prefer. In our example, we will place an if. . .else statement to check whether the user name and password are correct.

Take a look at the UserService.php script. It expects the user name and password pairs from the URL, and then it verifies and creates an XML response:

```php
<?php
$user = trim($_REQUEST['user']);
$password = trim($_REQUEST['password']);
```

```php
if ($user == "Elad" && $password == "123")
{
        $status = "true";
        $msg = "";
}
else
{
        $status = "false";
        $msg = "Incorrect user name or password!";
}

$response  = '< response >';
$response .= '<user>';
$response .= '<status>' . $status . '</status>';
$response .= '<message>' . $msg . '</message>';
$response .= '</user>';
$response .= '< /response >';

header("Content-type: text/xml");
echo $response;
?>
```

Post the script on a server (if you have one) or install a PHP engine on your local machine to test the service. Mac OS X 10.5 (Leopard) comes with both Apache and PHP installed. For computers running Windows Vista, you can just enable the service or install PHP under IIS 7 for Vista computers.

To test the service, navigate to the URL of the PHP file, and add the user name and password to the URL:

```
/UserService.php?user=Elad&password=123
```

The response looks like this:

```xml
<response>
    <user>
        <status>true</status>
        <message></message>
    </user>
</response>
```

You can also change the URL to have an incorrect user name and password, and you will get the following XML:

```xml
<response>
    <user>
        <status>false</status>
        <message>Incorrect user name or password!</message>
    </user>
</response>
```

We can now go back to Flex Builder and add the logic to make the request to the new service we just created. Start by creating a Script tag:

```
<Script>
        <![CDATA[
```

The verifyUser method will make the RPC request and set the listeners:

```
                private function verifyUser():void
                {
                        var service:HTTPService = new HTTPService();
                        service.url = " siteURL/UserService.php";
                        service.resultFormat = "e4x";

                        service.addEventListener(ResultEvent.RESULT, ➡
        onResultEvent);
                        service.addEventListener(FaultEvent.FAULT, ➡
        onFaultEvent);

                        service.send({user: userTextInput.text, ➡
        password: passTextInput.text});
                }
```

The onResultEvent method will handle the result using e4x syntax and display the result in an Alert component:

```
        private function onResultEvent(event:ResultEvent):void
                {
                        var xml:XML = event.result as XML;
                        var isVerify:Boolean = (xml.user.status ==  "true") ➡
        ? true : false;

                        var message:String = xml.user.message;

                        Alert.show("Verify: "+isVerify+", ➡
        message: "+message);
                }
```

We will also use an Alert component to handle error results:

```
                private function onFaultEvent(event:FaultEvent):void
                {
                        Alert.show(event.message.toString());
                }
        ]]>
</Script>
```

Last, add a click handler to call the verifyUser method in the loginBtn button:

```
<FxButton id="loginBtn" click="verifyUser()" />
```

Adding incorrect credential and logged in states

At this point, we can go back to Flash Catalyst to add a message to display the error information and create a new state after the user has logged in. To do that, we can export the project back to Flash Catalyst to complete the round-trip.

First, export the project as an FXP to Flash Catalyst. Select File ➤ Export FXP. Select the project location, and save it as LoginForm_3.fxp. Then, click Finish.

Once the project is saved, open the project in Flash Catalyst by double-clicking the LoginForm_3.fxp file.

Duplicate the LoginState state by selecting State on the Pages/States menu and selecting Duplicate State. Name the new state IncorrectUserState. To make room for the new text field for the user message, move the User Name and Password fields and the buttons a few pixels down. Also expand the rectangular box so it fits better (see Figure 12-9).

Notice that, as before, Flash Catalyst handles the animation between the different states. It adds an effect to expand the box and move the component as well as add the text.

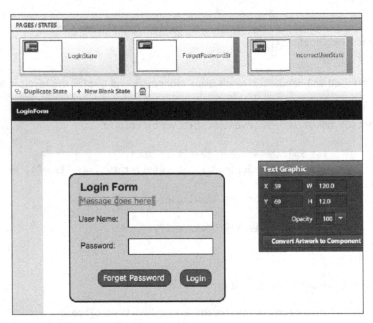

Figure 12-9. IncorrectUserState graphics

Create a new state to hold the graphics and the components you will display once the user has logged in. Call the new state UserLoggedState. Place a text label as a placeholder, so you can recognize that the new state has been added. The reason we leave the message as a placeholder is because we can set our service to return different error messages, based on a logic, such as "Incorrect user name or password," "Couldn't connect to service," or "Account is not active."

We are ready to return to Flex 4 to add logic so the application changes between the two states. Select File ➤ Save As ➤ LoginForm_4.fxp.

You can download and compare the complete application project from the friends of ED web site: http://www.friendsofed.com/downloads.html.

The project is LoginForm_4.fxp, and it's in the files for Chapter 12 of this book.

Open Flex 4, and import the project as a new project. Change the ID property of the new message text label in IncorrectUserState from textgraphic1 to formMessageText.

Change the onResultEvent event handler to change the current state based on the user verification. If the user is not verified, we'll change to the IncorrectUserState state. We'll go to the new placeholder if the user is verified.

```
private function onResultEvent(event:ResultEvent):void
{
    var xml:XML = event.result as XML;
    var isVerify:Boolean = (xml.user.status ==  "true") ➥
? true : false;
    var message:String = xml.user.message;

    if (!isVerify)
    {
        currentState='IncorrectUserState';
        formMessageText.text = message;
    }
    else
    {
        currentState='UserLoggedState';
    }
}
```

Run the application, and you can test different states. We just created a simple application that allows a user to log in and indicates when the user logs in or when login fails. This application can be used as a content management system (CMS) or any application that requires a user to log in.

Creating a mobile application with Catalyst and AIR

Now that you have practiced some of the basics of working with Flash Catalyst, let's work on a more real-life application. The application allows users to search the YouTube library and display the results, play a video, and download videos to watch while offline. The application can be deployed on a UMPC, a desktop, or a future mobile device that will support the Flash 10 platform.

We will be using a Photoshop graphic file in this example, so begin by downloading the SearchVideo. psd file from this book's Chapter 12 files on the friends of ED web site.

The graphic is very simple, and although I am not a designer, I managed to create it quickly, definitely more quickly than trying to create it as an MXML component. See Figure 12-10 for a screenshot of the application design composition in Photoshop.

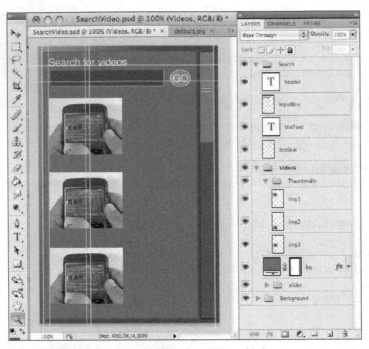

Figure 12-10. SearchVideo.psd's Photoshop CS4 graphic layers

Creating the Flash Catalyst project

Create a new Flash Catalyst project, and select the Adobe Photoshop PSD file import option in the welcome window. Browse to and select the SearchVideo.psd file. When the properties window opens, keep the layers editable, and change the background color to black, as shown in Figure 12-11.

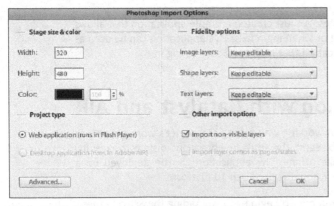

Figure 12-11. Importing an existing project into Flash Catylst

There is also an Advanced button that gives you more properties; if you click it, you can select the layers you would like to import and merge any duplicate layers using the window shown in Figure 12-12. In our application, we don't need to merge or disable any layers, but it's good to be aware of these options.

Explore your work area, which is shown in Figure 12-13. Notice that the layers in Flash Catalyst stay in the same order and structure as in Photoshop. You can see the layers, as well as change the order of each layer, just as you did in Photoshop.

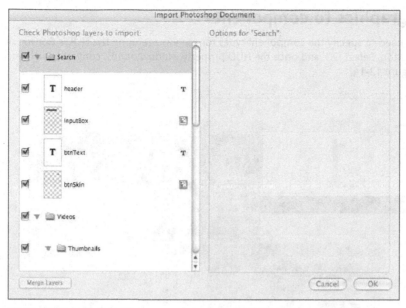

Figure 12-12. In Flash Catalyst, you can choose which layers to import.

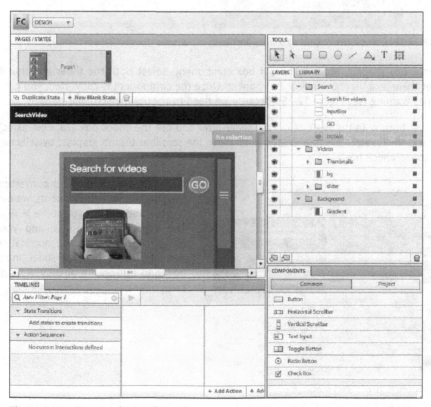

Figure 12-13. Flash Catalyst work area

503

Converting graphics to components

To continue, we need to specify the component types for each image using the HUD's Convert Artwork to Component button. Select GO, and once the HUD property window opens, convert the artwork into a button. See Figure 12-14.

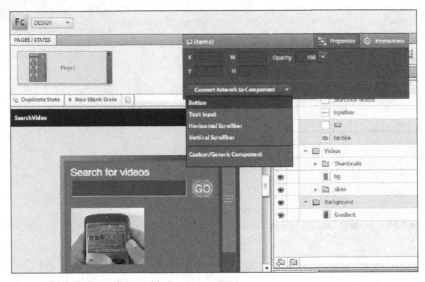

Figure 12-14. Convert the graphic to a component

Convert the input box graphic into a text input box component. Select both the slider and thumb graphics and set them as a Vertical Scrollbar component. Once the component is converted, you get a Component Issues warning (see Figure 12-15), because we need to specify the scrollbar parts.

Click the Edit Parts button. In the HUD, select the slider layer and use the check box Track (Required), to set as the track. Next, select the thumb layer, and assign the scrollbar thumb graphic, by selecting the Thumb (Required) check box.

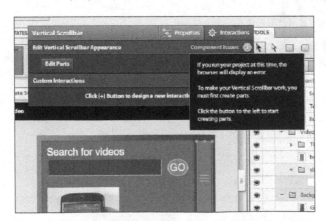

Now that we are finished converting the graphics into components, we can test the application. Select File ➤ Run. The application compiles, and your browser opens with the application running. Notice that the slider, input box, and button are already working components.

Figure 12-15. Component Issues alert message

If you want to change the color of the text input box, you have to switch to code mode using the option in the top-left corner, since design mode doesn't allow you to change the text color. Switch to code view, and change the color. Continue by selecting each text box and switching to code mode to change the colors. While in code mode, you can add the following line of code: color="white". See Figure 12-16.

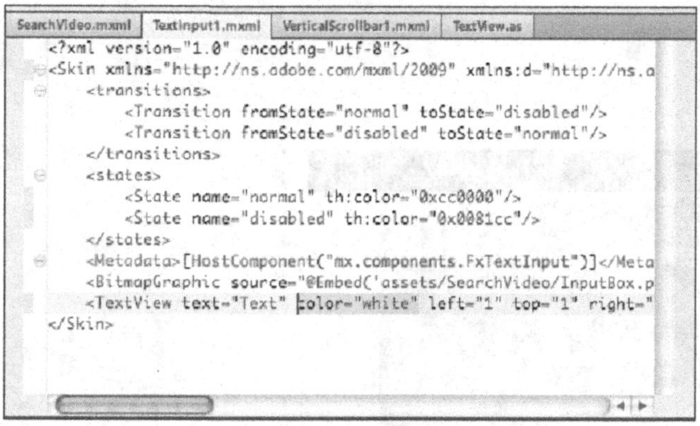

```
SearchVideo.mxml   TextInput1.mxml   VerticalScrollbar1.mxml   TextView.as
        <?xml version="1.0" encoding="utf-8"?>
       <Skin xmlns="http://ns.adobe.com/mxml/2009" xmlns:d="http://ns.a
           <transitions>
               <Transition fromState="normal" toState="disabled"/>
               <Transition fromState="disabled" toState="normal"/>
           </transitions>
           <states>
               <State name="normal" th:color="0xcc0000"/>
               <State name="disabled" th:color="0x0081cc"/>
           </states>
           <Metadata>[HostComponent("mx.components.FxTextInput")]</Meta
           <BitmapGraphic source="@Embed('assets/SearchVideo/InputBox.p
           <TextView text="Text" color="white" left="1" top="1" right="
       </Skin>
```

Figure 12-16. Flash Catalyst TextInput1 code view

Adding FXG graphic elements

For each video item, we need to add a title, a description, stars for reviews, and text that shows the number of users that viewed the video. Creating these items in Flash Catalyst ensures us that they will be created as vector graphics in FXG files using the Flash Drawing API, so we can manipulate them easily.

In order to create the elements follow these steps:

1. To create the title, click the text icon under the Tools pane. Position it on the stage pane, and use the HUD to adjust the following properties:

- Font size: 15
- Color: #fffefe
- Font family: Helvetica

2. Add the description text and set the following properties:

- Font size: 14
- Font color: #d2d2d2
- Font family: Helvetica

3. For the stars, select the star icon in the Tools pane, and position the star. Then, you can replicate the star five times.

4. For the viewed text, set these properties:

- Font color: #e1e1e1
- Font size: 12

5. Create a rectangle, and position it behind the image by moving the rectangle's layer behind the image layer. To move the layer, you can select the layer and use the arrows or drag and drop.

Your final result should look like Figure 12-17.

Figure 12-17. The application in Catalyst with graphics converted to components

Adding button state interactivity

Our next goal is to add buttons' interactivity to the layers. We will convert the buttons' graphics elements into a button component and create a mouse-over effect, as well as a click handler to allow us to play the video in a new page.

To do that, follow these steps:

1. First, we'll convert graphics to components. To convert the text graphic to a button, in the Layers pane, select the button graphic, right-click, and choose Convert selected artwork to. And then select Button.

2. Create states next. Double-click the button component we just created, or click it once and select Edit Button Appearance. Doing so will open the button's state mode, so we can make changes.

3. Next, create the mouse-over state. In the mouse-over state, let's change the background color of the rectangle to orange (#f99911) and change the title to orange.

4. Replicate the buttons. We need to create two more buttons. To do that, you can replicate the existing button by copying and pasting it.

Compile and run the project by selecting File ➤ Run Project, and you can see the changes in your browser. So far, the project in Catalyst should look like the one shown in Figure 12-18.

Figure 12-18.
Catalyst application running in the browser

Creating the detail state

Next, we need to add a new state, the detail state, to be used to play the video the user selects.

Before we can create the detail state, we need to create a new layer for it:

1. Duplicate the layer by selecting Duplicate State in the Pages/States pane.
2. Rename page1 to SearchPage and page2 to DetailPage.

In the detail page, we don't need the Videos layers and the Search layers anymore. We can remove them by deselecting the small blue square in the Layers pane, as shown in Figure 12-19.

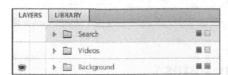

Figure 12-19.
Selecting the Layers pane

This detail state is simple, so we can create it in Flash Catalyst (you could also create it in Photoshop and import it into Catalyst). The detail state includes a placeholder for all these components: video player, title, description, viewed indicator, and stars. Create a new folder in the Layers pane, and call it DetailGraphics. Follow these steps to create the elements for the detail state:

1. To create the video player rectangle, create a black rectangle with a size of 320×240 pixels.

2. Next, we will import a placeholder image for the video player. Select File ➤ Import Artwork. You can find the placeholder in the graphic directory of Chapter 12, on this book's page at the friends of ED web site.

3. Add a title and description with "Lorem ipsum" text as a placeholder, stars for reviews, and more "Lorem ipsum" text for the viewed text component. We are using Helvetica with a light color code of #ebebeb.

> "Lorem ipsum" text is used as dummy text, often used as a placeholder in laying out pages for web sites, magazines, and newspapers.

Your detail page should look like Figure 12-20.

Figure 12-20. The detail page

Adding interactivity between states

At this point, we have completed creating the detail state. Next, we want to add interactivity so we will be able to switch between the search and detail pages.

We have three buttons that are identical and represent the results. To set up the interactions, go back to the search page, and select the first button out of the three. In the HUD, select the Interactions tab. Edit the button's appearance by clicking the plus button on the Custom Interactions line and selecting

On Click. From the Do Action drop-down, select Play transition to state, and from the Choose State drop-down shown in Figure 12-21, select DetailPage.

The first button interactivity is completed. Set the same custom interactions for the other two buttons.

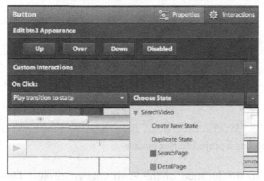

Figure 12-21. The Choose State drop-down

The next section is to create the choreography of the transition effects. We will be using the default transition of fading in and out, but feel free to create any transition you want by selecting the State Transitions and adding a custom action or an object. Next, select the Timelines pane, choose State Transitions from Search Page ➤ Detail Page and from Detail Page ➤ Search Page. Use Default Effects.

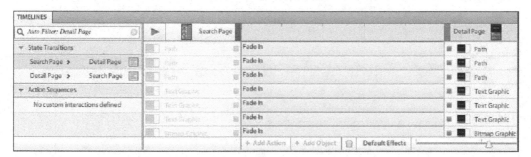

Figure 12-22. Creating transitions

Run the application to see the interactions we added. We can now import our Catalyst application to Flex 4 and add the logic.

Importing the FXP project into Flex Builder 4

Open Flex 4, and select File ➤ Import FXP, as shown in Figure 12-23.

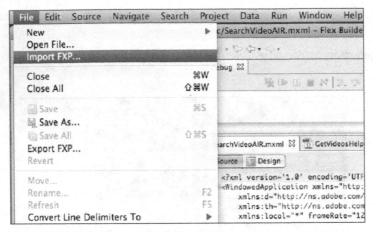

Figure 12-23. Importing a project to Flex Builder

In the next window, navigate to the location of the Flash Catalyst project file, SearchVideo.fxp, and click Finish. A new Flex project opens, and you can compile and run the project to open it in a browser; see Figure 12-24.

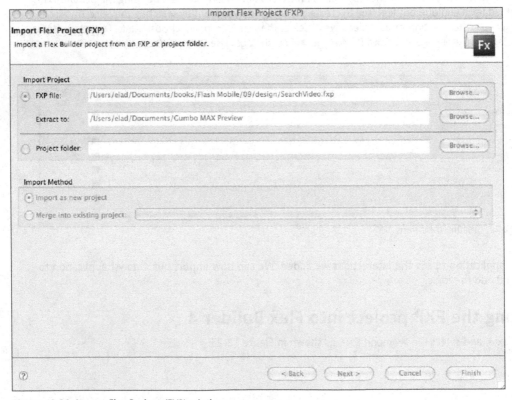

Figure 12-24. Import Flex Project (FXP) window

Converting the project to an Adobe AIR project

In the official release of Flash Catalyst, you will be able to create a project specifically for AIR. For now, we can easily convert the project to an AIR application using the following easy steps:

1. Create a new AIR project by selecting File ➤ New ➤ Flex Project, and call it SearchVideoMobile. Choose Desktop application using Flex 4, and click Finish.

2. Copy the content of the src folder from the Flex project to the AIR project, which should include the following files:

   ■ SearchVideo.mxml: Contains the application presentation layer folder

   ■ Components folder: Contains the component

   ■ Assets folder: Contains the images

3. In SearchVideoMobile.mxml, include the SearchVideo.mxml component <local:SearchVideo />. Make sure to include local in the application namespaces, as follows:

```
xmlns:local="*"
<WindowedApplication xmlns="http://ns.adobe.com/mxml/2009"
        width="320" height="495"
        backgroundColor="0x020303"
        layout="absolute" xmlns:local="*"
        color="0x020303"
        horizontalScrollPolicy="off" verticalScrollPolicy="off">
```

4. Open SearchVideo.mxml, and change the FxApplication tag to the Canvas tag, since we will embed the application in the Adobe AIR container. Once you try to compile, you will get an error message: Type 'BitmapGraphic' declaration must be contained within the <Declarations> tag. The reason is that we need to group these elements in a group container. Add a group container tag, <Group></Group>, after the canvas and before the canvas's ending tag. Make sure you move the states outside the Group tag.

The SearchVideo.mxml component will now contain the component we imported from Flash Catalyst and reflect our changes. Here's the complete code:

```
<?xml version='1.0' encoding='UTF-8'?>
<Canvas xmlns="http://ns.adobe.com/mxml/2009"
        xmlns:d="http://ns.adobe.com/fxg/2008/dt"
        width="320" height="480"
        backgroundColor="0x000000"
        xmlns:th="http://ns.adobe.com/thermo/2009">

        <states>
                <State name="SearchPage" th:color="0xcc0000"/>
                <State name="DetailPage" th:color="0x0081cc"/>
        </states>

        <Group>
            //  FXG graphic tags
        </Group>
</Canvas>
```

SearchVideoMobile.mxml can then be our entry application window and hold the SearchVideo component:

```xml
<?xml version="1.0" encoding="utf-8"?>
<WindowedApplication xmlns="http://ns.adobe.com/mxml/2009"
        width="320" height="495"
        backgroundColor="0x020303"
        layout="absolute" xmlns:local="*"
        color="0x020303"
        horizontalScrollPolicy="off" verticalScrollPolicy="off">

    <local:SearchVideo />

</WindowedApplication>
```

You can now compile and run the AIR application and see the work done in Flash Catalyst, all imported into Flex 4.

Getting the list of YouTube videos

The last step is to add the logic to the application that actually gets the list of videos. We want our application to be able to do a search in YouTube to find videos as well as play the selected videos.

To retrieve videos from YouTube, we will be using as3youtubelib, which you can download here: http://code.google.com/p/as3youtubelib/.

The as3youtubelib API uses YouTube feeds to get a list of videos based on criteria such as keywords, user, category, and popularity. The as3youtubelib API is packed with many packages that you don't really need, but you can copy only the ones you do need:

- Copy and paste the ca.newcommerce package under the src directory.
- You also need the JSON libraries which are included in the as3youtubelib file com.adobe. serialization.json.

Getting YouTube feeds with our utility class

We will implement the as3youtubelib API. To do that, we will create two utilities classes in the course of this section:

- GetVideoList.as: This class will retrieve the list of videos. It uses the as3youtubelib API to get a list of videos based on criteria such as keywords.
- ExtractFLVFromYouTube.as: This class will extract the URL of the FLV, since YouTube is hiding the URL of the videos. This class calls a proxy file created in PHP, which extracts the URL.

Let's take a look at these classes.

GetVideoList is the utility class that we will be using to call as3youtubelib to retrieve the video list. The class will extend the EventDispatcher so we can dispatch events once we complete our task.

The default constructor sets the event listeners from the YouTubeFeedClient class:

```
feedClient = YouTubeFeedClient.getInstance();
 feedClient.addEventListener(VideoFeedEvent.VIDEO_DATA_RECEIVED, ➡
feedsEventHandler);
feedClient.addEventListener(StandardVideoFeedEvent. ➡
STANDARD_VIDEO_DATA_RECEIVED,
```

Next, we have methods that are exposed to allow us to search for videos: GetVideosList, getTopRated, getMostViewed, getVideosBasedOnSearch, and getRecentlyFeatured. These methods call a request that will bring the YouTube feeds:

```
public function getMostViewed():void
{
        requestId = feedClient.getStandardFeed( ➡
YouTubeFeedClient.STD_MOST_VIEWED, "", 1, maxFeedLength);
}

public function getVideosBasedOnSearch(searchTerm:String):void
{
        requestId = feedClient.getVideos(searchTerm, "", ➡
null, null, null, null,"relevance", "exclude", 1, maxFeedLength);
}
```

When the request is completed, the feedsEventHandler method handles the event and sets a local value object (VO) that holds only the information we need to keep it lightweight.

```
private function feedsEventHandler(event:*):void
{
                    var feed:VideoFeed = event.feed;
                    var videoCollection:ArrayCollection = ➡
new ArrayCollection();
                    var videoData:VideoData;

                    while (videoData = feed.next())
                    {
                        var thumbnailIterator:ThumbnailIterator = ➡
videoData.media.thumbnails;
                        var thumbnailData:ThumbnailData;
                        var thumbArray:Array = [];

                        while(thumbnailData = ➡
thumbnailIterator.next() )
                        {
                                thumbArray.push(thumbnailData.url);
                        }

                        var youTubeVideo:YouTubeVideoVO = ➡
new YouTubeVideoVO(videoData.title, videoData.content , ➡
thumbArray[0], videoData.actualId, videoData.viewCount.toString()); ➡
                        videoCollection.addItem( youTubeVideo );
                    }
```

```
                                    if (videoCollection.length > 0)
                                    {
                                            this.dispatchEvent(new VideoListRetrievedEvent(➥
        VideoListRetrievedEvent.LIST_RETRIEVED, videoCollection));
                                    }
                }
```

Notice that we have created a simple custom event, so we can pass the video list collection:

```
        package com.elad.youtube.events
        {
                import flash.events.Event;

                public class FlvExtractedEvent extends Event
                {
                    public static var FLV_URL_EXTRACTED:String = ➥
        "flvURLExtracted";

                        public var flvURL:String;

                        public function FlvExtractedEvent(type:String, ➥
        flvURL:String)
                        {
                                super(type);
                                this.flvURL = flvURL;
                        }
                }
        }
```

Extracting the FLV from the YouTube utility class

Even though we've received the YouTube video information, we are not finished yet. YouTube services are hiding the video's URL. However, we can use a proxy to find the URL so we can play the videos as well as download them to watch once we go offline. Let's create a new class called ExtractFLVFromYouTube that will use a PHP proxy to extract the FLV file from YouTube. YouTube exposes an ID and then uses that ID as a primary key to find the video to play. Our proxy, getVideoId.php, does exactly the same thing. Take a look:

```php
<?php
$url = trim($_REQUEST['url']);
if (strpos($url, 'http://www.youtube.com/watch?v=') === 0)
{
    $ch = curl_init();

    curl_setopt($ch, CURLOPT_URL, $url);
    curl_setopt($ch, CURLOPT_HEADER, false);
    curl_setopt($ch, CURLOPT_RETURNTRANSFER, true);

    $info = curl_exec($ch);
```

```php
    $pos1 = strpos($info, "&video_id=", $pos1);
    $pos2 = strpos($info, "&t=", $pos2);

    $video_id = substr($info, $pos1 + 10, 11);
    $tag_t = substr($info, $pos2 + 3, 32);

    $response  = '<video>';
    $response .= '<id>' . $video_id . '</id>';
    $response .= '<t>' . $tag_t . '</t>';
    $response .= '</video>';

    header("Content-type: text/xml");

    echo $response;

    curl_close($ch);
} else
{
    die("Wrong URL / Parameters");
}
?>
```

Next, we need a simple utility class to which we can pass the YouTube ID and receive the parameters needed to get the video. We will be extending EventDispatcher, so we can dispatch an event once we are finished.

We need to expose only one method in the EventDispatcher class. The method we will be exposing will be using the remote procedure call (RPC) HTTP service to send a request to the PHP service script we created and receive the XML response back with the URL of the FLV file. The PHP scripts have extracted the exact URL of the FLV file in YouTube, which we can use in our Flex application to stream the video.

Notice that we are using the e4x result format, so we can easily get the parameters we need using object style notation:

```actionscript
public function getFLVURL(value:String):void
{
    service = new HTTPService();
    service.method = "GET";
    service.url = "http://YourServer/getVideoId.php?url= ➡
http://www.youtube.com/watch?v="+value;
    service.resultFormat="e4x";
    service.showBusyCursor=true;
    service.addEventListener(ResultEvent.RESULT, resultHandler);
    service.addEventListener(FaultEvent.FAULT, faultHandler);
    service.send();
}
```

Adding logic to the Flash Catalyst application

Now that we have everything we need, we can replace the placeholders with real information. The best approach would be to use test-driven development (TDD) with the presentation model, which we will cover in Chapter 14, but for now, we are going to implement this project with the fastest and easiest way since this is a proof-of-concept (POC) example and not production-grade code.

The two Bindable properties will hold the video URL and the video list collection:

```
[Bindable]
public var videoUrl:String;

[Bindable]
public var videoList:ArrayCollection = new ArrayCollection();
```

We are adding a method to allow us to retrieve the video list for the first time. The method will be used after both of these: the user runs the application and performs a search. Notice that we are referencing the keywordTextInput component, which is our text input. We have changed the text input ID to a more readable name. To change the ID number, you can search the code or use the design view in Flex Builder, as shown in Figure 12-25.

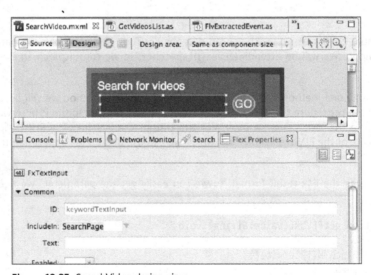

Figure 12-25. SearchVideo design view

In the following code, notice that we used the component subclass keywordTextInput.textView.text to get the text property from the component:

```
public function getVideoList():void
{
    var keywords:String = keywordTextInput.textView.text;
    var getVideo:GetVideosList = new GetVideosList();

    getVideo.addEventListener(VideoListRetrievedEvent.LIST_RETRIEVED, ➡
videoListRetrievedEventHandler);
```

```
        if (keywords == "")
           getVideo.getMostViewed();
        else
           getVideo.getVideosBasedOnSearch(keywords);
    }
```

Our next task is to handle the reply from the utility classes and set the information in the component. The videoListRetrievedEventHandler event handler sets the video list.

```
    private function videoListRetrievedEventHandler(event: ➡
    VideoListRetrievedEvent):void
    {
       videoList = event.videoList;
    }
```

The extractVideoURLEventHandler event handler sets the flv url.

```
    private function extractVideoURLEventHandler(event: ➡
    FlvExtractedEvent):void
    {
       videoUrl = event.flvURL;
    }
```

Our last method sets the detail page once a user clicks a video, based on the index of the video clicked. The method also calls the event to retrieve the video's URL:

```
    /*
     * Method gets video based on user interaction and sets detail page.
     */
    private function getVideo(index:Number):void
    {
       var extract:ExtractFlvFromYouTube = new ExtractFlvFromYouTube();
       var youTubeVideo:YouTubeVideoVO = videoList.getItemAt(index) ➡
    as YouTubeVideoVO;

       videoDetailTitle.text = youTubeVideo.title;
       detailPageDescription.text = youTubeVideo.description;
       videoDetailViewed.text = youTubeVideo.viewed + " viewed";

       extract.addEventListener( FlvExtractedEvent.FLV_URL_EXTRACTED, ➡
    extractVideoURLEventHandler);
       extract.getFLVURL(youTubeVideo.urlID);
    }
```

Notice that we set the following friendly ID names for the detail page:

- videoDetailTitle for the detail page title
- detailPageDescription for the description
- videoDetailViewed for the viewed text

We need to bind some properties in the FXG skins and components to display the data. In SearchResults.mxml, add the following code:

```
<DesignLayer d:userLabel="Thumbnails">
  <FxButton id="btn1" left="20" top="335"
    content="{videoList.getItemAt(0)}"
    skinClass="components.Button5"
   click="currentState='DetailPage';
   getVideo(0)" includeIn="SearchPage" />
  <FxButton id="btn2" left="22" top="211"
    content="{videoList.getItemAt(1)}"
    skinClass="components.Button5"
    click="currentState='DetailPage'; getVideo(1)"
    includeIn="SearchPage"/>
  <FxButton id="btn3" left="22" top="87"
    content="{videoList.getItemAt(2)}"
    skinClass="components.Button5"
    click="currentState='DetailPage'; getVideo(2)"
    includeIn="SearchPage"/>
</DesignLayer>
```

We are passing the video VO to the skin through the content property, and then, in the skin, we can assign the properties. Take a look at the skin class that was created automatically by Catalyst, components.Button5.

Using design view, we can easily identify the properties and assign the VO properties using the Bindable tag, for instance, {hostComponent.content.title}, which is shown in Figure 12-26.

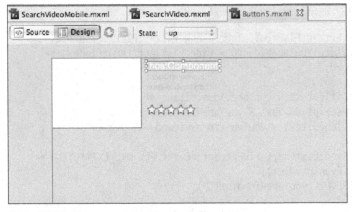

Figure 12-26. The components class in design view

Compile and run the application, and you can test the functionality; Figures 12-27 and 12-28 show the application's search results and detail pages.

Figure 12-27. The completed application's search results page

Figure 12-28. The completed application's detail page

Signing your AIR application

Now that we have completed our AIR application, we want to be able to ship and distribute it. AIR applications are distributed as an `.air` file that is basically a zipped folder containing the application and necessary files. To generate an AIR file, we must digitally sign the application. Singing the application allows developers (publishers) to deliver applications while ensuring that the client on the local machine will not be abused.

Here are your options for digitally signing the application:

- Sign your application with an untrusted certificate, which will result in a warning message when users install your application. This is a good option for testing purposes.

- Once your application is ready for release, we recommend that you sign it using an authorized certificate authority (CA).

- You can also create an AIR intermediate (AIRI) file, which can then be signed by someone within the organization who has the proper credentials. If someone else purchases the certification, that person needs to convert the AIRI file into a `.p12/pfx` file for the developer to use. An AIRI file can also be generated by a CA.

To test your application, you can either sign it yourself or use the AIR Debug Launcher (ADL) tool, which was shipped with Flex Builder to run the AIR application, as explained in the next section. To sign your application, you can also use the ADT command line, which was shipped with the Flex SDK.

Signing your application with Flex Builder

To sign and distribute your production-quality application, you can purchase a certificate. However, during development, you might not want to go through that process or pay the fee, so the easiest way for you sign the application is to use Flash Builder.

Select Project ➤ Export Release Version. The first window that opens, shown in Figure 12-29, allows you to include source code and other properties.

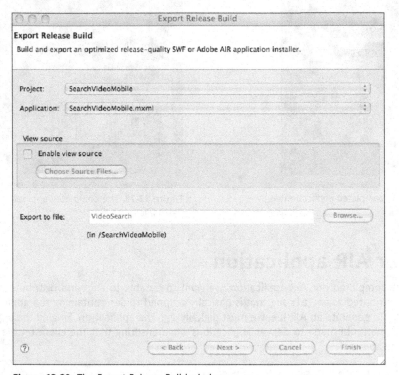

Figure 12-29. The Export Release Build window

After selecting your properties, such as Export to file location, click Next. The next window allows you to select the certificate you want to use; see Figure 12-30.

You can generate one of the three certificates: an untrusted certificate, a certificate from a CA, or an AIRI file. To sign the application using a CA, just browse to the certificate file. To generate an untrusted, self-signed certificate (see Figure 12-31), use the Generate button.

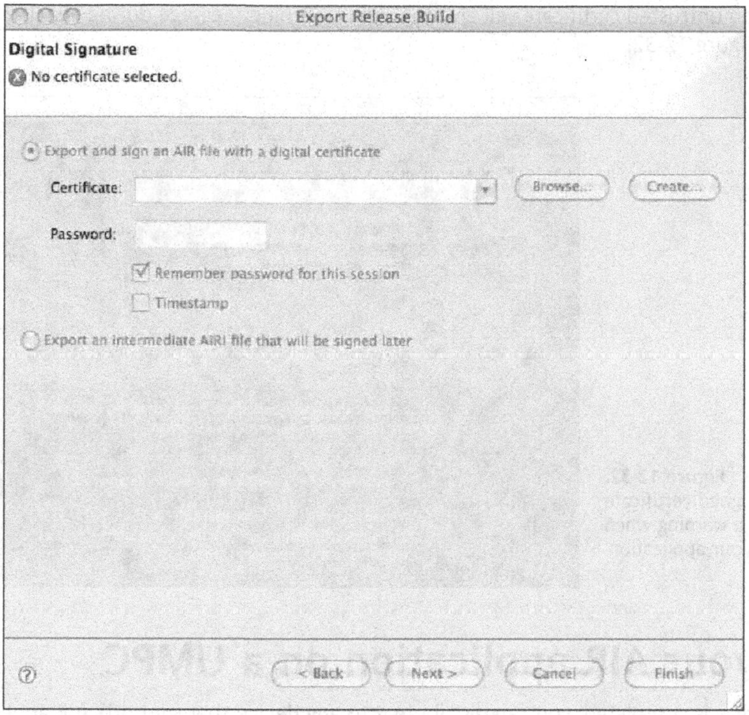

Figure 12-30. Selecting your certificate

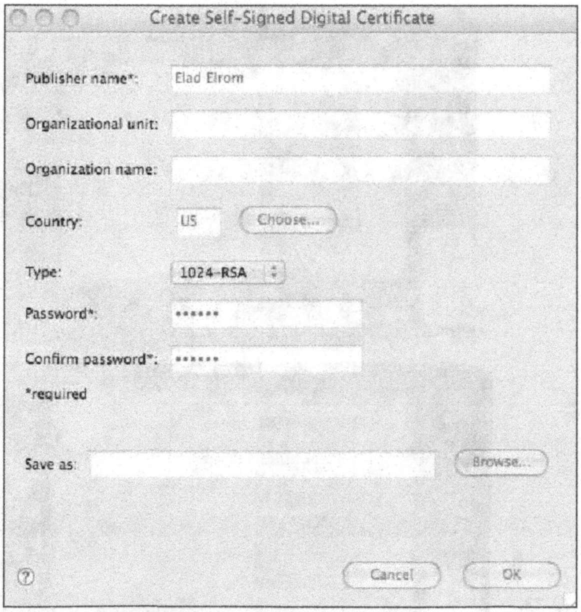

Figure 12-31. Signing your application

Keep in mind that an untrusted certificate will give the user a warning message during installation, like the one shown in Figure 12-32.

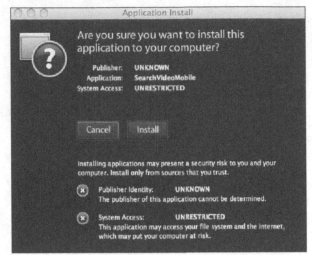

Figure 12-32.
Using a self-signed certificate will result in a warning when users install your application.

Deploying your AIR application on a UMPC

Once your application is completed, you can distribute it to any device that supports AIR applications, such as a UMPC or a Mac, Windows, or Linux desktop. The application is shown running on a UMPC in Figure 12-33.

Figure 12-33.
The video application installed on a UMPC

We've made the complete AIR application available for download at the following URL:

```
http://www.adobe.com/cfusion/exchange/index.cfm?
event=extensionDetail&loc=en_us&extid=1729023
```

Summary

Flash Catalyst, Adobe's new tool for creating FXP projects, can be used to build applications that follow the new design-centric development cycle. Using Flash Catalyst, a development cycle that consists of a round-trip workflow between Adobe CS4, Flash Catalyst, and Flex 4 is possible. Additionally, the development of interfaces becomes faster, easier, and more consistent with the graphic composition.

In this chapter, we started by giving you an overview of the tool, what panels are available and some basic capabilities. We continued by showing you how to create graphics and convert these graphics into components. Next, we showed you how to add actions to components and choreography to your application. After the design work was completed, we switched to Flex 4 and showed you how to add data, services, and logic, as well as how to complete a round-trip between Flex and Catalyst. Later in this chapter, we created a useful Adobe AIR application based on YouTube's library that allows users to search for videos and play selected videos.

In the next chapter, we will further explore how to adopt Flex and Catalyst for mobile devices. We will be creating an application that uses the same code and uses different dynamic graphical GUIs for different devices.

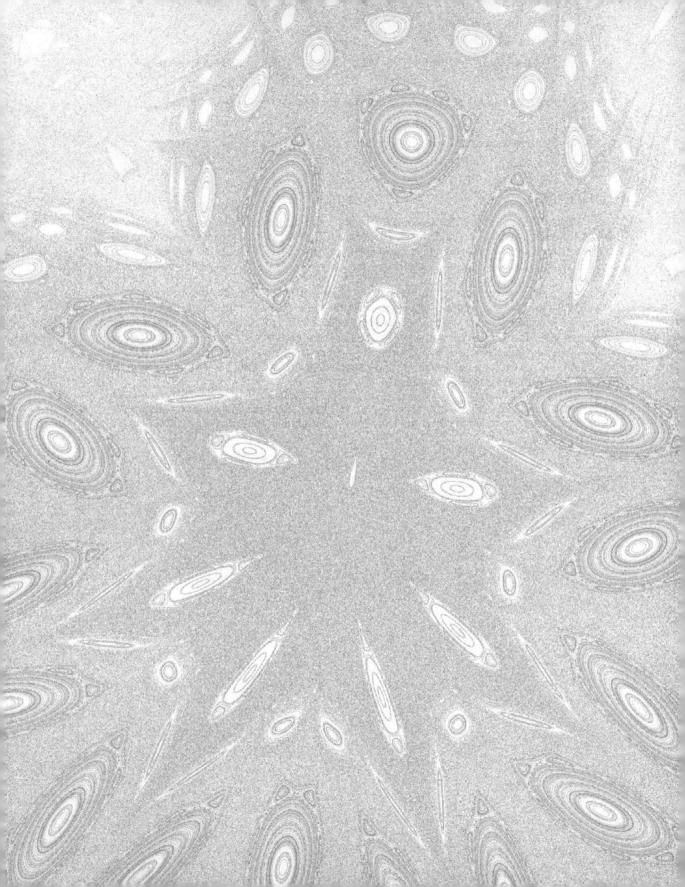

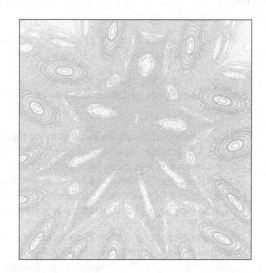

Chapter 13

ADOPTING FLEX FOR MULTIPLE DEVICES

Adobe announced at the GSM Association Mobile World Congress in 2009 that Flash Player 10 will be available on smart phones running Windows Mobile, Google Android, Nokia S60 Symbian, and Palm Pre.

These mobile devices with Flash Player 10 are expected to hit the market starting early in 2010. However, let's keep things in perspective. Flash Lite is deployed on 1.4 billion phones and not every phone will be Flash 10–capable; only a fraction of the mobile devices currently in use will support Flash 10. So although this is exciting news, it may be years before Flash 10 is fully adopted.

> *"GSM" stands for "Global System for Mobile communications"; the abbreviation was coined originally from Groupe Spécial Mobile. GSM represents the most popular standard today for mobile phones worldwide.*

You may be wondering, "Why didn't the iPhone make the list of Flash 10–capable devices?" Well, Adobe already has a version of Flash for the iPhone running on emulation software. And in a recent interview on Bloomberg Television, Shantanu Narayan, chief executive officer of Adobe, had this to say about integrating Flash 10 on the iPhone, "It's a hard technical challenge, and that's part of the reason Apple and Adobe are collaborating. . . The ball is in our court. The onus is on us to deliver."

We believe that the challenge in bringing Flash 10 to any mobile device lies primarily in the obvious mobile constraints we talked about in Chapter 10, such as limited resources, platform awareness, and adaptation.

Taking desktop applications and deploying them on a mobile device with the use of Flash 10 APIs such as the 3-D graphics, sound, and video (see Chapter 9 for an overview of Flash 10 APIs) can quickly drain the battery and cause poor performance. Adobe is working on creating a version of Flash 10 that has reduced functionality and has some additional APIs that will be able to tap into the touch screen as well as the GPS or other hardware devices. In fact, the Adobe Experience Team (XD) has already made some progress with multitouch screen applications.

In previous chapters, we covered Adobe AIR and creating an application that can be deployed on multiple devices. In this chapter, we will look at deploying Flex applications on mobile devices such as browsers and Flash 10–capable devices. Specifically, we will show you how to create an application for MID browsers capable of running Flash 9, and then we'll move on to create a dynamic GUI using Flash Catalyst for Flash 10.

Creating a Flex GUI for the Nokia N810 browser

Recall that, in Chapter 11, we created an AIR music player application based on the MP3Tunes service (www.mp3tunes.com). Our application was compiled using Flex to be deployed on a device that supports Flash 9. In this section, we will show how you can easily convert the application to Adobe Flex and deploy it to the Nokia N810, an MID. The deployment will be on the device's browser, which currently only supports Flash Player 9, so we will be using the Flex 3 SDK.

To convert the Adobe AIR application, MP3TunesAIR, to Adobe Flex, follow this simple process:

1. Create a new Flex project by selecting File ➤ New ➤ Flex Project. For the application name, use MusicPlayer.

2. Copy the MusicPlayer/src/com and MusicPlayer/src/asset folders from MP3TunesAIR to MusicPlayer.

3. Copy the MP3TunesAIR.mxml file's content to MusicPlayer.mxml.

4. In MusicPlayer.mxml change the root tag from mx:WindowedApplication to mx:Application.

5. As we will be creating different views, we will distinguish them according to the device width and height, so change the package name from desktop to W695H362.

Compile and run the application. The application is shown deployed on the Nokia N810 in Figure 13-1.

Figure 13-1. Music player application deployed on the Nokia N810

Creating dynamic GUIs using Flash Catalyst

So far, our application can accommodate Flash Player 9. In this section, we will use the same logic and create a view to be deployed on devices supporting Flash Player 10. Creating a Flash 10 application will allow us to use Flash Catalyst, a powerful tool that can help us address mobile device constraints by creating different skins and states with different functionalities and taking a round-trip between Illustrator and Flex builder. Taking a round-trip in Catalyst means that we can import a PSD or an AI file into Flash Catalyst and then export the project as a Flash XML Project (FXP). Flash Builder 4 beta allows importing FXP files so designers and developers can work in parallel.

Creating different views fits the new model of Flex 4 SDK and Catalyst, since we are moving to a designer-centric paradigm where we can easily take round-trips between Illustrator and Flex. The programmer is responsible for the model and logic, and the designer can create the visual design as well as the behavior of the component. See Chapter 12 for more information.

Using Illustrator, we will take the skin that we used previously and import it into Flash Catalyst. In Catalyst, we can generate an MXML file that includes the new declarative FXG language. The MXML will include the component skins as well as the behavior of the different components in the current view. Once we complete creating the MXML files in Catalyst, we will import them into Flash Builder and integrate them into the Passive Multiview design pattern.

> To use the techniques shown in this chapter, you will need to have Flash Catalyst and Flex Builder 4 (formerly code-named Gumbo). Installing Illustrator CS4 is optional but recommended.

Creating a GUI for a 320×480-pixel screen with Catalyst

The design document for this section's example was created in Adobe Illustrator CS4. The decision to choose Illustrator was driven by the advantage of importing vector art into Catalyst, which will allow creating vector paths using FXG. The vector path is then rendered using the Drawing API during runtime, which will increase performance compared to what we could get using images, since images have to be loaded.

To view the Illustrator file, you can download a trial version of Adobe Illustrator CS4 from the Adobe web site: http://www.adobe.com/products/illustrator/. Note that only Illustrator CS4 allows converting a pixel file into the FXG format, which you'll need to do for this example.

The first view we will be creating using Catalyst will be sized at 320×480 pixels, which will fit mobile devices with this screen size, including the Blackberry 9000, the iPhone, and the iPod Touch.

Importing the Illustrator file into Catalyst

We won't go into too many details on how the design document was created, since this is not a design book, but we do want you to notice that components are grouped together in their own layer. Once we import into Flash Catalyst, that layered structure will stay the same.

Download and open MusicPlayer320x480.ai in Adobe Illustrator. The MusicPlayer320x480.ai design document can be downloaded from this book's page on the friends of ED web site from the Chapter 13 ➤ Illustrator link.

Once you download the design document, you can open it in Illustrator (see Figure 13-2), though doing so is not necessary, since you can just import it into Flash Catalyst.

Figure 13-2. Music player in Illustrator CS4

Importing artwork into Flash Catalyst

Let's now import the artwork into Flash Catalyst:

1. Once the welcome page opens, select Create New Project from Design File ➤ From Adobe Illustrator AI File.

2. When the browser menu opens, browse to the AI file MusicPlayer320x480.ai.

3. In the Illustrator Import Options window, keep the default settings, and click OK to complete the import (see Figure 13-3).

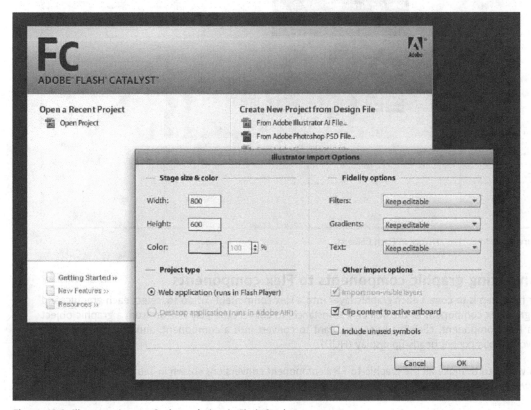

Figure 13-3. Illustrator Import Options window in Flash Catalyst

In the Tools window (see Figure 13-4), you can see that all the layers we created in Illustrator CS4 have been imported successfully into Flash Catalyst.

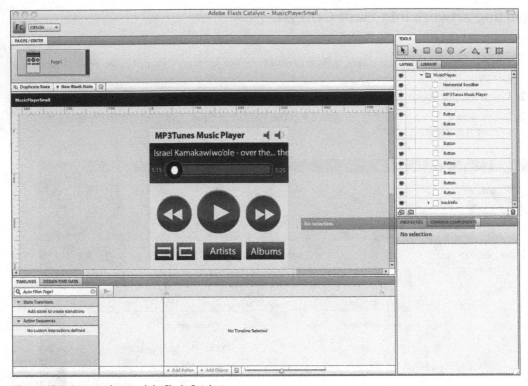

Figure 13-4. Imported artwork in Flash Catalyst

Converting graphic components to Flex components

Our next step is to covert each graphic layer into a Flex component. To do so, select each graphic, and assign a Flex component to the object. For instance, to convert the play button from a graphic object to a Flex component, click the layer you want to convert into a component, and select the Convert Artwork to component heads-up display (HUD).

You will need to make all the graphic-to-Flex component conversions shown in Table 13-1. Figure 13-5 shows the components highlighted within the view.

Table 13-1. Converting graphics to Flex components for the 320×480 view

Layer Name	Component Type	Functionality Description
MP3Tunes Music Player	Text graphic	Application header
volumeMin and volumeMax	Button	Volume adjustment
trackInfo	Group of text graphics	Track information
01:15 and 05:25	Text graphic	Track time information
rewindButton	Button	Rewind button
fastForwardButton	Button	Fast forward button

Layer Name	Component Type	Functionality Description
playButton	Button	Play button
randomButton	Button	Random song button
replayButton	Button	Replay song button
artistsButton	Button	Artist selection button
albumButton	Button	Album selection button

Note that each button component has four states: Up, Over, Down, and Disabled. Select the button, and in the HUD, you can set the different states. In our case, we will keep it simple and keep one state, instead of setting all four.

> For more information regarding how to convert graphics to Flex components, please refer to the previous chapter. Chapter 13 includes introductions as well as advanced topics that you should be familiar with before working through this section.

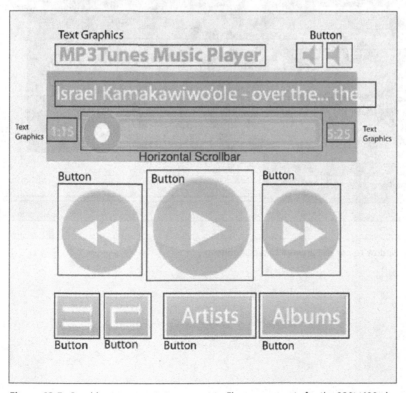

Figure 13-5. Graphic components to convert to Flex components for the 320×480 view

Converting the slider graphic into MXML components

In addition to the component specified in Table 13-1, we also need to create the slider for the song track, which will be created using the horizontal scrollbar control. To create the horizontal scrollbar, select the thumb and skin artwork using your keyboard or mouse, and in the HUD, select Convert Artwork to Component ➤ Horizontal Scrollbar (see Figure 13-6).

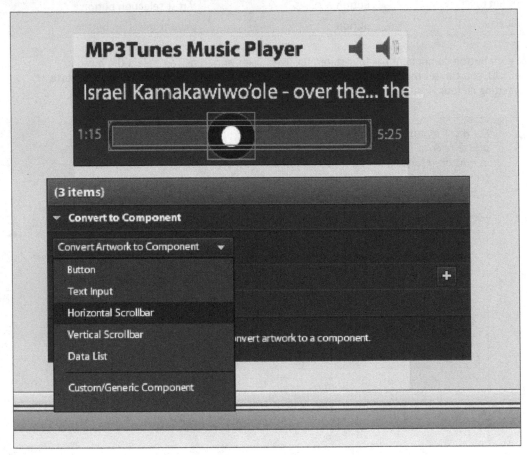

Figure 13-6. HUD window to convert artwork to a component

Once the graphic component is converted to a Flex component, we need to specify the thumb and the track graphics. Click Edit Parts. Once you zoom into the component, you can set the thumb and track. In the HUD, select Assign Parts ➤ Convert Artwork to Horizontal Scrollbar Part ➤ Thumb. Then do the same with the Track.

We have now finished the design part of our application, so we are ready to integrate this view with the music application. Save the project as MusicPlayer320x480.fxp. After creating the view for the 530×520-pixel screen size, we will take the FXP files and import them into Flash Builder 4 beta.

Creating a GUI for a 530×520-pixel screen with Catalyst

The next view we will create will fit into 530×520 pixels. We can deploy this view on larger screens such as Windows, Mac, or Linux desktops and laptops. To create the view in Illustrator, we can take the Illustrator file we previously created and stretch some of the graphics elements to fit a bigger size screen. Since we have more width, we will add a volume slider in addition to the volume increment/decrement buttons for a better user experience (see Figure 13-7). The artwork MusicPlayer530x520.ai is available from this book's page on the friends of ED web site, in Chapter 13's Illustrator folder (http://www.friendsofed.com/downloads.html).

Figure 13-7. Illustrator screenshot of the 530×520 pixel view

Open Flash Catalyst. Create a new application, name it MusicPlayer530x520.fxp, and import the Illustrator file into Catalyst (see Figure 13-8).

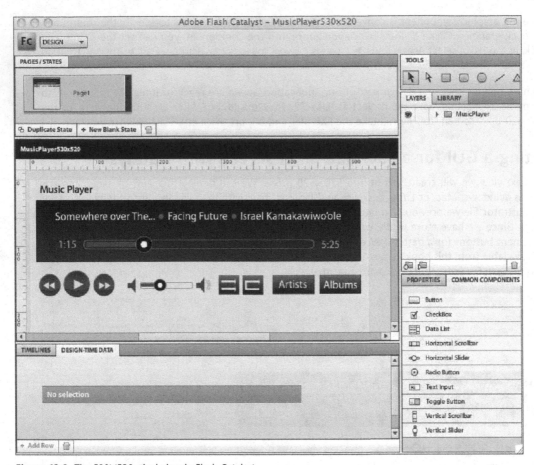

Figure 13-8. The 530×520-pixel view in Flash Catalyst

Converting graphic components to Flex components

To convert the graphic components to Flex components, follow the same process as for the 320×480-pixel view. Table 13-2 shows to what component you should convert each graphic, and the components are highlighted in Figure 13-9.

Table 13-2. Converting graphics into Flex components for the 530×520-pixel view

Layer Name	Component Type	Functionality Description
Music Player	Text graphic	Application header
trackInfo	Group of text graphics	Track information
01:15 and 05:25	Text graphic	Track time information
rewindButton	Button	Rewind button
fastForwardButton	Button	Fast forward button
playButton	Button	Play button
randomButton	Button	Random song button
replayButton	Button	Replay button
artistsButton	Button	Artists selection button
albumButton	Button	Album selection button
artistsButton	Button	Artist selection button
albumButton	Button	Album selection button

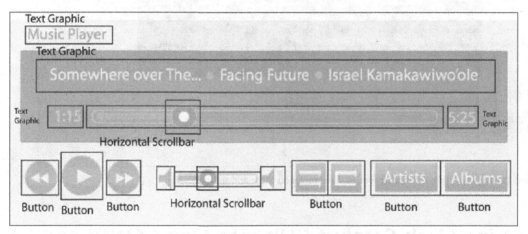

Figure 13-9. Graphic components to Flex component for the 530×520-pixel view

Converting sliders graphics into MXML components

As in the previous view, we need to create the horizontal scrollbar control for the song track slider. To create the horizontal scrollbar, select the thumb and skin artwork, and in the HUD, select Convert Artwork to Component ➤ Horizontal Scrollbar.

The main difference between the 320×480-pixel view and this one (other than different size graphics) is that, in this view, we create a volume slider to allow the user to control the volume in addition to the increment and decrement buttons. To convert the slider for the volume component, click Edit Parts. Once you zoom into the component, you can set the thumb and track. In the HUD, select Assign Parts ➤ Convert Artwork to Horizontal Scrollbar Part. Then, click the Thumb and Track options (see Figure 13-10).

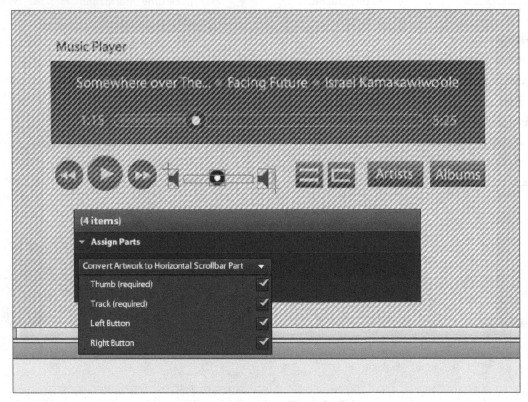

Figure 13-10. Converting graphic artwork to a horizontal scrollbar and splitting parts

Importing Flash Catalyst GUIs into Flex 4 SDK

Now that we have finished creating the design and views of our application, we are ready to integrate the views we created in Flash Catalyst into the application we built in Chapter 11. The integration between Flex 4 SDK and Catalyst is seamless, and we can import the entire project we created in Flash Catalyst. Once we have imported our application into Flex 4 SDK, we will take the Catalyst project and integrate the Passive Multiview pattern, so we can have the same application with different views to fit different screen sizes.

Importing the FXP project

The first step in the process is to import the FXP project we created in Flash Catalyst. We saved the Flash Catalyst projects as FXP files, and fortunately, Flex 4 SDK is capable of opening FXP files and importing them into the work area. Once the project is imported, you can compile and run it.

To import the FXP files into Flex 4 SDK to create projects, follow these steps:

1. Select File ➤ Import FXP.
2. Leave the default settings.
3. Select Finish.
4. Repeat steps 1 to 3 for both FXP applications (MusicPlayer530x520.fxp and MusicPlayer320x480.fxp) we completed in Flash Catalyst.

The file structure of the two projects is shown in Figure 13-11. Notice that the application contains the application entry point MusicPlayer320x480. mxml and a component folder that holds all the components skins and components we created in Flash Catalyst.

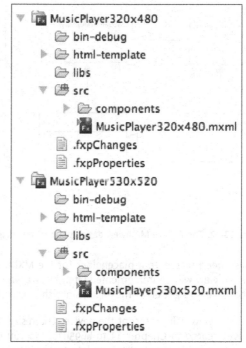

Figure 13-11. A tree view of the FXP projects imported into Flex 4 SDK

Implementing the Passive Multiview design pattern

Recall from Chapter 11 that we used the Passive Multiview design pattern to create the music player application. Figure 13-12 shows the UML diagram for this pattern. The creator uses the Factory pattern to find out which view (product) to use and pushes that view into the Presenter to create a composition. The SubPresenter and SubViews can be used by the main views.

The application we created in Flash Catalyst is the subview and will be referenced by the main view, which you can think of as a product in the Factory pattern. The creator will create a new composition based on the different main view we will include.

We will add two new packages for the views:

- src/com/elad/mp3tunes/view/W320H480
- src/com/elad/mp3tunes/view/W530H520

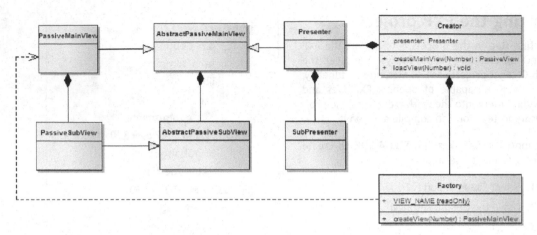

Figure 13-12. The Passive Multiview design pattern UML diagram

We also need to create a placeholder for the MXML component MusicPlayerMain in each package. The main view will be implemented later, but we want to insert a placeholder, so don't be surprised if you compile and get error messages, since the main view doesn't extend the abstract main view yet.

Each main view will represent the device screen size. We recommend refactoring the package for the view we created in Chapter 11 to W695H362, so you can easily find the view you want based on the device screen size. Here's the complete code for the MusicPlayerFactory:

```
package com.elad.mp3tunes.view
{
    import com.elad.mp3tunes.view.W320H480.MusicPlayerMain;
    import com.elad.mp3tunes.view.W530H520.MusicPlayerMain;
    import com.elad.mp3tunes.view.W695H362.MusicPlayerMain;

    import flash.errors.IllegalOperationError;

    public final class MusicPlayerFactory
    {

    /**
    * Music player types enums
    */
    public static const W320H480:int = 1;
    public static const W530H520:int = 2;
    public static const W695H362:int = 3;

    public static function createView(musicPlayerType:Number): ➡
    AbstractMusicPlayerMain
    {
        var retVal:AbstractMusicPlayerMain;
```

```
switch (musicPlayerType)
{
    case W320H480:
        retVal = ➥
        new com.elad.mp3tunes.view.W320H480.MusicPlayerMain;
    break;
    case W530H520:
        retVal = ➥
        new com.elad.mp3tunes.view.W530H520.MusicPlayerMain;
    break;
        case W695H362:
        retVal = ➥
        new com.elad.mp3tunes.view.W695H362.MusicPlayerMain;
    break;
        throw new IllegalOperationError ➥
("The view type " + musicPlayerType + " is not recognized.");
}

    return retVal;
            }
        }
    }
```

Notice that we are using the fully qualified package name, since we have three classes in different packages with the same component name, MusicPlayerMain.

For instance, to set the main view class to be a view of the size of 320✕480 pixels, we use the factory switch that represents the view in the size of 320✕480 pixels. We use the following statement:

```
retVal = new com.elad.mp3tunes.view.W320H480.MusicPlayerMain;
```

Next, we need to add the new views to the creator MusicApplication.mxml. The creator class was explained in detail in Chapter 11. Once the class is completed, the creationComplete method calls the creationCompleteHandler handler, which opens the LoginForm pop-up window. Once the user logs in, we can set the visibility of the HBox to true, so we can select the view we want.

Notice that, in the MusicApplication.mxml class, we created buttons that call the loadView method once the user clicks the buttons and pass the constant of the different views. Once the user chooses a view, we will be able to load it.

The loadView method is the same as the one we created in Chapter 11. We added the buttons, which call the method that allows creating different views based on constants. Once we complete creating our application based on the selected view, we can tie in the creator with the context awareness, so the application automatically chooses which view to use based on the device screen size. For instance, for a device that has a screen that's 1280✕1024 pixels, we can select the largest view available, which is 695✕362 pixels.

Here's the complete code of the MusicApplication.mxml class with buttons for two screen sizes we created in this project and the one we created previously in Chapter 11:

```
<?xml version="1.0" encoding="utf-8"?>
<mx:Application xmlns:mx="http://www.adobe.com/2006/mxml"
    backgroundColor="0xe6e6e6"
    x="0" y="0"
    verticalAlign="middle"
    creationComplete="creationCompleteHandler(event)">

<mx:Style source="assets/css/Main.css" />

<mx:Script>
<![CDATA[
    import com.elad.mp3tunes.view.presenter.MusicPlayerMainPresenter;
    import com.elad.mp3tunes.view.AbstractMusicPlayerMain;
    import com.elad.mp3tunes.view.LoginForm;
    import mx.managers.PopUpManager;
    import mx.containers.TitleWindow;
    import mx.events.FlexEvent;

    import com.elad.mp3tunes.view.MusicPlayerFactory;
    import com.elad.mp3tunes.view.AbstractMusicPlayerMain;

    private var loginForm:LoginForm;
    private var musicPlayerMainPresenter:MusicPlayerMainPresenter;

    // handler after creation complete
    protected function creationCompleteHandler(event:FlexEvent):void
    {
        loginForm = ➥
        LoginForm(PopUpManager.createPopUp(this, LoginForm, true));
        loginForm.addEventListener(LoginForm.LOGIN_SUCCESSFULL, ➥
onLogin);
    }

  // method to load the view
  protected function loadView(type:Number):void
  {
      hBox.visible = false;
      hBox = null;
      var musicPlayerView:AbstractMusicPlayerMain = ➥
      MusicPlayerFactory.createView(type);
      this.addChild(musicPlayerView);

      musicPlayerMainPresenter = ➥
      new MusicPlayerMainPresenter(musicPlayerView);
  }
```

```
            private function onLogin(event:Event):void
            {
                hBox.visible = true;
        }


            ]]>
        </mx:Script>

        <mx:HBox id="hBox" visible="false">
        <mx:Button label="320x480"
            click="loadView(MusicPlayerFactory.W320H480)" />
        <mx:Button label="530x520"
            click="loadView(MusicPlayerFactory.W530H520)" />
        <mx:Button label="695x362"
            click="loadView(MusicPlayerFactory.W695H362)" />
        </mx:HBox>

        </mx:Application>
```

Creating logic for Flash Catalyst applications

Flash Catalyst created for us the subview called MusicPlayer320x480.mxml and a folder named components where all the components we created were placed. The same is true for the other view: we have a subview class named MusicPlayer530x520.mxml and a components folder.

We need to copy all these classes to our existing application and do some name refactoring. We will copy the classes under the com.elad.framework.musicplayer.mp3tunes.view namespace package.

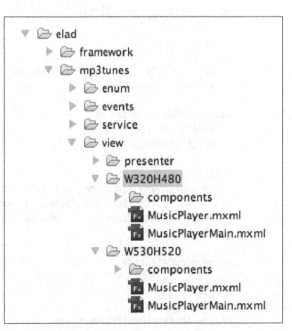

1. Create two new packages: W320H480 and W530H520.

2. Copy the classes and the components folders' content.

3. Rename the subviews MusicPlayer320x480.mxml and MusicPlayer530x520.mxml to the same name MusicPlayer.mxml (it's possible since they sit in different packages).

4. Create an empty Flex MXML component named MusicPlayerMain.mxml, if you haven't done so previously. This will be our main view. Figure 13-13 shows the namespace package structure as it now stands.

Figure 13-13. Tree view of two-view component

Creating the main view, MusicPlayerMain.mxml

The main view for the 530X520 application extends the AbstractMusicPlayerMain class. It includes the subview class MusicPlayer. Additionally, we include the components that are part of the view such as the HorizontalList and the AdvancedDataGrid, so we will be able to navigate between the different songs available.

The code uses the abstract class AbstractMusicPlayerMain and creates the component expected while setting the same ID names as in the abstract class, so the logic will be able to use these components. Notice that these components are passive, meaning have no logic, and are unaware that they are being manipulated.

```
<?xml version="1.0" encoding="utf-8"?>
<view:AbstractMusicPlayerMain xmlns="http://ns.adobe.com/mxml/2009"
   backgroundColor="0xe6e6e6"
   width="530" height="520" x="0" y="0"
   xmlns:view="com.elad.mp3tunes.view.*"
   xmlns:player="com.elad.mp3tunes.view.W530H520.*"
   borderStyle="solid" borderThickness="3"
   horizontalScrollPolicy="off"
   verticalScrollPolicy="off">

<player:MusicPlayer id="musicPlayer" />

<VBox y="190" x="10">

<HorizontalList id="tileList"
   columnWidth="125"
    rowHeight="125"
    columnCount="4"
   itemRenderer="com.elad.mp3tunes.view.W530H520.components. ➥
   TileResultRenderer"/>

<AdvancedDataGrid id="dg"
   width="500" height="180"
   sortExpertMode="true">

<columns>
   <AdvancedDataGridColumn dataField="trackTitle" />
   <AdvancedDataGridColumn dataField="artistName" />
   <AdvancedDataGridColumn dataField="albumTitle" />
</columns>

</AdvancedDataGrid>

</VBox>

</view:AbstractMusicPlayerMain>
```

Notice that we are using the AdvancedDataGrid control. The controller is part of the data visualization SWC; it expands the standard DataGrid control that is included in the Flex framework and adds much more control of the data display, aggregation, and formatting. We have also set the columns we will be using in advance.

The item renders for the HorizontalList points to the TileResultRenderer, which uses the VBox components and creates an image and labels.

Adobe Flex supports many controls to represent lists of items. The list controls are derived from the ListBase superclass, and each list-based class has a default item renderer defined for it, for instance, ListItemRenderer or TileListItemRenderer. The item renderer chooses how to represent each item in the list. The item can be represented in many ways, such as plain text or a combination of an image with text. You can also specify a custom item renderer to handle the representation of each item in the list. For example, this is how we represent the list in TileResultRenderer:

```
<?xml version="1.0" encoding="utf-8"?>
<VBox xmlns="http://ns.adobe.com/mxml/2009"
    horizontalAlign="center"
    verticalGap="0" borderStyle="none">

<Image id="image" width="60" height="60"
    source="assets/images/note.gif"/>
<Label text="{data.name}" width="120" textAlign="center"/>
<Label text="{data.count} song" fontWeight="bold"/>

</VBox>
```

The 320×480-pixel view, which has the same name MusicPlayerMain.mxml, is very similar to the 530×520-pixel view in many ways. It holds the same components and extends AbstractMusicPlayerMain. However, it uses the main view and subview for the 320×480-pixel presentation view and has different style properties and skins:

```
<?xml version="1.0" encoding="utf-8"?>
<view:AbstractMusicPlayerMain xmlns="http://ns.adobe.com/mxml/2009"
    backgroundColor="0xe6e6e6"
    width="320" height="480" x="0" y="0"
    xmlns:view="com.elad.mp3tunes.view.*"
    xmlns:player="com.elad.mp3tunes.view.W320H480.*"
    borderStyle="solid" borderThickness="3"
    horizontalScrollPolicy="off"
    verticalScrollPolicy="off">

<player:MusicPlayer id="musicPlayer" />

<VBox y="312" x="5" width="312">
```

```
<HorizontalList id="tileList"
          columnWidth="125"
          rowHeight="125"
          columnCount="4"
          itemRenderer = ➡
"com.elad.mp3tunes.view.W320H480.components.TileResultRenderer"
          width="309" height="74" y="7"/>


<AdvancedDataGrid id="dg"
          width="306" height="79"
          sortExpertMode="true">

<columns>
<AdvancedDataGridColumn dataField="trackTitle" />
<AdvancedDataGridColumn dataField="artistName" />
<AdvancedDataGridColumn dataField="albumTitle" />
</columns>

</AdvancedDataGrid>

</VBox>

</view:AbstractMusicPlayerMain>
```

Creating the subviews for MusicPlayer.mxml

The subview for the 530✕520-pixel view extends AbstractMusicPlayer and must override the methods we set in the abstract class; otherwise, we will get a compiler error message. The class was mostly created in Flash Catalyst, but we do need to make some changes: we need to set the id property for each component and make some changes to the skin component.

```
<?xml version='1.0' encoding='UTF-8'?>
<view:AbstractMusicPlayer xmlns="http://ns.adobe.com/mxml/2009"
    xmlns:lib="MusicPlayer_library.*"
    xmlns:d="http://ns.adobe.com/fxg/2008/dt"
    xmlns:th="http://ns.adobe.com/thermo/2009"
    xmlns:ai="http://ns.adobe.com/ai/2008"
    xmlns:view="com.elad.mp3tunes.view.*"
    backgroundColor="0xe6e6e6"
    width="530" height="520"
    horizontalScrollPolicy="off"
    verticalScrollPolicy="off">
```

```
<Group d:id="3" d:userLabel="trackInfoBackground"
    top="30.9" left="9.55">
<Group ai:knockout="0" top="0" left="0">
<Path winding="nonZero" ai:knockout="0"
    data="M 506.335 91.07 C 506.335 ➥
91.619 505.886 92.07 505.335 92.07 L ➥
0.975 92.07 C 0.425 92.07 -0.025 91.619 ➥
-0.025 91.07 L -0.025 0.975 C -0.025 0.425 ➥
0.425 -0.025 0.975 -0.025 L 505.335 ➥
-0.025 C 505.886 -0.025 506.335 0.425 ➥
506.335 0.975 L 506.335 91.07 Z"
        top="0.375" left="0.375">
<fill>
<LinearGradient x="252.532" y="94.1411"
    scaleX="116.959"
    rotation="-89.227">
<GradientEntry color="0x333333" ratio="0"/>
<GradientEntry color="0x1a1a1a" ratio="0.429813"/>
<GradientEntry ratio="0.807208"/>
</LinearGradient>
</fill>
</Path>
<Path winding="nonZero" ai:knockout="0" data="M 506.71 91.445 ➥
C 506.71 91.994 506.261 92.445 505.71 92.445 L 1.35 92.445 C ➥
0.8 92.445 0.35 91.994 0.35 91.445 L 0.35 1.35 C 0.35 0.8 0.8 ➥
0.35 1.35 0.35 L 505.71 0.35 C 506.261 0.35 506.71 0.8 506.71 ➥
 1.35 L 506.71 91.445 Z" top="0" left="0">
<stroke>
<SolidColorStroke caps="none" weight="0.75" joints="miter"
    miterLimit="4"/>
</stroke>
</Path>
</Group>
</Group>
```

> *Changes to ID names can be made in Flash Catalyst, but we wanted to show that you have the option to tweak your application in Flex when needed, so it's important to understand the underlying code that gets generated automatically in Flash Catalyst.*

The songInfoText holds the song title. Notice that we removed the following content tag:

```
<content><p><span></span></p></content>
```

The tag was generated in Flash Catalyst, so we will be able to match the Flash 9 format of text properties, since the abstract class expects to manipulate the text property.

```
<Group d:userLabel="trackInfo" top="48.15" left="39.75">
<TextGraphic id="songInfoText" fontFamily="Myriad Pro"
    fontSize="16.7445" text=""
    lineHeight="120%" color="0xe6e6e6"
    whiteSpaceCollapse="preserve"
    kerning="on" ai:knockout="0" top="0" left="0"
    d:userLabel="songInfoText">
</TextGraphic>
```

The currentTimeText and totalTimeText will show the user the total time and progress time. We have removed the content tag here as well to match what the abstract class expects.

```
<TextGraphic id="currentTimeText" fontFamily="Myriad Pro"
    fontSize="16.7445" lineHeight="120%"
    color="0xadacac" whiteSpaceCollapse="preserve"
    kerning="on"
    ai:knockout="0" d:userLabel="currentTimeText"
    top="40" left="0" text="00:00">
</TextGraphic>

<TextGraphic id="totalTimeText" fontFamily="Myriad Pro"
    fontSize="16.7445" lineHeight="120%"
    color="0xadacac"
    whiteSpaceCollapse="preserve" kerning="on"
    ai:knockout="0"
    d:userLabel="totalTimeText" top="40" left="411"
    text="00:00">
</TextGraphic>
</Group>
```

For the buttons we added buttonMode="true", so the component will be able to show the user a hand icon if the user is hovering over the button, since the hover state wasn't set in Flash Catalyst. Notice that the skin in each button component is pointing to the components created in Flash Catalyst.

```
<FxButton id="playButton" left="52" top="136"
    skinClass="com.elad.mp3tunes.view.W530H520.components.Button7"
    buttonMode="true"/>
<FxButton id="pauseButton" left="52" top="136"
    skinClass="com.elad.mp3tunes.view.W530H520.components.PauseButton"
    buttonMode="true"/>
<FxButton id="forwardButton" left="99" top="141"
    skinClass="com.elad.mp3tunes.view.W530H520.components.Button9"
    buttonMode="true"/>
```

```
<FxButton id="rewindButton" left="14" top="141"
    skinClass="com.elad.mp3tunes.view.W530H520.components.Button8"
    buttonMode="true"/>
<FxButton id="randomButton" left="295" top="144"
    skinClass="com.elad.mp3tunes.view.W530H520.components.Button10"
    buttonMode="true"/>
<FxButton id="replyButton" left="333" top="144"
    skinClass="com.elad.mp3tunes.view.W530H520.components.Button11" ➡
buttonMode="true"/>
<FxButton id="artistsButton" left="379" top="144"
    skinClass="com.elad.mp3tunes.view.W530H520.components.Button12"
    label="Artists" buttonMode="true"/>
<FxButton id="albumsButton" left="451" top="143"
    skinClass="com.elad.mp3tunes.view.W530H520.components.Button13"
    label="Albums" buttonMode="true"/>
```

The title for the music player stays the way it was created in Flash Catalyst:

```
<Group>
<TextGraphic fontFamily="Myriad Pro" fontSize="16" lineHeight="120%"
    whiteSpaceCollapse="preserve" kerning="on" ai:knockout="0"
    d:userLabel="headerLabel"
    color="0x000000" top="7.64" left="16">
<content><p><span>MP3Tunes Music Player</span></p></content>
</TextGraphic>
</Group>
```

The volume component consists of the FxHScrollBar for the slider as well as a ProgressBar that will represent the position of the volume.

```
<!-- Volume Slider -->
<Group>
<ProgressBar id="volumeProgressBar"
    left="170" top="155"
    barSkin="com.elad.mp3tunes.view.W530H520.components.➡
DownloadProgressBarSkin"
    trackSkin="com.elad.mp3tunes.view.W530H520.components.➡
VolumeProgressTrackSkin"
    minimum="0" maximum="100" labelWidth="0"
    direction="right" mode="manual" />

<FxHScrollBar id="volumeSlider"
    left="152" top="148" value="100"
    skinClass="com.elad.mp3tunes.view.W530H520. ➡
components.HorizontalScrollbar2"/>
</Group>
```

The track slider holds the components to display a few things:

- **Download progress**: Allows the user to monitor the download progress
- **Play progress**: Allows the user to see the progress of the song while it's playing
- **Thumb**: Thumb is part of the horizontal slider and allows live dragging
- **Track scrollbars**: Provides a scrollbar for the thumb and track to allow the user to change the position of the song

The following code creates these components:

```
<!-- Track Slider -->
<Group>
<ProgressBar id="downloadProgressBar"
    top="93.5" left="88.202" width="350"
    barSkin="com.elad.mp3tunes.view.W530H520.components.➥
DownloadProgressBarSkin"
    trackSkin="com.elad.mp3tunes.view.W530H520.components.➥
DownloadProgressTrackSkin"
    minimum="0" maximum="100"
    labelWidth="0"
    direction="right" mode="manual" />

<ProgressBar id="trackProgressBar" alpha="0.5"
        barSkin="com.elad.mp3tunes.view.W530H520.➥
components.TrackProgressBarSkin"
    trackSkin="com.elad.mp3tunes.view.W530H520.➥
components.TrackProgressTrackSkin"
    minimum="0" maximum="100"
    labelWidth="0"
    direction="right" mode="manual" />

<FxHScrollBar id="songSlider" left="84" top="85"
    minimum="0"
    maximum="250"
    value="0"
    skinClass="com.elad.mp3tunes.view.W530H520.components.➥
HorizontalScrollbar1"/>
</Group>
```

Finally, the private tag includes all the Illustrator vectors paths, which are rendered by the Drawing API in Flash 10:

```
<Private/>

</view:AbstractMusicPlayer>
```

Next, we need to edit the 320✕480-pixel view MusicPlayer.mxml component, which is very similar to the 530✕520-pixel view MusicPlayer.mxml. They both extend AbstractMusicPlayer and include the same controllers. Previously, we went through the code and set the id for all the controllers that the AbstractMusicPlayer expects, just as we did in the other view. One difference, other than changes in style properties, is that the view is smaller. Additionally, the slider for the volume is not visible, so there is no need for the progress bar. The approach we took was to still place the component, although it's not needed, since the abstract class expects it, but set the visibility to false:

```
<ProgressBar id="volumeProgressBar" visible="false" minimum="0" maximum="100"/>
```

Since the code is very similar, we don't need to explain it again (do pay attention to the similarities between the following code and the code for the previous view):

```
<?xml version='1.0' encoding='UTF-8'?>
<view:AbstractMusicPlayer xmlns="http://ns.adobe.com/mxml/2009"
    xmlns:lib="MusicPlayerSmall_library.*"
    xmlns:d="http://ns.adobe.com/fxg/2008/dt"
    xmlns:th="http://ns.adobe.com/thermo/2009"
    xmlns:ai="http://ns.adobe.com/ai/2008"
    xmlns:view="com.elad.mp3tunes.view.*"
    backgroundColor="0xe6e6e6"
    width="320" height="480"
    horizontalScrollPolicy="off"
    verticalScrollPolicy="off">

    <Group d:id="3" d:userLabel="trackInfoBackground"
    top="33.3" left="-0.6">
<Group ai:knockout="0" top="0" left="0">
<Path winding="nonZero" ai:knockout="0"
    data="M 319.471 88.108 C 319.471 ➥
 88.658 319.02 89.108 318.471 89.108 L ➥
0.975 89.108 C 0.425 89.108 -0.025 ➥
 88.658 -0.025 88.108 L -0.025 0.975 C ➥
-0.025 0.425 0.425 -0.025 0.975 -0.025 ➥
 L 318.471 -0.025 C 319.02 -0.025 319.471 ➥
0.425 319.471 0.975 L 319.471 ➥
88.108 Z" top="0.375" left="0.375">
<fill>
<LinearGradient x="159.135" y="89.9937"
    scaleX="110.474"
    rotation="-89.227">
<GradientEntry color="0x333333" ratio="0"/>
<GradientEntry color="0x1a1a1a" ratio="0.429813"/>
<GradientEntry ratio="0.807208"/>
</LinearGradient>
</fill>
</Path>
```

```
<Path winding="nonZero" ai:knockout="0"
   data="M 319.846 88.483 C 319.846 89.033 ➡
319.395 89.483 318.846 89.483 ➡
L 1.35 89.483 C 0.8 89.483 0.35 89.033 0.35 ➡
88.483 L 0.35 1.35 C 0.35 0.8 0.8 ➡
0.35 1.35 0.35 L 318.846 0.35 C 319.395 ➡
0.35 319.846 0.8 319.846 1.35 L ➡
319.846 88.483 Z" top="0" left="0">
<stroke>
<SolidColorStroke caps="none" weight="0.75"
   joints="miter" miterLimit="4"/>
</stroke>
</Path>
</Group>
</Group>

<Group>
<TextGraphic id="currentTimeText"
   fontFamily="Myriad Pro"
   fontSize="10" lineHeight="120%"
   color="0xadacac"
   whiteSpaceCollapse="preserve" kerning="on"
   ai:knockout="0" d:userLabel="1:15"
   top="87.092" left="4" text="0:00">
</TextGraphic>
<TextGraphic id="totalTimeText" fontFamily="Myriad Pro"
   fontSize="10" lineHeight="120%" color="0xadacac"
   whiteSpaceCollapse="preserve" kerning="on" ai:knockout="0"
   d:userLabel="5:25"
   top="87.092" left="288" text="0:00">
</TextGraphic>
</Group>

<Group d:userLabel="trackInfo" top="46.5" left="8.5">
<TextGraphic id="songInfoText" fontFamily="Myriad Pro" text=""
   fontSize="20" lineHeight="120%" color="0xe6e6e6"
   width="300" height="20"
   whiteSpaceCollapse="preserve" kerning="on"
   ai:knockout="0" top="0"
   left="0" d:userLabel="trackInfo">
</TextGraphic>
</Group>

<FxButton id="playButton" left="108" top="138"
   skinClass="com.elad.mp3tunes.view.W320H480.components.Button6"
   buttonMode="true"/>
<FxButton id="forwardButton" left="221" top="150"
   skinClass="com.elad.mp3tunes.view.W320H480.components.Button4"
   buttonMode="true"/>
```

```
<FxButton id="rewindButton" left="15" top="150"
    skinClass="com.elad.mp3tunes.view.W320H480.components.Button5"
    buttonMode="true"/>
<FxButton id="randomButton" left="10" top="256"
    skinClass="com.elad.mp3tunes.view.W320H480.components.Button10"
    buttonMode="true"/>
<FxButton id="replayButton" left="60" top="256"
    skinClass="com.elad.mp3tunes.view.W320H480.components.Button9"
    buttonMode="true"/>
<FxButton id="pauseButton" left="108" top="139"
    skinClass="com.elad.mp3tunes.view.W320H480.components.Button3"
    visible="false" buttonMode="true"/>
<FxButton id="artistsButton" left="122" top="256"
    skinClass="com.elad.mp3tunes.view.W320H480.components.Button8"
    label="Artists" buttonMode="true"/>
<FxButton id="albumsButton" left="221" top="255"
    skinClass="com.elad.mp3tunes.view.W320H480.components.Button7"
    label="Albums" buttonMode="true"/>

<Group>
<TextGraphic fontFamily="Myriad Pro" fontSize="20"
    fontWeight="bold" lineHeight="120%"
    whiteSpaceCollapse="preserve"
    kerning="on" ai:knockout="0"
    d:userLabel="MP3Tunes Music Player"
    color="0x000000" top="8.104" left="11.5">
<content>
<p><span>MP3Tunes Music Player</span></p>
</content>
</TextGraphic>
</Group>

<!-- Volume Slider -->
<Group>
<ProgressBar id="volumeProgressBar" visible="false"
    minimum="0" maximum="100"/>

<FxHScrollBar id="volumeSlider" left="263" top="5" value="100"
    skinClass="com.elad.mp3tunes.view.W320H480. ➡
components.HorizontalScrollbar2"/>
</Group>

<!-- Track Slider -->
<Group>
<ProgressBar id="downloadProgressBar"
    left="37" top="84"
    barSkin="com.elad.mp3tunes.view.W320H480.components. ➡
DownloadProgressBarSkin"
    trackSkin="com.elad.mp3tunes.view.W320H480.components. ➡
```

```
        DownloadProgressTrackSkin"
            minimum="0" maximum="100"
            labelWidth="0"
            direction="right" mode="manual" />

        <ProgressBar id="trackProgressBar" alpha="0.5"
            left="37" top="84"
            barSkin="com.elad.mp3tunes.view.W320H480.components. ➥
        TrackProgressBarSkin"
            trackSkin="com.elad.mp3tunes.view.W320H480.components. ➥
        TrackProgressTrackSkin"
            minimum="0" maximum="100"
            labelWidth="0"
            direction="right" mode="manual" />

        <FxHScrollBar id="songSlider" left="32" top="72"
            skinClass="com.elad.mp3tunes.view.W320H480.components. ➥
            HorizontalScrollbar1"/>
        </Group>

        <Private />

    </view:AbstractMusicPlayer>
```

Skinning the Flex components

Flex 4 offers a new component life cycle that includes the ability to manipulate the behavior of a component and the subcomponents. Each component associates itself with a particular skin class and manages itself in different states at the component level. Flex 4's new skinning architecture allows easier and more powerful visual customizations using the FXG declarative language.

In this section, we will take a look at the components created by Flash Catalyst and tweak them a little when needed to fit our application's needs. Note that, in an environment where you have a designer and developer, they can work in parallel and communicate regarding necessary changes.

We'll start with the progress bar. The component is using the bar skin and track skin. The DownloadProgressBarSkin.mxml skin holds the FXG data paths that were created in Flash Catalyst. The color that is used is a gray shade (0xe6e5e5).

```
        <?xml version="1.0" encoding="utf-8"?>
        <Group xmlns="http://ns.adobe.com/mxml/2009"
            xmlns:ai="http://ns.adobe.com/ai/2008"
            xmlns:d="http://ns.adobe.com/fxg/2008/dt" resizeMode="scale">

        <Pathwinding="nonZero" ai:knockout="0"
            d:userLabel="DownloadProgressBarSkin"
            data="M 81.615 4.98 C 81.615 7.443 81.615 9.44 ➥
        79.771 9.44 L 2.339 9.44 C 1.321 9.44 0.494 9.44 0.494 ➥
```

```
4.98 L 0.494 4.98 C 0.494 0.518 1.321 0.518 2.339 0.518 ➡
 L 79.771 0.518 C 81.615 0.518 81.615 2.516 81.615 4.98 ➡
 L 81.615 4.98 Z">
<fill>
    <SolidColor color="0xffffff "/>
</fill>
</Path>

</Group>
```

The `DownloadProgressTrackSkin.mxml` component is used for the bar skin in the progress bar. It holds the track skin and data path retrieved from Flash Catalyst.

```
<?xml version="1.0" encoding="utf-8"?>
<Group xmlns="http://ns.adobe.com/mxml/2009"
    xmlns:ai="http://ns.adobe.com/ai/2008"
    xmlns:d="http://ns.adobe.com/fxg/2008/dt"
    resizeMode="scale">

<Path alpha="0" winding="nonZero" ai:knockout="0"
    d:userLabel="DownloadProgressBarSkin"
    data="M 352.798 3.577 C 352.798 5.543 ➡
352.798 7.137 344.777 7.137 ➡
L 8.015 7.137 C 3.586 7.137 -0.004 7.137 ➡
-0.004 3.577 L -0.004 3.577 C -0.004 ➡
0.015 3.586 0.015 8.015 0.015 L 344.777 ➡
0.015 C 352.798 0.015 352.798 1.609 ➡
352.798 3.577 L 352.798 3.577 Z">
<fill>
<SolidColor color="0xffffff"/>
</fill>
</Path>

</Group>
```

`HorizontalScrollbar1.mxml` contains the track slider, states transition, and graphic. We point to the track and thumb buttons, which were created for us in Catalyst.

```
<?xml version="1.0" encoding="utf-8"?>
<Skin xmlns="http://ns.adobe.com/mxml/2009"
    xmlns:ai="http://ns.adobe.com/ai/2008"
    xmlns:d="http://ns.adobe.com/fxg/2008/dt"
    resizeMode="scale" xmlns:th="http://ns.adobe.com/thermo/2009">

<transitions>
<Transition fromState="normal" toState="disabled"/>
<Transition fromState="disabled" toState="normal"/>
</transitions>
```

```
<states>
<State name="normal" th:color="0xcc0000"/>
<State name="disabled" th:color="0x0081cc"/>
</states>

<Metadata>[HostComponent("mx.components.FxHScrollBar")]</Metadata>
<FxButton id="track" left="0" top="5"
    skinClass="com.elad.mp3tunes.view.W530H520.components.Button6"
    buttonMode="true" />
<FxButton id="thumb" left="81" top="0"
    skinClass="com.elad.mp3tunes.view. ➡
W530H520.components.Button5" />
</Skin>
```

HorizontalScrollbar2.mxml is the component of the volume control and contains the controls for the track and thumb as well as increment and decrement buttons.

```
<?xml version="1.0" encoding="utf-8"?>
<Skin xmlns="http://ns.adobe.com/mxml/2009"
    xmlns:ai="http://ns.adobe.com/ai/2008"
    xmlns:d="http://ns.adobe.com/fxg/2008/dt"
    resizeMode="scale"
    xmlns:th="http://ns.adobe.com/thermo/2009">

<transitions>
<Transition fromState="normal" toState="disabled"/>
<Transition fromState="disabled" toState="normal"/>
</transitions>

<states>
    <State name="normal" th:color="0xcc0000"/>
    <State name="disabled" th:color="0x0081cc"/>
</states>

<Metadata>[HostComponent("mx.components.FxHScrollBar")]</Metadata>
<FxButton left="20" top="6" skinClass=" ➡
com.elad.mp3tunes.view.W530H520.components.Button4" id="track"/>
<FxButton left="42" top="2" skinClass=" ➡
com.elad.mp3tunes.view.W530H520.components.Button3" id="thumb"/>
<FxButton left="107" top="0" skinClass=" ➡
com.elad.mp3tunes.view.W530H520.components.Button1" id=➡
"incrementButton"/>
<FxButton left="0" top="0" skinClass="➡
com.elad.mp3tunes.view.W530H520.components.Button2" id=➡
"decrementButton"/>

</Skin>
```

The pause button name was refactored to PauseButton.mxml; like any other Flex 4 button component, it can contain the transition between the states and the pixel.

The pixel is described in the FXG format and will be created using the Drawing API. We didn't set any states or transitions for the component, but you can bring the component back to Catalyst and create the different states just as easily as you can make the changes in Flex 4.

```
<?xml version="1.0" encoding="utf-8"?>
<Skin xmlns="http://ns.adobe.com/mxml/2009"
    xmlns:d="http://ns.adobe.com/fxg/2008/dt"
    xmlns:ai="http://ns.adobe.com/ai/2008" resizeMode="scale">

<transitions>
    <Transition fromState="up" toState="over"/>
    <Transition fromState="up" toState="down"/>
    <Transition fromState="up" toState="disabled"/>
    <Transition fromState="over" toState="up"/>
    <Transition fromState="over" toState="down"/>
    <Transition fromState="over" toState="disabled"/>
    <Transition fromState="down" toState="up"/>
    <Transition fromState="down" toState="over"/>
    <Transition fromState="down" toState="disabled"/>
    <Transition fromState="disabled" toState="up"/>
    <Transition fromState="disabled" toState="over"/>
    <Transition fromState="disabled" toState="down"/>
</transitions>

<states>
<State name="up"/>
<State name="over"/>
<State name="down"/>
<State name="disabled"/>
</states>

<Metadata>[HostComponent("mx.components.FxButton")]</Metadata>
<Group d:userLabel="pauseButton">
<Ellipse y="0.854492" blendMode="darken" width="41.3384"
    height="39.8027" ai:knockout="0">
<fill>
<SolidColor color="#3a3a3a"/>
</fill>
</Ellipse>
<Path alpha="0.6" winding="nonZero" ai:knockout="0"
    data="M38.5933 14.1792C38.6157 14.229 38.6294 14.2812 38.6479 ➥
14.3335 39.6216 15.8101 40.2144 17.5415 40.3315 19.3867 40.7202 ➥
20.3647 40.939 21.4121 41.0103 22.498 41.1968 22.251 41.3384 21.9941 ➥
 41.3384 21.7178 41.3384 15.7192 39.0249 10.2891
```

```
    35.2837 6.36084 31.5435 2.43066 26.3765 0 20.6694 0 9.25439 0 0 ➡
9.72217 0 21.7178 0 22.2061 0.299805 22.6523 0.809082 23.0635 ➡
0.742188 21.5684 0.899902 20.0615 1.33447 18.6279 1.34326 18.603 ➡
 1.35596 18.5806 1.36475 18.5557 1.52637 17.7397 1.76562
 16.9429 2.09863 16.1875 2.31396 15.103 2.68311 14.0454 3.25195 ➡
13.0571 6.92725 6.68115 13.7134 1.09668 21.1187 1.74316 28.7212 ➡
2.40771 35.2358 6.6543 38.5933 14.1792Z" >
<fill>
<SolidColor color="#999999"/>
</fill>
</Path>
<Group y="1.66016" d:id="3">
<Path alpha="0.6" winding="nonZero" ai:knockout="0"
data="M41.3384 20.2451C41.3384 31.4238 0 31.4238 0 20.2451 0 ➡
9.06299 9.25439 0 20.6694 0 32.0835 0 41.3384 9.06299 41.3384 ➡
 20.2451Z" >
<fill>
<LinearGradient x="20.7251" y="14.5273" scaleX="40.643"
    rotation="-89.418">
<GradientEntry color="#666666" ratio="0"/>
<GradientEntry color="#454545" alpha="0.83" ratio="0.20859"/>
<GradientEntry color="#0c0c0c" alpha="0.93" ratio="0.51534"/>
<GradientEntry ratio="0.57669"/>
<GradientEntry ratio="0.78528"/>
<GradientEntry alpha="0.83" ratio="0.99386"/>
</LinearGradient>
</fill>
</Path>
</Group>
<Rect x="12.8467" y="11.8706" width="4.125"
    height="19.3853" ai:knockout="0">
<fill>
<SolidColor color="#e6e6e6"/>
</fill>
</Rect>
<Rect x="23.8472" y="11.8706" width="4.125"
    height="19.3853" ai:knockout="0">
<fill>
<SolidColor color="#e6e6e6"/>
</fill>
</Rect>
</Group>
</Skin>
```

TrackProgressBarSkin.mxml contains the graphic for the song track progress bar. We set the color to 0x7f7f7f to create a shade of grey, but feel free to modify the color.

```
<?xml version="1.0" encoding="utf-8"?>
<Group xmlns="http://ns.adobe.com/mxml/2009"
    xmlns:ai="http://ns.adobe.com/ai/2008"
    xmlns:d="http://ns.adobe.com/fxg/2008/dt" resizeMode="scale">

<Path alpha="1" winding="nonZero" ai:knockout="0"
    d:userLabel="downloadProgress"
    data="M 352.798 3.577 C 352.798 5.543 352.798 7.137 ➥
344.777 7.137 L 8.015 7.137 C 3.586 7.137 -0.004 7.137 -0.004 3.577 ➥
L -0.004 3.577 C -0.004 0.015 3.586 0.015 8.015 0.015 L 344.777 ➥
0.015 C 352.798 0.015 352.798 1.609 352.798 3.577 L 352.798 3.577 Z">
<fill>
<SolidColor color="0x7f7f7f"/>
</fill>
</Path>

</Group>
```

The TrackProgressTrackSkin.mxml control holds the progress track skin. We have set the alpha to zero, since we don't want to display the progress bar track skin; we are only interested in the bar skin graphic as a placeholder, since the track skin is already created.

```
<?xml version="1.0" encoding="utf-8"?>
<Group xmlns="http://ns.adobe.com/mxml/2009"
    xmlns:ai="http://ns.adobe.com/ai/2008"
    xmlns:d="http://ns.adobe.com/fxg/2008/dt"
    resizeMode="scale">

<Path alpha="0" winding="nonZero" ai:knockout="0"
    d:userLabel="TrackProgressBarSkin"
    data="M 352.798 3.577 C 352.798 5.543 352.798 7.137 344.777 ➥
7.137 L 8.015 7.137 C 3.586 7.137 -0.004 7.137 -0.004 3.577 L -0.004 ➥
3.577 C -0.004 0.015 3.586 0.015 8.015 0.015 L 344.777 0.015 C 352.798 ➥
0.015 352.798 1.609 352.798 3.577 L 352.798 3.577 Z">
<fill>
<SolidColor color="0xffffff"/>
</fill>
</Path>

</Group>
```

Notice that the volume bar skin VolumeProgressBarSkin.mxml has the same data path as TrackProgressTrackSkin.mxml since they are going to overlap each other. The color is 0x3f3f3f, a different shade of grey than the TrackProgressTrackSkin.mxml. We would like to point out that the progress bar skin would keep changing as the presenter changes the progress bar position.

```
<?xml version="1.0" encoding="utf-8"?>
<Group xmlns="http://ns.adobe.com/mxml/2009"
    xmlns:ai="http://ns.adobe.com/ai/2008"
     xmlns:d="http://ns.adobe.com/fxg/2008/dt" resizeMode="scale">

<Path alpha="1" winding="nonZero" ai:knockout="0"
    d:userLabel="DownloadProgressBarSkin"
     data="M 352.798 3.577 C 352.798 5.543 352.798 7.137 344.777 ➥
7.137 L 8.015 7.137 C 3.586 7.137 -0.004 7.137 -0.004 3.577 L -0.004 ➥
3.577 C -0.004 0.015 3.586 0.015 8.015 0.015 L 344.777 0.015 C ➥
352.798 0.015 352.798 1.609 352.798 3.577 L 352.798 3.577 Z">
<fill>
<SolidColor color="0x3f3f3f"/>
</fill>
</Path>

</Group>
```

The volume track skin is described in VolumeProgressTrackSkin.mxml and will be visible:

```
<?xml version="1.0" encoding="utf-8"?>
<Skin xmlns="http://ns.adobe.com/mxml/2009"
      xmlns:d="http://ns.adobe.com/fxg/2008/dt"
      xmlns:ai="http://ns.adobe.com/ai/2008">

<Group d:userLabel="downloadProgress" left="0" top="0">
<Path winding="nonZero" ai:knockout="0"
    d:userLabel="downloadProgress"
     data="M 81.615 4.98 C 81.615 7.443 81.615 9.44 79.771 9.44 L 2.339 ➥
9.44 C 1.321 9.44 0.494 9.44 0.494 4.98 L 0.494 4.98 C 0.494 0.518 ➥
1.321 0.518 2.339 0.518 L 79.771 0.518 C 81.615 0.518 81.615 2.516 ➥
81.615 4.98 L 81.615 4.98 Z"
>
<fill>
<SolidColorcolor="0xe6e6e6"/>
</fill>
</Path>
</Group>
</Skin>
```

We have finished creating the different views for the music application. To compare your application with ours, download the application from the friends of ED web site in Chapter 13's MusicPlayer folder (http://www.friendsofed.com/downloads.html).

Once you compile and run the project, you can choose among the views we created in this chapter and Chapter 11 (see Figure 13-14).

Figure 13-14. Music application views created in Flash Catalyst integrated into Flex

Summary

In this chapter, we covered how to adopt Flex to be used on multiple devices. The chapter continues where we left off in Chapter 11, and we showed you how to create presentation views for additional devices.

We began by creating a Flex GUI for the Nokia N810 browser, which works with Flash 9 by making small changes in the Adobe AIR application we built in Chapter 11. We continued by giving you tutorials for creating powerful dynamic GUIs using Flash Catalyst. We then created the GUI for two additional views, for 320×480-pixel and 530×520-pixel screens. We used Flash Catalyst to import our graphic from Illustrator CS4.

When we completed importing the Flash Catalyst projects into Flex 4 SDK, we implemented the Passive Multiview design pattern and created the logic for the Catalyst views applications. The approach we took is one way to create multidevice applications using the same logic without repeating the same code twice. This example also showed how you could leverage the same logic to deploy different views to create a compelling application that fits the exact needs of a device. In the next chapter, we will explore building mobile applications using test-driven development techniques.

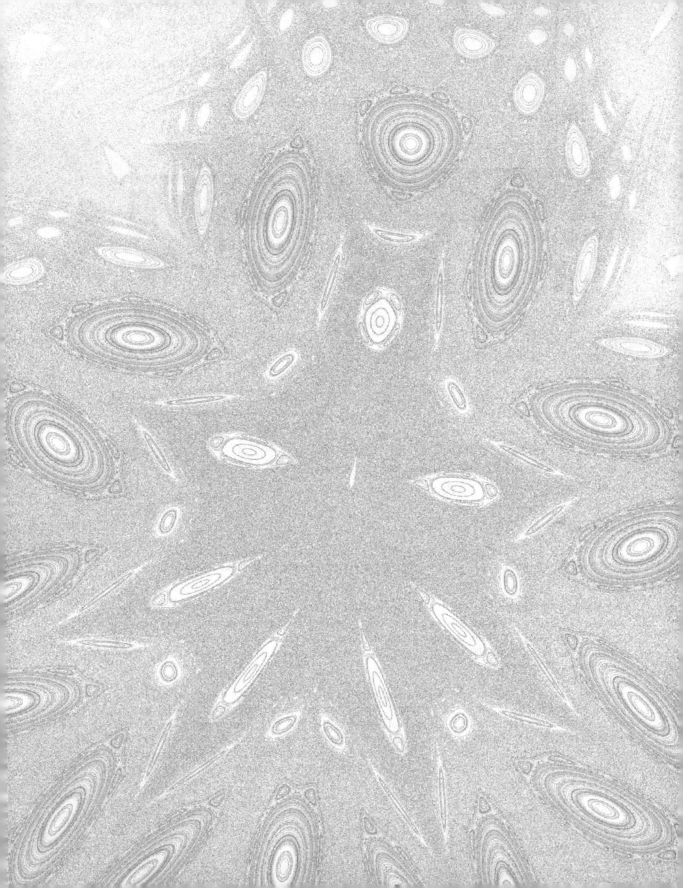

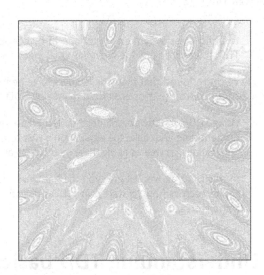

Chapter 14

BUILDING MOBILE APPLICATIONS USING TEST-DRIVEN DEVELOPMENT

Adobe's vision of separating the presentation layer from the logic and delegating more Flex applications to a design-centric application is underway with the new component architecture of Flash Catalyst and Flex 4. Removing some of the responsibility from developers will allow you to concentrate on creating smarter, more dynamic, and more complex Flash applications.

However, as the Flash applications become more complex and dynamic, particularly when business rules are changing rapidly, sometimes even during development, maintaining and scaling up Flash applications has become challenging. These challenges are common in any mobile, web, and desktop development, and many Flash developers are finding that even using a framework doesn't make the application easy to maintain and change.

For example, if a large application needs changes due to new business rules, how do you know that small changes you make won't break other parts of the application? How can you be assured that your code is bulletproof, especially if you are not the person who wrote the application initially?

Though somewhat new to Flash developers, this problem is not new to software engineers: Java and .NET developers challenged with the same issues have found test-driven development (TDD) a useful way to create applications that can be easily maintained.

Flash has grown from a small animation tool into a serious programming language and methodologies that are common in other programming languages are necessary to build large dynamic applications. In fact, Adobe and many other companies have found that using TDD solves many of the everyday challenges faced in all development cycles.

We have found that many developers have heard of TDD but are reluctant to use it, since they are not sure how to use it or are afraid that using TDD will increase development time.

Using TDD correctly doesn't necessarily increase development time. In fact, you may actually reduce development time and make the application easier to maintain. You can also implement and use TDD in existing applications, as well as apply these methods to any framework out there in some way or another.

In this chapter, we will give you the basics you need to know to get started, as well as more advanced topics such as how to start using TDD in existing applications and how to integrate TDD with popular frameworks.

Understanding TDD basics

What is TDD anyway? Test-driven development is a software development technique based on test cases that are completed during short development iterations (repetition). TDD started with programmers adding a test to their code after writing it. Then, in 1999, Extreme Programming (XP) came along.

> *XP is a school of thought that considers the development of dynamic projects with changing requirements and a development cycle that includes writing the tests before the code itself—that is test-driven development. Note that TDD is not the complete development cycle and is only part of the XP development paradigm.*

Preparing the tests before writing the code allows you to visualize the work in small steps, so you don't have to ask your customer to wait for the complete result to preview it.

The ability to test is an added benefit. The main benefit is that working in small increments allows your customers to make changes before you write the final code, as well as ensuring that things don't go wrong and that your code does what it needs to do and nothing more. It is important to mention that **the focus of the TDD technique is to produce code** and not to create a testing platform.

TDD relies on the concept that anything you build should be tested, and if you are unable to test it, you should think twice about whether you really want to build it.

Applying TDD involves using a short development process (each phase might last a couple of weeks) called iteration planning, which is based on user stories. Iteration planning begins with the user stories and then moves on to creating a test, which includes the code necessary to satisfy the user story. That code then becomes the test. Once the test is completed, the code is refactored to remove any extras and create cleaner code. At the end of each iteration planning cycle, the team delivers a working application.

> *A user story represents a business requirement. The customer explains the requirement to the software engineer and all those business requirements are user stories, which together are part of the specification of requirements. An example story might be "once the user logs in, a welcome window pops up."*

Let's explore the TDD technique, illustrated in Figure 14-1:

1. **Add tests**: The first step is to understand the business requirements (which turn into user stories) and think of all possible scenarios. If the requirements are not clear enough, you can raise the questions ahead of time instead of waiting until the software is completed and will require a large LOE (level of effort) to change.

2. **Write failed unit tests**: This phase is needed to ensure that the test unit itself is working correctly and does not pass, since you didn't write any code.

3. **Write code**: During this phase, you write the code in the simplest, most effective way to ensure that the test passes. There is no need to include any design patterns, think about the rest of the application, or try to clean up the code. Your goal is only to pass the test.

4. **Pass tests**: Once you write all the code and the test passes, you know that your test meets all the business requirements, and you can share the work with the customer or other members of the team.

5. **Refactor code**: Now that the test is completed and you confirmed that it meets the business requirements, you can ensure that the code is ready for production by replacing any temporary parameters, adding design patterns, removing duplicates, and creating classes to do the work. Ideally, once the refactor phase is completed, the code is given a code review, which is the key to ensuring that the code is in good standing and complies with the company's coding standard.

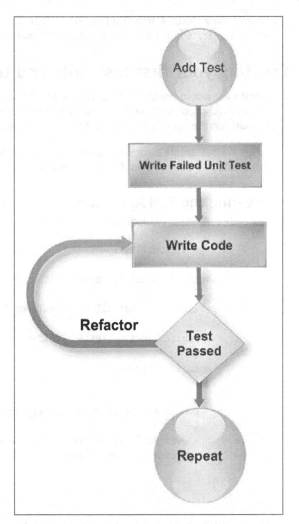

Figure 14-1. Test-driven development cycle

6. **Repeat**: Once the unit test is completed, you can move to the next unit test and publish your code to share with the customer or other members of the team.

Creating unit tests using FlexUnit

Adobe's recommended tool to use when working with TDD is a stand-alone open source tool called FlexUnit, which is hosted on Adobe's open source wiki. FlexUnit is based on JUnit, a Java tool for creating unit tests, and it allows testing ActionScript 3 code. With it, you can use unit testing in Flash Professional, Flex, or AIR projects.

To start using FlexUnit, download the FlexUnit SWC at http://opensource.adobe.com/wiki/display/flexunit/. Place it in your libs directory, and you are ready to get started.

Creating your first test suite and test case

A test suite is a composite of tests; it runs a collection of test cases. During development, we can create a collection of tests packaged into a test suite, and once we are done creating the test suite, we can just run the suite to ensure our code is still working correctly after changes have been made.

To get started, create a package, and call it flexUnitTests. Place it under the src directory. Then, we can create a test suite to hold all of our test suites and test cases.

Creating the TestSuite class

The code for TestSuite follows:

```
package flexUnitTests
{
    import flexunit.framework.TestSuite;

    public class TestSuiteClass extends TestSuite
    {
        public function TestSuiteClass(param:Object=null)
        {
            super(param);
        }

        public static function suite():TestSuite
        {
            var newTestSuite:TestSuite = new TestSuite();
            return newTestSuite;
        }
    }
}
```

Notice that it's necessary to create the constructor, since we will be using it in the test case, so the method will pass the name of the test method, which will be called by the test runner (i.e., the user interface).

Creating the TestCase class

A test case is our conditions or variables created to fulfill the business requirement. The TestCase class will be placed under the same package. Let's look at the minimum code needed to create a TestCase:

```
package flexUnitTests
{
    import com.elad.view.LogicClass;
    import flexunit.framework.TestCase;
```

```
public class TestCaseClass extends TestCase
{
  public function TestCaseClass(methodName:String=null)
  {
    super(methodName);
  }
}
}
```

The TestCase class doesn't hold any tests; it just holds the constructor, which is necessary since the test runner will pass the name from the test suite to the test case to determine which tests to run.

Create the TestRunner component

Our next step is to create the TestRunner class.

The test runner is a UI component that will create an instance of the test suite and allow us to add all the tests we would like to run. The test runner will display the tests' information in our browser.

The component runs, and onCreationComplete calls the test suite to create a new instance with all the tests. We then run the test runner:

```
testRunner.test = currentRunTestSuite();
testRunner.startTest();
```

We can then create a method to hold all the tests we want to run, currentRunTestSuite. The method just sets the test cases, and we can keep adding tests as we go through the TDD process.

```
var testsToRun:TestSuite = new TestSuite();
testsToRun.addTest(TestSuiteClass.suite());
```

Here is the complete TestRunner code:

```
<mx:Application xmlns:mx="http://www.adobe.com/2006/mxml"
  xmlns:flexunit="flexunit.flexui.*"
  creationComplete="onCreationComplete()"
  layout="absolute">

  <mx:Script>
    <![CDATA[

      import flexUnitTests.TestCaseClass;
      import flexUnitTests.TestSuiteClass;
      import flexunit.framework.TestSuite;

      private function onCreationComplete():void
      {
        testRunner.test = currentRunTestSuite();
        testRunner.startTest();
      }
```

```
                   public function currentRunTestSuite():TestSuite
                   {
                       var testsToRun:TestSuite = new TestSuite();

                       testsToRun.addTest(TestSuiteClass.suite());
                       return testsToRun;
                   }

               ]]>
           </mx:Script>

           <flexunit:TestRunnerBase id="testRunner"/>

       </mx:Application>
```

Run the application, and you will see the test runner UI with no test cases, since we haven't written any tests. See Figure 14-2.

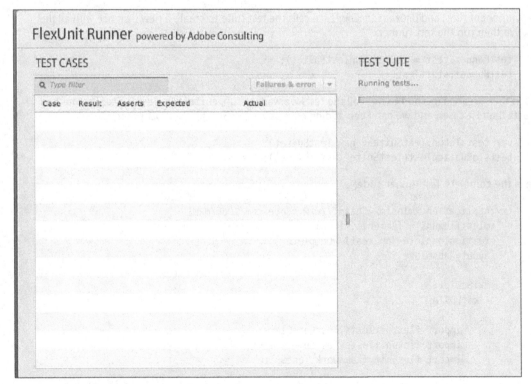

Figure 14-2. The test runner UI in the browser

Writing a failed unit test

Following the TDD process, we can now add an empty fail test to the test case class, TestCaseClass. Note that all tests method names must start with the word "test."

```
public function testFirstMethod():void
{
    fail("testFirstMethod fail method");
}
```

We also add a test to the TestRunner class, so it will add the test to the tests to run, FlexUnit.mxml:

```
public function currentRunTestSuite():TestSuite
{
    var testsToRun:TestSuite = new TestSuite();

    testsToRun.addTest(TestSuiteClass.suite());
    testsToRun.addTest(new TestCaseClass("testFirstMethod"));

    return testsToRun;
}
```

Run the FlexUnit application, and you can see the result in Figure 14-3: one method failed under our test suite TestSuiteClass.

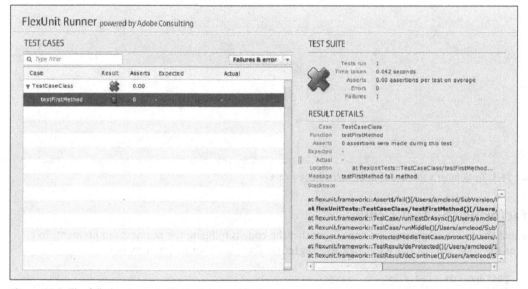

Figure 14-3. The failed test case in the test runner UI

Writing code to pass the test

Now that our test has failed, we want to write just enough code to pass the test. We don't care too much about the code, just passing the test.

This is an example, so we are using a basic method. Our method just asserts that we get zero as the result. In reality, that comparison can be made to anything in our application. For instance, the zero may stand for the application state in a stateful application or some computation we need to make.

Take a look at the code that implements our test case, TestCaseClass:

```
public function testFirstMethod():void
{
    var logic:LogicClass = new LogicClass();
    assertEquals( "Expecting zero here", 0, 0 );
}
```

Passing the test

Run TestRunner now, and you can see that the test has passed (see Figure 14-4).

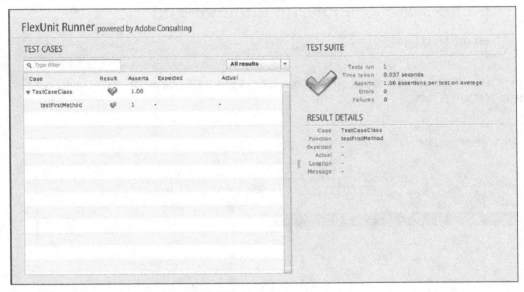

Figure 14-4. TestRunner's successful testFirstMethod test case

Refactoring the test's code

Now that the test is completed, we can ensure that the code is fulfilling the business requirement. To refactor the code, we will place the logic in a LogicClass.as class that just returns zero:

```
package com.elad.view
{
    public class LogicClass
    {
        public function LogicClass()
        {
            // constructor
        }
```

```
public function firstMethod():Number
{
    return 0;
}
}
}
```

And our `testFirstMethod` method in TestCaseClass needs to be changed to reflect the new changes:

```
public function testFirstMethod():void
{
    var logic:LogicClass = new LogicClass();
    assertEquals( "Expecting zero here", 0, logic.firstMethod() );
}
```

Run the application, and you can again see the green light, as shown in Figure 14-4.

Repeating this process

We can now create more test cases to complete business requirement. Take a look at Figure 14-5, the result of the `testNextMethod` class.

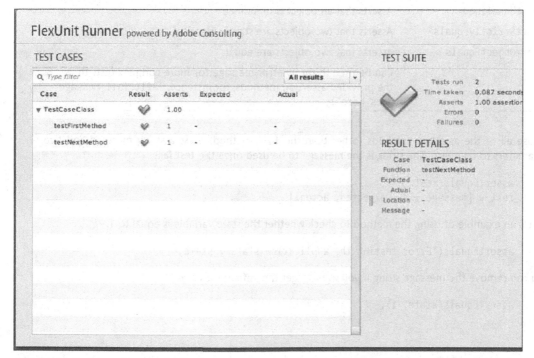

Figure 14-5. TestRunner's successful TestCases

Using assertion methods

So far, we used only the assertEquals assertion methods in our test cases assertEquals and failed, but there are many other assertion methods. Take a look at all the possible asserts available to us in Table 14-1.

Table 14-1. Available assertion methods

assertEquals	Asserts that two values are equal
assertContained	Asserts that the first string is contained in the second one
assertNotContained	Asserts that the first string is not contained in the second one
assertFalse	Asserts that a condition is false
assertTrue	Asserts that a condition is true
assertMatch	Asserts that a string matches a regular expression
assertNoMatch	Asserts that a string doesn't match a regular expression
assertNull	Asserts that an object is null
assertNotNull	Asserts that an object is not null
assertDefined	Asserts that an object is defined
assertUndefined	Asserts that an object is undefined
assertStrictlyEquals	Asserts that two objects are strictly identical
assertObjectEquals	Asserts that two objects are equal
fail	Can be used to throw error message for more complex tests then the provided assertion methods, for instance, fail("fail message goes here");

To use all of the assertion methods (other than the fail method), pass a string message and two parameters to compare. The string is the message to be used once the test fails.

```
assertEquals(rest…)
rest = [message = "", expected, actual]
```

Here's an example of using the method to check whether the state variable is equal to 1.

```
assertEquals("Error testing the application state", state, 1);
```

You can remove the message string if you want to get the default message:

```
assertEquals(state, 1);
```

Use the parent class's Assert method to see code hints, as shown in Figure 14-6.

```
Assert.assertEquals(state, 1);
```

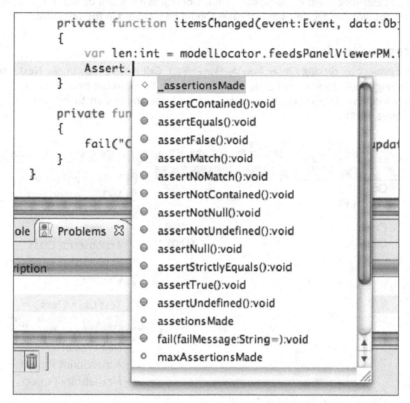

Figure 14-6. Assert code hinting showing all the methods avaliable

FlexUnit in Flex 4

Recently, Adobe has moved FlexUnit onto the Adobe web site as an open source project and they are using TDD in many of their projects in their consulting arm, Adobe Professional Services firm. Flex 4 includes FlexUnit built into Flex Builder and allows us to create the scaffolding of the test unit automatically, saving us time to create the same classes over and over again as well as ensuring we conform to best practices.

Flex 4 includes flexunit.swc and flexunitextended.swc. These SWCs are kept as part of the Flex 4 SDK, so there is no need to add them manually.

Let's take a look at how to use Flex 4 to create test suites and test cases.

Creating a test suite and test case in Flex 4

The key for creating unit testing using FlexUnit is creating test cases. A test case is a collection of conditions that help us determine whether our application is working as expected or not. A test suite is a collection of test cases. We can decide what test cases should be included in the test suite.

Creating a test suite class

Create a new Flex project by clicking File ➤ New ➤ Flex Project. Call it FlexUnitExample. Next, create a test suite by clicking File ➤ New ➤ Test Suite Class (see Figure 14-7). In the next window, call the class CalculatorTestSuite. We have no methods to include, so leave the option to include classes as unchecked (see Figure 14-8).

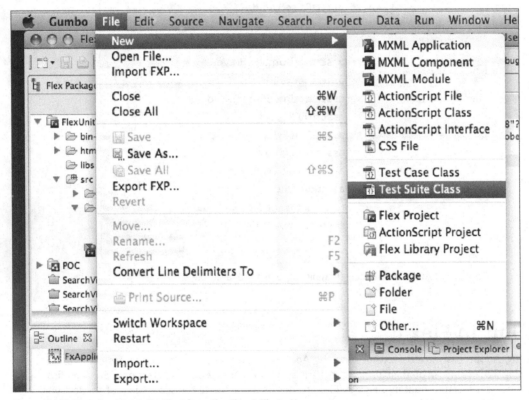

Figure 14-7. Choosing Test Suite Class from the Flex 4 File ➤ New menu

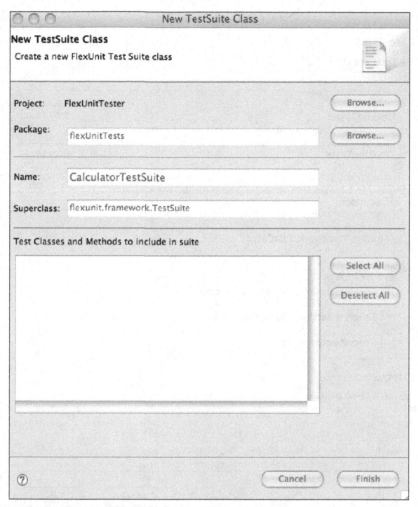

Figure 14-8. New TestSuite Class window options

Adding a test case class

Create a new test case class. Select File ➤ New ➤ Test Case Class, and then select Calculator as the class name. Keep the Generate constructor from superclass check, and for now there's no need to generate the setUp() and tearDown() stubs. We will explain about them later, so leave that option unchecked (see Figure 14-9).

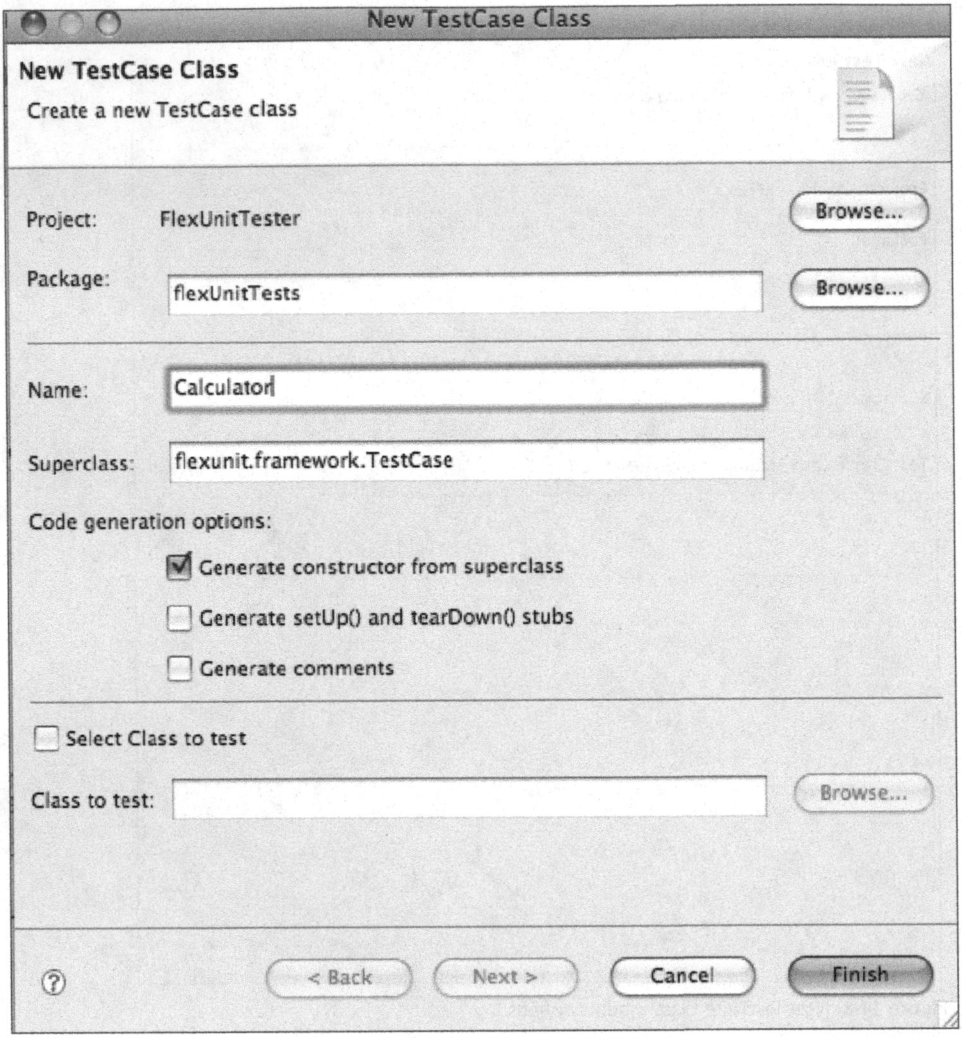

Figure 14-9. New TestCase Class window

And you are all done. Let's take a look at what was generated automatically for us. We have a package named FlexUnitTests that includes both the test case and test suite. The test runner was generated automatically for us, but it's not listed among the projects files in the library explorer view, since it gets created automatically every time we run the tests (see Figure 14-10).

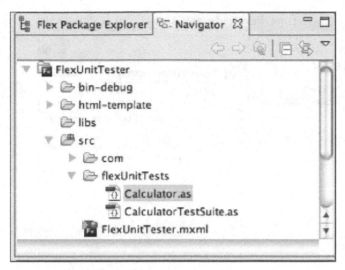

Figure 14-10. The folder structure and classes created automatically

Writing a failed unit test

We are ready to get started. Notice that a sample method was created automatically for us in the Calculator class we created.

```
/* sample test method
public function testSampleMethod():void
{
    // Add your test logic here
    fail("Test method Not yet implemented");
}
*/
```

> Recall that each method we create must start with the name test, in order for the test runner to be able to recognize the method. That is a requirement in FlexUnit 1. FlexUnit 4 beta addresses this limitation and is based on metadata, so you will not have to use the metadata if you use FlexUnit 4.

Remove the comment characters from the lines, and compile the project. After that, we can run the application by selecting the compile icon and choosing Execute FlexUnit Tests, as shown in Figure 14-11.

The next window allows you to select the test suite and unit you would like to test. Select all of them, and click OK (see Figure 14-12).

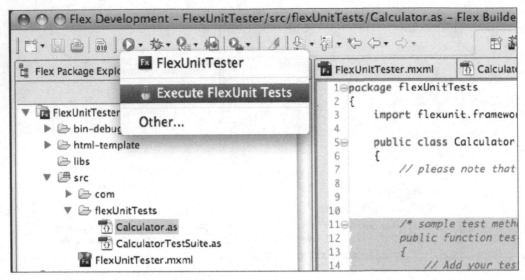

Figure 14-11. The Execute FlexUnit Tests option

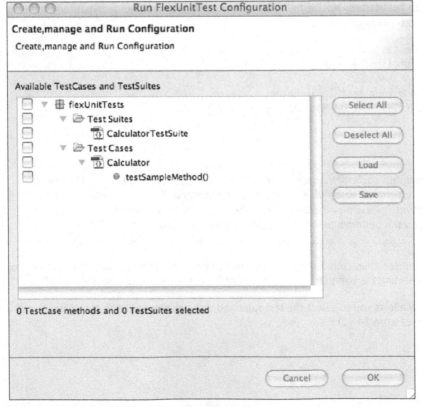

Figure 14-12. The Run FlexUnitTest Configuration window

Under the hood, an application named FlexUnitAutomaticallyGeneratedFile.mxml was created automatically and includes a test runner class called FlexUnitTestRunnerUI, which is similar in functionality to the FlexUnit TestRunner class. The application adds the entire test and runs the test in the UI.

Flex Builder hides the application. In order to be able to view the application, you need to generate an error message. For instance, remove the constructor from the test case, and try to execute the test (see Figure 14-13).

> Each time you run the application, the compiler automatically adds compiler arguments. To view these arguments, right-click the project, and select Properties ➤ Flex Compiler. *Here's an example of the syntax:* -locale en_US -includes flexUnitTests.ClassNameTestSuite -includes flexUnitTests. ClassNameTestCase.
>
> *It is important to be aware of how the compiler behaves, since if you remove the class you also need to remove the compiler argument.*

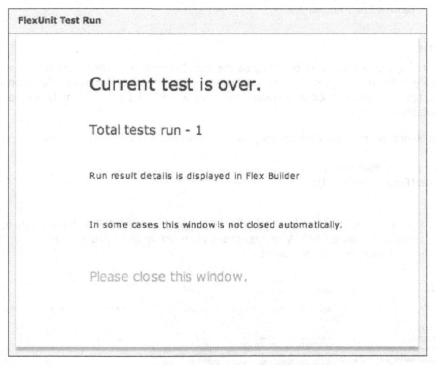

FlexUnit Test Run

Current test is over.

Total tests run - 1

Run result details is displayed in Flex Builder

In some cases this window is not closed automatically.

Please close this window.

Figure 14-13. FlexUnit Test Run result on browser

Once the application is completed, you will see a message in your browser and the test results in the FlexUnit Result View window (see Figure 14-14). As you can see, the test failed, since we had the following code:

```
fail("Test method Not yet implemented");
```

577

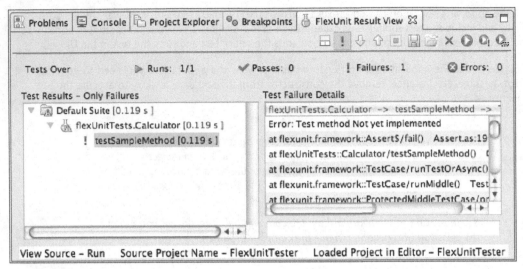

Figure 14-14. The FlexUnit Result View window

Writing code

Now that our test failed, we can write code to pass the test. The code we write should be the minimum code to get the test to pass. The first method we will write is for a simple calculation of two numbers. Let's call the method and rename the sample method from testSampleMethod to testAdditionMethod.

```
public function testAdditionMethod():void
{
    var result:Number = 10;
    assertEquals(result,8);
}
```

Take a look at assertEquals. The value is wrong, since 10 and 8 are not equal. Run the application, and it will fail, as shown in Figure 14-15. A message shows the problem and failed method: testAdditionMethod - > expected <10> but was <5>.

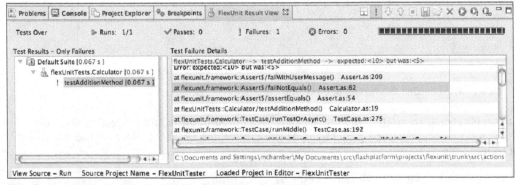

Figure 14-15. The FlexUnit Result View window showing the failed method

Passing the unit test assertion

Change the method, so we can pass the test and get a green light:

```
public function testAdditionMethod():void
{
    var result:Number = 10;
    assertEquals(result,10);
}
```

Refactoring our code

Now that our test passed, we can refactor our code to get it ready for production as well as present our code in small increments.

Create a utility class that actually gets two numbers and adds the values. When we created the unit test (testAdditionMethod) we created a result variable that holds the sum of the two numbers and checks to see if the result equals 10. In the addition method, we will implement code that adds two numbers together.

```
package com.elad.calculator.utils
{
    public final class calculatorLogicHelper
    {
        public static function addition➡
(value1:Number, value2:Number):Number
        {
            var retVal:Number = value1+value2;
            return retVal;
        }
    }
}
```

Now, update the testAdditionMethod method to use the addition method:

```
public function testAdditionMethod():void
{
    var result:Number = CalculatorLogicHelper.addition(5,5);
    assertEquals(result,10);
}
```

We can test the utility method we created in the unit test.

Creating a second unit test

Now that we've completed the first unit test and created an actual class and method to implement the functionality, we can continue and create the next unit test for the second method. The complete code for the methods we need for our calculator follow:

```
package com.elad.calculator.utils
{
    public final class CalculatorLogicHelper
```

```
    {
        public static function addition ➥
(value1:Number, value2:Number):Number
        {
            var retVal:Number = value1+value2;
            return retVal;
        }

        public static function subtraction ➥
(value1:Number, value2:Number):Number
        {
            var retVal:Number = value1-value2;
            return retVal;
        }

        public static function multiplication ➥
(value1:Number, value2:Number):Number
        {
            var retVal:Number = value1*value2;
            return retVal;
        }

        public static function division ➥
(value1:Number, value2:Number):Number
        {
            var retVal:Number = value1/value2;
            return retVal;
        }
    }
}
```

And here's the complete code for our unit test class:

```
package flexUnitTests
{
    import com.elad.calculator.utils.CalculatorLogicHelper;

    import flexunit.framework.TestCase;

    public class Calculator extends TestCase
    {
        public function Calculator(methodName:String=null)
        {
            super(methodName);
        }
```

```
public function testAdditionMethod():void
{
   var result:Number = CalculatorLogicHelper.addition(5,5);
   assertEquals(result,10);
}

public function testSubtractionMethod():void
{
   var result:Number = CalculatorLogicHelper.subtraction(5,5);
   assertEquals(result,0);
}

public function testMultiplicationMethod():void
{
   var result:Number = CalculatorLogicHelper.multiplication(5,5);
   assertEquals(result,25);
}

public function testDivisionMethod():void
{
   var result:Number = CalculatorLogicHelper.division(5,5);
   assertEquals(result,1);
}
   }
}
```

Writing asynchronous tests

The examples we have shown you so far are simple enough, but Flex is based on events, so in many cases, we need to perform event-driven tests; for instance, when loading data from an external source or checking a UIComponent once the creation complete event was dispatched. These asynchronous behaviors can be tested in FlexUnit using the addAsync() method.

Usually, FlexUnit performs our test cases and is unaware that we are listening to an event. Using the addAsync() calls, we instruct FlexUnit to wait until the event bubble is captured by our listener before determining whether the test was successful or not.

To create an asynchronous test, we will be using a timer to simulate an asynchronous behavior.

Create a new Flex 4 project, and call it FlexUnitAsynchronous, and create two classes within it as follows:

1. Select File ➤ New ➤ New TestSuite Class, and call the class AsyncTestSuite2.
2. Select File ➤ New ➤ New TestCase Class, and name the class AsyncTestCase. This time, also generate the tearDown() and setUp() methods by checking the Generate setUp() and tearDown() stubs in the TestCase Class window.

Run the compiler using the Execute FlexUnit Tests, and you will see the passed test.

Create a new test case, and call it TimerTestCase. This test case will wait until a timer event is dispatched before continuing and completing the test.

Set one timer and one interval flag:

```
private var timer:Timer;
private var timerIntervalFlag:Boolean;
```

We will be using the setUp() and tearDown() stubs for setting the timerIntervalFlag and stopping the timer. These methods will be called when the test case starts and ends. We set the interval to false, so we can track when the timer reaches the interval and ensure the timer stopped on tear down. We also want to clear the timer to ensure we don't have any memory leaks.

```
override public function setUp():void
{
        timerIntervalFlag = false;
}

override public function tearDown():void
{
     timer.stop();
     timer = null;
}
```

Our test will set a timer of 1,500 milliseconds with one interval. The timer will start, and after 1,500 milliseconds, a TIMER event will be dispatched to set the interval flag to true. Then, the timer will be completed and will be handled by the addAsync() method:

```
public function testTimer():void
{
    timer = new Timer(1500, 1);
    timer.addEventListener(TimerEvent.TIMER, function():void ➥
{ timerIntervalFlag = true } );
    timer.addEventListener(TimerEvent.TIMER_COMPLETE, ➥
 addAsync(onTimerCompleteEventHandler, 2000, {expectedResults: true}));
    timer.start();
}

private function onTimerCompleteEventHandler( ➥
timerEvent:TimerEvent, data:Object):void
{
    assertTrue("Interval flag should be true", timerIntervalFlag, ➥
            data.expectedResults);
}
```

FlexUnit's addAsync() method allows handling the request. The timeout is set to 2000, which tells FlexUnit to wait 2,000 milliseconds before creating a timeout error. The results may be either success or failure.

Success will pass the object information to the onTimerCompleteEventHandler method, and failures will be handled through the default event method in FlexUnit, since we didn't set any method to handle fail results.

Take a look at the complete code to test asynchronous calls:

```
package flexUnitTests
{
    import flash.events.TimerEvent;
    import flash.utils.Timer;

    import flexunit.framework.TestCase;

    public class TimerTestCase extends TestCase
    {
        private var timer:Timer;
        private var timerIntervalFlag:Boolean;

        public function TimerTestCase(methodName:String=null)
        {
            super(methodName);
        }

        override public function setUp():void
        {
            timerIntervalFlag = false;
        }

        override public function tearDown():void
        {
            timer.stop();
            timer = null;
        }

        public function testTimer():void
        {
            timer = new Timer(1500, 1);
            timer.addEventListener(TimerEvent.TIMER, function():void ➥
                { timerIntervalFlag = true } );
            timer.addEventListener(TimerEvent.TIMER_COMPLETE, ➥
    addAsync(verifyCount, 2000, {expectedResults: true}));
            timer.start();
        }

        private function verifyCount(timerEvent:TimerEvent, ➥
                            data:Object):void
        {
            assertTrue("Interval flag should be true", ➥
                    timerIntervalFlag, data.expectedResults);
        }
    }
}
```

Next, let's examine a more realistic example. In this example, we will be making a remote procedure call (RPC) to Adobe feeds (http://feeds.adobe.com/), and once we get a response, we ensure the call succeeded and that the results are what we expected.

Create a new test case class, and call it ServiceTestCase.

Set the service variable we will be using:

```
private var service:HTTPService;
```

Use the following code to set the set setUp() and tearDown() methods to the service properties we need and to empty the service var once we are finished with it:

```
override public function setUp():void
{
        service = new HTTPService();
        service.url = "http://rss.adobe.com/en/resources_flex.rss";
        service.resultFormat = "e4x";
}

override public function tearDown():void
{
        service = null;
}
```

The testServiceCall test method will set a listener and use the FlexUnit addAsync method to handle the call, just as we did with the timer example. We know that the feeds title is Flex News, so we will expect that once the service replies with the feeds:

```
public function testServiceCall():void
{
        service.addEventListener(ResultEvent.RESULT, ➥
addAsync(serviceResultEventHandler, 2000, {expectedResults: ➥
"Flex News"}));
        service.send();
}
```

In the success handler, we are using e4x to get the title node in the XML we received from the service call, and we can use assertTrue to compare the values:

```
private function serviceResultEventHandler( ➥
event:ResultEvent, data:Object):void
{
        var val:String = event.result[0].channel.title;
        assertTrue("Unable to retrieve Flex News feeds", ➥
                val, data.expectedResults);
}
```

Here's the complete code:

```
package flexUnitTests
```

```
{
    import flexunit.framework.TestCase;

    import mx.rpc.events.ResultEvent;
    import mx.rpc.http.HTTPService;

    public class ServiceTestCase extends TestCase
    {
        private var service:HTTPService;

        public function ServiceTestCase(methodName:String=null)
        {
            super(methodName);
        }

        override public function setUp():void
        {
            service = new HTTPService();
            service.url = "http://rss.adobe.com/en/resources_flex.rss";
            service.resultFormat = "e4x";
        }

        override public function tearDown():void
        {
            service = null;
        }

        public function testServiceCall():void
        {
            service.addEventListener(ResultEvent.RESULT, ➥
addAsync(serviceResultEventHandler, 2000, ➥
{expectedResults: "Flex News"}, failFunction));
            service.send();
        }

        private function serviceResultEventHandler➥
(event:ResultEvent, data:Object):void
        {
            var val:String = event.result[0].channel.title;
            assertTrue("Unable to retrieve Flex News feeds", val, ➥
                    data.expectedResults);
        }

        private function failFunction(data:Object):void
        {
            fail("Unable to connect to Flex News feeds");
        }
    }
}
```

Notice that, this time, we set a custom timeout-handling method to handle failed requests. The method we are using is called `failFunction`. With it, instead of using the default, built-in message, we provide a custom error message that identifies the problem in the application.

> We recommend that you set your own custom messages instead of using the default message, since your application will include much more than one method, and having a specific message will make tracking down errors easier.

Testing visual components with FlexUnit

Unit testing is typically for testing application logic and events, but in many cases, you also want to test the visual appearance and behavior of a component. Testing the visual aspects of components does not exactly fall under the unit testing category, and many will argue that it's not necessary to create unit tests for visuals. However, we decided to cover that subject, since Flex is very rich in graphic components and behavior.

You can use FlexUnit classes the way we did before to test visual components, but testing visual components quickly becomes complex, since many of the components' properties are the result of user interaction and may even contain complex changes, such as CSS properties applied only after user-generated events.

Basically, the testing of components is complicated by the richness of the Flex framework. The influence of states, styles, user interaction, and other containers can impact how a component behaves. Therefore, the testing of visual components can be better thought of as automated functional testing.

In order to test the behavior of a visual component often, we need to go through the various component life cycle steps. The Flex framework automatically handles this when a component is added to the display hierarchy.

Test cases are not visual components, which means that the component must be associated with an external object outside of the TestCase. This external association means that extra care must be taken to clean up after both failed and successful tests; otherwise, stray components could impact other tests.

We will be using a tool called FlexMonkey to test both the application visual appearance and visual behavior. FlexMonkey is an open source Flex library and can be downloaded at http://code.google.com/p/flexmonkey/. The tool uses the Flex Automation library to capture user gestures and allows you to replicate these gestures.

Let's take a look how it works by using a simple example:

1. Create a new project, and call it TestVisualUI.
2. Place FlexMonkeyUI.swc in the `libs` folder.
3. Right-click the project, and select Properties.
4. Under Flex Compiler, add the following arguments:

```
-include-libraries "${flexlib}/libs/automation_agent.swc" ➥
"${flexlib}/libs/automation.swc" "../libs/FlexMonkeyUI.swc"
```

We are ready to get started. We will create a simple application to show you how to create a test with FlexMonkey. The example has one text input and one button component. Once the user inserts a value and clicks the button, the width of the button changes accordingly.

Here is our complete code for the example application using FlexMonkey:

```xml
<?xml version="1.0" encoding="utf-8"?>
<mx:Application xmlns:mx="http://www.adobe.com/2006/mxml">

    <mx:Text text="Enter width size:" />
    <mx:TextInput id="textInput" />
    <mx:Button id="clickButton"
        click="clickButton.width=Number(textInput.text)"
        label="Change button width size"/>

</mx:Application>
```

If you run the application, the application and a window for FlexMonkey appear automatically (see Figure 14-16).

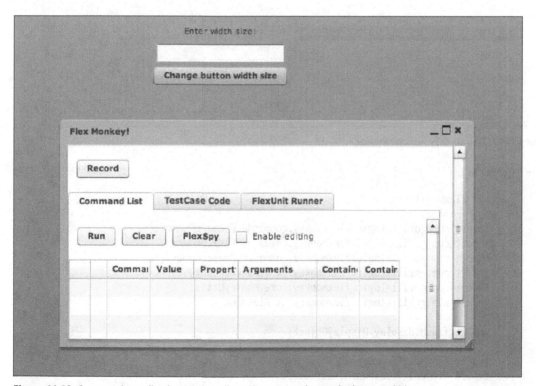

Figure 14-16. Our sample application UI that allows the user to change the button width

Click Record, and the commands you give will be recorded automatically. Type 300 in the text input box, and click the button. Now, you can switch the tab to TestCase Code, and copy the test case. Create a new test case, and call it UITestCase.flexUnitTests by selecting the file then copying and pasting the

587

test case code and modifying the class name. And now all you have to do is add the class to the compiler argument:

```
-includes flexUnitTests.UITestCase
```

Start the application again, and in the FlexMonkey window, select FlexUnit Runner to run the test (see Figure 14-17).

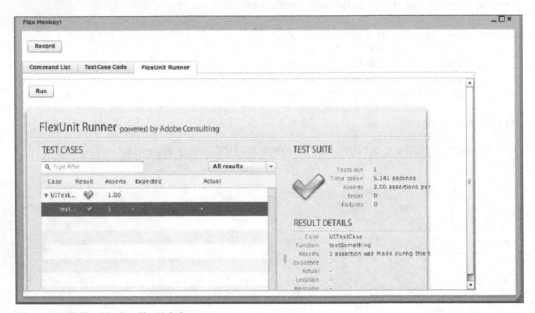

Figure 14-17. Flex Monkey FlexUnit Runner

Here's the code:

```
package flexUnitTests
{
    import com.gorillalogic.flexmonkey.commands.CommandRunner;
    import com.gorillalogic.flexmonkey.commands.FlexCommand;
    import com.gorillalogic.flexmonkey.commands.PauseCommand;
    import com.gorillalogic.flexmonkey.core.MonkeyEvent;
    import com.gorillalogic.flexmonkey.core.MonkeyUtils;
    import com.gorillalogic.flexmonkey.ui.FlexMonkey;

    import flash.display.DisplayObject;

    import flexunit.framework.Assert;
    import flexunit.framework.TestCase;

    import mx.controls.Button;
    import mx.controls.TextInput;
    import mx.events.FlexEvent;
```

```
[Mixin]
public class UITestCase extends TestCase
{
    public static function init(root:DisplayObject) : void
    {
        root.addEventListener(FlexEvent.APPLICATION_COMPLETE, ➥
function():void {
            FlexMonkey.addTestSuite(UITestCase);
        });
    }

    // Test test method
    public function testSomething():void
    {
        var cmdRunner:CommandRunner = new CommandRunner();
        cmdRunner.addEventListener( ➥
MonkeyEvent.READY_FOR_VALIDATION,➥
addAsync(verifySomething, 10000));
        cmdRunner.runCommands([
            new FlexCommand("textInput", "SelectText", ➥
["0", "0"], "automationName"),
            new FlexCommand("textInput", "Input", ["150"], ➥
"automationName"),
            new FlexCommand("Change button width size", "Click", ➥
["0"], "automationName"),
            new PauseCommand(2500)
            ]);
    }

    // Called after commands have been run
    private function verifySomething(event:MonkeyEvent):void
    {
        var btn:Button = MonkeyUtils.findComponentWith( ➥
"clickButton", "id") as Button;
        var txtInput:TextInput = MonkeyUtils.findComponentWith( ➥
"textInput") as TextInput;

        Assert.assertEquals(txtInput.text, btn.width);
    }

}
}
```

That concludes the creation and testing of our simple example. You can download a more complex example, which includes full tutorial document, from the FlexMonkey open source project. Testing your visual components is powerful and can help reduce your work during smoke testing and reduce the number of errors found by QA.

> *Smoke testing is the process of testing your application before submitting it for quality assurance (QA) testing, which ensures it behaves the way you expect and according to the business rules.*

Keep in mind that although XP preaches about building tests before creating the code, and ideally that's how we should work, in real life, there are many cases where we find ourselves writing the tests after the application. A good example is using TDD with auto-generated code. For instance, Flex 4 beta offers a plug-in for Cairngorm that generates code automatically, so it makes sense to write the code before the test.

TDD with MVC frameworks

Having completed the first part of this chapter, you now know the basics of working with FlexUnit and TDD. In this section, we are going to cover the more advanced topic of integrating TDD with existing frameworks such as MVC.

Model, View, Controller (MVC) frameworks, such as PureMVC (http://puremvc.org/) or Cairngorm (http://labs.adobe.com/wiki/index.php/Cairngorm), and TDD make a good marriage, since both MVC and TDD prefer the application logic to be separated from the front view and the data. TDD allows us to create test cases on only the logic and then to create a separate test case for the presentation layer.

What is the MVC pattern? Think about separating the three major parts of your application as follows:

- **Model**: The model is the application data.
- **View**: The view holds the presentation layer.
- **Controller**: The controller is the glue between the view and the model.

As MVC frameworks are often used in Flex projects, we think that it's worth spending the next several pages covering how to implement TDD in an MVC framework. We are not going to discuss which MVC framework is best; they each have their own advantages, but we'll cover integrating unit testing with these two common frameworks in this chapter:

- **Cairngorm**: You can use this vanilla-flavored, microarchitecture to develop an application with many user gestures. Cairngorm projects are easy to maintain in a large team. Though Cairngorm is Adobe's standard and is maintained as open source by Adobe, it doesn't support pure ActionScript 3.0 projects.
- **PureMVC**: This is a lightweight MVC architecture and a well-documented framework. It supports all ActionScript 3.0 code including Flex, AIR, and pure ActionScript 3.0, and it allows you to easily separate the view from its logic.

Creating tests with an existing framework may be challenging, and in some cases, it makes more sense to create the test after the code is completed rather that following traditional TDD practices. You may especially find writing the code before the test easier when you use plug-ins or code generator scripts to create your user gesture automatically. We recommend using your own judgment now that you've read about TDD and its advantages; just see what works best for you.

Using TDD with Cairngorm

In this section, we assume that you are familiar with basic development with Cairngorm, so we won't include a tutorial on how the Cairngorm framework works. Visit the Cairngorm open source documentation at http://opensource.adobe.com/wiki/display/site/Documentation to learn more about Cairngorm.

Cairngorm doesn't separate the model, view, and controller in each container by default. To use TDD, we recommend using the presentation model pattern, which separates the model and behavior of the presentation from the GUI controls used in the interface. The presentation model is a loosely coupled class that represents all the data and behavior of the component but without any of the controls used to render that UI on the screen.

These are the advantages of using the presentation model pattern:

- Allows you to test without the UI
- Allows you to create multiple views from the same UI
- Allows a component to be loosely coupled and thus easily reused

There are many ways to implement the presentation model. We will show you one way, but feel free to explore and try other ways.

Additionally, it is an important to point out that the following chapters are using FlexUnit 1, but currently, there is a new version of FlexUnit 4 beta, which improves the ability to test frameworks such as Cairngorm and PureMVC. To read more about FlexUnit 4, visit http://www.insideria.com/2009/05/flashbuilder4-will-support-fle.html.

Creating the use case

We are going to build a simple application with only three business rules:

1. Connect to Adobe feeds and retrieve the latest feeds related to Flex.
2. Display these results in a list.
3. When a user clicks an item on the list, display detailed information about that item.

Create an application test suite and two test cases. Open Flash Builder 4 beta, and select File ➤ New ➤ Test Case Class and then select Test Suite Case. Name the test classes ReadAdobeFeedsTestCase and UserSelectedFeedTestCase.

The ReadAdobeFeedsTestCase class is identical to ServiceTestCase, so you can take a look at the code of the ServiceTestCase class. The UserSelectedFeedTestCase class is a use case to ensure that, once the user selects an item, the selected item reaches the presentation model. In this specific example, it's easier to complete the test once the presentation model is completed.

The complete application is shown in Figure 14-18.

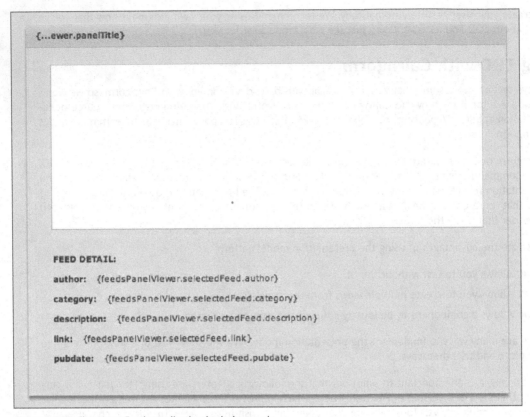

Figure 14-18. Flex News Feeds application in design mode

Creating the application model

We'll get started by looking at the application model. We are going to tweak the Model Locator pattern a little bit. Model Locator is one of the most criticized patterns in Cairngorm, because each component is based on the model locator, so one view cannot be pulled out of Cairngorm and placed in another application, since there is a strong dependency between the component and the model locator.

To break the dependency, one would have to go and check properties in the model locator and replicate these properties in a new Cairngorm application. If you want to pull a component away from a Cairngorm application, the job is even harder, since you will have to refactor your component.

Using the presentation model, we can adjust the model locator and use it as a locator to the application data instead of the storage class. We can split data into two types:

- **Domain data**: Data that is shared between different components and classes, for instance, user login information
- **Presentation data**: Data that is unique to a certain component, for instance, a list component data provider

The application is simple in nature and needs only two view components, our entry point and our panel that will hold the feeds and detail information.

Our model locator will reflect these views and will contain an instance of the two as well as the domain data. Under the model package, we will include three classes:

- feedsPanelViewerPM: Presentation model for the Adobe feeds' panel viewer
- mainPM: The main entry point for the application's presentation model
- libraryModel: Holds the application's shared data

The new modified ModelLocator class acts as a locator and creates an instance of the data classes the first time the class is called, so the data is persistence through the life cycle of the application:

```
package com.elad.application.model
{
    [Bindable]
    public final class ModelLocator implements IModelLocator
    {
        private static var instance:ModelLocator;
        public var libraryModel:LibraryModel;
        public var mainPM:MainPM;
        public var feedsPanelViewerPM:FeedsPanelViewerPM;

        public function ModelLocator(access:Private)
        {
            if ( access == null )
            {
                throw new CairngormError( ➥
CairngormMessageCodes.SINGLETON_EXCEPTION, "ModelLocator" );
            }
            instance = this;
        }

        public static function getInstance() : ModelLocator
        {
            if ( instance == null )
            {
                instance = new ModelLocator( new Private() );
                instance.libraryModel = new LibraryModel();
                instance.mainPM = new MainPM( instance.libraryModel );
                instance.feedsPanelViewerPM = new FeedsPanelViewerPM( ➥
                            instance.libraryModel );
            }
            return instance;
        }
    }
}

class Private {}
```

The LibraryModel class contains the application's shared data—any data that needs to be shared among the different classes will be stored in this data class. In our example, we are not sharing any information among classes and containers, so we will leave this class empty:

```
package com.elad.application.model.domain
{
    [Bindable]
    public class LibraryModel
    {
        // TODO: place all application data here
    }
}
```

AbstractPM is the abstract class for the presentation model and will be used in every presentation model class. The class takes care of common use cases. For instance, let's say we need to open a pop-up window the first time we run the application, but we don't need that window when the user calls the component again. The abstract class also has methods to handle preinitializing and initializing of the class. Keep in mind that the abstract class can have any logic that you think is needed, so feel free to create your own abstract class to fit your exact requirements.

```
package com.elad.application.model.presentation
{
    public class AbstractPM extends EventDispatcher
    {
        private var firstShow:Boolean = true;

        public function AbstractPM()
        {
        }

        public function handleShow():void
        {
            if( firstShow )
            {
                handleFirstShow();
                firstShow = false ;
            }

            else handleSubsequentShows();
        }

        public function preinitialize():void
        {
            handlePreInitialize();
        }
        public function initialize():void
        {
            handleInitialize();
        }
```

```
    protected function handlePreInitialize():void //to be overriden
    {
    }
    protected function handleInitialize():void //to be overriden
    {
    }
    protected function handleCompleted():void //to be overriden
    {
    }
    protected function handleFirstShow():void
    {
        // to be overriden
    }
    protected function handleSubsequentShows():void
    {
        // to be overriden
    }
    public function preInitializeCompletedHandler(event:Event):void
    {
        handleInitialize();
    }
    public function initializeCompletedHandler(event:Event):void
    {
        handleShow();
    }
        }
    }
```

Creating the Main.mxml class

Each container, including the main application class Main.mxml, includes the container and the data and logic.

The MainPM class will be used by our main application container and includes classes to handle initialization and preinitialization, which are common in large Cairngorm applications. The class allows us to keep the application class clean—containing only the UI containers—and no logic is needed in the view class, since the application logic is in the presentation model class.

```
    package com.elad.application.model.presentation
    {
        import com.adobe.cairngorm.control.CairngormEventDispatcher;
        import com.elad.application.events.InitializationCommandCompleted;
        import com.elad.application.events. ➡
                            PreInitializationCommandCompleted;
        import com.elad.application.events.StartupServicesEvent;
        import com.elad.application.model.ModelLocator;
        import com.elad.application.model.domain.LibraryModel;
```

```
[Bindable]
public class MainPM extends AbstractPM
{
    public var firstModulePM:FeedsPanelViewerPM;
    public var libraryModel:LibraryModel;

    public function MainPM(libraryModel:LibraryModel)
    {
        this.libraryModel = libraryModel;
        firstModulePM = new FeedsPanelViewerPM(libraryModel);
    }

    override protected function handlePreInitialize():void
    {
        // track once pre-initialize completed
        CairngormEventDispatcher.getInstance(). ➥
addEventListener( PreInitializationCommandCompleted.COMPLETED, ➥
preInitializeCompletedHandler );

        // call startup services
        new StartupServicesEvent().dispatch();
    }

    override protected function handleInitialize():void
    {
        // track once initialize completed
        CairngormEventDispatcher.getInstance(). ➥
addEventListener( InitializationCommandCompleted.COMPLETED,➥
 initializeCompletedHandler );

        new InitializationCommandCompleted().dispatch();
    }

    override protected function handleFirstShow():void
    {
        // implements or leave default
        handleCompleted();
    }

    override protected function handleSubsequentShows():void
    {
        // implements or leave default
        handleCompleted();
    }
```

```
        override protected function handleCompleted():void
        {
            // remove event listeners
            CairngormEventDispatcher.getInstance(). ➥
removeEventListener(    PreInitializationCommandCompleted.COMPLETED, ➥
preInitializeCompletedHandler );
            CairngormEventDispatcher.getInstance(). ➥
removeEventListener(    InitializationCommandCompleted.COMPLETED, ➥
initializeCompletedHandler );

            // TODO: implements changes in view
        }

    }
}
```

Notice that, once the initialize events are dispatched, the handleCompleted method is called, so we can place code that handles any changes we want to make in the application. For instance, we can wait until the services are done before changing the application state. Or we can set the mouse to an hourglass icon while the results are being dispatched using the CursorManager.setBusyCursor and remove the icon once the results are retrieve using the CursorManager.removeBusyCursor method.

Take a look at the application Main.mxml container. The code includes only the containers and reference to the presentation model we created previously, so all the initialization calls are handled in the presentation model.

```
<?xml version="1.0" encoding="utf-8"?>
<mx:Application xmlns:mx="http://www.adobe.com/2006/mxml"
    layout="absolute"
    xmlns:business="com.elad.application.business.*"
    xmlns:control="com.elad.application.control.*"
    xmlns:view="com.elad.application.view.*"
    preinitialize="modelLocator.mainPM.preinitialize()">

    <mx:Script>
        <![CDATA[

        import com.elad.application.model.ModelLocator;

        [Bindable]
        private var modelLocator:ModelLocator = ➥
                    ModelLocator.getInstance();
    ]]>
    </mx:Script>

    <mx:Style source="assets/main.css" />
```

```
<control:testController />
<business:Services />

<view:FeedsPanelViewer feedsPanelViewer= ➡
        "{modelLocator.feedsPanelViewerPM}"/>
```

```
</mx:Application>
```

Notice that we also have references to the front controller, services locator, and model locator, which are crucial so we have access to Cairngorm singletons for the following patterns:

- **Front controller**: Handle mapping of event and commands.
- **Model locator**: Gives us access to the data object.
- **Service locator**: Allows us to use services.

The container FeedsPanelViewer will hold the feeds viewer. Notice that we are passing the FeedsPanelViewer object, so the container will be completely independent and can be easily pulled out of our application.

Creating initialization events

The InitializationCommandCompleted and PreInitializationCommandCompleted events will be used to mark once the application is completed. These events extend the CairngormEvent class. In our application, we are really not handling anything after the application is completely loaded, but these will be used frequently in your real-life applications.

```
package com.elad.application.events
{
    import com.adobe.cairngorm.control.CairngormEvent;

    public class InitializationCommandCompleted extends CairngormEvent
    {

        public static const COMPLETED:String = ➡
"com.elad.application.events.InitializationCommandCompleted";

        public function InitializationCommandCompleted(type:String = ➡
InitializationCommandCompleted.COMPLETED, bubbles:Boolean=false, ➡
cancelable:Boolean=false)
        {
            super(type, bubbles, cancelable);
        }

    }
}
```

Creating the Adobe feeds container

The container will include all the classes needed to make a service call retrieve the feed information and store the information in an object.

FeedsPanelViewerPM   The FeedsPanelViewerPM is our presentation model for the feeds viewer and will include both the data and the logic necessary to handle the UI container.

In FeedsPanelViewerPM, we get a reference of the libraryModel in case we need to access any data properties that are shared across the application, and since the class is bindable and included in the model locator, we will be able to bind properties and get the binding from the libraryModel:

```
public var libraryModel:LibraryModel;
```

We need to include the following variables:

- feedsCollection: Holds the collection of feeds
- panelTitle: Holds the panel title name, which is based on the feed's name
- selectedFeed: User-selected feed that shows detail information

Take a look at the complete code of the FeedsPanelViewerPM class:

```
package com.elad.application.model.presentation
{
    import com.elad.application.events.UserSelectedFeedEvent;
    import com.elad.application.model.domain.LibraryModel;
    import com.elad.application.vo.FeedVO;
    import com.elad.application.vo.FeedsCollectionVO;

    [Bindable]
    public class FeedsPanelViewerPM extends AbstractPM
    {

        public var libraryModel:LibraryModel;

        public var panelTitle:String;
        public var selectedFeed:FeedVO;

        private var _feedsCollection:FeedsCollectionVO = ➥
new FeedsCollectionVO();
        public function set feedsCollection ➥
(value:FeedsCollectionVO):void
        {
            _feedsCollection = value;
        }
        public function get feedsCollection():FeedsCollectionVO
        {
            return _feedsCollection;
        }
```

```
        public function FeedsPanelViewerPM(libraryModel:LibraryModel)
        {
            this.libraryModel = libraryModel;
        }
        public function changeSelectedFeed(feed:FeedVO):void
        {
            new UserSelectedFeedEvent(feed).dispatch();
        }
    }
}
```

VO classes The presentation model for the feed viewer is using two VOs: FeedsCollectionVO and FeedVO. The collection holds all feed entries, and each feed has the properties that are given by the feeds:

```
[Bindable]
public class FeedsCollectionVO implements IValueObject
{
    public function FeedsCollectionVO() {
    }

    public var collection:ArrayCollection = new ArrayCollection;

    public function addItem(val:FeedVO):void
    {
        collection.addItem(val);
    }

    public function getItem(index:Number):FeedVO
    {
        var retVal:FeedVO = new FeedVO();
        retVal = collection.getItemAt(index) as FeedVO;
        return retVal;
    }
}

[Bindable]
public class FeedVO implements IValueObject
{
    public function FeedVO() {
    }

    public var title:String;
    public var link:String;
    public var author:String;
    public var description:String;
    public var pubdate:String;
    public var category:String;
}
```

FeedsPanelViewer class   The FeedsPanelViewer UI container holds only the UI without any logic or any data. The component holds a reference of the presentation model FeedsPanelViewerPM and binds the properties in the components to that class.

It consists of two components: one that displays a list of the feeds and one that displays information once the user selects an item in the list (see Figure 14-19).

```
<?xml version="1.0" encoding="utf-8"?>
<mx:Panel xmlns:mx="http://www.adobe.com/2006/mxml"
    title="{feedsPanelViewer.panelTitle}"
    styleName="panelView">

    <mx:Script>
        <![CDATA[
            [Bindable]
            public var feedsPanelViewer:FeedsPanelViewerPM;
        ]]>
    </mx:Script>

    <!-- Feeds List -->
    <mx:List
        id="feedList"
        dataProvider="{feedsPanelViewer.feedsCollection.collection}"
        change= ➡
"feedsPanelViewer.changeSelectedFeed(FeedVO( feedList.selectedItem ))"
        labelField="title"/>

    <!-- Detail information -->
    <mx:VBox width="540">
      <mx:HBox>
            <mx:Label text="author:" fontWeight="bold"/>
            <mx:Label text="{feedsPanelViewer.selectedFeed.author}"
                    width="100%"/>
      </mx:HBox>
    </mx:VBox>

</mx:Panel>
```

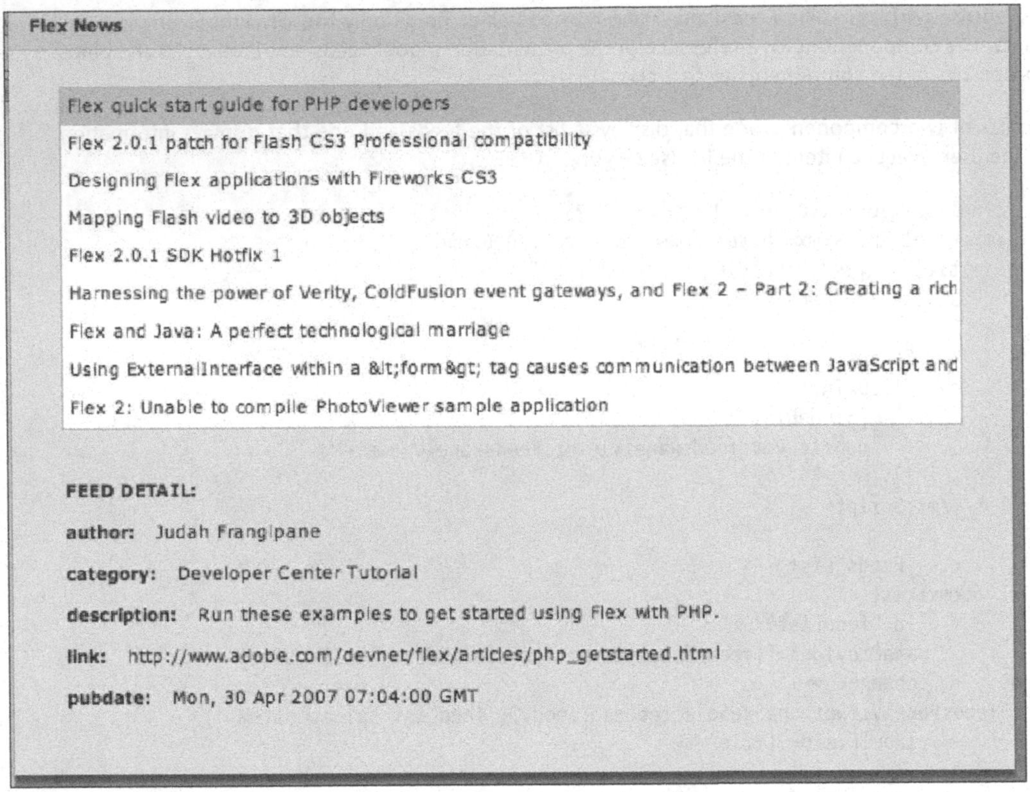

Figure 14-19. Flex News feeds application

Adding the service call

The Services.mxml class is the Cairngorm service locator singleton that holds all of the application's RPC components. We are using one service, and it's based on the feeds we used when we explained about asynchronous events in FlexUnit:

```xml
<?xml version="1.0" encoding="utf-8"?>
<cairngorm:ServiceLocator xmlns:mx="http://www.adobe.com/2006/mxml"
        xmlns:cairngorm="com.adobe.cairngorm.business.*" >
    <mx:Script>
        <![CDATA[
            public static var ADOBE_FEEDS:String = "adobe_feeds";
        ]]>
    </mx:Script>
    <mx:HTTPService id="adobe_feeds"
        url="http://rss.adobe.com/en/resources_flex.rss"
        resultFormat="e4x"/>
</cairngorm:ServiceLocator>
```

ReadAdobeFeedsDelegate is the delegate that will act as the bridge between the command and the service locator:

```
public function ReadAdobeFeedsDelegate(responder:IResponder)
{
    service = ServiceLocator.getInstance().getHTTPService ➡
                    (Services.ADOBE_FEEDS);
    this.responder = responder;
}

public function readAdobeFeeds():void
{
    var token:AsyncToken = service.send()
    token.addResponder( responder );
}
```

ReadAdobeFeedsCommand will pass the request to the delegate and than handle the results:

```
public function execute(event:CairngormEvent) : void
{
    var evt:ReadAdobeFeedsEvent = event as ReadAdobeFeedsEvent;
    var delegate:ReadAdobeFeedsDelegate = ➡
            new ReadAdobeFeedsDelegate( this );

    delegate.readAdobeFeeds();
}
```

The results are passed from the delegate back to the command class. We iterate through the class to create our feedsCollection VO, which holds each of the feeds using a FeedVO object:

```
public function result(data:Object) : void
{
    var result:ResultEvent = data as ResultEvent;
    var feed:FeedVO;
    var ob:Object;
    var len:int = result.result[0].channel.item.length();
    var collection:FeedsCollectionVO = new FeedsCollectionVO;

    for (var i:int=0; i<len; i++)
    {
        feed = new FeedVO();
        ob = result.result[0].channel.item[i];

        feed.author = ob.author;
        feed.category = ob.category;
        feed.description = ob.description;
        feed.link = ob.link;
        feed.pubdate = ob.pubdate;
        feed.title = ob.title;

        collection.addItem(feed);
    }
```

```
        modelLocator.feedsPanelViewerPM.feedsCollection = collection;
        modelLocator.feedsPanelViewerPM.panelTitle = ➥
            result.result.*[0].*[0];
        modelLocator.feedsPanelViewerPM.selectedFeed = ➥
    collection.collection.getItemAt(0) as FeedVO;

        // Initialization completed since we don't have any more services
        new PreInitializationCommandCompleted().dispatch();
    }
```

Once we complete setting objects in the model, we can call the PreInitializationCommandCompleted event:

```
    new PreInitializationCommandCompleted().dispatch();
```

Mark that services are completed and the main application can make changes if necessary by adding code to the handlePreInitialize method.

Now that our service classes are ready, we can set the StartupServicesCommand, which will be called when the application is initialized:

```
    public function execute(event:CairngormEvent) : void
    {
        var evt:StartupServicesEvent = event as StartupServicesEvent;
        new ReadAdobeFeedsCommand().execute(null);
    }
```

Responding to user selections of a feed

Once the user clicks a feed in the list, we want to display detailed information regarding the feed. UserSelectedFeedEvent and UserSelectedFeedCommand can easily handle that user gesture. The event expects a FeedVO to be passed with the feed item selected and the command just places it in the feedsPanelViewerPM.selectedFeed property.

```
    package com.elad.application.events
    {
        import com.adobe.cairngorm.control.CairngormEvent;
        import com.elad.application.vo.FeedVO;

        public final class UserSelectedFeedEvent extends CairngormEvent
        {

            public static const USERSELECTEDFEED_EVENT:String ➥
    = "com.elad.application.events.UserSelectedFeedEvent";

            public var selectedFeed:FeedVO;
```

```
    public function UserSelectedFeedEvent(selectedFeed:FeedVO)
    {
        this.selectedFeed = selectedFeed;
        super( USERSELECTEDFEED_EVENT );
    }
  }
}
```

The UserSelectedFeedCommand class sets the selectedFeed variable:

```
public function execute(event:CairngormEvent) : void
{
    var evt:UserSelectedFeedEvent = event as UserSelectedFeedEvent;
    modelLocator.feedsPanelViewerPM.selectedFeed = evt.selectedFeed;
}
```

As you'll recall, the presentation model class, FeedsPanelViewerPM, will be calling this event-command sequence:

```
public function changeSelectedFeed(feed:FeedVO):void
{
    new UserSelectedFeedEvent(feed).dispatch();
}
```

The sequence was originated from the FeedsPanelViewer view container:

```
<mx:List
        id="feedList"
        dataProvider="{feedsPanelViewer.feedsCollection.collection}"
        change="feedsPanelViewer.changeSelectedFeed ➡
                    (FeedVO( feedList.selectedItem ))"
        labelField="title"/>
```

Creating the application test suite and test cases

To create our test suite and test cases to test our application, we have to make some changes in the TestRunner.mxml container.

The reason is that we add the same references as we added in our main application to the single-ton classes: front controller and service locator. Otherwise, the application will not be able to map between the events and commands and will lack the ability to make service calls.

```
<?xml version="1.0" encoding="utf-8"?>
<mx:Application xmlns:mx="http://www.adobe.com/2006/mxml"
    xmlns:flexunit="flexunit.flexui.*"
    xmlns:business="com.elad.application.business.*"
    xmlns:control="com.elad.application.control.*"
    creationComplete="onCreationComplete()">
```

```
<mx:Script>
    <![CDATA[
        import flexUnitTests.GesturesTestSuite;

        import flexUnitTests.events.ReadAdobeFeedsTestCase;
        import flexUnitTests.events.UserSelectedFeedTestCase;
        import flexunit.framework.TestSuite;

        private function onCreationComplete():void
        {
            testRunner.test = currentRunTestSuite();
            testRunner.startTest();
        }

        public function currentRunTestSuite():TestSuite
        {
            var testsToRun:TestSuite = new TestSuite();

            testsToRun.addTest(GesturesTestSuite.suite());
            testsToRun.addTest( ➡
new UserSelectedFeedTestCase("testUserSelectedFeedEvent"));
            testsToRun.addTest( ➡
new ReadAdobeFeedsTestCase("testReadAdobeFeedsEvent"));
            return testsToRun;
        }

    ]]>
</mx:Script>

<control:testController />
<business:Services />
<flexunit:TestRunnerBase id="testRunner"/>

</mx:Application>
```

Ideally, we should create a test case for each Cairngorm user gesture, so the process of setting test cases for the Cairngorm gesture is as follows:

1. **Identify**: Understand the purpose of the user gesture and what data is affected.

2. **Track**: Dispatch the event, and watch changes in the model.

Additionally, it's helpful to create FlexMonkey tests to ensure the application view is changing according to our requirements, especially when you don't have QA resources available.

ReadAdobeFeedsTestCase is based on testing ReadAdobeFeedsEvent. Each Cairngorm event-command is based on a user gesture, and you need to identify all the user gestures based on the business requirement and user experience design.

In our case, we dispatch the event, and once the on-result method is called, we place the collection in the model. That way, we can dispatch the event and make sure the results reach the model. Here's the watcher:

```
watcherInstance = ➥
ChangeWatcher.watch(modelLocator.feedsPanelViewerPM,["feedsCollection"],
addAsync(itemsChanged, 2000, {compareResults: 0}, failFunc));
new ReadAdobeFeedsEvent().dispatch();
```

Once a change is made to the model, the binding method will dispatch an event automatically, and we can listen to that change and compare the results in the model:

```
private function itemsChanged(event:Event, data:Object):void
{
    var len:int = ➥
modelLocator.feedsPanelViewerPM.feedsCollection.collection.length;
    Assert.assertTrue("Collection is empty", ➥
len>data.compareResults);
}
```

Take a look at the complete ReadAdobeFeedsTestCase code:

```
package flexUnitTests.events
{
    import com.elad.application.events.ReadAdobeFeedsEvent;
    import com.elad.application.model.ModelLocator;

    import flash.events.Event;

    import flexunit.framework.Assert;
    import flexunit.framework.TestCase;

    import mx.binding.utils.ChangeWatcher;

    public class ReadAdobeFeedsTestCase extends TestCase
    {

        [Bindable]
        private var modelLocator:ModelLocator = ➥
                ModelLocator.getInstance();

        private var watcherInstance:ChangeWatcher;

        public function ReadAdobeFeedsTestCase(methodName:String=null)
        {
            super(methodName);
        }
```

```
                    public function testReadAdobeFeedsEvent():void
                    {
                        watcherInstance = ChangeWatcher.watch( ➥
                modelLocator.feedsPanelViewerPM,["feedsCollection"],
                        addAsync(itemsChanged, 2000, ➥
                {compareResults: 0}, failFunc));

                        new ReadAdobeFeedsEvent().dispatch();
                    }

                    private function itemsChanged(event:Event, data:Object):void
                    {
                        var len:int = ➥
                modelLocator.feedsPanelViewerPM.feedsCollection.collection.length;
                        Assert.assertTrue("Collection is empty", ➥
                            len>data.compareResults);
                    }

                    private function failFunc(data:Object):void
                    {
                        fail("Couldn't connect to Adobe feeds and ➥
                            update application model");
                    }
                }
            }
```

UserSelectedFeedTestCase follows the same type of methodology of listening to changes in the model. This time, though, once the user selects an item, the modelLocator.feedsPanelViewerPM.selectedFeed will change.

```
        var author:String = ➥
        modelLocator.feedsPanelViewerPM.selectedFeed.author;
        Assert.assertEquals(data.compareResults, author);
```

Take a look at the complete UserSelectedFeedTestCase code:

```
        package flexUnitTests.events
        {
            import com.elad.application.events.UserSelectedFeedEvent;
            import com.elad.application.model.ModelLocator;
            import com.elad.application.vo.FeedVO;

            import flash.events.Event;

            import flexunit.framework.Assert;
            import flexunit.framework.TestCase;

            import mx.binding.utils.ChangeWatcher;
```

```
public class UserSelectedFeedTestCase extends TestCase
{

    [Bindable]
    private var modelLocator:ModelLocator = ➡
ModelLocator.getInstance();

    private var watcherInstance:ChangeWatcher;

    public function UserSelectedFeedTestCase( ➡
methodName:String=null)
    {
        super(methodName);
    }

    public function testUserSelectedFeedEvent():void
    {
        watcherInstance = ChangeWatcher.watch( ➡
modelLocator.feedsPanelViewerPM,["selectedFeed"],
            addAsync(itemChanged, 2000, ➡
{compareResults: "Elad"}, failFunc));

        var feed:FeedVO = new FeedVO();
        feed.author = "Elad";

        new UserSelectedFeedEvent(feed).dispatch();
    }

    private function itemChanged(event:Event, data:Object):void
    {
        var author:String = ➡
modelLocator.feedsPanelViewerPM.selectedFeed.author;
        Assert.assertEquals(data.compareResults, author);
    }

    private function failFunc(data:Object):void
    {
        fail("Couldn't change selected feed");
    }
}
}
```

Using TDD with PureMVC

PureMVC is another popular framework. Let's take the application we created for Cairngorm and convert it to the PureMVC framework. This is a good exercise, since it shows you the differences between the two frameworks.

We can use the same FeedsPanelViewer.mxml view container we created for the Cairngorm application, but we need to make a few changes in the application. We'll remove the binding properties and let the mediator handle all the changes in the container to achieve a more loosely coupled architecture.

```
<?xml version="1.0" encoding="utf-8"?>
<mx:Panel xmlns:mx="http://www.adobe.com/2006/mxml"
    layout="vertical"
    width="600" height="450"
    styleName="panelView">

    <!-- Feeds List -->
    <mx:List
        id="feedList"
        change="dispatchEvent(new UserSelectedFeedEvent ➥
            (FeedVO( feedList.selectedItem )));"
        labelField="title"/>

    <!-- Detail information -->
    <mx:VBox width="540" horizontalScrollPolicy="off"
            verticalScrollPolicy="off">
        <mx:Spacer height="15" />
        <mx:HBox>
            <mx:Label text="FEED DETAIL:" fontWeight="bold"/>
        </mx:HBox>
        <mx:HBox>
            <mx:Label text="author:" fontWeight="bold"/>
            <mx:Label id="author" width="100%"/>
        </mx:HBox>
    </mx:VBox>

</mx:Panel>
```

Creating the mediator class

PureMVC uses the mediator class, which acts very similar to the presentation model we created in Caringorm. The mediator acts as an intermediary between the view containers and the data (proxy class). Our mediator class, FeedsPanelViewerMediator, listens to notifications regarding the data received from the proxy and sets the properties in the view container.

```
package com.elad.TDDPureMVC.view
{
    import com.elad.TDDPureMVC.events.UserSelectedFeedEvent;
    import com.elad.TDDPureMVC.model.FeedsPanelViewerProxy;
    import com.elad.TDDPureMVC.model.vo.FeedVO;
    import com.elad.TDDPureMVC.view.components.FeedsPanelViewer;

    import org.puremvc.as3.interfaces.IMediator;
    import org.puremvc.as3.interfaces.INotification;
    import org.puremvc.as3.patterns.mediator.Mediator;
```

```actionscript
public class FeedsPanelViewerMediator extends ➥
          Mediator implements IMediator
{
    public static const NAME:String = 'FeedsPanelViewerMediator';

    private var feedsPanelViewerProxy:FeedsPanelViewerProxy;

    public function FeedsPanelViewerMediator( ➥
              viewComponent:Object=null)
    {
        super(NAME, viewComponent);
        feedsPanelViewer.addEventListener( ➥
UserSelectedFeedEvent.USERSELECTEDFEED_EVENT, changeSelectedFeed);
    }

    private function changeSelectedFeed( ➥
              event:UserSelectedFeedEvent):void
    {
        setDetail(event.selectedFeed);
    }

    public function get feedsPanelViewer():FeedsPanelViewer
    {
        return viewComponent as FeedsPanelViewer;
    }

    override public function listNotificationInterests():Array
    {
        return [
            FeedsPanelViewerProxy.READ_ADOBE_FEEDS_SUCCESS,
              ];
    }

    private function setDetail(feed:FeedVO):void
    {
        feedsPanelViewer.author.text = feed.author;
        feedsPanelViewer.category.text = feed.category;
        feedsPanelViewer.description.text = feed.description;
        feedsPanelViewer.link.text = feed.link;
        feedsPanelViewer.pubdate.text = feed.pubdate;
    }

    override public function handleNotification( ➥
              notification:INotification):void
    {
        feedsPanelViewerProxy = facade.retrieveProxy( ➥
FeedsPanelViewerProxy.NAME) as FeedsPanelViewerProxy;
```

```
                            switch ( notification.getName() )
                            {
                                case FeedsPanelViewerProxy.READ_ADOBE_FEEDS_SUCCESS:
                                    feedsPanelViewer.feedList.dataProvider = ➥
    feedsPanelViewerProxy.feedsCollectionVO.collection;
                                    setDetail(feedsPanelViewerProxy.selectedFeed);
                                    feedsPanelViewer.title = ➥
    feedsPanelViewerProxy.panelTitle;

                                    break;
                            }
                        }
                    }
                }
```

Creating the proxy class

The proxy class serves a function similar to Cairngorm's command, delegate, and model classes together. Specifically, the proxy class encapsulates the service component, handles the onResult and onFault methods, and holds the data.

Take a look at FeedsPanelViewerProxy:

```
package com.elad.TDDPureMVC.model
{
    import com.elad.TDDPureMVC.model.vo.FeedVO;
    import com.elad.TDDPureMVC.model.vo.FeedsCollectionVO;

    import mx.rpc.events.FaultEvent;
    import mx.rpc.events.ResultEvent;
    import mx.rpc.http.HTTPService;

    import org.puremvc.as3.interfaces.IProxy;
    import org.puremvc.as3.patterns.proxy.Proxy;

    public class FeedsPanelViewerProxy extends Proxy implements IProxy
    {

        public static const NAME:String = "FeedsPanelViewerProxy";
        public static const READ_ADOBE_FEEDS_SUCCESS:String ➥
    = 'readAdobeFeedsSuccess';
        public static const READ_ADOBE_FEEDS_FAILED:String ➥
    = 'readAdobeFeedsFailed';
        public var service:HTTPService;

        public function FeedsPanelViewerProxy()
        {
            super(NAME, new FeedsCollectionVO() );
```

```
    service = new HTTPService();
  service.url = "http://rss.adobe.com/en/resources_flex.rss";
  service.resultFormat = "e4x";
   service.addEventListener( FaultEvent.FAULT, onFault );
   service.addEventListener( ResultEvent.RESULT, onResult );
}

public function getAdobeFeeds():void
{
    service.send();
}

// Cast data object with implicit getter
public function get feedsCollectionVO():FeedsCollectionVO
{
    return data.feedsCollectionVO as FeedsCollectionVO;
}

public function get selectedFeed():FeedVO
{
    return (data.feedsCollectionVO as FeedsCollectionVO). ➡
        collection.getItemAt(0) as FeedVO;
}

public function get panelTitle():String
{
    return data.panelTitle as String;
}

private function onResult( result:ResultEvent ) : void
{
    var feed:FeedVO;
    var item:Object;
    var len:int = result.result[0].channel.item.length();
    var collection:FeedsCollectionVO = new FeedsCollectionVO;
    var dataObject:Object = new Object();

    for (var i:int=0; i<len; i++)
    {
        feed = new FeedVO();
        item = result.result[0].channel.item[i];

        feed.author = item.author;
        feed.category = item.category;
        feed.description = item.description;
        feed.link = item.link;
        feed.pubdate = item.pubdate;
        feed.title = item.title;
```

```
                                collection.addItem(feed);
                    }

                    dataObject.feedsCollectionVO = collection;
                    dataObject.panelTitle = String(result.result.*[0].*[0]);

                    setData(dataObject);
                    sendNotification(READ_ADOBE_FEEDS_SUCCESS);
                }

                private function onFault( event:FaultEvent ) : void
                {
                    sendNotification( READ_ADOBE_FEEDS_FAILED, ➥
                        event.fault.faultString );
                }

            }
        }
```

Now that the proxy and mediator are ready, we can set the command ReadAdobeFeedsCommand:

```
        override public function execute(note:INotification):void
        {
            var feedsProxy:FeedsPanelViewerProxy = facade.retrieveProxy ➥
                    (FeedsPanelViewerProxy.NAME) as FeedsPanelViewerProxy;
            feedsProxy.getAdobeFeeds();
        }
```

Creating the test suite and test case to test PureMVC

Next, we need to create a test runner and test suite using FlexUnit default classes. We will assert changes in the proxy class by using helper classes from an open source library called PureMVC FlexUnit Testing (http://code.google.com/p/puremvc-flexunit-testing/).

Take a look at ReadAdobeFeedsTestCase. The setup() method registers the proxy class:

```
        override public function setUp():void
        {
            var facade:ApplicationFacade = ApplicationFacade.getInstance();
            facade.registerProxy( new FeedsPanelViewerProxy() );
        }
```

We need two methods to get an instance of the proxy and retrieve the container view:

```
        private function get proxy():FeedsPanelViewerProxy
        {
            var retVal:FeedsPanelViewerProxy = ➥
        ApplicationFacade.getInstance().retrieveProxy( ➥
                FeedsPanelViewerProxy.NAME) as FeedsPanelViewerProxy;
            return retVal;
        }
```

```
private function get view():IView
{
    return View.getInstance();
}
```

Our test calls the registerObserver method, which is used to listen for a PureMVC notification on the proxy. We pass the PureMVC view, proxy, and information for the AddSync() method, such as the callback method that sends the response and timeout:

```
public function testReadAdobeFeedsEvent():void
{
    registerObserver(this.view, this.proxy, ➡
        FeedsPanelViewerProxy.READ_ADOBE_FEEDS_SUCCESS, ➡
        handleResponse, 300);
    this.proxy.getAdobeFeeds();
}
```

Once the notification is captured the response method will be dispatched and we can assert our variable:

```
private function handleResponse(e:PureMVCNotificationEvent):void
{
    Assert.assertEquals("Feed title is incorrect", ➡
        proxy.panelTitle, "Flex News");
}
```

Here's the complete code:

```
package flexUnitTests.proxies
{
    import ➡
com.andculture.puremvcflexunittesting.PureMVCNotificationEvent;
    import com.andculture.puremvcflexunittesting.PureMVCTestCase;
    import com.elad.TDDPureMVC.model.FeedsPanelViewerProxy;

    import flexunit.framework.Assert;

    import org.puremvc.as3.core.View;
    import org.puremvc.as3.interfaces.IView;

    public class ReadAdobeFeedsTestCase extends PureMVCTestCase
    {
        override public function setUp():void
        {
            var facade:ApplicationFacade = ➡
                ApplicationFacade.getInstance();
            facade.registerProxy( new FeedsPanelViewerProxy() );
        }
```

```
        private function get proxy():FeedsPanelViewerProxy
        {
                var retVal:FeedsPanelViewerProxy = ➥
    ApplicationFacade.getInstance().retrieveProxy( ➥
    FeedsPanelViewerProxy.NAME) as FeedsPanelViewerProxy;
                return retVal;
        }

        private function get view():IView
        {
                return View.getInstance();
        }

        public function ReadAdobeFeedsTestCase(➥
                methodName:String=null)
        {
                super(methodName);
        }

        public function testReadAdobeFeedsEvent():void
        {
                registerObserver(this.view, this.proxy, ➥
    FeedsPanelViewerProxy.READ_ADOBE_FEEDS_SUCCESS, ➥
    handleResponse, 300);
                this.proxy.getAdobeFeeds();
        }

        private function handleResponse( ➥
            e:PureMVCNotificationEvent):void
        {
                Assert.assertEquals("Feed title is incorrect", ➥
                    proxy.panelTitle, "Flex News");
        }
    }
}
```

Summary

In this chapter, we covered unit testing and test-driven development (TDD). TDD and unit testing are among the hottest architectural subjects in the latest years, and they make development and scalability easier and less prone to errors.

We went through the development cycle of developing using TDD and gave you a complete overview on how to move your development cycle to TDD. We then showed you how to use FlexUnit to create test suites and test cases.

We continued by showing you the new Flex 4 plug-in. With it, you can create your scaffolding easily and simplify the process by having a view window in Eclipse to see tests. We also walked through creating asynchronous tests in FlexUnit and showed you some real life examples. You learned how to create tests for visual components utilizing FlexMonkey, and finally, we covered some advanced topics of using FlexUnit with existing frameworks and implementing the presentation model to separate the container from the logic and data.

We hope that this chapter will inspire you to change your development cycle for all Flash applications—mobile, web, or desktop—and will allow you to create better, more scalable code that can be moved from one application to another with little change to the code.

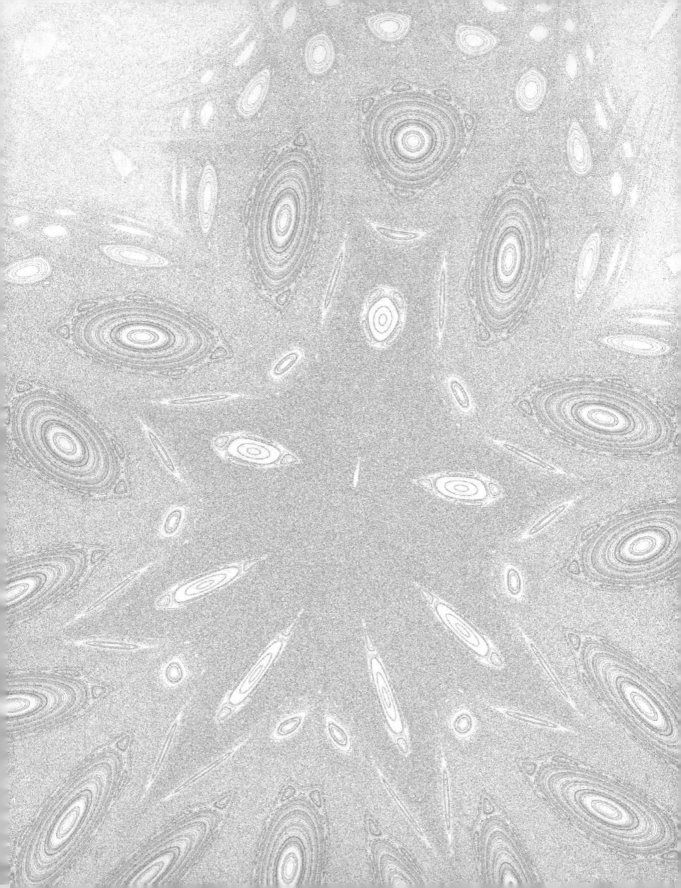

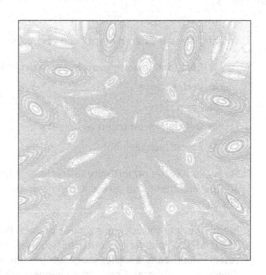

Chapter 15

CREATING A CROSS-PLATFORM VIDEO PLAYER AND OPTIMIZING CONTENT

Video is a key element of compelling web-based content. It is ubiquitous. It can convey and enhance news, blogs, music videos, web TV, and social media, as well as amateur and professional movie promotions. And more particularly, web content designers and developers *assume* quality video delivery is a resource that is readily available and treat it as a standard part of the vernacular when creating products and services.

Most mobile devices are equipped with video players to decode and render video for playback. Many device manufacturers and operators offer TV on-demand, such as Verizon V Cast, as well as streaming to consumers. In fact, most of today's mobile devices have the ability to play video files. In recent years bandwidth increased in mobile devices, and about 600 million such devices worldwide are connected to 3G networks with fast Internet connection of 144Kbps. What this means is that the user's expectation of viewing rich broadband video on their handhelds increases.

So how does Flash come into the picture?

Flash is the most used platform to view videos worldwide, with 80 percent of the videos based on Flash, according to Internet market research firm comScore. Flash 6 through Flash 10 has supported video playback across platforms. Flash on the mobile platform too has had the ability to render videos.

To date, motion video has not been very popular on mobile phones for the following reasons:

- Cost (data transmission and plan details)
- Performance
- Form factor
- Deficient production techniques
- Power management

Flash Lite has the opportunity to create a unified market that is big enough to support advancement and development and give entrepreneurs the chance to profitably innovate their way out of these difficulties.

Mobile devices include your mobile phones, PDAs, portable multimedia players (PMPs), Ultra Mobile PCs (UMPCs), and various other portable devices that support the playback of video files. Abundant research and early adopter usage analysis shows that, without question, the big early wins for small device application and content developers are likely to be in two areas: mobile TV (think live music and sports broadcasts) and gaming. Both are heavily reliant on video and audio.

Dealing with video for mobile devices is different than desktop or the Web. There are some key differences to take into account when doing design and development that targets small-screen battery-powered devices. Most of the video techniques that work well on big-screen, wall-powered devices that the typical Flash developer targets won't work for small-screen, battery-powered devices. This is not to say that video doesn't belong in small-device applications. On the contrary, using video presents perhaps the most extreme divergence from the typical circumstances:

- **Production**: In terms of production, it is recommended that video production be treated differently when the target is the small screen of a mobile device. This isn't simply a matter of cropping or scaling. To be successful, video capture techniques, the editing process, and story structure must be adjusted to account for the small image size, the cost of transferring data to a mobile device, and the highly interruptible nature of the content consumer's attention.
- **Device constraints**: Because mobile devices are highly constrained platforms, designers and developers must work harder to optimize content for small devices than is typically the case for video content targeting larger systems that are connected to wall power to ensure uninterruptable connection to the Internet. This may involve experimenting with different methods of encoding video clips to achieve the best balance between file size and video and audio quality.
- **Dynamic streaming and switching profiles**: Since mobile devices may often lose their connection to the network as well as change bandwidth connection when streaming videos, we recommend that you be able to stream videos as well as dynamically switch between profiles to increase user experience and avoid interruption.

Although Flash is as close to being a truly cross-platform mobile development and runtime environment as anything available today, there are still differences in execution environments for a couple of reasons. First, according to Adobe projections, 1 billion Flash Lite–enabled devices will have shipped worldwide by fourth-quarter 2010. In this population, there will remain at least three major versions of Flash Lite, and their video capabilities differ in important ways (possibly more, because device manufacturers have the option of modifying the behavior and capabilities of the Flash Lite engine to differentiate their devices, implement security strategies, or partner with carriers). For developers, this means that video-reliant applications must intelligently discern the status and characteristics of devices before blindly or naively downloading video files and launching playback.

In this chapter, we will cover the essentials for making a savvy desktop, web-oriented Flash video app developer rapidly functional in an environment where the aesthetic, technical, and cognitive rules are drastically modified by four things:

- Small form factors
- Inflexible power constraints
- Intermittent connection (or very short user attention spans)
- Fragmentation of the target device population

Additionally, we'll explore best practices for producing and delivering video content using Flash, video capabilities, and formats supported by Flash Mobile. We will see how Flash supports runtime detection of device characteristics so that applications can intelligently and appropriately send video to a user's phone. You'll learn about video production, encoding techniques, and application coding guidelines. We will explore building streaming and progressive download video players as well as optimization techniques. Finally, we will take a look at Adobe Strobe and Open Video Player and show how to reach as many devices as possible with a single, or at least very limited, number of versions of your content.

Initial strategy choices: reusing or creating video content

For *mobile* device video content to be engaging and compelling for content consumers, the key challenge is making video that works well on tiny screens.

Mobile devices seldom have the resolution, color depth, or backlighting intensity that designers and developers have come to expect. One of the paramount benefits Flash offers both developers and media consumers is that, of all the products available, it does the best job of bridging the technology chasms of the extraordinarily fragmented mobile device landscape.

Flash Lite is broadly compatible with its desktop progenitor, Flash, and so enjoys a vast equity in existing code and content that may reasonably be repurposed for small devices. Additionally, as more mobile devices support Flash 10 we will soon be able to use the same application used for the desktop in mobile devices.

But here's the challenge: leveraging existing video content is not usually going to be a "straight-across" process. Savvy editing, optimizing, and cutting will often be required in order to deliver a satisfactory user experience. Where it is an option, producing video content that specifically targets mobile devices is going to be the best and fastest bet, but again, production values and techniques, which fully account for the characteristics of small mobile devices, are a prerequisite to a great product.

The decision whether to create new video or reuse existing content might possibly be the key determinant of success for a project. Several factors influence effectiveness and smooth, efficient video playback on mobile devices. The first step in planning a mobile device targeting content project is to weigh the potential impacts of factors, which will ultimately determine the quality of the user experience you are able to create.

Tips for making great mobile device video content

Quality desktop or web video relies on great volumes of data, because of the large number of sequential images necessary to create the impression of fluid motion; because video is usually supported by audio, which is also requires voluminous data sets; and because lifelike color requires large color palettes. Taken together, these things could easily overwhelm both the bandwidth and the processing power of a small device if the uncompressed video files were naively streamed to it.

This isn't a new challenge. Early multimedia developers targeted desktop machines that would be considered both primitive and constrained in today's computing landscape had exactly the same limitations. The solution was the development of the *codec* (enCOder/DECoder) algorithm. (See the section "Video Codec 411," later in this chapter, to learn more about codecs, a key technology for web-based video and audio.) Codecs, as their name implies, are programs that compress and decompress data. (There are audio codecs as well as video codecs.) Compression has two main benefits: reduced file size speeds up transmission and reduces the needed data storage space on the destination device.

Most codecs are *lossy*, which means some of the data is lost during compression and cannot be recovered during decompression. *Lossless* codecs preserve all original data, and are therefore a 100 percent faithful transcription of the original data set when uncompressed. Lossless compression is not typically well suited to small devices and is therefore rarely used for deployment of videos for mobile devices.

Creating content for small devices is inherently a different process than creating content for large screen devices. Here's why: it might seem like belaboring the point to reiterate that small screen devices have. . .small screens! For purposes of content design and development, this is not simply a matter of scale and arithmetic. Cognitively, the human brain evaluates a palm-sized object very differently than one that has dimensions larger than the spacing between a typical pair of eyes. For this reason, mobile UI design demands an appreciation of how human cognition influences the gathering and absorption of information from small areas. Here are two biological considerations that influence the usability of small device applications and content:

- **Mobile devices have readability limitations, due to size, cognition issues, and the fact that ambient lighting can create glare**: Small displays aren't good for presenting extensive textual content. The reason is mainly due to the fact that reading is a highly integrative process, and not simply a sequential, linear traversal of words. Fluent readers iteratively scan a page, initially identifying nouns and noun phrases. Punctuation is a powerful cue in the scanning process, acting by pacing acquisition of information, telling the reader where to slow down, stop, or pay particular attention. Cognitively and visually, punctuation creates both rhythm and emphasis, not least because a noticeable area of white space typically follows it. In terms of reading comprehension and speed, white space is pivotal in showing the reader what information should be given focus. The interplay between white space and punctuation accounts for why small-display devices don't support high-level cognitive reading processes well: their limited scanning area is too small for discernable patterns of white space to emerge, so users must read each word, retain the sense of the string between screens, and synthesize data (words) into information.

  Put another way, tiny displays preclude using punctuation to determine emphasis and structure, because several sentences must be simultaneously visible to acquire punctuation cues. Forcing a competent reader to read very slowly produces extreme frustration and dramatically reduces both acuity and comprehension. The bottom line: highly textual interfaces don't work well on phones, and neither do deeply nested navigation models.

- **People have "blink limitations"**: A typical human normally blinks about once every 2–6 seconds. Confronted with a small object like a mobile phone screen, the brain assumes that it should be able to decode, interpret, and store information in a single blink cycle, or at most a few blink cycles. This cognitive presumption establishes sort of a nonrational baseline expectation about how fast and easy it should be to derive actionable information from the screen of a mobile device. Successful designs for content, navigation, and UI controls need to be speedy, visual, streamlined, and intuitive.

Given these usability and interaction influencers, it is a safe assertion that you can't produce good results on a small device simply by scaling down content or video originally produced for much larger formats. This is a critical consideration because usage pattern research suggests that consumers are ready to adopt mobile phones as entertainment devices, and would be willing to pay for content like live sports, Internet TV, and music performances. However, user expectations are high, and you'll never get a second chance at a first impression. On these constrained platforms, successes in the entertainment content niche will demand collaboration between software developers and graphics specialists. To help create satisfying and entertaining content that uses the best features of mobile devices but respects the inherent limitations of a small-display, battery-powered device, here are some usability fundamentals for video content architects and developers:

- Cognitively, intuitive understanding of visuals typically has as much to do with the *empty space* around the center of interest as with the actual depiction of the subject.

  Artists and designers call this empty area *negative space*, and it is often the defining feature of an effective visual design (for example, logos, and favicons often rely on negative space for visual impact). The small size of a mobile handset's display effectively eliminates the use of negative space as a major design element. For a graphical element to be effective across a range of mobile devices, follow these general rules to create high-impact visuals:

  - Focus on a single, simple subject.
  - Crop ruthlessly.
  - Limit the color palette to a small number of high-contrast colors.
  - Avoid subtle color transitions.
  - For linear features and embedded graphics, choose heavy, distinct lines, simple shapes, and uncomplicated designs.
  - For graphics, use fast drawing and filling methods and limit the use of transparency.
  - For text, use the bold san serif device font.

- Goodput (see the next section for an explanation of *goodput*) rates determine audio and video quality and, by extension, user experience satisfaction. Extensive research has shown that there are basic thresholds rates at which users consider quality acceptable. Most people consider video playback to be "good" at a sustained video frame rate of five frames per second and an audio rate of 12 kilobits per second. (For fast action, video requires higher frame rates to receive a "good" rating.) If the goodput falls below these rates, images appear blurry or blocky. Research has also shown that viewers are far more forgiving of temporary lapses in video quality than they are of audio breakups or dropouts. Here are some guidelines for creating high-quality video content for the small display:

  - Crop very tightly to the subject, and fill the frame.
  - Cut between shots to avoid panning.

- Wide-angle shots seldom work well on small screens, particularly those capable only of portrait mode. Use judiciously where they are absolutely necessary (e.g., to establish location).

- Use close-ups whenever possible.

- To shoot fast action, capture the subject moving directly toward or away from the camera. This helps reduce the frame rate required to depict action. Giving the viewer "stop action" and "replay" capability compensates for trade-offs made to hold frame rates down.

- Text features like signage and scoreboards probably won't be readable, so support shots using these features with explanatory audio.

- It *is* possible to reuse video captured for larger display formats, but rarely as a straight-across port. Expect to devote considerable effort to video editing and color palette compaction.

- Compression matters. Try different approaches to composition and storyboarding to make video files as small and efficient as possible. Computationally intensive jobs, high demand for screen backlighting, and antenna time are the three most battery-intensive tasks on the small device.

- Audio is the "make or break" element of a quality content consumer experience. A vast body of user acceptance research shows that consumers will forgive intermittently wavering video quality if visuals are buttressed by satisfactory audio. This is good news for content developers, because user acceptance plateaus at audio transmission rates of around 12 kilobits per second. Less than that is objectionable to most people, but more doesn't add significantly to user approval, which essentially means that the entire excess bandwidth above the audio requirement is available for moving video.

- Make small device content easily interruptible for the user. Usability research shows that most people are willing to watch video on mobile devices in short increments. They may not return to the subject for minutes or hours, much like a casual reader of a novel. For long formats like TV shows or movies, subdivide content into units a few minutes long, and put intense sequences in the middle of segments, so that there is no psychological "cliffhanger" penalty for viewing the work incrementally.

- Always optimize the app or the content so that it uses battery power as sparingly as possible, and do so based on the nature of workloads:

  - For incremental workloads (think discrete tasks undertaken once, like downloading a file), optimize for performance so that the task is finished as rapidly as possible. This allows the mobile device's CPU to step down to a lower power state, prolonging battery life.

  - For steady-state workloads (think video playback, where the file is already resident on the device), optimize to allow the CPU to constantly run at a lower power state. For video playback, you can induce power step-down by reducing video quality, lowering frame rate, or reducing the size of the window in which the video is displayed.

  - If you have to make quality trade-offs, always choose to maintain audio integrity and down-shift video frame rates, resolution, colors or window size.

Video Codec 411

A *codec* (the name is a portmanteau of the words enCOder/DECoder) can either be a physical device or a process that, on the encoding side, manages the compression of raw digital audio or video data into files of reduced size, optimizing both download and playback performance. On the decoding side, the process is reversed, with the codec uncompressing the file to produce a high-quality *facsimile* of the original content. Because the object of compression is to reduce the overall file size and streaming bandwidth requirements for a given segment of video, it is typically necessary or desirable to "throw away" some of the data during the compression process, meaning that when the codec reproduces content, it will have incrementally lower production values than the original.

> *Compression, which discards some data in the compression and optimization process, is called lossy data compression.*

At this point, we depart from the domain of science and cross over into craft and art, because to create an acceptable result, compression algorithms must strike a complex balance between the visual quality of video and the volume of data necessary to render it. For purposes of multimedia content, the key measure of codec performance is the **bit rate**. In the context of transmitting multimedia data over the Internet or mobile carrier connections, *bit rate* quantifies the number of bits required per increment of playback time in order for the viewer to see smooth, uninterrupted content. For streaming video, this degree of playback quality is also called **goodput**.

> *Goodput is the effective transmission rate supporting what the user actually sees on their device—in other words, it is the amount of data transferred after deducting things like Internet, Network, and Data Link layer protocol overhead; network congestion; and retransmission of data that was corrupted or lost in transit. The ability to empirically measure the performance of various codecs is key, because they have different strengths and therefore different applications.*

Essentially, codecs are optimization tools, and they are many and diverse, often with thriving application genres based on them. The choice of a particular codec is driven by what rendering or transmission characteristics are the focus of optimization, what codecs a developer can reasonably assume to be present on the target platforms, and what postprocessing tools the developer has available for converting raw data into a video file format. It's not surprising that there is a great deal of competition among the developers of codec technology, because achieving a big advance in compression without a loss of quality would have tremendous commercial value. But, on the other hand, if all codec technologies were secret, there would be crippling fragmentation resulting from dozens of incompatible proprietary file formats for encoded video. This problem is neatly solved by an extensive, widely embraced standards-making process for video encoding.

Video codec designs are precisely specified by the Motion Picture Experts Group (MPEG), an international body that includes 350 members representing media industries, universities, and research institutions. MPEG is chartered by the International Standards Organization (ISO) and is tasked with publishing standards documents that detail how various codecs work. What's interesting about this is that MPEG's published specifications assume that the compression of video files is *asymmetrical*.

> *In this sense, asymmetrical means that is it's far more complex and difficult to compress data than to decompress it.*

As a standards-making group, MPEG is exclusively interested in creating a framework for interoperability among various vendors' codecs and products. *This effectively means that only the decoding process needs to be enshrined in a public standard.* The encoding process is not constrained by a published MPEG standard. As long as the compressed video files can be decoded as described in the MPEG spec, innovators are encouraged to design new and better encoders, achieving advances in optimizations, while secure in the knowledge they'll reap the accompanying economic benefits. As encoder technology moves forward, the deployed decoder technology will continue to work, because the decoder side has no knowledge of encoder implementation and can't be broken by encoder evolution.

Since there is a great deal at stake, the exact strategies of popular encoder designs are not public, but the nature of general recent advances is an open secret. Most codecs have transitioned from logic that compresses video data frame-by-frame to an object-based model, where the encoder detects regions of frames that don't change rapidly and caches those semi-static portions. This is a tremendous advantage for bandwidth-constrained scenarios like mobile video, because it prevents transmission of redundant data.

Both transmission speed and quality of the video rendering produced by decoding the results of various encoders can differ dramatically from one encoder implementation to another. In addition, there can be significant trade-offs in video codecs' decoder runtime performance and resource utilization. It's a subtle point but an important one: codec standards enable interoperability, *but they do not imply uniformity of performance or quality across mobile devices*. This potentially complicates life for content designers and developers, because it is necessary to know what codec is going to play your content back in order to ensure that video files provide acceptable playback performance. On desktop and laptop computers, there are frequently a variety of codecs available, and the presence or absence of a single one is rarely an issue for content developers. In any case, a desktop video app can request the user to download a needed codec if it isn't already present. That's not the case with mobile devices.

Playback using device and Flash video

Most mobile devices in the smart phone class are capable of video file playback, but they aren't entirely symmetrical in terms of support for video file formats (encoding) or player technologies. Flash developers need to be concerned about two basic playback cases:

- **Device video**: This is the method of video file playback that is used when a device manufacturer includes a codec as a standard part of the exposed native programming interface. The app makes a call down to the handset video API, and then the handset reads the video file and renders the video frames. The advantage of device video is that typically the player is optimized to have the best quality, performance, and power conservation characteristics. The disadvantage is that device video is nonstandard, which makes content less portable or even nonportable.

- **Flash video**: Flash video (FLV) is a file format that is supported across newer Flash Lite versions and Flash 9 and 10. Video file decoding and rendering is handled entirely by the Flash runtime engine. The advantage of Flash video is that well-planned and executed content is seamlessly portable across the Flash platforms that support it. The disadvantage is that it is less optimized for specific devices than device video.

In practice, the relative performance advantages of device video over Flash video are less and less a consideration, because the technology of the codecs underlying Flash video has rapidly improved. The portability of content is generally such a powerful economic and time-to-market advantage that device video offers few incentives outside of highly custom applications where performance trumps every other consideration. On balance, in the absence of a compelling reason to do otherwise, FLV files are the method of choice for delivering video content to mobile devices that support them.

This said, it is necessary to recognize that of the billion Flash-enabled devices Adobe predicts by the end of 2010, one-half to one-third will be legacy Flash 2.0 devices, which don't support FLV playback. So developers must be aware that device video could still play a part in their application development plans if they can't afford to ignore the segment of their potential audiences that uses older mobile devices. For this reason, here's a recap of the version history of Flash, including information about the playback formats and codec standards each supports for mobile video:

- **Flash Lite 2.0 (2006)**: Device video is introduced. Some common device video formats are 3GP, 3G2 (or 3GPP2), and MPEG-4. Flash Lite 2.0 plays any video format that the target device supports because it calls out to the exposed functionality of the particular device. Flash Lite APIs make it possible to discover device characteristics, status, and bandwidth.

- **Flash Lite 3.0 (2007)**: Support is added for playing FLV files using ON2 (the Flash 7 codec) and Sorenson (the Flash 8 codec). Both are optimized versions specifically created for use on mobile phones. FLV files are decoded and rendered by Flash Lite 3.0 player, not the device.

- **Flash Lite 3.1 (2008)**: Support is added for Flash 9's H.264 video playback. H.264 encoding improves cross-platform portability of FLV video and supports video postprocessing for smoothing and de-blocking images. The quality of the video and the compactness of encoded files are closing the gap between FLV and device video playback.

- **Flash 10 (2009)**: Flash supports Flash video (.flv files). Flash Player 9 Update 3 supports MPEG-4 H.264, MP4, M4V, M4A, 3GP, MOV, as well as 3GP and 3G2 (or 3GPP2).

Knowing the sources and histories of the codec technologies is also useful, because it helps to form a picture of their relative strengths and ongoing vitality (see Table 15-1).

Table 15-1. Video codecs used in Flash Lite 3.0 and above

Codec	Format	Flash Player	Flash version	Used by
Sorenson	FLV file	Flash Player 6	Flash Lite 3.x	Apple QuickTime
ON2	VP6	FLV file	Flash Player 8 Flash Lite 3.x	Skype
H.264	H.264	Flash Player 9	Flash Lite 3.1 / Flex 3	MPEG-4 Published Video coding standard
Speex	Audio codec	Flash Player 10	Flex 4 (Gumbo)	Used for compressing audio

FLV, the most popular supported video format

FLV is the most popular video format available on the Internet, with some of the best web sites engaging their viewers with Flash-based videos. The Flash video format was made available on mobile phones with the release of the Flash Lite 3 player, thus making it possible for you to view video with the mobile web browser or in the Flash Lite stand-alone player.

An FLV file encodes synchronized audio and video streams. The audio and video data within FLV files are encoded in the same way as audio and video within SWF files. Starting with SWF files published for Flash Player 6, Flash Player can exchange audio, video, and data over Real-Time Messaging Protocol (RTMP) connections with Adobe Flash Media Server.

It is estimated that a one-minute video consumes 2–3MB of RAM, while a five-minute video consumes an average of 3–4MB. Longer videos play without requiring a linear increase in memory. This is true for progressive, streaming, local, and/or remote.

F4V format

F4V is associated with FLV, and many times you will see them attached together as the same format. F4V is simply Adobe's wrapper for the H.264 video. The reason a need for a wrapper even exists is to overcome the limitations that the H.264 format doesn't support, such as alpha channel or cue points. F4V is available from Flash Player 9.0.r115 and higher. The format maintains dimensions and frame rate of source. The format also eliminates black borders.

H.264 format

MPEG-4 is a collection of audio and video encoding. MPEG-4 is considered the standard for deployment of videos on desktops, as many software companies such as Apple and Microsoft support the format. MPEG-4 video codec and H.264 are the included standards for video coding and compression.

H.264 is video compression technology in the MPEG-4 standard, also known as MPEG-4 Part 10. H.264 delivers high-definition (HD) video quality across the entire bandwidth spectrum, from 3G to HD video players. This format is preferred because it produces high-quality video with the smallest amount of video data.

Flash Lite 3.1 supports H.264, which is a step to bringing HD to mobile, since Sorenson Squeeze codecs are good quality but may be a little fuzzy. The fact that FL 3.1 supports H.264 doesn't mean we can really use it on mobile devices. Network connection is improving for mobile devices, and around 600 million worldwide are connected to a 3G network with an Internet connection of 144Kpbs. However, Adobe recommends using H.264 with dual-core PCs and Macs, and even the latest smart phones are not capable enough to support that. With that said, a video application that can be deployed on multiple devices can be deployed on desktops and used then.

3GP format

As mentioned earlier, H.264 can be used for mobile, but since our smart phones are not as capable as those recommended by Adobe, 3GP is a simplified version of the MPEG-4 format; it is designed for mobile use. 3GP is based on MPEG-4 and H.263 video, and AAC or AMR audio. The format is designed to optimize the video content for mobile and specifically built to accommodate low bandwidths and little storage. 3GP format is a popular format in mobile devices and many support the 3GP format. The file extension is either .3gp for GSM-based phones or .3g2 for CDMA-based phones.

Dynamically discovering a device's available codecs

If you know exactly what device or devices your content will be targeting, identifying supported codecs is relatively easy. When you deploy an application to Flash 10, you don't have to be concerned about the Multipurpose Internet Mail Extensions (MIME) type since the player includes the codec for a defined set of formats. Deploying to mobile devices that support Flash Lite does not mean we know the codecs available on the device. Flash Lite allows you to look up the device's characteristics in Adobe Device Central using the Device Profiles tab (see Figure 15-1), or you can consult the device manufacturer's documentation at runtime.

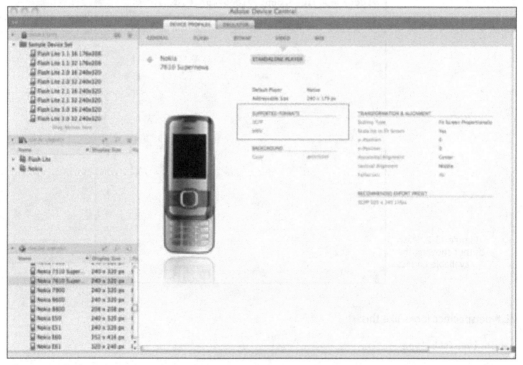

Figure 15-1. Adobe Device Central Device Profiles tab

If your audience and the types of devices they might be using are less easily identified, then discovering installed codecs will need to be handled dynamically at runtime.

Detecting device capabilities in Flash Lite

The API method for detecting device capabilities queries the ActionScript system.Capabilities. videoMIMETypes property: videoMIMETypes.

In the Action window, enter the following script, which uses the Capabilities API to find all the available codecs:

```
var mimeTypesCodecs = System.capabilities.videoMIMETypes;
trace(mimeTypesCodecs.toString());
```

To print the list of available codecs to the output window at development time, use this code and select Window ➤ Flash Output in Adobe Device Central CS4 to get the output shown in Figure 15-2.

You can check for the presence of a specific codec at runtime by checking for a specific MIME type. MIME content specifiers are defined for general use by the Internet Assigned Numbers Authority (IANA); you can see a list of all valid combinations at http://www.iana.org/assignments/media-types/.

Figure 15-2. Flash output showing the avaliable codecs

A MIME type specifier looks like this:

```
main_type/sub_type
```

For our purposes, here's the MIME type specifier that defines the H.264 video codec:

```
video/H264
```

The following is an ActionScript snippet that conditionally plays a video file if the 3GPP codec is present on the target device:

```
if (System.capabilities.videoMIMETypes["video/3gpp"]) {
    3gpp_video.play("movie.3gp");
}
```

Encoding video for Flash applications

Encoding videos for compression is a challenge since the compression needs to maintain the video quality and bitrate while decreasing the file size. Additionally, there are other factors to consider such as seeking, encoding, and decoding algorithms as well as speed of the network connection.

> *When we refer to bitrate in the context of video files, we mean the number of bits that are processed or transferred per second. The unit is bps or bit/s (bits per seconds).*

The software that handles the compression of the video file is called a video codec and has been used to deliver faster videos for web and desktop applications. Encoding video for mobile devices inherently involves optimizations that simply aren't as significant for desktop and web apps. Compression is key, and not only because effective compensation for device characteristics and limited bandwidth are fundamental to a good user experience. In many cases the user is paying incrementally for data they download, so there is an immediate disincentive if applications overuse bandwidth.

It's possible to switch videos while they are playing in any version of Flash Player, but the experience is not always seamless. Flash 10 supports seamless dynamic bitrate switching. The key for bitrate switching is to have enough profiles so we will be able to switch to a different video file once the user's bandwidth decreases.

You can create many different bitrate profiles, and later when you check the user's bandwidth, you will be able to determine which profile to use. Many online video file storage services offer the ability to load a video file and to encode the files to the various bitrate sizes automatically.

Here are some common video bitrate profiles:

- **Lowest quality**: 6Kbps, which is the minimum quality needed to see moving images
- **Medium quality**: Between 128 and 384Kbps; videoconferencing quality
- **VCD quality**: 1.25Mbps; VCD quality
- **DVD quality**: 5Mbps; DVD quality
- **HDTV quality**: 15Mbps; HDTV quality
- **HD quality**: 36Mbps; HD DVD quality
- **Blu-ray quality**: 54Mbps; Blu-ray disc quality

Delivering a compelling video experience to mobile devices requires placing the highest priority on compression, which means lossy data compression (sometimes very lossy). For best results, always begin the encoding process with raw files, because repetitive compression can destroy the integrity of video imagery.

Compressing video files using the Adobe Media Encoder

If your needs are simple (and this will particularly be true in cases where video was captured specifically with mobile devices in mind), you can use the Adobe Media Encoder (AME) to compress video and create video files for use in your application. AME is included in Flash CS4 (and several other Adobe products). AME integrates well with other elements of the Adobe toolset, and has an extensive set of predefined settings (presets) for importing in the most common formats. This is of particular value, because for encoding video, a surprising number of user-defined parameters customize and optimize codec output.

> *Adobe Media Encoder (AME) replaces the Flash Video Encoder that used to be bundled with Flash Professional. AME offers more than just an encoder, with features such as video manipulation, H.264 encoding, integration with other CS4 products such as Premiere Pro and After Effects, cue points, 2-pass variable bitrate encoding with the ON2 VP6 codec, as well as the ability to load directly to the server.*

AME has useful productivity features, including the ability to queue many files and then run them through the encoding process at night or some other convenient time. For files that are more than trivial in terms of window size or length, encoding can be an extremely lengthy process; therefore, queuing is definitely efficient. In addition, you can add prebuilt components that embed playback and volume controls in the FLV file, thus achieving content interactivity right out of the box. As well as compressing raw video, AME converts common video file formats to FLV, including QuickTime Movie, AVI, MPEG, digital video (.dv), and Windows Media.

Let's look at an example of working with AME. First we need to have a video file. You can use any video file that you have in your library or download free footage from sites like http:// stockfootageforfree.com.

Once you have the raw video file, open AME, located here:

- PC: C:\Program Files\Adobe\Adobe Media Encoder CS4
- Mac: Applications/Adobe Media Encoder CS4

Use the Add button to add a video (see Figure 15-3). Click the Duplicate button to create five identical profiles of the same video.

Let's set different files that we will be able to use with FMS. To change the bitrate settings, select Edit ➤ Export Settings. You'll see the screen shown in Figure 15-4.

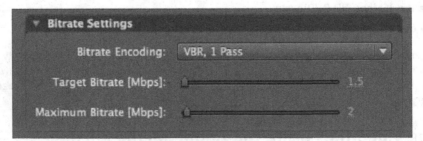

Figure 15-4. Adobe Media Encoder Bitrate Settings options

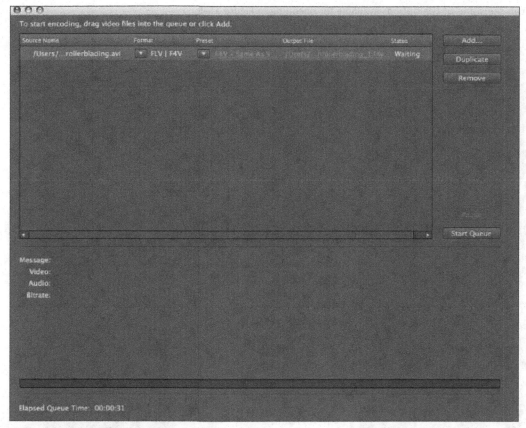

Figure 15-3. Adobe Media Encoder file added

Set the files names and bitrate values, as shown in Table 15-2.

Table 15-2. Files names and bitrates

File Name	Bitrate
videofile_16.flv	16kbps
videofile_128k.flv	0.128Mbit/s (minimum value)
videofile_384k.flv	0.385Mbit/s
videofile_500k.flv	0.500Mbit/s
videofile_1250k.flv	1.25Mbit/s
videofile_H264.mp4	3Mbit/s
videofile_H264.3gp	15fps
videofile_220x176.3gp	3GPP 220×176 15fps
videofile_320x240.gpg	3GPP 320×240 15fps

You can see some of the options available for encoding in Figure 15-5.

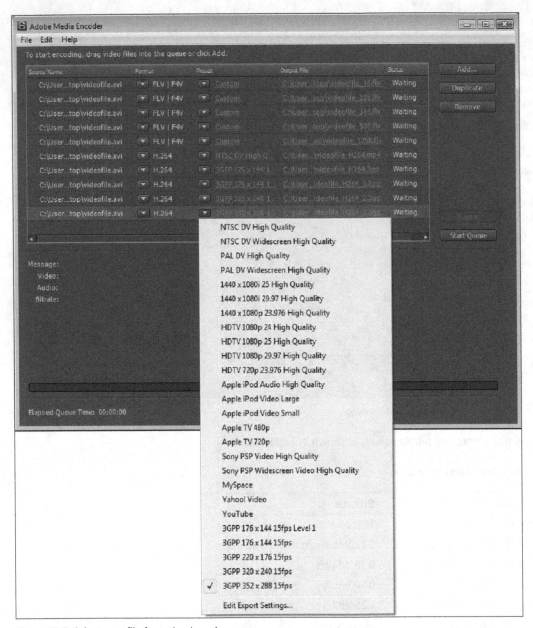

Figure 15-5. Select a profile from the drop-down menu.

You can click the Present button to view details regarding the export setting (see Figure 15-6). The detail page will allow you to set the bitrate to the desired bitrate.

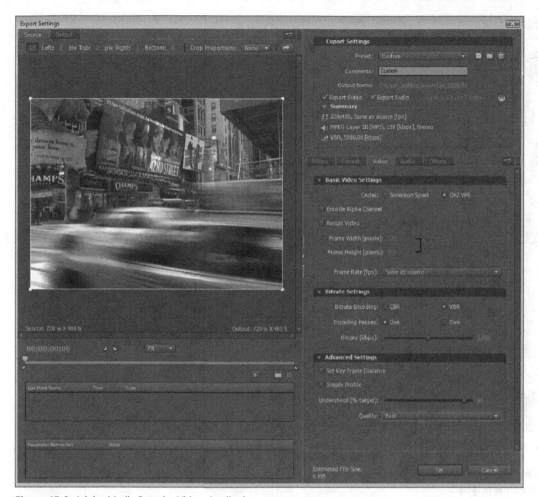

Figure 15-6. Adobe Media Encoder Video detail tab

Once all the profiles are added, click Start Queue and all the profiles you set will start decoding. See
Figure 15-7.

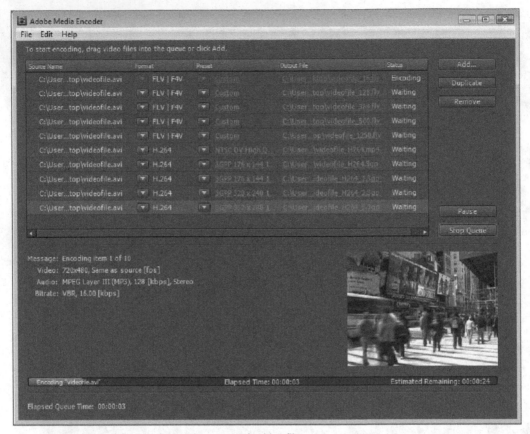

Figure 15-7. Adobe Media Encoder starting to encode video files

We have completed creating the profiles. In the next sections, we will be using the video profiles we created for playback.

We would like to point out that AME allows some manipulation of video files—for example, cropping and selecting subsets of a given clip for encoding—but if full-featured video editing is necessary, this won't be your only tool. Fortunately, there are a variety of professional-quality tools available, with a broad spectrum of capability and pricing. While some tools offer complete video production with effects, transitions, additions of callouts, pictures, and so forth, others are simpler with basic editing and converting abilities.

These tools optimize desktop video for mobile delivery and playback:

- **Adobe's Premiere Pro CS4 or Adobe Premiere Elements (lighter version of Adobe Premiere)**: Captures, edits, and delivers digital video online, on air, on disc, or on device. Premium toolset, but costly.

- **Nokia Multimedia Converter 2.0**: Converts common multimedia files (such as AVI, WAV, MPEG, and MP3) into standard 3GPP/AMR, H.263, wideband, and narrow-band-AMR-supported formats for use in mobile phone applications. Original and converted multimedia and 3GPP/AMR formats can be played on a PC. Available for free download at http://forum.nokia.com.

- **Apple QuickTime Pro**: Edits video clips using cut, copy, and paste; merges separate audio and video tracks; crops and rotates video; and saves and exports to codecs supported by QuickTime. Includes presets for exporting video to an iPod, Apple TV, and iPhone. Inexpensive, ($29.99) but heavily biased toward Apple technologies.

- **Windows Movie Maker**: Modest video-editing tool, but a free one bundled with Windows operating systems.

- **eRightSoft SUPER**: eRightSoft SUPER is a freeware converter recommended by Forum Nokia. It supports a variety of video formats, such as 3GP/3G2 and MP4 (H.263, H.264, and MPEG4).

- **VirtualDubMod**: A free, open source mobile video editor that Forum Nokia recommends for use in combination with the eRightSoft SUPER converter tool. Download from http:// virtualdubmod.sourceforge.net.

Understanding the difference between streaming and progressive download

There are two ways to deliver your video through a web server: streaming and progressive download. It's important to understand the difference between the two in order to successfully select the appropriate server.

Progressive download   Let's take an example. Say you want to deliver to a user the video we created previously in AME, which was encoded at 384Kbps, videofile_384k.flv. You can either place it on a server (or link a video component to the URL), or you can place it on a media server for streaming. When you place the video on your server and use the URL to link the video component to the video, what's happening is that the client downloads the file as soon as possible and the file seems to be streaming since it starts playing before the entire file is downloaded. The Flash interface is designed to start the video playback as soon as there is enough data. The limitation is that you cannot fast-forward (seek) to a part in the video file that isn't downloaded yet. The file is downloaded to a temporary location on the user's system so there will be no need to download the file again to replay the video.

In progressive download, the file is downloaded using HTTP, which uses Transport Control Protocol (TCP) to manage the transfer of data packets over the network and is built to handle large file sizes by allowing you to resend packets in case data gets lost. Once the download is completed, you can rest assured that the file is an exact copy of the original. However, TCP is not designed for real-time streaming and the time it takes to download the file, as well as ensuring the video is always playing, is not a concern of TCP.

Video streaming   As an alternative to HTTP connection, Flash Media Server (FMS) and its equivalents are software placed on a server that support a persistent connection with the server; this arrangement is specially designed for delivery of video. The server transfers the needed data to play the video at a predefined transfer rate. It is aware of the bandwidth and able to communicate with the player playing the video. Since the media server is aware of conditions such as bandwidth, it can adjust to changes as well as offer the ability to create ActionScript communication files (.asc extension), which can take into account the video's information. The video file is not stored on the user's computer and is discarded once the packet is not needed anymore. The file offers services for both users and content owners to monitor videos playing, enhanced seeking (so you don't have to wait until the video is downloaded), and video search, among other benefits. We will go into much more detail about media servers in the section "FMS architecture overview," later in this chapter.

The media server, unlike TCP, doesn't try to resend missing packets, and if any frames are dropped, the server just keeps sending data and sends notifications regarding the dropped frames, since the user prefers to see a small glitch in a media file (such as audio or video) than to stop the file until the missing data arrives. Additionally, some media servers (such as FMS) use multicast for delivery of live webcam, which enables more than one client to connect to a single stream as well as a two-way communication channel (client to user and user to client), allowing clients to communicate with one another. This type of technology saves bandwidth for the delivery of video on the server and provides a large number of connections at the same time.

Tips for selecting servers for your videos

Understanding the difference between streaming and progressive download allows you to better select the appropriate type of server. Keep in mind that a media server offers HTTP connections. It's also important to know that the cost for media servers is high.

Adobe offers two solutions, as of this writing:

- Adobe Flash Media Interactive Server
- Adobe Flash Media Streaming Server

Additionally, third-party vendors provide the service without the need to purchase the software directly.

Each case requires an assessment in order to decide whether the best approach is using FMS or progressive download. In general, FMS provides a better user experience, so usually small to mid-sized sites will use progressive download. For large sites that feature videos that are viewed by a large number of people, FMS is more common. Table 15-3 can help you decide what type of server you should use.

Table 15-3. Advantages of media and web servers

Advantage	Media server	Web server
* Plays short video?	No	Yes
Allows users to copy video?	No	Yes
Ensures data integrity?	No	Yes
Plays long video?	Yes	No
Provides interactivity?	Yes	No
Incorporates social features?	Yes	No
Offers live webcam?	Yes	No
Includes advanced user features?	Yes	No
Offers low cost?	No	Yes

* Mobile devices may often lose network connections as well as packets of data, so although we think short video should be deployed on web servers, streaming short videos may be worthwhile.

Building a progressive download video player for mobile devices

Whether you are creating a mobile application using Flash Lite or Flash 10, the same basic steps apply:

1. Create a streaming connection between the Flash Player and the file, which can be stored either on FMS or your local system.

2. Integrate the connection with the video object.

3. Play the video file.

Let's look at the code. We first create a NetConnection and establish connecting; then we create a NetStream streaming connection, integrate the connection to the video file, and play the video file:

```
// Create connection and net stream
connection = new NetConnection();
connection.connect(null);
netStream = new NetStream(connection);
video.attachVideo(netStream);

// play video
netStream.play("VideoFile.flv");
```

The process is as simple as that. In an ideal world that is all that you need in order to play a video file. However, creating a compelling video stream experience is much more complex since the characteristics of the system playing the video can change rapidly while the video is playing and we should be able to respond to these changes. We may also want to respond to messages coming from FMS as well as cue points placed on the video.

For instance, you may want to respond to a drop in users' bandwidth speed by dynamically switching to a different video file following a set of predefined rules so the stream is not interrupted. Or you may want to change the buffer size once it's filling up too quickly or too slowly. Additionally, you may want to respond to frame drops or insufficient bandwidth messages coming from the streaming server.

Creating video playback components in Flash Professional

In case you need to play back an external video file (using progressive download), Flash Professional offers a simple way to create a video component without writing one line of code:

1. To start, open Flash Professional CS4 and select File ➤ New ➤ Flash File. You can select either ActionScript 2.0 or ActionScript 3.0. Next, click Create. At this point you will have an FLA document.

2. Save the FLA file as videoPlaybackComponent.fla.

3. Choose Flash ➤ Import ➤ Import Video.

4. Select Load external video with playback component, as shown in Figure 15-8.

5. Select the video file you will be using. Begin by selecting the On your computer radio button and then click the Browse button to browse to the file's location.

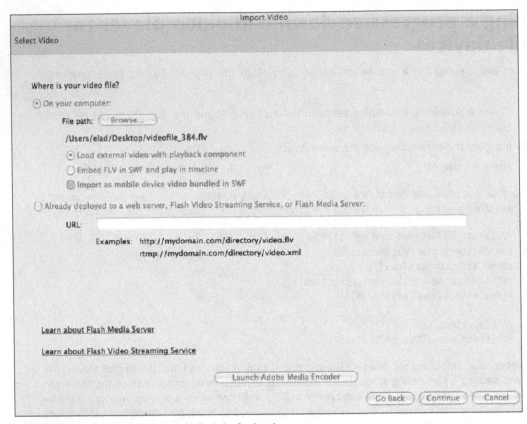

Figure 15-8. Import Video dialog box in Flash Professional

6. On the next page, you can select from a set of predefined skins, or you can create your own skin SWF and point to it (see Figure 15-9). Click Continue and complete the process.

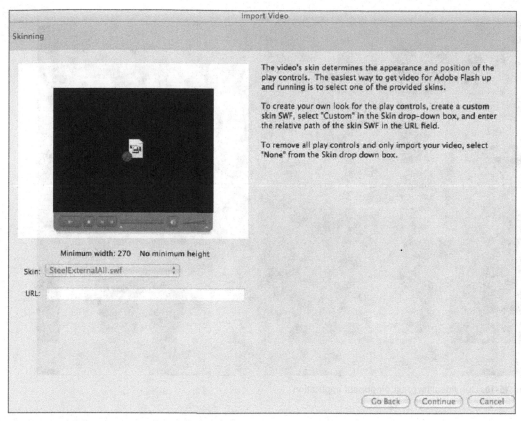

Figure 15-9. The Skinning page in Import Video

7. You can see the video in the timeline. Once you compile and run it, you will be able to play back the video (see Figure 15-10).

Figure 15-10. Our videoPlaybackComponent application

Creating a video player in Flash Lite

Now that you have a good understanding of how to build a simple video player using an external video file, we can put this knowledge to work and build a customized video player.

Open Flash Professional CS4 and create a new document by selecting File ➤ New. In the New Document window, select Flash File (Mobile), set Flash Lite Version to 3.0, and click Create in Device Central.

Ensure the Library window is open; if it's closed, select Window ➤ Library. Right-click in the Library window and select New Video (see Figure 15-11).

The Video Properties windows opens, as shown in Figure 15-12.

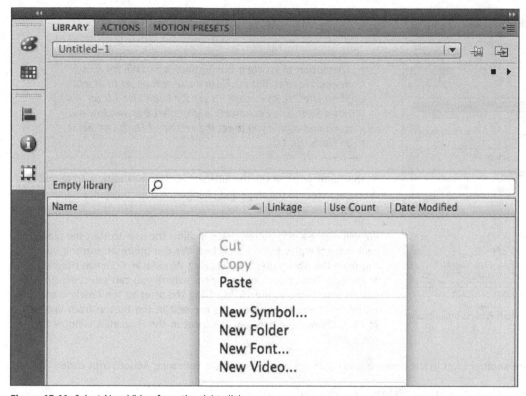

Figure 15-11. Select New Video from the right-click menu.

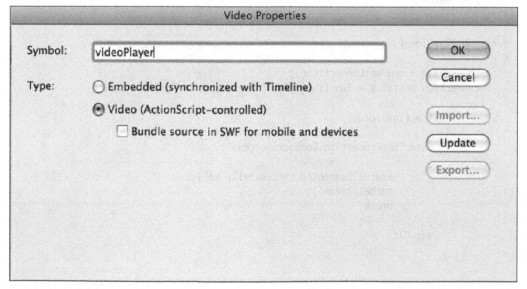

Figure 15-12. Video Properties window

Figure 15-13. Flash Professional library buttons

Type videoPlayer in the Symbol text box and select the Video (ActionScript-controlled) radio button.

> *The option to create a bundle source in SWF for mobile devices requires that the Flash document be set to at least Flash Lite 2.0, so in case it's set for Flash Lite 1.0 (or it's not a Flash Lite document), a pop alert box window will open and enable you to set the version of Flash Lite. Set it to Flash Lite 3.0.*

At this point you can see the video object in your library. Drag and drop the object to the stage and change the object instance name in the Properties window to video.

We will create a play button that will allow the user to start the playback once the play button is clicked. We can utilize an existing button from the library. Begin by clicking Window ➤ Common Libraries ➤ Buttons. The Library window opens, where you can select existing button assets (see Figure 15-13). Drag the asset to the timeline and double-click the asset to change the text in the button from Enter to Play. Change the name of the asset in the Properties window to playButton.

Create another layer in the timeline and name it actions. Paste in the following ActionScript code:

```
this.playButton.onRelease = function()
{
    playVideo();
}

function playVideo()
{
    connection = new NetConnection();
    connection.onStatus = function(info)
    {
        switch (info.code)
        {
            case "NetConnection.Connect.Success":
            {
                trace("Connected successfully to");
                setNetStream();
                break;
            }
            default:
```

```
                {
                        trace("Error with bandwidth check: "+info.code);
                }
            }
        };
        connection.connect(null);
    }

    function setNetStream()
    {
        netStream = new NetStream(connection);
        video.attachVideo(netStream);
        netStream.play("videofile_500.flv");
    }
```

Compile and run this code, and in Device Central you will be able to view the application in one of the emulators that support the FLV file format. See Figure 15-14.

Figure 15-14. A progressive download application deployed in the Device Central emulator

Let's examine the code. First, we set a method to handle the release of the button. Once the button is clicked and released, the playVideo method is called:

```
this.playButton.onRelease = function()
{
     playVideo();
}
```

The playVideo method creates the NetConnection and listens to onStatus events. In case there is a success event, we call the setNetStream method:

```
function playVideo()
{
     connection = new NetConnection();
     connection.onStatus = function(info)
   {
         switch (info.code)
         {
            case "NetConnection.Connect.Success":
            {
                 trace("Connected successfully to");
                 setNetStream();
                 break;
            }
            default:
            {
                 trace("Error with bandwidth check: "+info.code);
            }
         }
     };
     connection.connect(null);
}
```

The setNetStream method creates a new NetStream object and integrates the video object with the NetStream. We can now play the video:

```
function setNetStream()
{
     netStream = new NetStream(connection);
     video.attachVideo(netStream);
     netStream.play("videofile_500.flv");
}
```

Creating a video player for Flash 10

To create a customized video player for Flash 10, we will be using Flash Builder 4 Beta.

Open Flash Builder 4 Beta or Eclipse with the Flash Builder 4 Beta plug-in. Select File ➤ New ➤ Flex Project. Set the project name to VideoPlayerExample and make sure the project is set to use the Flex 4 SDK when you select the Flex SDK version. Click Finish to complete the creation of the project.

Paste the following code into the VideoPlayerExample.mxml file:

```
<?xml version="1.0" encoding="utf-8"?>
<s:Application xmlns:fx="http://ns.adobe.com/mxml/2009"
    xmlns:s="library://ns.adobe.com/flex/spark"
    xmlns:mx="library://ns.adobe.com/flex/halo"
    minWidth="1024" minHeight="768"
    creationComplete="creationCompleteHandler(event)">

    <fx:Script>
        <![CDATA[
            import mx.events.FlexEvent;
            import com.elad.CustomStreamClient;

            private var videoURL:String = "videofile_H264.mp4";
            private var connection:NetConnection;
            private var netStream:NetStream;

            protected function creationCompleteHandler(event:FlexEvent):void
            {
                connection = new NetConnection();
                connection.addEventListener(NetStatusEvent.NET_STATUS, ➥
netStatusHandler);
                                connection.addEventListener(SecurityErrorEvent.
SECURITY_ERROR, ➥
securityErrorHandler);
                connection.connect(null);
            }

            private function setNetStream():void
            {
                netStream = new NetStream(connection);
                netStream.addEventListener(NetStatusEvent.NET_STATUS,
netStatusHandler);
                netStream.addEventListener(IOErrorEvent.IO_ERROR,
onNetworkError);

                netStream.client = new CustomStreamClient();

                var video:Video = new Video();
                video.attachNetStream(netStream);

                netStream.play(videoURL);
                netStream.seek(0.01);
                netStream.pause();

                component.addChild(video);
            }
```

```
/********************************************************
 *
 *   Handlers
 *
 * ******************************************************/

private function netStatusHandler(event:NetStatusEvent):void
{
    switch (event.info.code)
    {
        case "NetConnection.Connect.Success":
        {
            playButton.enabled = true;
            this.setNetStream();
            break;
        }
        case "NetStream.Play.StreamNotFound":
        {
            trace("StreamNotFound: " + videoURL);
            break;
        }
        case "NetStream.Buffer.Full":
        {
            trace("bufferLength:"+netStream.bufferLength);
            break;
        }
        case "NetStream.Buffer.Flush":
        {
            trace(event.info.code);
            break;
        }
        case "NetStream.Seek.Notify":
        {
            trace(event.info.code);
            break;
        }
        case "NetStream.Buffer.Empty":
        {
            trace(event.info.code);
            break;
        }
    }
}

private function securityErrorHandler(event:SecurityErrorEvent):void
{
    trace( "securityError: " + event.toString() );
}
```

```
        private function onNetworkError(event:IOErrorEvent):void
    {
        trace( "NetworkError: " + event.toString() );
    }


    ]]>
</fx:Script>


<s:HGroup>
    <mx:UIComponent id="component" width="200" height="240" />
                <s:Button id="playButton" label="Play" click="netStream.
resume()"
            enabled="false" />
</s:HGroup>


</s:Application>
```

Once you compile and run the application, you will be able to view the video playback. Let's examine the code.

We first set the creationComplete event to call the creationCompleteHandler method:

```
<?xml version="1.0" encoding="utf-8"?>
<s:Application xmlns:fx="http://ns.adobe.com/mxml/2009"
    xmlns:s="library://ns.adobe.com/flex/spark"
    xmlns:mx="library://ns.adobe.com/flex/halo"
    minWidth="1024" minHeight="768"
    creationComplete="creationCompleteHandler(event)">

    <fx:Script>
        <![CDATA[
            import mx.events.FlexEvent;
            import com.elad.CustomStreamClient;
```

We set global parameters that we will be using in our application, such as the video URL location, the net connection, and the net stream:

```
        private var videoURL:String = "videofile_H264.mp4";
        private var connection:NetConnection;
        private var netStream:NetStream;
```

The creationCompleteHandler method is called once the component finishes the tasks of processing, measuring, layout, and drawing. At this point, we create the net connection and set event listeners for the messages to know when the connection is ready, as well as error messages resulting from security restrictions:

```
        protected function creationCompleteHandler( ➡
    event:FlexEvent):void
```

```
        {
            connection = new NetConnection();
            connection.addEventListener(NetStatusEvent.NET_STATUS, ➥
netStatusHandler);
            connection.addEventListener(SecurityErrorEvent. ➥
SECURITY_ERROR, securityErrorHandler);
            connection.connect(null);
        }
```

The netStatusHandler method will handle messages coming from the NetConnection object. We are using a switch to handle the different messages. We won't go into detail on these common messages now; the names of the event constants are self-explanatory.

```
        private function netStatusHandler( ➥
event:NetStatusEvent):void
        {
            switch (event.info.code)
            {
```

Once the connection is established, we call the setNetStream method. At this point, the user is able to play the video, so we set the playButton's enabled property to true so the user can click the play button and view the video:

```
        case "NetConnection.Connect.Success":
        {
            playButton.enabled = true;
            this.setNetStream();
            break;
        }
        case "NetStream.Play.StreamNotFound":
        {
            trace("StreamNotFound: " + videoURL);
            break;
        }
        case "NetStream.Buffer.Full":
        {
            trace("bufferLength:"+netStream.bufferLength);
            break;
        }
        case "NetStream.Buffer.Flush":
        {
            trace(event.info.code);
            break;
        }
        case "NetStream.Seek.Notify":
        {
            trace(event.info.code);
            break;
        }
```

```
case "NetStream.Buffer.Empty":
{
    trace(event.info.code);
    break;
}
        }
    }
```

The securityErrorHandler handler will let us know whether there are any security restrictions that block us from creating the connection:

```
private function securityErrorHandler( ➡
event:SecurityErrorEvent):void
{
    trace( "securityError: " + event.toString() );
}
```

The setNetStream method is called once we have established a connection. We can now create a new net stream and use the connection we established to listen to events and network errors. For the video, we set a new Video component.

```
private function setNetStream():void
{
    netStream = new NetStream(connection);
                        netStream.addEventListener(NetStatusEvent. ➡
NET_STATUS, netStatusHandler);
    netStream.addEventListener(IOErrorEvent.IO_ERROR, ➡
onNetworkError);
```

We can also specify a client property. This property allows us to direct all calls back to the client we define:

```
    netStream.client = new CustomStreamClient();

    var video:Video = new Video();
    video.attachNetStream(netStream);
```

Once we are ready, we will play the video, seek to the 0.01 seconds point, and pause it. The reason we do that is to display the first frame of the video and wait for user interaction to continue playing the video:

```
    netStream.play(videoURL);
    netStream.seek(0.01);
    netStream.pause();
```

We also add the video component we set in this method to a placeholder we defined:

```
    component.addChild(video);
}
```

Here is the handler for I/O network errors:

```
        private function onNetworkError(event:IOErrorEvent):void
    {
        trace( "NetworkError: " + event.toString() );
    }


        ]]>
    </ fx:Script>
```

We set a component as a placeholder so we can add the video object we are creating. The playButton button will allow us to play the video. Notice that we start the button as enabled="false" so the user will not be able to play it before the video component is ready for playback:

```
    <s:HGroup>
            <mx:UIComponent id="component"
                    width="200" height="240" />
            <s:Button id="playButton" label="Play" click="netStream.resume()"
                enabled="false" />
        </s:HGroup>

    </s:Application>
```

VideoDisplay for Flash 10

In Flash 10, Adobe has added a component for the Flex 4 beta SDK called the VideoDisplay spark class, which is in addition to the VideoDisplay mx component in Flex. The new video player component supports skinning, progressive download, multi-bitrate, and streaming of video right out of the box.

The MXML code allows us to create the VideoDisplay spark component looks like this:

```
    <s:VideoDisplay id="videoDisplay" />
```

To create a video player, you create the component and set the video file like so:

```
    <?xml version="1.0" encoding="utf-8"?>
    <s:Application xmlns:fx="http://ns.adobe.com/mxml/2009"
        xmlns:s="library://ns.adobe.com/flex/spark"
        xmlns:mx="library://ns.adobe.com/flex/halo"
        minWidth="1024" minHeight="768">

        <s:VideoPlayer id="videoDisplay"
            source="videofile.mp4" />

    </s:Application>
```

Once you compile and run the application, you'll see the result shown in Figure 15-15.

Figure 15-15. Flash 10 progressive download application deployed in a browser

As you can see, the component includes a toolbar with the controls Pause, Stop, Mute, Fullscreen, volume, and seek. The component can be skinned easily using VideoElement. Let's take a look.

Create a new Flex project and call it VideoPlayerGumboExample. In the entry point, VideoPlayerGumboExample.mxml, enter the following code:

```
<?xml version="1.0" encoding="utf-8"?>
<s:Application xmlns:fx="http://ns.adobe.com/mxml/2009"
    xmlns:s="library://ns.adobe.com/flex/spark"
    xmlns:mx="library://ns.adobe.com/flex/halo">

    <fx:Script>
        <![CDATA[
            import components.VideoSkin;
        ]]>
    </fx:Script>

    <s:VideoPlayer skinClass="{components.VideoSkin}"/>

</s:Application>
```

Notice that we included the spark VideoDisplay component and we set the skinClass property to point to a class we will create. The VideoSkin class we will be creating includes the VideoElement and the toolbar.

```xml
<?xml version="1.0" encoding="utf-8"?>
<s:Skin xmlns:fx="http://ns.adobe.com/mxml/2009"
    xmlns:s="library://ns.adobe.com/flex/spark"
    xmlns:mx="library://ns.adobe.com/flex/halo"
    width="348" height="276">

    <s:states>
        <mx:State name="loading"/>
    </s:states>

    <fx:Metadata>
        [HostComponent("spark.components.VideoPlayer")]
    </fx:Metadata>

    <s:VideoElement id="videoElement" autoPlay="true"
        source="http://bak.spc.org/abc/filth/mp4/768kbs/filthpt2-768kbs.mp4">
    </s:VideoElement>

    <s:Button id="playButton" skinClass="{PlayButton}"  x="6"  y="245"/>
    <s:Button id="stopButton" skinClass="{StopButton}"  x="86" y="245"/>

</s:Skin>
```

Let's examine the code. The component we are using is a Skin component, which is common when we create skins for Flex 4 beta components:

```xml
<?xml version="1.0" encoding="utf-8"?>
<s:Skin xmlns:fx="http://ns.adobe.com/mxml/2009"
    xmlns:s="library://ns.adobe.com/flex/spark"
    xmlns:mx="library://ns.adobe.com/flex/halo"
    width="348" height="276">
```

The HostComponent tag points to the component we are skinning:

```xml
<fx:Metadata>
        [HostComponent("spark.components.VideoPlayer")]
    </fx:Metadata>
```

VideoElement is necessary to skin the VideoDisplay component, and we point to the video file we are using. The location of the folder is relative to the FxVideoDisplay component that defines the skin, not to the skin itself:

```xml
<s:VideoElement id="videoElement" autoPlay="true"
        source="videofile.mp4">
    </s:VideoElement>
```

Next we can define all the subclasses that are used by the VideoDisplay spark component, such as pause(), play(), seek(), and volume(), as well as the various video states. We map the subcomponents by the id name. Each subcomponent needs to correspond to the expected id. Additionally, notice that each button points to another Skin class; for example, the playButton points to the PlayButton skin.

```
<s:Button id="playButton" skinClass="{PlayButton}"  x="6" y="245"/>
<s:Button id="stopButton" skinClass="{StopButton}"  x="86" y="245"/>
```

Finally, take a look at the playButton skin for the spark Button. We can define all the various states and the text graphic. For the graphic, we use a simple box with a border and a text field that holds the label text: play.

```
<?xml version="1.0" encoding="utf-8"?>
<s:Skin xmlns:fx="http://ns.adobe.com/mxml/2009"
    xmlns:s="library://ns.adobe.com/flex/spark"
    xmlns:mx="library://ns.adobe.com/flex/halo"
    xmlns:d="http://ns.adobe.com/fxg/2008/dt"
    xmlns:ai="http://ns.adobe.com/ai/2008">

    <s:states>
        <mx:State name="up"/>
        <mx:State name="over"/>
        <mx:State name="down"/>
        <mx:State name="disabled"/>
    </s:states>

    <fx:Metadata>
        [HostComponent("spark.components.Button")]
    </fx:Metadata>

    <s:Rect y="1.5" height="27" width="75" x="1.5" d:userLabel="playButton">
        <s:fill>
            <s:SolidColor color="0x3d3d3d"/>
        </s:fill>
        <s:stroke>
            <s:SolidColorStroke color="0xa5a7aa"
                caps="none" joints="miter" miterLimit="4" weight="3"/>
        </s:stroke>
    </s:Rect>

    <s:RichText width="44" height="14"
        fontFamily="Myriad Pro" lineHeight="120%"
        color="0xffffff" white spaceCollapse="preserve"
        kerning="on" x="20" y="10" ai:knockout="0"
        d:userLabel="Play" id="labelElement" text="Play">
        </s:RichText>
</s:Skin>
```

Create the same skin for the stopButton and name the class StopButton. The only difference is that the text field text property should be set to Stop.

Once the application is complete, you can compile and run it. You'll see the results shown in Figure 15-16.

Figure 15-16. Flash 10 progressive download application using Flash 10 skinning

Detecting connection status

We have created a streaming connection and played progressive download videos. We also listened to some basic messages coming from the NetStream object. Once the NetStream streaming connection is established, we listened to the NetStream.onStatus property. To create a complete playback user experience, you'll use certain messages:

- **Playback messages**: NetStream.Play.Start, NetStream.Play.Stop, and NetStream.Seek. Notify are simple and don't need much explanation. You are notified once the video starts or stops and while the seek operation is performed.

- **Buffer messages**: Buffer messages include the following:

  - NetStream.Buffer.Empty: This message is sent once to indicate that there is no data in the buffer. This message is a problem for the user, since it means that the user may experience disruption and that the movie playing may be paused until the end of a rebuffering session. The goal at this point is to fill the buffer as quickly as possible.

- `NetStream.Buffer.Full`: This message is received when the buffer is full. At this point, the video can begin playing.

- `NetStream.Buffer.Flush`: This is the message that the data has finished streaming. After the message is dispatched, the rest of the data in the buffer will be emptied.

- **Error messages**: There are two types of error messages:

  - `NetStream.Play.StreamNotFound`: This message is sent when the client tries to play back a stream that can't be found on the URL provided.

  - `NetStream.Seek.InvalidTime`: For progressive download video, this message indicates that the user has tried to play past the end of the downloaded video.

`NetStream` can generate additional messages. These messages can help us deliver a better user experience. Table 15-4 lists all the messages that `NetStream` can produce.

Table 15-4. NetStream messages

Code property	Property type	Meaning
NetStream.Buffer.Empty	Status	Empty buffer message. It means that the buffer is not filling up quickly enough.
NetStream.Buffer.Flush	Status	The data has finished streaming, and the remaining buffer will be emptied.
NetStream.Buffer.Full	Status	The buffer is full and the data can be played.
NetStream.Failed	Error	Failed error message.
NetStream.Pause.Notify	Status	Video is paused.
NetStream.Play.Complete	Status	Playback is complete.
NetStream.Play.Failed	Error	Playback has failed.
NetStream.Play.InsufficientBW	Warning	Data is playing at slower than the normal speed. Caused by low user bandwidth, or by the server sending data at a lower-than-expected speed.
NetStream.Play.PublishNotify	Status	Notifies all subscribers that publishing has begun.
NetStream.Play.Reset	Status	Playlist has been reset.
NetStream.Play.Start	Status	Playback has started.
NetStream.Play.Stop	Status	Playback has stopped.
NetStream.Play.StreamNotFound	Error	Client has tried to play a stream that can't be found.
NetStream.Play.Switch	Status	The playlist subscriber is switching from one stream to another.
NetStream.Play.UnpublishNotify	Status	Notifies all subscribers that publishing has stopped.
NetStream.Publish.BadName	Error	Client has tried to publish a stream that already exists.

continued

Table 15-4. Continued

Code property	Property type	Meaning
NetStream.Publish.Idle	Status	The stream's publisher has been idling for too long.
NetStream.Publish.Start	Status	Publishing has started.
NetStream.Record.Failed	Error	An error has occurred during recording.
NetStream.Record.NoAccess	Error	Either the client has tried to record a stream that is still playing, or the client has tried to overwrite an existing read-only stream.
NetStream.Record.Start	Status	Recording has started.
NetStream.Record.Stop	Status	Recording has stopped.
NetStream.Seek.Failed	Error	The seek operation has failed.
NetStream.Seek.Notify	Status	The seek operation is complete.
NetStream.Seek.InvalidTime	Error	For progressive download video, the user has tried to play past the end of the downloaded video.
NetStream.Unpause.Notify	Status	The subscriber has resumed playback.
NetStream.Unpublish.Success	Status	Publishing has stopped.

A streaming and optimizing technique for mobile devices

We've discussed the differences between progressive download and streaming; now let's explore how you can use a media server to stream videos for mobile devices. In this section, we'll show you how to use Adobe's FMS, and then give you tips and optimization techniques you can use with Flash Player 10. As you're going to discover in this section, creating a video player can be complex. So although it's important to understand how it all works, if creating a video player is not your main focus in your application, there are many products that can address many of the challenges that deploying a video player can bring. One of the solutions is an open source project that Akamai has started called the Open Video Player (OVP), which recently was adopted by Adobe and is now part of the Adobe Strobe initiative, which we will cover later on in this chapter.

FMS architecture overview

Adobe's FMS allows you to maintain a persistent connection with the server. A persistent connection is different from the typical connection, such as through a web server. A web server accepts HTTP requests from clients, such as your Flash Player or your browser, and then replies with a response that includes data. At this point, the connection with the web server is closed; to receive another response you would need to send a new request. A persistent connection, on the other hand, uses Real-Time Message Protocol (RTMP) requests from clients and keeps the connection open, which enables us to stream data between the client and the server. To close the connection, the user quits the application or sends a request to close the connection (see Figure 15-17). Since the server and clients keep a persistent connection, clients can potentially communicate with one another, live. In fact FMS offers services such as live chat or webcam chats and more. (Note that webcam and live chat are not in use for phones yet.)

FMS strongest feature is the ability to offer RTMP. However, keep in mind that you can also use HTTP connections with FMS.

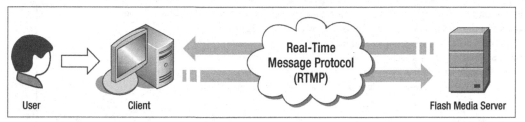

Figure 15-17. Adobe Flash Media Server architecture

Installing FMS 3.5 on Windows

Adobe (http://www.adobe.com/products/flashmediaserver/) offers two types of servers:

- **Flash Media Interactive Server 3.5**: A complete solution with both video delivery streaming and an environment for interactivity between clients. The solution includes out-of-the-box functionality such as social capabilities (chats, games, polls, etc.), dynamic streaming, DVR, HTTP delivery support, and HD H.264 support.

- **Flash Media Streaming Server 3.5**: A less expensive solution that offers the delivery of the video rather than communication between clients. The solution includes dynamic streaming, DVR, HTTP delivery support, and HD H.264 support.

As a developer, you can download a free version of FMS to use for testing purposes (see Figure 15-18). The developer version is fully functional but limits the number of connections. We will download and install Flash Media Interactive Server 3.5 on our local machine to act as a server.

There are currently two versions for Linux and Windows. We will show you how to install the server on a PC, so download the Windows version.

To download FMS, go to the following URL:

http://www.adobe.com/products/flashmediainteractive/

> Currently FMS 3.x is available only on Windows or Linux OS; however, you can develop your application on a Mac and install FMS 3.x on a version of Mac running Windows or Linux OS in parallel. The Flash application can run on the Mac, and FMS runs on a Windows or Linux virtual machine. Additionally, you can use FMS 3.x installed on a Windows machine, using the network connection to test your application.

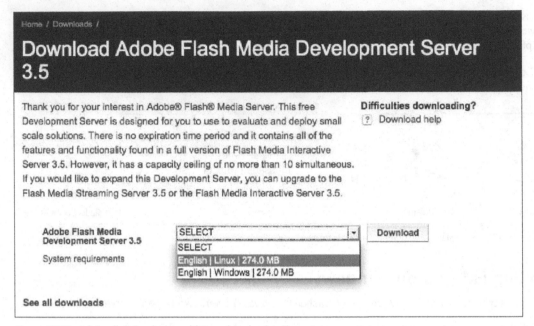

Figure 15-18. Adobe download page with two download options

Download the file to your computer. Unzip and run the setup file `FlashMediaServer3.5.exe`. The installation process is simple, so feel free to skip this part and use the default settings if you prefer:

1. The welcome window pops up. Click Next to continue to the next window.

2. The agreement window comes up. Select Accept the agreement and then click Next.

3. The Enter your serial number window opens. Leave the serial number field blank and click Next. Without the serial number, a developer version is installed.

4. In the next window you are asked to set your destination location to install FMS. The default will leave the software under Program Files. We recommend using the default location.

5. The Window installing additional component window opens and will install Apache 2.2 as an additional tool. Click Next twice.

6. The Flash Media Administration Services window is next. This page requires that you set a username and password. Set your admin username and password and keep a copy since you will need them later on.

7. The next window, Configure Flash Media Server 3.5.1 ports, allows you to set the port of the server you will be using. Keep the default values, unless you want to customize a specific port (see Figure 15-19).

8. Click Install. The installation process begins.

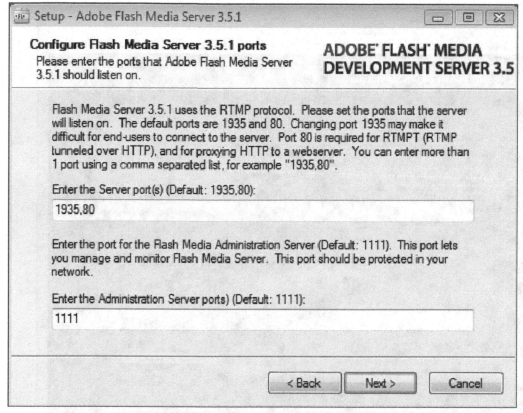

Figure 15-19. Configuring Flash Media Server ports

Once you complete installation, the index.html page opens, which is located here:

```
file:///C:/Program Files/Adobe/Flash Media Server 3.5/➥
webroot/index.html
```

The FMS local home page (see Figure 15-20) provides links to many useful pages, including sample applications, documentation, and useful tools, as well as a link to the Administration Console. You should bookmark this URL.

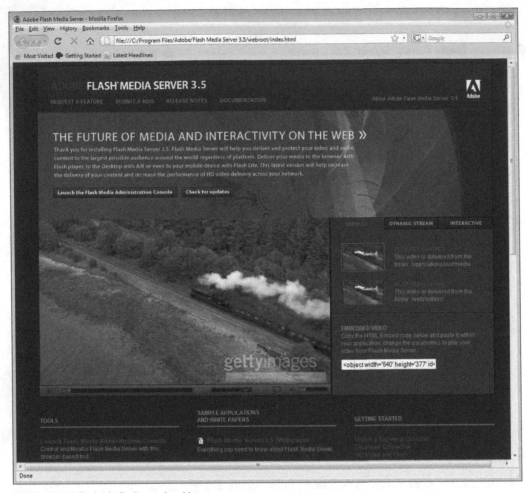

Figure 15-20. Flash Media Server local home page

Streaming video to a mobile device using FMS 3.5

Remember that simple application we created for progressive download? We will take that application and stream the video into a mobile device. Note that since we are using a developer version of FMS and the server is not available online, we will not be able to test the app on a real mobile device, as we cannot point to an Internet URL. But we can use Device Central to emulate a device and see a video playing.

The application we are using was described in the earlier section "Creating a Video Player in Flash Lite." The only change we need to make to the script is to change the URL we are connecting to and set it to the FMS server:

```
this.playButton.onRelease = function() {
    playVideo();
}

function playVideo()
{
    nc = new NetConnection();
    nc.connect("rtmp://127.0.0.1/vod");
    ns = new NetStream(nc);
    video.attachVideo(ns);
    ns.play("sample2");
}
```

The script creates an instance of the NetConnection class connecting to the FMS using RTMP. Then it creates a NetStream class based on the NetConnection and attaches the NetStream to the video object. We can then play the video.

Here are some things to note:

- You set the server based on the IP address: 127.0.0.1. Otherwise, the code may not work for mobile devices through the emulator.
- The FLV file sample2.flv doesn't include the extension name.
- The device must support the video file format to play the video.
- The NetConnection is connecting to the folder vod, but feel free to create a different folder and set the NetStream to a new location.

Next we need to copy the FLV video to the FMS folder. The default location is

```
C:\Program Files\Adobe\Flash Media Server 3.5\webroot\vod
```

You can download the sample FLV from the folder FMS sample.zip.

You can now start Adobe Device Central by selecting Control ➤ Test Movie. Select the Flash Lite 3.0 16 240x320 profile, and you can play the video. See Figure 15-21.

You can log in to the FMS Administration Console (see Figure 15-22) and view the connected video as well as see reports such as Active Applications and Bandwidth.

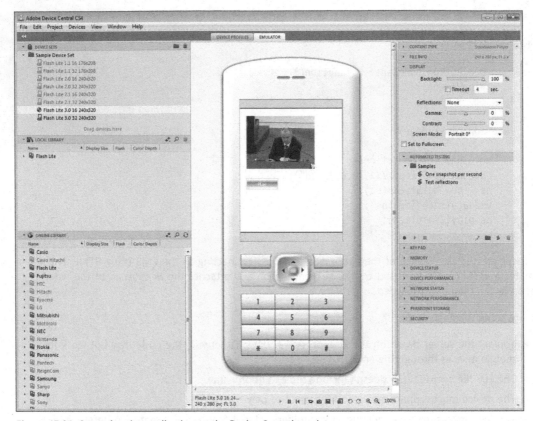

Figure 15-21. Streaming the application on the Device Central emulator

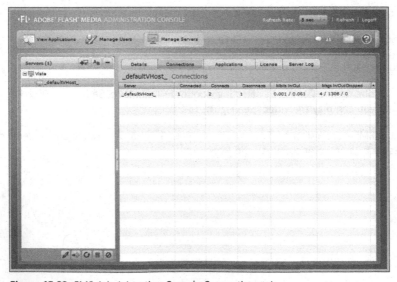

Figure 15-22. FMS Administration Console Connections tab

Setting a smart buffer policy

An appropriate profile can provide a consistent user experience across many platforms with different hardware and different connection speeds. It's important to be able to determine how to handle buffer bandwidth fluctuations as well as switch video files, which are created with different bitrates.

Let's start by explaining what a buffer is. A buffer is a temporary holding pen in the system memory for data until the process handles the data. For instance, when you send a job to your printer the job is held in a buffer until the printer can handle the data and print your page. In video streaming, the buffer allows the media player to save part of the file to the user's local storage; that way, a video can be played back without interruption since the subsequent data needed is already stored in the buffer.

Here's how the Flash Player works. Once it receives the data stream, it starts archiving the data in the buffer until it is full. When that happens, the movie starts to play and the Flash Player tries to keep the buffer full to the chosen length. During the playback of the movie, in case the bandwidth goes below the value required by the current stream, the amount of data available in the buffer slowly decreases. This is because the data rate at which FMS feeds the buffer becomes lower than the data rate at which the Flash Player fetches data from the buffer. If the buffer becomes empty, the movie stops playing until the buffer fills up again. You can control the amount of data the server sends to each client by providing an approximate bandwidth capacity.

In an ideal world, the user's bandwidth would be sufficient to play back a video in real time; however, in reality, changes in the user's bandwidth can cause interruptions. The NetStream API includes a property called bufferTime, which allows you to set how long buffer messages should display before starting to display the stream. You're specifying how long the first seconds of the stream will play without interruption. The stream starts playing only after the number of seconds you specified is filled in the buffer. Another property, called bufferLength, allows you to check how many seconds' worth of video are currently in the buffer. In deciding on the best approach, consider three things:

- A small buffer of up to a couple of seconds fills up quickly, allowing the movie to start quickly; however, a change in bandwidth will easily empty the buffer, causing movie playing to pause until the end of a *re-buffering*, when new data fills the buffer.

- On the other hand, a large buffer can help ensure the buffer is not easily emptied and playback is less likely to be interrupted; however, we will have to prompt the user to wait until the buffer is filled (known as *pre-buffering*).

- Before Flash Player 9 Update 3, the Flash Player waited for the buffer to fill before resuming playback, which often caused a delay (for instance, if the buffer size was large the user would have to wait). Starting with Flash Player 9 Update 3, the Flash Player no longer clears the buffer when we pause the playback by calling NetStream.pause().

The recommended approach is to set a dual-threshold buffering policy, which allows you to switch between two thresholds when needed:

1. Before the video starts, keep the default buffer at 0.1 second.
2. Once the video starts, increase the buffer based on the user's bandwidth.
3. Once the video pauses and play again, treat the buffer as if you are starting the video again.
4. Once the user performs a seek, treat the buffer as if you are starting the video again.

To implement that policy, you can listen to the NetStatusEvent messages and change the buffer size accordingly:

- NetStream.Buffer.Full: Indicates that the movie has data to play.
- NetStream.Buffer.Empty: Indicates that the media player has no data to play and the playback may be interrupted. At this point, you need to modify the buffer length again to the starting value.
- NetStream.Play.InsufficientBW: Using FMS, you can listen to a status message from NetStream, which indicates that the bandwidth is insufficient and that you should replace the profile with a lower bitrate profile if possible.
- NetStream.Pause.Notify: Indicates that the pause method was called.
- NetStream.Seek.Notify: Indicates that the user is performing a seek.

Once you are ready to change the buffer size to a higher value, you can use the setBufferTime method on the NetStream object. Here's the syntax: netStream.setBufferTime(NumberInSeconds);.

You can also configure the capacity of the Flash Media Server in the configuration file called Application.xml.

Bandwidth Detection

Another important aspect when you're trying to increase the level of sophistication for your video player is the ability to detect bandwidth changes. To improve the user experience, we must have a way to identify the user's bandwidth and select the correct bitrate video profile.

Earlier we created different profiles using the Adobe Media Encoder, and now it's time to start using these profiles. The reason we need to use different profiles is that the bandwidth between the server and the Flash client often changes due to many reasons, such as

- Server usage increase.
- A mobile user can lose service.
- Hardware constraints on the client's system.
- Decrease in bandwidth due to the Internet connection.

The assumption we need to make when building a video player for mobile devices is that we are dealing with an unstable bandwidth connection. Without moderation of the user's bandwidth and corresponding adjustments, we may have scenarios where playback is disrupted and a stream can even be terminated altogether.

A common place to locate all the different profiles is an XML file called a Synchronized Multimedia Integration Language (SMIL) file, which provides links to profiles of video files with different bitrates. Many video content management systems provide the ability to create SMIL files for each video file.

We are capable of listening to messages from FMS, which indicate when the slower-than-normal bandwidth speed occurs. We should be able to use a lower bitrate video the next time we are playing a video or switching the video dynamically.

There are two methods to detect the client's bandwidth:

- **Native bandwidth detection**: This method is faster than server-side scripting since the code is written in C and C++; additionally, the detection is done using edge servers, which provide better and more accurate information. The detection is enabled by default.
- **Server-side script**: This method is written in the ActionScript Communication file (.asc extension), which allows you to program the script on your own in Flash Professional CS; you can also configure the settings easily. The server sends packets of data to the client to detect the bandwidth.

We will show you how to use the server-side script method. The first step is to enable the detection of the user's bandwidth. Using server-side scripting, we can enable the service on the FMS server. To begin, open the Application.xml file, located here:

```
C:\Program Files\Adobe\Flash Media Server 3.5\ ➥
applications\vod\Application.xml
```

Add the following node:

```
<BandwidthDetection enabled="true">
        <MaxRate>-1</MaxRate>
        <DataSize>16384</DataSize>
        <MaxWait>3</MaxWait>
</BandwidthDetection>
```

You can customize the XML to fit your needs better. Let's see what the node elements mean (Table 15-5).

Table 15-5. Application.xml bandwidth detection elements and their purpose

Element	Purpose
BandwidthDetection	Enables you to turn the feature on or off.
MaxRate	Indicates the maximum rate in Kbps that the server sends data to the client. The default value is –1, which means that data will be sent using the necessary rate to measure bandwidth.
DataSize	Indicates the amount of data in bytes that the server sends to the client. In order to detect the client's bandwidth, the server tries to send random packets of data to the client player. For instance, x bytes are sent, then $2x$ bytes, then $3x$ bytes, and so on until the MaxWait time has occurred.
MaxWait	Indicates the number of seconds the server sends data to the client. The more time you allow the detection to occur, the more accurate your results will be, but the user will have to wait until the check is completed.

Once you have completed updating the application.xml file, you will need to restart FMS. To do so, navigate to the following URL:

```
file:///C:/Program Files/Adobe/Flash Media Server 3.5/webroot/
```

After you log in, click the Stop Server icon (see Figure 15-23) and then click the Connect to Server icon.

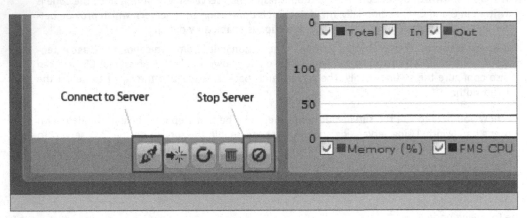

Figure 15-23. Click the Stop Server icon and then the Connect to Server icon.

Next, you place the script on the server. Create a new folder called bwcheck in the following location:

```
C:\Program Files\Adobe\Flash Media Server 3.5\applications\bwcheck\
```

Macromedia developed the script we will be using to calculate the user's bandwidth for Flash Communication Server MX 1.5, but it still does the work.

Create the file bwcheck.asc and paste in this script:

```
application.onConnect = function(p_client, p_autoSenseBW)
{
        //Add security here

        this.acceptConnection(p_client);

        if (p_autoSenseBW)
                this.calculateClientBw(p_client);
        else
                p_client.call("onBWDone");
}

Client.prototype.getStreamLength = function(p_streamName) {
        return Stream.length(p_streamName);
}

Client.prototype.checkBandwidth = function() {
        application.calculateClientBw(this);
}
```

```
application.calculateClientBw = function(p_client)
{
      p_client.payload = new Array();
      for (var i=0; i<1200; i++){
            p_client.payload[i] = Math.random();        //16K approx
      }

      var res = new Object();
      res.latency = 0;
      res.cumLatency = 1;
      res.bwTime = 0;
      res.count = 0;
      res.sent = 0;
      res.client = p_client;
      var stats = p_client.getStats();
      var now = (new Date()).getTime()/1;
      res.pakSent = new Array();
      res.pakRecv = new Array();
         res.beginningValues = ➡
{b_down:stats.bytes_out, b_up:stats.bytes_in, time:now};
      res.onResult = function(p_val) {

             var now = (new Date()).getTime()/1;
             this.pakRecv[this.count] = now;
             //trace( "Packet interval = " + (this.pakRecv[this.count] -
             //              this.pakSent[this.count])*1  );
             this.count++;
             var timePassed = (now - this.beginningValues.time);

             if (this.count == 1) {
                  this.latency = Math.min(timePassed, 800);
                  this.latency = Math.max(this.latency, 10);
             }

             //trace("count = " + this.count + ", sent = " + this.sent +
             //   ", timePassed = " + timePassed);

             // If we have a hi-speed network with low latency send more
             // to determine better bandwidth numbers, send no more
             // than 6 packets
             if ( this.count == 2 && (timePassed<2000))
             {
                  this.pakSent[res.sent++] = now;
                  this.cumLatency++;
                  this.client.call("onBWCheck", res,
this.client.payload);
             }
```

```
                    else if ( this.sent == this.count )
                    {
                            // See if we need to normalize latency
                            if ( this.latency >= 100 )
                            { // make sure we detect correctly
                                    if ( this.pakRecv[1] - this.pakRecv[0] > 1000)
                                    {
                                            this.latency = 100;
                                    }
                            }

                            delete this.client.payload;
                            // Got back responses for all the packets
                            // compute the bandwidth.
                            var stats = this.client.getStats();
                            var deltaDown = (stats.bytes_out - ➥
this.beginningValues.b_down)*8/1000;
                            var deltaTime = ((now - this.beginningValues.time) - ➥
(this.latency * this.cumLatency) )/1000;
                            if ( deltaTime <= 0 )
                                    deltaTime = ➥
(now - this.beginningValues.time)/1000;

                            var kbitDown = Math.round(deltaDown/deltaTime);

                            trace("onBWDone: kbitDown = " + kbitDown + ", deltaDown= " + ➥
deltaDown + ", deltaTime = " + deltaTime + ", latency = " + this.latency + ➥
"KBytes " + (stats.bytes_out - this.beginningValues.b_down)/1024) ;

                            this.client.call("onBWDone", null, kbitDown, ➥
deltaDown, deltaTime, this.latency );
                    }
            }
            res.pakSent[res.sent++] = now;
            p_client.call("onBWCheck", res, "");
            res.pakSent[res.sent++] = now;
            p_client.call("onBWCheck", res, p_client.payload);

    }
```

Copy and paste the file under the directory we created, bwcheck (see Figure 15-24).

Once the server starts, you should be able to see the application we added to the bwcheck folder, as shown in Figure 15-25.

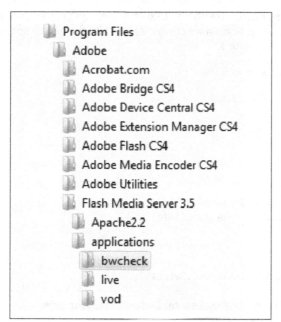

Figure 15-24. FMS folder structure

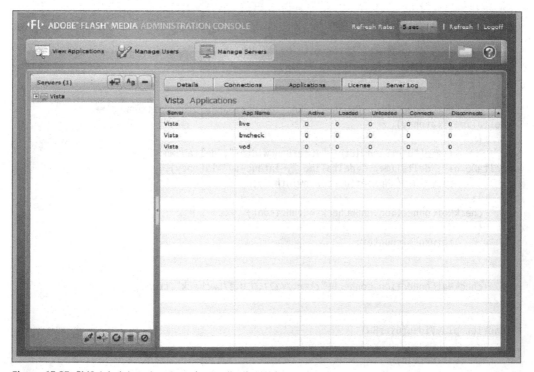

Figure 15-25. FMS Administration Console, Applications tab

To test that the bandwidth check is performed correctly and to switch between profiles once we start our application, we will be using the same application we created earlier with the button and video (in the section "Creating a Video Player in Flash Lite").

In the action layer, replace the existing code with this:

```
 this.playButton.onRelease = function()
{
     checkUserBandwidth();
}

function checkUserBandwidth()
{
     checkNetConnection = new NetConnection();
     checkNetConnection.onStatus = function(info)
     {
         switch (info.code)
         {
             case "NetConnection.Connect.Success":
             {
                 trace("Connected successfully to: "+this.uri+ ➥
" in order to do bandwidth check.");
                 break;
             }
             default:
             {
                 trace("Error with bandwidth check: "+info.code);
             }
         }
     };
     checkNetConnection.onBWDone = function(userBandwidth, deltaDown, ➥
 deltaTime, latency)
     {
         trace("userBandwidth: "+userBandwidth+", deltaDown: " ➥
+deltaDown+", deltaTime: "+deltaTime+", latency: "+latency);
         playVideo( Number(userBandwidth) );
     };
     checkNetConnection.onBWCheck = function()
     {
         return ++counter;
     };

     checkNetConnection.connect("rtmp://127.0.0.1/bwcheck",true);
};

function playVideo(userBW)
{
     if (userBW<=16)
```

```
    {
        trace("bandwidth too low!");
        break;
    }

    if (userBW>16 && userBW<=135)
    {
        useVideoBitrate = "16";
        buffer = 0.1;
    }
    else if (userBW>135 && userBW<=360)
    {
        uscVideoBitrate = "128";
        buffer = 0.3;
    }
    else if (userBW>360 && userBW<=450)
    {
        useVideoBitrate = "384";
        buffer = 0.5;
    }
    else if (userBW>450 && userBW<=1100)
    {
        useVideoBitrate = "500";
        buffer = 1;
    }
    else if (userBW>1100)
    {
        useVideoBitrate = "1250";
        buffer = 2;
    }

    videofile = "videofile_"+useVideoBitrate;
    trace("display video: "+videofile);

    videoNetConnection = new NetConnection();
    videoNetConnection.connect("rtmp://127.0.0.1/vod/");
    videoNetStream = new NetStream(videoNetConnection);

    videoNetStream.onStatus = function(info)
    {
        trace("onStatus: "+info.level+" Code: "+info.code);
    };

    videoNetStream.setBufferTime(buffer);
    video.attachVideo(video_ns);
    videoNetStream.play(videofile);
}
```

Let's examine the code. The playButton button calls the checkUserBandwidth method once a release event is detected:

```
this.playButton.onRelease = function()
{
    checkUserBandwidth();
}
```

The checkUserBandwidth method creates a NetConnection object that will be used for the bandwidth check only:

```
function checkUserBandwidth()
{
    checkNetConnection = new NetConnection();
```

We need to listen to messages coming from the NetConnection object, so we identify once the connection has been established and determine if there are any error messages:

```
checkNetConnection.onStatus = function(info)
{
    switch (info.code)
    {
        case "NetConnection.Connect.Success":
        {
            trace("Connected successfully to: "+this.uri+ ➡
" in order to do bandwidth check.");
            break;
        }
        default:
        {
            trace("Error with bandwidth check: "+info.code);
        }
    }
};
```

Once the bandwidth check is completed, we set a method that will display the information and call the playVideos method to play the video. Notice that we're also counting how many times we tried to send data to the client:

```
checkNetConnection.onBWDone = ➡
function(userBandwidth, deltaDown, deltaTime, latency)
{
    trace("userBandwidth: "+userBandwidth+", deltaDown: " ➡
+deltaDown+", deltaTime: "+deltaTime+", latency: "+latency);
    playVideo( Number(userBandwidth) );
};
checkNetConnection.onBWCheck = function()
{
    return ++counter;
};
```

Now that everything is set, we can connect to the bwcheck script:

```
checkNetConnection.connect("rtmp://127.0.0.1/bwcheck",true);
};
```

The playVideo method will determine which profile file to use based on the user bandwidth results we've received:

```
function playVideo(userBW)
{
    if (userBW<=16)
    {
        trace("bandwidth too low!");
        break;
    }

    if (userBW>16 && userBW<=135)
    {
        useVideoBitrate = "16";
        buffer = 0.1;
    }
    else if (userBW>135 && userBW<=360)
    {
        useVideoBitrate = "128";
        buffer = 0.3;
    }
    else if (userBW>360 && userBW<=450)
    {
        useVideoBitrate = "384";
        buffer = 0.5;
    }
    else if (userBW>450 && userBW<=1100)
    {
        useVideoBitrate = "500";
        buffer = 1;
    }
    else if (userBW>1100)
    {
        useVideoBitrate = "1250";
        buffer = 2;
    }
```

At this point, we received the user's bandwidth information, and we can set the video file we will be using. As you recall, the video files are based on the name; for instance: videofile_16 will point to the 16Kbps file. Keep in mind that we don't need to indicate the file extension since it's not needed by the FMS server; however, we do need to ensure the device support the file extension we are trying to play back.

> You should use video formats that are natively supported by the device you are targeting. Otherwise, your application will not be able to play the video.

```
videofile = "videofile_"+useVideoBitrate;
trace("display video: "+videofile);

videoNetConnection = new NetConnection();
videoNetConnection.connect("rtmp://127.0.0.1/vod/");
videoNetStream = new NetStream(videoNetConnection);
```

We can set onStatus to capture NetStream messages:

```
videoNetStream.onStatus = function(info)
{
    trace("onStatus: "+info.level+" Code: "+info.code);
};
```

The setBufferTime method will set the buffer size:

```
videoNetStream.setBufferTime(buffer);
video.attachVideo(video_ns);
videoNetStream.play(videofile);
}
```

Dynamically switching between different video profiles

Now that we know how to check the user's bandwidth and select the appropriate profile, we can take it one step further and switch the video profile seamlessly while the video is playing. To achieve that we can set logic to check frame drops, buffer policy, and bandwidth, and once we recognize a change that requires changing the video, we can switch the video.

Up until Flash 10, switching of video profile files was done by seeking the new profile file to the same time the old profile was playing and then stop playing, stopping the old profile, and beginning the new file. This type of approach is not seamless and the user can experience a small glitch. However, the glitch is not so bad when using FMS streaming, since you don't have to wait for the file to be completely downloaded so that section will play the video.

Starting with Flash Player 10, Adobe added a method to the NetStream class called play2(). The new method allows you to switch profiles as well as create a playlist. You can add video files in queues, and once the client requests that the FMS switch the media file or play a different video file in the playlist, the transition is seamless. We can use the info() method, which gets cast as NetStreamInfo, to monitor network conditions. See the section "Dynamic switching of video profiles," later in this chapter, to see a sample implementation.

To implement the switching, Adobe created a custom class called DynamicStream (to download the class and documentation, visit http://www.adobe.com/go/fms_tools) that extends the superclass NetStream and allows dynamic switching of streams and detects network conditions and changes. You can also create your own dynamic streaming class that complies with your own logic and metrics. You can then use software that emulate different Internet connections such as NetLimiter (http://www.netlimiter.com/) to test the switching mechanism.

FMS 3.5 DVR using Flash Media Live Encoder 3.0

Adobe Flash Media Live Encoder allows you to capture live audio and video while streaming it in real time to FMS. You can download Flash Media Live Encoder 3.0 here:

http://www.adobe.com/products/flashmediaserver/flashmediaencoder/

Install the software by selecting the defaults.

Embedding video techniques

There are times when you would prefer to embed your video file into your application. These are special cases, and most of the time it's better to load the file as an external file after the application has started. You don't want users to wait until the video file loads to start the application, since it has an advantage over progressive download or streaming, which allows the video to play after a portion of it is loaded.

However, there are some use cases when we might prefer to package our SWF with the video file and embed it into the movie. That way, once the SWF is loaded, the video file will be available and we don't need to attach it with our application. Here are some reasons you'd use this approach:

- **Small size**: The video file size is small.
- **Offline playback**: You intend to support the playback without a network connection.
- **Quicker playback**: You would like to load the video to the user's machine and play back the video with no interruptions.
- **Better control**: You have absolute control over distribution of video: security, privacy, and chain of custody.

The process of embedding videos works as follows. The video is cut into separate frames. Each frame is an image that is displayed over a short time so that it creates the illusion of an animation. (Think of the children's flipbook concept.) The video can stop and start just like any SWF movie. We will explore your options for embedding your video file using Flash Lite and Flash 10.

Embedding a video file in a Flash Lite application

To begin, open Flash Professional and choose Flash ➤ Import ➤ Import Video. As you can see, there are four ways to import a video:

- Load the external video with the playback component.
- Embed the FLV in the SWF and play it in the timeline.
- Import the video as a mobile device video bundled in the SWF.
- Deploy the video to a web server, Flash Video Streaming Service, or Flash Media Server.

We already covered how to load an external video with the playback component. That option loads the video during runtime as an external file; we will now explore the option Bundle source in SWF for mobile devices:

> *The option Bundle source in SWF for mobile devices can be used with Flash Lite 2.0 or higher. It creates an embedded copy of the video file within our SWF, and we don't need to point to any external link to have the video play back.*

1. Open Flash Professional CS4 and create a new Flash document by selecting File ➤ New ➤ Flash File (Mobile).

2. Once the Flash document is created, Adobe Device Central opens so you can select the device profile. Select Player version 3.0 and Flash Lite 3.0 240x320, and then click Create to create a profile using Flash Lite 3.0.

3. Next we need to import the video file we will be using. To do so, select File ➤ Import ➤ Import Video.

4. A window opens where you can select the video file. On your computer, browse to the location of the file location.

5. Select Import as mobile device video bundled in SWF. Click Finish (see Figure 15-26).

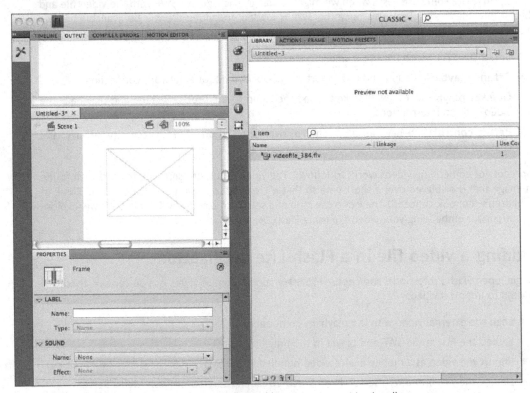

Figure 15-26. Flash Professional CS4 stage, including a video component with a bundle source

Drag and drop the video component to the stage, and in the properties, set the name to video. Create another layer and call it actions. The last step is to add a method to play the video; call it video. play();. Then you can compile and run the application.

Embedding a video file in Flash 10

So far we created a video player in Flex. However, the asset was loaded at runtime as an external file and you had to provide the video file with your application or point to a separate URL. Flex allows you to embed assets into your applications. When you use the <embed> tag, the assets are compiled into the SWF file of your Flex application and there's no need to provide the assets with the application. Once the application is loaded, the asset will be available automatically. The content of the SWF file can be an application just like the one we created earlier for Flash Professional.

Unfortunately, Flex doesn't support embedding video files as it does with images or SWFs. Until it does we have to create a SWF and embed it into our application:

```
<?xml version="1.0" encoding="utf-8"?>
<s:Application xmlns:fx="http://ns.adobe.com/mxml/2009"
    xmlns:s="library://ns.adobe.com/flex/spark"
    xmlns:mx="library://ns.adobe.com/flex/halo"
    minWidth="1024" minHeight="768">

    <fx:Script>
        <![CDATA[
            import mx.events.VideoEvent;
            import mx.events.FlexEvent;

            [Embed(source="assets/videofile_384.swf")]
            [Bindable]
            public var videoFile:Class;

        ]]>
    </fx:Script>

    <mx:SWFLoader source="{videoFile}" />

</s:Application>
```

We will be using the SWFLoader component, which is used to load SWFs. We created a class to hold the asset and used the <bindable> tag so that once the asset is loaded, we will be able to attach it automatically to the component's source property.

There is another, simpler way to embed an asset. You can replace the code with the following MXML tag:

```
<mx:SWFLoader source="@Embed('assets/videofile_384.swf')" />
```

Use the first approach when you want to create a class to hold all the assets or when you need to listen to changes and be notified once the class has changed. Otherwise, we recommend using the MXML tag approach.

Adobe Strobe and Open Video Player (OVP) initiatives

In this chapter we've covered many of the challenges involved in building video players:

- User bandwidth detection
- Support of streaming and progressive download
- Dynamic switching of bitrate profiles
- Buffer policy
- Monitoring of NetStream messages
- Improvement of seeking
- DVR integration
- Playlists
- Frame drop policy
- DRM
- Ways to overcome network proxy issues
- Error handling
- Live streams

As you can tell, the evolving complexity of the video player is difficult to implement, not to mention a tedious task that some of the most sophisticated developers out there will be glad to avoid. It can become pretty challenging to create a smart video player that takes into account these features as well as new ones.

In 2008 Akamai started an open source project called the Open Video Player (OVP) (http://openvideoplayer.sourceforge.net/). OVP is an open source video player that addresses many of the challenges involved in building a high-quality video player. Adobe recently announced that they would adopt the OVP project and include it as part of the Adobe Strobe framework (http://www.adobe.com/products/strobe/).

Dynamic switching of video profiles

To understand how the OVP works, let's take a look at the business diagram in Figure 15-27.

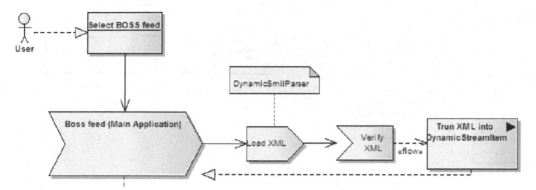

Figure 15-27. OVP business diagram for loading a SMIL file

Getting the video information The implementation or entry point will begin with a media XML file, the SMIL file, that the user selects. The SMIL file can be hosted on a CMS. Once the user selects a video file, we can call the SMIL file, which will contain all the information we need, such as the host name and the different profile files. The DynamicSmilParser is based on ParserBase and includes URLLoader, which loads the SMIL file as well as a method for checking the integrity of the XML nodes.

> *A SMIL file is based on XML and has a file extension of .smil. The SMIL file contains all the information needed to describe a multimedia presentation: the layout presentation, the timeline of presentation, and the source of multimedia elements.*

Once the SMIL is loaded, it is turned into a class called DynamicStreamItem, which holds the stream's URLs and points to the video files and the bitrate of each video file.

Creating a NetConnection Once the SMIL file is loaded, the AkamaiConnection (which is the implementation of the superclass OvpConnection) connects to the host name we received from the SMIL. OvpConnection builds an array of connection strings to be used in streaming and tries to connect to determine available connections.

> *FMS tries by default to use RTMP over port 1935. If it fails, it will try ports 443 and 80. The reason for these attempts is to work around the user's firewalls, and this approach will solve about 96 percent of firewall issues, according to Adobe. This approach stops any attempt to make a TCP connection over unconventional ports. To close the gap even further, use a server proxy or HTTP tunneling (which involves the transmission of RTMP packets over HTTP).*

Once a connection has been found (see Figure 15-28), the OvpConnection.handleGoodConnect method calls the NetConnection.Connect.Success event. The event will reach the AkamaiDynamicNetStream, which is a wrapper for the NetStream. At this point we can play the video.

The AkamaiDynamicNetStream.play method calls the superclass OvpDynamicNetStream.play method, which calls the startPlay method to begin playing the video in addition to starting a timer. The timer has an event listener that checks the switching rules every 500 ms.

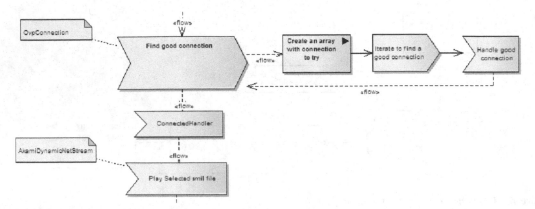

Figure 15-28. OVP business diagram for finding a good connection

Switching rules   During the first time the video is playing, the application checks for the user's bandwidth and adjusts to the appropriate profile. Every 500 ms there are three rules currently available with the OPV that will be examined:

- **Bandwidth rule**: Holds the switching rule for bandwidth detection
- **Frame drop rule**: Holds the switching rule for detecting dropped frames
- **Buffer rule**: Holds the switching rule for buffer detection

Each rule is based on the `ISwitchingRule` contract and can be configured, created, or replaced easily. The rules use a metric provider, which listens to `NetStatusEvent` messages such as `NetStream.Buffer.Full` or `NetStream.Buffer.Empty` as well as `NetStreamInfo`. It also has an update method, which keeps information regarding the health of the stream so we can make a better decision every time we examine the switching rules.

Switching of video   Once the logic indicates that there is a need to switch the video with a different profile, the `NetStream.play2` method is used (see Figure 15-29).

Let's take a look at part of implementation of the OVP core classes:

```
<?xml version="1.0" encoding="utf-8"?>
<s:Application xmlns:fx="http://ns.adobe.com/mxml/2009"
          xmlns:s="library://ns.adobe.com/flex/spark"
          xmlns:mx="library://ns.adobe.com/flex/halo"
          minWidth="1024" minHeight="768"
          backgroundColor="#000000"
          applicationComplete="init()">

<fx:Script>
        <![CDATA[
            import mx.core.UIComponent;
            import mx.events.SliderEvent;
            import mx.controls.Alert;
```

```
import org.openvideoplayer.events.*;
import org.openvideoplayer.net.*;
import org.openvideoplayer.rss.*;
import org.openvideoplayer.parsers.*;

import com.akamai.net.*

// Define private variables
private var _nc:AkamaiConnection;
private var _ns:AkamaiDynamicNetStream;
private var _smilMetafile:DynamicSmilParser;
private var _sliderDragging:Boolean;
private var _waitForSeek:Boolean;
private var _video:Video;
private var _videoHolder:UIComponent;
private var _hasEnded:Boolean;
private var _videoSettings:Object;
private var _streamLength:Number;
private var _transitionMsgTimer:Timer;
private var _lastSwitch:int;

private const _DEFAULT_SMIL_FILE_:String = ➥
"http://mediapm.edgesuite.net/ovp/content/demo/smil/elephants_dream.smil";
private const _SWITCH_REQUEST_MSG_:String = "Requesting
switch...";
private const _SWITCH_UNDERWAY_MSG_:String = ➥
"Starting stream transition...";
private const _SWITCH_COMPLETE_MSG_:String = "Stream transition
complete.";
private const _STREAM_TRANSITION_AT_HIGHEST_:String = ➥
"Already playing the highest quality stream.";
private const _STREAM_TRANSITION_AT_LOWEST_:String = ➥
"Already playing the lowest quality stream.";
private const _TRANSITION_MSG_DISPLAY_TIME_:int = 2000;
```

Once the application is created, the init method is called, which creates new instances and adds event listeners to some of the class variables such as the SMIL parser and the AkamaiConnection. It also adds the video to the stage and sets the transition timer and location:

```
private function init():void {
        stage.addEventListener(FullScreenEvent.FULL_SCREEN, ➥
handleReturnFromFullScreen);

        _smilMetafile = new DynamicSmilParser();
        _smilMetafile.addEventListener(OvpEvent.PARSED,bossParsedHandler);
        _smilMetafile.addEventListener(OvpEvent.ERROR,errorHandler);
```

```
        _nc = new AkamaiConnection();
        _nc.addEventListener(OvpEvent.ERROR,errorHandler);
        _nc.addEventListener(NetStatusEvent.NET_STATUS,netStatusHandler);

        addVideoToStage();

        _transitionMsgTimer = new Timer(_TRANSITION_MSG_DISPLAY_TIME_);
        _transitionMsgTimer.addEventListener(TimerEvent.TIMER, ➥
onTransitionMsgTimer);
        var pt:Point = videoWindow.contentToGlobal(new Point(videoWindow.x, ➥
videoWindow.y));
        pt = transitionInfoContainer.globalToContent(pt);
        transitionInfoContainer.x = pt.x;
        transitionInfoContainer.y = pt.y + videoWindow.height - ➥
transitionInfoContainer.height ;
        _lastSwitch = 0;
    }
```

The addVideoToStage method will attach the video to the stage using the videoHolder placeholder that was set:

```
    private function addVideoToStage():void {
        _videoHolder= new UIComponent();
        _video = new Video(480, 270);
        _video.smoothing = true;
        _video.visible = false;
        _video.x = (_videoHolder.width-_video.width) / 2;
        _video.y = (_videoHolder.height-_video.height) / 2;
        _videoHolder.addChild(_video);
       videoWindow.addChild(_videoHolder);
    }
```

The startPlayback method is called from a load button and clears the old session in addition to starting the load process of the SMIL file:

```
    private function startPlayback():void {
        output.text = "";
        bPlayPause.enabled = false;
        bFullscreen.enabled = false;
        _hasEnded = false;
        multiBRCtrls.visible = false;

        // Clean up from previous session, if it exists
        if (_nc.netConnection is NetConnection) {
            _ns.useFastStartBuffer = false;
            _nc.close();
        }

        // Start parsing the SMIL file
        _smilMetafile.load(bossLink.text)
    }
```

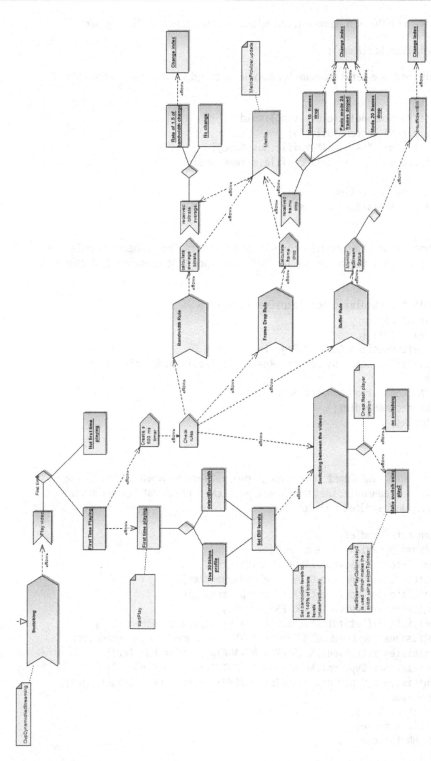

Figure 15-29. OVP business diagram for dynamic switching of bitrate videos

Once the SMIL file is loaded, we have the host name and can establish a connection to the FMS Server:

```
_nc.connect(_smilMetafile.hostName);
```

When the connection is established, the netStatusHandler handler is called since it is set in the init method:

```
private function bossParsedHandler(e:OvpEvent):void {
        write("SMIL parsed successfully:");
        write("  Host name: " + _smilMetafile.hostName);
        write("  Stream name: " + _smilMetafile.streamName);

        // Establish the connection
        _nc.connect(_smilMetafile.hostName);
    }
```

The netStatusHandler method listens to a successful connection and errors. The connectedHandler method sends a request to play the video based on the SMIL file. Once that is achieved, it calls connectedHandler:

```
private function netStatusHandler(e:NetStatusEvent):void {
        write(e.info.code);
        switch (e.info.code) {
            case "NetConnection.Connect.Rejected":
                write("Rejected by server. Reason is "+e.info.description);
                break;
            case "NetConnection.Connect.Success":
                connectedHandler();
                break;
        }
    }
```

Once a connection is found and established (overcoming proxy firewalls when needed), the connectedHandler is called. connectedHandler uses the AkamaiDynamicNetStream instance and passes the SMIL file information: _ns.play(_smilMetafile.dsi);.

```
private function connectedHandler():void {
        _ns = new AkamaiDynamicNetStream(_nc);
        _ns.addEventListener(OvpEvent.ERROR,errorHandler);
        _ns.addEventListener(OvpEvent.DEBUG, debugMsgHandler);
        _ns.addEventListener(OvpEvent.COMPLETE,completeHandler);
        _ns.addEventListener(OvpEvent.PROGRESS,update);
        _ns.addEventListener(NetStatusEvent.NET_STATUS,streamStatusHandler);
        _ns.addEventListener(OvpEvent.NETSTREAM_PLAYSTATUS,streamPlayStatusHandler);
        _ns.addEventListener(OvpEvent.NETSTREAM_METADATA,metadataHandler);
        _ns.addEventListener(OvpEvent.NETSTREAM_CUEPOINT,cuepointHandler);
        _ns.addEventListener(OvpEvent.SUBSCRIBE_ATTEMPT, handleSubscribeAttempt);
        _ns.isLive = true;
        _ns.maxBufferLength = 10;
        _video.visible = false;
        _video.attachNetStream(_ns);
```

```
        write("Successfully connected to: " + _nc.netConnection.uri);
        write("Port: " + _nc.actualPort);
        write("Protocol: " + _nc.actualProtocol);
        write("Server IP address: " + _nc.serverIPaddress);
        _ns.play(_smilMetafile.dsi);
    }
```

The errorHandler method will handle all the error events generated from the SMIL parser (DynamicSmilParser), NetStream (AkamaiDynamicNetStream), and NetConnection (AkamaiConnection).

```
    private function errorHandler(e:OvpEvent):void {
        switch(e.data.errorNumber) {
            case OvpError.INVALID_INDEX:
                handleInvalidIndexError();
                break;
            case OvpError.STREAM_NOT_FOUND:
                Alert.show("Connected to the server at " + _nc.serverIPaddress + ➡
    " but timed-out trying to locate the live stream " + ➡
    _smilMetafile.streamName, "UNABLE TO FIND STREAM ", Alert.OK);
                break;
            default:
                Alert.show("Error #" + e.data.errorNumber+": " + ➡
    e.data.errorDescription, "ERROR", Alert.OK);
                break;
        }
    }
```

Compile and run the example, as shown in Figure 15-30.

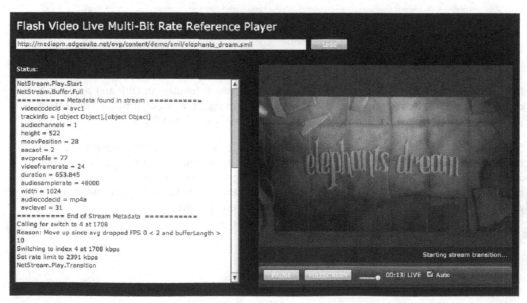

Figure 15-30. OVP implementation displaying in the browser

You can download the complete open source implementation from here:

```
http://openvideoplayer.sourceforge.net/
```

Enhancing progressive download seeking

We showed how the OVP handles dynamic switching of bitrates profiles. Additionally, OVP includes a service called Akamai JumpPoint, which lets you instantly seek progressively delivered FLV files beyond the point at which they have been downloaded and also prevents the FLV data from being cached in the client system. This feature is a major enhancement since it allows you to overcome disadvantages of the HTTP service. Keep in mind that the Akamai JumpPoint service will not function properly when run against a standard HTTP server. The JumpPoint service can be used with the AkamaiEnhancedNetStream class, which extends the AkamaiNetStream class.

Adobe Strobe framework

We pointed out the complexity of creating a video player, but it doesn't end there. There are other elements that make a video player a complete composition, such as advertising elements, social network elements, reporting, content management, and DRM. Adobe recently announced a new framework called Adobe Strobe that is aimed at solving these issues.

Strobe is an open source (vanity license) AS3 media framework that supports the workflow around video playback and monetization. Video players have different feature sets. The skins, integration, and architecture workflow are different. But they do essentially the same thing and can be created using the Strobe framework. The framework is based on the quality of the video player (OVP) and addresses the common challenges.

> Adobe vanity license *means that it's OK to use and redistribute. Modifications can be submitted to Adobe for redistribution.*

The foundation of the framework is QoS (quality of service), which focuses on OVP and provides a quick start for playing videos (the smallest buffer size needed to start the video), efficient connection logic, and switching bitrates dynamically (recall the metric monitor service in OVP).

The framework by itself is not powerful without having the content distribution networks (CDNs) and the publishers onboard. Adobe is currently trying to get them onboard and is getting positive responses. The idea is that each CDN will integrate their plug-ins to the Strobe framework and the publisher will be able to easily switch CDNs. This type of pluggable component can allow publishers to easily switch as well as test performance and services over different CDNs.

Here are the advantages to this scenario:

- **Reduces the barrier of entry for new publishers**: By offering a framework to integrate the different pieces of the video player, new publishers can get started quickly and with fewer resources, and scale up as requirements increase.

- **Provides a flexible framework**: Strobe provides an easy way to extend each component and allows these components to act as a building block that can be extensible and *compositable* (this term, borrowed from Java, means you can apply a multimedia mode, such as image or video operations, to the data that this object is presenting).

- **Leverages existing code**: The Strobe framework uses the Flash Player from OVP.

- **Drives standards and allows custom workflows**: Many of the elements that connect to a video player are not standard yet, and Adobe Strobe will help standardize these components as well as allow them to be configured.

- **No runtimes or framework dependency**: The framework is based on Flash 10 AS3 and is not dependent on any framework such as Flex SDK, Cairngorm, or others. With that said, some integrated elements may be created using a framework, but these are loosely coupled and can be replaced if needed.

- **Partners can focus**: There are two partners: CDNs and publishers. CDNs can focus on services and integration, and publishers can focus on user experience.

- **Integrates with existing Adobe tools**: Adobe Strobe will be integrated with other Adobe Suite tools and services such as Catalyst, Illustrator, FMS 3.5, and FMRMS.

- **Optimizes performance**: With the ability to separate the core framework and each element as a separate SWC, you can increase performance by keeping file size to a minimum.

The Adobe Strobe framework can be represented as an MVC pattern, as follows:

- **Model (media elements)**: The media element (based on IMediaElement) may be video, image, SWF, or others. Every media element has defined capabilities (traits based on IMediaTrait) and a life cycle; they are called *regions*—for instance Region 1 (Image), Region 2 (Video), and so on. Each media element implements the IMediaElement contract, which contains the dynamic media traits (capabilities), and you can add or modify a trait. The traits are the building blocks, and they can be set once and be reused.

- **Controller (media compositions)**: A media composition (IMediaFactory) is a collection of media elements. Each media can be rendered based on a set of rules as well as a media region that defines how to use the capability and the life cycle.

- **View (media configurations)**: A collection of media regions with properties that map to defined capabilities. Each media region can render each media element and can be spatially arranged. The entire media configuration can be the stage.

Let's take a closer look at the higher architecture (see Figure 15-31). The UI management is the set of tools we use to create our video player and skin it, such as Flash Professional and Flex. (Soon we will be able to use Flash Catalyst for Flash 10 applications.) Advertising companies such as DoubleClick or EyeWonder allow us to add rich advertisement elements such as pre-, mid-, and post-roll ads in playlists, or as companion ads or overlay ads. Applications provided by sites such as KickApps and Gigya allow embedding of the video player in social networks such as Facebook. The Flash platform enables playback of video files. Companies such as Level 3 Communications (http://www.level3.com/) and Akamai (http://www.akamai.com/) provide syndications of feeds that can be consumed by other APIs. Finally, stream management is available through Adobe's server.

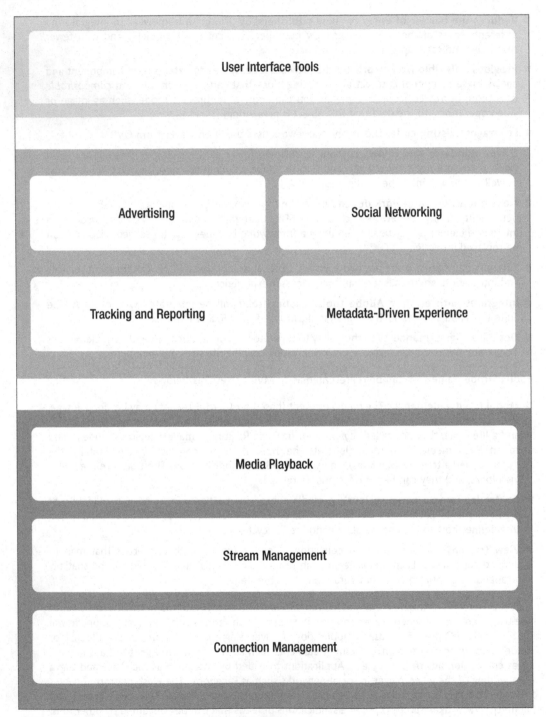

Figure 15-31. Strobe framework higher-level architecture

The framework architecture was designed to allow you to integrate at multiple points and support different use cases. It also allows you to use only the pieces you need and to scale up when ready. There are three types of implementation you may find useful (see Figure 15-32):

- **Media Framework (level 1 integration)**: Small in size and includes basic integration, such as the video player by OVP and pluggable CDNs. It allows you to hook into your higher-level API, tweak the UI, and access the needed classes and methods you define, such as play and pause.

- **Media Framework and Composition Framework (level 2 integration)**: In addition to level 1 features, level 2 allows you to create a composition framework, which includes the ability to integrate to plug-ins that can provide monetization workflow for ads and tracking.

- **Configuration Framework, Media Framework, and Composition Framework (level 3 integration)**: In addition to the features that level 2 and level 1 offer, the level 3 integration offers dynamic chrome and syndication.

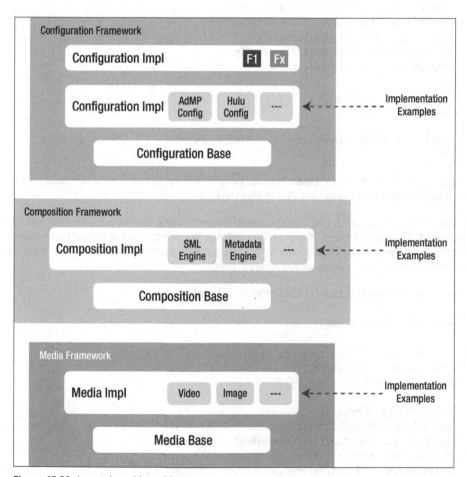

Figure 15-32. Layer pluggable architecture

Currently, the product is available for beta testers only. Version 1 of Adobe Strobe is scheduled to be released in third-quarter 2009 and should include a stable version of the framework and APIs as well as integration with FMS 3.5 features (such as dynamic streaming of live DVR and dynamic switching of bitrate profiles). Three to four months after the release of version 1, Adobe Strobe is expected to provide support for the Adobe tools, multiscreen, and additional plug-ins and services, as well as support to external configurable SWFs.

The framework in action   Let's take a look at a simple implementation of the framework provided by Adobe. Keep in mind that the implementation was provided by Adobe and it's under the Adobe licensing agreement:

```
package com.adobe.strobe.player
{
    import com.adobe.strobe.loaders.*;
    import com.adobe.strobe.media.*;
    import com.adobe.strobe.media.events.*;
    import com.adobe.strobe.traits.*;
    import com.adobe.strobe.traits.events.*;
    import com.adobe.strobe.view.*;

    import flash.events.*;
    import flash.net.*;

    public class MainWindow extends MainWindowLayout
    {
```

The childrenCreated method will be called automatically by the component once the child objects are created, since it's replacing the default UIComponent method.

We create the MediaFactory, which holds all the media elements using IMediaInfo. We then call the registerDefaultMedia and add event listeners to the buttons. We bring back the mediaPlayer object, which is capable of playing any type of media by holding a media element that has all the traits we need (such as IPausible, which pauses and resumes playing).

```
override protected function childrenCreated():void
{
    super.childrenCreated();

    // Construct a loader factory:
     factory = new MediaFactory();
    registerDefaultMedia(factory);

    // Add button handlers:
    buttonStop.addEventListener(MouseEvent.CLICK,onStopClick);
    buttonPlay.addEventListener(MouseEvent.CLICK,onPlayClick);
    buttonPause.addEventListener(MouseEvent.CLICK,onPauseClick);
    buttonResume.addEventListener(MouseEvent.CLICK,onResumeClick);
    buttonToggleMute.addEventListener(MouseEvent.CLICK,onToggleMuteClick);
    buttonLoad.addEventListener(MouseEvent.CLICK,onLoadClick);
```

```
        // Get a reference to our player:
        player = flexMediaPlayer.mediaPlayer;
        player.scaleMode = ScaleMode.LETTERBOX;
    }
```

The registerDefaultMedia method creates all the media elements that our application will be supporting, such as progressive download, streaming, audio files, images, and SWFs:

```
    private function registerDefaultMedia(factory:IMediaFactory):void
    {
        var loader:ILoader = new VideoLoader();
        factory.addMediaInfo
( new MediaInfo
    ( "progressive"
    , loader as IMediaResourceHandler
    , VideoElement
    , [VideoLoader]
    )
);

        loader = new RTMPLoader();
        factory.addMediaInfo
( new MediaInfo
    ( "streaming"
    , loader as IMediaResourceHandler
    , VideoElement
    , [RTMPLoader]
    )
);

        loader = new SoundLoader();
        factory.addMediaInfo
( new MediaInfo
    ( "audio"
    , loader as IMediaResourceHandler
    , SoundElement
    , [SoundLoader]
    )
);

        loader = new ImageLoader();
        factory.addMediaInfo
( new MediaInfo
    ( "image"
    , loader as IMediaResourceHandler
    , ImageElement
    , [new ImageLoader()]
    )
);
```

```
            loader = new SWFLoader();
            factory.addMediaInfo
( new MediaInfo
            ( "swf"
            , loader as IMediaResourceHandler
            , ImageElement
            , [SWFLoader]
            )
);
}
```

The loadMediaByURL method creates a new media element based on the URL the user provided. We add a listener and set it in our player component:

```
private function loadMediaByURL(url:IURLResource):void
{
     // Stop listening to the current media, if any.
     toggleMediaListeners(player.media,false);

     // Create the new media.
     var media:IMediaElement = factory.createMediaElement(url);

     // Listen for events related to the new media.
     toggleMediaListeners(media,true);

     // Set it on our media player.
     player.media = media;
}
```

The toggleMediaListeners method adds the event listeners to the media. Once the states have changed and the on flag is set to true, it will call the event handler onMediaStateChange. The media element has a trait for loading the asset, and once the onLoadableStateChange is captured, the text field will display the information.

```
private function toggleMediaListeners(media:IMediaElement,on:Boolean):void
{
     if (media != null)
     {
if (on)
{
     media.addEventListener(MediaStateChangeEvent.STATE_CHANGE, ➥
onMediaStateChange);
}
else
{
     media.removeEventListener(MediaStateChangeEvent.STATE_CHANGE, ➥
onMediaStateChange);
}
```

```
var loadable:ILoadable = media.getTrait(ILoadable) as ILoadable;
if (loadable)
{
    if (on)
    {
loadable.addEventListener(LoadableEvent.LOADABLE_STATE_CHANGE, ➥
onLoadableStateChange);
    }
    else
    {
loadable.removeEventListener(LoadableEvent.LOADABLE_STATE_CHANGE, ➥
onLoadableStateChange);
    }
}
    }
}
```

The event listener will handle the interaction with the media element based on the traits that are assigned to the media:

```
private function onStopClick(event:MouseEvent):void
{
    player.stop();
}

private function onPlayClick(event:MouseEvent):void
{
    player.play();
}

private function onLoadClick(event:MouseEvent):void
{
    var url:String = urlInput.text;
    if (url.length > 0)
    {
player.unload();
loadMediaByURL(new URLResource(url));
    }
}

private function onLoadableStateChange(event:LoadableEvent):void
{
    loadState.text = event.newState.toString();
}
```

The onMediaStateChange event handler will handle the display and hiding of the toolbar:

```
private function onMediaStateChange(event:MediaStateChangeEvent):void
{
    if (player.media)
    {
buttonStop.visible = buttonPlay.visible = ➥
player.media.getTrait(IPlayable) != null;
buttonPause.visible = buttonResume.visible  = ➥
player.media.getTrait(IPlayable) != null;
buttonToggleMute.visible = player.media.getTrait(IAudible) != null;
    }
}

private var factory:IMediaFactory;
private var media:IMediaElement;
private var player:MediaPlayer;
```

We can test constants to hold the different media files:

```
private static const REMOTE_PROGRESSIVE:String = ➥
"http://flipside.corp.adobe.com/pirates3/Pirates3-1.flv";
private static const REMOTE_MP3:String  = ➥
"http://flipside.corp.adobe.com/brian/strobe/media/Remember.mp3";
private static const REMOTE_STREAM:String = ➥
"rtmp://flipside.corp.adobe.com/trailers/EvanAlmighty";
private static const REMOTE_IMAGE:String = ➥
"http://www.adobe.com/products/mediaplayer/assets/images/amp_icon.jpg";
private static const REMOTE_SWF:String  = ➥
"http://flipside.corp.adobe.com/testing/swfPlayback/as3/Objects/ ➥
Color/ObjClr_setRGB.swf"
    }
```

Figure 15-33 shows Strobe playing a sample video.

Figure 15-33. Strobe playing a video example

Summary

In this chapter we covered basic as well as advanced topics related to creating cross-platform video players for Flash Lite and Flash 10. We compared reusing and creating video content, and gave you tips for creating mobile device content. We talked about the difference between progressive download and dynamic streaming and how to encode using the Adobe Media Encoder.

We explored how to create a customized progressive download video player for Flash Lite and Flash 10 players, and you learned about the connection status messages. We covered Flash Media Server and optimization techniques, and showed you how to embed a video file into Flash Lite and Flash 10 applications. Finally, we talked about some of the new features in Flash 10 and FMS 3.5, such as dynamic switching of video profiles and enhanced progressive download, as well as the OVP and Adobe Strobe initiatives.

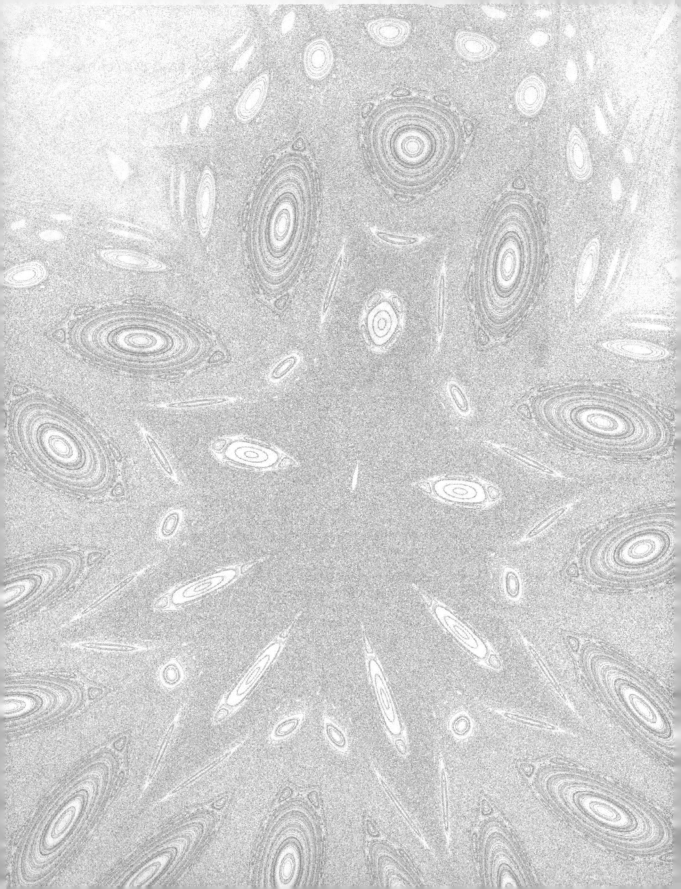

INDEX

XML for Flash   Actionscript Animation   Flash 8   ASP.NET 2.0 for Flash   Flash 8 Video

1-59059-543-2 $39.99 [US]   1-59059-518-1 $39.99 [US]   1-59059-542-4 $36.99 [US]   1-59059-517-3 $39.99 [US]   1-59059-651-X $44.99 [US]

EXPERIENCE THE DESIGNER TO DESIGNER™ DIFFERENCE

Flash Applications for Mobile Devices   New Masters of Flash   New Masters of Photoshop

1-59059-558-0 $49.99 [US]   1-59059-314-6 $59.99 [US]   1-59059-315-4 $59.99 [US]

Object-Oriented ActionScript for Flash 8   Extending Flash MX 2004   Apache Essentials   Dreamweaver MX 2004 Design Projects   From After Effects to Flash

1-59059-619-6 $44.99 [US]   1-59059-304-9 $49.99 [US]   1-59059-355-3 $24.99 [US]   1-59059-409-6 $39.99 [US]   1-59059-748-6 $49.99 [US]

AdvancED ActionScript Components   AdvancED Flash Interface Design   DOM Scripting   Web Accessibility   HTML Mastery

1-59059-593-9 $49.99 [US]   1-59059-555-6 $44.99 [US]   1-59059-533-5 $34.99 [US]   1-59059-638-2 $49.99 [US]   1-59059-765-6 $34.99 [US]

Blog Design Solutions   CSS Mastery   Flash Application Design Solutions   Web Standards Solutions   Podcast Solutions

1-59059-581-5 $39.99 [US]   1-59059-614-5 $34.99 [US]   1-59059-594-7 $39.99 [US]   1-59059-381-2 $34.99 [US]   1-59059-554-8 $24.99 [US]